THE OXFORD HISTORY OF LIFE-WRITING

Volume 2

Early Modern

THE OXFORD HISTORY OF LIFE-WRITING

General Editor: Zachary Leader

1. *The Middle Ages*
   Karen A. Winstead
2. *Early Modern*
   Alan Stewart
3. *Eighteenth Century*
   Rebecca Bullard
4. *Romantic*
5. *Nineteenth Century*
6. *Modernist*
7. *Later Twentieth Century and Contemporary*
   Patrick Hayes

THE OXFORD HISTORY OF LIFE-WRITING

Volume 2

Early Modern

ALAN STEWART

OXFORD
UNIVERSITY PRESS

OXFORD
UNIVERSITY PRESS

Great Clarendon Street, Oxford, OX2 6DP,
United Kingdom

Oxford University Press is a department of the University of Oxford.
It furthers the University's objective of excellence in research, scholarship, and education by publishing worldwide. Oxford is a registered trade mark of Oxford University Press in the UK and in certain other countries

First Edition published in 2018

Impression: 1

Published in the United States of America by Oxford University Press
198 Madison Avenue, New York, NY 10016, United States of America

British Library Cataloguing in Publication Data
Data available

Library of Congress Control Number: 2017964398

ISBN 978-0-19-968407-6

Printed and bound by
CPI Group (UK) Ltd, Croydon, CR0 4YY

To Lisa Jardine

Acknowledgements

I didn't realize it at the time, but I started thinking about this book over twenty years ago, when Lisa Jardine asked if I'd consider co-authoring a biography of Francis Bacon. Two more early modern lives followed, of Philip Sidney and James VI and I, before I started teaching courses on life-writing, at the Centre for Editing Lives and Letters (CELL), then at Queen Mary, University of London. But it was not until Zachary Leader asked me to contribute to a 2012 conference at the Huntington Library that I started to consider life-writing more deeply: I am grateful to him and to Jacqueline Norton at Oxford University Press for the invitation to contribute this volume to OUP's *History of Life-Writing*, and for their support while I wrote it.

I started work at the Folger Shakespeare Library, which gave me two short-term fellowships in 2012 and 2016 for entirely different projects—but which always supported me in my pursuit of this book in its collections. Warm thanks to Andy Boyle, Kim Coles, Chris Highley, Kathleen Lynch, Christia Mercer, Richard Schoch, Alexandra Walsham, Mike Witmore, and Heather Wolfe, and the reading room staff headed by the much-missed Betsy Walsh. Initial research was supported by the John Simon Guggenheim Foundation, to which I am deeply grateful. David Scott Kastan and James Shapiro championed this project from the outset. Lehua Yim read countless first drafts and shaped countless second drafts. Kate Bennett, Daniel Blank, Julie Crawford, Danielle Clarke, Katie Gucer, Katy Mair, Jeffrey Miller, Joe Moshenska, and Molly Murray gave valuable advice on particular chapters. Brian Lockey guided me to the manuscript by Tobie Matthew that anchors Chapter 9; Alan Nelson generously gave me his transcripts of the diaries of Richard Stonley; Jason Scott-Warren was incredibly gracious in commenting on my work on Stonley, about whom he knows far more than I. Special thanks go to Daniel Ebalo, Andrew Gordon, Zachary Leader, and James Shapiro, who commented on the book in its entirety; and to Steven Zwicker, Andrew Hadfield, and the other, anonymous reviewers at OUP, who truly influenced its contents. I am grateful to the Department of English and Comparative Literature at Columbia, and especially its chairs Nicholas Dames, Jean Howard, and Sarah Cole, for supporting my work on this book.

Sincere thanks go to librarians and archivists of the Bibliothèque nationale de France in Paris; the British Library, Dr Williams's Library, and the Jesuit Archives in London; the National Archives in Kew; the Bodleian Library, Oxford; Emmanuel College, Cambridge; Boston Public Library and the Massachusetts Historical Society in Boston; and, in New York, Columbia University Libraries and the Burke Library at Union Theological Seminary. For help with images, I am also indebted to the Pepys Library, Magdalene College, Cambridge; Cambridge University Library; the Kunstmuseum, Basel; the National Portrait Library, London; the Beinecke Library, Yale University; and the Henry E. Huntington Library. An earlier version of Chapter 6 was published in *On Life-Writing*, edited by Zachary Leader. I am grateful to Oxford University Press for permission to use this material.

Teaching undergraduate and graduate classes on life-writing at CELL and at Columbia, I learned a huge amount from my students' enthusiastic responses to these sometimes arcane materials. I led a seminar on life-writing at the 2013 meeting of the Shakespeare Association of America in Toronto, and thank all the participants for their insights, especially Adam Smyth for his response. Parts of this book were tried out as papers at the Henry E. Huntington Library, the London Renaissance Seminar at Birkbeck College London, the Wolfe Institute at Brooklyn College, the National University of Ireland at Galway, the Folger Shakespeare Library, the University of Fribourg, the Columbia University Seminar in the Renaissance, the Renaissance Society of America (Chicago), and the University of Sussex's Centre for Medieval and Early Modern Studies: I am grateful for the invitations from Zachary Leader, Susan Wiseman, Christopher Ebert, Daniel Carey, Kathleen Lynch, Derek Dunne and Indira Ghose, Cynthia M. Pyle, and Matthew Dimmock and Andrew Hadfield, and to all the comments and suggestions offered by the audience members.

For equally sustaining dialogue, albeit in less formally academic venues, I thank especially Chris Ross, Christopher Ebert, Lehua Yim, James Daybell, Andrew Gordon, Diana Barnes, John Kuhn, András Kiséry, Seth Williams, Jerry Passannante, David Simon, Molly Murray, Jenny Davidson, Seth Kimmel, and Patricia and David Brewerton.

At Oxford University Press, I have benefitted from the professionalism and care of Jacqueline Norton, Eleanor Collins, and Aimee Wright, the copy-editing of Ian Brookes, the proof-reading of Sally Evans-Darby, and the project supervision of Suryajeet Mullick.

This book is dedicated to Lisa Jardine.

General Editor's Preface

'Life-writing' is a generic term meant to encompass a range of writings about lives or parts of lives, or which provide materials out of which lives or parts of lives are composed. These writings include not only memoir, autobiography, biography, diaries, autobiographical fiction, and biographical fiction, but letters, writs, wills, written anecdotes, depositions, court proceedings (*narratio* first existed not as a literary but as a legal term), marginalia, lyric poems, scientific and historical writings, and digital forms (including blogs, tweets, and Facebook entries). Some theoreticians and historians of life-writing distinguish between shorter forms, conceived of as source material, and 'life-writing proper' or 'extended life narratives' or 'formal biography and autobiography'; others distinguish between life-writing that is exemplary or formulaic, often associated with older periods, and the sort that seems or seeks to express qualities thought of as modern: authenticity, sincerity, interiority, individuality. More commonly, at least since the 1970s, theoreticians and historians of life-writing fuse or meld sub-genres, as in the neologisms 'auto/biography', 'bio-fiction', 'biografiction', 'autonarration', and 'autobiografiction' (this last, surprisingly, the most venerable as well as the most ungainly of coinages, having first appeared in print in 1906). The blurring of distinctions may help to account for life-writing's growing acceptance as a field of study, conforming to a wider academic distrust of fixed forms, simple or single truths or meanings, narrative transparency, objectivity, and 'literature' as opposed to writing.

The larger aim of *The Oxford History of Life-Writing* is to focus and consolidate recent academic research and debate, providing a multi-volume history of this newly recognized genre. Constituent volumes will often focus on the lives of writers, but they will also consider the lives of non-writers, especially in cases when these lives have altered or influenced literary life-writing, or when they are *by* literary figures. Some attention may also be given to works about forms of life-writing, or about topics obviously related to life-writing, such as Hume's *Treatise of Human Nature* or Carlyle's *On Heroes, Hero-Worship and the Heroic in History*, or to novels and plays about real-life figures, or fictional writers, including memoirists, letter writers, and biographers.

The constituent volumes of the *History* provide selective surveys of the range of life-writing in a period, giving extended attention to the most important or influential authors and works within the genre. The advantages of contextualizing influential works through a broad survey should be clear, but individual authors will carve out their own narrative accounts of the field, in the process producing discoveries, obscure or unjustly neglected works and authors, themselves worthy of extended treatment. Although the primary focus of the *History* will be on life-writing in English, when relevant, influential works in other languages will be discussed.

Inevitably there will be variation in structure and approach from volume to volume (as well as over particulars, including decisions about old spelling or versions quoted). But all volumes will contain some discussion of the following topics: the range of life-writing in the period, in terms of different schools, traditions, types, themes, forms, and functions; detailed accounts of those writers or writings deemed most important or influential or innovative in the period, either by contemporaries, or by literary history, or by the authors of the individual volumes themselves; the production and consumption of life-writing in the period, including discussion of the nature of the audience, the rewards of authorship, and the standing of the genre; the genre's debt to the wider culture of its period, for example to dominant notions of personal identity, nationhood, political and religious authority, authorship, creativity, literary criticism, and literary value; some reference, where relevant, to developments in life-writing in contemporaneous non-English-speaking cultures and to national distinctions within the English-speaking world; and the accuracy or usefulness of influential characterizations of life-writing in the period.

Individual volumes will take clear or distinctive lines and approaches, but the *History* as a whole will not, thus avoiding both predictability and authorial constraint. Not all volumes will be structured chronologically, but all will make clear the importance of a historical understanding of the genre. All authors will be encouraged to consider the needs of a general as well as an academic audience, in keeping with the comparatively broad-based readership of the most prominent types of the genre (biography, autobiography, memoir). For similar reasons, strong narrative will be encouraged, as will the avoidance of abstruse terminology. The seven volumes in the series are divided along roughly traditional literary-historical lines, though there may be some overlap between adjacent volumes and some innovation both in nomenclature and in beginning and ending dates, particularly in the case of later volumes.

Zachary Leader

Contents

List of Figures

Abbreviations

BL	British Library, London
Bodl.	Bodleian Library, Oxford
CELM	*Catalogue of English Literary Manuscripts*
CP	Hatfield House, Cecil Papers
CUL	Cambridge University Library
DNB	*Dictionary of National Biography*, ed. Leslie Stephen and Sidney Lee, 63 vols (London, 1885–1900)
Folger	Folger Shakespeare Library, Washington, DC
HMC	Historical Manuscripts Commission
HMSO	His/Her Majesty's Stationery Office
Huntington	Henry E. Huntington Library, San Marino, CA
MS	manuscript
OED	*The Oxford English Dictionary*, ed. J. A. Simpson and E. S. C. Weiner, 2nd edn, 20 vols (Oxford: Oxford University Press, 1989) and online version
ODNB	*Oxford Dictionary of National Biography*, ed. H. C. G. Matthew and Brian Harrison, 61 vols (Oxford: Oxford University Press, 2004) and online version
PROB	Records of the Prerogative Court of Canterbury
SP	State Papers
STAC	Star Chamber
STC	*A Short-Title Catalogue of Books Printed in England, Scotland, & Ireland and of English Books Printed Abroad 1475–1640*, ed. A. W. Pollard and G. R. Redgrave, rev. W. A. Jackson, F. S. Ferguson, Katharine F. Pantzer, and Philip K. Rider, 2nd edn, 3 vols (London: The Bibliographical Society, 1976–1991)
TNA	The National Archives, Kew
Wing	*Short-Title Catalogue of Books Printed in England, Scotland, Ireland, Wales, and British America, and of English Books Printed in Other Countries, 1641–1700*, ed. Donald Wing (New York: Index Society, 1945–1951)

Note on Transcription

Many of the life-writings quoted in this book feature highly idiosyncratic spelling and punctuation. In order to preserve the individual characteristics of each writer, the spelling, capitalization, and punctuation in early modern texts have been retained, unless indicated otherwise (by the use of square brackets). Standard contractions in manuscript and early printed texts have been expanded, and the supplied letters indicated in italics. In the writings of Thomas Whythorne (Chapter 4), who developed his own phonetic orthography, the idiosyncrasy reaches a new level. In this case, I have modernized the fossil thorn (þ) as 'th', and the fossil yogh (ʒ) as 'g' or 'j'. Whythorne's attempt to render the long vowel by the use of 'pricks' above or below the letter (e.g. ạ, ẏ) has been returned to the standard use of the terminal -e: so 'cạm' is rendered as 'came'. (For an explanation of Whythorne's orthography, see pp. 79–80.) Thanks to the efforts of previous editors, the shorthands of Samuel Pepys and others (Chapter 14) have been transliterated.

Introduction

I start this book with a story about a death and a 'life'. On 29 January 1613, Thomas Bodley, the intelligencer, diplomat, and re-founder of Oxford's University Library, died after a lengthy illness. News quickly spread that the rich man's last will and testament had some scandalous omissions.[1] The newsletter-writer John Chamberlain claimed that while £7000 had been given to the library that would bear his name, and £200 bequeathed to Merton College, in whose chapel he would be buried, Bodley had 'dealt very mechanically' with his servants, giving no more than £20 even to those who had served the family for over twenty-two years, and nothing at all to many of his friends (including, it should be said, Chamberlain) and to members of his wife's family.[2] Worse, his long-time follower William Gent received nothing; when Gent died in June, Chamberlain opined that his demise 'I make no doubt but was hastened by Sir Thomas Bodleys vnkindnes'.[3] A lavish funeral–held two months later and budgeted at a phenomenal £666 14s 6d–was 'the last act of Sir Thomas Bodleys vanitie'. Chamberlain was appalled: 'though I neuer had any excellent conceit of him, yet I did not thincke he had ben so vainly ambitious as he discouers himself many wayes'.[4] In short, he concluded, 'the truth is he was so druncke with the applause and vanitie of his librarie that he made no conscience to rob Peter (as they say) to pay Paul'. The only comfort was that this self-financed adulation would soon die down: while now the university heaped verses and orations on Bodley, 'I make no question but they will quickly vanish, and in short time come to stop mustardpots'.[5]

Beyond the paltry legacies and the self-indulgent exequies, there was yet more devastating gossip, which Chamberlain passed on to Bodley's son-in-law, Ralph Winwood, *sub rosa*:

> One argument of his vanitie I will adventure to communicate unto you, though yt were in a manner committed to me *sub sigillo confessionis* [under the seal of confession], and so I pray you let yt remaine till you hear more. He hath written his owne life in seven sheetes of paper, and not leaving out the least *minutezze*, or omitting nothing that may tend to his owne glorie or commendation.[6]

These seven sheets of paper told a very particular version of Thomas Bodley's life. After giving the facts of his parentage, birth, upbringing, and education, Bodley dedicates considerable space to an account of his diplomatic successes, assuring his reader that 'approbation was given of my painefull endeavours by the Queene, Lords in England, by the States of the Country there, and by all the English Souldiery'. Finding his career stalled by the court factionalism of the 1590s, as he tells it, Bodley abandoned the political scene in order to work on his library: 'I concluded at the last to set up my Staffe at the Library doore in *Oxford;* being th[o]roughly perswaded, that in my solitude and surcease from the Common-wealth affaires, I could not busy my selfe to better purpose, then by reducing that place (which then in every part lay ruined and wast) to the publique use of Students.' This final instalment of his life is dealt with summarily because, as Bodley points out, what he had achieved 'will testifie so truly and aboundantly for me, as I need not be the publisher of the dignity and worth of mine owne Institution'. He ended the account with a declaration and a signature: 'Written with my owne hand Anno 1609. December the 15. Tho: Bodley'.[7]

For Chamberlain, the scandal did not stop with the vainglorious *minutezze*. For while Bodley had left out 'nothing that may tend to his owne glorie or commendation', he had skimped on certain other details. The names of Sir Francis Walsingham and Robert Dudley, earl of Leicester were notably absent, in spite of the fact that they were 'his maine raisers', the men on whom he had built his career. And just as he had cut his wife's family out of his will, Bodley had cut them out of 'his owne life'–indeed, 'he hath not so much as made mention of his wife or that he was maried, wherby you may see what a mind he caried, and what account he made of his best benefactors'.[8] This omission was all the more shocking because the one thing everybody knew about Thomas Bodley is that he owed his personal fortune to his wife, 'a riche widdowe', as the Middle Temple lawyer John Manningham recorded in his diary, whose previous husband 'grewe to a greate quantity of wealth in a short space, specially by trading for pilcheres [pilchards]'.[9] But in his 'owne life', Bodley remained unmarried. Most shocking of all to Chamberlain, there was talk that this life was to be published in print, although he had hopes it would not come to pass: 'this treatise is commended to the hands of the prime prelate'–Archbishop of Canterbury George Abbot, a member of the Court of High Commission which licensed books for printing, who 'hath too much judgement to let yt be published'.[10]

Whether or not Abbot suppressed the publication, Bodley's 'life' did not make it into print in 1613.[11] But, for all Chamberlain's outrage, Bodley's 'life' was not to remain a thing to be whispered under the seal of confession. In 1647, *The Life of Sir Thomas Bodley* was published in civil-war Oxford by the University's printer Henry Hall, with a preface probably composed by the provost of Queen's,

Gerard Langbaine. In stark contrast to Chamberlain three decades earlier, Langbaine found nothing odd about Bodley writing his own life, or indeed about that life's publication in print, remarking only a certain stylistic simplicity about Bodley's writing—'the nakednesse of this relation'—which was now taken to vouch for its authenticity: 'That I may speake the worke above all scorne, above all praise; it was his Owne. Not durst we call that draught in question, which felt the hand of so exact a Master; but with awe lookt on it, as on the fabrique of an ancient Temple, where the ruine furthers our Devotion; and gaudy ornaments doe but prophane the sad religion of the place.'[12]

Bodley's *Life* was now a relic to be worshipped. And from that time forward, it remained firmly in the public sphere: his cousin George Hakewill translated it into Latin;[13] David Lloyd included a redacted version of 'Observations on the life of Sir *Thomas Bodley*, by himself' in his two compendia of *States-men and Favourites* (1665, 1670); Anthony Wood drew heavily on it for his account of Bodley's life for his dictionary of Oxford alumni, the *Athenæ Oxonienses* (1691);[14] and Thomas Hearne published it again in his 1703 edition of *Reliquiæ Bodleianæ*, after finding Bodley's papers at the Bodleian: 'I immediately took a Transcript of them, and sent them to the *Press*; that others imitating Sir *Thomas*'s Zeal and Industry for the good of *Learning*, might become *Benefactors* themselves to such a noble *Repository*.'[15] Hearne later deplored previous generations' attitude to life-writing: he must 'lament, that some other of our ancient Worthies had not left us Memoirs of their Lives'. He appreciated that this task had been 'neglected by them, as disagreeable to the Rules of Modesty', but their fears were unjustified: this 'was a false notion, especially if they took care to conceal what they committed to writing of that kind 'till after their death, and put it into the hands of some faithfull Friends, that might make use of it in defence of their posthumous Fame against malicious Enemies'. In building his case, Hearne pointed out that 'Some of the greatest Men did not look upon it as immodest to do themselves this piece of Justice'. And his first modern example was Sir Thomas Bodley, who 'was pleased also to leave behind him an Account written by himself of his own Life'.[16]

Thomas Bodley's life-writing falls near the midpoint of the two centuries treated by this book, two centuries that saw remarkable innovations in—and a quantitative explosion of—life-writing. At the start of the sixteenth century, the only biographies being written in England were of significant religious figures, alongside character sketches of rulers and military commanders; a century later, in 1605, Bodley's friend Francis Bacon still opined that 'I doe finde strange that these times haue so litle esteemed the vertues of the times, as that the Writings of liues should be no more frequent', since there were 'many worthy personages, that deserue better then dispersed reports, or barren *Elogies*'.[17] Yet by the end of the seventeenth century men, women, and even children from almost every rank and occupation were deemed worthy, at least by some, of having their lives written: as Thomas Manton insisted, 'The Lives of Gods *precious Saints*, (how *private* so ever their station be) are very well worthy of *record* and *publick notice*.'[18] Diaries were once the preserve of those holding office or on special missions—military, diplomatic, naval—but gradually various practices of daily writing took hold across society. An 'owne life' such as Bodley's was an even scarcer commodity in sixteenth-century England, but by 1700 a remarkable number of women and men were finding their own lives worth writing. By the opening decades of the eighteenth century, Edmund Calamy and Roger North would write lengthy disquisitions on life-writing, and even suggest a brief canon of recent British life-writers.[19]

This undoubted increase in life-writing between 1500 and 1700 has led many critics to insist that it was only in the last half of the seventeenth century that we see the first glimpses of great English life-writing in a very few special cases. In this narrative, Izaak Walton's collected *Lives* (1670) typically constituted 'certainly the most important biographical work in English literature prior to [Samuel] Johnson' a century later, since Walton was 'the first Englishman consciously to write artistic biography' (John Aubrey's *Brief Lives* merited an honourable mention).[20] The eighteenth century was similarly cast as 'the classical age of autobiography' with its predecessor only feeling its way with works by Edward, Lord Herbert of Cherbury and Thomas Hobbes, and above all, John Bunyan's *Grace Abounding* (1666).[21] And it was only with Samuel Pepys's diary, written between 1660 and 1669, that England attained a '"pure" diary-writing', with John Evelyn's much more sustained journal receiving some grudging attention.[22] Over the past half century these assumptions about chronology—and the predominantly elite, male-authored, secular and literary canon they created and sustained—have been happily unsettled. Mid-Tudor lives of Cardinal Thomas Wolsey and Thomas More by George Cavendish and William Roper have been championed as the 'first sign' of biography in which 'human detail and character kept breaking through';[23] the discovery of composer Thomas Whythorne's *c.* 1576 self-narrative has allowed us to see that 'the beginnings of English autobiography' predated the seventeenth century;[24] and the publication of Elizabethan-era godly diaries by Richard Rogers, Samuel Ward, and Lady Margaret Hoby belied the confident assertion that the form commenced with Pepys.[25] The dominance of 'literary' life-writing has been challenged by an increased willingness to examine less obviously crafted works, such as spiritual autobiographies and conversion narratives.[26] The geographical range has been widened to include the life-writings emanating from New England and the English Catholic houses on the Continent.[27] The overwhelmingly male bias of earlier studies has been dented by a wide-ranging interest in the writings of women, in print and especially in manuscript;[28] and while life-writings from the lowest ranks of early modern English society remain rare, the few that have surfaced—by London artisan Nehemiah Wallington and the sailor Edward Barlow, for example—have been revelatory.[29]

But despite the broadening of scope, the critical consensus remains that life-writing expanded across the sixteenth and seventeenth centuries as part of a march towards modernity: because of increased rates of literacy; because 'the climate was favourable to self-assertion, self-scrutiny, self-revelation' (Margaret Bottrall); because 'with the accepted stress on the individual which accompanied the Reformation, and with the rise of scientific empiricism, there was more curiosity about the mainsprings of human character' (James L. Clifford); because of 'the increasing individualism of the Puritan movement' (Dean Ebner); because it provides 'evidence of a form of cultural production related to the manifestation in England during the early modern period of the individual self' (Michael Mascuch).[30] There is of course some truth to each of these—but, as I hope to demonstrate, there is no single grand narrative that can explain, or explain away, the phenomenal growth in life-writing in early modern England.

Instead, what I trace here are a number of factors—many of them highly local and specific—that led to, and sometimes demanded, new forms of life-writing. These include the attempt to explain a personal religious conversion from Catholicism to Protestantism, and vice versa; the move to create Catholic 'martyrs' and Protestant 'saints' of men and women who had been persecuted for their faith; the impulse to understand one's daily life through scrupulous financial accounting or constant moral self-examination; the attempt to memorialize one's own life or the life of another; the telling of a family's fortunes (interpreted in multiple ways); the drive to create new communities; the need to separate out and cover up parts of a life; and the overwhelming need to preserve what would otherwise be ephemeral. Together they tell a new story of early modern English life-writing.

Life-writing

While the standard modern terminology of biography, autobiography, and diary inevitably permeates this book, I prefer to think of my subject as 'life-writing'. Partly this is to avoid anachronism: by the end of the seventeenth century, only 'biography' and its cognates could claim a limited currency, their learned users probably inspired by the neo-Latin 'biographia',[31] while what we term 'autobiography' had no equivalent in the period (early attempts such as 'self Story' and 'idiography' failed to catch on,[32] and 'autobiography' itself was not used until 1796).[33] But I also want to read these writings as what they say they are, rather than as imagined embryonic versions of what will become modern biography or autobiography. Early modern life-writings describe themselves in a bewildering variety of terms: memoir, memoirs, epitaph, memorial, journal, course of examination, observation, receipts and payments, confessions, history, adventures, juvenile rambles, minutes, vocation, book of accounts and remembrances, book of songs and sonnets, true historical relation—to name just a few. What Meredith Anne Skura and Adam Smyth have recently demonstrated of autobiographies is true for early modern life-writings more generally: they partake of literary genres and material forms that we might not now recognize as life-writing—anything from sermons to account books to picaresque novels to poetic miscellanies to commonplace books. Like Skura and Smyth, I read texts that lie beyond the genres that we might now readily see as life-writing, but whereas Skura is not concerned to 'distinguish between "true" and fictional autobiographies', and Smyth includes genres such as parish registers that accidentally bear autobiographical traces, I am interested in authors who deliberately set out to *write lives*, whether their own or others'.[34]

By returning to this concept of *writing lives* or *life-writing*,[35] I also break with the critical practice of separating out biography from autobiography, which has held sway for most of the last century. While Donald A. Stauffer's 1930 study of *English Biography before 1700* found room for a chapter on autobiography, virtually every scholarly book that followed has devoted itself to one genre or the other—so, for example, Paul Delany's fine 1969 survey of seventeenth-century 'British autobiography' deliberately eschews any discussion of biography, while, in an elegant symmetry, Allan Pritchard in his 2005 'critical survey' of seventeenth-century 'English biography' writes, 'Like Delany, I view autobiography as a form separate from biography, and do not include it in the present study.'[36] In a further move, the serially written diary or journal has been cleaved from the narrative autobiography, with many scholars citing Georges Gusdorf's influential dictum that whereas '[t]he author of a private journal, noting his impressions and mental states from day to day, fixes the portrait of his daily reality without any concern for continuity', the act of autobiography 'requires a man to take a distance with regard to himself in order to reconstitute himself in the focus of his special unity and identity across time'.[37]

However sophisticated the theoretical distinctions, the evidence from the period simply does not support the imposition of these hard-and-fast generic divisions. The astrologer and physician Simon Forman left no fewer than six writings that we would today call autobiographical, but they are bewilderingly diverse. As Lauren Kassell describes, his 'The bocke of the life and generation of Simon' (1600) 'is in the third person, and it reports Forman's life as though he were a character cavorting through a combination of the Bible, the Golden Legend, and an Elizabethan romance'; his so-called 'Diary', commenced in 1603, takes the form of astrological figures charting the position of planets, with accompanying lists of the 'accidents' of his life—resulting in what Kassell calls 'a retrospective version of a luxury horoscope with yearly revolutions'; a 1604 account of Forman's run-ins with the College of Physicians takes the form of a psalm; while in 1605, he attempted a family genealogy and history, starting in the year 1028. What to call any of these? They are, as Kassell puts it nicely, 'nimble species of texts'.[38]

Other figures constantly blur any distinction between biography, autobiography, and diary. The seventeenth-century clergyman Henry Newcome opens his own manuscript life by praising others for writing theirs, claiming that 'what men have so writ of themselves hath made posterity a truer and more exact account of passages of divine providence towards them than could be done by any other that hath come after them, that hath taken in hand the lives of men deceased and gone'. He is not concerned here to value autobiography over biography—rather to establish that autobiography is the necessary precursor to great biography: 'it is little question but those lives that have been so written by others, had been much fuller representations of goodness and admirable providence if some remembrances had been made thereof by themselves, who were the parties concerned'. Newcome himself can write his own life only because he had long kept a diary: 'having had some account of things all along from my younger years', he is able 'to contract and methodize some of those accounts into this entire narrative'.[39] His diary-keeping was prompted by the example of his Cambridge college head, Dr Samuel Ward, and Newcome continues to take inspiration from the manuscript diaries of others ('I read in Mr. Angier's Diary to my great advantage').[40] Newcome's diary and narrative are both studded with references to other life-writings—by Franciscus Junius and Bishop Joseph Hall, John Foxe's 'Booke of Martyrs', David Lloyd's 'Book of English Statesmen', 'Dr. Staunton's Life', 'Mr. Allein's Excellent Life', 'the Lives of holy men'[41]—which can sometimes suggest the shape of his own life-writing: 'When I read the lives of some of the German divines, that notice was taken of their inclinations in their youth, and the delight that one had when he was a child to sit aloft above his companions, and to seem to read to them, was taken for a presage of his being a Doctor of the chair, &c., I cannot but remember that my fancy ran much after preaching, it being my ordinary play and office to act the minister amongst my playfellows.'[42] And when Newcome's life-writing ends, his son Henry writes, 'He died the same day and month as Bullinger died.—Melc. Adami. Vit. Germ. Theol. p. 505'—dating his father's death with a precise reference to Melchior Adam's collection of lives of German theologians.[43] What we would separate out as biography, autobiography, and diary—and what he would call the reading and writing of lives—are inextricably linked for Newcome.

Writing Lives

Henry Newcome's papers also reveal that what we might perceive as an early modern written 'life', in the sense of a honed, polished diary, autobiography, or biography, was likely to be only one stage in a sequence of notes, fragments, and previous (and future) attempts. Processes of revision and rewriting reveal connections between diary, autobiography, and biography: lists of expenses in almanacs get rewritten as diary entries, diary entries are re-read and meditated on in the writing of spiritual autobiography, diaries are quoted in biographies, autobiographies are absorbed into personal memoirs and biographies, which act in turn as models for future life-writers.[44] The sheer porousness of early modern life-writing is everywhere evident in its material remains. Elizabeth Isham's 'Booke of Remembrance' (1638), 'a discursive spiritual and biographical reflection' bequeathed to her family, needs to be understood in relationship to her idiosyncratic diary, in which she has one entry per year from the age of four; but we also know that the 'Booke' went through various versions, since draft sections have survived on unused sides of letters that she had received.[45] When Essex clergyman Ralph Josselin started his diary in August 1644, he first reconstructed his first twenty-eight years, noting 'many things I have omitted that may be found in my notes, almanacks, etc.'.[46] John Evelyn was an inveterate diary-keeper, filling the spaces in a printed almanac from the age of eleven,[47] but he was also a reviser and a compiler: what we now know as Evelyn's 'Diary' was in fact collated in the 1680s, drawing on these earlier notes but including material drawn from books printed after the events described.[48] Lady Anne Halkett, who compiled her memoirs in the 1680s, left some twenty-one folio and quarto manuscripts dating from 1644 to the late 1690s, and 'about thirty stitched Books, some in Folio, some in 4to [quarto] most of them of 10 or 12 sheets, all containing occasional Meditations'.[49] The minister Oliver Heywood's 'autobiography'—which he termed 'A relation of the most considerable passages of my life from my infancy hitherto'—is drawn from, and shares space with, a diary, memoranda, and 'Observations Experimental', all housed in small pocket books.[50] And so on—the examples could multiply endlessly.

In pursuing these myriad life-writings, then, I pay particular attention to their *writing*—the material ways in which early modern women and men penned their lives in the sixteenth and seventeenth centuries. When and where did these authors write? How did they use paper, ink, the page's layout, and different hands to signal to the reader how to read their lives? Why do we have these texts? Where did they come from? Who got to read them? I want to recapture the important differences between works that were promptly published in print, those that circulated in manuscript, and those that remained locked in a family chest or muninents room. In many cases, this entails paying attention to the manuscript sources—materials that have for centuries been at the mercy of editors and publishers who selected what to include, and exclude, when fashioning a manuscript text for print publication. When Samuel Bury published his late wife Elizabeth's diary in 1720, he admitted that he had been forced 'to leave out at least Nine Parts in Ten of what I thought was truly valuable, and thereby to break the Connection, Dependance, and Consistency of the whole *Diary*', but 'it was absolutely necessary, or else the Volume must have swell'd to such a bigness as to have been Useless to many for whom it was especially design'd'.[51] Women's writings have been particularly vulnerable to intervention by editors with 'a marked preference for female piety'—as Sara Heller Mendelson reveals by comparing nineteenth-century editions of the autobiographies of Sarah Savage, Mary Rich, countess of Warwick, and Alice Thornton with the surviving manuscripts;[52] the standard edition of even a work as famous as Lucy Hutchinson's *The Life of John Hutchinson* omitted some 9,000 words.[53] In their endeavours, editors also routinely ignored, and effectively effaced, the meaningful qualities of their document's format. It is well known that what is today published as Samuel Pepys's diary is in fact a transliteration of six volumes that Pepys wrote in a shorthand. But readers of successive editions of John Dee's *Private Diary* could well remain unaware this so-called 'diary' is in fact a transcript of notes Dee wrote in printed 'ephemerides', tables showing the predicted movement of heavenly bodies; by lifting the notes out of this context, editors stripped the recorded events of what Dee took to be their astrological significance.[54] Wherever possible, then, I have returned to the manuscript sources—often to find much more messy, complicated, and fascinating texts than the standard printed editions offer.

The story of Thomas Bodley's 'Life' raises many of the issues that this book will explore. Firstly, life-writing of this period was created for, with, and by other people, and usually with a goal in mind: to establish or rehabilitate a reputation, to make a claim for a legacy, to join a particular community or congregation. The life-writings in this book are highly social and often political in their orientation; if, in their focus on a single person, they suggest a heightened interest in individualism, then that individualism needs to be understood within the social frameworks—familial, parochial, civic, confessional, national—that gave rise to that life-writing. Bodley's 'Life' clearly values certain frameworks (Oxford, Merton College, his library) over others (notably his family and friends).

Secondly, while all life-writings originate in highly particular and local social, political, and religious contexts, those contexts are subsequently, almost inevitably, challenged and overtaken. Bodley's 'Life', a handwritten manuscript precisely referred to as 'seven sheetes of paper' deposited in his own library, becomes in turn a printed pamphlet in Royalist civil-war Oxford, and then, at the turn of the eighteenth century, part of a substantial printed volume of Bodley's 'genuine remaines', at each appearance adapting itself to the requirements of a new historical moment and a new readership. For John Chamberlain, the 'Life' forms part of a battery of charges against Bodley; for Henry Hill and Gerard Langbaine, a record of a high point in Oxford's history; for Thomas Hearne, a relic of the great man, Thomas Bodley.

Thirdly, a piece of life-writing never stands on its own: it is inextricably linked to other texts that shape how it is created, defined, and interpreted. In Bodley's case, the 'Life' becomes a scandal in relation to the vanity and selfishness of his last will and testament, another text only posthumously circulated and read. (Wills are a feature in several of this book's chapters, one of the most widespread and undervalued forms of life-writing.) Although a first-person autobiography, the 'Life' is reworked, in another language, into a third-person funeral panegyric,[55] and then into a series of biographical accounts that seek to place Bodley among different groups, such as state worthies, or Oxford alumni.

Fourthly, we must ask what it is we're looking at in a piece of early modern life-writing, and how we come to be looking at it. All the documents surviving from the sixteenth and seventeenth centuries have a story to tell: why were they produced? what format do they take? where have they been in the three or four centuries since they were written? what was their journey after their initial function was exhausted? and what might that journey mean for our understanding of them? All the seventeenth-century writers insist that Bodley's 'Life' is a manuscript, 'seven sheetes of paper', as Chamberlain specifies, written in Bodley's hand and signed by him, 'being kept as a choice rarity in the archives of his Library', to quote Anthony Wood. In short, Bodley arranged for his life-writing to have a quasi-official status as a foundational document for his library, vouchsafed by his own hand and signature, and deposited in that archive. (And yet, those seven sheets of paper appear to be missing from the Bodleian today; in order to reconstruct the document, I am dependent on early transcriptions in manuscript and later publications in print.[56])

Fifthly, and perhaps most crucially, the story of Bodley's 'Life'—a shocking scandal at one historical moment, and a revered artefact at another, only a few decades later—speaks to the high emotions that this writing provokes. Life-writing in early modern England can just as easily be the object of disparagement, scorn, and ridicule as it is the object of praise. For every Thomas Hearne lamenting that worthies had not left memoirs of their lives, there is a John Chamberlain to denounce such memoirs as the last word in vanity. And, as we shall see, certain life-writings could have the very highest of 'real-life' stakes—for their writers, their publishers, even their readers.

Life-Writing in Early Modern England

This book takes the form of fifteen chapters, each telling the story of one individual's or group's life-writings. Without observing the strictest chronology, or attempting an exhaustive survey, each chapter broadly advances the historical account from 1500 to 1700. This 'case-study' model runs the risk of accentuating the idiosyncratic and eccentric—and indeed, some of these life-writings are quite unique. But there are broader trends at work. The story told here is peculiarly English. The expected landmarks of Renaissance life-writing—Giorgio Vasari's *Lives of the Most Excellent Painters, Sculptors, and Architects, from Cimabue to Our Times* (1550), and the lives written by Benvenuto Cellini (1558–63) and Girolamo Cardano (1575), for example—had little or no impact in England at the time.[57] The vaunted self-exploration of Michel de Montaigne's *Essais* left its trace in many English writings, but not obviously in life-writings: when Montaigne is invoked by Sir Henry Slingsby in his diary, it is to praise Montaigne's *father* for his advice on keeping a journal (Michel de Montaigne never kept one).[58] As we shall see, the autobiography of St Teresa de Avila stands as something of an exception, but its appeal was perhaps greatest to English women and men in exile from their homeland.[59] This is not to say that English life-writing has no international connections: many of the individuals I discuss spent considerable time overseas. But the story I tell here is a specific and insular affair, responding to largely local concerns.

England at the turn of the sixteenth century was still part of Catholic Christendom, largely looking to the past for long-established traditions of life-writing. From the ancient world, it inherited the exemplary lives written by classical authors: Plutarch's paired biographies of famous Greeks and Romans, the *Parallel Lives*, which focused largely on character; Suetonius' lives of Roman rulers, more concerned with deeds; Quintus Curtius Rufus' life of Alexander the Great; and Diogenes Laertius' lives of Greek philosophers. The *viri illustres* genre—a writer's life with a list of his writings—derived from Suetonius and entered the Christian world via St Jerome. Augustine's *Confessions* remained a hugely influential writing of one's own life. The early humanist Renaissance produced the *vita* of a celebrated individual, such as Giovanni Boccaccio's life of Dante, and Leonardo Bruni's lives of Dante Alighieri and Francesco Petrarca, as well as collections of lives, including Petrarca's *De viris illustribus*, and Boccaccio's *De casibus virorum illustrium* and *De mulieribus claris*. But in 1500 all these texts were largely the preserve of the educated, Latin-reading class; they would only be published in English from the late sixteenth century onwards.[60]

Much more widely known than any of these were the lives of the saints, the hagiography or 'sacred biography' of the medieval Roman Catholic Church, the goal of which was 'to teach the truth of the faith through the principle of individual example'.[61] With the introduction of the printing press, some vernacular lives—such as the translated collection of saints' lives known as the *Legenda aurea (Golden Legend)* (from 1483), to which printer William Caxton added some English lives, and the autobiographical writings of Margery Kempe (1501)—enjoyed a new and wider readership; and there were additions to the canon, such as Henry Bradshaw's verse lives of St Werburg (1521) and St Radegunde (1525).[62] And yet this flourishing tradition would have startlingly little traction past the 1520s. For the history of early modern English life-writing is in many ways the history of post-Reformation English life-writing. It was the Reformation, its politics and policies, that provoked innovations in how English men and women wrote their lives. The *Legenda aurea* was published for the last time in England in 1527,[63] and within years the worship of saints was officially suppressed.

This Reformation turning point can be seen quite vividly in the life-story of the enterprising humanist scholar Thomas More. More was himself a life-writer: in the first two decades of the sixteenth century, he introduced to the English language the Latin life of Pico della Mirandola, excerpting it firmly to serve as a pious exemplar for his friend's sister Joyce Lee, as a token of his 'desire to haue [her] godly prosperous'; and wrote his own histories (in English and Latin) of the recently killed Yorkist king, Richard III.[64] But after a glittering career during which he rose to be Lord Chancellor, More would lose his life to the English Reformation, executed in 1535 for refusing to accept the king, Henry VIII, as head of the Church of England, and reviled by Protestant writers as a traitor. Not until the reign of the Catholic Mary Tudor (1553–8) was there an attempt to rehabilitate some of the major figures whose reputation had been thus besmirched.[65] More then became the subject of two biographies, by his son-in-law William Roper and Catholic propagandist Nicholas Harpsfield, which form the focus of Chapter 1. Writing in 1557, the same year that saw the publication of a major volume of More's English works, Roper wrote to establish his credentials as conveyor of More's legacy, while Harpsfield offered More as a great Catholic 'protomartyr'—but within a year, the Protestant Elizabeth had come to the throne, and their writings could circulate only clandestinely. Indeed, the hunt for the manuscript writings of men such as Harpsfield was intense and often violent.

While More stood by his allegiance to the Pope, the Carmelite friar John Bale, the subject of Chapter 2, during the 1530s left his order, married, and became a propagandist for the Reformation cause. Bale is an extraordinary figure in the history of English life-writing: once a Carmelite hagiographer and biographer, he was to become an influential Protestant biographer—and indeed hagiographer. But almost alone among the millions of men and women who converted to Protestantism, Bale attempted to describe the process by telling his own life-story. Between the late 1530s and the late 1550s, he wrote his autobiography four times, and the four very different versions reveal much about the ever-changing nature of England's Reformation. It was Bale, too, who wrote what has been described as the first printed autobiography in English, *The Vocacyon of Iohan Bale* (1553), detailing the challenges of his time as bishop of Ossory in an Ireland that still held to the traditional religion, and his subsequent enforced flight to the safety of Protestant Europe.

While autobiographical treatments are rare, biographical writing was used by both Protestants and Catholics to present positive images of their respective confessional heroes. Bale, who as a Carmelite historian had been a long-time writer of the short biographies known as *viri illustres* as well as saints' lives, now pioneered the writing of the first Protestant and proto-Protestant martyrs' lives, in his 1540s works on the Wyclif supporter John Oldcastle, baron Cobham, and the Henrician martyr Anne Askew, published during the last years of Henry's reign, when Bale was in exile in Europe. While Bale had pointed the way to the Protestant martyr's life with his work on Oldcastle and Askew (and, less convincingly, himself), it was his friend and collaborator John Foxe who brought the genre to its fruition, with his massive and massively influential *Actes and Monuments* (first edition 1563), which modelled an exemplary Protestant suffering under the tyranny of the Roman Catholic Church. Widely and repeatedly read over the next two centuries, Foxe's 'Book of Martyrs', the subject of Chapter 3, is probably the most important collection of biographical life-writing in early modern England. It provided its readers not only with a sense of an ancient English Church that had been persecuted for centuries under the oppressive Roman Church, but also with a set of role-models to be emulated for their courage, resilience, and determination in the face of imprisonment, interrogation, and death at the stake.

Not all sixteenth-century life-writing is explicitly concerned with churchmen and martyrs. Around 1576, the musician, composer, and teacher Thomas Whythorne wrote his life-story in a manuscript 'Book of songs and sonetts', in which he revealed the real-life motivation behind the writing of hundreds of songs. While that life-story, the subject of Chapter 4, may not be entirely convincing—Whythorne has a suspicious tendency to present himself as the irresistible target for women's affections—the 'Book of songs and sonetts' certainly seems miles away from the heated clashes of the likes of Bale, Foxe, and Harpsfield. And yet Whythorne's life-story also reveals him as very close to some controversial figures whose doctrinal and political disputes are here strategically downplayed, and makes a bid for a new status for beleaguered English musicians suffering in the wake of the English Reformation's attack on ecclesiastical music-making.

One practical area that the Reformation affected severely was the remembrance of the dead. Traditionally, the dead had been commemorated by chantries and guilds praying for their souls in Purgatory and, as such, commemoration of the dead had been a key part of the economy, belief, and practice of the Catholic Church. With the abolition of Purgatory, the need to pray for the dead was, theoretically, eradicated—but there remained a strong affective desire to commemorate the dead. William Lambe, the subject of Chapter 5, serves as a test-case for the limitations of post-Reformation memorialization. Preparing for his death in 1580, Lambe mobilized every conceivable form of commemoration—almsgiving, the founding of a school and almshouses, charitable gifts and bequests to individuals, churches, companies, and the public at large, a funeral sermon and memorial sermons, a monument in the chancel—and in order to draw attention to those acts, Lambe also commissioned the writing of his life, in both verse and prose, broadsheet and book. But his many good works prompted whispers of papism that his life-writings could not silence.

The few diaries that survive from the earlier decades of the sixteenth century are either accounts of short periods of time (journeys, campaigns, pilgrimages) or professional records, largely financial. The late Elizabethan period, however, saw two innovations in the genre of the diary, startlingly different in kind. Three volumes of the diaries of the Exchequer teller Richard Stonley (1520–99) survive, ranging from 1581 to 1598, and share a common format: each day's entry includes the transcription of moral sayings from Scripture or classical learning, a set of financial accounts, and a brief narrative telling of the day's events. Stonley's diaries, the subject of Chapter 6, are a gold mine for historians wanting to track the price of commodities in late Elizabethan London, and his appetite for buying books makes him an appealing figure to literary historians. But in his insistent shaping of his days, Stonley reveals himself as something of a pioneer in the recording of domestic life. For his diaries—despite being meticulously kept—reveal very little of the most remarkable aspect of his career, one that eventually saw him lose his position and die in jail.

Stonley's diaries have almost nothing in common with the spiritual self-examination undertaken at the same time by Essex minister Richard Rogers, the subject of Chapter 7, which would become a model for so many godly men and women in the century that followed. Richard Rogers is a key figure in this book, the earliest surviving example of a Puritan minister keeping a daily journal of self-examination, a genre that was to spread quite widely—usually, I shall suggest, by personal example—and would establish itself as a standard feature of a certain strain of puritan life in areas of England and especially in New England. A substantial fragment of Rogers's own diary from the late 1580s survives, and reveals that Rogers returned to his diary repeatedly, comparing his current situation with his situation at various moments in the past—in other words, what appears to be a serial act of writing, in daily or near-daily form, is also an early form of sustained autobiographical writing. Rogers also expected this diary to be read: we see him reading the diary of one of his close friends, and carefully arranging for his own diary to be inherited and used by three of his minister relatives.

The late sixteenth century also saw the beginning of another trend that would peak in the seventeenth century, explored in Chapter 8: that of the funeral sermon, which often contained a biographical component. It was, in many ways, a controversial genre: some reformers deplored the practice as intrinsically popish, deeming its speaking of the dead as a sneaky form of intercession for them. And yet, within decades, it had become a highly popular form of commemoration. Ralph Houlbrooke has calculated that while only some twenty funeral sermons were printed during the Elizabethan period, by the end of the 1630s, the number had reached nearly 200, and by the end of the seventeenth century over a hundred sermons per decade were being published. Given that '[o]nly a miniscule proportion of the sermons preached found their way into print', it follows that the funeral sermon constitutes one of the most generative forms of life-writing in early modern England.[66] Among the most popular of printed sermons were the two written for Katherine Brettergh, a Lancashire puritan gentlewoman who died young in 1601, and whose struggle with Satan was to remain a touchstone of female piety for the next century. Yet their printed form betrays the anxieties felt about the funeral sermon, as a 'life' is appended to fill out the biographical portrait; and Brettergh's personal battle stands in for a concerted campaign against Lancashire Catholics.

There is a dominant strand of criticism that identifies the puritan diary as the foundation for the English autobiographical tradition—and indeed, as early as 1614, portions of Richard Kilby's diary were included in his *Hallelu-iah: Praise Yee the Lord, for the Unburthening of a Loaden Conscience*, which recounted his struggle with a serious illness.[67] The first half of the seventeenth century certainly saw the beginnings of the rise of what has been studied as 'Protestant autobiography'. In some cases, this took the form of an autobiographical narrative preceding the opening of a diary: in November 1634, Richard Rogers's grandson Samuel Rogers admitted that 'I have long bene thinking of a general view of my life; and some hurrying thoughts, or other have caused mee to desist often', but now, as he turned twenty-one, he was determined to 'begin then, and dally no longer',[68] while Ralph Josselin provided 'a summary view of my life' before embarking on his diary on 8 August 1644.[69] Other writings documented an important personal conversion. In the mid-1630s in heavily puritan Colchester, and under the influence of local preachers, two women—Cicely Johnson and Rose Thurgood—wrote accounts of their realization that they were among the chosen: Johnson in an 'ecstatic moment when she received assurance of her elect status while taking communion'; the poverty-stricken Thurgood in a 'sweet flash' as she lies ill and despairing in bed.[70] A few years later in Bermuda, the surveyor Richard Norwood wrote his 'Confessions', an account of his eventful life where the conversion was away from his Catholic tendencies.[71]

There is, however, a strong case to be made for the prior claim of Catholic life-writing, most often spurred by the dictates of an institutional director or spiritual confessor. The English Catholic Church had started to commission and collect the life-stories of its members—both spiritual and lay—as early as the 1580s.[72] Persecuted priests, including John Gerard and William Weston, wrote accounts of their sufferings at the hands of the Protestant authorities.[73] Novitiates at the English College in Rome told their life-stories in a set form prompted by a questionnaire; English nuns in continental houses were encouraged to record their conversions, again to a formula.[74] Tobie Matthew, the subject of Chapter 9, brought together many of these practices during his intriguing life. In 1611, he wrote an account of his conversion in the form of a letter to Dame Mary Gage, an English Benedictine nun in Brussels; over the next three decades, he would adapt and expand the letter as his life-story took some unexpected directions. Matthew also translated important Catholic life-writings, by Augustine and Teresa de Avila among others, for an English audience; in his later years, acting as a spiritual confessor to English nuns in the Low Countries, he encouraged them to write their own lives, with the models of Teresa and others to guide them.

While spiritual impulses and religious allegiances spark many life-writings of the period, other factors remained important. A good number of life-writings that have survived are, in effect, family histories: biographical or autobiographical accounts of a particular lineage, detailing the exploits of previous generations, usually for an intended readership of the family's future generations. But some life-writings speak to alternative family relationships. Chapter 10 explores three of them: the thrice-widowed Martha Moulsworth's poem about her life; Elizabeth Lucy's biography of her mother-in-law, Lady Constance Lucy; and the life of Elizabeth Lucy by her daughter Martha Eyre. It shows how Elizabeth Lucy sought to depict Lady Lucy as a ward, stepmother, mother-in-law, and intimate friend rather than daughter, wife, and mother; and how Moulsworth's poem obscures her very active role, during her widowhood, as a stepmother.

The turmoil from 1640 of civil war, commonwealth, interregnum, and restoration was another massive spur to life-writing. Many people found themselves displaced, both geographically and affectively, and writing their life-stories was one mechanism for dealing with that dislocation.[75] Notably, following the Restoration, several elite women attempted to rehabilitate their own or their husband's ruined reputations through life-writing: Lady Ann Fanshawe's *Memoirs* give an account of the travels she and her husband undertook during the Second Civil War and the Interregnum; Margaret Cavendish's *The Life of William Cavendish* re-presented the royalist military career of her husband; Lucy Hutchinson wrote to clear the name of her husband John Hutchinson, a parliamentarian officer who signed the death warrant for Charles I; and Lady Anne Halkett sought to rid herself of the accusation that she had known that her suitor, the royalist agent Colonel Joseph Bampfield, was already married.[76] But perhaps the most immediately felt impact was the sudden explosion in the early 1650s of printed biographies and autobiographies, especially the so-called 'enthusiastic' autobiography, from the likes of tailor Arise Evans, shoemaker Nicholas Smith, self-styled prophet Anna Trapnel, and nonconformist minister Richard Coppin;[77] many Quakers, Baptists, Muggletonians, and other nonconformists followed suit.[78] It was these publications that gave rise to the most famous of all seventeenth-century English autobiographies, John Bunyan's *Grace Abounding*, first published in 1666, which—according to some critics—led eventually to the novels of Daniel Defoe.[79]

Another phenomenon of the middle years of the seventeenth century was the rise of the new 'gathered churches'. These churches constituted themselves through the 'confessions' of their members, in which they related their conversion narratives—some of which were then published, as a collection, by their ministers.[80] This gathering of lives into collections would become a notable feature of the latter half of the century. In 1650, London saw the publication of minister Samuel Clarke's first collection of lives, covering both church fathers and modern divines. For his anthology, Clarke, the subject of Chapter 11, drew on whatever he could get his hands on: biographies appended to collected works, autobiographies, funeral sermons. From these materials he sculpted not only a series of lives, but, as he called it, the very 'marrow of ecclesiastical historie'. Readers were urged to contribute to the collection, and enough did to keep Clarke busy adding to his collections until his death in 1683: in the process he also encouraged a new genre of collected lives—worthies of England, Oxford alumni, Royalist loyalists, statesmen and favourites, poets, and playwrights.

Two of the most famous of such collections were compiled by Izaak Walton and John Aubrey, the subjects of Chapters 12 and 13 respectively. Walton claimed that he never intended to pen some of the lives for which he is famous: he saw himself more as a researcher and editor. But in his much-revised life of John Donne, initially designed as the preface for a collection of sermons, Walton contributed something new to English life-writing: the interweaving of a subject's speeches, letters, and literary works into the very fabric of the telling of his life. In the 1650s, John

Aubrey intended to write a life of his hero Sir Francis Bacon, but was beaten to it by Bacon's editor William Rawley. In later years, however, Aubrey set out not to write lives, but to collect a supplementary repository to be saved for posterity: what he called 'minutes of lives'—the kind of details that would otherwise be lost forever. Sometimes prurient and even scatological, Aubrey's 'minutes' not only record the sometimes ephemeral details of the lives of the great and good, but also insist on the importance of his informants, who might otherwise be utterly forgotten.

As the seventeenth century progressed, the diary became an increasingly popular genre. Men and women from all walks of life started to write daily records of their lives—not just their expenses and their activities, as earlier journal-keepers had done, but also their thoughts, their emotions, their dreams.[81] Following the lead of Richard Rogers, many were kept by churchmen: perhaps the best-known spiritual diary, brought to prominence in the 1970s by historian Alan Macfarlane, was written by Ralph Josselin, vicar of Earls Colne in Essex.[82] But from the Cambridge-trained ministers of Essex, the habit soon spread across the literate classes. We have surviving diaries from a Northampton town clerk (Robert Woodford), an East Anglian iconoclast (William Dowsing), a London artisan (Nehemiah Wallington), and a godly woman from Flintshire who was still writing her diary into her eighties (Sarah Savage).[83] And while the vast majority of diaries were kept by the aristocracy, gentry, and middling classes, there are signs of a wider appeal: Roger Lowe, apprentice to a mercer in Ashton-in-Makerfield, south Lancashire, started his diary in 1663, and kept it—irregularly, with sometimes long intervals between entries—for the next eleven years,[84] while the prophet Anne Bathurst's journal of mystical visions 'reveals her to have been on the very edge of illiteracy'.[85]

Not all diaries were designed to be morally edifying. Anne Clifford's surviving diaries are predominantly a record of her attempts to regain the lands and titles that her father had bequeathed away from her, while Katherine Austen's 'Book M' documents her long legal battles to gain control of her husband's estate.[86] Inner Temple student John Manningham's journal is at heart a jest book; the student Simonds D'Ewes kept a diary of gossip long before he kept his oft-cited parliamentary diary; Henry Slingsby admitted he regarded his diary as 'a recreation at vacant times, without observing any time, method, or order in my wrighting, or rather scribbling; et quicquid in Buccam venerit effutire [and blurt out whatever came into my mouth]'.[87] Some lasted a lifetime: John Evelyn's diary covers the period from 1620 to 1697, and is as much a record of the news of the world as it is the activities of its writer.[88] Yet, to some observers, the practice would remain ludicrous: in Ben Jonson's play *Volpone*, the ridiculous traveller Sir Politick Would-Be boasts of 'my *Diary*, | Wherein I note my actions of the day', which include noting that a rat has 'gnawne my spur-lethers', buying toothpicks, getting his silk stockings mended, 'and at St *Markes*, I vrin'd'.[89]

The most famous diary of seventeenth-century England—undertaken by Samuel Pepys at a moment of acute uncertainty just before the Restoration—is famed for its apparent spontaneity. Although famously frank in its detailing of Pepys's illicit sexual exploits, its form—written almost entirely in a painstaking shorthand—forces us to rethink Pepys's intentions. Pepys was hardly alone in writing in shorthand: the New England puritan minister Michael Wigglesworth and his Harvard contemporary, alchemist George Starkey, both turn to shorthand when detailing their sins, especially their sexual sins; and several women in the later seventeenth century are known to have kept diaries in shorthand—largely, it would seem, to prevent their husbands from reading them. And yet, as Chapter 14 makes clear, Pepys took the practice to new lengths: writing in shorthand, then in shorthand foreign languages, then in a shorthand polyglot, and finally in a shorthand polyglot-cum-babytalk. This escalation of obscurity parallels Pepys's increasingly reckless philandering—and the diary comes to an abrupt end as he realizes that he can no longer juggle the massively time-consuming activities of both adultery and writing about his adultery.

Several critics have noted the ways in which some seventeenth-century life-writing took on features from fictional writing, most notably romance, the perennially popular form to which Philip Sidney gave renewed impetus in his *Arcadia* (first published in 1591), and which remained in vogue throughout the century, thanks in part to an influx of French imports. With its convoluted and sensational plotting, its sudden reverses of fortune, and its improbable coincidences, romance provided a welcome heightening of the mundanities of real life. And since readers often read romance *à clef*—assuming that the fictional characters masked real-life figures—it made sense to render real life-writings as romance. So Sir Kenelm Digby cast himself as Theagenes and his wife Venetia Stanley as Stelliana in 'Loose fantasies', a romance allegedly drafted on the Mediterranean island of Milo in August 1628, and artfully revised thereafter.[90] The twenty-one-year-old Robert Boyle wrote the story of his first sixteen years as a third-person biography, 'An account of Philaretus during his minority', in which young Philaretus suffers 'Disasters', 'Afflictions', 'Contagion', and 'Accidents', but escapes death by drowning, a collapsing wall, and an apothecary's error through 'Providence'. Philaretus is himself prone to reading romances, which send him into a 'raving', but while travelling on the Continent he has a 'Conversion' during a storm at Geneva, and abandons his bad literary habits.[91] And the mode proved particularly popular with women: Julie Eckerle has traced romantic motifs and reader expectations in the life-writings of women as diverse as Dorothy Calthorpe, Lady Anne Halkett, Lady Ann Fanshawe, and the puritan

Mary Rich, countess of Warwick.[92] One even finds romance pushing through the seams of Lucy Hutchinson's life of her husband, as she has to tamp down its traces: 'If it were a Romance, wee should say...but...wee are relating wonders of Providence'.[93]

But perhaps the most extreme case of life meeting life-writing is that of Thomas Dangerfield, the subject of Chapter 15. The mid-seventeenth century saw the rise of a kind of 'rogue biography', inspired by Spanish picaresque novels with their seductive anti-heroes, in which the exploits of career criminals were related in a heightened form. Some, such as highwayman George Fidge and con artist Mary Carleton, were real figures; others, like Meriton Latroon, had a more complex relationship with reality. Thomas Dangerfield complicated the genre even further. His many criminal exploits were turned into something approaching fiction in *Don Tomazo* (1680), a work that melded criminal biography with the picaresque novel. But *Don Tomazo* came back to bite Dangerfield in real life, as it led readers to misinterpret his published diary, *Dangerfield's Memoires*, in 1685. In a final twist, Dangerfield's life, and especially his death—a bizarre event, stranger than any fiction—prompted reflections that influenced two of the most important life-writers of the early eighteenth century: John Dunton and Daniel Defoe.

Taken together, the case studies in this book show us that the critical stories told of life-writing in early modern England are overly simplistic. They do not support grandiose narratives of increased literacy, or emergent individualism, or the birth of a modern introspection, or the rise of the novel by other means. Instead, they show that innovations in life-writing occur in response to often very local political challenges and religious fluctuations. This book aims to listen to the contexts that gave rise to these early modern texts, and to pay attention to the diverse material writing practices that brought these heterogeneous genres into being—to look again at how lives were written in early modern England.

1

The Dangerous Lives of Sir Thomas More

In the spring of 1582, a pursuivant named Richard Topcliffe sat down to read a small vellum-bound manuscript, some eight by six inches. This manuscript, now in the library of Emmanuel College, Cambridge, bears the traces of its travels inscribed inside its front cover:

This booke was fovnde by Rich: Topclyff in M[r] Tho: Moares studdye emongs other bookes at Greenstreet M[r] wayfarers hovse when M[r] Moare was apprehended: the xiij[th] of Aprill 1582.[1]

In a new clampdown on English Catholic writings, Topcliffe had raided Greenstreet, a house in the parish of East Ham, supposedly occupied by Arden Waferer, a rich Catholic lawyer expelled from the Inner Temple in 1570 for his recusancy.[2] Greenstreet was no doubt targeted because it had recently been the site of a surreptitious, illegal printing press run by the Jesuit Robert Persons, dedicated to publishing books for the English Catholic community. There, in a study apparently used by a local recusant named Thomas More, Topcliffe found this manuscript, filled with writings by the Catholic controversialist Nicholas Harpsfield, who had died six years earlier. Among them was one that was especially pertinent to this Thomas More: a life of his grandfather, Sir Thomas More, the man who refused to accept Henry VIII as the Supreme Head of the Church of England, and as a consequence was executed for treason in 1535.[3]

Topcliffe's seizure of Harpsfield's manuscript was part of a campaign to eradicate a dangerous new phenomenon: the printing of books for English Catholics. In 1581, Edmund Campion, one of the first Jesuits to join the English Mission, had been captured, interrogated, tried, and then executed at Tyburn in December. While the English government put out an official publication denouncing Campion as a traitor, in the first week of Lent in 1582 a counter-narrative appeared, 'commending of

Campion and of his fellowes / and of theire deathe', a death which the title page referred to as a 'martyrdome'.[4] The authorities knew they had to suppress the book. William Fleetwood, the Recorder of London, launched an investigation to find those responsible for its writing and printing, working with pursuivant Topcliffe: he reported back to Lord Treasurer William Cecil, Lord Burghley that 'I pursued the matter so nere that I found the presse / the lettres the figures and a nosmber of the bookes', sending the Lord Treasurer 'a boxe of popish stampes [i.e. type]' as evidence of his diligence.[5] No materials related to the Campion publication were found at Greenstreet, but Topcliffe was equally interested in this prose life of Thomas More, known to be circulating clandestinely in manuscript.[6] The real-life connection of the manuscript with More's grandson at Greenstreet was suspicious enough to ensure that More was thrown into the Marshalsea prison for four years.

When he raided Greenstreet, Topcliffe, although fifty years old, was little known, but it would not be long before he became a byword for his zeal in pursuing Catholics and his sadism in interrogating them.[7] A typical eyewitness account comes from the Jesuit John Gerard, who in 1594 was questioned by a man 'who for many years now had conducted examinations under torture. His name was Topcliffe. He was a cruel creature and thirsted for the blood of Catholics. He had an uncommon cunning and slyness...He was old and hoary and a veteran in evil. Topcliffe looked up at me and glared. "You know who I am? I am Topcliffe. No doubt you have often heard people talk about me?"'[8] No doubt Gerard had. It was rumoured that Topcliffe had set up a torture chamber in his own residence; that he had impregnated a female prisoner and then used her to trap her own father; that he had sued a colleague for failing to pay him for promised services in killing his father and brother (who had died before Topcliffe could dispatch them).[9] In 1595, Topcliffe would boast to Queen Elizabeth herself–and probably justifiably–that 'I have helpt more traitors [to hang at Tyburn] than all the noblemen and gentlemen of the court, your counsellers excepted'.[10]

In April 1582, Topcliffe was just on the threshold of this ignoble career, but his habits were already starting to form. In later years, he would annotate his manuscripts and printed books with exuberant marginalia that bespeak a twisted mind. To help find the pages of printed Catholic books on which he had written vituperative marginal notes, he threaded blood-coloured silk.[11] On a series of examination reports of Jesuits in 1587, he doodled a tiny gallows next to each man condemned to die.[12] Now, as he read, Topcliffe filled the margins of the Harpsfield manuscript with pointed exclamations deriding its account.

In his 'Life of Sir Thomas More', Harpsfield's agenda is clear: to present More as 'the first as any whatsoeuer laye man in Englande that dyed a martyr for the defence and preseruation of the vnitie of the Catholike Churche'. Even when the English 'forsooke the vnitie of the Catholike Churche, and gaue the Popes spirituall supremacie to a temporall king', Henry VIII, Harpsfield writes, God was good enough to provide 'that euen in this Realme also should be those that should first of all people in the world confirme and seale the vnitie of the said Churche with their innocent bloud'—and of those laymen that died 'the very first was our woorthy Sir Thomas More'. More is thus 'our blessed Protomartyr of all the laitie for the preseruation of the vnitie of Christes Churche', 'a blessed martyr and happie martyr' whose name could be uttered alongside 'the blessed martyrs St Thomas of Douer and St Thomas of Caunterbury'—Thomas of Dover, who died defending his Benedictine priory under French attack in 1295, and Thomas Becket, assassinated in Canterbury Cathedral in 1170. While More's severed head might have been placed on a pole among the traitors on London Bridge, 'yet Sir Thomas Mores head had not so high a place vpon the pole as had his blessed soule among the celestiall holy martyrs in heauen'.[13]

Some of Topcliffe's comments correct the manuscript's admittedly wayward Greek and Latin transcriptions, but most provide a running commentary on the supposed qualities of its subject. When More reads Augustine's *City of God* in the church of St Laurence in London, Topcliffe protests, 'Master More a Lay man, to reade in the Church!'. When More says 'by our Ladye, for my part', Topcliffe congratulates him: 'well sworn sir'; and when More's wife says 'by God goe forwarde', Topcliffe gleefully notes 'Then Sr Tho: Mores wife could sweare too!' A reference to 'this worthy man, of whose storye we be in hande' prompts an angry 'All traytors!'. When Harpsfield writes that 'I suppose verilye he [More] was of himselfe very vnwilling to take vpon him' the office of Lord Chancellor, Topcliffe is not convinced: 'So doe not I'. When Harpsfield tells of how More 'would goe to the Churche and be confessed', Topcliffe retorts, 'He had better have gone to bed in prayer!'. A rare moment of approbation—and black humour—comes in response to the revelation that More mortified his body by self-flagellation: 'Whipp on! & smart enough.'[14] One passage in particular, in which More describes his fears for a Protestant future, truly galled the annotator:

> Then, saith he [More], shall Luthers Gospell come in, then shall Tindalls Testament be taken vp, then shall false heresies be preached, then shall the Sacramentes be sett at naught, then shall fasting and prayer be neglected, then shall holy Saintes be blasphemed, then shall Almightie God be displeased, then shall he withdrawe his grace and lett all runne to ruine, then shall all vertue be had in derision, then shall all vice reigne and runne forth vnbridled…

'No Sir,' protests Topcliffe, 'tis Christs gospell & Christs Testam*ent*', not Luther's and Tyndale's, before setting to work rewriting More's prediction: 'then shall the Sacramentes be *esteemed*, then shall fasting and prayer be *frequented*, then shall holy

Saintes be *honored*, then shall Almightie God be *appeased*…'. The thought that 'all vice' would 'reigne and runne forth' is branded 'a vile sclaunder', while More's impudence in foreseeing the future is mocked: 'w*ha*t then! was Sir Thom*as* More a prophet?'.[15]

These marginalia reveal 1582 as a particularly fraught moment in English religious history when the Protestant establishment felt itself under acute threat from Catholics: although More has been dead for over forty years, and Harpsfield's 'Life' is a quarter of a century old, for a man like Topcliffe that 'Life' is freshly dangerous, subversive, and heretical. And yet it was not written to be dangerous, subversive, or heretical. When Harpsfield composed his life of More in 1557, he wrote from a position of strength. The Catholic Mary I was on the throne, England had been saved from its unfortunate flirtation with Lutheranism, and the reputation of Thomas More was being rehabilitated, with a folio edition of his *English Workes* underway. Harpsfield also wrote with the personal imprimatur of More's inner circle: as his dedicatory epistle reveals, Harpsfield was charged with writing the life by More's own son-in-law, William Roper: 'if I haue erred', he jokes, then Roper has erred 'in *your* choyse, in that you appointed no meeter person'.[16] Roper not only commissioned Harpsfield to write the life, but gave him materials with which to do it, 'the good instructions diligently and truely by your industrie gathered, and whereof many ye knowe well by your owne experience, which ye haue imparted to me, and furnished me withall'.[17]

More's foremost biographer R. W. Chambers claimed in 1932 that Harpsfield has 'the honour of being the first modern to compile, in the English tongue, a complete biography, and thus to present an all-round picture of his hero' and that Roper was 'merely supplying, for Harpsfield's use, notes of what he himself knew'.[18] But few would now refer to Roper's work as 'notes'. It has become clear that it had a distinct life of its own: while Harpsfield's text survives in eight early modern manuscripts, Roper's is extant in a phenomenal twenty-seven (and was printed in 1626).[19] Roper's 'good instructions' are acknowledged as having influenced not only Harpsfield, but other early lives of More by Thomas Stapleton, 'Ro: Ba:', and Thomas More II's son Cresacre More.[20] And Roper's 'Life' has won plaudits from modern critics: C. S. Lewis praised it (at Harpsfield's expense), judging that Roper 'in small compass produced a masterpiece'; while Robert Gittings claimed that it was in Roper's 'More' 'that the welding of scientific observation with imaginative art, which is biography, showed its first sign', as 'human detail and character kept breaking through'.[21] And yet the praise of Roper's 'Life' is often linked to his distance from Harpsfield's all-too-clear ideological agenda: Michael A. Anderegg claims that while Harpsfield 'wishes to portray the martyr, the first layman in England to die for the unity of the Catholic church', Roper 'was satisfied with simply portraying the man'.[22] To see Roper's 'Life' as 'simply portraying the man', I shall suggest, is both to underestimate and to misunderstand it. In writing his life of Thomas More, William Roper had his own distinct agenda.

'I, William Roper'

Roper's 'Life of Sir Thomas More' opens with a remarkably long sentence that contains within it the key to the entire work:

> fforasmuche as Sir *Thomas Moore* knighte sometyme lorde Chauncelor of England, a man of singular virtue, & of a cleere vnspotted consciens, as witnessethe *Erasmus*, more pure & white then the whitest snowe, & of such an angelicall witt, as England (he saith) neuer had the like before, nor neuer shall againe, vnyvarsaly, aswell in the Lawes of our owne realme, a study in effecte able to occupy the whole life of a man, as in all other sciences right well studied, was in his dayes accompted a man worthy perpetuall famous memory: I, *William Roper* (thoughe most vnworthy) his sonne in lawe, by mariage of his eldest daughter, knowing no man that of him, & of his doings vnderstood so much as my self, for that I was contynually resident in his house, by the space of xvj yeares and more, thought it therefore my parte, to sett forth such matters towching his life, as I could at this present call to remembraunce.[23]

While More, his character and accomplishments, may appear to dominate the sentence, the subject is 'I, William Roper'—both grammatically and visually, for in the manuscript the 'fforasmuche', 'Thomas Moore', and 'I, William Roper' are penned in a larger hand, and inked in heavily. As much as sketching More, Roper uses his first sentence to assert his *bona fides* for writing the 'Life'. Closely related by marriage, living in the same house as More, Roper has the kind of personal access to his subject that 'no man', some twenty-odd years after More's death, can boast.[24] While More 'was in his dayes accompted a man worthy perpetuall famous memory', that famous memory has turned out not to be perpetual: he now needs Roper to write this life by 'call[ing] to remembraunce' the 'very many notable things (not meete to haue bine forgotten)', at the request of friends, 'to thentent the same should not at all vtterley perishe' (1).

As various critics have made clear, Roper's 'Life' is highly crafted.[25] In a move typical of both classical biography and medieval hagiography, Roper identifies moments in More's early life that prefigure his later character: when he was being raised in the household of Cardinal Morton,

> thoughe he was younge of yeares, yeat wold he at Christmas tyde soddenly sometimes steppe in among the players & neuer studying for the matter, make a parte of his owne there

presently among them, w*h*ich made the lookers on more sporte then all the plaiers aside. In whose witt & towardnes the Cardinall muche delightynge, wold often say of him vnto the nobles that divers tymes dined with him: This child here wayting at the table, whosoeu*er* shall liue to see it, will proue a mervailous man. (5)

Studied mention is made of his piety: after time spent at Lincoln's Inn and Furnival's Inn (which is skimmed over quickly), 'he gaue himselfe to devotion & prayer in the Charter house of London, religious lyvinge there, without vowe, about iiij^{er} yeares' (6). Although More falls in love with Master Colte's second daughter, 'yeat when he considered that it wold be both greate greif & some shame also to the eldest to see her yonger sister in mariage preferred before her, he then of a certayne pity framed his fancy towards her, & soone after [maryed] her' (6). The stand against his sovereign that ultimately costs him his life is prefigured in a stand-off with Henry VII, where More argues in parliament against a proposed heavy subsidy: the king is told that 'a beardless boy had disapointed all his purpose' (7). In revenge, since More had nothing to seize, the king 'devised a cawseles quarrel against [his] father, keeping him in the tower vntill he had made him pay to him an hundrethe pounds fyne' (7–8); and so on. More's moral and ethical credentials are established so that his eventual downfall appears to be the natural outcome of his accustomed principled behaviour. Throughout the 'Life', much is made of More as a devoted family man, and only a reluctant success in public life. And as is dictated by the genre of the *ars moriendi*, the art of dying well, his execution finds him cheerfully facing the next life, joking with the Lieutenant of the Tower, 'I pray you, m*aster* Leieutenaunte, see me salf vppe, & for my cominge downe let me shifte for my self', and begging his executioner, 'Plucke vpp thy spirites, man, & be not afrayde to do thine office; my necke is very shorte; take heede therefore thow strike not awrye, for savinge of thine honestye' (103).

Roper's 'Life' is often prized for its author's first-hand reminiscences of his father-in-law. But Roper himself seems less than certain about his ability to remember, and much of his narrative is dependent, sometimes explicitly, on other sources. He notes at the outset that 'very many notable things (not meete to haue bine forgotten) throughe neckligens & long contynuans [continuation] of tyme are slipped out of my mynde' (1–2). Despite his sixteen years of intimacy with More, he has no personal access to More's childhood and youth. At times he signals the gaps in his knowledge: details of More's early life are 'as I haue hearde reported' (7), while others are vouchsafed by More himself, 'as I haue herd him say' (8–9). Some elements are presumably transcribed from existing written accounts: one speech made by More asking to be discharged from the post of speaker is 'not nowe extant' (12) whereas the next speech is given *in extenso* over three manuscript pages. Roper admits that he was not present at More's arraignment, one of the crucial set pieces of his narrative, but instead his account 'haue I by the credyble reporte of the right worshipp*full* Sir Anthony Seintleger, knight, & p*ar*tely of Ric*hard* Heywood, & John webbe gentlemen, withe others of good creditt, at the hearing thereof present themselves, as farre as my poore witt & memory wold serue me, here truly rehersed vnto you' (96–7).

In fact, there is ample evidence that Roper turned to written documents, and especially More's own letters, to inform his biography.[26] Roper quotes 'the most godly word*es*' that Henry VIII spoke to More 'at his first coming into his noble service, the most vertuous lesson that euer prince taught his servant, willing him first to looke vnto god, & after god to him' (50). This lesson is to be found in three letters that More wrote (to Thomas Cromwell, his daughter Margaret, and Dr Nicholas Watson), all of which were printed in More's 1557 *Workes*: the closest match is in the letter to his daughter Margaret Roper, where he tells her that during his Tower interrogation, he answered 'that I had alway fro the begynning truely vsed my self, lookyng fyrst vppon god, and next vpon the king, accordinge to the lesson that hys hyghnes taught me at my fyrst cumming to his noble seruice, the most verteous lesson that euer prince taughte his seruante'.[27] Given that More recycled this *bon mot* in his letters so enthusiastically, it is entirely possible, of course, that Roper heard him say something similar—but in other cases, the debt to written documents is more clear-cut.

Roper goes on to relate that 'so pleased it his highnes further to say vnto him, that for the service that he before had done hym, in anye sute w*hi*ch he should after haue vnto him, that either should concerne his honor (for that word it liked his highnes to use vnto him) or that should app*er*taine vnto his p*ro*fitt, he should find his highnes good and gratious Lord vnto him' (52). This sentence is clearly drawn from a letter that More sent to Henry VIII where he asked the king to recall the conversation in which he had accepted More's resignation as Chancellor: 'It pleased your Highnes ferther to say un to me, that for the service which I had before done you (which it than liked your goodnes far above my deserving to commend) that in eny suit that I should after have unto your Highnes, which either should concerne myn honor (that word it liked your Highnes to use un to me) or that should perteyne unto my profit, I should fynd your Highnes good and graciouse lord un to me'.[28]

Roper writes himself into several scenes. Seeing Henry VIII walking with More in a garden at More's Chelsea home, 'holdinge his arme aboute his necke', Roper 'told Sir Thom*as* Moore, howe happy he was, whom the king had so familiarly entertayned, as I had neuer seene him to doe to any before, excepte Cardinall Wolsey, whom I once sawe him walke with, arme in arme' (21). He reports a conversation with More, 'on a tyme walking with me alonge the teames [Thames] side at

Chelsey' (24). In this way, Roper can lay claim to More's more private utterances. He tells of how More, hearing how some judges disliked his injunctions as Lord Chancellor, called them to dine in the council chamber at Westminster, and said 'fforasmuch as your selves my lordes, drive me to that necessity, for awardinge out Iniunctions, to releive the peoples iniury, you canot hereafter any more iustly blame me'. But '[a]fter that he said secreatly vnto me, I perceiue (sonne) why they like not so to doe: ffor they see that they may by the verdict of the Iurye cast of [i.e. off] all quarrells from them selves, vppon them which they accompte their chief defens, & therefore am I compelled to abide thadventure of all such reportes' (45). The intimacy between the two men is shown to increase, as they walk and talk in increasingly private spaces. Leaving his family at Chelsea, More takes a boat towards Lambeth 'with me and our foure servantes'. '[S]itting still sadly a while', More finally 'rounded me in the yeare'—whispering directly into Roper's ear—and said, 'Sonne Roper I thancke our Lord, the field is wonne.' Not knowing what More means, 'yeat loth to seeme ignorant', Roper answers, 'Sir I am thereof very glad.' But he decides that More meant that 'the love he had to god, wrought in him so effectually, that it conquered all his carnall affections vtterlye' (73). To C. S. Lewis, this display of ignorance can be read as a sign of Roper's humility—'he will cast himself for the fool's part if the anecdote demands it'[29]—but it also serves to underline the physical and emotional intimacy of More and Roper.

A Battle for Inheritance

Roper's centrality in the narrative is further ensured by the role taken by his wife, Margaret, notably during an incident he identifies as 'a manifest miraculous token of [God's] speciall favour towardes' More. Roper's wife, along with many others, was taken ill with the sweating sickness, and was despaired of by her many 'experte wise & wel learned' doctors. More 'by praier at gods hand sought to get her remedy'. Going into his chapel, 'vppon his knees, with teares most devoutly, besought all mighty god, that it wold like his goodnes, vnto whom nothinge was impossible, if it were his blessed will, at his mediation to vouchsafe gratiously to heare his petition; Where incontynent came into his mynd, that a glister [enema] shold be thonly way to helpe her'. When he told the physicians, 'they by & by confessed, that if there were any hope of health, that *that* was the very best helpe indead, much marvalinge of themselfes, that they had not before remembred it'. Administered to Margaret sleeping—Roper notes that his wife 'could by no meanes haue bine brought vnto wakinge'—the enema served to wake her (28–9). Roper's wife thus becomes the embodied evidence that More's prayers are directly answered by God.

Margaret's (and therefore William's) privileged access to More extends to his body. While his fine outer clothing befitted his elevated post, 'inwardly he no such vanityes esteeming, secreatly next his body ware he a shirte of heare', and 'vsed sometimes to pvnishe his body with whippes, the cordes knotted, *which* was knowen only to my wife his eldest daughter, whom for secrecy aboue all other he specially trusted, causing her, as need required, to washe the same shirte of heare'. This hair shirt figures in an anecdote that Roper uses to stress both Margaret's knowledge and the ignorance of a rival in-law, the wife of More's son John:

> my sister Moore, a yong gentlewoman, in the sommer, as he sate at supper singly in his doublet & hose, wearing thervppo*n* a plaine shirte, without ruffe or coller, chauncing to spye it, began to laughe at it: my wife not ignorant of his manner p*er*ceyuinge the same, pryvily told him of it. And he beinge sory that she sawe it presently amended the same. (48–9)

The slight against his sister-in-law is not unique and far from accidental. Roper has already reported how, during More's Lord Chancellorship, 'one of his sonnes in lawe said merily vnto him' that when Cardinal Thomas Wolsey was Lord Chancellor, various members of his privy chamber and door-keepers 'gatt greate gayne'. Roper explains that since this son-in-law 'had married one of [More's] daughters, &'–like Wolsey's chamberers and door-keepers–'gaue still attendaunce vppon him, he thought he mighte of reason look for som*me*; where he indeed…could find none, *which* was to him a great discourage'. The son-in-law was obliged not to accept gifts from those wanting to be brought into More's presence–who 'wold gladly haue his furtheraunce'–and while he found this refusal to be influenced by gifts 'very comendable' in his father-in-law, 'yeat to him said he being his sonne he found it nothing p*ro*fitable'. More responds with a homily on justice that quashes any suggestion of familial favouritism: if 'my father stood on the one side, and the divill on the tother, his cause being good, the divill should have right'. Another son-in-law, Giles Heron, saw this in practice, Roper continues, when 'presuming to[o] much on his favour' when he had a suit in the court of Chancery, More 'wold by him in no wise be p*er*swaded, to agre to anye indifferent order, then made he in conclusion a flatt decre against him' (42–3). In each case, Roper hints, and none too subtly, that the other sons- and daughters-in-law are more interested in the social advantage More can bring to them than genuinely sympathetic to him.

The implicit favour displayed by More towards the Ropers culminates in the arrangements he makes for their inheritance. After giving over his office and worldly affairs, Roper writes, More made 'a conveyaunce for *th*e dispositio*n* [disposing] of all his land*es*, reseruinge to himself an estate thereof only for tearme of his owne life & after his decease, assuringe some p*ar*te of the same to his wife, some to his sonnes wife for a Joynture, in consideracion that she was an inheretrice in possession of more then an houndred poundes landes by the yeare, & some to me & my wife in recompence of our marriage money, with divers remaynders ouer'. Roper is at pains to insist that '[a]ll which conveyaunce & assurance was parfitelye finished, longe before that matter (wherevppon he was attainted) was made an offence'—that is, before More was accused of treason, a charge that carried with it not only the death of the traitor but also the disinheritance of his family. But despite this careful deed of feoffment, More's wishes did not come to pass. The conveyance was 'after by statute clearly avoided [made void]. And so were all his landes, that he had to his wife & children, by the said conveyaunce in such sorte assured, contrary to thorder [the order] of lawe, taken away from them, & brought into the kings handes'. The only exception was 'that porcion that he had apointed to my wife and me in possession' (69).[30] This was because the statute in question 'had vndone onely the firste conveyaunce, geeving no more to the kinge, but so much as passed by that', while '[t]he seconde conveyaunce, whereby it was geeven to my wife & me, being dated two dayes after was without [beyond] the compasse of the statute. And so was our porcion to vs by that meanes clearely reserved' (80). What this meant, in practice, was that the Ropers (and after Margaret's death in 1544, William) were able to stay on More's Chelsea estate in a house known as Butts Close.

This detailed attention to the legal transactions that allow the Ropers, alone among More's children, to maintain their property is only the most material example of Roper's concern for how Thomas More will be bequeathed to future generations. It can also be seen in his arrangement of documents and objects in the telling of More's life. There is only one document that Roper explicitly quotes: 'a letter written with a coale' sent from prison by More to Margaret the day before his death 'plainely expressing the fervent desire he had to suffer in the morowe [i.e. die on the next day]'. Roper reports its direct address to his wife:

> I comber you, good Margaret much, but I wold be sory if it should be any longer then to morowe, ffor to morowe is St Thomas even, & the vtas of St Peeter. And therefore too morowe, longe I to goe to god, it were a daye very meete & convenient for me, &c. I neuer liked your manners better, then when you kissed me last. ffor I like when daughterly loue, & deere charitye, hath no leysure to looke to worldly curtesye. (99–100)

More is here referring to the memorable and touching incident, also recorded by Roper, when More made his final journey from Westminster down the river to the Tower of London. Margaret, knowing this would be her last chance to see her father, waited on Tower Wharf. 'Assone as she sawe him, after his blessing on her knees reuerently receaued, Shee hastinge towards him, & without consideracion or care of her self, pressinge amonge the thronge and company of the garde, that with halberds & bills wente round aboute him, hastely ranne to him, & there openly, in the sight of them all, imbraced him, tooke him about the neck & kissed him.' More, 'well liking her moste naturall & deere daughterlye affection towardes him, gaue her his fatherly blessing, & many goodly wordes of comforte besides' (98). But Margaret is 'not satisfied' with this, and 'having respecte neyther to her self, nor to the presse of people & multitude, that were aboute him, sodainely retorned back againe, ranne to him (as before) tooke him about the neck, & divers tymes together most lovingly kissed him'.[31] Only then did Margaret take her leave. The spectacle of such intense daughterly affection in turn affected its audience: 'The beholding whereof was to many of them that were present thereat so lamentable, that it made them for very sorowe to mourne and weape' (98–9). This letter therefore places Margaret and her intense relationship with More at the centre of More's penultimate day. Moreover, with this letter 'he sent his shirte of heare (not willing to haue it seene) to my wife his deerely beloved daughter' (99): Margaret thus becomes the recipient and guardian of the testimony to More's most secret pious habits.

That last letter, as Roper notes, is 'contayned in the foresaid booke of his workes' (99)—and indeed, in the *Workes* it is billed as 'the laste thynge that euer [More] wrote'. In excerpting a single paragraph from the letter, Roper implies that it is focused exclusively on his wife Margaret. As printed in the *Workes*, by contrast, the letter instead reads like More's last will and testament. It opens with an invocation that God should bless Margaret 'and youre good housbande, and youre lyttle boye, and all yours, and all my children, and all my Goddechyldren, and all oure frendes'. The bulk of the letter is a litany of requests for Margaret to act as an intermediary for messages and gifts to multiple members of More's household. Daughter Cecily is sent a handkerchief. Daughter Elizabeth is given instructions about what to do with a 'picture in parchemente'. Maids Dorothy Coly and Joan Aleyne are singled out. Foster-daughter Margaret is sent back 'her algorisme stone'. And the final paragraph is devoted not to the recipient, but to More's son John and his wife and family:

> I praye yow at time conuenient recommende me to my good sonne John More. I liked wel his naturall fashion. Our lorde blesse hym & his good wyfe my louing doughter, to whom I praye him be goode as he hathe greate cause: and that yf the lande of myne come to his hande, he breake not my wyll concernynge his sister Daunce. And oure Lorde blisse Thomas and Austen and all that they shal haue.[32]

So Thomas More's last writing ends with the firm desire that his son John should inherit a parcel of his father's land, and a blessing for his grandsons Thomas and Austin—the same Thomas who will be arrested by Richard Topcliffe in 1582.

The More Legacies

Roper's life, however, ends with a very different view of the More family. The news of More's death is brought to the Holy Roman Emperor Charles V by the English ambassador, Sir Thomas Elyot. After Elyot confirms the news of the execution, the emperor says, '[W]ell... it is too true: And this will we say, that if we had bine maister of such a servante, of whose doings our selfe haue had these many yeares no small experience, we wold rather haue lost, the best city of our dominions, then haue lost such a worthy councell*our*' (104). At one level, this anecdote neatly reverses More's own prophecy that, despite his intimacy with the king, 'if my head wold winne him a castle in ffraunce... it should not faile to goe' (21). Roper's account of the emperor's praise gripped the imagination of the biographers that followed him, but, as several critics have pointed out, the story is a historical impossibility: Elyot's stint as ambassador ended in April 1532, and at the time of More's death in 1535, Elyot was in Oxfordshire.[33] So it seems that Roper has confected this pivotal scene, to include not only the praise of a major Catholic ruler but also the words of the man who by the time Roper came to pen his treatise had become England's most prominent humanist scholar, Sir Thomas Elyot.

But more important to Roper is the scene he provides for the story's retelling: this praise 'was by the same Sir Thomas Eliott to my self, to my wife, to maister Clement, & his wife, to m*aster* John Haywood, & his wife, and diuers other his ffriends accordingly reported' (104). Here the 'Life of More' ends: but with a new cast to pass Thomas More to posterity. William Roper, John Clement, and John Heywood represent More's next generation, thanks to their unnamed wives: respectively, More's daughter Margaret, More's foster-daughter Margaret Giggs, and More's niece Joan Rastell. But they constitute a very partial representation of More's posterity. To see how odd this gathering is, one need only look at how More's family and household were represented visually during the sixteenth century. In 1527–8, Hans Holbein executed a portrait of the More family; while it was destroyed in the eighteenth century, a surviving sketch shows what it contained (Fig. 1). Holbein painted More with his father John, his second wife Lady Alice, his four children (Margaret, Elizabeth, Cecily, and John), and three quasi-children: the family 'fool' Henry Pattenson, the foster-daughter Margaret Giggs, and the ward Anne Cresacre, who would marry John More. More's three sons-in-law, including Roper, are notably absent from the family portrait. Compare that with Rowland Lockey's 1590s representation of the More family, now in London's National Portrait Gallery, clearly based on the Holbein portrait (Fig. 2). Lockey's rendition deletes from the 1527 grouping Lady Alice, Pattenson, and Margaret Giggs, and presents, instead of a

Figure 1. Hans Holbein, Study for the family portrait of Thomas More, 1527-8. Kupferstichkabinett, Öffentliche Kunstsammlung, Basel.

Figure 2. Rowland Lockey, The More family, 1590s. © National Portrait Gallery, London.

household, a celebration of bloodlines. A second group, to the right of the painting, is anchored by John More's son Thomas (the owner of the Harpsfield manuscript) and comprises his wife Maria and his sons John and Christopher Cresacre; Thomas's mother Anne Cresacre More appears again in a portrait hanging on the wall. Taken together, the two groups present the More legacy through the dynastic male line.

By contrast, the closing image of Roper's life of More suggests a different legacy for his hero. William and Margaret Roper, John and Margaret Clement, John and Joan Heywood: these are figures close to More as martyr, and the key figures in his planned rehabilitation. As we have seen, Roper represented his wife Margaret as the dominant figure in More's life; John Clement had been imprisoned in the Tower with More, and he and his wife fled to Louvain during the reign of Edward VI, staying with More's friend Antonio Bonvisi. The Clements' daughter Winifred died in exile in Louvain in 1553, but her husband William Rastell, Joan Heywood's brother, returned to England when Mary came to the throne. There in 1555 he became a serjeant-at-law, his two patrons for the post being Cardinal Reginald Pole and William Roper, a fellow bencher of Lincoln's Inn; in 1556, again with Roper's assistance, he became standing counsel to the city of Canterbury; and in 1557 he would publish More's *English Workes*. In other words, these are the figures that witnessed the most profound sufferings of Thomas More, and were now leading the rehabilitation of his reputation in print.

Nicholas Harpsfield was also an integral part of this group. Like the Clements, he spent the Edwardian years with Bonvisi in Louvain; under Mary, he worked closely with William Rastell in Canterbury—it is by no means inconceivable that his life of More was intended for inclusion in the 1557 *English Workes*. Certainly, it remains scrupulously on-message in relaying Roper's instructions. The account of the land transfers to the Ropers is repeated verbatim. The praise of Margaret Roper is, if anything, amplified. In Harpsfield's life, the erasure of John More is even more marked. He appears precisely once—as he is born, as Harpsfield relates that More had by his first wife 'three daughters and one sonne, called John More, to whom *Erasmus* did dedicate Aristotles workes printed by Bebelius'.[34]

But Harpsfield gives Roper another role to play. Having recounted—again almost verbatim from Roper—the miraculous recovery of Margaret Roper, Harpsfield mentions Roper's children, and then has 'occasion somewhat to interlace of the saide *Master* William Roper'. He recounts how at the time of his marriage, Roper was 'a meruailous zealous Protestant', 'so feruent... that he tooke the brydle into the teeth, and ranne forth like a headstronge horse, harde to be plucked backe againe'. Speaking publicly of 'his newe doctrine', even at Paul's Cross, Roper skipped close to the wind, spending time with merchants who were 'openly for heresie at Paules Crosse abiured' by Cardinal Wolsey: Roper, 'for loue borne by the Cardinall to Sir Thomas More his father in lawe, was with a frendly warning discharged'.[35] In his dedicatory epistle to Roper, Harpsfield insists that 'I am not ignorant, that ye come of a woorthye pedigree, both by the ffather and mothers side' and traces that pedigree to important actions as far back as the Norman Conquest. 'But yet', he continues, 'you and your familie are by no one thing more adorned, illustred, and beautified, then by this woorthy man Sir Thomas More, in marying his daughter, the excellent, learned, and vertuous matrone mistris Margaret More: He was your woorthy ffather in lawe: what say I? your father in lawe? nay, rather your verye father in deede; and though a temporall man, yet your very spirituall father'—a spiritual father who 'recouered your lost soule', who in effect converted him, when the youthful Roper was 'ouerwhelmed, and full deepe drowned in the deadly dreadfull depth of horrible heresies'.[36] In a brilliant move, Harpsfield not only makes explicit what Roper pushes at with such insistence—that it is he, William Roper, who is the true son of Sir Thomas More—but recasts the story as a conversion narrative in which More miraculously reclaims the soul of his lost son Roper, the layman becoming a 'spirituall father'.

Topcliffe and Harpsfield

The heretic-hunter and life-annotator Richard Topcliffe, scribbling in the margins a quarter of a century after Harpsfield wrote, did not care about William Roper's claim to be More's son. Indeed, despite the angry marginalia, he was not primarily interested in Sir Thomas More—but in the author of the 'Life', Nicholas Harpsfield. During the reign of Mary I (1553–8), Harpsfield had risen spectacularly in the Catholic Church to become archdeacon of Canterbury and vicar-general of London.[37] He used his powers to attack Protestants, undertaking a visitation of London that prosecuted about 400 offenders, and instigating multiple heresy trials in Canterbury: it was due to Harpsfield's 'unmercifull nature and agrest [rough] disposition', recalled the Protestant historian John Foxe, that 'very many were put to death in that dioces of Canterbury'.[38] It was from this position of institutional strength that Harpsfield wrote to establish More among the 'celestiall holy martyrs in heauen' whose 'hartie deuout' intercession had, in effect, ensured the current victory of the cause: 'God of late hath the sooner cast his pitifull eye to reduce vs againe by his blessed minister and Queene, Lady Mary, and by the noble, virtuous, excellent Prelate, Cardinall Poole, to the vnitie of the Churche that we had before abandoned.'[39] With hindsight, of course, we know the Marian glory days were numbered: within twenty-four hours, on 17 November 1558, both Mary and Reginald Pole died; months later, Harpsfield was stripped of his offices, and placed in the Fleet prison, where he would remain for twelve years.

Although he was deemed dangerous enough in 1562 to be denied visitors, Harpsfield still managed to pen a vast attack on the new Protestant martyrologies, which was smuggled out and published pseudonymously in 1566, and his writings were the basis of printed books by Nicholas Sander and Girolamo Pollini.[40] Harpsfield's power to fuel the Catholic propaganda machine, even from within prison walls, was of particular annoyance to Topcliffe—as we know, once again, because he told us about it in his marginalia. His copy of Pollini's *L'historia ecclesiastica della Rivoluzion d'Inghilterra* (1594)—a work that drew directly on Harpsfield's writings—survives in Exeter University Library, and Topcliffe's notes refer to Harpsfield constantly.[41] Despite the fact that Harpsfield is nowhere mentioned on the title page, Topcliffe inscribes his copy with the information that Harpsfield is 'a hateful Enemy to Queen Elizabeth', and later elaborates that 'owt of this doctor Nicolass Harpsfildes Englishe written Booke, All the veanom & poysonne matter within this Booke doth Springe to his Imortall shayme'.[42] The 'Englishe written Booke' to which Topcliffe refers was 'A Treatise of Doctor Nicholas Harpesfeilds Concerning Marriage, occasioned by the pretended Diuourse betweene King Henry the Eight and Queene Katherine', which retold the story of the English Reformation from a decidedly unsympathetic perspective;[43] Topcliffe claimed that this was the work of Harpsfield, Bishop Edmund Bonner, Sir Thomas Fitzherbert, and Dr Nicholas Sander—'Ohe rabell of tratowrs'—'who did Compile together *the* English history whiche I have Extant, writen by doctor harpesfild when *they* together All were presoners in *the* fleet [Fleet prison] & In the Marshallsee, A*nno* 1: and 2: Elyza*beth*' (i.e. 1558–60).[44] After a sober assessment of the case for the king's divorce, Harpsfield's 'Treatise' descends into entertaining scurrility, claiming that Anne Boleyn had six fingers on each hand, and that Henry VIII could have been Anne's father, since he had an affair with her mother; with particular venom reserved for Archbishop Thomas Cranmer who, Harpsfield claims, was secretly married and 'sometymes Carried [his wife] about him with him in a greate Chest full of holes that his prittie Nobsey might take breath at'.[45]

This kind of out-and-out propaganda might seem to be in a different register to his hagiographic life of Thomas More, but Harpsfield himself opens the 'Treatise' by linking the two firmly: 'fforasmuch as this matter is incident to the life and dooinges of Sir Thomas Moore, And forasmuch as wee haue for causes before by vs rehearsed obliged our selues by promise for this treatise wee haue now to discharge and disburden vs of the said promise taken the matter in hand and after some sort perfected and finished it'.[46] In other words, the 'Treatise...occasioned by the pretended Diuourse' is a sequel to his life of More—or perhaps more pertinently, the life of More is the first instalment in Nicholas Harpsfield's Catholic history of the English Reformation. Although the reputation of Thomas More himself was 'still very much up for grabs' in the 1580s,[47] Topcliffe certainly regarded Harpsfield's life of More as itself a piece of heretical treason.

The cost of this writing was extreme. After the raid on Greenstreet, Topcliffe turned his attention in July 1582 to a house in London's Hart Street, home to a printer named William Carter. This was no random choice: in his marginalia, Topcliffe explains that Carter had lived with Harpsfield, 'who did bringe hym vp *with* ovld Caw[ood,] printer', apprenticing him to the Queen's printer John Cawood. Carter became 'skillfvll in *the* arte of printing, was Learned in *the* Tunges: hee did printe many tratoroos Books', including *The Treatise of Schism*.[48] This time Topcliffe struck gold, uncovering manuscripts of Campion's debates in prison, which had been copied for Carter to publish.[49] Within weeks, most of those involved in the Campion book had been apprehended and punished: the poet Stephen Vallenger, who contributed some verses, was fined, imprisoned, and lost both his ears; its author Thomas Alfield would later be hanged for the 'dispersing of slaunderous bookes against the execution of justice'; only the printer, Richard Rowlande *alias* Verstegan, was able to flee to the Continent.[50] Carter's fate was perhaps worst. Topcliffe alleged that he had been selling manuscript copies of Harpsfield's treatise for £20: 'That same Orygenall written Booke By doct*o*r Nicolas harppesfild I did fynde in this William Carters Cvstodye, whiche the *Queenes* Maie*st*y hath Seene, & hath Redde of, & her highnes did Com*m*ande mee to keepe, which I have Extant still for her maie*sties* Service.'[51] William Carter would spend the next two years in prison, being interrogated by Topcliffe and his men, before being hanged, drawn, and quartered at Tyburn on 11 January 1584. For his sufferings, he was claimed as a Catholic martyr: the second edition of the anonymously published *Concertatio ecclesiae Catholicae in Anglia* (1588), a documentary account of the persecution of Catholics in England, featured a lengthy biography of William Carter alongside those of Thomas More and Edmund Campion.[52]

The fortunes of men such as Harpsfield and Carter show us quite vividly what could be at stake in the writing, copying, printing, and publishing of controversial Catholic life-writings during the reign of Elizabeth. But these high stakes were not a perennial feature. For Roper writing in 1557, the life is the means by which he lays claim to the legacy of his father-in-law. For Harpsfield in the same year, the life of More is a mainstream work of hagiography. It is only for Topcliffe twenty-five years later that a life of More is a dangerously seditious tract. And these life-writings retained their political potency into the twentieth century, when Elsie Vaughan

Hitchcock edited the lives by Harpsfield and Roper in 1932 and 1935 respectively, as her collaborator R. W. Chambers was completing his 1935 biography of More. When on 19 May 1935, four centuries after his execution, Thomas More was canonized, Pope Pius XI sent a medallion to Hitchcock and Chambers 'in appreciation of the work they did, and the honour they paid to the memory of St. Thomas More'.[53]

2

The Reformed Lives of John Bale

John Bale (1495–1563) is remembered for many things, as 'a prolific author, editor, preacher, dramatist, controversialist, antiquary, scholar, collector of books and manuscripts, bibliographer, historian, biblical commentator, and evangelical bishop'.[1] To that list we need to add 'life-writer', for Bale was perhaps the most prolific English life-writer of the sixteenth century. He spent years recording the lives and achievements of British writers in a series of massive catalogues that present Bale not only as prolific biographer, but also serial autobiographer: in each iteration of his catalogue of learned men he included an entry on himself. He justified this move in the first iteration: 'I insert myself among the others–though I am the least of them all–so that those that come after know that I, like them, have not been always idle.'[2] And in 1553, he authored what has been claimed as 'the first separately printed autobiography in English', *The Vocacyon of Iohan Bale*.[3]

When the seventeenth-century collector of lives Thomas Fuller included Bale among his *Worthies of England*, he placed him at the head of the list of Suffolk writers 'Since the Reformation',[4] and in many ways Bale embodied the spirit of the early English Reformation–angry, outspoken, iconoclastic.[5] In a torrent of prose works and plays, he created a new history for the Reformed Church of England, casting the Roman Church as a belated, foreign perversion of an ancient true British Church, and providing scurrilous anti-clerical polemics in which he gleefully exposed the alleged doctrinal and sexual misconduct of Catholic friars, monks, and nuns, in a splenetic, vituperative, prurient, scatological rant that led Fuller to dub him 'Biliosus Balæus'.[6] But Bale was not only '*Since* the Reformation', as Fuller puts it. He also spent almost thirty years within the Roman Catholic Church as a committed Carmelite friar; it was only when he broke his vows, left the order, and married that he embarked on his career as a Protestant propagandist. The life of John Bale is broken across the English Reformation.

Although the Carmelite Bale collected and wrote saints' lives,[7] the bulk of his output was not hagiographic. Instead, he put his considerable energies into composing *viri illustres*, the lives of famous men,[8] a genre usually traced to the Roman historian Suetonius, whose *De viris illustribus* (*On Famous Men*) comprised short sketches of grammarians, rhetoricians, poets, and historians that also mentioned their principal works. Bale cited as his main influences the churchmen who had co-opted the genre for Catholicism: St Jerome, whose fifth-century *De viris illustribus* commemorating 135 Christian figures was continued by Gennadius of Massilia; John Trisse, a fourteenth-century Carmelite from Nîmes, who produced a list of priors general of the order;[9] and the German Benedictine abbot Johannes Trithemius, whose *Liber de scriptoribus ecclesiasticis* (1494) provided Bale with his more detailed format—a brief 'life' of the author, a list of works giving each title, the number of books in the work, and the 'incipit' (first line) of the work (although many of these are missing), with perhaps a short comment following.[10]

Bale's early research naturally took as its focus the lives of learned English Carmelites. Surviving manuscripts reveal that he toured houses of the order, in England and abroad, taking notes from the documents they held, and gathering information first-hand from the friars.[11] As Bale later recalled, the impending Reformation prompted an intensifying of his research:

> [S]ince in 1533 I had foreseen by means of true arguments that the most just destruction of the monasteries of England was near at hand on account of the abominable sins of their inhabitants and their contempt for truth, through the singular gift of God I immediately betook myself to libraries of the Austins and Carmelites, who were familiar to me and welcoming...I would have done the same at the Dominicans and Minorites, Carthusians, Brigittines, and other orders too if they had not rudely refused me entrance.[12]

'For three years', Bale recalled, 'I laboured, collecting the authors and titles of various books, along with the incipits of certain of them'.[13] Those three years witnessed seismic changes in his life. In 1533, Bale was prior of the Carmelite house at Ipswich; the following year, he would become prior at Doncaster. But in 1536, Bale left the order after almost thirty years, becoming a stipendiary priest at Thorndon in Suffolk. That summer, he completed a work he called 'Anglorum Heliades', dedicating it to the antiquarian scholar John Leland (1503?–53), who had received a royal license 'to peruse and dylygently to searche all the lybraryes of monasteryes and collegies' in England to research his own *De uiris illustribus*, a planned four-volume history of 'them who hathe been lernid, and who hath writen from tyme to tyme in this realme'.[14] Bale reminded Leland that 'you have assigned me the task to describe for you the coming into England of the Carmelites, and how the order has grown since then, and to compile for you a catalogue of its illustrious men'.[15] But Leland made less use of his labours than Bale hoped,[16] and ultimately abandoned the project when he suffered a breakdown in 1547. As Bale was told, 'Maistre Ley[l]ande... is in such a frenesy at thys present, that lytle hope I haue of hys recouer... It hath pleased god that he shuld thus be depryued of hys wyttes'.[17]

With Leland incapacitated, Bale attempted to bring his *De uiris illustribus* to fruition himself; a version of his labours survives in the library of Trinity College, Cambridge. But, as James Carley has shown, by the late 1540s, Bale was unable or unwilling to let some of Leland's verdicts pass. For Bale, the English Reformation did not start in the 1520s, but must be projected back through history. This meant that the learned men of the past were not above reproach: those who had attacked the proto-reformer John Wyclif in the early fifteenth century were to be treated with the same contempt as those who attacked William Tyndale one hundred years later. To take just one example, Leland had devoted a short entry to one John Sharpe:

> As old libraries reveal, John Sharpe was highly regarded among the philosophers and theologians of his time; the great dispute he had with the Wycliffites added something to the renown of his name. For he struck fiercely with the sword of the Gospel against those loathsome hydras who were rearing on high new heads of virulent disquisitions over the sacrament of the Eucharist.[18]

Bale not only presented a different picture of Sharpe, but attacked Leland's praise head-on:

> Weigh carefully the preposterous judgement of Leland here. He says that the most barbarous sophist is a famous theologian. Pious doctors he calls hydras. And he says that the most frigid—actually the most iniquitous glosses of the papists are the sword of the Gospel. Observe, however, what sort of people Sharpe and his peers were from their writings.[19]

Unable to let the matter go, Bale was still pursuing it in his printed *Catalogus* of 1557–9, liberally quoting Leland only to cut him down.[20] But in rewriting the history of pre-Reformation England, Bale would also need to rewrite himself.

Bale's Conversions

Over the course of the sixteenth century, many practising English Catholics became Protestants. One might imagine that these conversions would give rise to a corresponding multitude of written life-stories, tracking this momentous change.

But while 'conversion narratives' would become common in the seventeenth century, almost no sixteenth-century English man or woman wrote such a life.[21] Judith Pollman has proposed that 'Sixteenth-century conversions took place in a cultural and emotional setting that radically differed from that of the Protestant soul-searchers of the seventeenth century; sixteenth-century converts probably had good reasons for experiencing a conversion without turning it into a conversion experience of the Pauline and Augustinian type'.[22] There is an exception, however, and he wrote not one account of his conversion, but four.

The four sketches of John Bale's life, written between *c.* 1539 and 1558, awkwardly reflect the uneven developments of the English Reformations. In 1539, when he wrote the 'Fasciculus Carmelitarum' and the 'Anglorum Heliades', he had recently left the Carmelite order, and was working for Henry VIII's leading counsellor, Thomas Cromwell, writing and acting in a series of propagandistic plays. But when Cromwell fell in 1540 and the king reneged on some of his reformist policies, Bale fled to the Continent, launching a prolific new career as a Protestant polemicist. His third life appeared in his *Illustrium maioris Britanniae...summarium*, a catalogue of British writers, published in Wesel in 1548, and dedicated to the new king, Edward VI, in a bid for royal favour. That patronage was granted only belatedly in 1552, when Bale was nominated to the Irish see of Ossory, an appointment whose unhappy tale he recounted in the *Vocacyon*. Forced out of Ireland after Mary I's accession in 1553, Bale once again fled abroad, and it was in Basel that he wrote his fourth life, for the two-volume *Scriptorum illustrium maioris Brytannicae...catalogus*, published in 1557–9. After Elizabeth succeeded Mary in November 1558, Bale returned to England for the last time, spending his final years as a prebendary in Canterbury, where he died in 1563.

Above and beyond any necessary updating required from 1539 to 1548 to 1557, Bale radically revised his autobiography each time, adding and subtracting details, and casting events in a new light. The facts of his early life are consistent in all four sketches, although Bale's presentation of them varies pointedly. Bale was born in Covehithe on the Suffolk coast, the eldest of many children to Henry and Margaret Bale. At twelve, he was placed in the Carmelite house at Norwich, being educated there and at Cambridge. In the earliest sketches, Bale writes of how he 'devoted his labour at Cambridge, Louvain, and Toulouse to the liberal arts', and took up positions in Carmelite houses in Maldon, Ipswich, and Doncaster.[23] By 1548, however, any pride taken in his Carmelite work has been replaced by a visceral hatred for the experience. He was placed in 'the Carmelite monk-pit in Norwich' because his parents were 'deceived by the pseudo-prophets' illusions'. At Norwich and Cambridge, 'I wandered through the whirlwinds of dogma with neither tutor nor

Maecenas'.[24] There is now no mention of the fact that he rose to high office in the Carmelites.

Bale's conversion to the Reformed faith also undergoes considerable change. In the 'Fasciculus', writing of himself in the third person, he departs the Carmelites as part of a general movement:

> At last, when the truth of the Gospel shone out, he changed the rule of his papist vow... Certain other fellow fighters in this Babylon abandoned their papist vows... For Christian men could not endure the evils which at that time were done among them... In AD 1538 our lord eradicated them in England utterly by his command, to cast them out, according to Christ's prophecy, Mt. 15 [Matthew 15:13].[25]

In 'Anglorum Heliades', Bale specifies that one of those 'fellow fighters' was of particular importance: 'At last the truth of the Gospel began to shine forth. From love of its burning flame I also exchanged the course of my improper vows with the aforesaid Barret [fellow Carmelite John Barret], preferring divine law to the traditions of men.'[26]

By the time he published his *Summarium* in 1548, Bale had adopted a new rhetoric, as he elaborates his individual response to the Gospel:

> With the exposure of God's word the churches began to turn to the founts of true theology. In that light, or rather the splendour of the rising new Jerusalem, I saw my deformity, and through God's goodness, I was taken to the harbour, where all things were brought on solid rock. The accursed mark of the terrible beast or detestable Antichrist I eradicated, extirpated, utterly destroyed. For I took my most faithful wife, not from man, nor through man, but from the particular word and gift of Christ, that I might be the Pope's creature no longer, but under God's command: He who cannot contain himself, let him marry in the Lord [1 Corinthians 7:9].[27]

Bale moves away from being the 'Pope's creature' by taking a wife, unmentioned in 1539. In his 1557 telling, the underlying logic here becomes clearer: Bale marries, he tells us, 'lest thereafter I might be any such execrable creature of the beast'.[28] He sets in place a choice between godly marriage to a woman, and beastly, sodomitical subjection in the monastery, a theme he elaborates, insistently and with relish, in a wide array of his writings.[29]

Like his 'most faithful wife', other figures come and go in the various iterations. In the 1557 *Catalogus*, Bale specifies that he was 'called neither by monk nor sacrificial priest but by the famous Lord Wentworth': Sir Thomas Wentworth from Nettlestead near Ipswich, a courtier in the circle of the king's sister, Mary Brandon, duchess of Suffolk. Wentworth was a known Protestant sympathizer: a surviving 1537 appeal by

Bale to Cromwell cites Wentworth as someone who could vouch for his integrity.[30] Here, Bale explicitly contrasts Wentworth to the other possibilities for his personal conversion, a monk or a priest: whereas once he was part of a communal reformation, or the particular influence of fellow votary John Barret, now the impetus to convert comes from a secular patron. But why is Barret mentioned only in the 1530s and Wentworth not until the late 1550s? The answer lies in these men's shifting positions. In 1548, Bale knew that Wentworth had been responsible for sending two Protestants to the stake three years earlier. Subsequently, however, Wentworth was rehabilitated by his appointment to Edward VI's Privy Council—and by dying in 1551, he had not needed to compromise with the Marian regime.[31] By contrast, in 1557 Bale announced that his supposedly lifelong friend Barret was lost to him, after he had re-embraced Catholicism: Barret, he wrote sadly, was 'among the first to take up the Gospel doctrine… But now, led by what giddy spirit I do not know, he has returned, like the vilest dog, to his own vomit.'[32]

In the retellings, Bale's conversion takes on increasingly far-reaching qualities. In the late 1530s, the power of the gospel allows Bale and his fellow votaries to see the degeneration of the order, and to leave it, yet he maintains respect for the Carmelites, and proudly lists the centres of Carmelite learning where he has studied, and the houses where he has held office. By 1548, Bale writes only of himself, not of his fellow troopers. No longer a learned international community, the Carmelite order is reduced to the 'monkish hell-pit' in Norwich where his life was ruined. The nature of that hell is indicated by his taking of a wife, by which he is saved from the sexual incontinence of those houses.[33] And by 1557, he is called not simply by the gospel, but by a secular patron. These four lives tell us a good deal not only about Bale but about the challenges facing life-writers of the English Reformation. Within the span of a single life, his Catholic past had to be written off variously as monkish, barbaric, sodomitical, and foreign, in order to allow the present to be reformed, civilized, happily married, and English. But Bale of all people knew that this re-writing cloaked an essential continuity.

The Vocation of John Bale

Bale's autobiographical writings did not end with the sketches he provided for his *viri illustres*. In 1553, he published *The Vocacyon of Iohan Bale to the Bishoprick of Ossorie in Irelande*, covering the period when Bale was called (hence 'vocation') to the bishopric of Ossory in Ireland, the challenges that he faced there and during his escape from Ireland, and ultimately his 'deliveraunce' to Germany, from where he writes and publishes the *Vocacyon*.[34] While, as several critics have noted, the *Vocacyon* does not attempt to cover Bale's entire life, it does, I shall suggest, attempt to present a model for Bale's entire life—albeit, only to fail.[35]

The timeline of the *Vocacyon* maps onto a particularly unsettled and unsettling period in Anglo-Irish religious history: the final months of the reign of Edward VI, and the uncertainty that followed his death, in which Lady Jane Grey was placed on the throne for nine days, only to be deposed by Edward's elder half-sister, Mary. During this time, England and Ireland, in theory, swung from Protestantism back to Roman Catholicism, although Bale's narrative makes clear that on the ground, especially in Ireland, the situation was considerably more muddled. The narrative of the *Vocacyon* is sensational, bristling with the plot devices of romance—this year in the life of John Bale encompasses persecution, conspiracy, murder, kidnap, and a lengthy sojourn with pirates. Coincidences punctuate the story, which starts conveniently on the day Bale is delivered from a 'mortal ague'; his raising to the bishopric happens because King Edward catches sight of him from a window in Southampton—surprised to see a man whom he had been told was 'bothe dead & buried' (B8^r). And yet Bale's narrative can be surprisingly precise: he sometimes supplies dates, days of the week, and even hours of the day in placing his important events. He also gives a certain weight to documentary evidence: the Privy Council letter appointing him to his bishopric is proudly reprinted, and Bale specifies its date, its signatories, and even its amanuensis, council clerk B. Hampton (B8^v).

Bale's nomination formed part of a concerted effort to bring the Reformation to a recalcitrant Ireland, and he does not miss a chance to portray the sorry state of religious practice in his adopted country. Landing in Waterford, he saw 'many abhomynable ydolatryes mainteined by *the* Epicurysh prestes / for their wicked bellies sake'. Communion was 'altogyther vsed lyke a popysh masse / with the olde apysh toyes of Antichrist / in bowynges and beckynges / knelinges and knockinges. There wawled they ouer *the* dead / with prodigyouse howlynges and patterynges' (C1^v). Stopping overnight in Knocktopher, Bale meets a parish priest, Sir Philip, who boasts that the last prior of the local Whitefriars was 'his naturall father'—and indeed that it was considered 'an honour in this lande / to have a spirituall man / as a bishop / an Abbot / a Monke / a Fryre / or a Prest to father' (C2^r). This is a country where the bishop of Galway can 'gadde from towne to towne over the English part / confirminge yonge children for .ii. pens a pece'—and be so drunk doing it that he inadvertedly confirmed a 'dogge wrapped in a shete' brought by a gallowglass 'for a mocke'. But then, 'this beastly bishop,' as Bale notes, is 'more fit to confirme dogs / than christen mennes children' (D4^r).

Things seem to look up when, on his arrival in Dublin, Bale finds his friends Hugh Goodacre elected archbishop of Armagh and David Coper appointed parson of Callan: 'Much of the people ded greatly reioyce of our comminge thidre', Bale claims, 'thinking by our preachinges / the popes superstitions wolde diminish & the true Christen religion increace' (C2^{r-v}). But immediately he encounters resistance from 'that greate Epicure the Archebishop' of Dublin, George Browne, who attempts to defer their consecration in order to maximize his own profits (C2^{r}),[36] and from the dean of the cathedral church, Thomas Lockwood ('Blockheade he might wel be called'), who insists that the ceremony should not follow the new, second Book of Common Prayer—because, according to Bale, he thought the new regime would 'hindre his kychin and bellye' (C3^{r}). Only Bale 'stepped fourth' to object to Lockwood's plan, declaring that 'If Englande and Irelande be undre one kinge / they are both bounde to the obedience of one lawe undre him'; foiled in his attempt, 'the asse-headed deane' went 'awaie more than halfe confused'. Bale proudly remarks that 'Neyther folowed there any tumulte amonge the people / but every man saveinge the prestes / was wele contented' (C3^{r-v}).

Despite these minor victories, Bale's Irish ministry in Kilkenny is an uphill struggle: among his clergy, he finds no 'helpars', 'but adversiaries a great nombre' (C4^{r}). While seeking 'to distroye the ydolatries / & dissolve the hypocrites yockes', he provokes 'angers / slaunders / conspiricyes / & in the ende the slaughter of men'. He urges the local clergy 'not to occupie so muche of the tyme in chauntynge / pypynge / and syngynge' (C4^{v}), but fails to persuade them to follow the new Book of Common Prayer: the Irish Parliament had not ratified that version, and the clergy cite 'the lewde example of the Archebysship of Dublyne', who did not follow it himself (C5^{v}). In particular, Bale angers Irish churchmen by telling them to marry, '& to leave the unshamefast occupienge / of other mennes wyves / doughters / and servauntes'. They counter by asking why should they marry 'for halfe a yeare / & so loose our livynges?' (C4^{v}–C5^{r})—as if they knew that the religious regime would change in six months' time at the death of Edward VI. 'Thinke ye not that these men were ghostly inspired?' Bale asks his readers, or 'yet had knowledge of some secrete mischefe wurkinge in Englande?' Finally, he realizes that Scripture had told him 'that the impenitent ydolatour must therwith be also a fylthie adulterer or most detestable sodomite. It is his just plague (Rom*ans* 1). We can not stoppe it' (C5^{r}).

On 25 July, while Bale was spending time at Holmes Court, five miles away from Kilkenny, the clergy showed some uncharacteristic enthusiasm, as the *Vocacyon* recalls: 'the prestes were as plesauntly disposed as might be / and went by heapes from tavern to tavern / to seke the best Rob davie and aqua vite / which are their speciall drinkes there. Thei cawsed all their cuppes to be filled in / with Gaudeamus in dolio [let us rejoice in sorrow] / the misterie therof only knowne to them / and at that to none other els' (C6^{r}). The mystery of their good mood is soon revealed: news had reached Ireland that Edward VI had died at Greenwich Palace on 6 July. The Irish clergy, Bale believed, were now 'in hope to have their maskynge masses againe', and started to flex their muscles (C6^{v}). The following day, two local dignitaries, justice Thomas Hothe and Richard Butler, viscount Mountgarret, son of the earl of Ormond, demanded that a communion in honour of St Anne be held at the cathedral church, a request that flew in the face of Bale's prohibition of such celebrations except on Sundays. Hothe informed the priests that he discharged them of their obedience to Bale on this point—to Bale's fury. But the situation was by no means as settled as Hothe may have hoped. On 27 July, the Protestant Lady Jane Grey was proclaimed queen in Ireland; Bale was absent from the solemnities, doubting that the matter was settled (C7^{r})—and indeed, back in England, her nine-day reign was already well over.

Finally, on 20 August, Mary Tudor was proclaimed queen at Kilkenny. With an ardent Catholic now on the throne, local resistance to Bale's strictures was legitimized—and the *Vocacyon* registers his frustration and increasing exhaustion: 'What a do I had that daye with the prebendaryes and prestes abought wearing the cope / croser [crozier] / and myter in procession / it were to muche to write.' Refusing to be party to the sacraments and ceremonies, Bale, testament in hand, marched to Kilkenny's marketplace to preach on Romans 13. The prelates tried to undermine him by using two 'disgysed prestes' to walk in front of Bale, one bearing the mitre, the other the crozier; Bale retaliated by having a group of young men put on at the market cross performances of his plays *Gods Promises* and *John Baptistes Preachinge*, complete with organ playing and songs—'to the small contentacion of the prestes and other papistes there', as he puts it, with rare understatement (C8^{r}).

The following Thursday, St Bartholomew's Day, Bale preached on Romans 1 ('I am not ashamed of the Gospell. And whie? For it is the power of God into salvacion / to all them that believe it') and spoke against transubstantiation and the saying of prayers for the dead (C8^{r}-D1^{r}). Every move was calculated to incense the local priests—and they clashed again that evening, when Bale dined with the mayor. After dinner, the priests 'began very hotely to dispute with me concerninge their purgatorye & suffrages of the dead' (D1^{v})—and claimed that Romans 1 was wrong. Bale's rebuke was devastating:

> Then sayde I unto them, Ye have set me fourth a newe lesson / and taught me this daye / to knowe a good man from an hipocrite / & to discerne a true Christiane from a wicked papist. The good man (sayd I) beleueth a truthe in the scriptures / the hipocrit denieth it / the christian embraceth it / the papist doubteth & disputeth against it / as ded that devill in the wildernesse with Christe / whan he sought by one scripture to confounde an other. (D2^{r})

No longer Protestant versus Catholic: Bale cast the battle as Christian versus papist.

Tensions had reached a new level. Earlier in the year, after Easter, Bale had heard that Goodacre, the new archbishop of Armagh, had been 'poysened at Dubline / by procurement of certen prestes of his diocese / for preaching Gods verite & rebukinge their commen vices'. Friends sent letters to Bale begging him to beware of something similar happening to him (C6^{r}). But once the king was dead, the situation worsened. English forts were assailed, with nine Englishmen slain at one. On 13 August, the wife of an English clerk named Matthew King, living in a nearby castle, fled towards Kilkenny with her family and goods in a cart, but 'in the hygh waye was spoyled of all / to her very petycote', and four of her company slain by kerns and gallowglasses (C7^{r}-C8^{r}). On 26 August, back at Holmes Court, Bale learned that two priests of his diocese, Richard Routh, treasurer of the Kilkenny church, and James Joys, his own chaplain, with the help of his neighbour and tenant Barnabe Bolgar, had hired kerns from Mountgarret and his brother-in-law Barnaby Fitzpatrick, barn (or baron) of Upper Ossory, men 'whom they knewe to be most desperate theves and murtherers / to slea me'—a slaying which would benefit both the priests and the local gentry, who wanted his lands. At the same time, Bale alleged, Fitzpatrick was molesting his tenants; Bolgar had married his daughter to one of the 'murderers', hoping to get his hands on Holmes Court after Bale's death; Mountgarret's groom came into Bale's court and bragged to Bale's servants that he would steal his horses, 'and also that he would have my heade if I cam abroade' (D2^{v}). Bale's appeals to Mountgarret fell on deaf ears: he 'had but a slendre answere / with no redresse at all' (D3^{r}).

On the following Thursday, with Bale safely out of town, the Kilkenny clergy, urged on by Hothe, resumed Catholic forms of worship. Bale captures the scene vividly: 'They ronge all the belles in the cathedral ministre and parrish churches, they flonge up their cappes to the battlement of the great temple / with smylinges and laughinges most dissolutely'—even Hothe was offended. 'They brought forth their coopes / candelstickes / holy waterstocke / crosse and sensers. They mustered fourth in generall procession most gorgeously / all the towne over / with Sancta Maria ora pro nobis [Holy Mary pray for us] / & the rest of the latine Letanie. They chattered it / they chaunted it / with great noyse and devocion' (D3^{r-v}). Now, Bale alleged, they can 'without checke / have other mennes wives in occupienge / or kepe whores in their chambers / or els playe the buggery knaves / as they have done alwayes / and be at an utter defiaunce with marriage'. Whatever crimes they commit, confession, so they boast, would make them 'so white as snowe' (D3^{v}).

The tone of the *Vocacyon* changes abruptly on Friday 8 September. Between eight and nine in the morning, five of Bale's household servants went about half a mile from Holmes Court to make hay, among them 'a yonge mayde of .xvi. yeares of age' (D4^{r-v}). At the entrance to the meadow, they were ambushed by more than twenty 'cruell murtherers', who 'leaped out of their lurkynge bushes with sweardes and with dartes / and cowardly slewe them all unarmed & unweaponed / without mercye', before stealing all Bale's horses (D4^{v}). According to Bale, the attackers had been watching and waiting for a month, hoping to kill him; subsequently the priests let it be known that God had slain Bale's servants for going to work on the holy day of Our Lady's Nativity (D5^{r}). The suffren (mayor) of Kilkenny came that afternoon with a defensive force of 100 horsemen and 300 footmen to escort Bale in safety to Kilkenny, 'the yonge men syngynge psalms and other godly songes all the waye / in rejoyce of my deliveraunce' (D4^{v}).

Despite the rescue, matters did not improve in Kilkenny. On the Saturday following the attack, the treasurer came to Bale demanding that he sing a requiem mass and dirige for Edward VI; Bale refused, and asked for the solemnities to be deferred so that he could get official confirmation from Queen Mary's commissioners at Dublin that he was indeed discharged of the oath he took to abolish the Catholic mass (D6^{r}–D7^{v}). On the next day, it was proclaimed that hearing mass would not be compulsory, which Bale took as a hopeful sign that 'Thus was that buyldynge clearly overthroowne / and that practyse of blasphemye wolde not take at that tyme / as God wolde'. But other signs told a different story. Bale overheard mutterings that priests were still conspiring his death; the bishop of Galway and others were saying that the Pope would once again head the Church of Ireland; priests were setting up altars and icons in the cathedral church. With no English deputy or governor to complain to, Bale decided it was time to take his leave: 'I shoke the dust of my fete against those wicked collignyers [collegians] and prestes accordinge to Christes commaundement / (Math. 10)' (D7^{v}). And so, with the help of friends, he fled to the nearby castle at Leighlinbridge, and from there to Dublin.

The archbishop of Dublin, George Browne, let it be known that he would never let Bale preach in his city. 'But this neded not,' Bale assures us. 'For I thought nothinge lesse at that time / than to poure out the preciouse pearles of the Gospell afore so brockish a swine as he was / becomminge than of a dissembling proselite / a very perniciouse papiste.' Warming to his theme, Bale paints a priceless picture of the archbishop. While Browne 'muche boasted am*onge* his cuppes' of his learning, 'I knowe none *that* he hath so perfightly exercised / as he hath *the* knowne practises of Sardinapal*us*', the notoriously dissolute king of the Assyrians. Browne preached only twice a year—'of *the* plough ma*n* in wi*n*ter / by Exit qui seminat / & of *the* shepeherde i*n* somer / by Ego su*m* pastor bon*us*'—so that his repertoire was 'now so wele knowne by rott [rote] of euery gossipp i*n* Dubline *that* afore he co*m*meth vp into *the* pulpet / they ca*n* tell his sermo*n*'. Unlike Bale, Browne had shown his willingness to dissolve his marriage in order to save his career,[37] and would do the same again, if need be: 'as for his wife / if *the* mariage of prestes endureth not / he hath already prouided his olde shifte of conueyaunce / by one of his seruauntes' (D8r). There was a deep irony here: 'About thre yeares ago / he made interpellacyon to the Kynge in hys lente sermon for his daughter Irelande / but now he commaundeth her to go a whoringe aganie / and to folowe the same deuyll that she folowed afore' ($D8^{r-v}$).

Despite the dates and places, there is a lack of specificity about much of Bale's time in Ireland. Some key characters are not named. There is little (if any) explanation of the complex religious situation in Ossory, which Bale paints in bold sweeps of black and white, evil versus good. We are not told, for example, that the clergy of Kilkenny had been summoned to meet with the Lord Deputy and council of Ireland in 1549 and directed to 'abolish the mass';[38] that his see of Ossory had been empty for over two years, after various bids by Irish magnates to place their own candidates had been rejected by the Privy Council;[39] and that William Turner, dean of Wells, had turned down the appointment.[40] Perhaps most surprisingly, Bale does not make anything of what he would later talk of as the greatest injury inflicted by Ireland: the loss of much of his library. Writing in 1560 to Matthew Parker, archbishop of Canterbury, he claimed that 'I had in Irelande more than ii great wayne [wagon] loades' of books, but that he was 'depryued of all that I had, by the papystes vndre quene Marye, and hauock was made of the bokes, by an other wurke of the Deuyll, that they shulde not yet come to lyghte'. He claimed then that many books were left at Kilkenny, 'amonge the prebendars there', and more than eighty volumes remained in the keeping of Nicholas Hearne (or Heron), the captain of Lechlinbridge, where he had broken his final journey from Kilkenny to Dublin.[41] But none of this appears in the *Vocacyon*.

As Bale looks to leave Ireland, the *Vocacyon* enters its second phase. Bale comes to terms with a young Essex man named Thomas, who is looking after the affairs of his Scottish master, to pay half the charges of a pickard (a small ship) ($D8^{v}$). But while the two men are waiting for the tide, an Irish pirate named Walter, working as a pilot or lodesman in a Fleming ship-of-war, makes his captain believe that Bale is a Frenchman carrying 'innumerable treasure'. The captain invades the pickard, and takes Thomas and Bale on board his ship, searching them 'to the very skinnes', and seizing their money, books, and clothing ($E1^{r}$). Despite Bale's repeated pleas to be set ashore, the ship sets sail from Dublin to Waterford, and gets halfway to Cornwall, before it is driven back by a storm to Waterford. The captain overhears Bale talking to a Dutchman, and 'hearde [him] wishe [him]selfe in Duchelande [Germany]'. The captain assures him: 'I promise yow / we will honestly brynge yow thydre / and not longe tarry by the waye' ($E2^{r}$). But there is a long enough tarry ahead. Driven into St Ives in Cornwall, Walter gets ashore first and denounces Bale as 'an haynouse traitor' fleeing from Ireland; a local man named Downings, 'the most cruell termagaunt of that shire' (E2^{v}), comes to investigate, but Walter ultimately has to admit that all he knows of Bale is that he was attempting to get to Scotland—which Downings angrily points out isn't treason. Walter 'stode still / and was able to saye nothinge / for he was as dronke as an ape / in hope of a bone viage' (E3^{r}).

By the time Bale reaches England, Catholicism is back in full force. He attends church on Sunday to find the mass is now in Latin and only the litany in English. The priest, Sir James, is no better than those Bale encountered in Ireland. At dinner, Sir James rails upon his bishop, Miles Coverdale; Bale is about to defend Coverdale when a local gentleman rubs him on the elbow, and 'bad me in mine eare / to lete him alone / and I shulde heare wonders'. Wonders indeed. The priest boasts that in the past he had impregnated two of his parishioners' wives, a cunning ploy 'to encreace the churches profyght in crisymes and offeringes', and that he uses the communion wafer as fishbait; Bale's fellow mariners later complain that the priest had played 'an uncomly part' with their piper: 'he had pyssed in his mouthe / beinge gapinge a slepe in the church after evensonge'. 'This', Bale declares to his reader, 'is the bewteouse face of our Irishe and Englishe churches at this present. The poore people are not taught / but mocked of their mynysters / their servauntes abused / their wives and doughters defyled / and all christen ordre confounded' (E4^{r-v}).

After this unedifying glimpse of Marian England, Bale spends the next few months prisoner on the ship, as the captain tries to work out how best to make money out of him, and goes 'roving', performing acts of piracy (E5^{r-v}). Once they reach Dover, Bale and Thomas are not allowed ashore, but Bale learns that a French-born English pirate named Martin had spread 'most prodigious lyes' that Bale had 'put downe the masse in Englande', caused Stephen Gardiner, bishop of Winchester, 'to be kepte so longe in the tower', and that he poisoned King Edward, 'whome I loved & reverenced above all mortal men' (E6^{r}). Finally, they come to a deal whereby the captain takes Bale to Flanders for a considerable sum—which only comes to pass after they spend twenty-four days 'folowinge prises / as they call their roberies'. The shipbound Bale was, he recalls, 'by that time / so full of lyce / as I could swarme' (E8^{v}). Landing in Zeeland, Bale finds sanctuary in the house of one of the ship's owners, the god-fearing Lambert and his wife.[42] Once again, there is a delay of three weeks while Bale's future is hotly debated before he is allowed to go free for a payment of thirty pounds: 'Thus hath my lorde God most miraculously delivered me from all these dangerouse parels / and from the gredye mouthes of devourynge lions / into the wurthie lande of Germanye yet ones againe' (F1^{v}). Finally, Bale achieves 'deliveraunce'.

A Second St Paul

Despite the text's clear message of 'deliveraunce', most readers come away from the *Vocacyon* with a different image—for Bale gives his narrative a frame that proves powerful. The account of Bale's time in Ireland and his subsequent flight is spliced between two other sections—a lengthy 'Preface' in which Bale speaks directly 'to the folowers of Christes Gospell', and a shorter 'Conclusion'. The purpose of the *Vocacyon* is made clear in the 'Conclusion', a direct address to 'thu sorowfull churche of England', urging that 'in the middes of thy afflictions thu shouldest not despayre'. God has delivered Bale, 'his most unworthie servaunt of all men / and an excedinge great sinner', and the church is vexed by 'no noble men': 'They are but pilde peltinge prestes / knightes of the dongehill / thought they be sir Swepestretes / maistre doctors / and lorde bishopppes' (F3^{r}). But the 'Preface' has a more original, and more personal, purpose.

The 'Preface' provides a model for reading Bale's narrative—one that is not suggested in the narrative itself. Bale is here forthright about why he has written about 'these 3. matters of vocacion / persecucion / & deliveraunce' (A3^{r}): 'Neyther am I ashamed to tell my bretherne / what God hath most graciously done for me / nomore than s. Paule was for hymselfe in hys owne Epistles / and Luke in the Actes for saint Peter / though I be farre unlike them.' In contrast to the papists, who 'rejoyce in helthe / prosperite / riches and worldly pleasures for their bellies sake', we rejoyce 'in our infirmytees / afflictions / losses / and sorrowful crostes / for Christes veritees sake' (A3^{v}). And we—and therefore Bale—are entitled to 'boast of it without offence / for so ded the forenamed S. Paule (2 Cor. 11) and earnestly willed us to be his folowers (Phil. 3)' (A3^{v}–A4^{r}).

Since Paul 'boasted of his vocacion / and sayde, God sorted me out and appointed me from my mothers wombe/ and also he called me by his grace / to preache his lively gospel amonge the heathen / (Gal. 1)', Bale then asks, somewhat rhetorically, 'What if I shoulde in like case boaste / that he by his grace had also called me in this age / to preache the same Gospel to the Irishe heathens / which never heard of it afore / to knowledge?' The answer is 'I shulde not do other wise than the truthe is' (A4^{r}). Paul 'boasted muche of his persecucions'; 'If I have lyke wyse / felte a great meanie of the same afflictions,' Bale asks, 'as I have done in dede / maye not I also with him reioyce in them?' (A4^{v}). And if Paul 'rejoiced / that God had so miraculously delivered him from so manye daungerouse jeopardyes / and spareth not so to report them', it follows for Bale that 'Whie shulde I than shrinke or be ashamed to do the lyke / havinge at Gods hande the lyke miraculouse deliveraunce?' (A5^{r}). So when Paul in Damascus, with the lieutenant of King Aretas lying in wait for him, escaped by being let down at a window in a basket (Acts 9), Bale 'in the cytie of Dubline / beinge assaulted of papistes / was convayed awaye in the nyght in mariners apparell / & so escaped that daunger by Gods helpe' (A5^{r}). When Paul was in mortal danger from some Jews in Jerusalem, the captain there ordered two under-captains to convey him to Caesarea with 200 soldiers, 70 horsemen, and 200 spear-men (Acts 23); Bale had an escape 'In lycke case' when he was rescued from Holmes Court after the murder of his servants, by Kilkenny's suffren with 100 horsemen and 300 footmen (A5^{v}). And so on—Bale finds such parallels throughout his story. Summing up, he writes, 'Thus had I in my troublous journaye from Irelande into Germanye all those chaunces in a maner that S. Paul had in his journaie of no lesse trouble / from Jerusalem to Rome / saving that we lost not our shippe by the waye' (A6^{v}–A7^{r}).

Bale plays up this reading on the title page, which he adorns with two scriptural verses: 'God hath deliuered me from the snare of the hunter / & from the noisome pestilence' (Psalm 21), and 'If I must nedes reioyce / I will reioyce of myne infirmities' (2 Corinthians 11).[43] The title page also features a woodcut of 'The English Christian' with a cowering lamb threatened by 'The Irishe Papist', strangely inhuman with birdlike features, drawing his sword, accompanied by a wolvish, fanged dog (Fig. 3). It is a striking image of the struggle Bale will recount—but it was not designed to depict the Irish. In fact, the picture had been used a decade earlier by Bale's printer Joos Lambrecht, in Andries van der Muelen's 1543 Dutch translation of a tract on asceticism, *De miseria humanae conditionis*, written (ironically enough) by Pope Innocent III; Bale simply appropriated it, opportunistically, to depict 'the hunter' of his scriptural citation.

Something similar happens, I would suggest, with his self-comparison with Paul. Some critics have seen the *Vocacyon* as his attempt at a Protestant saint's life.[44] Certainly, Bale lards his story with elements of the miraculous: ill with a 'mortall ague', he metaphorically rises from the dead to see King Edward VI and take up his bishopric (B8^{r}); when he is held prisoner in Zeeland for three weeks, the parson of the town, 'a most cruell monke... and an inquisitor of heretykes' falls ill, 'and never came out of his bedde so longe as I was there'—'a most wondrefull wurke of God', in Bale's estimation (F1^{v}). But, as Meredith Skura has shown in a perceptive analysis, the resemblances are at best superficial: Bale's exploits may sometimes echo the letter of Paul's actions, but never the spirit.[45] The comparison certainly annoyed one of Mary I's chaplains, James Cancellar, so much so that he dedicated over seven pages of his 1556 publication *The Pathe of Obedience* to the *Vocacyon*. 'That presumpteous heretike Iohn Bale', according to Cancellar, did 'not sham[e] to compare himselfe with holy saincte Paul in troubles, in labours, in perill of shipe wracke, in perill of the sea, in perill of false brethren, in peril of pirates, robbers

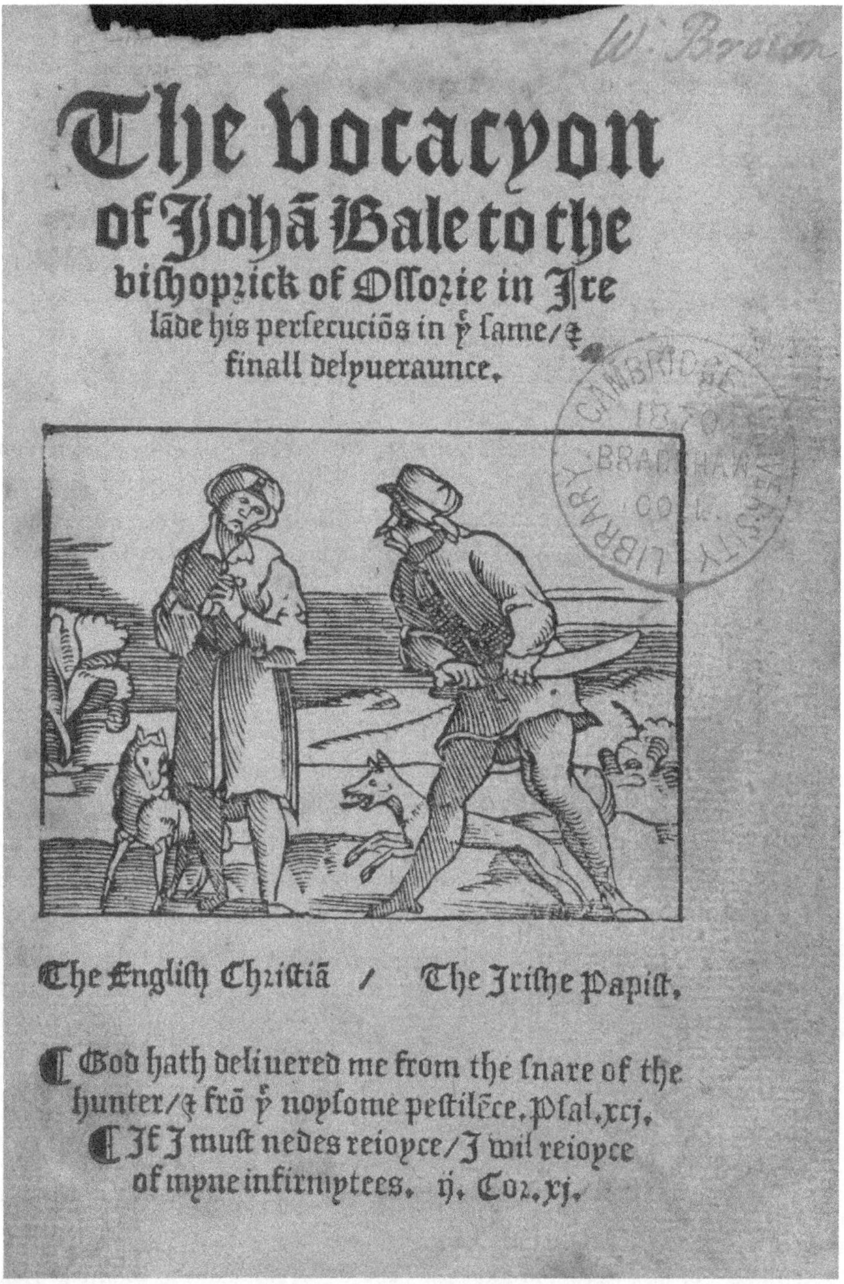

The vocacyon
of Iohā Bale to the
bishoprick of Ossorie in Ire
lāde his persecuciōs in ye same/ &
finall delyueraunce.

The English Christiā / The Irishe Papist.

¶ God hath deliuered me from the snare of the
hunter/ & frō ye noysome pestilēce. Psal. xci.
¶ If I must nedes reioyce/ I wil reioyce
of myne infirmytees. ii. Cor. xi.

Figure 3. Title page of John Bale, *The Vocacyon of Iohan Bale* (1553). Reproduced by kind permission of the Syndics of Cambridge University Library, Hib.8.55.1.

and murtherers'–'lyke a mad harehead'. The comparison is, in Cancellar's view, entirely self-serving: 'Here Frier Bale beginneth craftely to perswade with the poore Christians that GOD hath deliuered him fro*m* peril of death by miracle as thoughe he were called of god in these daies to set vp a light in his churche.' Cancellar counters that 'If you had been as you saye a true disciple of Christ and as felow lyke with Sainct Paule as you wryght your self to be, when you by chaunce of wether were dryuen into Douer rode woulde lyke as Paule did at Philippus haue set youre fote on lande & preached Christe but contrary wyse...you were more desirous to sette youre hande to a bill of fyfty poundes more the*n* you were able to pay to that ende you myghte be set on lande in flaunders'. In reality, Bale is not Paul, but rather 'that notable heretyke Cerinthus', the first-century gnostic who, in Cancellar's telling, 'did labour to put oute of the Churche of God the true lyght of the gospell in the time of the holy apostle Saint Iohn'. Bale is 'compelled of necessite to runne with *the* thefe or murtherer fro*m* Citie to Citie and from contrie to contrie for the assuraunce of your lyfe' because he is 'a notable heretike a postata [apostate] and runagate [renegade]'.[46] (Bale later responded to this attack, in a still-unpublished manuscript tract.[47])

While Cancellar is motivated by his anti-Protestantism, it can be argued that Bale's comparison with Paul fails because it was an afterthought: the 'Preface', which recapitulates points from the main narrative, was written after the rest of the book and no doubt printed last (bibliographically it forms a separate signature, A). At the end of the Preface, seeking to conclude his *Vocacyon*, Bale writes that God 'finally will delyver' the faithful, in one of two ways: 'eyther from tyrannouse molestacions / as he hath done me' or 'els into martirdome for his truthes sake'. This is the first–and only–time that Bale suggests that deliverance might come in the form of death, but he disavows it as a possibility for himself. Although he takes on the mantle of Paul, and makes Paul's journey from Jerusalem to Rome, that story ends with Paul's martyrdom in Rome, and Bale has no intention to follow it through. He concludes the Preface by quoting Psalm 118–'I called uppon the Lorde in my trouble / and the Lorde hearde me at large. The Lorde is my helper / I wyll not feare what man doeth to me' (A8^{r})–but it is a singularly inappropriate epitaph for John Bale, who has spent much of his *Vocacyon* on the run, from Ireland, from England, from pirates. Bale is not martyr material: he is motivated by survival. But the work that would answer Bale's call for a new history of England would indeed need to be a book of martyrs.

3

John Foxe's Lives of the Saints

Grace Sharington was raised in the 1560s with somewhat restricted reading matter. Her mother 'thought it euer dangerous to suffer young people to reade or study bookes wherein was good & euill mingled togither; for *that* by nature we are inclyned rather to learne & retayne the euill then the good', so she prescribed a limited shortlist for Grace: 'The Bible, Musculus common places, the imitation of Christ, & Mr ffoxes Bookes of Martirs were the onely books she layed before me.' The lasting influence of that reading was evident decades later when Grace Sharington, now the widowed Grace, Lady Mildmay, wrote an autobiographical letter of advice to her grandchildren, beginning, 'I haue found by experience [and] I commend vnto my children as approoued this is to be the best course to set our selues in from the begin*n*ing vnto the end of our lyues'. Scripture, read every day, 'from the first of Genesis vnto the last of the Reuelation' over and over, came first, as well as the English chronicles, the statutes and laws, and 'the wyse & wittie sentences of the philosophers'. But directly after Scripture, Lady Mildmay advised her grandchildren that we must 'make our selues expert in the knowledge of the histories contayned in the booke of Acts & Monuments of the church', so that 'our faithfull zeale may be increased & strengthened & our hartes encouraged manfully to suffer death & to giue our lyues for the testimony of the truth of God wherin we are thus confirmed, and sealed by the death & bloud of Christ'.[1]

This chapter tells the story not of an individual life-writer, but of a book of lives. Even today, the 1563 volume of *Actes and Monuments* that Grace Sharington read as a child is an impressive tome, vastly more ambitious than anything previously printed in England. John Foxe's text—itself drawing on the work of many other writers—not only tells the stories of the men and women persecuted by the Roman Catholic Church, but prints vast amounts of documentary support in the form of letters, interrogations, and debates, while its publisher John Day saw to it that Foxe's text is set off by wonderfully vivid illustrations depicting the martyrs' agonies in prison and at the stake. It is still possible for a reader to lose herself in this dense, imposing volume. *Actes and Monuments* is many things: as the leading Foxe scholars Elizabeth Evenden and Thomas Freeman explain, it 'is a complicated book with numerous overlapping messages–it is at once a book of didactic advice on how to live the Christian life, a book of spiritual consolation for troubled souls, a history of the Church in its many facets, a history of England, and an exegesis of the Apocalypse unfolding through the history of the world'.[2] It is also, I would suggest, the single most important body of biographical life-writing in post-Reformation Britain. Although initially conceived as a new ecclesiastical history for the English Protestant Church, and as a repository for the documentary evidence for that history, *Actes and Monuments* became most celebrated as a collection of martyrs' lives, a *Book of Martyrs*, as it became popularly known. Grace Sharington, eleven years old in 1563, stands for a generation that was raised on these lives. Revised and expanded many times, and read intensively over the following century (and beyond), they became part of the common language of many religious-minded English men and women, and the individual lives served as reference points and indeed role-models for how to live.

But, even before *Actes and Monuments* appeared, Foxe realized that there was a problem with presenting it as a collection of lives. In a Latin epistle to the reader in that first 1563 edition he writes that in the long months it had taken to bring the volume to completion, people had started to refer to it as 'our *Golden Legend*'.[3] It is a barbed joke. As all his readers knew, the *Golden Legend* (*Legenda aurea*) was the hugely popular compendium of Catholic saints' lives put together by the thirteenth-century Dominican friar Jacobus de Voragine. Read over centuries throughout Europe in Latin and many vernacular languages, in an England the collection had received a boost by being printed in an English translation by William Caxton in multiple editions;[4] it even found its way into parish churches.[5] But as the English Reformation took hold, and the new Protestant Church abolished the worship of saints, the *Legenda aurea* became a source of derision. In 1536, Wilhelm Gnapheus classed 'the tales of legenda aurea' as 'fantasies & dreames';[6] in 1538, Nicholas Wyse asked his reader that when God bids you 'seke and ye shal fynd', where will you look? 'Wyll ye seke it in the bysshops of romes decretals and in Legenda aurea as your fathers dyd?'[7] With its institutional support undermined, the *Legenda aurea* went out of print, seeing its last full English edition in 1527.[8] In theory, Foxe's *Actes and Monuments* was the antithesis of the *Legenda aurea*. In practice, the similarities were hard to deny. Like the *Legenda aurea*, the *Actes and Monuments* was organized primarily around individual lives. Like the *Legenda aurea*, *Actes and Monuments* was kept in churches, featured vivid illustrations, and claimed for itself a quasi-liturgical function. And there were perhaps more fundamental reasons why its Protestant martyrs smacked of the *Legenda aurea*'s Catholic saints.

When Foxe Met Bale

While the 1563 *Actes and Monuments* carries the name of John Foxe, in its conception and ideology it bears the unmistakable influence of the man Foxe first encountered in the summer of 1548. Foxe was working at Mountjoy House, the home of Mary Fitzroy, duchess of Richmond, as tutor to the children of her recently executed brother, the poet Henry Howard, earl of Surrey, when he met John Bale, recently returned from his first period of exile, and still four years away from his promotion to the bishopric of Ossory. Together Bale and Foxe discussed how best to conceive and write a history of the Reformed English Church that they both championed. From Bale, Foxe derived the idea of reading the Protestant and Catholic churches as the 'two churches' predicted in the Book of Revelation, the true and the false, corresponding to the Bride of Christ and the Whore of Babylon. And from Bale, he saw the possibilities of Protestant martyrs—a new class of English saints, a line of victims of Church persecution that stretched from at least as far back as the early fifteenth century to the present day.

It comes as no surprise to find John Bale among those attacking the *Legenda aurea*. In his final days as a Carmelite in Doncaster, Bale was examined for preaching against 'honourynge and prayenge to sayntes'.[9] By 1545, he would dismiss the entire martyrology of the Roman Catholic Church: 'Nothynge els are youre histories of the Saintes but fables / lyes / and fantasyes taken out of Legenda aurea made by fryre Iames de voragine.'[10] But, as with so much for Bale, 'youre histories of the Saintes' had an awkward personal resonance. In the two lists of his works that survive from the 1530s, the recent Carmelite proudly includes his 'Diue Anne vitam' ('Life of St Anne', mother of the Virgin Mary), a work which survives in a manuscript at the Bodleian Library, and which contains all the features that Reformers attacked in the *Legenda aurea*: miracles (pregnancy at sixty-one, divine conception) and risible evidence (in this case, a non-existent genealogy).[11] When Bale updated his bibliography in 1547, the life of St Anne had disappeared. But by then, Bale had some new saints to promote.

In 1544, Bale published *A Brefe Chronycle Concernynge the Examinacyon and Death of the Blessed Martyr of Christ Syr Iohan Oldecastell the Lorde Cobham*, a supporter of John Wyclif who was executed as a heretic in 1415.[12] As Bale notes, William Tyndale had published on the same topic fourteen years earlier, but whereas Tyndale used an account written by a friend of Oldcastle's, Bale excitedly claims to have something more potent: 'sens that tyme I haue founde it in theyr owne wrytynges (which were than his vttre enemyes) in a moche more ample fourme than there'. Bale redeploys the Catholic Church's 'owne wrytynges' against Wyclif and his associates, collected as part of his Carmelite researches, to attack the Catholic Church. He has, he boasts, the archbishop of Canterbury's 'great processe' against Oldcastle, 'wrytten by his owne notaryes and clarkes', signed and sealed by the archbishop for publication throughout the realm. Most importantly, he has the writings of the king's confessor Thomas Netter of Walden, who was 'present at [Wyclif's] examinacyon / condempnacyon / & execracyon' and 'regestred it amonge other processes more / in his boke called Fasciculus zizaniorum Wicleui'.[13] (A scribal copy of the 'Fasciculus zizaniorum Wicleui'—the list of alleged erroneous opinions to be found in Wyclif's writings—survives in the Bodleian, annotated and indexed in Bale's hand.[14]) From these Catholic materials, Bale fashions a new Protestant martyr.

Bale's technique is always combative. At the end of *A Brefe Chronycle*, he compares Oldcastle's death with that of the celebrated English Catholic saint, Thomas Becket, assassinated in Canterbury Cathedral in 1170; while Becket was the saint with whom Nicholas Harpsfield would draw comparisons to Thomas More, to Bale he is a false martyr. 'Conferre [Compare] the causes of this godlye mannys death with the poyntes that Thomas Becket dyed for and other Popishe martyrs besydes', Bale instructs his reader, '& ye shall fynde them farre dyfferent and vnlyke.' Becket was slain 'in his Prelates aparell / in the head churche / before the hygh aultre / amonge relygyouse Monkes and Prestes / and in the holye tyme of Christmas / by his owne sekynge'—all of which 'is gloryouse vnto worldlye iudgementes'. By contrast, Oldcastle 'was brent [burned] in cheanes / at London in saynct Gyles felde / vndre the galowes / amonge the laye people / & vpon the prophane workynge daye / at the Bysshoppes procurement'—all of which 'is vngloryouse / yea & verye despyscable [*sic*] vnto those worldlye eyes'. Oldcastle's death is much more like Jesus Christ's, 'for he was crucyfyed at Hierusalem / without [outside] the cyte & without the holye synagoge / a cursed out of churche / amonge the prophane multytude / in the myddest of theues / in the place where as theues were commonlye hanged / and not vpon the feastfull daye but afore yt / by the Bysshoppes procurement also'. Bale rhetorically demands of his reader: 'tell me which of these two semeth rather to be the martyr of Christ / and which the Popes martyr?', and then answers his own question with a marginal note: 'No popysh martyr is Cobham'[15]—Cobham is a martyr of a superior cast.

Two years after claiming Oldcastle, Bale salvaged another martyr, but this time a contemporary. Anne Askew was a young Lincolnshire gentlewoman who had developed Protestant beliefs, left her husband, and moved to London. In 1545 and 1546 she was twice interrogated by the ecclesiastical authorities about her heterodox opinions; in June 1546 she was arraigned for heresy, found guilty, then on

16 July, at the age of twenty-five, burned at the stake in Smithfield alongside three men. Askew's two examinations became the subject of publications by Bale: in 1546, he published *The First Examinacyon of Anne Askewe, Latelye Martyred in Smythfelde*; a year later *The Lattre Examinacyon* followed, with the two publications subsequently paired in four further editions.[16] Bale presents what he claims is Askew's own handwritten account of the 'examinacyons' or interrogations, split into small sections, with each section followed by a (usually longer) 'elucydacyon', or commentary, by Bale. For those with no knowledge of Askew's case, these books can be opaque. After the opening remark that 'In Lyncolne shyre was she borne of a verye auncyent and noble stocke, Sir Wyllyam Askewe a worthye knyght beynge her father',[17] biographical information is only proffered by Bale when he deems it absolutely necessary. It is not until Askew mentions a 'master kyme' in *The Lattre Examinacyon* that Bale feels it necessary to provide the history that led to Askew's imprisonment–that Anne had been married against her will to comply with a deal struck between her father and her husband's father, old Master Kyme. Despite her reservations she 'demeaned her selfe lyke a Christen wife' and bore Kyme two children. Over time, however, Anne's Bible reading led her to reject Catholicism; at the priests' urging, Kyme 'vyolently drove her oute of hys howse', at which point Anne 'thought her selfe free from that uncomelye kynde of coacted [enforced] marryage', following Paul's dictum in 1 Corinthians 7 ('If a faytfull woman have an unbelevynge husbande, whych wyll not tarrye with her, she may leave hym'), and sought a divorce. As a result, Bale writes, 'Of thys matter was she first examined (I thynke) at hys instaunt laboure and sute'.[18] Bale's uncharacteristic hesitations–he is 'infourmed' that she has two children, he 'thynke[s]' it was Kyme who brought Askew to this situation–suggest not only a lack of first-hand knowledge, but a lack of concern. Bale is not here interested in giving us a 'life' of Anne Askew, but only what is needed to explain the account she gives of her examinations.

Instead, in his introductory remarks Bale turns again to analogy, comparing Askew to Blandina, a slave martyred in the second century in Lyon, France. Like Blandina, Askew was young and tender. Like Blandina, Askew was put to death with three companions for her Christian belief; the faithful brethren in France wrote to the brethren in the lands of Asia and Phrygia, as Bale does now writing 'unto yow in Englande' (from exile in Europe). Blandina 'never faynted in torment', and neither did Askew, 'when she was so terrybly racked...that the strynges of her armes and eyes were peryshed'. Blandina had burning plates of iron and brass put to her sides; Askew had 'the flamynge brandes of fyre'. Blandina was given 'to wylde beastes to be devoured'; Askew was given 'to cruell Byshoppes and prestes, whom Christ calleth ravenynge wolves, devourers, and theves'. On the scaffold, Blandina rebuked the pagan priests for their error; '[s]o ded Anne Askewe whan she was fast tyed to the stake, with stomack rebuke that blasphemouse apostata Shaxton [Nicholas Shaxton, who had recanted his Protestant faith] with the Bishoppes and prestes generacyon, for their manifest mayntenaunce of ydolatrye'– and so on and so on.

Bale believed that the example of Anne Askew would inevitably draw people away from the Catholic Church: 'I dare boldlie saye vnto them, that by burnynge Anne Askewe and her .iii. companyons, they haue one thousande lesse of their popishe beleue than they hade afore', he writes confidently.[19] But Bale never reckoned on isolated figures such as Oldcastle and Askew being enough. In the second Askew book, addressing his 'Christen readers', Bale recalls how, during the persecutions of the primitive Church, 'manye dylygent wryters collected the godlye answers and tryumphaunt sufferynges of the martyrs, as necessarye examples of Christen constancy to be folowed of other'. Now there is a similar need to collect, since nothing can be more comforting 'than to knowe the ernest constancy of their troubled companyons in that kyngdome of pacyence...or to marke in them the stronge workynge of faythe, and beholde the myghtye mageste of God in their agonyes'. Many have suffered in recent years at the hands of 'Antichristes fuyrouse advocates': their confessions, causes, and answers, Bale proposes, 'are a great deale more notable and godlye, if they be ryghtyle wayed, than ever were the confessyons, causes and answers of the olde canonysed martyrs, which in the popes Englysh churche have had so manye solempntyees, servyces, and sensynges'.

Bale develops his theme of 'conferring' (comparing) these martyrs, 'the olde with the newe'. He separates out those of what he calls 'the Brytayne churche, or the prymatyve churche of thys realme', which was never under the Roman pope– these are Christ's 'true martyrs' which need to be discerned from 'the popes and Mahometes counterfett martyrs'. Since Augustine of Canterbury had founded 'the popes Englysh churche' in England, there had been two kinds of martyr: first, 'monasterye buylders and chauntrye founders' put to death for disobedience or treason–men like Becket; and second, 'preachers of the Gospell, or poore teachers therof in corners, whan the persecucyon was syche, that it might not be taught abroade', who were put to death for heresy and 'lollerye' (Wyclif's followers being known as 'Lollards'). Becket and his ilk have been lionized–'The ymages of these have bene sett up in their temples, lyke the olde goddes of the paganes, and have had ther vygyls, holye dayes, ryngynges, sacryfysynges, candels, offerynges, feastynges, and moch a do besydes'–but no such solemnity greeted the real 'Christen martyr': 'No, they had not so moch as penye dyrge or a grote masse of Requiem'–but instead 'have bene holden for condemned heretykes ever sens'. The old supposed English martyrs can present 'verye fewe coloures or yet tokens' of martyrdom, 'unlesse', Bale notes wryly, 'ye take pylgrymages, pompes rellyckes, women, battels, huntynges, ydelnesse, monkeryes, moneye, treasure, worldlye kyngedomes, contempt of marryage, superstytcyons and soch other vanytees for them'. By contrast, Askew and her companions exhibit 'the expresse tokens that Christe sealeth hys martyrs with. They apered as shepe amonge wolves. They were throwne into stronge preson. They were brought forth into counsels and synagoges. Their answers were out of Gods sprete...and not out of their owne. They were revyled, mocked, stocked, racked, execrated, condempned, and murthered...By a spirtualte also, as he promised they shuld be, Math. 23 and 24.' These are the new, true English Christian martyrs, role-models for Bale's 'Christen readers'—and the crucial inspiration for John Foxe.

Foxe's Histories of the Church

It was in Strasbourg that Foxe published his first Protestant history, in Latin: *Commentarii rerum in ecclesia gestarum* (*Commentaries on the History of the Church*), a small octavo volume of 212 leaves, telling of the persecution of the true Church from the time of John Wyclif through to Reginald Peacock, who lost his episcopal see for heresy in 1458, largely focused on England (although Foxe finds room for Savanarola).[20] By now Foxe was alone: he and Bale had been separated when Bale left for Ireland in late 1552, and a year later, Foxe—ousted from his teaching position once Mary came to the throne—was forced into exile in Strasbourg.[21] But although he was no longer with Foxe, Bale's influence was evident: Evenden and Freeman calculate that about three quarters of the *Commentarii* was based on two sources, of which one was Bale's copy of the 'Fasciculi Zizaniorum', the collection of Carmelite documents which he had copiously annotated with notes on Lollard biography and history—so even at a distance Bale was helping to write Foxe's book.[22]

Foxe then expected to work on a volume devoted to the continental counterparts to the persecuted Englishmen, but events in England forced him to change plans. On 4 February 1555, the biblical scholar and one-time lecturer in divinity in St Paul's John Rogers was 'burned for erroneous opinions' at Smithfield, as the diarist Henry Machyn put it.[23] Within five days, London preacher Lawrence Saunders had been executed in Coventry, John Hooper, bishop of Gloucester and Worcester, was burned at Gloucester, and Suffolk clergyman Rowland Taylor was killed at Aldham Common. By the time Mary died on 17 November 1558, close to 300 people had lost their lives at the stake: men and women, clergy and secular, from bishops to the indigent. Foxe set to work, expanding the *Commentarii* into a 1559 volume entitled *Rerum in ecclesia gestarum*, using chronicle materials to trace the history of the true Church until the death of Edward VI in 1553, drawing again on publications and notes by Bale, and including a Latin translation of Bale's tract on Anne Askew. Evidently pressed for time, Foxe gives only a patchy and necessarily second-hand account of the 'Marian martyrs' up to the execution of Cranmer on 20 March 1556, merely listing the victims that followed.[24]

But Foxe remained committed to producing a martyrology that would span the persecuted Church from the late medieval period to the end of Mary's reign. In October 1559, he arrived back in England, and within a month had published—with the printer John Day—a teaser for his grand project: *A Frendly Farewell*, written by the bishop of London Nicholas Ridley to his friends from prison shortly before his execution. In a letter 'to the gentle Reader', Foxe describes 'this litell treatis of Doct. Nicholas Ridley' as one '[a]mongest manye other worthy & sundrie Histories, and notable acts which we haue in hande, and ente*n*de (by the grace of Christe oure Lorde) shortly to set abrode, of such as of late daies haue ben persecuted, murthered, & martyred for the trewe Gospell of Christ, in Quene Maries raigne'. In these 'Histories wha*n* they shal come to light, (I suppose) thou shalt see as horrible a slaughter of the Sainctes, ioyned with as much crueltie of some English hertes, as euer in anye one realme before Christe, or after was sene'.[25] Foxe was not the first to focus attention on the Marian martyrs as a group: in 1559, Thomas Brice published a martyrs' calendar in rhyme that devoted a stanza to each month of the recent massacre, each finishing with an appeal to Elizabeth, whose accession would stop the suffering.[26] But Foxe was the first to insist on the Marian martyrs, this 'slaughter of the Sainctes', as the latest instalment of an ecclesiastical history based on the persecution of Protestants.

It was not until March 1563 that the work was published, just months ahead of the death in Canterbury of Foxe's collaborator, John Bale. The impressive folio volume boasted a suitably grandiose title: *Actes and Monuments of these latter and perillous dayes touching matters of the Church, wherein ar comprehended and described the great persecutions & horrible troubles, that haue bene wrought and practised by the Romishe prelates, speciallye in this realme of England and Scotlande, from the yeare of our Lorde a thousande, vnto the tyme nowe present* (Fig. 4). On the title page, God sits at the top, with angels on either side sounding their trumpets towards Him. But underneath the banks of angels the two churches are depicted in stark contrast. In the bottom-left corner, we see a Protestant preacher in the pulpit, addressing a congregation of men and women holding books in their hands, and a man leading a group of kneeling men in prayer, gazing up at the tetragrammaton. Above them we see a group of seven burning martyrs, sounding their trumpets upwards; in the image above that, they have been transposed into seven saints in heaven. In the bottom-right corner, a Catholic priest addresses a group of men and women, indifferently toying with their rosaries, while an impressive procession of tonsured men accompanies a canopied prelate. Above them, instead of burning martyrs, we have monks trumpeting during a communion mass, with

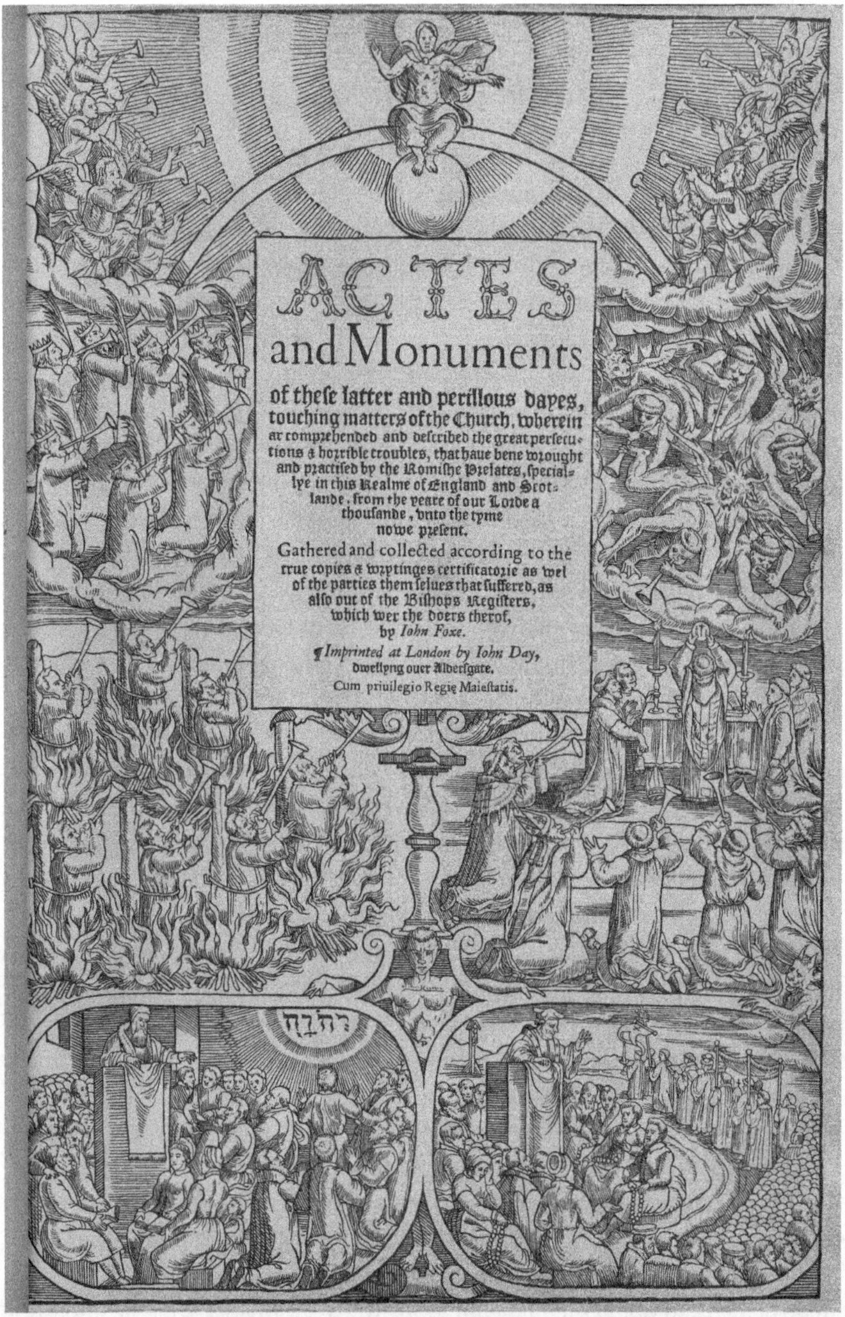

Figure 4. Title page of John Foxe, *Actes and Monuments* (1563). Beinecke Rare Book and Manuscript Library, Yale University.

the host lifted upwards. And in the higher space, instead of saints, we have devils, trumpeting downwards.

Inside the book, the prefatory materials feature a 'Kalendar' in which most days of the year are given a martyr to commemorate, some of them highlighted as red-letter days: so 1 January and 6 January are still the traditional 'Circumcision' and 'Epiphany', but 2 January is now 'John Wicklef preacher, martyr' (*3^r), Oldcastle is assigned to 6 February (*3^r), while Askew and the men executed with her occupy 1 and 2 June (*4^r). Most of the named martyrs and confessors are English, mainly from the Marian years, but Foxe finds room for a few Continental figures, including Martin Luther and Jan Hus. Foxe then writes a dedicatory epistle to Queen Elizabeth, another, in Latin, 'ad lectorem [to the reader]', before a third 'To the Persecutors of Gods truth, commonlye called Papistes'. And then he embarks on some 1800 pages, in six parts, of the *Actes and Monuments*.

Foxe believed he was writing a history of the Church, in the spirit of Eusebius, the fourth-century Greek bishop of Caesarea who composed the first surviving account of early Christianity. But what many people read was a 'booke of Martyrs'—much to his annoyance: 'I wrote no such booke bearyng the title of the booke of Martyrs', he complained in the 1570 edition. 'I wrote a booke called the Actes and Monumentes, of thinges passed in the churche, &c. Wherin many other matters bee contayned beside the Martyrs of Christ.'[27] But it was the martyrs and their martyrdoms that hooked readers: and it was Foxe himself, along with his publisher John Day, who rendered them so compelling. To understand what Foxe contributed, we can look to his treatment of Anne Askew, which he took from Bale's books. Foxe strips away Bale's 'elucidacyons' and his characteristic recourse to analogies and comparisons, leaving what appears to be largely an autobiographical text. Bale is notably reluctant to discuss the execution: 'Now to conclude with Anne Askewe as the argument of thys booke requyreth', he notes that 'she suffered most cruell deathe' at Smithfield, with Lassells, Adam, and a priest 'whose name at thys tyme I had not'. In Bale's telling, the execution is notable for a supernatural event: 'Credyblye am I infourmed by dyuerse duche marchauntes whych were there present, that in *the* time of their sufferynges, the skye abhorrynge so wicked an acte, sodenly altered coloure, and the cloudes from above gave a thunder clappe, not all unlyke to that is written, Psal. 76'—the elements thus conveyed 'the hygh displeasure of God for so tyrannouse a murther of innocentes'.[28] By contrast Foxe's account of Askew's 'end and martyrdom' does away with the editorializing, and provides much more detail. Askew, he tells us, was brought into Smithfield in a chair, 'because she could not go on her feete, by meanes of her great tormentes'. At the stake, 'she was tied by *the* middle with a chaine, that helde vp her body' (2P3^r). Later editions become even more specific. Foxe describes the dignitaries on the bench, and how 'the multitude and concourse of the people was exceeding, the place where they stood being railed about to keep out the press'. One of those on the bench, 'hearing that they had gunpouder about them, and being afeard least the fagots by strength of the gunpouder would come flying about their eares, began to bee afrayde', but he was assured by the earl of Bedford that 'the gunpouder was not layde vnder the fagots, but onely about their bodies, to ryd the*m* out of their payne, which hauing vent, there was no daunger to them of the fagots'.[29]

While Foxe had to make over earlier material such as that on Askew, with the Marian martyrs he stamped his signature from the outset, and in so doing developed a new, distinctive model of life-writing. Foxe opens up the types of person treated to include, as John Jewel, bishop of Salisbury, put it, 'Married, Unmarried, Learned, Unlearned, Olde, Yonge, Boies, Maides, Laiemenne, Priestes, Bishoppes, Archebishoppes'.[30] He gives a short account of the subject's birth and education (which Bale does not). From Bale he takes the emphasis on documentary evidence—the title page boasts the volume is based on 'the true copies [and] wrytinges certificatorie, as wel of the parties them selues that suffered, as also out of the bishops registers, which wer the doers therof'—but whereas Bale is interested in debate, Foxe stresses suffering, and, most notably, he gives a vast amount of attention to the deaths. Among the earlier martyrs, Richard Bayfield's macabre end in 1531 is dealt with in two sentences: 'for lacke of a speady fire', Bayfield 'was iii. quarters of an houre a liue. And when the left arme was on fyre and burned, he rubbed it with his right hand, and it fel from his bodye, and he continued in prayer to the ende wythout mouyng' (2X3^{r}). This kind of sickening physical detail is elaborated much more pruriently when Foxe describes the fates of the Marian martyrs. The final suffering and death of each martyr occupies a privileged position within each narrative, often singled out with a subtitle: 'The cruell burning of W. Flower' (3I3^{v}). Foxe consistently draws attention to the mechanics of burning at the stake, a particularly cruel form of execution whose victims were often forced to suffer at length before finally expiring. Fires could take a long time to reach the necessary momentum if the wind was in the wrong direction, or if inappropriate or wet materials were used as kindling. Although the condemned were made to carry faggots (bundles of twigs or sticks) as a sign of their heresy, these faggots were meant to catch light and hasten their deaths. George Marsh was chained with 'a number of Fagots vnder hym, & a thing made like a firkin wi*th* pitch and tarre in the same ouer his head'; but despite this, because 'the fier was vnskilfully made' and 'the wind dyd driue the flame to and for', he still 'suffered great extremitie in his death, whiche notwi*th*standing he abode very pacie*n*tly' (3H3^{v}). Laurence Saunders was burned 'with greene woode, and other smothteryng [*sic*] rather then burnyng fewel, which put hym to much more pain' (3B2^{v}), while Robert Ferrar, bishop of

St David's, 'for lacke of wood & other fuel...was burned wyth turffes & soddes, which was to him a more greuous torment' (3F4^{v}).

Many came prepared. Bishop John Hooper, allowed to wear only his shirt, hid bladders filled with gunpowder between his legs and under each arm. Holding two bundles of reeds, he 'embraced them, kissed them, & put vnder either arme one of them, and shewed with his hand how the rest shoulde be bestowed, and pointed to the place where any dyd lacke'. But when the fire was put to the green faggots, they did not kindle, and it 'was a prety while also before it tooke the reedes vpon the faggotes'. Finally, the fire got going, 'but the wind hauing full strength in that place (it was also a louring and a cold morning) it blewe the flame from him'. More dry faggots were added, which 'burned at the nether partes', but the wind meant that 'it did burne his heare & swel his skin a litle'. As only his lower extremities burned, Hooper's prayers escalated until he was beginning 'with an indifferent loude voice: For gods loue (good people) let me haue more fire'. When a third, stronger fire was added, 'the bledders of gonnepowder brake, which did him small good, they were so put, and the wind had such power'. The last words he was heard to speak were 'Lord Iesu haue mercy vpon me: Lorde Iesu haue mercy vpon me. Lord Iesus receaue my spirite', but 'when he was blacke in the mouth, and his tonge swollen, that he could not speake: yet his lippes went, till they wer shrounke to the gommes: & he did knocke his brest with his hands vntill one of his armes fel of, and then knocked still with the other, what time the fat, water, and bloud dropped out at his fingers endes, vntil by renewing of the fire, his strength was gonne, and his hand did cleaue fast in knocking, to the yron vpon his brest. So immediatly bowing forwardes, he yelded vp his spirite' (3C3^{r-v}).

The focus on the horrible sufferings and deaths was exacerbated by the sensational woodcuts. These seem to have been the contribution of Foxe's publisher, John Day, who as early as 1548 had printed a woodcut of the execution at Smithfield of Anne Askew and her associates. Askew and her fellow sufferers, however, are shown here at a distance; in the *Actes and Monuments*, the martyrs are given the print equivalent of a close-up. The images gave Foxe's work a readership well beyond those literate in English. Sir Francis Drake, who took a copy on board the *Golden Hind* during his voyage around the world from 1577 to 1580, put the illustrations to use. In Holy Week of 1579, at the Mexican port of Guatulco, Drake was observed reading Foxe's volume for some time. A factor named Francisco Gomez Rengifo claimed that Drake produced 'a book of the size of the *Lives of the Saints*'—a telling comparison—and the Spanish cleric Simon de Miranda testified that Drake 'had a large book brought to him and read it for some time. He said it was to them what the Bible is to us. It contained many illuminated pictures of the Lutherans who had been burnt in Spain.' Since none of the Spanish in Mexico could read English,

Drake deployed the illustrations to score points against their faith and against Spain. Showing 'a figure representing a fire and a man' to Rengifo, Drake said, 'Look at this book. You can see here those who were martyred in Castille'; 'turning over the pages of the book' he pointed out another picture which, he claimed, 'figured the astounding [arrogance] of the Supreme Pontiff'.[31]

Those present at the executions—and those reading Foxe's book—are taught to look for signs of God's providence even in these most excruciating scenes. At his burning, Thomas Hawkes's supporters asked him to give them 'some toke*n*' while he was burning 'whereby they might be more certaine, whether that in that kynde of punishment: there wer so great pain and greefe, that a man mighte not keepe hys minde constant therein'. It was agreed that if he found the flame to be 'tolerable', he would 'lyft vp hys handes aboue his heade towarde the heauen, before hee gaue vp the ghost'. At the stake, after a long burning which consumed his fingers, Hawkes not only 'dyd lift vp his hands halfe burned, & burning with heate aboue his head, to the liuing God', but 'eue*n* in a sodain, and with great reioycing striketh them three tymes together: By which thing, contrary to all mens expectation beyng sene, there followed so great reioycing and crye of the multitude gathered together, that you would haue thought heauen & earth to haue com together' (3L5^{v}).

There is no doubt that the sufferings at the stake were a focus for most readers. As John Wolton, one of the cathedral church in Exeter, wrote in 1577, 'Many of vs haue séene with our eyes, and those that haue not séene, maye reade in the booke of Martyrs: of the constancie and patience, of Christes seruantes, in the flames of fyre, so straunglye, and aboue all humane strength, that they wearied and appaled the cruell tormentors'. But, despite claiming the constancy of Christ's servants, Wolton is ultimately unsure. 'What doeth it shew?' he asks. Is this indeed 'an heauenlie gyfte of tollerancie, and patience', or simply 'a sencelesnesse of payne', pain numbing all sensation?[32]

That Huge Dongehill of Your Stinking Martyrs: The Catholic Backlash

Foxe's *Actes and Monuments* was too substantial an achievement for Roman Catholics to ignore, and they very soon went to town on it, heaping abuse on the volume. In 1565, Thomas Harding protested that Foxe had exaggerated the numbers of recent martyrs, so that 'scores be hundreds, hundreds be thousands, thousands be millions'; moreover, the fact that these men and women were burned did not mean that they had 'borne witness vnto truth' but rather 'shewed their desperate obstinacie against the truth'. And yet 'this is the chiefe argument ye make in all that huge dongehill of your stinking martyrs, which ye haue intituled Actes and monuments. But we tell you, It is not death that iustifieth the cause of dying. But it is the cause of dying that justifieth the death.'[33] Two years later, Harding attacked the calendar of martyrs with which Foxe prefaced his work: 'Wheras as you wil nedes haue them to be called Martyrs, and now be canonizate a Gods name by M. Foxe, and set in a solemne Calender, that holy daies and hye feastes be kept for them, who can otherwise do, but laugh at you?' He advised, 'Let M. Foxe make no Martyrs'–or if he must, 'let him be warned to vse a more discretion, then heretofore he hath vsed, els his huge booke of Actes and Monumentes can not long kepe credit. For what wil wisemen thinke, euen they of your owne side, when they shal consider, what persons he hath canonizate, and registred for Martyrs?' Some of his martyrs were hanged for felonies, not heresy: a parade of 'murderers, theeues, Churcherobbers, rebelles, and Traitours, and by your owne confession detestable heretiques, haue ye made Martyrs'.[34]

Some critics grudgingly admitted that Foxe's work was uncommonly effective, with the Jesuit Robert Persons writing that the 'lyinge Actes and Monuments hath done more hurt alone to simple soules in our countrey by infecting and poysoninge them unawares under the bayte of pleasant histories, fayre pictures and painted pageants than many other the most pestilent bookes togeather'. Persons identified several key elements: first, 'the variety of the history it selfe, draweth many to read yt'; second, the 'spectacle and representation of martyrdomes (as they are called) delighteth many to gaze on, who cannot read'; third, 'the hypocrisy of the wryter, making those protestations which before haue byn mentioned, and otherwise, gayninge opinion of piety with the common people, by a certayne affected simplicity of life'; and fourth, 'certayne tender speaches attributed by him to sectaryes at their deathes, with his owne sanctifying & canonizinge them for Saints'–combined 'with the very greatnes of the booke yt selfe, obtruded to be read in very many parish Churches, and other publike places'.[35]

Of all the horrors in Foxe's book, one stood out for readers, then and now–and attracted the most virulent attacks. In May 1556, a Guernsey woman named Perotine Massey was arrested alongside her mother and sister for the harbouring of stolen goods. Although the criminal charges came to nothing, it was discovered that the three women had not been attending mass. On 1 July, they were once again arrested and interrogated about their religious beliefs, and in short order found guilty of heresy and sentenced to death at the stake. As usual, Foxe devotes considerable attention to their final sufferings which, in Massey's case, were extreme. When the Guernsey women

> were burning in the fyrye flames aboute them, the wombe of the sayde Paratine, shee beyng great with childe, brake with the heate of the sayd fyre, and thereby issued foorthe of her

bodye a goodlye man chylde which was taken vp, and handled by the cruell tormentours, and after they threw most spightfullye the same chylde into the fyre agayne, wher it was burned with the sely Mother, Graundmother, and Aunt, very pitifully to behold.

The outrage is depicted in a woodcut headed 'A Lamentable Spectacle' (Fig. 5), and prompts a rare outburst by narrator Foxe:

Oh cruel Papistes, that euer suche a foule murther vpon earth should be committed. The Lorde hym selfe wyll reuenge it no doubt, to your perpetual shame, although in this world neither the complaint was greatlye regarded, nor the cause condignly pondered, nor the cruel murther as yet reuenged. &c.

But Foxe also knows that, due to 'the horrible straungenes of the fact', this story 'wyl be hardly beleued of some, but rather thoughte to bee forged, or els amplified

Figure 5. 'A Lamentable Spectacle of three women, with a sely infant brasting out of the Mothers Wombe', in Foxe, *Actes and Monumentes* (1570). Beinecke Rare Book and Manuscript Library, Yale University.

of vs' (*3Vv4^{v}). He therefore presents as evidence a supplication made by various Guernsey men (including the brother of the two sisters) to the Queen's commissioners, complaining of the child's murder; he also proudly states that the commissioners found there was a case to answer, and imprisoned and dispossessed the dean. The murder charge remains 'further to be examined & decised' but Foxe states, 'I know that gods high iustice and reuenging hand wyl not suffer that gyltles bloude and detestable facte to escape vnreuenged, excepte greter repentance come' (*3Vv5^{r}).

The episode caught the imagination of the book's readers. The bishop of Salisbury, John Jewel, charged Thomas Harding that 'Ye scourged them with roddes: ye sette burninge torches to their handes, ye cutte of their tongues, ye hanged them, ye beheadded them, ye burnte them to ashes, ye tooke the poore innocent babe fallinge from the mothers wombe, and threwe it cruelly into the fier. Briefly, ye did with them, what so euer your pleasure was.'[36] Jewel evidently expected Harding to recognize the reference, and Harding did: 'Concerninge the manner of their executions and punishmentes, you describe it so, as a man may point vnto you, and say, there goeth a scholer of Iohn Foxes. In his lying Actes and Monumentes you seme to haue ben a great student.'[37]

Harding goes to great lengths to undo Foxe's story about Perotine Massey. First, he claims that the story 'wil not to any wise man appeare very probable'. Even assuming it were true, did the fault lie 'in the officer, that tooke not the childe out of the fier, or in the vnnatural mother, that brought it into the fier'? Harding notes that 'there is no woorde spoken' of the child's father, so the child was presumably illegitimate, and that although the mother could have pleaded for 'the benefite of her belly', and delayed her punishment until the child was born, 'your pratteling parrat Paratine' did not tell the judge. By keeping her pregnancy quiet from the magistrates, Perotine 'now not only like an harlot or Heretique, but like a Murtherer went desperatly to the fier, and murdered bothe her selfe, and her childe conceiued within her'. In 'suffering the childe to fal from her wombe, in the sight of al that stoode by', God was therefore delivering His 'condemnation bothe of her, and of the cause for which she dyed'. Harding asks his reader to judge who was to blame—the ministers of justice who simply executed the law, or 'the woman, that for auoiding a worldly shame, conceeling her owne turpitude, became a murtherer of her owne babe, before it came to perfection. So that she died gilty of three heinous crimes, of heresie, lecherie, and murther. And to these thefte may be added for the fourth'—given that 'Foxe him selfe' tells us 'that she was a thefe, as being accessorie to the honest woman Vincent Gosser, that stole a siluer gobblet'. Hardly 'a fitte vessel to receiue the glorie of these newe inuented Martyrdomes'. And what could Jewel have done better for 'that vnperfite and dead childe'?

If they had taken it out of the fyer, what should that haue auailed? Life it had none, and therfore was it not to be baptized. Sense it had none: and therfore had it not ben holpen by sauing it from burning. As for burial, sith it was neither Christened, nor come to be perfite man: it was aswel burnt, and buried in earth, yea in some respecte better, bicause being burnt with the wicked mother, besides the more detestation of the horrible crime to the example of others, it was a testimonie against the mothers vnnaturalnes.

And so, Harding triumphantly concludes, 'the mother your Syster in the Lorde, is fownd but a meane Martyr, and witnesse of the truth. Of the fruite of such Martyrdome, the famous Tree of Tybourne bringeth forth good stoare.'[38]

Characteristically, Foxe did what he could to answer even these criticisms. In the 1570 edition, he urges Harding to 'surcease from this vncharitable raylyng and brawlyng, especially agaynst the dead which can not aunswere him', and chides him for 'accus[ing] of murder the parties that were murdered'. But he also rescues Perotine from Harding's libel by naming her husband, a Protestant minister from Normandy named David Jores, and for good measure providing the name and present location of the minister who married them.[39] And, rather than in any way retracting his claims, Foxe exacerbates his attack by focusing on the baby:

And so the infant Baptised in his owne bloud, to fill vp the number of Gods innocent Saintes, was both borne and dyed a Martyr, leauing behind it to the world, which it neuer saw, a spectacle wherein the whole world may see the Herodian crueltie of this graceles generation of Catholicke tormentors, Ad perpetuam rei infamiam [to the eternal infamy of the matter].[40]

Not now the accidental victim of his mother's martyrdom, the baby is a martyr in his own right, a Christ-like figure fallen victim to the Catholics' Herodian cruelty.

Reading the *Book of Martyrs*

Despite some complaints about its size and cost–and, of course, the Catholic attacks on it–Foxe's *Book of Martyrs* was a huge success. Foxe returned to the project several times, producing ever vaster tomes, and more than doubling the level of illustrations. (The 1583 edition, the last to which he contributed, included 153.[41]) When the second edition was produced in 1570, the Privy Council urged England's leading churchmen to place copies of the volume in all churches, since the book 'was very profitable to bringing her majesties subiects into good opinion, understending and dere liking of the present gouernment'.[42]

As Grace Mildmay's instructions suggest, the *Actes and Monuments* took its place in importance somewhere between the Bible and the English Chronicles. In 'A Faithfull Memoriall of my owne Mother that is Deceaced', the puritan London artisan Nehemiah Wallington recalled that God had given Elizabeth Wallington 'a pregnant witt and an excellent memory. She was verye rife [i.e. rich] and perfitt in all the stories of the Bible, likewise in all the stories of the Martyres, and could readily turne to them. Shee was also perfitt and well seene in the English chronicles and the Discentes of the Kings of England.'[43] And in 1690, almost 130 years after its first appearance, the clergyman Anthony Walker recalled that, after introducing her daughters to the Bible, his late wife Elizabeth Walker 'would give them other Books, and often hear them read them, and would make a prudent choice of Books of Instruction, and Devotion, and sometimes usefull Histories; as the Book of Martyrs, and Abbreviations of our English Chronicles, and Lives of Holy, Exemplary Persons, especially of those who were so while Young, that she might doe several things at once; both perfect their Reading, and inform their Judgments, and inflame their Affections to an imitation of their early Piety'.[44]

But *how* exactly did early modern men and women read Foxe's *Actes and Monuments?* As Foxe himself noted, readers could hardly aim to be martyrs. But '[i]f theyre blessednes be moste certayne and sure', he urged, 'let vs also direct the course of our lyfe to the same felicity':

> Those men haue put of[f] this lyfe, which they might haue kept. But albeit that we cannot put of[f] our lyfe, let vs not be slowe to amend, and correct the same: and though we cannot dye with them in lyke martyrdom yet let vs mortify the worldly and prophane affections of the fleshe, which stryve against the spirite: & at *the* least take hede that we run not into the licentious desires of the world. (316^{v})

It was commonly advertised as having unspecified salutary effects: in one of the many texts encouraging women to read Foxe, Thomas Salter in 1579 recommended for his female reader 'aboue all for delight, if shee loue to bee delighted in vertue, let her reade that worthie booke of Martyrs, compiled by that famous Father and worthie man of God maister Foxe'.[45] From the scattered references to contemporary reading practices, it would seem that Foxe's volume was treated akin to the Bible: a text to be read and re-read.[46] Ignatius Jordan, MP for and mayor of Exeter in the 1630s, 'took so much delight in reading that voluminous and excellent Book of the *Acts and Monuments* of the Church, that upon occasion he told a Friend that he had read it seven times over'.[47] The parliamentarian army officer Adam Eyre noted in his diary on 15 December 1647 that he had 'finished the first reading of the first vol. of *the* Booke of Martyrs', clearly indicating that he did not intend this to be the last reading; two months later, on 27 February 1647/8, he lent the volume to Reginald Appleyard to read.[48] The Lancashire apprentice Roger Lowe visited his friend James Wood on Thursday 8 March 1666 and recorded in his diary that 'I stayd till noone reading in the *Booke of Martirs*'.[49]

Not all reading of Foxe was solitary: in her diary, the Yorkshire gentlewoman Lady Margaret Hoby records how on Friday 28 September 1599 she 'hard one of the men read of the book of Marters', as she did again the following Thursday, presumably one of her male servants reading aloud to the household; on 11 June 1601, she records how 'After priuat prairs I went about the house and wrought amonge my Maides, and hard one read of the Booke of Marters' (Hoby and her husband owned at least three different editions of Foxe's work).[50] On 4 September 1637 the Northampton lawyer Robert Woodford had dinner with five friends, including the minister Daniel Rogers. In his diary he noted how 'I was much affected with the story of Crow (that so carefully kept his new testam*ent* in his p*er*ills) in the booke of Acts & mon*uments* related by Mr Rogers, blessed be thy name oh Lord for the comfort of good freinds thou art pleased to afford us' (Foxe tells how Gregory Crow was forced to throw away all his belongings when he was shipwrecked, but kept hold of his New Testament).[51]

Reading of Foxe's work was so common that it could be used as a shorthand, as when Dr Robert Harris, the rector of Hanwell, added a codicil to his will in 1636: 'First for you, my dear Wife, you shall finde the substance of that I would say to you printed to your hand in the Book of *Martyrs*, Vol. 2. p. 1744, to wit, in *John Careless* his Letter to his Wife; keep the Book, and often read the Letter.'[52] The East Anglian yeoman-farmer and iconoclast William Dowsing owned three different editions of *Actes and Monuments*, and compulsively annotated volumes of his substantial library with cross-references to both the Bible and Foxe. He also expected his correspondents to do likewise. Writing to the Dedham lecturer Matthew Newcomen in 1643, he advised him it was a good time to pull down all the 'reliques of popery' in Cambridge: as justification, he adds simply, 'I only reffere [*sic*] you to that famous story in Ed[ward VI's reign] how the English got the victory against the Scots in Museleborough field the same day & hower the reformation was wrought in London and images burnt—A&M edit last'—that is, the most recent (1610) edition of *Actes and Monuments*, from which he had lifted the previous sentence.[53] Even the prominent Catholic recusant Sir Thomas Tresham turned to Foxe after being arrested in 1581 for harbouring the fugitive Jesuit priest Edmund Campion in his Middlesex house: he defended his 'refusal' by citing the precedent not only of 'ancient Catholic' authorities but 'of late protestant writers, by the precedents of blessed martyrs in the primitive church and by the martyrs mentioned in Mr. Fox'.[54]

But above all, the lives in *Actes and Monuments* were to be meditated upon. The Cornish gentleman William Carnsew recorded in his diary for 1575–6 how he 'reed rydlyes end and Latymers and hys frendly farewell' (referring to bishop of London Nicholas Ridley and bishop of Worcester Hugh Latimer) before moving on to '[Stephen Gardiner, bishop of] Wynchesters sermons before Ky: Edwarde'; two days later, he 'reed[s] Wynchesters sermon before Ky: E 6 and hys ende'. While he is clearly reading his Foxe for its historical materials, Carnsew follows Foxe's emphases by registering in particular the importance of each man's 'end', his death.[55] But death need not be the defining characteristic of every figure in the *Actes and Monuments*: eighty years later, the clergyman Henry Newcome noted in his diary for Thursday 16 March 1653/4 that 'I meditated this night after reading in the Book of Martyrs all day. A wonderful weaver was John Careless'—Careless being one of the few included 'martyrs' who managed to escape actual martyrdom.[56]

To return to that early reader of Foxe: Lady Mildmay made clear the reading practice in which she had been encouraged as a girl. In the manuscript directed to her daughter and grandchildren, she recommends 'the excellent Booke of actes & Monuments of the Martyrs' because it 'contayneth a liuely demonstration & testimonie of the true church, and theyr constancie in confession of suffering for the sincere word & truth of God. Euen the onely true doctrine of our saluation in our onely sauiour Jesus Christ, with their true and inviolable faith in him sealed with their death and bloud. Which is a most liuely spectacle, & example vnto all posterities, euen to the end of the world'.[57] Later in the manuscript, she demonstrates how the *Actes and Monuments* might be used, discussing a series of historical figures who appear in Foxe's work, giving a page reference in the margin. So, alluding to what 'Ignatius that famous Martyr sayde before his martirdome', she notes 'Actes & Monuments Folio 36' (2:15); 'Iustinus a famous philosopher' on folio 44 (2: 16), his martyrdom in AD 154 on folio 40, and so on. As Kate Narveson has detailed, after Mildmay has summarized a life from Foxe, she uses Scripture to apply the moral of the life and death in more general terms, producing what she elsewhere describes as a 'meditation'.[58] One group of early French Christians 'refused to be called Martirs, & confessed that the name of Martirdome was to be geuen to Christ, the faithfull & true Martir & witnesse *the* first borne of the dead, & the captayne of lyfe'—and here Mildmay is quoting verbatim from Foxe ('Actes & mon: fol.45'). But she takes this as a starting point for her own meditation:

Christ suffered as an innocent vndeseruedly; & that voluntarily for vs, whereby to free vs from eternall tortures, & to strengthen vs in our sufferings.

But all we mortall & sinfull men are guilty of our sinnes & deserue our punishmentes, & are worthy of them whatsoever can be layed vppon vs.

Yet in our sufferings for Christ our vnworthynesse of his suffering is not imputed; but our faith in Christ is accepted, and we are crowned with Christ in his triumphant victory.

As a result, 'It is Certaine that the true religion of Christ cannot be impaired by persecucons but rather encreased thereby'—a conclusion hooked to 'Actes & Mon: fol.50' (2:18).

Before too long, Mildmay seems to tire of her task. 'Reading the Booke of Martirs, I purposed to haue gathered some of the principall poyntes & to haue aplyed them to myne own instructi*on* comfort & increase of Fayth', she tells her daughter and grandchildren, but she was 'interrupted in proceeding therein bycause my sight did sodaynely goe from me'.[59] But her infirmity allows her to pass the task to succeeding generations: 'Wherefore I left it off to them which succeed mee, to performe it in a better manner then myne abilitie could afford yet I trust God will accept of his owne giftes according to the measure thereof' (2:20). Over the decades to come, it would fall to readers to find new ways to interpret the lives of the martyrs—and to live those lives for themselves.

4

Thomas Whythorne's Life in Songs and Sonnets

We don't know how we come to have the life of Thomas Whythorne. In 1955, Major H. C. Foley found in a wooden box at his Herefordshire estate, Stoke Edith, a substantial volume wrapped in brown paper, bearing the title 'A book of songs and sonetts, with longe discoorses sett with them, of the chylds lyfe, togyther with A young mans lyfe, and entering into the old mans lyfe. devysed and written with A new Orthografye by Thomas Whythorne, gent.'.[1] Appraising Foley's collection, Sotheby's cataloguer Peter Crofts realized that the manuscript was an autobiographical narrative by a sixteenth-century English musician, generously punctuated with the lyrics of over 200 songs he had composed and, in some cases, published. Why Whythorne's manuscript should have ended up at Stoke Edith, the family seat of the Foleys since the seventeenth century, remains a mystery: a nonplussed Major Foley suggested that his collector father 'might have picked it up at some sale' or his musician grandmother 'may have bought it somewhere'.[2] James M. Osborn purchased the manuscript for his home institution, Yale University; when the British government designated the manuscript a national treasure and refused to let it out of the country, Osborn donated the manuscript to the Bodleian Library as the foundational contribution to the American Friends of the Bodleian.[3] The discovery vastly increased our knowledge of an important moment in English musical history, and gave us the most sustained English autobiographical writing of the Tudor period.

Half a century earlier, Thomas Whythorne barely merited an entry in the *Dictionary of National Biography*, dismissed as a 'musical amateur', albeit 'an amateur with an inordinate belief in his own powers'.[4] His two printed collections, *Songes for Three, Fower, and Fiue Voyces* (1571) and *Duos or Songs for Two Voices* (1590),[5] had been routinely denigrated by musical authorities since Charles Burney declared in 1789 that 'Both the words and the music of these Songs... are truly barbarous'.[6] Between the wars, however, Whythorne underwent something of a renaissance. Rejecting this 'sneering criticism' as 'wholly unwarranted', madrigal expert Edmund Horace Fellowes scored a half-dozen songs in 1921, and claimed Whythorne as 'an important pioneer in the history of English Part-song'.[7] Four years later, the early music aficionado Philip Heseltine, writing as Peter Warlock, claimed that Whythorne's books contain 'some of the most original and attractive specimens of English sixteenth-century music', concluding that 'one acclaims Whythorne as a composer of real genius who has been too long neglected'.[8] While not accepting him as a 'real genius', scholars since Warlock have seen Whythorne as an important early figure in English musical history with a number of firsts: his 1571 *Songes*, the first book of English songs in almost fifty years, providing a stepping stone to William Byrd's *Psalmes, Sonets & Songs* in 1588;[9] his 1590 *Duos* the first English duets to be published;[10] and his 'Buy New Broom' the first printed English solo song with instrumental accompaniment.[11] And his manuscript has been used by music historians, notably Katie Nelson and Christopher Page, to demonstrate that Whythorne was not an 'amateur' but a long-term professional music-teacher, working in private households before becoming master of music at Lambeth Palace, a forward-looking musician who experimented with the gittern and the sittern, and a pioneer in music publication, who grappled with a London printing trade unfamiliar with the concept.[12]

Above all, Whythorne's 'Book of songs and sonetts' reveals an Englishman in the 1570s experimenting with the writing of his life. It was James M. Osborn who edited the manuscript, entitled it *Autobiography*, and made it the centrepiece of his 1959 Clark Library lecture in which he claimed Whythorne's manuscript was 'the beginnings of autobiography in England', a cue followed by several critics.[13] But that reassuringly modern title distorts the contents of the manuscript. Certainly, there are aspects of the text that deal with the details of Whythorne's life—a narrative about himself that touches on specific places and events, an individualized portrait of himself, even a personalized orthography; but equally, there are many features that are, at best, utterly commonplace—an 'ages of man' schema lifted from classical and humanist sources, a reliance on proverbial wisdom to interpret his experiences, a life filled by episodes that are so generically similar as to defy belief. This, I shall suggest, is no accident. Whythorne is experimenting with ways of writing a life, but not simply to produce the idiosyncratic individuality that is the hallmark of autobiography to modern readers: he is simultaneously attempting to write the lives of every man that he deems to be, like himself, a true musician.[14]

Devysed and Written with a New Orthografye

Any reader opening Whythorne's manuscript is immediately struck by its spelling (Fig. 6). Whythorne opted to pen his 'Book' in his own orthography, which he adopts, he explains, 'becaws I do find more reasone in it than in that which is now commonelye vsed' (4). Debates about orthography had exercised Whythorne's learned countrymen for the past three decades, developing from a controversy between Cambridge academics about the correct pronunciation of ancient Greek into a more widespread discussion about the pronunciation and spelling of English.[15] Whythorne himself cites John Hart's 1569 *An Orthographie*, which argued that English spelling was in 'such confusion and disorder, as it may be accounted rather a kinde of ciphring, or such a darke kinde of writing' that reading it was 'a long and tedious labour', and it was 'vnfit and wrong shapen for the proportion of the voice'. But while Hart's orthography aimed to standardize English across the country, Whythorne, musician that he was, aimed to capture sound, to 'wryte wurds as they be sownded in speech' (6). Rather than flattening English to a single pronunciation, his standardized spelling system is able instead to convey the variations of dialect: among his poems is a mock 'Testiminiall' voiced by a poor servant woman, Sibbel Sluis, that captures her rural Gloucestershire accent, rendering 'far' as 'var', 'soon' as 'zoon', and 'serve' as 'zarv' (167–70).

Whythorne found that some conventional features of English spelling gravitated against the capturing of sound, so he simply corrected them. The soft 's' becomes 'z'. Long vowels are designated by placing a 'prick' underneath, so 'same' becomes 'sạm'; since it is spatially impossible to put a 'prick' under 'y', he places the prick

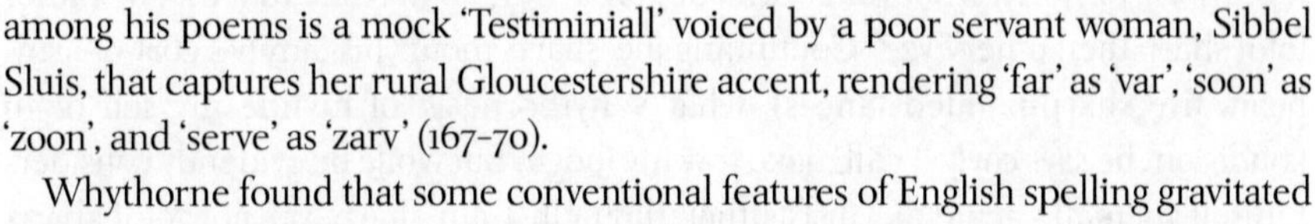
De pleazurz pat I tak
Now in my yowthfull yeerz
De sam shall mee forsak
When hoery az appeerz

Figure 6. Detail from Thomas Whythorne, 'Book of Songs and Sonetts'. The Bodleian Libraries, The University of Oxford, MS. Eng, Misc. c. 330, fo. 7[r].

above 'y' to produce 'ẏ'. The soft 'g' in 'age' is designated by the old Saxon yogh (ȝ), and 'th' in 'the' by the thorn (þ). Here we find Whythorne sharing the linguistic interests of his final employer, Matthew Parker, archbishop of Canterbury: he borrows the pricked y, the yogh, and the thorn from the first printed book to develop an Anglo-Saxon type, the 1567 A *Testimonie of Antiquitie*, a sermon by Aelfric, abbot of Eynsham, printed with an English facing-page translation, co-edited by Parker, and published by John Day (who also published Whythorne's 1571 *Songes*); Whythorne reasoned that 'I had rather vse the olde maner then any new' (5).[16] To render the entire 'Book' in this orthography was quite an undertaking: a surviving slip of paper containing an earlier draft reveals that Whythorne first wrote his text in what might pass for standard spelling in the 1570s, and then re-wrote all ninety-plus pages in his own spelling.[17] (In the interests of readability, I have here depricked, dethorned, and deyoghed Whythorne's verse and prose into a more manageable but still suitably idiosyncratic orthography.)

Whythorne turns this orthography on himself to probe his surname: is it Whyþorne (Why-thorne, with the 'th' joined together) or Whythorne (Whyt-horne with the 't' and 'h' separated)? But ultimately, he concludes, it does not matter which it is, 'thorn, or horn': whoever is 'prikt or gored' by it 'shall fynde that thei be rather to[o] sharp then otherwyze'. Continuing the 'sharp' motif (his family's coat-of-arms bears five sharp-pointed lances), what Whythorne is 'of mynde my self or in kondision', he says coyly, 'I will make yow my iudge'. But while he evidently considers himself mentally acute, he insists that 'tho[ug]h I am sharp, yet not to[o] sharp' (212)—the Italian form of which he takes as his motto, *Aspra mà non troppo* (213). This interaction between Whythorne's name and his own orthography is indicative of his punning humour: Whythorne claims back both thorn and horn as evidence of his sharpness, but then claims he's not *too* sharp—just as well for a musician.

'Thomas Whythorne'

Running through the manuscript is an account of the life of its author. But that life is not straightforwardly told: specific dates and names are scarce, and one can glean only a fraction of what is now known of Whythorne's biography. His first and last masters are clearly identified as John Heywood and Matthew Parker, archbishop of Canterbury. Other events and figures, however, have been obscured by Whythorne who often cites only a person's rank (nobleman, gentleman, duke's wife); for the identification of most of them, we are indebted to the researches of editor James Osborn.[18]

According to the manuscript, Thomas is initially raised at his father's house and 'sent to skools evry day for the moste part where I first learned to read, to wryte, and also to sing Muzik' (7). Elsewhere, Whythorne mentions that he is from 'the furthest part of Somerset sheer' (170), and archival research has revealed that he was son to John Whythorne and Joan Cabell, who lived in Ilminster. At ten, he moves to live with his uncle five miles from Oxford, a priest whose identity remains unknown. This uncle asks him what he wants to be when he grows up: young Thomas rejects the idea of being a physician or a lawyer, or studying grammar and Latin, but agrees to study music, so that he can 'learn to sing, and to play on the Organs, the which be good qualities and be much esteemed in these daies. and by them many men do lyve very well, and do cum to preferment therby' (11). To pursue this path, he goes to what he calls 'the muzik skooll', Oxford's Magdalene College School, for six years as a chorister, moving on for one year to 'the grammar skooll' there. (Whythorne's name appears in the register as a 'Demi' in 1544 at the age of sixteen.[19])

When his uncle dies, Thomas departs for London, where a friend places him in the household of poet and musician John Heywood, 'to be bothe hiz servant and skoller, for hee waz not only very well skylled in Muzik, and playeng on the virginals but also such an english *poet*, az the lyke, for hiz witt and invension, with the quantite that hee wrote, waz not az then in England, nor before hiz tyme sinse Chawsers tyme' (13). During Whythorne's three years with him, Heywood composes 'diverz dittiez to bee sung vnto muzikall instruments', and Whythorne learns to play the virginals and the lute, and to 'make English verses', while serving as an amanuensis: 'I did wryte owt for him diverz songs and sonets' made by Henry Howard, earl of Surrey, Sir Thomas Wyatt the elder, and 'mr Moor the exsellent Harper', as well as psalms by Wyatt and 'also mr Sternhold'. Here Whythorne lets us catch a glimpse of a vibrant manuscript verse culture in the last years of Henry VIII's reign. Both Wyatt's penitential psalms and Thomas Sternhold's psalm translations would make it into print in December 1549, while the 'songs and sonets' of Surrey and Wyatt would be famously published under that title by Richard Tottel in 1557.[20] Whythorne is copying these for Heywood 'before thei were publishd', and does not hesitate to read and transcribe them for himself: 'I have the copiez of most of them in A book at this present of mye own wryteing', he writes—a book now sadly lost. Moreover, this 'wryting & reading' inspires his own efforts: 'I afterward gave my self to imitate and follow their trades and devyses in wryting az okkazions moved me' (14).

Leaving Heywood's service, Whythorne takes a chamber in London, and determines 'to live of my self by teaching' music (18), a decision that leads him into a series of often fraught household positions. For some years he is employed by a widowed gentlewoman, turning down a more prestigious offer by a 'A duches or diuks wyfe', whom Osborn identifies as Jane, countess of Northumberland, to teach 'A yoong lady and daughter of hers' to play the virginals (55). When the widow's estate suddenly changes 'from hy to low', however, Whythorne discovers that 'shee doted not on mee', and decides instead 'to spend A tyme in forrein and straing kuntriez the better to digest all the chainges that hitherto I had felt and tasted' (60). Whythorne's foreign travels take him through the Netherlands, Germany, Italy, and France; on his return he writes 'in proze A book of my travel and of the things that I noted in the tyme of my travel, and also of the originall, and beginning of peopull of thoze kuntreyz', another lost book (65–6). After an unsuccessful attempt to win the hand of a lawyer's daughter, he finds a new position with a nobleman, identified by Osborn as Lord Ambrose Dudley, whose wife Elizabeth 'waz my skoller' (83). Called to military service overseas at St Quentin in 1557, Dudley 'konsiumed much of hiz ladies land and substans', and, as a result, shortly after his return was forced 'to break vp hows keeping' and dispense with many of his servants (85).[21] Although Whythorne stays on for a while, Dudley fails to deliver his promised annuity, and eventually agrees to let Whythorne go.

Whythorne then enters the service of a privy councillor (who remains unidentified), serving as 'skoolmaster vnto his childern' (86) in his country house. When 'sertain trobles' befall his new master, his wife and Whythorne 'fell at A jar', as a result of which, he notes tartly, 'I had leav to depart from hiz servis'. Returning to London, 'which sitty is alwaiz, my cheef worldly refiuge at such tymes of need' (92), Whythorne tutors the children of a gentleman living five miles out of town; Whythorne enjoys the company of the gentleman's wife, who 'bin sum tyme A koortier' (93). When he becomes aware that the gentleman has begun 'to wax wery of my being in his hows' (97), Whythorne takes on another family's children, about eight miles away. But, equally, this master 'waxed wery' of the expense of a schoolmaster, and Whythorne returns to London. There he meets a gentleman with a son at Cambridge (115), identified by Osborn as Lieutenant of the Ordnance William Bromfield; Whythorne travels to Cambridge to tutor Bromfield's son, another William. After about six months, he witnesses a remarkable event: 'the resurreksion of doktor *Bucer*' (120–1), when the body of the German Protestant reformer Martin Bucer, which had been publicly burned during Mary's reign, was solemnly reburied; this we can date to July 1560.

After two years at Cambridge, Whythorne and William move to Bromfield's house in London. Called to serve the queen 'in her warz beyond the seaz' (136), Bromfield commits both his son and his many business ventures to Whythorne, before being mortally wounded at Le Havre in 1563. With the son also now abroad, Whythorne continues to serve the Bromfield family interests in London, which was soon 'sore vizited with the plage of pestilens' (145); fearing that he would die, Whythorne turns to religion, reworking some of his secular verse in a spiritual vein–'Sins I embrase | mi ladies grase' (42), for example, becomes 'Sins I embras | the heavnly gras | In sort az I wold have – | Rejois I must | till I for dust | do yeeld mi korps to grave' (157). When Bromfield junior returns, over half a year later,

Whythorne is discharged from his duties, and finds himself once again the tutor of a gentleman's daughter, teaching her 'to play sumwhat on the virginals, and the liut, and also to sing priksong' (165).

Finally realizing that there could be 'no such sekiurite and stabilite in any way' in music-teaching, Whythorne decides 'to gyve my self wholey to the profession' of music. He concludes that to 'make my self to be known of many in the shortest tyme', there is 'no better way for that purpoze then to sett and publish sum miuzik of myne own making in print' (173). Briefly waylaid by a return to a previous country appointment—which yet again does not work out—Whythorne prepares his songs for publication, while residing in 'A gentilmans hows' in London (214). With Latin commendatory verses penned by a number of friends, including Thomas Barnam, a fellow Latin tutor in the household,[22] Whythorne publishes his volume, but soon complains to his printer that it did not sell fast because it was 'very fals printed' (220); that printer was John Day, who had previously set music by Thomas Tallis for Matthew Parker's 1567 metrical psalter, but delayed work on Whythorne's book because he was busy with a much more significant project, the second edition of John Foxe's *Actes and Monuments*.[23] Despite this setback, Whythorne continues to plan for a new volume. Finally, he is approached 'to serv Doktor [Matthew] parker of late Archbyshop of *Cantorbery*' as 'the master of the muizik of hiz chappell' (254–5); that is, at Lambeth Palace. Whythorne accepts with alacrity, knowing that 'by hiz plase hee waz the most honorabl man in this realm next vnto the Queen' (255). He determines to write more songs, and pen more verse—and with many examples of this, the manuscript ends.

Readers of the manuscript, however, might barely be aware of the biographical throughline I have just identified, since Whythorne plays a clever game with naming and not naming the figures in his life—in what is, I would argue, a deliberate attempt to avoid some charged figures and events of England's Reformations. For example, Whythorne presents his time with John Heywood as a useful apprenticeship that taught him how to play and write music. What he fails to tell us is that Heywood was a staunch Catholic, who at the time of Whythorne's writing had been in exile in Mechelen (in the Low Countries) for over a decade.[24] His wife Joan was the daughter of the playwright John Rastell and Elizabeth More, Thomas More's sister. In 1542–3, Heywood had been involved in the so-called Prebendary Plot to de-seat Archbishop of Canterbury Thomas Cranmer, and only extricated himself, it seems, through his writings: Sir John Harington claimed Heywood 'scaped hanging with his mirth', since the king could not believe 'that a man that wrate so pleasant and harmelesse verses, could not haue any harmefull conceit against his proceedings'.[25] But, perhaps as a gesture of reconciliation, Heywood wrote 'A komedy or play' entitled 'the partes of man' to be played for Cranmer (13–14), a portion of which

Whythorne transcribed in his 'Book', the only lines of the play that have survived (74).[26] Whythorne's time in Heywood's household in the 1540s could therefore be construed as a close association with a known Catholic activist; it is significant that he promptly left Heywood's service when the Protestant Edward VI came to the throne in 1547.

When Whythorne claims that he turns down a job offer from 'A duches or diuks wyfe' to teach her daughter, the duchess in question is Jane, wife of John Dudley, earl of Northumberland. It was Northumberland who, at the death of Edward VI, manoeuvred his daughter-in-law Lady Jane Grey to the throne for nine days, and was subsequently executed for treason, as were Grey and her husband, Northumberland's eldest son Guildford. Since Whythorne refuses the duchess's job offer, he steers clear of the calamitous collapse of the Dudley fortunes, and yet he returns to the family around 1555, when a younger son of Northumberland's, Ambrose Dudley, is pardoned for his involvement in the Jane Grey affair. Given Whythorne's associations with the Dudley family, it is suggestive that he chooses the years 1553 to 1555, when most of the Dudleys are in jail and the Catholic Mary comes to the throne, to head overseas to Europe—as did many Protestants who feared the new Marian regime. Whythorne's studied vagueness about names and dates repeatedly lifts him free of the religious, political, and military battles in which Heywood, the Dudleys, William Bromfield, and his printer John Day were so heavily implicated. Instead, Whythorne encourages us to see his life in a range of different modes that are not pre-determined by confessional allegiance or household loyalty—as a poetic miscellany, a collection of proverbs, an analysis of the ages of man, and a gallery of portraits.

A Book of Songs and Sonetts

In describing his life-writing as 'A book of songs and sonetts', Whythorne was identifying himself with a thriving tradition of poetic publication in mid-sixteenth-century England. In 1557, a legal publisher named Richard Tottel brought out a poetic miscellany entitled *Songes and Sonettes, Written by the Right Honorable Lorde Henry Haward late Earle of Surrey, and Other*, the 'other' including Thomas Wyatt and Nicholas Grimald. In an unsigned preface to the reader, Tottel—or an unnamed editor—explained that the purpose of the volume was to bring the verse that had been locked up in the houses of the elite to public view for the delectation and edification of the masses. In so doing, however, the editor of *Songes and Sonettes* provided some light interpretation of the volume's contents. Poems that had circulated in manuscript without title were now given headings that described the supposed occasion of their composition: 'Descripcion of the restlesse state of a louer, with sute to his ladie, to rue on his diyng hart', 'Complaint of a louer, that defied loue, and was by loue after the more tormented', 'Complaint that his ladie after she knew of his loue kept her face alway hidden from him', and so on.[27] Tottel's *Songes and Sonettes* was a huge success, with nine further editions by 1587,[28] and inspired other poets to publish their own miscellanies: in 1563, Barnabe Googe released his *Eglogs Epytaphes, and Sonettes*, which was answered by George Turbeville's 1567 *Epitaphes, Epigrams, Songs and Sonets*.[29] And then in 1573, another poet took the genre a step further. George Gascoigne published an anthology of his verse entitled *A Hundreth Sundry Flowres*–but presented it as the work of a group of poets (including Gascoigne) leaked to the press by a well-meaning friend. To launch this conceit, Gascoigne concocted a story about a Master F. J. whose poems are 'explained' by a narrative, written by a self-appointed editor H. W., in which F. J. vies for the love of a married woman named Elinor.

Whythorne's 'Book of songs and sonetts' bears intriguing similarities to Gascoigne's collection, which was published perhaps two or three years before Whythorne penned his manuscript.[30] Like the 'editor' H. W., the friend of Master F. J. who contextualizes each verse by explaining 'the very proper occasion whereuppon it was written',[31] Whythorne sets out to describe the supposed 'occasions' that gave rise to the composition of his songs and sonnets. Echoing Gascoigne's circle of gentlemen poets, Whythorne's 'Book' opens with an address to 'My good frend' (3),[32] to whom he has promised 'the copies of such songs and sonetts, as I have made from tyme to tyme' until the present day. This is a reciprocal arrangement: the friend 'did impart vnto mee at owr last being togyther, sum of yowr pryvat and secret affayrs past, & also sum of the secret purposes and entents the which have lyen hidd and byn as it were entombed in yowr hart', and so Whythorne has decided to follow suit: '[I] do now lay open vnto yow the most part of all my pryvatt affayres, and secrets accomplished from my childhood vnto the day of the date heerof.' Some of the accompanying 'discourses' he wrote at the time of penning the verse, he explains, and others were put down later. A pattern is set whereby Whythorne recounts a situation, or describes some reading he undertakes, and then provides the verse that was inspired by that occasion. Even this opening prose explanation is subsequently rendered in 102 decasyllabic lines that commence 'My faithfull frend, sins that thow didst impart | The secrets that lay hid within thy hart' (14). Ostensibly part of a private gift-giving, an exchange between friends of their verses and life-stories, the manuscript is nonetheless clearly aimed at a wider audience than the unnamed 'faithfull frend'.

Also like Gascoigne's F. J., Whythorne spends a remarkable amount of time getting entangled with amorous ladies of the households in which he works, and then writing poems about the dilemma. His first employment is with a widowed gentlewoman, who wants him 'to bee bothe her servant and also her skoolmaster' (36). Experienced in 'the fashions of the world', the widow toys with her new tutor: 'her joy waz to have men to bee in loov with her, and to brag sumtymes how shee kowld handl such az were so, az how shee kowld fetch them in, and then how shee kowld with a frown make them look pale, and how with A mery look she kowld make them to joy again' (38). When he is out of her sight, or speaking with another woman, the widow acts jealous; while Whythorne believes her to be pretending, he decides to play along, since 'to dissembull with A dissembler waz no dissimulasion'—and 'if shee ment goodwill in deed, then I waz not willing to loos it bekawz of the kommodities that myht [might] be gotten by such A one as shee either by mariag or otherwyze' (40). So he writes her a poem that describes how his 'hart is burnd in loou' for an unnamed woman: he makes the song 'sumwhat dark & dowtfull of sens, not knowing how she would take it or who might read it thereafter'. The widow responds by making 'sum what more of mee then shee did before' (41), telling him how 'to apparell my self, az of what stoff, and how she wold have it made' and 'what manner of rings wold bekum my hand to wear, and also what jewell'; Whythorne points out that 'my purs waz thin lyned' to buy such a jewel, but that if she gave him one, he would 'wear it for her sake'. By these means, Whythorne receives money and cloth from the widow, and reciprocates with another verse: 'Sins I embrase mi ladies grase [grace] in sort az I dezier, | I will rejois with pleazant vois Sins quenched is this fier' (42). Whythorne reprimands any 'Suspiciows headz' who might imagine that the quenching of his fire came through 'A konjiunksion kopiulatyue [conjunction copulative]': to this accusation, 'I must say, and say trewly, that neyther my hand nor any other part of myne did ons towch that parte of herz where the konjiunksion is made' (43).

The schoolmaster doth protest too much. In Whythorne's heavy-handed astrological sexual punning, we find the implication that underlies much of his 'Book'—that music masters have an unsettling degree of intimacy with their female students. The same expectation fuels Gascoigne's narrative where a visiting poet (F. J.) and a domestic male secretary vie for the (freely given) sexual favours of their married mistress. But with a music master, the tension is stronger, because the teaching relationship is fuelled by the writing and singing together of love songs—and indeed, the flirtation of Whythorne and the widow continues through the dropping of short lyrics in places where the other will find them. The relationship only ends when the widow's fortunes decline precipitously at the accession of Mary I, for reasons that are, typically, unexplained. But she is quickly replaced by a succession of wives, daughters, female friends, and neighbours who make advances to Whythorne, often to his expressed discomfort, but always to the benefit of his poetic and musical creativity. This means, however, that the abiding impression of Whythorne's 'Book' is not the narrative of his own life-story but rather a set of variations on a cliché whereby the music-teacher becomes the object of erotic attention from various ladies.

This sense of the generic is deepened by Whythorne's reliance on proverbs. While Whythorne was living with John Heywood, his master 'cawzed to be printed A book made vpon owr englysh proverbz' (13). *A dialogue conteinyng the nomber in effect of all the prouerbes in the englishe tongue compacte in a matter concernyng two maner of mariages* took the form of a verse conversation between two men in couplets, almost entirely compiled of English proverbial phrases. First published in 1546, and reprinted by itself and in Heywood's collected works throughout the sixteenth century, the *Dialogue* influenced Whythorne greatly: his own 'Book' contains hundreds of proverbial allusions. Given his subject matter, it is not surprising that many are concerned with romance between men and women—'jon waz az good az my lady (az the adag[e] saieth)' (52); 'A faint hart never got fair lady' (47); 'the falling owt of loverz waz the renewal of loov' (81–2)—nor that just as many are openly misogynist: women 'will turn az the wynd and wetherkok' (23); 'fair be sluttish, and fowl be prowd' (23), 'A shrew profitabull may be born withal of A man reazonable' (79).

Whythorne turns to proverbs to explain his own predicament. 'It iz A kommen saing, that who so hath bin entangled in the snarse of loov, and hath gotten owt of the same again, that hiz gawll is broken' (57), or 'It is A kommen saieng & an old, that hee that killeth A man when hee is drunk hee shalbe hanged when hee iz sober' (61)—common and old: Whythorne seems buoyed by the notion that this wisdom is generally accepted and proved by long experience. Stymied in his suit to marry a lawyer's daughter, he reasons that 'the proverb saith that lyke will to lyke': if that's true, 'then how shiuld I have brought hiz goodwill on my syde', he asks, since musicians live through 'them that do delyte in korkord', while lawyers 'lyve chiefly by thoze that do delyte in diskord'. It helps him that 'being perswadid that the proverb is trew which saith that. *Be it far or be it ny, mariag[e] iz alwaiz destiny*', it would follow 'that my destiny waz not to have her to my wyfe' (82). Yet another proverb gives him further sustenance: 'to furder my konseit and help mee now at A pinch, I kalled to my remembrans an old proverb which saith that absens kawzeth forgetfulness, which saeing iz to be embrased emong thoze loverz which kannot enjoy their loovz. and I warrant yow I having sum kawz at that prezent to remember it, I for my parte wold not dispyze the same. for az the old proverb saith, I thank God & my kunning' (83).

The net effect of this endless recourse to proverbs is to flatten out any individuality in the events of Whythorne's life. Everything that happens to him is old and common. But then, life itself for Whythorne is a set pattern. As his title explains, the 'songs and sonetts' come accompanied 'with longe discoorses...of the chylds lyfe, togyther with A yoong mans lyfe, and entring into the old mans lyfe' (1). As he explains to the friend to whom the work is ostensibly directed,

> as I have byn chaynged from tyme to tyme, by tyme, so altered myne affections and delyghts. when I was A chylde, I did as A chylde, and when I was A yoong man, weening [believing] then, that yong men were as wyse as the olde experienced men be...but now I wott [know] though I am not verye olde that there remayns many follies in yoong men[,] the which I dare warrant yow, ye may soon espye by my doings in my yoong life. (4)

During 'the tyme of my infansy', young Thomas 'was suffred by my parents and gardons [guardians] to lyve the wanton and idl lyfe that belongs to that age, bekawz that the memories of those of that age are not apt to retain and carry or bear any long tyme' (4). Later, he establishes that 'chyldhod...kontyneweth from the infancy vntill fyfteen', and is then succeeded by 'the ag[e] named *Adolescency*[,] which kontineweth vntill twenty and fyve'. This is 'the first part of the yoong mans ag[e]' (19).

There were several schema of the 'ages of man' available to Whythorne, dating back to the classical canon. Pythagoras names four ages (childhood, youth, manhood, old age), Aristotle's *Rhetoric* specifies three (childhood, flourishing man-age, old age), and Hippocrates seven—the same number that Jaques in Shakespeare's *As You Like It* will present two decades after Whythorne.[33] But a closer model is Thomas Elyot's *The Castel of Helth* (1539), which states firmly that 'Ages be foure':

> Adolescency to .xxv. yeres, hotte and moyst, in the whiche tyme the body groweth.
>
> Iuuentute vnto .xl. yeres, hotte and dry, wherin the body is in perfyte growthe.
>
> Senectute, vnto .lx. yeres colde and drie, wherein the bodye begynneth to decreace.
>
> Age decrepite, vntil the last time of lyfe, accidently moist, but naturally colde & drye, wherin the powers and strength of the body be more and more minished.[34]

Whythorne elsewhere cites Elyot's book (239), and his use of the rare term 'juventute' adds weight to the notion that it is Elyot's scheme on which he draws. But Whythorne adapts as he appropriates, dividing Elyot's 'Adolesency' into two categories, 'the chyldish yeerz' (lasting until 15), and 'the adlessensy', before moving to 'the *jiuventiut* or yoongmans ag[e]' (135). He also develops Elyot's notion that certain 'hiumorz have moste dominion' in each of 'the ages of mankynde': 'the blood raineth [reigns] cheefly in the jiuventiut' (25 to 40 years), 'so the hiumour named koler doth cheef rain in this second and last part of the yoongmans age' (80).

Having chosen this 'ages of man' schema, however, Whythorne fails to do much with it, beyond aligning what happens to him with the humoral characteristics of each age. Instead, he turns to another mode of tracking his age: the record of visual representation. Whythorne commissioned and sat for his portrait at least four times.[35] It was around 1549 that he became interested in visual depictions: 'I took sum pleasur in the painterz arte', and decided to 'sett owt my fantazy in koolorz'. He records how 'I kawzed A tabull to be made to hang in my chamber wheron was painted (in oyll kolowrz) the fygure and imag[e] of a yoong woman plaing vpon A Liut, who I gave to name *Terpsicore*' (whom he identifies as the muse of song and music-making, rather than dance), alongside images of 'A virginall but also of the Gittern, and Sittern, and also A book wherin iz bothe pricksong, and tabulature for the lute', as well as a six-line sonnet, 'The muzic tewns of vois or string | Doth help the earz…'. Inspired by this, he then commissioned a picture of himself to be painted in 'A pair of virginals', with himself taking up the Terpsichore pose, 'lykewyze playng vpon A lute', also with a verse: 'The pleaziurz that I take | Now in my yowthfull yeerz | The same shall mee forsake | When hoery ag[e] appeerz' (20). His 'yowthfull yeerz' proved to be short, for only two years later after a serious illness, Whythorne had his picture painted again 'to see how I waz chainged by Sir Jon Agew and hiz impryzonments'—that is, the personified illness 'Sir John Ague'—'sins the tyme I made the other piktiur of myn' (49).

Two years after returning to London from Cambridge, Whythorne visited his old acquaintance the painter, in whose house he sees many pictures both of 'those that were much elder then I, az of sum such that were of my yeerz. yee, and much yoonger then I waz' (133–4). He pondered that while young people commissioned paintings for themselves for the 'pleaziur to behold their bewtiez & favorz', older people—lacking such pulchritude—'did kawz their piktiurz or kounterfets to be painted from tyme to tyme to see how tyme doth alter them'. Whythorne foresees his reader's objection—'peradventiur yow wold say that thei may see themselvz when thei will in A looking glas'—and dismisses it on several grounds. First, your mirror tells us only about now: 'the glas sheweth but the dizpozision of the fase for the tyme present, and not az it waz in tyme past'. Second, your mirror presents you in reverse: 'it sheweth the fase the contrary way'. And third, the image is fleeting: 'the perfeksion of the fase that iz seen in A glas doth remain in the memory of the beholder, littl lenger then hee iz of beholding the same, for so soon as hee looketh of from the glas hee forgetteth the dispozision and grase of hiz fase'. By having their pictures made, and comparing how they had altered, people could consider 'how thei owht [ought] to alter their kondisions' and to pray to God that 'thei may be the more ready to dye in such sort az bekummeth trew kristiens'. There is also an element of bequest: they are able to leave to young children, 'who when thei do kum to yeerz of diskresion, thoh their fatherz be dead yet may thei see what maner of favor thei had, and also therby put in mynde that if thei left A good report of their vertewz behynd them, thei may embrase and follow the same' (or not follow, if 'their report were otherwyze') (134).

Comparing the two 'kowntefeitz', twelve years part, Whythorne realized 'that I waz much chainged from that I waz at that tyme, az by the long and fulnes of my beard, the wrinkels on my fase, and the holonez of myne eyez, and also that my fase waz altered'. Faced with this alteration, 'so were the delihts of my mynd chainged', and he had the picture inscribed with the lines 'Az tyme doth alter evry wiht [man] | So evri age hath hiz deliht'—which, predictably enough, inspired another sonnet (135).

Given the amount of time Whythorne devotes to these pictures in his 'Book', it is odd that he neglects to mention the portrait he had painted in 1569, when he was forty-one, now in Yale University's Beinecke collection (Fig. 7).[36] Portrayed next to his coat of arms, Whythorne is indeed bearded, gaunt, and by now with receding black hair—his widow's peak is particularly distinctive. This may well have been the model for the woodcut he included in his 1571 *Songes*, recycled in his 1590 *Duos*, and had sewn in to the front cover of his 'Book' (Fig. 8). It was extremely unusual for English books of this period to bear the image of a living author, but Whythorne reasoned with himself 'that seing the books with the miuzik in them shiuld bee, az my childern, bekawz thei konteined that which my hed brought forth...Also bekawz thei shiuld bear my name, I kowld do no les then sett in evry one of them, their fatherz piktiur or kounterfet, to represent vnto thoze who shiuld ywz [use] the childern, the form and favor of their parent' (211). Ironically for a man keen to track the ageing process, the 1571 image claimed he was forty years old, a year younger than he had been two years before; and in 1590, at the age of sixty-two, he remained an eternal forty.

Thomas Whythorne, Gent.

Whythorne had another motive for placing his portrait in his books: that their users 'shiuld see that az in the beginning of them I do ad vnto my name the tytle of A gentilman, so I mean to shew my self to be one azwell in the outward marks, az in the inward man'. While the inward man would be demonstrated through 'the muiuzik with the dittiez and songs & sonets', he also intended 'to shew my self' through 'owtward marks': 'I will set with my kownterfet such armes, az I have fownd to be left vnto mee by my poor Aunseterz with the which although thei have left mee no great revenewz to support and maintain them withall, yet tharby thei have left mee A remembrans that I am az free A man born both by father and mothers syde, az hee that mai dispend thowzandz of powndz, of yeerly inheritans' (211–12).

While Whythorne remains vague about the men and women who employed and patronized him, he is consistently determined to register their social status—nobleman, gentleman, gentlewoman—and to insist on his title page that he is 'Thomas Whythorne, gent.' (1). Whythorne was born into a reasonably prosperous

Figure 7. George Gower?, portrait of Thomas Whythorne, *c.* 1569. Beinecke Rare Book and Manuscript Library, Yale University.

family, but there were limits to their wealth, as his uncle makes brutally clear to Thomas as a child:

> Althoh . . . yowr father iz abull to lyve of him self, yet hee iz not habull to keep yow and the rest of hiz childern in such sort az yee may lyve idelly and at eaz. and althoh yee shall have sertain howzes and landz after the deseas of yowr parents, it iz easily seen that whyll the gras groweth the hors starveth, and hee that looketh to wear dead folks shows [shoes] had need to bee shod with iron. (12)

Figure 8. Unknown artist, portrait of Thomas Whythorne, 1571, stitched into his 'Book of Songs and Sonetts'. The Bodleian Libraries, The University of Oxford, MS. Eng. Misc. c. 330, fo. 1^{v}.

It is this consideration that sets Thomas on his musical training, but when it becomes time to 'keep my self withowt penury and need', he discovers that he is 'brouht to have A kare of myne own kreditt, and estimasion, with the maintenans therof az of A master and not az either servant or skoller' (18). Forced 'to lyve of my self', he had to 'cast my witts so many waiz, and they being never trobled somuch that way before, az I waz almost at my witts end' (18–19). Among the ways he finds to set himself up is to master the favoured 'exersyzes and qualyties' of the right sort of 'yoong folks', so he 'went to the daunsing skool, and fens skooll'. In particular, he learns two new instruments, the gittern and sittern, which he characterizes as 'then strang[e] in England, and therfore the more dezyred and esteemed' (19). That desire and esteem derive from social rank: the gittern 'waz an instriument much esteemed and yvzed [used] of gentilmen, and of the best sort in thoz dayz', and as Christopher Page notes, both gittern and sittern were 'associated with a free and companionable amateurism' as practised by gentlemen.[37] Whythorne tellingly treats his gittern as 'A sytting mate, lieng mate, and walking mate' (30)—a gentleman friend with whom he sits, walks, and shares a bed, ensuring, in turn, that Whythorne is himself a gentleman.

Despite Whythorne's insistence on his status, it soon becomes painfully clear that some clients see him simply as a servant.[38] As he puts it, 'to be A skoolmaster I did not mislyk, but to bee A serving kreatiur or serving man, it was so lyke the lyfe of A water spannell that must be at kommaundement to fetch or bring heer or karry thare, with all kynd of drudgery, that I kowld not lyke of that lyfe' (37). To demonstrate that he is no water spaniel, Whythorne constantly asserts his own status relative to his employers and their (other) servants. When a neighbouring gentleman invites all the serving men of Whythorne's house to dinner, he notes, rather pathetically, that 'emong the which I (az one nothing inferior vnto them, and an ase [ace] aboov them by the means of my teaching of the yoong gentilfolks in the hows) waz also solemly bidden' (87)—in Whythorne's logic, teaching gentlefolk makes you one of them. He then proudly records that with another couple 'I did kovenant…that I wold be with them but by the week, and also that I wold be ywzed az A frend, and not A servant'. In practice this meant that 'thei did not only allow mee to sitt at their tabull, but also at their own mes'—sharing their food—'az long az ther were not any to okkiupy the room and plase that were A great deall my betterz'. The arrangement supposedly encourages a different level of communication—'I being thare but by the week, and to be ywzed as A frend, made mee the bolder to speak my fantazy sumtymes, when I thouht good' (94)—but Whythorne is only used as a friend on weekdays when there's nobody better around.

At Cambridge, he offends his student William Bromfield's existing tutor who 'envied mee very much bekawz I waz appointed to be also A tiutor to hiz piupull, and also bekawz that I wold not do to him such reverens and kap kurtezy az hee looked for'. By 'kap kurtezy', Whythorne meant the social niceties of allowing someone to walk away from the road and next to the wall when you pass him in the street: 'A thing much ywzed and looked for', he remarks, 'espesiall of such as kum vp to Degreez from the plow and kart, & such base okkiupasions'. Whythorne would perform such niceties, but only out of courtesy, not duty, 'bekawz that I kame thither to lyve with him and not by him at hiz charges [expenses]', and not as a scholar or pupil, but as a schoolmaster and tutor. Moreover, Whythorne points out, he was in the 'fellowz kommens in the hows where he waz remaining' alongside 'both lordz soons, knihts soons, and gentilmans soons', so he did not owe him any special reverence (115).

And yet on occasion, Whythorne claims his gentility through his music, making high-handed claims about the inherent nobility of his profession 'to teach one of the sevan sienses liberall' (58). It is not simply that those who do not appreciate music are, a priori, 'blokhedz, and dolts': 'Ther iz none that do dispyze it, but such az be either delyted to drudg[e] and toil for their lyvings in servill, and filthy tradez, or els be ingnorant [*sic*] in all sorts of learnings' (248). Rather, Whythorne asserts that 'I do think that the teacherz therof (if thei will) may esteem somuch of them selvs az to be free and not bownd, much les to be made slave lyk' (58–9). Indeed, in pursuing this claim, he cites Gerard Legh's heraldry manual *The Accedens of Armory*, which states that 'A king of *Heralts* may gyve arms to any that iz exsellently skilled in ani of the seven liberall sienses (wherof miuzik iz one) althouh hee nor hiz aunsetorz miht never gyve any before' (243).[39] So which is it? Is Whythorne entitled to the coat-of-arms so prominently displayed on his portrait by his birth or by his profession?

'Miuzik in This Tyme Prezent'

This dilemma lies at the heart of what Whythorne is trying to achieve with his 'Book of songs and sonetts'. Whythorne last writes of himself as working for the archbishop of Canterbury, Matthew Parker, sometime after his *Songes* is published in 1571; Parker died on 17 May 1575, and Whythorne is listed among the 'yeomen of his household' at his burial on 6 June.[40] Presumably Whythorne was then looking for employment, so the manuscript may have been designed as a *curriculum vitae* to show off his literary accomplishments. But equally, Whythorne may have intended to further his reputation in print—in the final pages, he claims to have penned forty '*Diuos*, or songs of ij partes', and intended to write forty matching 'songs of three parts' to match, plus twenty-six more songs in four parts, the genre which was 'most in request', and twenty-five more songs in five parts—as well as some songs in six and seven parts. Ultimately, Whythorne's 'Book' did not reach print: perhaps it was his May 1577 marriage to Elizabeth Stoughton that rendered such a plan unviable, as she may not have welcomed the publication of his endless tales of the romantic attentions of female patrons.

But there are signs that the manuscript that survives was not Whythorne's final word. A scrap of paper inside the volume (foliated as 67^{v}) appears to be a planned insertion for fo. 68^{r} (as indicated by a leaf symbol on both). The scrap includes a list 'Of Doktorz and Bachelarz of Miuzik in England'—on one side, 'Those of aunsient tyme', on the other, those 'of late tyme'. This second list derives from the final years of Whythorne's life—it mentions the organist and composer John Bull as 'Doktor Bull' and identifies Thomas Morley as 'of the queens magesties chappell', a doctorate and appointment that both date from 1592. Whythorne evidently intended to absorb this list into a further revision of his piece, and points, I believe, to his agenda in writing the 'Book of songs and sonetts'. When he published his *Songes* in 1571, he claimed in his preface that 'What I cowld write in Musicks prays [praise] I will at this time stay'.[41] Now, in his 'Book', he makes good his promise to his reader, 'to make yow A witness what I kan say for miuzik in kommendasion therof' (221). This is a cue for a quite extraordinary twenty-four-page digression from his life-story, an apologia for music, which starts with the argument 'miuzik was ywzed in heavn before the world began' (221), and works through a vast trove of scriptural, classical, and near-contemporary authorities to prove music's exalted place 'in the middell between the seven liberall sienses': grammar, logic, rhetoric, music, arithmetic, geometry, and astronomy (237–8).[42]

There is a determinedly political edge to this discussion. In Italy, Whythorne writes, he was 'kredibli enformed' that the state and magistrates gave over 300 crowns per annum to the Flemish composer Adrian Weillert 'to kompoze and to make the miuzik that was sung in their Chiurch' (229–30); indeed, any Italian organist was making 100 crowns a year. In 'tyme past' in England, he continues, music was maintained by cathedral churches, abbeys, colleges, parish churches, chantries, guilds, and fraternities; but when the abbeys and colleges were put down during the Reformation, 'then went miuzik to decay'; at the same time, various noblemen and women stopped employing organists and singing men in their private chapels (243–4). Now, 'the Raskall and of skymm [offscum] of that profession'—minstrels, not musicians, in Whythorne's view—'did and do make it kommen by offring of it to evry jak[e], going abowt evry plas and kuntrey for the same purpoze' (244).

Earlier in the digression, Whythorne draws attention to the last of the Queen's Injunctions, drafted by his last employer, Matthew Parker, where 'shee with the consent of all her klargy, do allow both of singing and also of sownding of miuzikall instriuments to be ywzed in the Chiurch'—as indeed, Elizabeth daily used in her own chapel, he adds (229). This topic is picked up in the final section where, Whythorne announces, 'I will speak of the yws of miuzik in this tyme prezent'. Music, he claims, is now only 'slenderly maintained' by the Church, so that 'when the old store of the miuzisians be worn owt'—those who were 'bred' when the Church maintained music—'(which is lyke to bee in short tyme) yee shall have few or none remaining' except some singing men and players of instruments, very few of whom would be about to 'make A good lesson of deskant'. Such men would call themselves 'miuzicians', but to Whythorne 'ther be none wurthi of thatt name except thei kan make songs of ij, iij, iiij parts and so vpward akkording to the trew rewls therof'. He discounts what he calls the '*speculators*' who have become musicians 'by studye withowt any praktis', who write songs without being able to sing them (245). He is also at pains to establish 'the diffrens of degreez, and names of professions of thoze that do after sum sorts profess miuzik' (232), moving down from doctors and bachelors of music, 'miuzisians vnkomenced', organists, schoolmasters (who teach music, pricksong, and various instruments), singers in churches, those who teach and serve in private houses, and lastly itinerant minstrels, banned by statute (232–4).

Whythorne is here explicitly attempting to construct a post-Reformation profession for English musicians, who must be composer-musicians, comparable to those for physicians and lawyers, with its own codes, hierarchies, and exclusions, its guaranteed and institutionalized royal and ecclesiastical patronage. While the benefit of this formal recognition for Whythorne himself goes without saying, what is crucial here is that in this supposed 'autobiography' Whythorne stops making an individualized case for Thomas Whythorne—to which all his previous efforts, as a teacher, a musician, and a published composer have led—and instead makes a case for musicians as a group, and for music as a profession. The social prestige that he at first claims as a born gentleman now accrues to his profession of musician. Instead of the autobiography of Thomas Whythorne, what he leaves us is the life of every man who can produce a book of songs and sonnets, who can truly claim to be a musician.

5

The Memorials of William Lambe

At six o'clock in the evening on the Wednesday of Easter week, 7 April 1580, a 'sudden earthquake' hit London. The great clock bell in Westminster Palace struck by itself; gentlemen taking supper in the Temple ran out of their hall, knives in hand, to encounter the unknown threat; playgoers in the recently built Theatre, fearing that the galleries would collapse, fled the playhouse. City chimneys collapsed and stones from churches fell down, killing an apprentice outright and fatally injuring a female servant as they attended a sermon at Christ's Church near Newgate market. Aftershocks were still felt late at night, as far away as Dover, where 'a peece of the cliffe fell into the sea' along with part of the castle wall. And then, a few weeks later, at midnight on 1 May, Kent suffered another earthquake, causing inhabitants to ponder what 'naughtie filthinesse of the flesh (full of lusts and infirmities)' had caused God to correct 'natures inclination' by making 'Douer, Sandwich, Canturburie, Grauesend, and sundrie other places tremble and shake'.[1]

These unexpected and worrying events made their way into the revised and expanded 1587 edition of Raphael Holinshed's *Chronicles*. But true to the *Chronicles*' chronological organization, the April and May earthquakes are separated by an account of an event that happened between the two: the death on 21 April 1580 of a London citizen and Clothworker, William Lambe, that prompts the telling of his life and works, specifically his 'almesdéeds and manifold charities'. Whereas the newsworthy earthquakes are dispatched in 623 words, Lambe merits a massive 2,644, the detailed description of his 'almesdéeds' apparently designed to prompt similar philanthropy in other wealthy men.[2] But how—and why—did this Clothworker, by no means among London's most prominent or even richest men, come to be part of a chronicle history?

The inclusion of the life of William Lambe in Holinshed's *Chronicles* was just the last, albeit unforeseen, step on a carefully coordinated plan for Lambe's memorialization that had been decades in the making—by Lambe himself.

William Lambe wanted to be remembered through the means that had worked for his ancestors: through charitable giving in life and bequests in death, and through his memorialization in stone and metal in the chancel of his church. But with the Reformation, the character of commemoration had been radically altered. As John Morrill explains,

> The first Reformation was firmly directed against the doctrine of the communion of saints, the doctrine that bound together the living and the dead as a community of believers helping one another in preparation for the Day of Judgement. The living prayed constantly for those members of their family and local community who had gone before them, and even enlisted them into their fraternities. They also benefited from the chantries others had founded. They looked to the saints and the host of heaven to watch over and protect the living and to intercede for them with the Father. Every *active* manifestation of that communion of the living and the dead was destroyed in the first generation of the Reformation: the side altars, the chantries, the reliquaries, the shrines, the Doom and the paintings that illuminated that theme.[3]

The latter half of the sixteenth century saw English men and women grappling with the changed nature of commemoration, looking for new ways of memorializing themselves and others that would not smack of outlawed Catholic practices.[4] William Lambe went further than most, turning in his final months to the medium of print to tell his story, producing, as the *Chronicles* record, 'a memoriall recorded in print, agreeing in truth with his last will and testament'.[5] But this 'memoriall recorded in print' itself betrayed the shifting nature of memorialization in post-Reformation England. The writer whom Lambe commissioned to write his life was not so impressed by his subject's good works, and the life he tells never shakes off the hint of papism that his fellow Londoners detected in Lambe. This chapter tells a story of the forms of memorialization in Elizabethan London, and how they gave rise to a new genre of life-writing.

William Lambe, Philanthropist

William Lambe was born in the last years of the fifteenth century, the son of a gentleman of Sutton Valence in Kent. He later claimed to have been a 'Gentleman of the Royal Chapel', but records suggest he was a Man of the Vestry of the Chapel, appearing on vestry lists in 1520 and 1524.[6] Subsidy assessments in 1541 and 1571 show him to have been a moderately wealthy Londoner. By 1541, he was living in Mugwell or Monkwell Street, next to the hermitage chapel of St James at London Wall.[7] In 1543 he bought thirty parcels of land in the capital, mostly former monastic properties that had belonged to the foundations of Rowley, St John Jerusalem, and St Bartholomew, Smithfield. In 1568, by now in his early seventies, he entered the Clothworkers' Company by redemption, and became its Master the following year. These are the archival traces of Lambe's life as laid out by his recent biographer Ian Archer, but, as Archer points out, Lambe is 'A man about whom, had it not been for his acts of philanthropy, little at all would have been known'.[8] Charitable giving is the activity for which Lambe is now remembered, if at all; his *Oxford Dictionary of National Biography* entry describes him simply as 'philanthropist'.[9]

Although he married three times, Lambe died childless; as a result, he was in a position to give away most of his wealth either before or at his death. Lambe's acts of philanthropy were many and various, but a sequence of events is evident. His entry into the Clothworkers' Company in 1568, and his almost instantaneous rise to Master, were possible because Lambe used the Company to administer his bequests, including the provision of ministers to lead divine service and preach sermons, and distributions of food, money, and clothing to the poor. In his home town of Sutton Valence, he founded a free school in 1576, providing salaries in perpetuity for the master and usher, and founded and maintained six almshouses, with an orchard and garden.[10] After his death, £10 per annum was assigned to maintain a free school in Maidstone, Kent, while the Shropshire towns of Ludlow and Bridgnorth were each to receive £100 to provide labour opportunities for poor clothiers.[11] The Clothworkers administered these bequests assiduously, maintaining responsibility for the Sutton Valence school for over three centuries.[12] In return, properties passed to the Clothworkers on Lambe's death, notably the buildings on the site of the medieval hermitage of St James on London's city wall north-west of Cripplegate, including a chapel that was adopted by the Clothworkers and henceforth known as Lambe's Chapel.[13]

In addition, Lambe specified that Christ's Hospital and St Thomas's Hospital were to receive parts of his estate and annual income after his death, while the Stationers' Company was required to distribute twelvepence in money and twelvepence in bread every week to twelve poor people in the parish church of St Faith under St Paul's (where he would be buried). Lambe's most prominent gift, however, was the rebuilding of a vital public utility, the Holborn conduit, work on which commenced on 26 March 1577 and was completed the following 24 August, at a cost of some £1500. Water was conveyed in lead pipes from a variety of springs to a single head, and from there through a conduit of over 2000 yards to the vertical 'standart' on Holborn bridge, with a cock to dispense the water; Lambe even bestowed 120 pails on poor women to carry water from the standard. With water renowned for its purity, Lambe's Conduit, as it was popularly known, quickly became a landmark of the city.

More striking than the philanthropy itself, however, were the ways in which it was trumpeted to the public. As the eighty-five-year-old Lambe neared his death in early 1580, he put his affairs in order: on 10 March he wrote a new will, supplementing one from seven years earlier, and on 5 April he added a codicil. Lambe died on 21 April and was buried in St Faith under St Paul's on 6 May; his will was proved on 2 June, and the charitable bequests began to flow forth. But simultaneously, his memorialization in print got underway, with the publishing of a broadsheet ballad entitled *An Epitaph, or Funerall Inscription, vpon the Godlie Life and Death of the Right Worshipfull Maister William Lambe Esquire* (Fig. 9).[14] Whereas the broadsheet epitaph was the limit of the print memorialization of most luminaries, Lambe's life was also written at greater length.[15] On 28 April 1580, a week after Lambe's death, Thomas Turner entered in the Stationers' Register 'A Memoriall of the famous monuments and charitable almesdeedes of the Right worshipfull Maister William Lambe Esquire, somtime Gentleman of the Chappell, in the reigne of the most renowmed [*sic*] King Henrie the eight, &c. And late Citizen of London, and free of the Right worshipfull companie of Clothworkers: deceased the 21. of April. An. 1580';[16] the title soon appeared in print as a tiny sextodecimo pamphlet (Fig. 10).[17] Even at a glance, the *Epitaph* and *Memoriall* are clearly identifiable as elements in a coordinated campaign. Both are printed by Henry Denham for the stationer Thomas Turner, and both feature the striking device of a lamb, with the motto 'Sacrifizio agnello salvazione mvndo' ('Sacrifice of the lamb, salvation of the world'). But more notably, both are credited to a single writer: Abraham Fleming. Fleming, a graduate of Peterhouse in Cambridge and an accomplished Latinist, has been identified as that new phenomenon, the 'professional' print-market author, who wrote for as many as fifteen publishers and printers, most often to commission.[18] And the Lambe memorials were commissioned in a very particular manner. Fleming, we are told, 'deuised' the verse of the *Epitaph*; but for the *Memoriall*, he 'Recorded in print, according to the tenour and trueth of his [Lambe's] last will and testament'. In other words, in writing Lambe's biographical *Memoriall*, Fleming is channelling Lambe's autobiographical will.

Epitaph and Memoriall

The genre of the broadside epitaph had blossomed in the early years of Elizabeth's reign.[19] The anonymous *An Epytaphe vpon the Death of M. Rycharde Goodricke Esquier*, celebrating the life of a lawyer and ecclesiastical commissioner, was printed in 1562; John Awdelay's *An Epitaphe vpon the Death [of] Mayster Iohn Viron Preacher* appeared in 1563, and was followed by comparable 'epitaphs' on various divines (Edmund

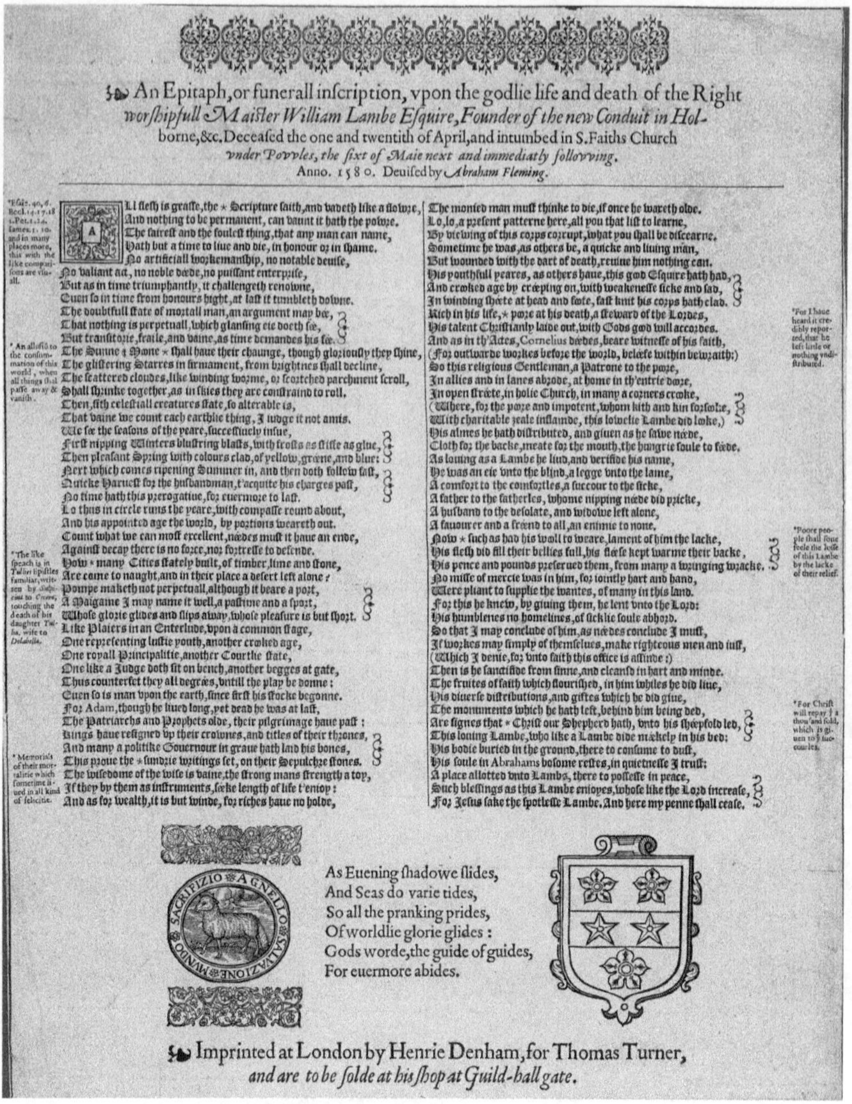

An Epitaph, or funerall inſcription, vpon the godlie life and death of the Right *worſhipfull Maiſter William Lambe Eſquire, Founder of the new Conduit in Hol-* borne, &c. Deceaſed the one and twentith of April, and intumbed in S. Faiths Church *vnder Povvles, the ſixt of Maie next and immediatly follovving.* Anno. 1580. Deuiſed by *Abraham Fleming.*

*Esai. 40, 6. Eccl. 14. 17. 18. 1. Pet. 1. 24. James. 1. 10. and in many places more, this with the like comparisons are visuall.

All flesh is grasse, the * Scripture saith, and vadeth like a flowre,
And nothing to be permanent, can vaunt it hath the powre.
The fairest and the foulest thing, that any man can name,
Hath but a time to liue and die, in honour or in shame.
No artificiall workemanship, no notable deuise,
No valiant act, no noble deede, no puissant enterprise,
But as in time triumphantly, it challengeth renowne,
Euen so in time from honours hight, at last it tumbleth downe.
The doubtfull state of mortall man, an argument may bee,
That nothing is perpetuall, which glansing eie doeth see,
But transitorie, fraile, and vaine, as time demandes his fee.

* An allusion to the consummation of this world, when all things shall passe away & vanish.

The Sunne & Moone * shall haue their chaunge, though gloriously they shine,
The glistering Starres in firmament, from brightnes shall decline,
The scattered cloudes, like winding worme, or scorched parchment scroll,
Shall shrinke together, as in skies they are constraind to roll.
Then, sith celestiall creatures state, so alterable is,
That vaine we count each earthlie thing, I iudge it not amis.
We see the seasons of the yeare, successiuely insue,
First nipping Winters blustring blasts, with frosts as stiffe as glue,
Then pleasant Spring with colours clad, of yellow, greene, and blue:
Next which comes ripening Summer in, and then doth follow fast,
Quicke Haruest for the husbandman, t'acquite his charges past,
No time hath this prerogatiue, for euermore to last.
Lo thus in circle runs the yeare, with compasse round about,
And his appointed age the world, by portions weareth out.
Count what we can most excellent, neede must it haue an ende,
Against decay there is no force, nor fortresse to defende.

* The like speach is in *Tullies* Epistles familiar, written by *Sulpicius* to *Cicero*, touching the death of his daughter *Tullia*, wife to *Dolabella*.

How * many Cities stately built, of timber, lime and stone,
Are come to naught, and in their place a desert left alone?
Pompe maketh not perpetuall, although it beare a port,
A Maigame I may name it well, a pastime and a sport,
Whose glorie glides and slips away, whose pleasure is but short.
Like Plaiers in an Enterlude, vpon a common stage,
One representing lustie youth, another crooked age,
One royall Principalitie, another Courtlie state,
One like a Iudge doth sit on bench, another begges at gate,
Thus counterfet they all degrees, vntill the play be donne:
Euen so is man vpon the earth, since first his stocke begonne.
For Adam, though he liued long, yet dead he was at last,
The Patriarchs and Prophets olde, their pilgrimage haue past:
Kings haue resigned vp their crownes, and titles of their thrones,
And many a politike Gouernour in graue hath laid his bones,

* Memorials of their mortalitie which sometime liued in all kind of felicitie.

This proue the * sundrie writings set, on their Sepulchre stones.
The wisedome of the wise is vaine, the strong mans strength a toy,
If they by them as instruments, seeke length of life t'enioy:
And as for wealth, it is but winde, for riches haue no holde,
The monied man must thinke to die, if once he wareth olde.
Lo, lo, a present patterne here, all you that list to learne,
By viewing of this corps corrupt, what you shall be discearne.
Sometime he was, as others be, a quicke and liuing man,
But wounded with the dart of death, reuiue him nothing can.
His youthfull yeares, as others haue, this good Esquire hath had,
And crooked age by creeping on, with weakenesse sicke and sad,
In winding sheete at head and foote, fast knit his corps hath clad.

* For I haue heard it credibly reported, that he left little or nothing vndistributed.

Rich in his life, * poore at his death, a steward of the Lordes,
His talent Christianly laide out, with Gods good will accordes.
And as in th'Actes, Cornelius deedes, beare witnesse of his faith,
(For outwarde workes before the world, beleefe within bewraith:)
So this religious Gentleman, a Patrone to the poore,
In allies and in lanes abroode, at home in th'entrie doore,
In open streete, in holie Church, in many a corners crooke,
(Where, for the poore and impotent, whom kith and kin forsooke,
With charitable zeale inflamde, this lowelie Lambe did looke,)
His almes he hath distributed, and giuen as he sawe neede,
Cloth for the backe, meate for the mouth, the hungrie soule to feede.
As louing as a Lambe he liud, and verifide his name,
He was an eie vnto the blind, a legge vnto the lame,
A comfort to the comfortles, a succour to the sicke,
A father to the fatherles, whome nipping neede did pricke,
A husband to the desolate, and widowe left alone,
A fauourer and a freend to all, an enimie to none.

* Poore people shall soone feele the losse of this Lambe by the lacke of their relief.

Now * such as had his wooll to weare, lament of him the lacke,
His flesh did fill their bellies full, his fleese kept warme their backe,
His pence and pounds preserued them, from many a wringing wracke.
No misse of mercie was in him, for iointly hart and hand,
Were pliant to supplie the wantes, of many in this land.
For this he knew, by giuing them, he lent vnto the Lord:
His humblenes no homelines, of sicklie soule abhord.
So that I may conclude of him, as needes conclude I must,
If workes may simply of themselues, make righteous men and iust,
(Which I denie, for vnto faith this office is assinde:)
Then is he sanctifide from sinne, and cleansd in hart and minde.
The fruites of faith which flourished, in him whiles he did liue,
His diuerse distributions, and giftes which he did giue,

* For Christ will repay ye a thou'and fold, which is giuen to ye succourles.

The monuments which he hath left, behind him being ded,
Are signes that * Christ our Shepherd hath, vnto his sheepfold led,
This louing Lambe, who like a Lambe dide meekely in his bed:
His bodie buried in the ground, there to consume to dust,
His soule in Abrahams bosome restes, in quietnesse I trust:
A place allotted vnto Lambs, there to possesse in peace,
Such blessings as this Lambe enioyes, whose like the Lord increase,
For Iesus sake the spotlesse Lambe. And here my penne shall cease.

SACRIFIZIO AGNELLO SALVAZIONE MVNDO

As Euening ſhadowe ſlides,
And Seas do varie tides,
So all the pranking prides,
Of worldlie glorie glides:
Gods worde, the guide of guides,
For euermore abides.

Imprinted at London by Henrie Denham, for Thomas Turner, *and are to be ſolde at his ſhop at Guild-hall gate.*

Figure 9. Abraham Fleming, *An Epitaph, or Funerall Inscription, vpon the Godlie Life and Death of the Right Worshipfull Maister Wiliam Lambe Esquire* (1580). Henry E. Huntington Library.

Bonner, John Jewel), aristocrats (Lady Catherine Knollys, and the earls of Pembroke, Arundel, and Southampton), high-ranking politicians (the Chief Baron of the Exchequer), and civic luminaries (a lord mayor's wife).[20] In time the genre became available to lesser mortals. In 1587, John Charlewood published an epitaph to one Richard Price Esquire, described as 'the second sonne of Sir Iohn Price Knight'

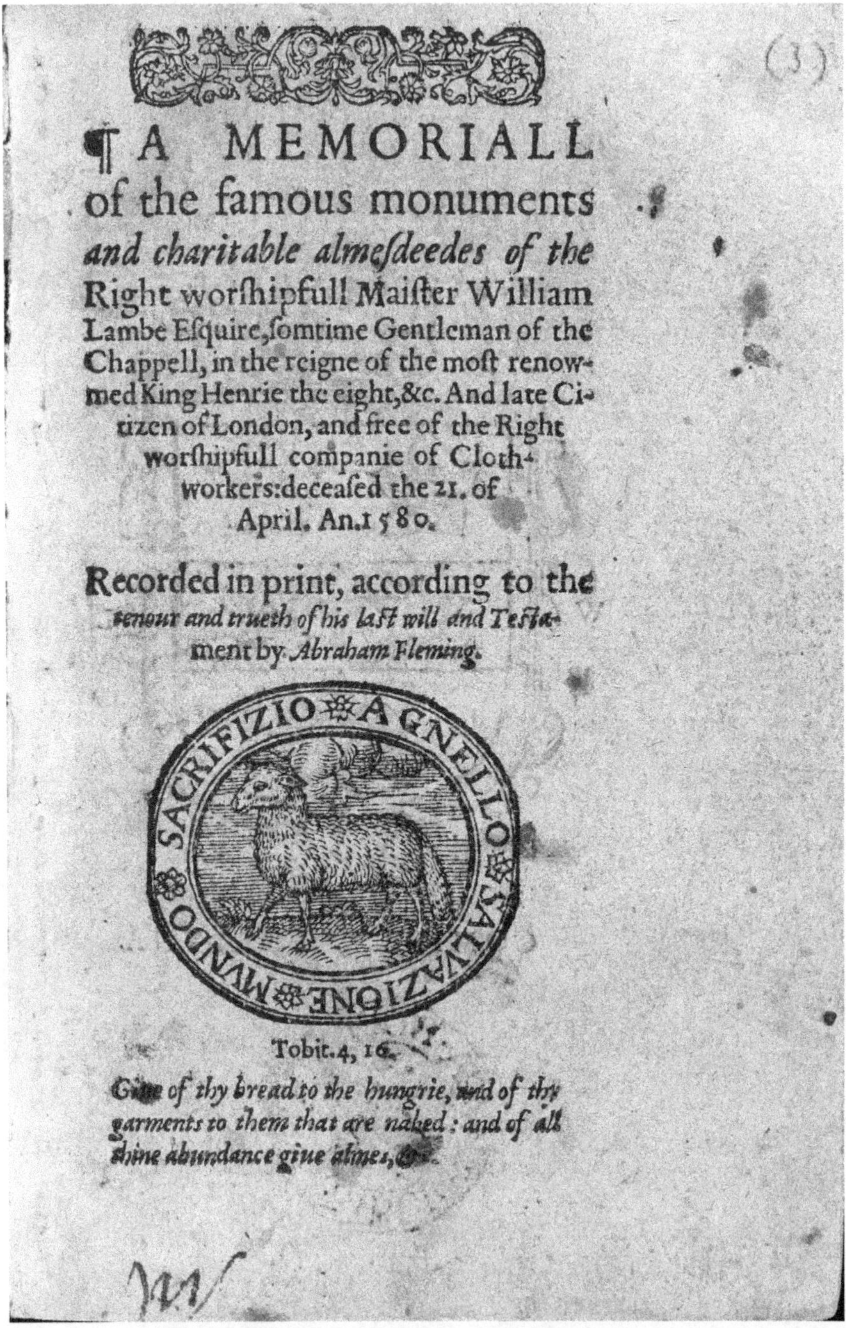

¶ A MEMORIALL
of the famous monuments
and charitable almesdeedes of the
Right worshipfull Maister William
Lambe Esquire, somtime Gentleman of the
Chappell, in the reigne of the most renow-
med King Henrie the eight, &c. And late Ci-
tizen of London, and free of the Right
worshipfull companie of Cloth-
workers: deceased the 21. of
April. An. 1580.

Recorded in print, according to the
tenour and trueth of his last will and Testa-
ment by *Abraham Fleming.*

Tobit. 4, 16.

Giue of thy bread to the hungrie, and of thy garments to them that are naked: and of all thine abundance giue almes, &c.

Figure 10. Title page of Abraham Fleming, *A Memorial of the Famous Monuments and Charitable Almesdeedes of the Right Worshipfull Maister William Lambe Esquire* (1580). The Bodleian Libraries, The University of Oxford, 8° W22 (3) Art, title page.

(though it is not clear how far the readership reached: the sole surviving copy has the annotation 'Epitaph of my Unckle & godfather m^{r} Richard Price').[21] The London Merchant Adventurer and Leatherseller Robert Rogers would be immortalized in 1601 in *A Liuing Remembrance of Master Robert Rogers*.[22] But the *Epitaph* on Lambe perhaps inaugurates the tradition of non-élite epitaph broadsheets.

The verse memorializing William Lambe is in rhyming fourteeners, the standard metre of the period's popular ballads. Printed in two columns, the *Epitaph* also divides its content in two. The first half develops the general theme with which the poem opens: 'All flesh is grasse, the Scripture saith, and vadeth [*sic*] like a flowre'. The second half turns to Lambe, and suggests—still in quite general terms—the nature of his philanthropy. '[T]his religious Gentleman', we're told, was 'a Patrone to the poore, | In allies and in lanes abrode, at home in th'entrie doore, | In open stréete, in holie Church, in many a corners crooke'; he was 'an eie vnto the blind, a legge vnto the lame, | A comfort to the comfortles, a succour to the sicke, | A father to the fatherles,... | A husband to the desolate, and widowe left alone, | A fauourer and a fréend to all, an enimie to none'. The name 'Lambe' naturally triggers Christological associations: Lambe is 'this lowelie Lambe', 'the spotlesse Lambe', 'Christ our Shepherd hath, vnto his shéepfold led, | This louing Lambe, who like a Lambe dide [died] méekely in his bed'. But it also calls up the ecological benefits of the animal: Lambe provided 'Cloth for the backe, meate for the mouth, the hungrie soule to féede', and with his death 'Now such as had his wooll to weare, lament of him the lacke, | His flesh did fill their bellies full, his fléese kept warme their backe'.

Like the *Epitaph*, the *Memoriall* spends about two-fifths of its forty-page length dealing with generalities before turning to William Lambe. In the first half, Fleming expatiates on the very notion of memorialization. '[A] custome it hath béene both ancient and famous', he notes, 'not onely among Pagans...but also among people fearing God, and addicted to the extolling of his name, that the notable actes of such persons as were singular, shoulde not sléepe in obliuion, but by one monument or other [be] made immortall.' Ultimately, the precedent is scriptural: 'the holie Ghost hath vouchsafed some such speciall and souereigne dignitie, as to haue their names registred euen in the Bible, their vertues extolled, their déedes aduaunced: partly that the remembrance of them should neuer die, and partly to be prouocations vnto vs to walke worthie of our calling' (A3^{v}–A4^{r}). By the same token, the names of the wicked are recorded, so that 'Few fathers that loue their children, will baptize them by the name of *Absalon*, of *Achitophel*, of *Hamman*, of *Iudas*' (B1^{r}). For a wealthy man, inclusion in the register of the righteous is not easy, but there is a way: 'Will riche men so die, that they may liue in the Lorde? Then let them be charitable and pitifull, liberall and bountifull' (B3^{v}). Lambe serves as a shining example: 'A rare testimonie hereof may be séene in this famous Citie, euen at this instant, in a notable Gentleman, whose good déedes bare witnes of his Christianitie in his life, and shall continue the memorie of his charitie after death' (B4^{r}).

Supposedly writing Lambe's 'life', Fleming gives as a narrative only the faintest outline of a man whose 'knowledge & vnderstanding...remoued him from a mean estate, to a worshipfull calling: from the Countrie, to the Court: where being placed euen in the Chappell, to serue his souereigne Lord King *Henrie* the eight of immortall memorie, of whome he was well liked, and béeloued, he spent his time appointed in such séemelinesse as might be thought requisite for his degrée and person' (B4^{r-v}). With Lambe's life thus dispatched, Fleming moves on directly to the good deeds: 'And remembring that learning bringeth preferment, yea euen to them which are but basely borne, as it pleased God to moue him by his good and gratious spirite, he proued himselfe by testimonials of his doings, a louer of learning, and a fauourer of euerie honest profession' (B4^{v}).

Fleming makes clear the reason that he skimps on the biographical detail: 'I will say no more than I haue laide before me in writing, and maie boldely exemplifie' (B4^{r}). And the writing he has laid before him, as a marginal comment declares earlier, is 'the Testators owne last will & testament' (A3^{r}). As a result, most of Fleming's *Memoriall* is simply a recounting of Lambe's itemized will—which has survived—re-couched in the third person.[23] There are glimpses of a literate playfulness in Fleming's use of imagery inspired by the Holborn conduit. Lambe's Kentish school foundations are 'séede-plots of learning...watered with the springs of his bountie'; after detailing his funding of Shropshire clothiers, we move to London with the line, 'the well of his wel-doing not yet waxing drie, but yéelding liquor of reliefe verie largely, hath watered other places'; and so on (C1^{v}, C2^{r}). But Fleming's presence is felt more powerfully in a running commentary on the will's bequests. On the whole, the editorializing is positive: when Lambe gives ten shillings each to forty 'poor maides...in good name and fame' on the day of their marriage, Fleming adds, 'It were iniurie offered, to let slip vnremembred his mindfulnesse of poore maides marriages: & how willing he was to helpe them.' Noting that Lambe added the caveat that the maids should be 'in good name and fame', Fleming writes, approvingly: 'marke how in all his bequests, wisedome is ioined as a yokfellowe with his bountie'. Similarly, as Lambe provides for his servants during the difficult six months after his death, Fleming praises the way in which 'this discréete Gentleman, caried away with the zeale of a good conscience, tendering the state of his seruantes, left them also at a reasonable good stay...alas! these sorrowfull seruants doe not a little lament the losse of so louing a Maister' (D3^{r}).

On occasion, however, Fleming is provoked to some heavy-handed moralizing. Lambe's bequest to prisoners in seven of London's prisons simply lays out the gifts of mattresses and money for each jail, but Fleming cannot resist registering some resistance to the bequest. '[O]ffenders', he declares, 'deserue rather to be punished than fauoured, whervpon by politike gouernement it is prouided, that their bodies apprehended, be committed to apointed places of emprisonment.' Despite this, 'this good Gentleman remembring that the holie Ghost willeth vs not to withdraw our hand from any of our brethren in distresse, considering that charitie should not be parciall but indifferent, hath for the relief of the poore prisoners of the *Two Counters*, of *Newgate*, of *Ludgate*, of the *Marshall seas*, of the *Kings bench*, & of the *white Lion*, dealt very bountifully, and discréetely...'–and he goes on to detail the bequest, before editorializing again: 'of which charitable déed, how déepely they [the prisoners] are bound, if they haue any sparkle of grace, to thanke God for his goodnes shewed vnto them by the ministerie of this Gentleman, all the world may perceiue' (D2^{r-v}). One becomes aware that Lambe's is not the only will being itemized in his *Memoriall*.

Yet, for all Fleming's evident input, there are indications that Lambe was decidedly proactive in the writing of his *Memoriall*, above and beyond penning the will on which it is based, as the following passage suggests:

> And here by the way it is to bée noted, that whereas it is recorded in the summarie of English Chronicles, that he gaue to the hospitall, commonly called *The Sauoy*, founded by K. Henrie the seuenth, to purchase lands for the behoofe of the said hospitall, one hundred pounds in monie: it is nothing so. For his beneficence towards that hospitall was staid, not through any default in him, but because such agréements could not be concluded vpon, as he reasonably required. Wherefore his contribution that way ceased, sore (I dare say) against his godlie will. Thus much I was desired to speake touching that matter, to the intent that nothing but plaine truth might be reported, with the contrarie whereof he was not a litle offended. (D2^{r})

The awkwardness of the final sentences shows Fleming claiming he has no access to Lambe's feelings on the subject ('sore (I dare say) against his godlie will'), while admitting that he is acting under Lambe's instructions ('I was desired to speake...he was not a litle offended'). The offending passage in 'the summarie of English Chronicles' to which this refers occurs in John Stow's 1579 updating of his *The Summarie of the Chronicles of England*, where it forms part of what might be seen as a proleptic version of the *Memoriall*. The impetus for Lambe's inclusion in the *Summarie* was the beginning of work, on 26 March 1577, on 'the new Conduit neere vnto *Oldborne*, and a Standart with one Cocke at *Oldborne* bridge', 'founded by *William Lambe*, somtime Gentleman of the Chappel to King *Henrie* the eyght, now Citizen and Clothworker of *London*'. But the conduit also served as an excuse for Stow to record his fellow citizen's bequests–to the Clothworkers' and Stationers' companies, Christ's, St Thomas's and the Savoy hospitals, the free schools in Sutton

Valence and Maidstone, and funds 'to sette poore Clothiers aworke' in Ludlow and Bridgnorth. The passage in Stow to which Fleming draws attention states quite briefly: 'Item to the Hospitall called the Sauoye founded by king H. 7. one C. li [£100] in money to purchase lands for the same hospitall'.[24] When Stow produced another edition of his *Chronicles* in 1580, however, the same entry showed Lambe's editorial intervention:

> Item, to the Hospitall called the *Sauoy*, founded by King *Henrie* the seauenth, he minded to haue giuen one hundred pounde in money, to purchase lands for the same Hospital, but bycause suche agréementes coulde not be concluded vpon as he reasonablye required, hys contribution that waye ceased, sore against his wil, as manifestly appeareth by his charitable giftes to the saide Hospitall somtyme ten pound at once to buy bedding with.[25]

The detail given by Stow—and the fact that he knows of a bequest that did not happen—demonstrates that he also had access to the text of Lambe's will, and presumably therefore Lambe's cooperation. The wording employed by Stow and Fleming is strikingly similar: Stow writes that 'bycause suche agréementes coulde not be concluded vpon as he reasonablye required, hys contribution that waye ceased, sore against his wil', while Fleming phrases it, 'because such agréements could not be concluded vpon, as he reasonably required. Wherefore his contribution that way ceased, sore (I dare say) against his godlie wil'. Do we here see Fleming adapting Stow, and characteristically adding 'godlie', or are they both quoting a draft by Lambe? Either way, it is clear that Lambe is actively intervening in his memorialization in print *during his lifetime*, expressing 'his will' and desiring his memorial writer to speak his truth.[26]

The *Memoriall* contains another indication that Lambe's plan for memorialization in print was some time in the making. In his concern to consider not only body but 'the safetie of the soule', Fleming asserts, Lambe made it his 'daily custome…to meditate vpon a Praier booke, called *The Conduit of Comfort*, published vnder his name: that with the water thereof his soule, as with the other his bodie, might be refreshed' (C3^{v}). *Lambes Conduit of Comfort* (1579) was, as Fleming slyly suggests, only 'published vnder' Lambe's name—it was in fact the work of Fleming himself.[27] And Fleming doesn't miss the opportunity to push his year-old book: since *The Conduit of Comfort* could be 'bought for a litle monie', he urges, its benefits were 'generall, euen as the Conduit which he founded not seuerall but common' (a7^{v}–a8^{r}). The tiny pocketbook (no more than three inches by two and a half) describes its 'Anatomie' as 'The Conduit of Comfort, The Contemplation of a Christian', and claims that it will expound the Lord's Prayer, the Common Creed, and the Ten Commandments 'by Sentence and Example'. The 'appurtenances to this Conduit' are a cistern, a pipe, a lock, and a key, which correspond, respectively, to conscience, peace, love, and knowledge. In his dedicatory epistle to Lambe, Fleming suggests that he had himself invented this unlikely piece of theological plumbing and then decided to whom to dedicate it: 'Meditating this Manuell, intituled, *The Conduit of Comfort*, and deliberating with my selfe (according to common custome,) vnder whose sheeld it might bee safely shadowed: and entering into a reckoning of your meritorious deedes, (wherein you haue left witnesse to the world, that you are a true Christian Almoner,) I rested vpon this resolution, euen to committe this my Manuell to your protection' ($a3^v$–$a4^r$). But this is disingenuous at best. It seems much more likely that Lambe commissioned Fleming to produce *Lambes Conduit of Comforte* as a print tie-in to bring his financing of the charitable water project to the attention of the reading public.[28]

But Stow's volumes and *Lambes Conduit of Comforte* were not the only instances of pre-mortem memorialization that Lambe undertook. In the *Memoriall*, Fleming transcribes what he describes as an 'Epitaph enigmaticall' engraved on Lambe's tomb. 'It is a spéech Prosopopoicall', he explains, 'as if he personally spake vnto vs aliue, to put vs in mind by his example, of our transitorie state':

As I was, so are ye:
As I am, you shall be:
That I had, that I gaue:
That I gaue, that I haue:
Thus I end, all my cost:
That I left, that I lost.
($E2^v$–$E3^r$)

The epitaph plays on the difference between past and present, living and dead, past giving and present having, past keeping and present losing. But while the trick is meant to be that the dead Lambe speaks 'as if he personally spake vnto vs aliue', in truth it predated Lambe's death: 'by probable coniectures', writes Fleming, 'it may be thought, that it hath béene there any day this fourtéene or fiftéene yeares: for so long at least his almes hath béene giuen in that parish Church' ($E2^r$). Lambe's last will confirms this: he asks that 'my bodye shalbe buried in the parrish church of St ffaith vnder Paules church in London in a vawte vnder a tombe which I lately erected and made there'.[29] So for some fourteen or fifteen years, Lambe's tomb spoke to the worshippers at St Faith about the state of being dead, while Lambe himself was still very much alive. In this respect, Lambe was far from unique: Nigel Llewellyn has calculated that at least thirty per cent of funeral monuments were constructed while their subjects were still alive, conjuring the bizarre scene where

'In church after church across the early modern realm and on countless occasions through this period, members of the local gentry and their spouses must have knelt down in prayer alongside their own effigies'.[30] But in taking on the voice of his own corpse, Lambe is pushing the convention to an extreme.

According to William Dugdale's account of the chapel of St Faith under St Paul's, this inscription was placed on a raised tomb in the nave of the church ('Super Tumulum elevatum in navi Ecclesiæ'), and a plan drawn up by Wenceslaus Hollar has that tomb next to a column in the centre of the church, affixed to which was yet another self-memorialization–what Fleming terms a 'remembrance of his person', engraved in bronze ('In Lamina ænea, columpnæ juxta præfatum Tumulum affixa'):[31]

> *William Lambe*, so sometime was my name,
> Whiles I aliue did runne my mortall race,
> Seruing a Prince of most immortall fame,
> The eight *Henrie*, who of his princelie grace,
> In his Chappell allowed me a place,
> By whose fauour, from Gentleman t' Esquire,
> I was preferd with worship for mine hire.
>
> With wiues three I ioyned wedlocke bande,
> Which all aliue true louers were to mee,
> *Ione, Al[i]ce*, and *Ione*, for so they came to hande,
> What needeth praise, regarding their degree?
> In wifelie truth none stedfast more could bee,
> Who though in earth deaths force did once disseuer,
> Heauen yet I trust shall ioyne vs all for euer.
>
> O Lamb of God, which sinne didst take away,
> And as a Lamb wast offered vp for sinne,
> Where I (poore Lamb) went from thy flocke astray,
> Yet thou (good Lord) vouchsafe thy Lamb to winne,
> Home to thy fold: and hold thy Lamb therein,
> That at the day when Lambs and Goates shal seuer,
> Of thy choice Lambs, Lamb may be one for euer.[32]

Here we find the scanty biographical arc that Fleming invokes and the easy punning on 'lamb of God' that he exploits in the *Memoriall*–although notably he chose not to dwell on Lambe's three marriages (for which this is the only evidence).[33] Under this 'remembrance' were two further lines, 'I pray you all that receiue breade and pence, | To say the Lordes praier before ye go hence', which Fleming explains as 'a petition with an iniunction of dutie to the poore, who wéekely receiued their allowance at the handes of the worshipful Stationers' (E2^{v}). For the last fourteen or fifteen years of his life, Lambe had been 'pitifull to the poore of the parish of Saint *Faiths*', bequeathing £6 13s 4d per annum 'for the perpetuall succour of the poore and impotent...euen to the worldes end'. The distribution of 'twelue pence in monie, and twelue pence in bread' to twelve poor people every Friday at St Faith under St Paul was undertaken by 'the worshipfull companie of the Stationers', 'to whom he bearing great affection, and hauing also no small affiance, made them his disposers or stewardes in that behalfe'.[34] The choice of the Stationers was not random. St Faith under St Paul was the *de facto* parish church for many of the print professionals who worked in the cathedral precinct. Lambe constructed his tomb close to those of stationers Richard Waterson (d. 1563) and John Cawood (d. 1572); in future years the vault would also contain the remains of William Norton (d. 1593), Simon Waterson (d. 1599), Francis Coldock (d. 1602), John Norton (d. 1612), and Bonham Norton (d. 1635).[35] But Lambe's generosity to the Society came with strings: the Company's records reveal that every 6 May, the anniversary of Lambe's funeral, the Company paid a preacher six shillings and eightpence to deliver 'a sermon...in memoriall of the benefitte of master Lambe'. From 1591, this practice was supplemented for a few years by a dinner 'at the polle head for the lyvery after the sermon', with the notably more generous outlay of thirty-seven shillings and sixpence.[36]

The Limitations of Good Works

We might then see the *Memoriall* as the pinnacle of a well-organized and successful campaign by which Lambe ensured that he would be remembered through his almsgiving, his conduit and its print companion, *Lambes Conduit of Comfort*, his memorials in St Faith's, and his print *Epitaph* and *Memoriall*. But even within Fleming's two memorial texts, there are signs that the operation did not run smoothly. As Fleming concludes his *Epitaph*, he writes four lines that cast doubt on the narrative that he has been telling up to this point:

> So that I may conclude of him, as néedes conclude I must,
> If workes may simply of themselues, make righteous men and iust,
> (Which I denie, for vnto faith this office is assinde [assigned]:)
> Then is he sanctifide from sinne, and cleansd in hart and minde.

Good works alone, asserts Fleming, do not make men righteous and just; for that, faith is required. This is in line with the consistently 'godly' approach detectable across Fleming's writings, from his translations and editions of the works of various

Continental divines to his providentialist readings of comets and earthquakes in pamphlets—but there is a mismatch between Fleming's sense of how one gets to heaven and the material he has been given here to write with, and he outright 'denie[s]' that good works are adequate for salvation. He goes on to suggest a compromise that Lambe's 'diuerse distributions, and giftes' and 'The monuments which he hath left' can be considered as 'The fruits of faith which flourished, in him whiles he did liue' and 'signes that Christ our Shepherd hath, vnto his sheepfold led, | This louing Lambe'.[37] But the fact remains that the writer of this epitaph has trouble with his remit.

Fleming's hesitation also here speaks to a wider debate in Elizabethan England: after the Reformation had banished Purgatory and intercessory prayer, how could one memorialize and commemorate the dead? Previously, the dead were remembered through their charitable giving: one could found a chantry, support a chantry priest, give vessels or Eucharistic ornaments, buy a membership in a fraternity. With all these channels suddenly blocked, those wishing to be remembered needed to find new paths. As Ian Archer writes, 'the reformers, appropriating the cause of the poor in their struggle against the Antichrist, urged the duty of charity on their congregations, and giving, much of it directed through companies and parishes, surged through the Reformation years'.[38] Archer's account would certainly tally with Lambe's behaviour in the final two decades of his life—but Fleming's *Memoriall* suggests there may have been a more specific and pressing need to establish Lambe as a properly godly man.

Despite all Lambe's good works, Fleming alleges, 'a number there are, that wanting discretion, beare small good will to deuotion, which in their priuie whisperings and open méetings, call this Christian Gentlemans religion in question'. The 'suspicion', he continues, is 'not grounded vpon anie probable cause', but should 'be vtterly suppressed, and no longer vndeseruedly conceiued'; Fleming himself undertakes to 'render good reasons, and so discharge him of that Papisticall opinion, whereof manie lacking the light of iudgement, and indéede scarse Christianly affected, partlie supposed, and partly reported he was a fauourer' (D4^{r}). First, Lambe was 'a hearer of the worde preached', sometimes 'séene and marked at Powles crosse, to haue continued from eight of the clocke, vntill eleuen, attentiuely listening to the Preachers voice, and to haue endured the ende, being weake and aged, when others both strong and lustie went away'. To fill the time 'before the Sermon began, he spent the same in reading some part of the holie Bible'. At Little St Bartholomew's, he was 'noted zealous and earnest in praier': 'he hath not had his eies occupied in gazing about the Church: but his minde meditating vpon heauenlie mysteries'. And to judge by the day of his death, 'if a quiet conscience, if desire to forsake this world, if stedfast beliefe in Christ Iesus, and other fruites of Christianitie may be taken for the testimonials of a mans religion: then, not mine, but the report of reuerend, learned, graue, and wise Preachers, shall be sufficient confirmations in this behalfe: and to their iudgement and knowledge I appeale'. The 'sufficient confirmations' with reformist credentials beyond reproach who 'visited him in his sicknesse' are none other than Alexander Nowell, the dean of St Paul's, and martyrologist John Foxe (who had shared rooms at Brasenose half a century earlier) (E1^{r}). After itemizing Lambe's gifts, Fleming concludes,

> And thus you sée what monuments this Gentleman hath left behinde him, to beare witnesse to the worlde of the fruitfulnesse of his faith: which if (as Saint *Iames* saith) it may be iudged by workes, and that it is a dead and a barren faith which declareth not it selfe by déedes: then the sequele may be this, that the faith wherewith he (of whome we haue written) was indued [endowed], sheweth it selfe to be the same faith which is wished, and I woulde to God were in the heart of euerie Christian. (D3^{v})

Despite his evident doubts, then, Fleming finds multiple ways to recuperate Lambe's good works and to complete his commission.

But, as we have already seen, this was not the end for William Lambe's project of memorialization—although it may be fairly doubted that he had any idea that he would end up in Holinshed's *Chronicles* seven years after his death. Here we witness one of history's happy accidents: the for-hire print-market writer whom Lambe commissioned in 1579 became the leading editor (as it is now generally accepted) of the 1587 revision and expansion of the *Chronicles*.[39] In this important role, Fleming missed no opportunity to advertise his back catalogue.[40] While discussing the tomb of King Alfred, he notes that 'in memorie of him a certeine learned clarke made an epitaph in Latine, which for the woorthinesse thereof, is likewise (verse for verse, and in a maner word for word), translated by *Abraham Fleming* into English, whose no litle labor hath beene diligently imploied in suppleing sundrie insufficiencies found in of [*sic*] this huge volume'.[41] While Harold II was awaiting the Norman force that would defeat him at Hastings, a 'blasing starre' appeared in the skies for seven nights. Assuring his readers that such stars 'neuer appeare but as prognosticats of afterclaps', Fleming advises them, 'To be resolutelie instructed herein: doo but peruse a treatise entituled; A doctrine generall of comets or blasing starres published by a bishop of Mentz in Latine, and set foorth in English by *Abraham Fleming* vpon the apparition of a blasing starre seene in the southwest, on the 10 of Nouember 1577, and dedicated to the right worshipfull sir William Cordell knight, then maister of her maiesties rolles, &c.'.[42] Just as he could not pass up the chance to advertise a ten-year-old pamphlet when supposedly focusing on the eve of the Norman Conquest, so Fleming could not resist inserting into his account of 1580 'an extract' of 'a memoriall recorded in print'–one that he just happened to have written himself.[43]

In shoehorning his own *Memoriall* into a chronicle history, however, Fleming made some minor but significant emendations. This was his standard practice: Fleming revised, extended, and amplified Holinshed's text, and notably elaborated the narrative by adding moralizing passages, brief edifying commentaries, capped by classical verse *sententiae*. His editorial touch was not impersonal. As Matthew Woodcock has noted, Fleming 'frequently interposes his own voice to comment on and judge a historical figure or source, and signals his interventions with a diacritical textual marker ("¶") and a marginal attribution'. The result is an 'active, directed form of didacticism that seeks to extract transferable precepts provided by the bountiful lessons of history, and one which also insists upon the importance of recognizing the workings of providence'.[44] Much of the Holinshed Lambe is a verbatim reprint of Fleming's *Memoriall*, so digressions from that text are all the more notable. There are two crucial cuts: Lambe's past with Henry VIII is not mentioned, and the rumours of papism are notably absent. But two short passages are introduced, each leading to a Latin tag (one by Palingenius, one by Hieronimo Wolf) which is typographically set apart, prompting the reader to read it as the concluding moral of Lambe's tale:

> So litle esteemed he the mucke of this world, in respect of doing good, speciallie when he saw old age drawing him to his graue: of which mind it were to be wished all richmen would be (whom God hath made his stewards) when they wax crooked & bow backt, and (as the poet saith)
>
> Obrepit canis rugosa senecta capillis [wrinkled age creeps in with white hair].[45]

and

> Thus regarded he not so much his priuate thrift, as the common good, giuing therein to the world a testimonie of christian prudence, whose nature is to prefer the benefit of manie before the profit of one, according to that of the poet:
>
> Publica priuatis qui sapit anteferet [he who is wise prefers the public before the private].[46]

Note here how Fleming has recast his account of William Lambe. No longer tinged with the traces of his Catholic past, Lambe's good works can now become an exemplar of how rich men, God's stewards of wealth, should prefer the common good over private thrift. And placed between the two earthquakes–Fleming has been noted for his penchant for sensational or supernatural materials–William Lambe becomes the lost exemplar of 'Christian prudence' against whom the rest of the world, punished by natural disasters, can be measured. 'Thus much hath at large beene spoken for others example, whome as God hath indued with riches', as Fleming writes in his final comment on the life of William Lambe; 'so it were to be wished they would vse them no woorse'.

The Fate of the Monuments

Fleming's rousing praise of the 'monuments' Lambe had 'left behinde him' lacked the benefit of hindsight: Lambe was soon enough forgotten by most people. *Lambes Conduit of Comforte* was republished in the seventeenth century—but with all references to Lambe stripped from it.[47] As was typical with broadsheets, the single-sheet *Epitaph* soon disappeared: only one exemplar survived, thanks to a collector of the genre, and the tiny *Memoriall* had a similar fate. Even the stone and bronze memorials in St Faiths could not survive the Great Fire of 1666; we are dependent on Anthony Munday's, Dugdale's, and Hollar's records of them.

The philanthropic gestures that bore his name fared a little better. The Clothworkers heard sermons in Lambe's Chapel every quarter-day: the first sermon, in 1581, was given by Richard Hakluyt, later known as the editor of the *Principal Navigations*.[48] During the reign of Charles I, the Company chose the puritan minister Arthur Jackson to preach there, only to have Archbishop of Canterbury William Laud take him to task for using 'a turn-up table' to celebrate communion. Jackson weathered that storm,[49] but a report in 1648 painted a depressing picture of the chapel. Lambe had directed that only prayers and sermons should take place there, but marriages of strangers were being celebrated, 'oppugneing that comaund'; there was no surplice, a pewter basin was serving as a font, and the communion table was still a chair-stool that provided a seat during most of the service, 'but when the holye Sacrament is to be celebrated the back of that chairestoole is turned downe and made their Comunion table'. Part of the chapel had been cordoned off, and was occupied by 'one Bagshawe'; some of the walls had been torn down to make 'greate folding windowes into their Chambers'; and a cellar had been dug out under the chapel—allowing the occupants of two adjoining tenements to store their coal and beer—and in so doing, the corpses buried there had been 'carried awaye'. Lambe's picture remained, 'painted to *the* life in an Ovall circle', but the picture was now blasphemously 'sett over the place where the Comunion Table should stand at the vpper end of that Chappell'—an effect not at all mitigated by the fact that 'the Picture of a lamb is set vnder him'.[50]

Lambe's Chapel was demolished in 1873, as the Clothworkers moved their church to St James's in Islington, where an effigy of Lambe, dated 1612, survives.[51]

Lambe's Conduit itself was already defunct by the end of the seventeenth century, and the site of the well-head is today marked only by a nondescript inscription.[52] But the bequest did give its name to Lamb's Conduit Street–and, belatedly, to The Lamb, the public house on that street, founded in 1727, that does excellent business to the present day.

6

The Receipts and Payments of Richard Stonley

On 23 April 1973, the Folger Shakespeare Library announced a momentous Shakespearean discovery. While perusing a recent acquisition of three volumes of a manuscript diary, curator Dr Laetitia Yeandle had come across the earliest known record of a purchase of a book written by William Shakespeare.[1] On Tuesday 12 June 1593, the diary's writer, Richard Stonley, laid out twelvepence, recording the transaction in this entry (Fig. 11):

Bookes	for the Survey of ffraunce with the Venus & Adhonay per Shakespere[2]	xij d

From this it appears that Shakespeare's recently published erotic poem *Venus and Adonis* was sold alongside a very different volume, John Eliot's *The Suruay or Topographical Description of France*, published in the previous spring of 1592.[3] Thanks

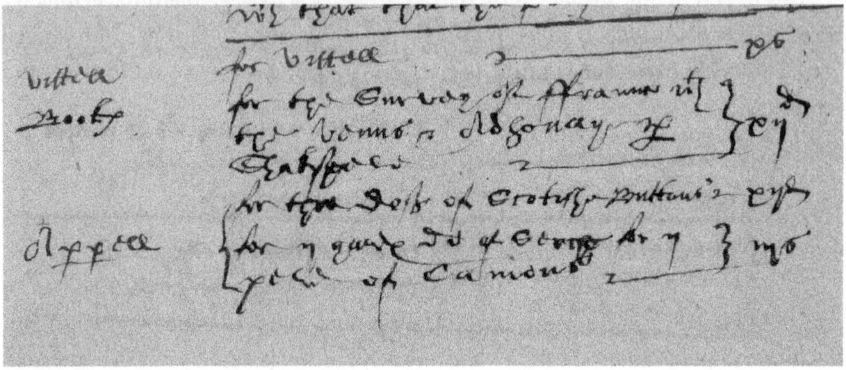

Figure 11. Detail from entry for 12 June 1593, diary of Richard Stonley. By permission of the Folger Shakespeare Library.

to this entry, Stonley wins the prize, or as Samuel Schoenbaum puts it, 'the minor distinction of being the first recorded purchaser of Shakespeare's first publication'.[4] Despite the fanfare in 1973, the entry containing Stonley's purchase was not in fact news—it had been known by Shakespeare editors Edmond Malone and George Steevens in the mid-1790s, when the relevant volume was in the possession of their friend, the collector Francis Douce.[5] But the source of the information disappeared as the diaries remained in private hands for the next 175 years.[6]

Richard Stonley opened each volume of his diary with the words 'Recept*e*s and payment*e*s', and inside he recorded his expenditure on all kinds of commodities. This would suggest that the books are primarily financial account books—and one could hardly expect anything else from a man like Stonley, a lifelong employee of the Exchequer, whose job depended on the accurate and detailed recording of receipts and payments. But, just as Stonley's career at the Exchequer turned out to have a vexed relationship with receipts and payments, so his diaries are much more than a crude double-entry bookkeeping. For these receipts and payments are only part of a diary that aims to record many different aspects of his life—domestic and professional, spiritual and secular—within the limited format of its pages.

Self Accounting: The Rise of the Diary

William Matthews's 1950 catalogue of British diaries designates all pre-1600 'diaries' under subcategories that qualify their status as diaries: daily notes of embassy, diplomatic diary, family diary, travel diary, public diary, military diary, astrologer's diary, prison diary, medical diary, war diary, theatre diary, ecclesiastical diary, yeoman's diary, legal diary, country diary, farming diary.[7] It is true that most of the surviving sixteenth-century documents designated as 'diaries' record only a circumscribed period of time, usually related to a particular activity—a pilgrimage, military campaign, or sea-voyage. Others may be kept for longer periods, but are, in effect, professional diaries that record the duties of the writer or the finances of the writer's post. So we have the diary that Master of the Ordnance Sir Richard Guylforde made during his 1506–7 pilgrimage to the Holy Land (he died in Jersualem);[8] John Taylor's daily journal of a 1513 military campaign;[9] Sir Richard Torkington's 1516–17 account of his travels from Rye to Jerusalem via Rome;[10] an account by an anonymous Lyddington steward of the summer 1544 military expedition against Calais;[11] and All Souls' fellow Richard Madox's diary recounting his voyage with Edward Fenton in 1582.[12] A few others are records of the professional duties of their writers: such a diary was kept by King Edward VI between 1549 and 1552, and by secretary of state Sir Francis Walsingham between 1570 and 1583—or rather by his secretary.[13]

Perhaps the most famous of these 'professional' diaries is by Henry Machyn, the parish clerk of Holy-Trinity-the-Less: a daily record of events from 1550 to 1563 that focuses on public processions, especially funerals, in London. It is a fascinating document for historians of London—but a very frustrating read for anyone interested in Henry Machyn. Although Machyn is implicated in what is being described, he makes only one explicit appearance in his diary. On 13 November 1561, St Clement's Day, Machyn recorded the day's Paul's Cross sermon given by Michael Reniger, as was his custom. But he also recorded that 'monser henry de machyn' paid penance for an alleged offence: Jean Veron, the French Huguenot minister, had been slandered by Machyn, who was repeating gossip he had received from William Laurence, clerk of St Mary Magdalen's in Milk Street. As required, Machyn writes, there 'dyd [sit] all the sermon tyme monser henry de machyn', but despite the fact that '*the* sam hare [the same Harry] knellyd down [be]ffor M veron & *the* bysshope' they 'yet wold nott for[give] hym' despite, 'all is [his] frynd*es that* he had worshephull'.[14] Although Machyn himself, the same Harry, here features prominently in his journal, he casts himself in the third person. That sense of distance is characteristic of many sixteenth-century diaries.

It is only in the 1570s that we find the earliest surviving continually kept English diaries that appear to track a person's life rather than chronicle his job. Some were made possible by printed books that provided spaces in which to write. At the top end of the market, expensive 'ephemerides'—which provided details of each day's planetary positions—acted as a diary for the scholar and magus John Dee. In his autobiographical 'The compendious rehearsal of John Dee his dutifull declaracion' in 1592, Dee recalled how in 1547, 'I began to make observations (very many to the houre and minute) of the heavenly influences and operations actuall in this elementall portion of the world'. This seems to refer to the notes, starting on 1 November 1547 in Louvain, that Dee entered in the blank back pages of a volume, in which he attempted to map the current weather onto the planetary configurations of the day.[15] From then, he continues, 'Of which sort [of observations] I made some thousands in the yeares then following: as may appeare by my owne writing in my *Ephemerides*, and in sundry other bookes purposely recorded'. Later he went beyond the weather, making notes about events in his life, still in relation to the 'heavenly influences'. Two volumes survive: on 15 January 1577 he started making notes in the margins of a copy of Georg Stadius' *Ephemerides* for 1554–1600 (Cologne, 1570), and continued in a copy of Giovanni Magini's *Ephemerides coelestium motuum* for 1581 to 1620 (Venice, 1582), keeping up the practice until April 1601.[16] Dee's remarkable life ensures that his entries contain their fair share of name-dropping—'The Queen's Majesty had conference with me at Richmond inter 9 et 11 ante meridiem', he noted on 8 October 1578—but he was not above chronicling more domestic excitement: on

2 September 1595 he immortalized 'The spider, at 10 of the clock at night suddenly, on my desk, and suddenly gone; a most rare one in bigness and length of feet, &c. I was in a great study at my desk, &c.'.[17]

But most writers turned to a much less costly option. For decades, almanacs had been one of the most popular of cheap printed books, with their month-by-month lists of saint's days, fairs, moons, and tides. In 1565, however, Henry Denham printed for William Pickering *An Almanacke, and Prognostication* by Joachim Hubrigh, an almanac that left blank spaces against a list of dates, in which the owner could write his or her own information (Fig. 12).[18] Others soon followed suit, with title pages often suggesting that almanac-owners should make use of them in this way: Thomas Purfoote's 1566 *A Blanke and Perpetuall Almanacke* notes that the book can serve 'as a memoriall...for any...that will make & keepe notes of any actes, deedes, or thinges that passeth from time to time (Worthy of memory to be registered)', while Thomas Hill's 1571 *An Almanack* specified what kind of 'sundry affayres' might be noted: 'receytes, payments, or sych lyke'.[19] Adam Smyth, who has undertaken the most comprehensive study of the autobiographical use of early modern almanacs, states

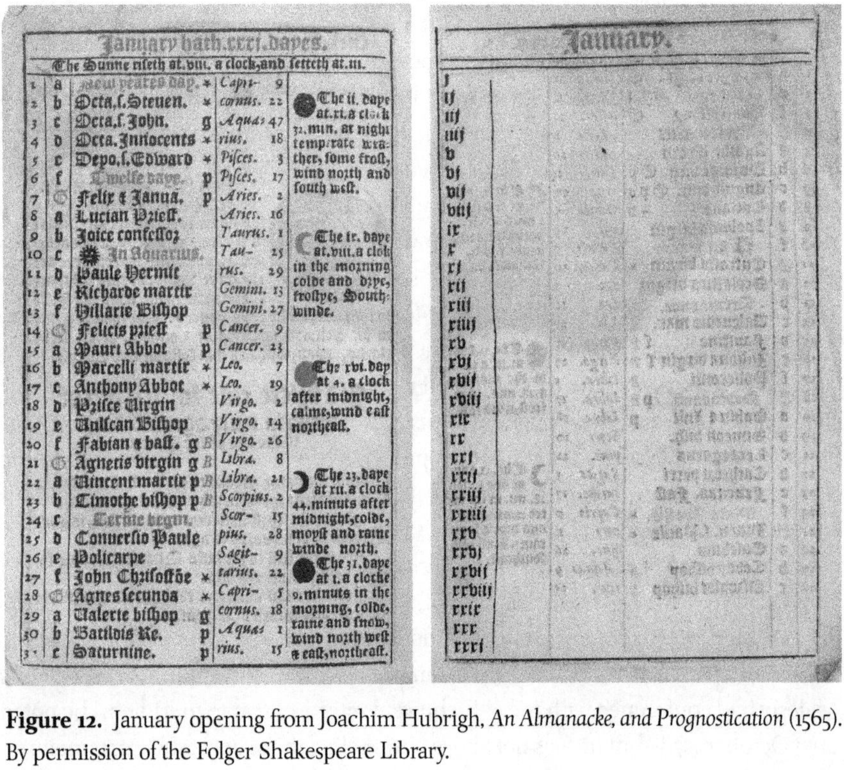

Figure 12. January opening from Joachim Hubrigh, *An Almanacke, and Prognostication* (1565). By permission of the Folger Shakespeare Library.

that 'Certainly, by the seventeenth century annotations were widely and systematically added: about one in seven almanacs I have examined contains some form of sustained handwritten additions'.[20] Sometimes these almanac entries were compiled to form other autobiographical documents: the Monmouthshire gentleman Walter Powell of Llantilio Crossenny (1581–1656) produced what he called 'a booke of ould remembrances collected by me Walter Powell of the ages of me & my ffrindes and children', including in it 'matters happening in my occasions, collected out of my ould Almanacks, which I have filed togeather from yeare to yeare, as in the blanks thereof they are written more at large'. Rather than replacing the almanacs, this new book was designed as 'a shorte breviat to be caried about me to helpe my memorie concerning those things & vpon all occasions', to be cross-referenced with the almanacs when required.[21]

As Peter Stallybrass has pointed out, although we tend to assume that manuscript precedes print, some of the period's most widespread manuscript forms were in fact prompted by print innovations—and the printed almanac form certainly influenced some people's manuscript diaries.[22] In researching his 1941 book *Tudor Cornwall*, the historian A. L. Rowse brought to light a portion of a small (6⅛ × 8¼ inches) manuscript diary for 1576–7, belonging to a Cornish gentleman named William Carnsew of Bokelly (*c.* 1530–89). In it, day by day, Carnsew records the weather; details of his frequent travels; his farming, estate activities, and mining enterprises; his wide reading; the letters he sends and receives; his attempts to minister medical cures and treatments; and news—local, national, and international—that he has heard and read (with false information sometimes corrected with the note 'A lie').[23] But the diary also aped aspects of the printed almanac form. Each opening covered a month, with Carnsew copying the first two columns of an almanac such as Hubrigh's, to give the date and day of the week. He then wrote across what remained of the two pages (Fig. 13). (Carnsew's son Richard at university in Oxford kept a manuscript book with a strikingly similar format, largely to keep track of his expenses, but also to record his and his brother Matthew's reading.[24]) Carnsew's diary provides an interesting comparison against which to view Richard Stonley's volumes. While the two men were writing diaries at the same time, Carnsew is following an established format, albeit one that usually existed in print. With Stonley, however, we come to an entirely new way of writing a diary.

The Diaries of Richard Stonley

The Folger's Stonley diaries constitute three volumes, which presumably derived from a longer run, since they are not chronologically consecutive. All three are

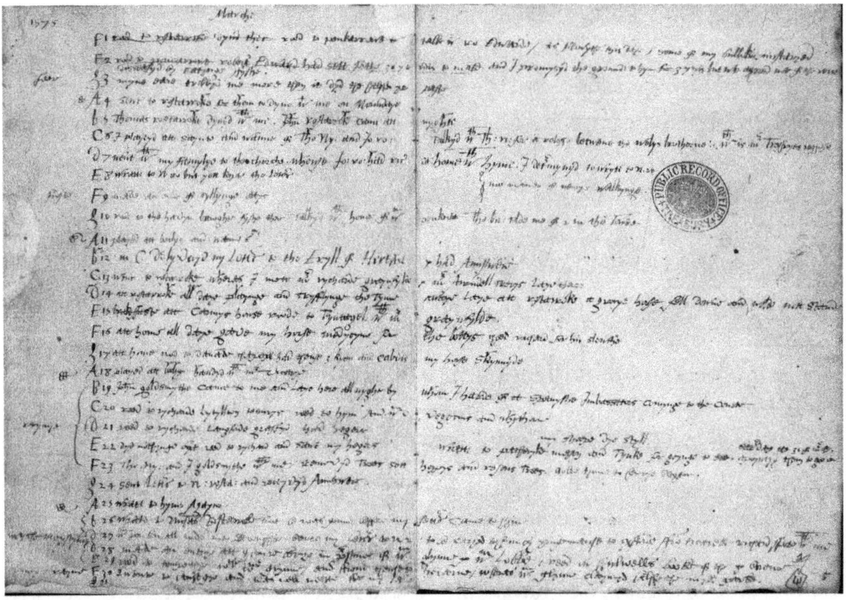

Figure 13. Opening from diary of William Carnsew of Knollys. The National Archives.

small paper books, purchased already sewn, but blank and unformatted. The earliest volume (now Folger MS V.a.459), of one hundred leaves, runs from 15 June 1581 to 31 December 1582; the second (V.a.460), ninety-two leaves long, from 14 May 1593 to 24 May 1594; and the latest (V.a.461), some seventy-seven leaves, from 14 March 1596/7 to 18 May 1598. Stonley writes in his diaries in a remarkably consistent manner. In the first surviving volume (1581–2), there is no evidence of fumbling to find a format, which suggests that Stonley had been keeping diaries for some time.

On the first two-page opening of this first volume, for example (Fig. 14), Stonley adopts a very clear layout, in which each page is effectively divided into two columns. The second column, which takes up about three quarters of the space, contains the body of the text; the first column serves as a kind of marginal indicator of what is in that text. Each new day is signalled with the date in Latin centred on the page as if it were a title. Following the date, each day's entry begins with a sentence or two of text. In the diary of 1581–2, these sentences are taken from Scripture, starting with Psalm 136 and progressing verse by verse through the Bible—and Stonley even copies out verbatim the marginal commentaries from his Bible. (In the second volume, Stonley has moved on to Erasmus' edition of Cato's *Disticha moralia* in an English version by Richard Taverner, quoting first the Latin and then Taverner's English. In the third he moves to another of Taverner's collections, the section of *The Garden of Wysdome* based on Erasmus' *Apophthegmata*.[25])

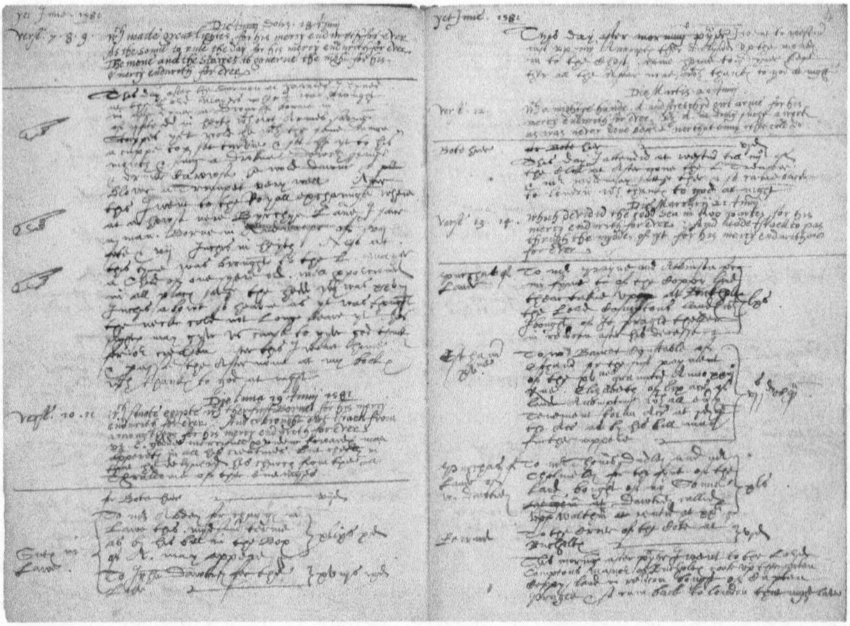

Figure 14. Opening from diary of Richard Stonley, June 1581. By permission of the Folger Shakespeare Library.

The first portion of each day's entry, therefore, is an act of verbatim copying. After the copied passage Stonley rules a line, and takes a different tack. On most days (but not Sunday, the Lord's day), this involves financial expenditure. On Monday, for example, Stonley lists: 'for Bote hire–viijd [eightpence]; To Mr Abdey for charges in Lawe this mydsym*er* terme as by his bill in the Box of A. may appere–xlixs xd [49 shillings and tenpence]; To John dawtrey for the Law–xviijs ixd [18 shillings and ninepence]'–the latter three charges bracketed together as 'Sut*es* in Lawe', denoting Stonley's legal expenses. ('Box of A' presumably denotes one of the boxes in which Stonley keeps his financial papers.) These financial outgoings are followed by a narrative of the day, which on Monday reaches only two sentences: 'This day after morning pr*a*yers I went to Westm*inster* cast vp my Accompt*es* ther Delyu*er*d vp the money in to the Chest. came home to Dyner kept ther all the After none with thank*es* to god at night.'

This entry follows a formula that becomes very familiar as the manuscript progresses. But within that formula, as should already be apparent, there are multiple different ways of writing Stonley's life on display. One is financial, in the form of his itemized outgoings. But another thread might be called spiritual, as suggested by the act of scriptural quotation and the emphasis on prayer. Another reaches towards narrative, with the sequential account of the day, split up into regular portions and activities: morning prayer; morning work, quite often at Westminster; dinner (a midday meal in the period) at home; activities at home—most often 'with my books'; and then 'thanks to God at night'. But does one of these dominate? Is the point of keeping the diary to record his expenses, or to document his activities? Is the quoting of Scripture merely a rote activity of copying? And, most fundamentally, what is the relationship between these three?

In the top left-hand corner of that first opening, Stonley writes 'yet June 1581' (i.e. still June 1581), to let himself know the month and the year in which he is writing his entries. That detail suggests that Stonley expected to come back to these entries, and required a quick reminder of where certain years and months were in his books. Similarly the marginal notes on these pages constitute a quick guide to the contents of the main text. The symbols in the margin, usually now called manicules, might be best understood here as a pointing index finger that serves literally to *index* the entries in the inner column. We find fingers pointing to entries such as 'Purchase of land', 'Reward', 'Owt rent', 'Rep*ara*cions', 'Servant*es* wag*es*', 'Apparrell', 'watching', 'Stable charg*es*', 'Barber', 'Scoll*ers* Charges' (at Oxford, where Stonley paid for his stepsons' education), 'Bok*es*', 'Iren work', 'Vittell', and so on. Stonley apparently used these index descriptions to calculate the totals of expenditure in certain categories. At the end of the earliest volume, we find a tally entitled 'The Some of the Totall Charge of the Book' which runs from 1 January 1581/2 to 1 January 1582/3. Returning to the start date in the diary, 1 January 1581/2, we find that Stonley has gone through each marginal note and scored it out—presumably as he transferred the individual amounts to a running total.

A number of critics have recently drawn attention to the importance of the rise of double-entry bookkeeping in the early modern period.[26] After Luca Pacioli included a section on bookkeeping in his 1494 Venetian book on arithmetic, tracts on accountancy were published in Europe's vernacular languages—first in Italian, then in French, Dutch, and German, and from 1543 in English.[27] These popular bookkeeping manuals aimed to instil long-established mercantile practices among the population. As a result, it has been argued by Adam Smyth, the rhetoric, habits, and mindset of mercantile accountancy can be found in forms of life-writing in the period, as the writer tallies incomings versus outgoings.[28] When confronted with this sort of evidence, the temptation is to assume that Stonley's diaries are primarily financial in nature: that the record of certain purchases might prompt a brief narrative account of the day, but that at heart the function of these diaries was to keep track of money. So for Alec Ryrie, for example, despite its evident piety Stonley's diary is 'less a spiritual journal than an account-book containing brief notes of Stonley's actions and devotions'.[29] For some critics, the ostentatious piety of a diary-writer like Stonley can seem bogus. Jason Scott-Warren suggests that, in mercantile ledgers, the 'sometimes elaborate religious formulas... aimed to demonstrate the piety and probity of the merchant and to redeem their profits from the taint of usury'. In this case, Scott-Warren continues,

> Stonley's rote use of moral and scriptural excerpts to frame his daily accounts suggests that he too saw the utility of contemporary book-keeping practice in sublimating the worldliness of his everyday experience. Put simply, a massive tailor's bill looks less sinful when it is prefaced by a biblical excerpt about the calamities that God sent to his church in order to test his children.

In this reading, 'Stonley's diaries are an accountant's fictions, a means for securing creditworthiness in the wider community'.[30]

Scott-Warren's argument here implies that the 'wider community' might be reading these volumes, which seems doubtful; there is no evidence that anybody else saw Stonley's diaries—until his final months, at least. I would also be very wary of prioritizing the financial over the spiritual here, as if the latter simply serves as a cover for the former. Far from being in opposition, these two registers often meet in the period, with the language of accountancy permeating even the most pious writings. William Perkins, perhaps the most popular English Calvinist writer, explicitly calls for the godly to 'take a fore-hand reckoning of our selues in the time of this our life' ahead of the final reckoning at the Day of Judgement:

> First, we must draw out the bill of our receipts and expenses. The bills of receipt are framed thus: we must call to remembrance what graces, blessings, and gifts we have received of God, whether temporall or spirituall... That done, we are next to frame our bills of expences: which are nothing els, but large considerations of our sinnes... Tradesmen for their temporal estates, keepe in their shoppes bookes of receipts and expences: shall we not then much more doe the like for our spirituall estates?

Ultimately, 'we shal appeare before the great God of all the world, to give vp our account'.[31] The recurring phrase here 'receipts and expences' is, of course, a version of the title Stonley gave to his diaries—but is he balancing the books of his temporal estate, or of his spiritual estate? Or is he doing both in one document?

The Life of Richard Stonley

I have deliberately refrained from introducing the writer of these volumes, for good reason. Even before his diaries were rediscovered by historians, enough was known about Richard Stonley to furnish a detailed biographical account by Nora

Fuidge for the History of Parliament Trust.[32] Born around 1520, Richard Stonley lived on Aldersgate Street in the parish of St Botolph's without Aldersgate in London. There is no record that he attended university or the Inns of Court. In his professional life, Richard Stonley was an official of the Exchequer, one of four tellers whose responsibilities included the receiving of monies owed to the Crown. Stonley became a teller in his early twenties, in 1554, during the reign of Mary I, and remained in the post until the late 1590s, a remarkable fifty-year career. He was well connected in City circles thanks to his marriage to Anne Branche Dun, the widow of Robert Dun, who died in 1552 or 1553. Anne's brothers, John and Thomas Branche, were both prominent London drapers (John became Lord Mayor in 1580); she brought three sons into her second marriage, including Dr Daniel Dun (or Donne) who became Master of Requests and the principal of New Inn,[33] and the physician William Donne. Together the Stonleys had two daughters: Anne, who married William Heigham of East Ham, and Dorothy, who married William Dawtrey of More in Sussex; the Donnes, Heighams, and Dawtreys make frequent appearances in the diaries. Stonley owned property in several counties, although his primary country estate was at Doddinghurst in Essex. Richard Stonley was, in short, a well-established official.

The longevity of that Exchequer career is all the more remarkable given that, for the last fifteen years, Stonley was under investigation for defrauding the Crown. As G. R. Elton writes, Exchequer officers 'drew their income from three sources: they had official salaries, took fees from revenue officers and others for such requirements of the accounting process as the making out of documents or of certified copies from the record, and could hope for perquisites and bribes intended to dispose them favourably to those who got involved in the Exchequer's machinery'. But tellers like Stonley found a further aspect to the job. Since the tellers received all the monies being paid into the Exchequer of Receipt, as Elton notes, 'The essential problem in the Receipt consisted in controlling the tellers who alone handled the money for which they rendered half-yearly accounts'.[34] Apparently, when he 'went to Westminster cast vp my Accomptes ther Delyuerd vp the money in to the Chest', Stonley did not deliver all the money. Like other Exchequer officials, Stonley saw one of the unofficial perks of his job as the ability to use the cash he was holding—and he claimed to be holding about £300,000 per annum—in order to speculate in property, and to lend money at interest.

There is a long paper-trail of enquiries into Stonley's conduct. In 1584, Thomas Lichfield, auditing the Exchequer, alleged that Stonley 'had defrauded the Crown by concealing fines and by other means, [and] that his denial of the charges, and demands to be allowed to answer them in a court of law, were subterfuges'.[35]

A year later, in August 1585, Stonley was required to produce an inventory of his 'estate', the monies he had in his hands and the reasons for his losses, in which he describes himself as 'being now in case to beg in his old days, being 65 years of age'. Worse was to come in August 1586, when the Exchequer auditor Robert Petre had to tell Lord Treasurer Burghley that Stonley was 'unable to make up his accounts by £16,000' and had 'been forced to lay the burthen on the other three tellers'.[36] In February 1588, Stonley attempted to explain the shortfall with a litany of excuses—he had been overwhelmed; there had been 'sundry falls' in the value of coin; he had 'double charged' himself with certain sums—and to sell off his lands in Essex, Berkshire, and Buckinghamshire to make up about £14,000 of what he owed.[37] In the autumn of 1588, it was again revealed that massive amounts of money were missing from the Exchequer. This time, another teller, Robert Taillor, claimed to Burghley that while he admitted to 'over-boldnes in vsinge monye in my Office', it was in fact his clerk William Raven who was guilty of a 'horryble practyse' in that he 'hath treacherouslye conveyed awaye her Ma*iesties* monye owte of the Cheste once Locked vp by your honors order';[38] Raven's version of events, predictably enough, reversed the story. Around the same time, Stonley was forbidden to make any payments—an order that became increasingly difficult to observe as the end of the year approached.[39] This business, Elton writes, 'lasted at least from 1588 to 1593', but as long as Burghley was willing to trust his man Robert Petre as auditor of the receipt, Stonley seems to have been safe.

However, in the latter half of 1593 the situation changed—as the second Folger volume records.[40] On 20 September, the elderly Robert Petre died, and shortly after, long-time Burghley servant Vincent Skinner was appointed as his replacement. Skinner was soon putting pressure on Stonley, by now the most senior of the tellers. On 3 October 1593, Stonley records in his diary that 'This day after morninge p*r*ayer I went to westm*inster* kept ther till xj [eleven] conferrid with Mr Skyner of my recept*es* & payment*es*'.[41] On the 10th, 'This day after morning p*r*ayer I went to westm*inster* sent from thenc the state of my Accompts to my *Lord* Treasorer at the Courte'.[42] On Friday 12th, in a departure from the usual procedure, Stonley received a visit at his London home:

> And this After none my *Lord* Treasorer sent Mr Skynner & Edmond English [Petre's man] to conferr with me towching my Charge in my office wherof I made my Lord a declaracion the day before & p*ro*mised to sertefye his honou*r* fully.

But Stonley was able to buy some time: he promised to certify Burghley fully 'vpon my returne from the funerall of Mr Ro*bert* Peter after Tewsday next so as on the Monday after I ment to c*u*m to London & so to my Lorde'; this answer apparently 'contentyd them'.[43] The following day, Stonley travelled to his Essex estate of Doddinghurst, and on Tuesday 16 October was one of the chief mourners at Petre's funeral at nearby Ingatestone. On 24 October, he went 'to Mr Skynner at westm*in-ster* to conferre with hym touchinge my Accompt*es* and to satesfy my *Lord* Treasorers *Lettres*'. The following day, 'I occupied my self in making bok*es* to my *Lord* Treasorer for the state of the office', and on the 26th, 'I kept home makinge vp my book*es* to the Lord Treasorer at the Courte'. It was on the 27th that Stonley 'went to westm*inster* attendid ther till xj Answerid the Lord Treasorers *Lettres* & d*elivere*d them to Mr Skynner'.[44] The Cecil Papers contain a letter dated 27 October 1593 from Skinner to Burghley in which he includes 'a packet from Mr. Stoneley, in answer of your Lordship's letter to him, wherein he saith he hath included the state and rates of his lands, towards the satisfaction of your Lordship therein'.[45] At that point, the issue seems to retreat—although on 21 January 1593/4, Stonley notes that 'This day after morning p*raye*r I kept home at my book*es* preparing to Answer all p*er*sons agenst [in preparation for] this terme especially my *Lord* Treasorer who sercheth earnestly my dealings in my office as reason for his owne discharge';[46] this suggests that Stonley believed that Burghley was scapegoating him to cover his own tracks. Despite Skinner's investigation, Stonley again kept his job, remaining in post until May 1597 when his luck finally ran out, his property was sequestered by the Crown, and Stonley himself was jailed in the Fleet Prison. He died there on 19 February 1600, at the age of seventy-nine.

Reading the Page

Knowing this fascinating life-story is something of a poisoned chalice for the reader of Stonley's diaries. With the exception of the Skinner investigation, the diaries bear almost no trace of his professional woes.[47] From this perspective, it would seem that these diaries provide only a slim slice of the life Stonley led. For those wishing to investigate Stonley's conduct in his Exchequer role, the diaries are either: (a) pretty much useless, or (b) a compelling piece of negative evidence to show that Stonley was a thoroughgoing dissembler who lied even to his diary. For Scott-Warren, for example, there is an irresistible continuity between Stonley's embezzling at work and his account-keeping at home: 'just as his public account-keeping material unravelled...so (one senses) might these "privy purse" accounts have been a fragile façade'.[48]

I would like to suggest a third scenario. These diaries are an important record of a means by which Stonley attempted to make sense of his daily life. They represent what he wanted to record and to remember, perhaps simply for himself. Certainly they do not include the details of his professional financial dealings. But that omission may suggest that Stonley was able to, or at least trying to, separate out parts of his life. In order to pursue this, we might look again at Stonley's page—but rather than reading the text, analysing instead how he places his text on the page.

The spiritual, financial, and narrative jostle for room on the page—or rather, they try not to jostle, because Stonley is clearly attempting to impose some order and separation on the aspects of his life he has brought together. While the text is divided into days, as one would expect, blocks of text are also divided by ruled lines that do not coincide with the transition from one day to the text; instead, those ruled lines bisect the entry of a single day. So while Stonley groups together his scriptural quotations, financial accounts, and narrative through the unit of the day, he works against that day-unit in his use of ruled lines, which separate the scriptural quotation (and commentary) from the next item, be it the accounts or the narrative. Stonley also deliberately writes in two different hands: the scriptural quotations and the marginal notes against them are in a Roman hand, whereas the rest of the entries are in the more common secretary hand—a move that serves visually to highlight the verses.[49] Does this mean that we should not relegate the scriptural verses to a secondary, 'copied' status, but instead see them as importantly constitutive of Stonley's day?

Even within the 'narrative' element of each day, there emerge some insistent patterns and separations. It is not difficult to perceive a correlation between the shape of Stonley's day, in his relating of it, and the daily entries in the manuscript. Each entry starts with a scriptural quotation, echoing the morning prayer; it then moves to business; and lastly to what is effectively a short narrative account of the day, which finishes with 'thankes to god at night'—both a record of the thanks Stonley offers to God in prayer, and a reiterated thanks in written form. But the entry also distinguishes between what happens in his house (morning prayer, time spent with his books, dinner, supper, evening prayer) and what happens elsewhere (at Westminster, church, at Doddinghurst). Even within the house, we are made aware of irruptions into the domestic scene, as Stonley painstakingly lists the names of 'Strangers at dyner and supper', with 'Strangers' denoting those not of his household.

Other aspects of the diaries are thrown into relief when one focuses attention on the layout. Returning to that first opening of the 1581 volume, perhaps the most striking feature visually is the excessively long narrative entry on Sunday 18 June, in which Stonley writes:

This day after the Sarmon at Paules I dyned at the Lord Mayers where was brought in after dyner a dwarf borne in [*lacuna*] of ij fote ded in heyth [i.e. height] without Armes savinge Stomppes yet wold he with the same daunce a cuppe top set turvie and set yt to his mowth & sing a drunken dowch songe and drinke Carowse & wold daunce & blowe a Trumpt very well After this I went to the Royall exchaunge where at a house nere Byrchyn Lane I saw a man Borne in Andwarpe of vij fote & vij Inches in hyeth Also at this tme was brought to the *Lord* Mayor a Child of one yere old, well *pro*porcioned in all places save the hedd w*hi*ch was xxviij Inches abowt so heavie as yt was thought the necke cold not longe beare yt Thes sight*es* may gyve vs cause to gyve god thank*es* for *ou*r creason [creation]. After this I went home & passed the Afternone at my book*es* with thank*es* to god at night.[50]

In stark contrast to so many of Stonley's terse entries, this offers a wonderfully vivid evocation of early modern London's foremost venues: the Sunday sermon at Paul's Cross in the churchyard of St Paul's Cathedral; the Lord Mayor's residence (a visit not as remarkable as it might seem, since Lord Mayor John Branche was Stonley's brother-in-law); and the merchants' meeting place, the Royal Exchange, opened ten years earlier. The entry is not entirely alone in recording what we might describe as 'public events': on Friday 30 June 1581, for example, Stonley records 'a disord*er* abowt Smythfeld in taking a way of one Butcher from the Cart that was ponyshed ther for sturringe vp the people to make a rebelli*on* about gentlemen & *Ser*vingmen', and on 21 July he registers the pillorying of those who had rescued Butcher.[51] Two days later, he records how the Jesuit Edmund Campion was paraded through Cheapside to the Tower, and later notes his arraignment (16 November) and execution (1 December). But such occurrences are the exception. Then why this emphasis on Sunday 18 June on what we might see, in comparison, as rather inconsequential sideshows?

In this entry, Stonley brings together three sightings of what he deems sensational human figures: a 'dwarf', a very tall man, and a baby with an oversized head. Interestingly, a month later, the 'dwarf' and the tall man appear in the chronicles of John Stow and Raphael Holinshed, by which time they have formed a double act of somewhat limited versatility—they sit side-by-side to show off their difference, and the smaller man walks between the legs of the taller while wearing a feathered hat.[52] But for Stonley, these sights have a specific purpose: they are to 'gyve us cause to gyve god thank*es* for *ou*r creason': they serve as a salutary contrast to Stonley's state, an interruption to the order that Stonley is so keen to find in his life and in his life-writing. The sheer length of this Sunday's entry—longer than any other in the diaries—serves to make it pop out of the page as something uncommon and outsized, echoing the monstrous nature of the information it contains. By contrast, Stonley's entries for the following Monday, Tuesday, and Wednesday evince a reassuring sense of proper balance and order.[53]

Strikingly, Stonley's layout and format remain the same throughout the three volumes, despite a major change in the author's circumstances. By the time Stonley embarks on the final volume in 1598, he is a prisoner in the Fleet. Relieved of his duties at the Exchequer, he has a daily routine that is, of necessity, radically altered—and yet his diary's account of each day is notably similar to what it has always been. Each day is still headed by a quotation, although by now, having presumably worked through the Bible, the text is not scriptural, but from the collection of Latin apophthegms by Erasmus, with its English commentary by Richard Taverner.[54] Stonley continues to record his outgoings: once a week, his 'flete charges' are registered, usually with an entry written by Stonley, for example, 'To John Hore deputie to the warden of the fleete for one fortnights Chamber rent endinge this daye', thirty shillings. The recipient then countersigns his book in proof of payment—and here the book truly becomes a record of 'Recept*es* and payment*es*'.[55] There is usually a one-line account of the day, either 'I kept my Chamber' or 'I occupied my self abrode in the Citie', the latter betraying the fact that Stonley was not required to remain in jail twenty-four hours a day. This too came at a price: there are entries 'To the same [John Hore] for my libertie abrode during that tyme', six shillings and eightpence with a further payment 'To m*aste*r wever my keeper for that tyme' of five shillings. And Stonley keeps up the practice of listing 'strangers' at dinner—usually his son-in-law Heigham, grandson Henry (Harry) Dawtrey, and 'the boy', presumably his servant—although the scene is no longer his household, and the strangers are listed no doubt partly as a way of keeping track of Stonley's prison expenses.

In other words, the same set of groupings and demarcations is still in evidence, and the shape of Stonley's day remains the same. There is, however, one late entry which speaks to a heightened awareness of the way in which the diary is crafted. We have already seen how Stonley uses his diary as a ready reckoner to calculate annual expenses, but on 29 June 1597 he proposes that, starting on that day, his system would become more complex:

> [F]rom this day ther is a nother booke w*hi*ch I terme the weekboke or kytchin book wherin I notte all thyng*es* & somes of money laid out all kynde of weyes. what ys spent besid*es* of provicion what presents & what stranger resort to me that in the end of the yere I may voyd owt eu*er*y thinge in ther p*ro*per plac*es*.[56]

Stonley introduces a preliminary book, into which 'all thynges' (including all expenses, all visitors, etc.) would be noted, to allow for the end-of-year calculations, in which he 'voyd[s] owt eu*er*y thinge in ther p*ro*per plac*es*'. (A 'week book' is the weekly version of a daybook, 'in which the occurrences or transactions of the day are entered', and a 'kytchin book' provides an inventory of victuals bought for the household.[57]) This shows that Stonley's 'diary' is in fact one document in a series of 'multiple, interconnected notebooks', a phenomenon which Adam Smyth has shown to be a feature both of early modern accountancy and early modern autobiography.[58] But it also reveals the extent to which the volumes now at the Folger are *not* a week book or a kitchen book, not the first 'catch-all' manuscript in which 'all thyng*es*' are jotted down, but a meditated redaction of those things, 'in ther p*ro*per places'.

In the diaries, there may not be a trace of the thousands that passed through Stonley's hands as a teller—but not necessarily because Stonley was hiding those transactions, which were of course recorded in their own 'proper place'. Instead, we might consider the diaries as a telling exploration of what was important to Stonley, what he wanted to record, and how he wanted to understand the elements of his own life. The evidence of the diary pages suggests that Stonley had found a way to conceive of his spiritual, financial, and domestic lives together as part of his day; but the insistent separating out of those elements—by ruled lines, by a change in hand—equally suggests that the utter absence of his Exchequer activities was not necessarily the devious deception of a criminal mastermind, but rather the textual effect of a man who separated his domestic and professional lives. And I would tentatively suggest that what ultimately mattered to Richard Stonley, according to this, was not his post at the Exchequer, or his embezzlement, but his morning prayer, his dinner with the Lord Mayor, his occasional indulgence in an erotic pamphlet 'per Shakespere', and his thanks to God at night.

7

Richard Rogers's Course of Examination

John Bradford was among the first of the Marian martyrs, imprisoned within the first month of Mary's reign, and burned at Smithfield in July 1555. John Foxe portrays him as an exceptionally bookish man, who 'slept not co*m*menly aboue .iiii. [four] howers a nighte: and in his bed till slepe came, his booke went not out of his hand… he counted that houre not well spent, wherin he did not some good, either wi*th* his pen, studie or exhortacio*n* to others &c.'.[1] In a posthumous edition of Bradford's sermons, his friend Thomas Sampson elaborated on what Bradford was doing with his book and pen. '[O]ur *Bradford*', he wrote, 'had his dayly exercises and practices of repentance.' Among his habits was

> to make to hym selfe a Cataloge of all the grossest & most enorme synnes which in his lyfe of ignorance he had committed, and to lay the same before hys eyes when hee went to priuate praier, that by the sight and remembraunce of them, he might be stirred vp to offer to God the sacrifice of a contrite hart, seeke assurance of saluation in Christ by faith, thanke God for his calling from the waies of wickednes, and praye for increase of grace to bee conducted in holy lyfe acceptable and pleasing to God.

By a 'Cataloge', Sampson here seems to mean a listing of past sins which Bradford must keep before his eyes in praying for his future 'holy lyfe', but another of Bradford's 'exercises' was more dynamic: 'He vsed to make vnto him selfe an *Ephemeris* or a *Iournal*, in which hee vsed to write all such notable thinges as either hee did see or heare eche day that passed.' This journal was not, however, merely a recording of external acts witnessed by Bradford, but a means by which he might assess himself: 'what so euer he did heare or see, he did so pen it, that a man might see, in that booke the signes of his smitten hart. For if he did see or heare any good in any man, by that sight he found & noted the want thereof in hym selfe, and added a short prayer, crauing mercye and grace to amende.' Conversely, '[i]f he dyd heare or see any plague or misery, he noted it as a thing procured by his own syns, and styl added: *Domine miserere mei, Lord haue mercy vpon me*'. In this way, both the good he saw and the misery he saw were transformed, by his penning of them, into means of appreciating his own flaws and sins. In addition, Bradford used the journal to log his inner feelings: 'He vsed in the same booke to note such euyll thoughtes as did ryse in him', whether it be 'enuying the good of other men, thoughtes of vnthankfulnes, of not considering God in his works, of hardnes and vnsensiblenes of hart when he dyd see other moued and affected'. Sampson sums up by claiming that in this way, Bradford 'made to him selfe and of himselfe a booke of daily practices of repentance'.[2] *To him selfe and of himselfe*: that strange phrase neatly captures the ways in which Bradford's ephemeris or journal operates, providing himself with a record of the outside world, with which to chart his own spiritual progress, and to enable his repentance. And, crucially, this works 'daily', with 'eche day that passed'.[3]

Bradford's sermons were republished frequently, and Sampson's brief sketch proved remarkably influential. Its language is still detectable in John Clarke's 1634 injunctions to readers to 'Keepe a Catalogue of all thy grossest knowne sinnes, not balking any, but dealing truely with thy selfe', and to 'summe up thy accounts, and make all straight twixt God and thee... In the *end* of every *day*' by asking: 'What have I *done*? What have I *done* amisse? What have I *left* undone?'[4] By the early seventeenth century, Puritan writers were routinely advocating the keeping of written records to monitor one's spiritual life. In 1622 Nicholas Byfield suggests that in order to 'wisely consider of [God's] workes', we 'should do well for this purpose to *keepe Records and Register* vp the special glorious works of God'.[5] Robert Harris in 1624 urges his reader, 'when thou has prayed, doe... as *Daniel cap.* 9.1. take notice of thine enlargements in prayer, and of thy successe after, write down time and place as the Prophet doth, and so helpe thy selfe in future times by former experiments'.[6] And Bradford is explicitly cited by Daniel Dyke in 1616: 'The practice of *Bradford* that worthy Repentant in this kind was very memorable: who to this purpose booked euery notable accident each day that passed; and that so, that in the penning a [he] might see the signes of his smitten heart.'[7]

Perhaps most influentially, Bradford's practice was held up as an example in one of the most important of early English puritan texts, *Seuen Treatises*, which offered a direction that 'may be called the practise of Christianitie'. Written by Richard Rogers, 'preacher of the Word of God at Wethersfield in Essex', and published with the imprimatur of fellow ministers Stephen Egerton, Ezekiel Culverwell, and Francis Marbury, *Seuen Treatises* aimed to show Christians 'how to leade a godly and comfortable life euery day'—or, as Tom Webster puts it, it details 'the most spiritually effective way for the aspiring saint to lead his or her life'.[8] Hugely popular, it went through eight editions by 1630, and was excerpted in the even more popular 1609 *Garden of Spirituall Flowers.*[9] In the words of William Haller, *Seuen Treatises* 'was the first important exposition of the code of behavior which expressed the English Calvinist, or, more broadly speaking, the Puritan, conception of the spiritual and moral life. As such it inaugurated a literature the extent and influence of which in all departments of life can hardly be exaggerated.'[10] In it, Rogers wrote, 'we reade it written of Maister *Bradford*, (who had much inward communion with God) that he was neuer satisfied in the duties he did through the day, and namely in praying at the Chappell (when he was fellow of a colledge) and in his chamber with his puples, vntill he had also powred out his heart to the Lord by himselfe alone'. Later, like Sampson's Bradford, Rogers points to two textual means of doing this. One is that the Christian should 'set downe many parts of his life in writing . . . such as principally to be kept in record (as Gods benefits and his owne sinnes) as he is able, and all to helpe him to [be?] better directed in it'–a version of Bradford's 'Cataloge of all the grossest & most enorme synnes'. But Rogers's energies are directed primarily at something closer to Bradford's ephemeris. In describing this, Rogers turns to what may appear a secular example:

> as the Steward of some Noble mans house doth not make a generall reckoning and account of much money laid out, but writeth the particulars, daily and hourely as he giueth out and receiueth, that hee may not bee deceiued: so and much more (as the Christian life is more precious then all earthly treasure) doth the wise man looke daily to his waies, and through the day, that his account may the lesse trouble him at his lying downe, and consequently at the day of his death.[11]

The figure of the steward conjures Luke 12:42–'And the Lord saide: Who is a faythfull and wyse stewarde, whom his lorde shall make ruler ouer his housholde, to geue them their portion of meate in due season?'–but the crucial point here is that it is not enough to write a general log of outgoings and incomings, but rather one that pays attention to the 'particulars, daily and hourely'. This is a constant, ongoing process that does not leave evaluation even until the end of a day, and certainly not until 'the day of his death'.

Elsewhere in the *Seuen Treatises*, Rogers essays a more complex version of this self-reckoning. Citing the injunction of Hebrews 3:22 that 'we tak heede that there be not at any time, and so any part of the day in vs an euill heart', he urges that to combat forgetfulness and a lack of observance, 'we should sometime looke backe to see how we haue regarded the charge that is giuen vs'. The fittest time for this is 'wh*en* we haue ended the day'–unless, of course, 'some speciall sinne committed in the day do require a more speedie examining of our selues before'. He offers the example of Job (1:9) who 'did euery day of his childrens banquetting together, offer sacrifice to God and pray for them, and command them to cleanse their hearts and sanctify the*m*selues' before turning again to a secular example to explain how this might work:

> For euen as men who are in great occupyings, do not onely write their takings and their layings out, but do also at euen [evening] conferre them together, lest any delay of time should cause forgetfulnesse (and yet this labour they thinke needful about things that shall perish:) so is it much more necessarie in the accounts of our soules that we should do; that is, daily looke what we gaine or loose, that we may procure to our selues therby most sound safetie, and prouide also the better for the time to come to do the like, and that with more ease...[12]

In what appears to be a throwaway sentence, Rogers then reveals the importance of this regime for life-writing: 'Yea, and more then that, so will hee euen set downe many parts of his life in writing also, such as are principally to be kept in record (as Gods benefits, and his owne sinnes) as he is able, and all to helpe him to be better directed.'[13]

By the time Rogers published *Seuen Treatises* in 1603, he had already been 'set[ting] downe many parts of his life in writing' for several years, keeping a journal in which he examined himself, if not daily, then at least very frequently. A portion of his diary survives in the Dr Williams' Library in London, as Baxter MS 61.13. It is a small (5.75 × 7.75 inches) paper book comprising forty-one leaves, notably scuffed and frayed, and missing the bottom inch of its first four leaves. The pagination (13–46 and 51–98) reveals that several folios are missing.[14] What remains covers a period from 28 February 1586/7 to 26 August 1590. The volume is anonymous, but internal references to places and people allowed editor M. M. Knappen to identify the author as Richard Rogers.[15] This remarkable document survives as the first spiritual diary in English.

My State in My Christian Practice

Essex-born Richard Rogers (1551–1618) was educated at Christ's College and Gonville and Caius, Cambridge, before serving as curate at Radwinter in Essex. He was appointed lecturer in nearby Wethersfield in 1577, and was probably a founding member of the Braintree conference of Presbyterian ministers. His nonconformist conduct came to the attention of the bishop of London John Aylmer in the 1580s, and he was suspended for thirty weeks for refusing archbishop of Canterbury John Whitgift's three articles requiring ministerial conformity in 1584. During the period covered by the diary, his conduct was under particular scrutiny. In 1589, he was ordered to use the surplice, and to administer the sacraments according to the Book of Common Prayer. In court on 25 November, he admitted that he had not administered communion since he had last appeared there, but was able to produce a letter from Thomas Whythorne's erstwhile employer, Ambrose Dudley, earl of Warwick (conveniently, if suspiciously, dated only a day earlier), which claimed that Rogers was required to perform duties as his chaplain.[16]

Although dating from the same decade, Rogers's diary bears almost no relation to Richard Stonley's.[17] Here we get no sense of a daily rhythm, little acknowledgement of place, and no attention to financial matters. In his will, Rogers refers to these writings as 'my state in my christian practize'—and that describes perfectly what is at stake. Focusing on his Christian practice, Rogers lets family events slip by almost unnoted. The birth of his son Ezekiel in February 1588 is signalled by a marginal note: 'Nat*us* est Ezech[iel] meus. ffeb. 1º & my w[ife] hardly escaped',[18] which may (or may not) explain the main text which records 'By labour I have tried, & espec[ially] here of late *that* god hath made harde thing*es*, & such as I durst hardly venture to preach of them...' (15^{v}). (Is his wife's near-death experience one of the 'harde thing*es*'?) The death of his son Nathaniel in August 1588 is again relegated to a marginal note ('Nath[aniel] bur[ied]') while the text reflects on the dual threat posed 'by o*ur* enem[ies] *the* Span[ish] & at home papist*es* in multitud*es* ready to come vppon vs vnawares' (20^{r}). The birth of his daughter Mary on 7 January 1590 is recorded in the main text ('nata est mar[ia] mea'), but largely because her baptism, a week later, was the cause of a three-day visit by a fellow minister from Cuckfield in Suffolk, John Knewstubs, during which 'we 2. had veary comfort[table] & p*ro*fitable com[panyings?] in prayer & confer[ence] togith*er*' (33^{v}). The visit provokes a lengthy meditation on 'The exampl of mr. knew[stubs]' (34^{r}) in which Knewstubs' 'unwearyed' praying, his 'merveilous love to all', his humility, knowledge, wisdom, bearing of wrongs, bountiful liberality, mercifulness, his 'litl account makeing of any thinge that he hath, or keeping any stock', and his 'contentation in a sol[itary] lif[e]' only serve to make Rogers 'see my case exceedingly differinge from his'—with the usual conclusion that 'my sin must needs be great' (33^{v}–34^{r}).

Although the text focuses on 'my state', Rogers is by no means cut off from the outside world. In April 1588, he spends ten days in London, where he visits the poor at the Bridewell prison (17^{v}), and at the end of November, he rides to Cambridge (23^{r}). There are moments where national and international events intrude: on 13 August 1588, he notes that 'we are now in peril of goodes, liberty, life, by our enemies the Span[ish]' (20^{r}), and on 26 October following, he muses that 'I have been oft times well moved with thinckine on our late deliv[erance] from the rage of Spain' (22^{r}). He fails to record that the threat of the Spanish Armada has been neutralized, news he presumably received in September—but the news is not important here: what is being calibrated is the effect of the threat and the deliverance on the estate of his Christian practice. So on 13 August, the Spanish and domestic threats prompt this:

> For my part I am so resolutly perswaded that god wil visit us some way, that if he should not by some universal calam[ity] sweepe us away, I protest that I should be in a most woefull case if I shoulde not…come to a more frutful and christian like estate then lately heretofore. I meane both to set lesse by the world, to have lesse dealing in it, to spende more time in study, to prepare better for afflic[tion], and to loath that detestable bayt which so much snareth. (20^{r})

And on 26 October, the deliverance provokes him to praise God: 'Blessed be his name for ever. I trust I have much use for it. For, even now and ever since, I say, as Israel, and I uttere it to others, If god had not then been on our side, we had not been here to inioy his blessings, but had been swallowed upp' (22^{r}).

As it was for John Bradford, writing is an important part of Rogers's daily routine: 'I continue my riseinge in morn[ing] about 5', he writes on 4 December 1587, 'and ether in my study, or about myne hart, and the bettering of my life in writing this, and such like thin[gs], I thanck god, my tyme is bestowed' (12^{r}). However, from the evidence of this diary, Rogers did not write at the end of each day, but sometimes at the end of a month. On 28 February 1586/7, he opens, 'Of thinges worth the remembr*ance* in this month this was one: a most sweet iorney with mr. Cul [Ezekiel Culverwell]…' (1^{r}). In the following June, after recounting the traumatic experience of 'goeing amonge a company of bad felowes', he reflects on the act of writing: 'Thus have I sett downe some part of those thinges which have fallen out this month and the sweet peace which I finde and feele since I wrot this…' (5v). There are moments, though, when Rogers does not wait for the end of the month, but records events with greater urgency. Writing immediately becomes a way of dealing with temptations. On 12 September 1587, he records that

> this after noone I felt stronge desire to inioy more liberty in thinckinge uppon some vaine thinges which I had lately weaned my selfe from. Me thought it great bondage to be tyed from delighting in such thinges as I tooke pleasure in, and if I had not either written this immediately, or by some other means met with it, I had allmost been gone from this course and become plainely minded and idle as before. (8^{r})

It is not clear whether 'written this' refers simply to the act of writing the present entry, or whether Rogers wrote elsewhere. There are signs that he is writing in multiple books. Lamenting the 'Great liberty I have geven my selfe' on 2 September 1587, for example, Rogers refrains from elaborating: 'I neede not here set downe *the* partic[ulars] w*hich* in my book are lardgly set downe' (7^{v})—presumably 'my book' is a separate volume. He sometimes refers to his 'meditations': on 17 July 1590, he records that, after a day of fasting, his mind is now 'well seasoned, chiefly by reading my med[itations], 40 or 50 of them, though I felt it disordred and confounded veary much' (40^{r}). Eight days later, he tells how he decided to be contented 'in the matter about loss of lib[erty]'; in coming to this conclusion, he writes, 'To this I was well moved by reading a med[itation], March 17, 1582. I resolve to be cheerful in my lif' (40^{v}). Again, the meditations would seem to have been in a separate book.

Rogers is not only writing his life but *reading* his own life-writing. The margins of his diaries are peppered with instructions to 'note', and more extensive assessments that something was 'A good speech' (7^{v}) or 'Worth *the* note' (8^{r}), or injunctions to 'Thinke of this oftimes in disgrace' (8^{v}) or 'Read this oft & make good vse of it' (9^{r}). Sometimes this is merely a matter of reading back over recent entries. On 20 September 1589, he remarks, 'Consideringe then what complaints I have made in the former pages, good cause I see there is whi I should pray, lord keep me in mine old age as thou hast in my youth…' (29^{r}). Following his account of a difficult month on 22 July 1587, he writes, 'I thanck god at the setting downe hereof I was well affected, and mine hart since yesterday was greeved to see such a decay of grac as partly now I have set downe. And in deed I am glad that I may see with grief when there is any declineing in my lif, seing it cannot be avoided but such shalbe, but yet that thei are so often, and that so few times of grace may be redde in these papers to have been inioyed of me, it is no meane grief unto me' (6^{r}). Reading over his entries allows him to 'see such a decay of grac', to 'see…any declineing in my lif…' (the verbs he uses are insistently visual). On occasion, he detects a mismatch between what he finds on the pages and his own sense of recent events: 'though I have no great thin[ges] to sett downe to accuse me', he writes on 30 August 1589, 'yet, seing the time was not filled with frutes of christian[ity], even that is enough against me' (29^{r}). At other times, the activity is compelling enough to persuade him to a course of action. On 18 November 1589, when the likelihood that he will be suspended as a preacher makes him '*per*ceiv[e] my mind not so cheerful nor of so good courage as to be readily disposed to duty', he decides to 'frame my mind wil[lingly] to goe vnder it', 'after *the* reading of some pa*r*t of my wri[tings]' (31^{v}).

We would be wrong to assume that Rogers merely writes then reads over what he has written. He is not simply recording past events, but providing a way of engaging with his past in order to mould his future—not just reading the past, but commenting on it, and rewriting it. Each manuscript page shows a complex pattern of writing and annotation, rewriting and expansion. Particularly charged occasions can be the cause of repeated rereading and annotation, sometimes over decades. On 23 June 1590, Rogers reacts to the news that his 'liberty in p*r*eching was stayed by Sta'—perhaps

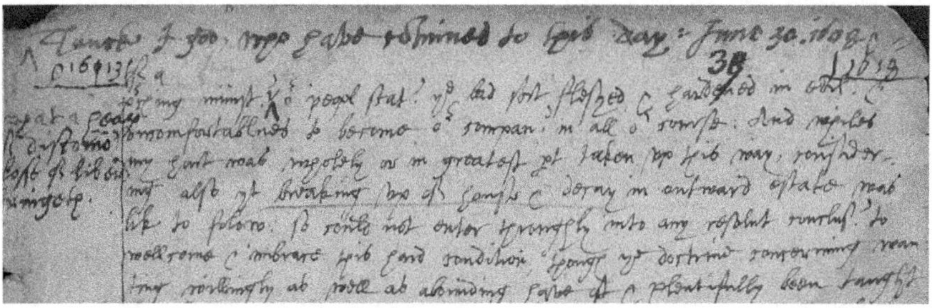

Figure 15. Page from Richard Rogers's diary. © Trustees of Dr Williams's Library, London.

by Edward Stanhope, a member of the High Commission.[19] Rogers's reaction is extreme:

> the sodainnes of it, & vnlooked for restraint, or short continuaunce of lib[erty] with so hard condic[ion], as to be bound over to consist[ory], this I say did bewray much weakn[ess] in me, & taught me *that* my strenghth was not great. ffor I was cast therby into a deep heav[iness], *which* did stay me in m[ine] owne feeling from cheerfuln[ess] & frut in comp[any], & oth[ers] did espye it as I was too much touched with grief in thincking *that* we must bidde farewell to all our sweet comp[any] & commu[nion] pub[lic] & privat, void of a preching minist[ry], our peopl scat[tered]… (38^{v}–39^{r})

The despair of this passage seems to have hit Rogers hard in future years. A marginal note instructs him 'This & the next sect[ions] read oft'. Another notes the subject matter: 'how losse of lib[erty] was taken'. Eighteen years later, with the left margin full, Rogers is forced to write in the top margin, 'Thanck I god, who have continued to this day: June 30. 1608' (39^{r}). But still he adds, appending that comment with '1613'. And again, '1618'. Given that Rogers died in April 1618, he must have revisited this low point in his final weeks (Fig. 15).

The habit of reading over what he has written forces the writing to evolve in particular ways. The diary takes on a cumulative effect, as Rogers decides he does not need to record every instance of a particular phenomenon. On 22 December 1587, he notes that 'here in these 2. months I have more partic[ularly] set downe thinges, not to observe the same course throughout, for *that* were infinit, but where any part of my life hereafter shall agree *with* any of this, *which* I have here set downe, *that* I may mak relation of it, to som of this: & not allwaies sett downe the same thinges againe' (13^{r}). Thus, on 11 April 1589, he writes, 'I litle looked to have stuffed my booke with such matters, as now to my great grief, I see I must. Since *the* last time I have been much after *that* *which* I have set downe last decemb[er] 21. And withall not reformed *the* abuze, *which* was last of all sett downe 6 lynes before' (25v). Here, the reader is required to consult the entry for 21 December 1588, and six lines before that entry, in order to understand what Rogers refers to as '*that* w*hi*ch I have set downe' and '*the* abuze, w*hi*ch was last of all sett downe 6 lynes before'. But the very act of cross-reference—and of reconsulting past entries—allows Rogers to map his spiritual journey. As he writes on 26 August 1590, 'I desire to have daily before mine eies *the* times, & yeares past of my life: w*hi*ch doe not a litle rouze me vp to care if it were neglected' (41^{v}). This 'rousing up to care' can be achieved through the contrast of the present day with times past: thus, on 29 November 1587, he records how 'this morne in my med[itation] I read my writeing*es* in Octob[er] 1582. wherby, I p*er*ceived how daungerously I am broken from *the* holy league w*hi*ch there I finde *that* most faithfully I entred into with *the* lord' (23^{r}). On other occasions, it can give him a sense of the continuity of his sins. On 9 July 1589, he is in particular despair, claiming

I remember no such bad estat these many month*es*. I have set downe oft, how such distemp*er*ature ariseth, namely, by being vnwil[ling] to take paine about *the* weaning of my self from secret outstrainge [outstraying] into vnlawful liberty. My purpose is (if god bless us in it) to drive out this devil by fasting, & prayer. god forgev such coldnes. *the* particulars have been *the* scurfie of all *the* sinnes w*hi*ch I in this book set my self against, leaning too much, & inclineing toward*es* them, but not abideing in any: onely this except, that knowledge seeking hath been for the most part neglected, except study for sermons.[20] (27^{r})

On this difficult occasion, 'this book' becomes ammunition against himself, a constant, undeniable reminder of his 'secret outstrainge' and 'coldnes' towards God.

Rogers's most extended discussion of this process occurs in an entry in mid-December 1587, when he recalls that 'I had this med[itation] one morn[ing]':

comp*ar*ing this course, in w*hi*ch I vew my life continually, with *the* form*er* wherin I did it by fits & so was oft vnsetled, out of order, & then eth*er* not seeing my self, though I had been vnwatchefull [*sic* - presumably he means watchful], walked in great daung*er* by every occas[ion] or seeinge it, could not easily recover my selfe: & so went unfit (many houres, & sometime dayes) for my calleinge: sometime dumpish & too heavy: sometime loose: & many such frutes folowinge: as no study, but vnprof[itableness], I saw an vnmeasurable difference: & said with my selfe, *that* as this was *the* life of a chr*ist*ian, so I desired *that* it myght ever be my compan[ion]. Oh lord, say I to my selfe, when I deeply weigh the benefit of such a course keeping, how litle a man doth tast of *the* bitter cupp of other men, who runn their course in foly & licentiousnes. What should be so regarded of me, *that* for the seekinge after it, I should deprive my selfe of this comfort & happines? (12^{v})

For Rogers, the key to 'comfort & happines' is precisely the maintenance of his course of self-examination, in which 'I vew my life continually': doing it in 'fits' does not produce the same results. Now, seeing 'an vnmeasurable difference', he vows to stick to this 'life of a christian'.

It is tempting to assume that writing so focused on 'I' must be an inward, solipsistic affair. But for all its apparent inwardness, this writing is not solely a private exercise. Much of Rogers's solitary meditation is explicitly inspired by external elements, with his relationships with other godly men to the fore. As the extant diary opens in February 1586/7, we find him becoming close to the preacher at Felsted: 'a most sweet iorney with mr. Cu[lverwe]l 2 dayes & much time bestowed on the way about *our* christian estat of god*es* mercy in *our* calleing to *the* felowsh[ip] in the gospel of the true testemonies of faith & of [the] great comfort w*hi*ch by continuing herein doth come vnto godes peo[ple]' (1^{r}). The following month, March 1587, it is presumably the classis meeting to which he approvingly refers when he claims 'I never enioied *the* like with any neighbor or broth*er* at any time, for it is not out of season at any time, to be occupied eith*er* in confer[ence] about knowl[edge] atteininge or groweinge in godlines' (1^{r}). When he writes down 'the exemple of mr. knew[stubs]', following the visit in January 1589/90, he notes that 'as it was my purpose to make p*ro*fit of his comp[any] so for *the* bett*er* tyinge of my selfe to reape it in deede, I have sett downe some p*ar*tic[ular] thing*es* wherein I desire to better mine estate by him' (33^{v})—even a personal encounter can be enhanced by a written record for future self-betterment.

The communion of his fellow local clergymen is of crucial importance to him and to his spiritual well-being. Francis J. Bremer has tracked how 'clerical friendship' among groups of ministers reinforced each man's 'godliness'.[21] Rogers records of his conference how 'we fasted betwixt our selves, to the stirring upp our selves to greater godliness...and then we determined to bringe into writing a direction for our lives, which might be both for our selves and others'—this 'direction for our lives' evolved into the *Seuen Treatises* of 1603. And there is reason to believe that part of what bound these men together was the reading of each other's writings. Rogers imagines a reader for what he has written: on 30 August 1587 he notes that 'He *that* should read my former writeing woulde thinck *that* I might have continued a month after in veary gracious & godly manner' (7^{r}). And he was certainly perusing similar writings by other godly men: on 9 July 1589, he records that 'Reading *the* writeing*es* of an oth*er* broth[er] about his estat, an houre & longuer, I was moved to write, & to bring my hart into a better frame: which in *the* beginning was impos[sible] to me: but I thanck god, I feel a sensibl chaung of *that*, & will set downe after, how myne hart groweth better seasoned' (27^{r}). Crucially here, it is the act of reading the brother's 'writeing*es*...about his estat'—the reading of another's life-writing—that moves Rogers to write about his own estate.[22]

The Spread of the Spiritual Examination

As Owen Watkins writes, Rogers's confessional diary 'embodies the essential features of the Puritan tradition of self-examination, which were to remain basically unchanged until well into the eighteenth century'.[23] A survey of those later seventeenth-century men and women who were known to keep a spiritual diary would fill a book in itself. But historians have been bemused by the rise of this genre.[24] Although there is ample evidence that many people kept such diaries, no published guide on how to do so appears before the mid-seventeenth century, when the ejected Lancashire minister Isaac Ambrose published his *Media* (1649), including a few sample entries,[25] and then John Beadle published a much more thorough guide to spiritual diary-keeping, his *Journal or Diary of a Thankful Christian* (1656). Even at that point, some seventy years after we know Richard Rogers to have been keeping a diary, Beadle can claim that 'this work here commended, is very usefull, though the duty be seldome practised, because the subject is rarely handled. It is as untroden a path, as ever I have gone; who have had scarce a little day hole of light to direct me, much lesse a Cloud of witnesses, or a Pillar of fire, or a Star to guide me'.[26] But how then did this practice spread?

The late Elizabethan and Jacobean periods have left surprisingly few spiritual journals. Samuel Ward kept a diary and sermon notebook from 1592 to 1601, while he was a student at Christ's College: this survives at Sidney Sussex College, of which he was eventually master.[27] The Yorkshire gentlewoman Lady Margaret Hoby kept a diary from 1599 to 1605, now at the British Library.[28] Extracts from a journal charting an illness (and concomitant despair) were printed in minister Richard Kilby's *Hallelu-iah: Praise Yee the Lord, for the Vnburthening of a Loaden Conscience*, published in 1618.[29] Other diaries are lost, but we have accounts of their keeping. According to his brother Jeremiah, Daniel Dyke, who died young in 1614, maintained 'his holie and religious course; which was, to keepe a catalogue or diary of his sinnes against God: and euery night, or the next morning, to reuiew the faults of the day past: Euerie Saboth morning, or night before, to reuiew the faults of the whole weeke: and at the ende of euery moneth to suruay the whole moneths transgressions'.[30] According to his funeral sermon, John Harington, second baron Harington of Exton, who also died young in 1614, embarked on a 'priuate exercise & course of pietie' which included one activity 'markeable aboue many other things':

> hee withdrew himselfe from his seruants and friends, and there in a booke which hee kept for the account of his life, hee set down what he had done al that day, how he had either

> offended or done good, and how he was tempted, and with stood them, and according to his account, he humbled himselfe; and such was his wisedome, that such temptations as were not fit (as I suppose) to come to any mans view but his owne, and his Gods, he writ in a peculiar Caracter knowne to none.[31]

The clergyman Samuel Fairclough (1594–1677) had 'his own *Diary*, which he kept *constantly*, from his age of *twenty* years'—that is, from *c.* 1614—'and (daily almost) wrote down in it a full History of all God's *dealing* with him, and of the daily *frame* of his own *heart*, and of *Satans* temptations (and of the *assistances* of Gods Spirit in them) and his *victory over* them'.[32] And as his son recalled, the Suffolk minister John Carter (1554–1635) 'kept a constant Diary, or day-book, in which he set down every day Gods extraordinary dispensations, his own actions, and whatsoever memorable things hee heard or read that day'.[33]

What prompted these men and women to start keeping such a 'constant Diary'? Given the absence of any printed guide, such as John Beadle's, the answer must be that this practice was disseminated on the local level, as ministers encouraged each other to keep diaries, and then urged their congregations to follow suit. Although Beadle may not have published his *Journal or Diary of a Thankful Christian* until 1656, he had long exhorted his parishioners to keep such a diary. The playwright and historian Arthur Wilson (1595–1652) recalled how 'Mr. Beadle of Banston preached at Leeze' on Sunday 21 July 1644, on Numbers 33:1, '*Theise are the journies of the children of Israel*, &c, insisting upon this. That every Christian ought to keep a record of his owne actions & ways, being full of dangers & hazards; that God might have the glorie.' By so doing, 'everie man, though of the meanest qualitie, may see the hand of the Divine Goodnes working for him in the many occurrences of his life. Which, as it may be a register to his owne memorie, so it may bee an example of gratitude to those who shall read or heare it, when they shall reflect upon themselves; & make a like collection of God's mercie towards them.' Beadle's advice to 'keep a record of his owne actions & ways' prompted Wilson to do precisely that: 'This made mee run backe to the beginning of my life, assisted by my memorie & some small notes; wherein I have given a true, though a meane deleniation [*sic*], of eight & forty yeares progresse in the world'—a manuscript that Wilson would work on for the next five years, entitled 'Observations of God's Providence, in the tract of my life'.[34] So Beadle's sermon inspired Wilson's life-writing—and I would suggest that it is in this kind of personal example, rather than printed exhortation, that explains the initial spread of spiritual journal-keeping.

Ellen McKay has previously suggested that 'a form of network existed between many of the diarists who wrote during the sixteenth, and principally the seventeenth centuries'.[35] While McKay does not cover them, it is also true that virtually all the surviving early Puritan self-examination diaries I have mentioned can be tracked to a narrow circle of godly men in Cambridge.[36] The surviving manuscripts of Samuel Ward, like Rogers educated at Christ's, show him to be very much under the spell of William Perkins and Laurence Chaderton.[37] Two of the known Jacobean diary-keepers were at Sidney Sussex under Ward: Daniel Dyke proceeded BA in 1595/6 and MA 1599, becoming a fellow in 1606;[38] John Harington of Exton joined him there in 1607–8 (not coincidentally, among the treatises Harrington read 'at the time of his sicknes' were 'the workes of a reuerend man now liuing, one *Master Rogers*').[39] Even posthumously, Ward's example could inspire the young Henry Newcome (1627–95), who recalled that in 1646, after two years at Cambridge, 'I was induced to begin a diary. It was chiefly begun upon the occasion of hearing that Dr. Ward (the late Master of Sydney, and Margaret professor in Cambridge,) had left a diary of his life in his study, from his being sixteen years of age. I thought it was a very brave thing to have such a thing left from so early a time of his life, and so set upon it.'[40] Samuel Fairclough started his diary while an undergraduate at Queens' College;[41] John Carter was an early follower of Laurence Chaderton, Lancelot Andrewes, and Ezekiel Culverwell at Cambridge.[42] And John Beadle was raised in the parish of Bramford in Suffolk, where Carter was the local minister.

The diary of Lady Margaret Hoby may seem an outlier here: Hoby did not attend Cambridge, and lived in Yorkshire, far from the Essex and Suffolk parishes where the diary-keeping puritans preached. But it is notable that the diary lasts from 1599 to 1605, the period during which Hoby was attended as chaplain by Richard Rhodes. Rhodes was of the same Cambridge generation as Samuel Ward, a sizar at St John's College from 1591, who received his BA in 1595 and MA in 1598, and was ordained in 1597: when he moved on from the Hoby household to become perpetual curate in Hackness in 1605, Lady Margaret's diary peters out.[43] As Andrew Cambers suggests, 'It is worth speculating that the diary was part of the regime of self-examination which Richard Rhodes brought to her as chaplain'.[44] It is also a regime that did not stick: after the first couple of years, Hoby records less of her spiritual life, and more of her managerial and political life, as Julie Crawford has traced.[45]

Lionized in his own time, Richard Rogers may well have had such influence among his congregation. His grandson William Jenkyn, pastor of the church at Blackfriars, wrote of him: 'That blessed saint now with God, Mr. *Richard Rogers* (who was another *Enoch* in his age, a man whose *walking with God* appeared by that incomparable directory of a Christian life, his book called the *Seven Treatises*, woven out of Scripture and his own experimental practise)'.[46] New England historian Cotton Mather tells of how the future Boston minister John Wilson, who was 'forestalled with prejudices against the Puritans of those times', was converted by Rogers: 'going to a bookseller's shop, to augment his well-furnished library, he lighted upon that famous book of Mr. Richard Rogers', called "*The Seven Treatises*;" which when he had read, he so affected, not only the matter, but also the author of the book, that he took a journey unto Wethersfield, on purpose to hear a sermon from that Boanerges', and there 'heard the heavenly passages that fell from the lips of that worthy man, privately as well as publickly'; as a result, he realized that 'they who were nicknamed Puritans, were like to be the desirablest companions for one that intended his own everlasting happiness'. When he was invited to preach at Sudbury, Wilson 'cheerfully complied, and the more cheerfully because of his opportunity to be near old Mr. Richard Rogers, from whom afterwards, when dying, he received a blessing among his children'.[47] Thomas Shepard described 'old Rogers's Seven Treatises, and the Practices of Christianity', as 'the book which did first work upon my heart'.[48]

But the influence of his diaries, I suggest, was more tangible. Rogers's will is more careful than most of the period about the dispersal of his books and papers. His son Ezekiel was to be given 'all my latten and Hebrew and greeke bookes', unless his son Daniel did not already have the works of Augustine, in which case those were to go to him. Daniel was also to receive his manuscript sermons on Kings, Samuel, and Acts, with the hope 'if he think good to take some paynes to correct and sett some of them forth'. All 'my written lectures and papers' were to be given to Daniel and Ezekiel and 'my Cosen Rogers of Dedham', along with 'those w*h*ich concerne my state in my christian practize w*h*ich are seaven'–that is, his diary, now in seven volumes. These were to be divided as his heirs thought fit: 'I will some to vse some of them and other some other of them as they please.'[49] The key word here is *use*: Rogers did not intend for his manuscripts to sit on a shelf as family heirlooms, but to be made use of. And here it is not any coincidence that the volumes are not bequeathed to his named executors (his widow Susan, his 'beloved cousin' John Wright, and his son-in-law Francis Longe), but to three men who, though indeed family members, were all themselves godly ministers. (Rogers was not alone in this ambition: two decades later, the London merchant John Parker went further, giving 'order in his *will*, to have all his *spirituall journals*, his *meditations* and *remembrances*, gathered together, digested and reduced into a methode, by some two godly *Divines*, unto whom also he hath assigned a very liberall consideration for their paines therein taken: and severall *Copies* thereof to be transcribed and made up for the use of each of his *Children*'.[50])

Tracking Rogers's manuscript diaries through his heirs, we can see the practice of diary-writing spreading not simply through exhortation, but also through the keeping and reading of others' diaries. Richard's eldest son Daniel Rogers had followed his father to Christ's College, Cambridge, and in time would also become lecturer at Wethersfield; Daniel's son Samuel Rogers attended Emmanuel, and kept a diary from 1634 to 1638, which has survived.[51] The 'Cosen Rogers of Dedham' to whom Rogers bequeathed the third part of his diaries was his nephew John Rogers (*c.* 1570–1637), who had attended Emmanuel from 1588, and became lecturer of Dedham, in the Stour valley, in 1605. Among his parishioners was the future nonconformist minister John Angier (who also kept a diary): he told his biographer, Henry Newcome, that in his thirty-two-year career there, Rogers became something of a celebrity with his histrionicism, drawing crowds to his sermons—'it was wont to be said, Come let's go to *Dedham* to get a little fire'.[52] Rogers certainly adopted much of his uncle's programme of self-examination: in his 'Sixty Memorials for a Godly Life', he wrote that 'He that makes Conscience of his Ways, and to please God his *only Way*, is to take him to a *Daily Direction*, and some *set Rules*, thereby looking constantly to his Heart all the Day'. Each evening, the day's activities and meditations should be drawn together, 'shutting up the Day in *Examination*, and viewing it over'.[53]

Richard's younger son, Ezekiel Rogers, another Christ's man, would in 1639 leave for New England; a fire 'consumed the good library that he had broght out of England', including presumably the volumes of his father's diaries.[54] And it was in New England, with its heavily puritan population, that the practice of daily self-examination really took hold in a significant way. As Catherine A. Brekus has written, British settlers set sail with paper, quills, and inkwells: John Winthrop (1587/8–1649), future governor of the Massachusetts Bay Colony, composed a volume of 'Annals', which described the events about ship, and another, of 'Experiencia', which described his interior spiritual life.[55] The British colonies produced some of the most striking spiritual diaries of the seventeenth century, including those of ministers Thomas Shepard, Michael Wigglesworth, Increase Mather, Jonathan Mitchel, and Cotton Mather, whose great history of New England figures quotes extensively from diaries of his subjects, to which he had access.[56]

Here, too, the influence of the circle around Rogers is easily seen. At eighteen, as he recounts, John Winthrop 'married into a family under Mr. Culverwell his ministry in Essex; & living there sometimes I first found the ministry of the Word to come home to my heart with power'.[57] At Emmanuel College, Thomas Shepard's first spiritual awakening came listening to sermons by the master, 'old Doctor Chadderton'.[58] Rogers's own family were also influential. His stepson Nathaniel Ward, rector of Stondon Massey in Essex, set out for America in 1637, achieving some fame as the author of the satirical *The Simple Cobbler of Aggawam*; his daughter would marry another emigrant, Giles Firmin, who recorded tales of Rogers and Ward family members in his *The Real Christian*.[59] John Rogers of Dedham's son Nathaniel Rogers left for New England in 1636, founding a dynasty of ministers, among them his son John (1630/1–84), who became president of Harvard College.[60] Cotton Mather laments of Nathaniel Rogers that 'He was known to keep a *diary*;

but he kept it with so much reservation, that it is not known that ever any one but himself *did* read one word of it: and he determined that none ever *should*; for he ordered a couple of his intimate friends to cast it all into the fire, without even looking into the *contents* of it'. This passage is telling: like Richard Rogers, Mather expects a personal diary to be read by others and to be preserved for the use of others after the diary-writer's death. With that expectation, Nathaniel Rogers's 'Reservation' is seen as extreme. 'Surely', Mather continues, 'with the loss of so incomparable a person, the survivors must lament the loss of those *experiences*, which might in these *rich papers*, have kept him, after a sort, still *alive* unto us!'[61]

Patrick Collinson has written of 'the godly Emmanuel mafia of "painful preachers" which spread itself across Essex and its borders', in which Rogers's tight-knit family had a widespread influence not only in the parishes of Essex, but far beyond;[62] Rogers was 'one of the founder-members of a godly clan whose influence on the future of English Calvinism and the history of New England is beyond parallel'.[63] And, I would add, to the history of life-writing. For Cotton Mather, the diaries inspired by Rogers's example were a rich source for biography. But the writing of diaries also led, almost inevitably, to some other form of autobiographical writing. For Rogers, the iterative process of writing, reading, and annotating his journal led to the creation of something like a life-narrative for those wishing to read for one. For Arthur Wilson, John Beadle's sermon is an invitation to go home and write an account from 'the beginning of my life'. Many surviving diaries commence with a recapitulation of the subject's life unto the point of commencing the diary—usually listing past events now seen by the author as providential. The taking up of a course of examination was a spur to life-writings of many kinds, which would become a familiar feature in England and New England in the seventeenth century.

8

The Christian Life and Godly Death of Katherine Brettergh

In May 1600, the church at Childwall, near Liverpool, witnessed the burials of two local women.[1] On 16 May, the wife of Ralph Hitchmough–her Christian name is not recorded in the parish register–was laid to rest, but not without incident. As was customary, family and friends carried the corpse to the churchyard, but they then refused to enter the church to hear the service. At the burial, the minister Edmund Hopwood noted that the covering sheet over the breast bore a large cross of red cloth, and two further crosses had been made using a burning iron. These signs of Catholicism were strictly forbidden at funerals, and Hopwood reprimanded the widower for his 'blindness and folly'; Hitchmough was unrepentant, and informed Hopwood that 'he would have a cross as long as he lived'. Four days later, another known Catholic, Katherine Chaloner, was taken to be buried at the same church. This time Hopwood refused to perform the burial unless the corpse was brought into the church: her friends and family were forced to bury the body themselves.[2]

These messy and no doubt upsetting burials are known to us because they were investigated in the Star Chamber and left a goodly paper trail, well studied by historian Roy Dottie.[3] The parish registers make no note of the disturbances, or even of the heterodox confessional allegiances of the dead women. But another burial, a year later, does stand out. In May 1601, the interment of Katherine, the wife of the gentleman William Brettergh, is recorded in a distinctive, larger hand, indicating her death was somehow more significant.[4] Partly this was a matter of social rank: Katherine Brettergh came from an armorial family, and her death therefore warranted a funeral certificate from the College of Arms.[5] But the entry also prefigured the significance that would be attached to Katherine Brettergh in the days, years, and indeed decades after her death. Brettergh was afforded two funeral sermons, delivered not by the parish priest, but by two ministers brought in from outside: William Harrison of Huyton preached a sermon before the burial; William Leigh of Standish after it. Their sermons, with an 'annexed' account of her

'Christian life and godly death', were put into print in 1602, and proved to be among the most republished funeral sermons of the century:[6] the entire volume was reprinted in 1606, twice in 1612, and again in 1617, while the biography was printed alone in 1612, 1634, and twice in 1641.[7] And even then, Brettergh's life continued to be told, as Samuel Clarke in 1650 included a redacted version in his 'lives of Christians of an Inferiour Rank'–the only non-aristocratic woman in the collection.[8]

While her funeral was not marked by the violence that scarred those of her neighbours, the impetus for the attention given to Katherine Brettergh came, as Patricia Phillippy has shown, from those funerals of her fellow Childwall women in May 1601, and from the very local battles in which Brettergh and her family had become embroiled.[9] Both the fight over Brettergh's death in 1601, and the commemorative volume containing her funeral sermons published in 1602, need to be understood in the context of these battles. The life-writing of Katherine Brettergh bears the scars of raging debates over the proper way to speak, or not to speak, of the dead.

The Funeral Sermon Controversy

In many ways, what happened in Childwall at the end of Elizabeth's reign was the inevitable outcome of debates that had been rumbling since the early years of the Reformation. Attacks on the Church of England's prescribed forms of burial and memorialization came not only from recusant Catholics, but from its puritan-leaning critics. The Book of Common Prayer gave instructions for 'The ordre for the Buryall of the Deade' in which the priest should meet the corpse, borne by the deceased's friends, at the church stile, and intone a prescribed form of words at the graveside, before earth was cast on the body by those standing by, and the priest would commit the body to the ground.[10] But critics claimed that, according to Leviticus, the priest should not officiate at the burial, and certainly should not deliver a sermon. Praises of the dead smacked too much of Catholic intercession for the dead in purgatory.[11]

Until the Jacobean era, at least, doubts about funeral sermons seem to have prevailed. Fewer than twenty printed sermons survive from the Elizabethan period, and their sometimes bizarre content bears testimony to the notion that the genre was highly contested. As Anthony Anderson, the parson of Medburne in Leicestershire, put it at the funeral of the elderly lawyer Robert Keylwey in March 1580,

> It hath beene from auncient time receiued, and verie long vsed in the Church of God (right worshipfull and Christian audience) at the Funerals of the godly to haue the worde preached

to the people: Not thereby to profite the deade (which no way after life can change this departing state) but by it to instruct the lyuing, that they may learne to die in the Lorde: and so rest from the labour of sinne and hell. And why may not the godly preacher, take occasion at funerals to preach the worde of God? Nay: why shoulde they omitte any occasion? but rather with Christ and his Apostles waste oportunitie to preach the worde, whensoeuer the people be gathered together?[12]

The defensive stance of Anderson's rhetorical questions ('And why may not…? Nay: why should they omitte…?') reveals some of the contested territory of the funeral sermon. To what extent was this a custom of the ancient church? Was the funeral sermon really just to 'instruct the lyuing' or might it also 'profite the deade', by acting as some kind of intercessory prayer for the deceased? Anderson seems very sure of himself in his opening pages, but in his eighty-page sermon he is careful never to mention the late Robert Keylwey.

The few other printed sermons of the 1580s are barely more forthcoming. Thomas Sparke's September 1585 funeral sermon on Francis Russell, second earl of Bedford, devotes under four pages of his 112-page sermon to 'A briefe report & testimony of the Earle of Bedfords life and death', focused entirely on 'his later daies', and even then seems to resent the time spent discussing the man: 'let vs proceed in the text', he resumes, 'In the handling whereof I wil be *the* briefer, because I haue bin *the* longer in this'.[13] Although Thomas White is not shy about praising Sir Henry Sidney in his June 1586 funeral sermon, he devotes only two of thirty-six pages to the man.[14] Bartholomew Chamberlain's funeral sermon for Anne Dudley, countess of Warwick, in 1587 similarly turns to its subject only briefly, giving us only six of the blandest details about her:

Here is a spectacle, a Ladie by birth, a Countes by mariage, by title right honorable, a widow of a vertuous life, a woman of many yeares, a mother of good children, whose bodie death hath killed, whose soule Christ hath taken, whose bodie must to the earth, whose soule is in the hands of God. Beholde in her the ende of all flesh: for as we are, so was she: and as she is, so shal we be.[15]

In 1595, Gervase Babington, then bishop of Llandaff, preached a sermon for 'Maister T. L. Esquire'. 'T. L.' is unidentified—and the efforts to which Babington goes to avoid telling his auditors anything about the dead man are almost comic. T. L., he claims, is

a Gentleman so well-knowne vnto euery man here, that any speech of mine concerning him shall not neede…His birth and discent by Father and Mother, hys kindred and friends by either side, his Allyances by marriage, with such like, they are things known euen to the very younglings here...The actions also of the life of this Gent. haue beene still before your eyes, (beeing most remaining at home, and little delighted to trauell abroad,) so that euery man may make his best profit of them towardes his owne reformation, without any speech of mine...

Even the dead man's demise—usually a set-piece in funeral sermons—flashes by in a half-sentence: 'concerning his death and end amongst vs, it was so quicke with him, that his best friends, I think, sawe it not so neere, till it was euen past and finished'.[16]

Even as the genre became more common in the seventeenth century, the dilemma—should the sermon evoke the virtues of the departed, or simply edify the congregation?—made its mark on the sermon's very form. The bulk of the sermon was given over to exegesis of a scriptural text: if a biographical portrait was included, it was tacked on to that exegesis, often with a peculiarly rusty hinge. As the minister Nathaniel Shute put it nicely in May 1625, while delivering the funeral sermon of merchant Richard Fishburn, 'And so I fall downe from the text to the occasion'.[17] Yet many sermons betray the fact that, as far as the congregation was concerned, the occasion outweighed the text. At the funeral of Sir Anthony Cope in 1622, Charles Fitz-Geffry admitted that his audience needed him to come to the point: 'Time, and your expectation, summoneth me to the sad occasion of this dayes sorrowful solemnitie.'[18] 'And now my Friends, having done with one Text, I know it will be expected I should apply my self unto another, namely to speak something touching our dear Sister', announced Christopher Scott at the funeral of Margery Fisher in 1672.[19] The congregation had spent the better part of an hour staring at a shrouded corpse, as Nicholas Guy noted at the funeral of Elizabeth Gouge: '*Thus much of my Text.* Giue mee leaue to adde a few words about the particular occasion of this our meeting, which is euident by the obiect here before our eyes, and maketh vnto vs a visible Sermon of our mortalitie. For it is a dead corps, which was within these few dayes the receptacle of the euer-liuing soule of Mistris *Elizabeth Gouge*...'[20] It was a rare preacher who could make something witty of the dilemma—like George Ferebe, at the funeral of the gentleman John Drew at St John's in Devizes, Wiltshire, in 1614, who toyed with the mourners: 'But I have abused your patience too long with nothing, by making too much adoe about nothing. Let me now end with something of this late something, new nothing, now nothing, as nothing'—namely, 'a true and deserued testimony of his vertuous and Christian carriage, worthily manifesting his liuely faith working by charity'.[21] While the physical presence of the corpse could perhaps justify the biographical component of the sermon, the printed version lacked that excuse. So when Daniel Featley led a group of preachers in publishing some forty-seven funeral sermons as *ΘΡΗΝΟΙΚΟΣ. The House of*

Mourning in 1640, they stripped the texts of their biographical coordinates, so that only one dead person is named ('our deceased Brother, Master *John Moulson*'), and a full nineteen of the sermons say nothing at all about the deceased.[22]

Katherine Brettergh in Print

The 1602 volume on Katherine Brettergh remains one of the most elaborate commemorative books of the period. It contains the two funeral sermons preached at Childwall on 3 June 1601: William Harrison's *Deaths Advantage Little Regarded* and William Leigh's *The Soules Solace against Sorrow*. Both adopt the lop-sided form of a lengthy interpretation of scripture plus a brief, slightly begrudging mini-biography. Of eighty-four pages in Harrison's sermon, seventy-four are devoted to his text (Isaiah 57:1, 'The righteous perisheth, and no man considereth it in heart'); only in the final ten do we turn to 'A *righteous* woman is *perished*' (F6^{v}); and only in the last six do we learn anything specific about Katherine Brettergh, despite the fact that Harrison claims that 'I knew both the course of her life, and the manner of her death' (F7^{r}). Leigh's sermon devotes sixty-nine of his seventy-seven pages to Psalm 126:5–6 ('They that sowe in teares, shall reape in ioy') before moving to Brettergh, with the usual inelegant transition: 'And now breathren beloued and longed for (I say now) that I haue finished my course, ended the text, and closed vp the booke, giue me leaue a little to turne me to the dead...' (L7^{r}). Leigh clearly did not know Brettergh: whereas Harrison tells us that Brettergh 'gaue her selfe much to reading', reading 'euery day eight chapters in the bible' (F7^{r}); praying 'both morning and euening' with her family (F7^{v}); attending 'the publick exercises in the Church', and being 'greatly grieued, if shee might not heare one or two Sermons' every Sabbath, despite living far from the church (F8^{v}), Leigh merely paraphrases what he had heard Harrison say in the morning ('You heard in the former Sermon, how eight chapters a day, was her taske...'; L7^{v}).

But there are signs in Harrison's sermon that this subject is more important than most, thanks to the nature of her deathbed experience. Visiting her '[n]ot long after the beginning of her sicknes', about a week before her death, he found her 'somewhat troubled in conscience; the enemy had then begun to assault her: but within a while, by conference with me and others and also by prayer, she was comforted'. After he and the others left, however, 'the enemy did more strongly & strangely assault her againe, as might appeare to them which were present: for she neither would, nor yet could conceale it'. Harrison thus misses the central struggle, appearing again only as Brettergh wins out: 'Though I was not present at this conflict, yet was I present at the conquest.' On the day before her death, he 'found her exceedingly rauished with the ioyes of heauen, praying God most cheerefully for his great mercies, and wonderfull works of God toward her, repeating many verses of the Psalmes, and other places of Scripture, to expresse the worke of the Lord vnto her, and to set forth her thankfulnes vnto him'. Although he claims to be unable to rehearse much of what Brettergh said, Harrison does quote her as saying '*the path was smooth, and strowed with flowers where she did treade, that she was as it were in Paradice, and felt a sweete smell, as in the garden of Eden: that the ioyes which she felt were wonderfull, wonderfull!* repeating that word oftentimes together' (G1^r). The following morning, a Sunday, she was unable to speak so much, but still asked for those present to pray for her; and as Harrison left the house to go to church, 'she caused mee to bee called backe, to pray once again with her' (G1^v). By contrast, Leigh speaks in general terms: 'I leaue her life and come to her death, whereunto (as I am tolde) she walked, as Christ did to *Caluary*, with much care, and many agonies' (L8^r)—a death he describes as 'the firie triall which did befall this Gentlewoman, to prooue her at her end' (M1^v).

What is striking about Harrison's account is that he takes for granted that the congregation knows about Brettergh being 'troubled in conscience' on her deathbed, and that she had suffered an 'assault' by 'the enemy'. He is also keen to explain how when he is with Brettergh, she is either 'comforted' or at a time of 'conquest' over her enemy. The reader becomes aware that Harrison is addressing an unspoken knowledge about Brettergh and, sure enough, he eventually alludes to rumours: 'I haue heard that some speake very uncharitably of her, by reason of her temptation, and thereupon mutter much against religion itselfe: but such should remember that which I haue spoken before, that the Deuill most assaulteth them which be most godly, thinking to hinder all religion, if he may preuaile with such' (G1^v). Instead, he claims, 'her enemie for a while seemed to preuaile, but in the end was trodden downe under her feete. Wee should rather praise God for the victory, then speake euill of her for the combate: & feare least he who tempted her so strongly will also tempt vs' (G2^r).

On the day of her burial, then, 3 June 1601, Katherine Brettergh's piety is vouchsafed by two Puritan ministers, one of whom explicitly seeks to dispel rumours that Brettergh lost her faith on her deathbed. But it was apparently not enough. When the two were published together in 1602, the sermons are bolstered by several other materials. Harrison's sermon is prefaced by a letter from him 'To the Christian Reader', and comes accompanied by a pull-out Ramist chart of his sermon; Leigh's sermon is prefaced by a letter from Katherine's widower, William Brettergh, explaining that he persuaded Leigh to give him a copy of the sermon, and is publishing it without his express permission. A 'Post-script to Papists' addresses the Catholics of Lancashire:

Peace and truth to as many of you as pertaine to God. I am moued in conscience to deale with you, by this manner of writing, because of the false and slanderous reporte which (I heare) some of your faction haue blazed and diuulged abroade, concerning the death of Mistresse *Katherin Brettergh*, a Christian Gentlewoman, whose life indeed was holy, and death most comfortable. (N1^{r})

Although well aware that 'It is no noueltie, or new thing, to heare a lye from a *Papist*, but rather a principle of your religion' (N1^{r}), the biographer is writing because of a particular papist lie: that '*If a man dye like a lambe, and passe out of the world like a bird in a shell, he is certainely saued*, although neither holines were in his life, nor God in his mouth; grace in heart, nor yet repentance, faith, or feeling at his death' (N1^{v}). If, by contrast, the death is a struggle, 'if the violence of any disease stirre vp impatience in a man at his death', then 'our country-Papists' immediately charge that '*there is a iudgement of God, seruing either to discouer an hypocrite, or plague a wicked man* (especially, if they professe the truth of *Iesus Christ*, as this Gentlewoman did)' and 'cry, and shout; *see the effect of this religion, see the end of these men*: where as indeed the truth is farre otherwise' (N2^{r}). As a result, he claims, 'some of your Romish faction haue bragged' about Brettergh's death, 'as though an oracle had come from heauen to proue you Catholicks, and vs Hereticks' (N2^{v}). But in fact, 'the Diuell and you are all deceiued, and God, euen our mightie *Iehouah*, hath you in derision, and shall laugh you to skorne, who hath not only frustrate your fond expectations, but made your follie manifest to all men. This Gentlewomans life being more holie, and her death more comfortable, then possiblie any of yours can be, so long as you continue *Papists*. The trueth whereof, I haue compendiously set foorth in this present treatise following, as will be testified in persons of honester none and condition, then any of your generation' (N2^{v}–N3^{r}). The reader is then presented with materials that aim to stop 'the mouth of the sclanderer': four pieces of verse 'to be fixed nigh her Hearse', including an epitaph by 'both an eye and eare-witnesse' of Brettergh's death (N3^{v}).

The most important element, however, with its own title page, is *A brief discovrse of the Christian life and death, of Mistris Katherin Brettergh, late wife of Master William Brettergh of Bretterghoult, in the Countie of Lancaster Gentleman; who departed this world the last of May.* 1601, which occupies thirty-eight pages. The title's continuation gives no doubt about the most salient point of Brettergh's 'Christian life and death': 'With the manner of a bitter conflict she had with Satan, and blessed conquest by Christ before her death, to the great glorie of God, and comfort of all beholders' (M4^{r}).

A further, unsigned prefatory address 'To the Christian Reader' explains the occasion: 'I considered the vngodly and vncharitable tongues of the *Papists* abiding in our countrey, who, since her death, haue not ceased to giue it out that she died despairing, and by her comfortles end, shewed that she professed a comfortless Religion' (M7$^{r\text{-}v}$). The biography seeks to achieve what the funeral sermons have signally failed to do–to put an end to the rumour, and to allow the memory of Katherine Brettergh to rest in peace.

In the *Brief Discovrse*, we follow Katherine from her birth, 'well descended, and of an auncient house', the daughter of John Bruen of Bruen Stapleford in Cheshire, to her burial. Her upbringing was a pattern of godliness: 'The Scriptures she knew from a childe, and by reading thereof, gained such knowledge, that she was able readily to applie them when occasion was offered, as wee may see at the time of her death, and that so fitly, and effectually, that she seemed to haue made them her daily meditation. For the things of this world she was moderate, and sober' (N5^{r}). The Sabbath 'was alwaies deere and welcome to her, what time she would not be without the word preached, though many times she went farre for it'; 'her heart was so tender, and full of compassion, that oftentimes she was seene to heare Sermons, reade, pray, and meditate with tears' (N5^{v}). Katherine 'made conscience of all sinne', no matter how small, never swearing, never using 'vaine or vnseemely speeches; not somuch as a iest-lye, or immodest word', nor taking the Lord's name in vain (N5^{v}–N6^{r}). In short, 'To reade, to pray, to sing, to meditate, was her daily exercise; and her chiefest delight was in the holie societie of the Saints vpon earth . . . the precepts of the Lord were precious vnto her, for from her childhood she feared God and walked before him' (N6^{r}).

The biographer often casts Brettergh as a scriptural type. In her youth, he records, 'She vsed not to gad abroad with wandring *Dinah*, to dancing greenes, markets, or publike assemblies; but rather with *Hannah* did chuse to tread vpon the dust of the sanctuarie, and walke in the ways of *Sion*; yea, with *Dauid rather to be a doore keeper in the house of God, then to haue societie with the wicked, or to dwell in the tents and Tabernacles of the vngodlie*' (N5^{v}); printed marginal notes alert us to the relevant scriptural passages (Genesis 34:1, 1 Samuel 1:9–12, Psalms 84:10). The effect is to abstract Katherine from such local English surroundings as dancing greens, markets, and public assemblies, and place her in a timeless biblical setting of tents and tabernacles. But in so doing, the biography also shies away from conveying the singular nature of her upbringing at Bruen Stapleford, which we can construct from another source.

Katherine was eight years old when her father died, and she and ten of her siblings were raised by her elder brother, John Bruen, who decades later had his own life written by the minister William Hinde (and who, like his sister, was featured in Samuel Clarke's collection of Christian lives).[23] Coming into his inheritance, Bruen determined to lead his household in a pious life. He instituted a regime wherein psalms were sung, Scripture read, and prayers said seven times a day, and by 1590 had built a pulpit in his house. But his household comprised more than family and servants; according to Hinde, it 'was as the common Inne, or constant harbour of the Church, and of Gods children, and himselfe as *Gaius*, a godly and good Hoste, to give them liberall, and cheerfull entertainment, as they came unto him'–travellers from as far afield as London and Ireland.[24] While Hinde paints Bruen as an exemplar of hospitality, the ecclesiastical authorities took a less benign view, seeing the household's devotions as illegal conventicles.[25]

Bruen's piety was public and theatrical. Every Sunday, he led his entire household the mile to church on foot, singing psalms as they went. He arrived at church before the service, 'so hee might more comfortably joyne with Gods Minister and people, in confession of sins, in prayer, and praise, reading and hearing of the Word, singing of Psalmes, and partaking of the Sacraments'. After the service, he stayed in the church, to 'bestow himselfe...in Gods Service...by repeating the Sermon, which hee had taken very exactly (as usually hée did) with his owne hand, and by singing of Psalmes, and by wholy and wholesome conference in, and about good things'. Once these 'publique duties of the Sabbath' were completed, Bruen 'returned homewards with his company,...repeating, and conferring of the Evening Sermon, and...singing of Psalmes a fresh'.[26]

There are glimpses, even in Hinde's hagiographic account, of a violent side to Bruen's piety. When he turned to religion, Hinde relates, Bruen's first move was to give up his favourite pastime of hunting: he 'laid away Hawkes and Hounds, and cast off for ever his wide mouth'd Dogs, and utterly ceased any longer, to follow them, or their followers'. But the manner of doing this was alarming: in order 'to cut off all occasions of wastefull and riotous expence both of time and other things', Bruen turned to the park he owned behind his house, 'well stored and furnished with fallow Deere', and 'presently killed up the game, and disparked the Parke'. Only by the mass slaughter of the deer could he prevent himself from hunting them. The severity of his reformation presaged his later actions. Hinde reports sympathetically how, seeing in the local parish church of Tarvin 'many superstitious images, and idolatrous pictures in the painted windowes, and they so thicke, and darke that there was, as he himselfe saith, scarce the breadth of a groat of white glasse amongst them', Bruen took it on himself to banish the 'painted puppets, and popish idols'. This he did, Hinde assures us, 'in a warrantable and peaceable manner, and of his owne cost and charge, repaired the breaches, and beautified the windows with white and bright glasse again', acting on the Queen's Injunctions, 'utterly to extinguish and destroy all pictures, paintings, and all other monuments of idolatry and superstition' in church buildings, and 'by the authority of a Commission sent down into the countrey to the Earle of *Darby*, the Major of *Chester*, and others, to the same purpose, at the same time'.[27] In truth, in 1603 seven of Bruen's servants were brought before the bishop of Chester and admitted 'they did with their staves throw down a stone cross standing in the churchyard of Warton' and that two of them 'did break down about three or four foot of glass of the great window in the chancel of the parish church of Tarvin, wherein was the image of St Andrew and Lazarus'. While they denied that they had been encouraged to do so by their master, there can be no doubt that Bruen set the tone for his household. As R. C. Richardson puts it, Bruen 'set up a miniature religious community and created the atmosphere which it breathed. Iconoclasm was no more than a natural result of this situation... indirect responsibility for the outbursts of iconoclasm still rests with Bruen.'[28] This is the milieu in which Katherine Brettergh was raised.

In the *Brief Discovrse*, Brettergh's biographer writes that 'When she was about twentie yeeres old (by the consent of her selfe, & her friends) shee was married to a young *Lancashire Gentleman, Master William Brettergh of Bretterghoult* neere *Liuerpoole*: one that likewise embraced Religion sincerely' ($N5^v$–$N6^r$). Once again, this tells half the story. In Hinde's account, her brother John Bruen spoke of how he 'faithfully discharged himselfe of his fathers charge, paying his brethren and sisters all their portions, and placing them in marriage, and otherwise very comfortably...This charge through Gods assistance (saith he) I well discharged. And married well all my sisters, and preferred all my brothers, and none of them offended.'[29] By 'married well', Bruen refers less to the spouses' financial security, and more to their suitable godliness: he deployed marriage to strengthen the links between a group of godly families. He had himself met his second wife Anne, daughter of William Foxe of Rhodes, at a prayer meeting in Manchester. On 24 June 1599 Anne's brother William Foxe married Scholastica Brettergh in Childwall's parish church,[30] and probably around the same time, Scholastica's older brother William Brettergh married Bruen's younger sister Katherine.[31] (Later, Anne and William's sister Margaret Foxe was married to the man who would write Bruen's life, William Hinde, from 1603 a preacher at Bunbury.[32]) While Katherine may have given her 'consent', there was little chance of her marrying outside a very limited selection of godly men chosen by her brother.

Grievances at the Hands of Papists

As William Brettergh is introduced, we are told not only that he 'likewise embraced Religion sincerely' but also that he had 'for the same indured many grieuances at the hands of Papists'. While the newly wed Bretterghs 'liued together in such mutuall ioy and comfort, as well beseemed the children of God, which make profession of his trueth' for two years, with their only child, a daughter Anna, the biographer paints the marital home of Brettergholt once again in biblical terms. Katherine 'came from the habitations of *Abraham*, to dwell in *Sodome*, amidst the tents of *Kedar*, that is to say, among inhumane bands of brutish Papists'. Once married to William, Katherine too 'indur[ed] many temporal grieuances from them; yet her knowledge, patience, mild inclination, and constancie for the trueth was such, as that her husband was farther building vp in Religion by her meanes, and his face daily more and more hardened against the diuell, and all his plaguie agents; the *Popish Recusants, Church Papists, prophane Atheists, and carnall Protestants*, which swarmed together like Hornets in those parts' ($N7^r$). One particular attack from these 'plaguie agents' is detailed, which 'fell out not long after shee was married to him': 'It is not vnknowne to *Lancashire*, what horses and cattell of her husbands were killed vpon his grounds in the night, most barbarously at two seuerall times by Seminarie Priests (no question) and Recusants that lurked thereabouts. And what a losse and hinderance it was vnto him, being all the stocke hee had on his grounds to any purpose' ($N7^{r-v}$). No more is made of this attack on Brettergh's livestock, but, again, extant documents tell a more complex, two-sided story than the one the biographer is willing to recount.

Lancashire had been identified as a region with dangerously recalcitrant religious politics, pockets of the county still fiercely loyal to the traditional faith.[33] A report signed by seventeen Lancashire preachers in 1590 described 'the manifold enormities of the ecclesiastical state' and laid out the challenges posed by recusancy.[34] As the century ended, the situation intensified: Christopher Haigh writes of six years of 'intermittent resistance by local Catholics',[35] and in part, this resistance was responding to an intensification of anti-Catholic activism. In the early 1590s, Sir Thomas Heneage, chancellor of the duchy of Lancaster, reported to the queen that in the county palatine there were 'few or no incumbents of learning or credit' in the parsonages, and as a result, 'priests creeping in drew the people from their duty'.[36] But it was Heneage's successor Sir Robert Cecil, serving as chancellor from 1595 to 1601, who freed up funds to allow the bishop of Chester, Richard Vaughan, to take action to address the issue. (Vaughan thanked him for showing 'rare mercy to many miserable soules, ready to be devoured by popishe woulves'.[37]) As the bishop wrote to Cecil in February 1600, four 'Queen's Preachers' were to be placed in the parts of the county where there was a concentration of recusants[38]—so Richard Midgeley, William Harrison, William Forster, and Barnard Adams (of whom at least the first three were firmly puritan-leaning) were placed in, respectively, Leigh, Huyton, Garstang, and Ormskirk, with the goal of preaching against Catholicism, and converting Catholics to the Church of England.[39]

When Katherine married, she found herself at the centre of these troubles. Her husband William was recruited by Queen's Preacher William Harrison in April

1600 as High Constable of West Derby Hundred, and soon gained a reputation for his activism against recusants, and his hard-line views.[40] One of Brettergh's first actions came during the week in May 1600 that saw the two Catholic women buried at Childwall church. On Monday 16 May, Ralph Hitchmough's wife was buried. Only four days later, on Friday May 20, Brettergh decided to detain Hitchmough while he was working on his lands. The timing was deliberately provocative: the attempt came during the time that Katherine Chaloner's body was being brought to Childwall church for burial. Brettergh botched the arrest, failing to apprehend Hitchmough but instead striking him with his staff, an action that caught the attention of the eighty-strong procession accompanying Chaloner's body. With all but five abandoning the corpse, many of the men ran to Hitchmough's aid, and during a messy fracas, Hitchmough escaped to his house, and subsequently sought shelter with a friend.[41]

It was following this incident, on 22 May, that Brettergh had 'three oxen and one horse killed in the night'; the bishop of Chester blamed recusant gentlemen, led by Edward Norris of Speke.[42] After these 'riots' were reported to the Privy Council,[43] leading Lancashire recusants were called before the Council in late June; while they were away, during the night of 25 June, 'sixe kyne and one Bull' belonging to the Bretterghs' friend and kinsman Justice of the Peace John Wrightington were 'hurt and mangled, whereof one died'.[44] And immediately after Brettergh indicted some of Hitchmough's rescuers at the assizes in August, his losses escalated: during the night of 15 August, Brettergh 'had two oxen three kyne two geldinges and one more hought [hurt?] cutt and mangled wherof they all died, but one cowe'.[45] In the same month, more than twenty people, 'all in Armor with muskett*es*, and other weapons' marched to the vicar's house, where they 'purposed to haue massacred her Mai*es*ties Preacher [Forster], the vicar, and one of the Messengers attendinge on the Co*m*mission Eccl*esiasti*call'.[46] In September, there were further attacks as the seminarian Middleton was moved from Preston to jail in Lancaster. Another seminary priest, Thurstan Hunt, was arrested around the same time, and executed in April 1601.[47]

Brettergh's biographer devotes only three sentences to these attacks on the horses and cattle. He is more concerned to describe Katherine's reaction:

> This fell out not long after shee was married to him; yet this was so farre from dismaying her, or working such passions in her, as are common to her sex, that she rather * *reioyced, then sorrowed*; turning it into matter of praising God, and submitting her selfe to his good prouidence. (N7[v])

The asterisk and italicized text refer us to the page's margin, where the biographer cites not the scriptural chapter and verse we might expect, but instead names of the individuals who have informed him that Brettergh 'rather *reioyced, then sorrowed*' at the attacks on their livestock, namely '*John Wrightington Esquier. Richard Orme. Raph Heaton &c. and many moe*' (N7^{v}, margin). With this, the biographer introduces a new form of authority to complement the scriptural: the men and women who observed Brettergh during her life.

Brettergh's habitual piety is quickly sketched, building on Harrison's portrait in his sermon: pitiful and bountiful, constantly praying, meditating, and reading—'eight chapters a day at the least' of Scripture (N8^{v}), plus 'some godly writer, or expositer of Scripture, or in the booke of Martyrs'. Foxe's volume affected her especially: Brettergh 'was seene to weepe most bitterly, when either shee had read of that which touched her affections neere, or of the cruel matrydome [*sic*], which the deere children of God were put vnto, by the cruell and wicked tyrants of former daies'. Katherine is consistently contrasted with Catholic women: 'She was not like the simple Popish women of our daies, which *are euer learning, and neuer able to come to the knowledge of the truth*...For Poperie, she saw it too grosse and foolish, that shee would not once *name* it, except it were to argue against it, but neuer for it' (N6^{v}, O1^{r}).

The biographer portrays Katherine as providing an important example to her husband. She prays that God will forgive their enemies and cause them to repent: 'and she would call vpon her husband, that he would doe the like, and *blesse them that cursed him.* And for feare least her husband should faile in that point through infirmitie and weakenes...she...daily prayed vnto the Lord to sanctifie her husbands thoughts, and direct his heart aright, only to seeke Gods glorie, without either desire of reuenge, or satisfying his owne affections' (N8^{r}). He also shows her as being 'grieued' at the sight of '[s]inne' in others:

> On a time, as her husband and shee were riding toward the Church, he was angry with his man: *Alas husband* (quoth she) *I feare your heart is not right towards God, that it can be thus angry for a trifle*: And weeping she said further *you must pray against this your affection, and always bee sure your anger be of God, for else how dare you appeare this day before his minister? And offer vp your prayers in the publike congregation of the saints of God?* (O1^{r-v})

On another occasion, when one of her husband's tenants was behind with his rent,

> she desired [Brettergh] to beare yet with him a quarter of a yeere, which he did: and when the man brought his money, with teares she said to her husband: *I feare you doe not well to take it of him, though it bee your right. for I doubt he is not well able to pay it, and then you oppresse the poore.* (O1^{v})

In these brief anecdotes, Katherine Brettergh is established as an unassailable paragon of godly virtue: after she married, 'she continued in the things she had learned, and held her profession with such sinceritie, that the common enemies to our religion (the verie Papists) had nothing to say against her, but confessed her life was vnreproouable' (O1^{v}).

All this was to be challenged by her final illness, which occupies a full twenty-eight pages of the thirty-eight-page life. The biographer takes his readers through its progress. On the Saturday before Whitsunday, Brettergh contracted '*a hot burning Ague*, which made her…now and then to talke somewhat idly, and through the tempters subtiltie, which abused the infirmitie of her bodie to that end, as he oftentimes vseth to do in many, from idle words, to descend into a heauie conflict, with the infirmitie of her owne spirit'. She fretted how 'the seueritie of Gods iustice' would deal with 'the greatnes of her sinnes'; she accused herself of pride, 'delight[ing] too much in her selfe, and her beautie'; she felt she had no faith, and sometimes would 'cast her Bible from her', claiming that 'she had read the same vnprofitably, and therefore feared it was become to her the booke of death'. She wept, believing her sins made her 'a pray to Satan; a spectacle to the world; a disgrace to religion; and a shame to her husband, kinred, and all true Christians'. Burning up with fever, 'it seemed the sorrowes of death hemmed her in, and the griefes of hell laid hold vpon her'. Trying to complete the Lord's Prayer, she could not say 'Leade vs not into temptation', '*being interrupted, as she said, by Satan*'. Among 'these firie darts of Satan', weak and unable to sleep, she was heard to utter 'vaine speeches' about 'her child, the killing of her husbands cattell, that she thought shee saw a fire by her'. She 'soone ouercame' the initial attack on Sunday, but on Monday night 'it increased vpon her, and the assault of the enemie began to be sharp' until Tuesday afternoon, at 'what time God deliuered her, and sent her peace, and comfort of conscience' (O2^{r-v}), in which state of mind she continued until her death the following Sunday.

During this struggle the marginal witnesses come into their own. As he starts his account of Brettergh's illness, the biographer names a host of witnesses: her husband William Brettergh and other Brettergh family members, John and Maud; her brother-in-law William Foxe and his wife Scholastica; neighbours Edward Aspinall (later described as 'a faithfull professor of the truth, and *a true Israelite*'; O4^{v}),[48] William Woodward ('[a] Christian friend'; O4^{v}), and Elizabeth Challoner (O2^{v}). Later visitors include her brother John Bruen (O7^{v}), John Holland (O8^{r}), and 'Master *William Harrison the Preacher*' (P5^{v}). Some observations are vouchsafed by a single witness: William Brettergh testifies that 'Once after a great conflict with Satan, she said: *Satan reason not with me, I am but a weake woman, if thou haue any thing to say, say it to my Christ; he is my aduocate, my strength, and my redeemer, and he shall pleade for mee*'. John Brettergh provides the information that she 'would with many a pittifull sob and much weeping, *pray to the Lord Iesus Christ to helpe and comfort her, a poore, wofull, distressed woman*'. Edward Aspinall describes how she would 'make confession of her faith' (O4[r]). Sometimes they prompt her: William Foxe asks her '*whether she did beleeue the promises of God, nor no? and whether she could pray?*' (O3[r]).

At the most charged moments, however, they act as communal silent testimony to Brettergh's suffering. William Harrison, along with William Brettergh, William Foxe, John Brettergh, and William Woodward, serve as witnesses for the most extended transcription of Katherine's speech—a shorter version of which appears in Harrison's sermon. When Harrison visits her on the Saturday evening, Brettergh exclaims:

> *Oh Master Harrison, my soule hath been compassed about with terrors of death, feare within, and feare without, the sorrowes of hell were vpon me, knots and knorres were vpon my soule,* (which twice or thrice she repeated) *and a roring wildnernesee of woe was within me; but blessed, blessed, blessed be the Lord my God, who hath not left me comfortles, but like a good shepheard, hath he brought me into a place of rest, euen to the sweete running waters of life, that flowe out of the sanctuarie of God, and he hath lead me into the greene pastures, where I am fed, and exceedingly comforted: yea, he hath restored my soule, and lead me into the plaine and easie paths of righteousnes. The way that now I goe in is a sweete and easie way; yea, it is more easie and soft then the sand, for I goe and tread vpon wheate, euen vpon the finest flower of wheate: Oh blessed be the Lord; O blessed be the Lord, that hath thus comforted me, & hath brought me to a place, more sweeter vnto me, then the Garden of Eden. Oh the ioy! the ioy, the delightsome ioy that I feele! Oh how wonderfull, how wonderfull, how wonderfull is this ioy! O praise the Lord for his mercies, and for this ioy, which my soule feeleth ful wel, praise his name for euermore.* (P5[v]–P6[r])

This is a finely wrought passage, full of neat alliteration ('knots and knorres'), emphatic repetition, and invocations to praise. These praises, the biographer writes, 'she soundeth forth, like *Dauids harmonie*, being indued with *Dauids* spirit' (P6[r])—and, of course, in the midst of this outburst, with the skill of a preacher, Brettergh channels Psalms 23:2–3 and 147:14. As Brettergh nears the end, her exclamations become shorter and more random ('as one awaking out of sleepe'; P6[v]), until her final moments. Saying the Lord's Prayer with the assembled company, she falters at 'thine is thy kingdome':

> her strength then being gone, her tongue failed her, and so she lay silent for a while, euery one iudging her then to be neere death, her strength and speech failing her: yet after a while lifting vp her eyes with a sweet countenance and still voice, said: *My warrefare is accomplished, and my inquities are pardoned. Lord, whom haue I in heauen but thee? and I haue none in earth but thee: my flesh faileth, and my heart also, but God is the strength of my heart, and my portion for euer. He that preserueth Iacob, and defendeth his Israel, he is my God, and will guide me vnto death: guide me O Lord my God, and suffer me not to faint, but keepe my soule in safetie.* (P7[r])

The biographer records that 'with that she presently fell a sleepe in the Lord, passing away in peace, without any motion at all; and so yielded vp the Ghost', at around four in the afternoon of Whitsunday, 'a sweete Sabboaths sacrifice' (P7[r]).

This, he writes, was '[a] sure testimonie of the truth of our profession... It must needes be a diuine Religion, and a truth comming from God, that thus can fille the heart and mouth of a weake woman, at the time of death, with such admirable comfort' (P7^{r-v}). And conversely, 'a wretched conceit, and mere antichristian is that religion, which so hateth and persecuteth this faith, which is thus able to leade the true-hearted professors thereof, with such vnspeakable peace vnto their graues' (P7^{v}).

The volume ends with the words of Solomon in Proverbs 10:7: '*The memorial of the iust shall be blessed: but the name of the wicked shall rot*' (P7^{v}). This speaks to the letter 'To the Christian Reader' which opens the volume, which charges the 'crueltie, and lyes' of the Papists, 'in murthering the Martyrs, in persecuting the Protestants, and now of late in these parts, in beating and wounding the bodies, in killing & spoyling the cattell of those which withstand them by publike authoritie' (A4^{r}). The lies take many forms, but especially 'spreading abroad false reports against our best professors to hinder their doctrine: as they haue bitterly reuiled them for the course of their liues; so haue they most shamefully slaundered them for the manner of their death'. He cites 'malitious slaunders and manifest vntruths' published by 'some of the Romish faction' about the deaths of many Protestants, from Luther to the Guernsey martyr Perotine Massey—all of whom 'sealed the truth of Christ with their owne blood' (A4^{r}).

This, then, is the context for the volume commemorating Katherine Brettergh. Brettergh's final days have been 'bitterly reuiled' and 'shamefully slaundered', a standard tactic of 'the Romish faction', and so the biographer is forced to retaliate in order to rehabilitate her. But the charge does not bear scrutiny: there is no trace of any written attack on Katherine Brettergh. The biographer is not taking on a printed work that has broadcast Catholic lies about his subject, and responding in kind. Instead, he seems to be ventriloquizing those lies—possibly even inventing them—in order to promote Katherine Brettergh as an exemplar of puritan piety, a model to be emulated.

The Author of Brettergh's Life

Who, then, wrote this much-read life of Katherine Brettergh? The name most often advanced is the minister William Hinde, on the grounds that he was related by marriage to the Bruens, and authored the life of Brettergh's brother John Bruen.[49] But this is unlikely: while in time, Hinde was indeed appointed as preacher at Bunbury in Cheshire, some forty miles away, and married John Bruen's wife's sister, in 1601–2 he was still at Queen's College, Oxford, and had no connection to the Brettergh-Bruen-Foxe clan.[50] Moreover, the distinctive style and content of Hinde's

Faithfull Remonstrance bears very little resemblance to the *Brief Discovrse*. Another faint possibility might be the second preacher, William Leigh of Standish. Local to the area since the 1580s, he was married to Mary Wrightington, daughter of the Bretterghs' friend and kinsman John Wrightington, and like them had links to the household of Henry Stanley, fourth earl of Derby, a prominent godly patron. But Leigh is demonstrably distant from the publication of the sermons and life: indeed, Katherine's widower goes so far as to preface the printed version of Leigh's sermon with a letter he wrote to Leigh, dated 20 November 1601, in which he effectively declares that he is publishing the sermon without Leigh's prior knowledge.[51]

I would argue instead that there can be little doubt that it was William Harrison who coordinated the publication, and most likely wrote the *Brief Discovrse*.[52] Harrison knew Katherine Brettergh, visited her in her final days, and delivered the first of the two funeral sermons. Although the *Brief Discovrse* is unsigned and speaks of 'Master *William Harrison the Preacher*' in the third person ($P5^v$, $P6^r$), in the volume's opening epistle 'To the Christian Reader', Harrison writes that, in addition to publishing his funeral sermon 'by the importunitie of some, who hearing it preached, earnestly desired to haue it printed' ($A3^r$), he was 'Moreouer…willing to giue a publike testimonie of that godly Gentlewomans death, at whose buriall it was preached: to cleere her from the slanderous reports of her popish neighbors, who will not suffer her to rest in her graue, but seeke to disgrace her after her death' ($A3^v$). The *Brief Discovrse* is presumably that 'publike testimonie'. The volume also contains 'A Post-script to Papistes', a device that Harrison was to use again in *The Difference of Hearers*, a 1614 collection of sermons given at Huyton.[53]

As a result, we need to understand this 1602 life-writing as an integral part of the campaign against Catholics in the duchy of Lancaster. William Harrison was the most local of the Queen's Preachers; it was Harrison who appointed William Brettergh to act as his agent in arresting Catholic recusants. In mid-April 1601, Bishop Vaughan sent Harrison to Sir Robert Cecil in London to report first-hand on the state of religion in Lancashire, vouching that Harrison has 'Learnynge, honestye, and good discretion' and 'hath traveyled [travailed] with good successe in his place'.[54] Did Cecil urge Harrison to seek out new ways of making his case? Katherine Brettergh's struggle with Satan was not without precedent: a decade earlier, Philip Stubbes had published his wife Katherine's 'most heauenly confession of the Christian faith, which shee made a little before her departure' which involved 'a wonderfull combate betwixt Sathan and her soule', as *A Christal Glasse for Christian Women*, a short tract that would prove wildly popular, running through twenty-four editions by 1640. The widower Stubbes wrote of 'the godly life and Christian death of Mistresse Katherine Stubs'; now Harrison, with the widower Brettergh's cooperation, wrote of 'the Christian life and godly death' of Mistress Katherine Brettergh.[55] The title was entered into the Stationers' Register on 16 December 1601, and was probably ready for sale early in the new year.[56]

Harrison took a parochial Lancashire battle and, through the London book market, made it speak to the nation. It was a timely propaganda coup—but it had an unexpected side effect: the immortalizing of Katherine Brettergh. Robert Bolton quoted 'Blessed Mistris *Brettergh* upon Her last Bed' in a 1631 lecture on afflicted consciences.[57] James Nalton exhorted his congregation to 'Do as that blessed Saint *Katharine Bretter*, when she was continually haunted with Satans temptations'.[58] In 1669, Thomas Brooks in his *A Cabinet of Choice Jewels* reminded readers of 'When Mrs. *Katherine Brettergh* was upon her dying bed, and most grievously assaulted by temptations'.[59] William Traughton devoted eight pages of his 1677 *Of the Causes and Cure of Sad Disconsolate Thoughts in Christians* to a summary of her story.[60] Shorn of its charged Lancashire religious politics, Brettergh's became the archetypal story of a dying woman assaulted by Satan—and joyously winning, as John Glascock recalled in his 1658 funeral sermon for Anne Petter: 'Oh the joyes! the joyes! the joyes! that I feel in my soul! they be wonderful, they be wonderful, they be wonderful; were the words of Mistresse *Katherine Brettergh*.'[61]

9

The Revised Lives of Tobie Matthew

On 8 September 1640 in London, Sir Tobie Matthew signed and dated a manuscript which contained, as its title page claimed, 'A true historicall Relation of the Conuersion of Tobie Matthew to the holie Catholick Fayth'.[1] Declaring that 'I take God humbly to wittness, *that* all this Relation aforesaid, is entirely true', Matthew signed the manuscript in two places, and sealed it with his ring (2:21). But he was not alone. Under his first signature is written the following statement:

> Wee heer vnderwritten affirme, that we haue heard Sir Toby Matthew declare, and take it vpon his Soule, that both the Relation of his Conuersion, which is heer sett downe in this Booke; as also the following Short Discourse which he calls by the name of *Posthumus, or the Suruiuer*, are entyrely true, to the best of his Vnderstanding, and Memory. Both which are signed, by his owne hand. He also holds the following fiue and twenty considerations, in order to Religion, to be very considerable, and true. (232–3)

There follow ten signatures, of Elizabeth and Anne Mordaunt, George Wintour, Edward Sulyard, Edward Guildford, Thomas James, Elizabeth and Francis Petre, and Edward Young—all members of noted English Catholic families (Fig. 16).

The manuscript, which survives in the Folger Shakespeare Library, thus advertises, in insistent fashion, that it belongs to the London of the autumn of 1640, a place and a time, as we shall see, of particular tension and danger for Sir Tobie Matthew. But, in truth, only a fraction of the manuscript addresses Matthew's present situation, and then only obliquely. It primarily focuses on earlier periods of his life, dating back over thirty years, and is confusingly addressed to a 'deare Friend' who is nowhere identified in the manuscript, and who drops out of sight after the opening pages. What appears to be Tobie Matthew's 1640 life-writing is, in fact, the last surviving version of a life that was rewritten several times over multiple decades, as Matthew's own life underwent some startling changes. From

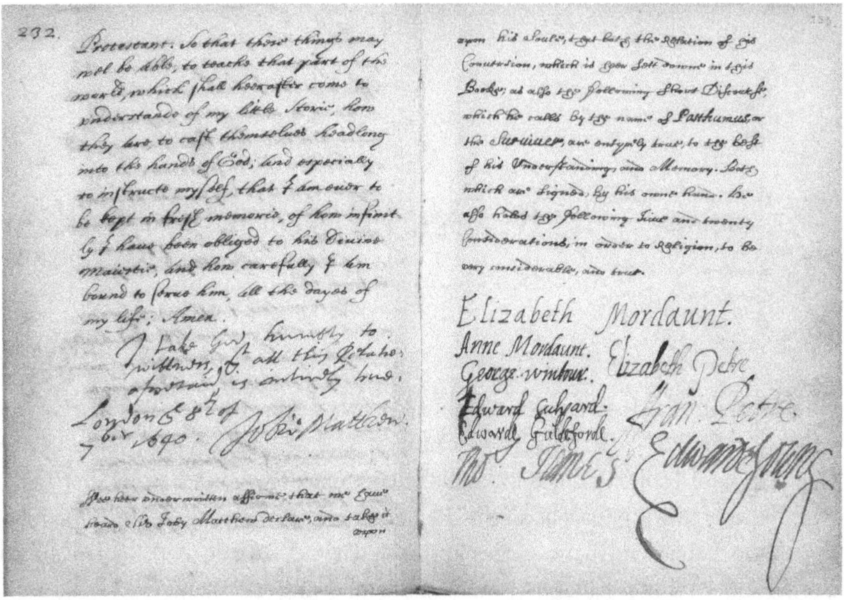

Figure 16. The signatures of nine witnesses to Matthew's 'A true historicall Relation'. By permission of the Folger Shakespeare Library.

the survival of a manuscript in the Jesuit Archives, we know that the first ninety-five pages of the Folger manuscript are a revised version of a letter sent by Matthew in 1611 in which he celebrates his conversion to Roman Catholicism. I speculate, from internal evidence, that another version was written sometime in or after 1629, when his position in English society seemed finally secure; and that the text was finally expanded to encompass events in 1640, when that sense of security proved deceptive.

In 1640, Matthew's decision to write his own life was hardly surprising: over the past two decades, he had demonstrated an abiding interest in life-writing, translating Catholic biographies and autobiographies from Italian, Spanish, and Latin, most notably—and controversially—the first English translation of Augustine's *Confessions*.[2] In his later years, he wrote the lives of English women living in monastic houses in the Low Countries, and embarked on a life of Augustine, in whom Matthew found a model to emulate—but also a model from whom he was constantly forced to part company. But it was as early as 1611—two years before Thomas Bodley was excoriated for writing his life-story—that Tobie Matthew thought his life worth writing—and its myriad changes meant it was worth rewriting.[3]

1611: Conuersion to the Catholick Fayth

The Folger manuscript of Matthew's 'Relation' specifies that the text is written 'To a deare Friend': 'At your request, or rather vpon your commandment,' Matthew opens, 'I will heer declare that, in brief manner, which passed between God and me, in order to my Conuersion to the Catholick Fayth' (1). In responding to the command of a figure within the Roman Catholic Church, Matthew's narrative shares common ground with other Catholic life-stories of the early seventeenth century. The Jesuit priest John Gerard (1564–1637) wrote a Latin account of his life on the England mission, probably in spring 1609, when he was in Louvain, training novices of the Society of Jesus. He makes clear that he wrote it at the order of his Superiors, and that it 'must not, then, be thought an unusual or remarkable thing to do'; although what he achieved was relatively insignificant, nonetheless, 'it is a "praiseworthy thing to make known the works of God", and, on this account too, I need have no bashfulness in recording the results of my own poor efforts'.[4] Two years later, in 1611, William Weston (1555–1615) similarly penned an autobiographical account of his mission in England at the request of his general.[5]

The impetus to write such a life-story was firmly institutionalized. As Molly Murray has shown, the English College in Rome enforced a rudimentary form of life-writing on its acolytes through an internal questionnaire divided into six 'chapters' concerning the student's identity, condition, education, health, whether he had lived in heresy, and whether he felt able and willing to embrace an ecclesiastical life.[6] In some cases, this questioning prompted further autobiographical activities: the poet and convert William Alabaster (1568–1640), for example, produced an account of his life of over 100 pages, which Robert Persons undertook to translate into Latin.[7] More generally, as James S. Amelang notes, 'Early modern Catholics were used to a spiritual director's command to transform a general auricular confession into a written one. Such was the stimulus behind numerous spiritual autobiographies, especially by female mystics, whose visions and other claims to divine favors could be more closely scrutinized by male superiors after being consigned to paper.'[8] Matthew was especially drawn to such writings: he translated and published the life of future saint Maria Magdalena de' Pazzi, recounted by her confessor Vincenzio Puccini; the life of repentant bandit Troilo Savelli, executed in 1592 for rapes and murders, as told by his confessor Giuseppe Biondi; and the collection *Audi filia* (*Listen, Daughter*) written for the nun Doña Sancha Carillo by her spiritual father Juan de Avila.[9]

Many of these narratives include a moment of conversion—either from another confession to the Roman Catholic faith, or from a life of impiety to one of repentance and prayer. Matthew's 'Conuersion to the Catholick Fayth', as told to his 'deare Friend', fits both models. But as we read the Folger manuscript, we find no further mention made of this 'deare Friend' who has sworn to keep Matthew's secrets—and for good reason: by 1640, the friend had been dead for twenty-six years. The first hundred pages of the 1640 'Relation' are in fact a revision, with some significant additions and deletions, of an older text: a letter that Matthew wrote on 16 August 1611 from Paris to his 'deare Friend' Dame Mary Gage at the English Benedictine monastery in Brussels; a copy of this letter survives in the Archivum Britannicum Societatis Iesu (the Jesuit Archives in Britain).[10] Matthew had probably met Dame Mary a year earlier when he passed through Brussels; she was the sister of George Gage, the man known as his 'inseparable companion', his 'fidus Achates', 'his Damon', to whom he wrote several sonnets and to whom in his 1614 will he left a bequest of 400 crowns of gold per annum, as 'my most dearest and most entire frynd'.[11] (Matthew's intimacy with the Gage family continued: the Elizabeth Petre who witnessed his 'Relation' in 1640 was born Elizabeth Gage.) Dame Mary died three years after Matthew wrote the letter.[12]

Even in its 1611 incarnation, Matthew's account is quite substantial: he excuses 'this relation upon relation' by claiming it was required 'to let you see, and to make you feel the extreme necessity which I have of your holy prayers' (351). Matthew's letter begins his narrative '[w]hen I came to have about seven and twenty years of age', around the beginning of the reign of James I, as he used a licensed journey to France to head south to Florence, where God 'did...vouchsafe to call me to the communion of His Church'. In Matthew's account, the conversion came slowly. He was approached by 'divers Catholic gentlemen of my acquaintance' who tried 'divers discourses of me, in favour of the Catholic religion' but 'the ears of my soul were made deaf with the noise of vanity'—indeed, 'I had a much greater ambition to speak like an Italian, than to believe like a Christian'. But strange events had a greater impact on Matthew. Swept off his horse into a river on his way to Naples, he was miraculously saved from death. Then in that city he heard 'a procession of children, singing the litanies of our Blessed Lady':

I know not by what chance or rather providence of almighty God, the tune of that sweet verse Sancta Maria ora pro nobis [Holy Mary, pray for us] came so often into mine ears, and did so extraordinarily delight me, that at last my tongue took it up not as a prayer (such was my misfortune for it is a misery to have been at any time any other than our *Blessed* Lady's humble servant) but as a song whose ditty fell sweetly to the air; and so when I found myself alone, my ordinary entertainment was to sing Sancta Maria ora pro nobis in the tune of those babes and sucklings who shewed forth her praise. (314)

In time, Matthew grew interested in theological issues, under the tuition of Father Robert Persons, the leading English Jesuit. In Rome, 'a certain Cardinal' encouraged him to 'be careful not only to view the antiquities of the decayed Roman Empire, but of the Catholick Roman Church' (324–5), and Matthew was spellbound by the tombs of St Sebastian and St Pancratius:

the sight of those most ancient Crosses, Altars, Sepulchres, and other marks of Catholick religion having been planted there in the persecution of the primitive Church (which might be of more than fifteen hundred years ago and could not be of less than thirteen hundred) did strike me with a kind of reverent awe, and repress my insolent discourse against the Catholick religion ever after. (325)

Back in Florence, Matthew started attending sermons 'out of curiosity' (327), and settled into 'a more virtuous, moral course of life…recommending my soul to God by prayer (though it were but seldom and faintly made)'; as a result, God turned his gaze 'inward, by causing me to consider what I was, how I lived, what I believed, what account I were able to make, if then I should be called to give it up'. Asking '*Domine, quid me vis facere?* [*Lord, what wilt thou have me to do?*; Acts 9:6]' (327–8), Matthew found some answers in that 'excellent tract of St. Augustine, *De unitate ecclesiæ* [*On the Unity of the Church*]', discovering that Augustine's fourth-century arguments against the Donatists strongly resembled the Catholic Church's arguments against the Protestants of his own time. Determining that 'I would instantly humble myself to the yoke of Christ', Matthew was taken by a Jesuit to the Inquisitor, who 'instantly absolved [him] of all heresies', an occasion also marked by 'an accident which happened at the instant of my reconciliation' in which the 'fair day did suddenly change itself into such a dark tempest of rain and thunder, as the eldest of us had not seen a greater'; the Inquisitor, 'smiling, said that the Devil was angry to see a soul return to God'. A month later, Matthew made his general confession and was received 'to the Blessed Sacrament of the Altar'. From that moment, Matthew writes, 'I have found myself free, by the space of some whole years, from so much as the thought of some one particular sin, to which, until I had been nourished with the Bread of Angels, I was so abandoned, that I remember well, when I have apprehended it, as the sentence of death to be restrained from committing it, I say, not for the space of years or months, but even of two or three days' (345). We are not further illuminated as to the nature of Matthew's chronic and 'particular sin'.

For the informed reader, Matthew's narrative contains obvious echoes of the most influential autobiography of the Christian tradition: the *Confessions* of St Augustine. Like Matthew, Augustine was familiar with Scripture long before he believed in it; like Matthew, his path to conversion started in his late twenties, was protracted, and contained some uncanny, inexplicable episodes like Matthew's escape from drowning. The most explicit point of comparison comes when Matthew hears children singing 'Sancta Maria ora pro nobis [Blessed Mary, pray for us]' a clear allusion to Augustine hearing a child say 'Tolle, lege [Pick up and read]', the instruction that leads him to discover Paul's epistle to the Romans. In Matthew's conversion, the crucial text is *De unitate ecclesiæ* by Augustine himself; and he also relates how, 'whilst I was yet an heretic', Robert Persons 'put into my hands…that divine book of his *Confessions*', urging him 'that I would make it my inseparable companion'. In his valediction to Dame Mary, Matthew again quotes from the *Confessions*, describing how Augustine complains to God, 'Sero te amaui pulchritudo tam antiqua et tam nova, sero te amaui [Late have I loved you, beauty so old and so new, late have I loved you]', noting 'O that my soul could truly speak thereof as a virtue, whereof that great and glorious Saint did accuse himself as of a fault!' (351–2).

The comparison with Augustine reaches only so far, however. In *Confessions*, Augustine initially rejects the Christian faith of his mother, Monica, and is reunited with her when he converts. In Matthew's account, by contrast, his parents block his path to Catholicism, at first forbidding any foreign travel, and then yielding when he agrees not to visit Italy or Spain (although 'I meant nothing less than what I said') (307–8). And there is no reunion after his conversion, as Matthew recounts at the conclusion of the letter: 'The only thing which threatened me, by way of hindering my conversion, and which still doth urge me, is that consideration of my parents, though it touch me now in a different kind from what I thought of at that time' (348–9). While as an obedient son, he understands their grief, in fact

> The greatest cross which I bear concerning them is to see the little use they make of the example of the conversion of me their son; whereof howsoever they may esteem but lightly, I beseech God that it lie not heavily upon their souls in that fearful day of Judgment. Well; yet they are both alive. As the trees fall so they shall lie, but as long as they stand upon their roots I will hope even beyond hope, and pray both by myself and all the charitable friends I have, that they may fall in a fair ground. (349)

The letter thus comes full circle to the parents, with whom it started.

Despite this emphasis on his parents, what is notably missing from this relation is any trace of Matthew's life before the age of twenty-seven, and any specific detail about those parents. Tobie had an impeccable Church of England pedigree. His father, also

Tobie Matthew, was at the time of his eldest son's birth a career academic, dean of Christ Church in Oxford, but he soon became bishop of Durham and later archbishop of York. His mother Frances was the daughter of William Barlow, late bishop of Chichester, and the widow of Matthew Parker, son to the archbishop of Canterbury of the same name; her sisters married the bishops of Coventry and Lichfield, Hereford, and two successive bishops of Winchester—indeed, her lengthy memorial in York Minster concludes 'a Bishop was her Father, | An Archbishop her Father-in-Law; | She had Four Bishops, her Brethren, | And an Archbishop her husband'.[13] Frances Matthew recorded the births of her children in a manuscript: her firstborn, Tobias, was born 'Octob. 3, 1577, a little after three of the Clock in the afternoon'[14]—his first appearance in a life-writing.

In the decade before his narrative commences, Matthew had been in sharp conflict with his parents. While studying for his MA at Christ Church, he suffered what appears to have been a complete physical and mental breakdown. The details, gleaned from letters between his Oxford contemporary Dudley Carleton and various correspondents, remain opaque, but we can gain a general impression. On 18 December 1596, Matthew suffered an epileptic seizure, which was attributed both to a stomach condition and the 'cure' he had received for it.[15] The vice-chancellor used Matthew's friend Carleton to send word to Matthew's father, now bishop of Durham, but the bishop let Carleton know 'that he had rather haue heard of his sonnes death then his sicknes although this [i.e. his sickness] doth somwhat please him in that he sees God hath harkened to his praiers'. He went on to say that Tobie would 'neuer recouer his fauour': 'he is a reprobate, a castaway, an example aboue example of an irreuerent and disobedient child, and to conclude One, quem ipsa salus seruare non potest [whom salvation itself cannot save]'. The bishop also claimed that Tobie 'did impiouslie practise against his mother, his deare (and chast) mother, whose life he doth tender aboue seauen sonnes yea seauentie seauen sonnes'. Finally, he entreated the vice-chancellor to show Tobie 'no comfort, to vndertake nothing for him, nor to be deceaued with his Hyppocriticall shewes, and malenchollie sicknes'.[16]

To a friend, Carleton related that Tobie's father had laid 'so mightie a burden on his sonne[s] neck as his weaknes could not beare'. Specifically, the bishop, he wrote ironically, 'like a bonus paterfamilias [good head of the household] refers strangers to the shame of his own house, to the sight of a schedule in *wh*ich is breeflie sett down and wisely compiled, his sonnes endightment [indictment]'. This 'schedule' seems to have been a particularly punitive form of life-writing, in which 'his [Tobie's] faultes fro*m* his infancie were enrolled, his wordes, wrested fro*m* him, esteemed as deedes'. When Carleton writes of Tobie's 'wordes' being 'wrested fro*m* him', is he referring to a diary or other life-writing in which Tobie had confided his feelings, as Richard Rogers did, that is now being recast as a biographical 'schedule'? For his part, Tobie declared that 'his father erred in iudgment in making a fire to burne his owne house with by framing his sonnes arrainement and aggrauating the smallest matters as yf he had rather haue these accusations pass for current then be disproued'. The 'schedule', Carleton reports, 'was burnt in my sight with these wordes that the world should not be acquainted with that *which* yf he dide [died] would be to his shame, and *which* yf he liud he could not recall [i.e. take back]'.[17]

Despite his vociferousness, it is not clear from the bishop's fulminations what exactly his son had done. Clearly, someone had accused Tobie of something: he describes himself to Carleton as 'so weaklie backed and so mightelie opposed by those that malice it, as that an opinion intimated by the*m*, is as disaduantageable to me, as if it were a truth'. Faced with this 'hard case', Tobie is unsure what response to make: 'silence would argue my consent, answearing would in their opinion accuse me of vntruth, since what I must denie is deposed by the oath of a periuriouse knau[e]'.[18] But it is significant that Tobie Matthew senior felt that the best way of dealing with this misdemeanour was to produce such a 'schedule', a written account of what his son was supposed to have done; and that his son was outraged by that writing, and burned it ceremoniously. The episode speaks to the power of life-writing to record for posterity—and to harm its subject.

1629: A Visible Marke of Particular Honour

Matthew's letter to Dame Mary Gage hints briefly at what happened after his conversion, in the years between 1607 and 1611: he mentions losing the support of a powerful man who had been his friend, and he alludes, in passing, to having been in prison. But this is strictly superfluous to the account of his conversion. At some point, however, he revised and extended his account quite considerably. Internal evidence would suggest that this version dates from around 1629. Whereas the 1611 account was firmly focused on Matthew's conversion, the 1629 version is emphatically about Matthew's love/hate relationship with his native land, England.

In the continuation (which we have from the 1640 manuscript), Matthew recounts his first return to England in the autumn of 1607 (although no dates are given in the 'Relation'). Having made contact with an old friend, Sir Francis Bacon, he meets with the archbishop of Canterbury, Richard Bancroft, and debates the papal supremacy and the invocation of saints. Initially friendly, Bancroft soon becomes angry at Matthew's answers, and places him in the Fleet prison, where Matthew is visited by a remarkable series of prominent men, sent to talk him out of his heresy. Matthew's treatment of his would-be interlocutors is sometimes harsh, sometimes irreverent. His 'deare friend' Sir Maurice Berkeley was 'withall, a most honest man, if Puritanisme would haue let him alone' (147, 148); of the Protestant controversialist, and future bishop of Durham, Dr Thomas Morton, 'I was much vexed by him, in person; and much abused, by his ill reports of me' (144–5); the good-natured courtier Sir Henry Goodere seemed not to understand the rules of the game, and 'would ingenuously confesse, whensoeuer in discourse he thought, I had the better reason of the two' (148); the barrister Richard Martin and the poet John Donne (then starting his own journey to the ministry) 'were meer libertines in themselues … they thought me too sawcie, for presuming to shew them the right way, in which they liked not then to goe' (149); the one-time Catholic diplomat Sir Christopher Perkins 'loued Musick very much; and had a boy, whome he was yet suspected, to loue more' (121). The parliamentarian Sir Edwin Sandys failed to impress: 'the tediousnes of his discourse, the solemnes of his vnderstanding; the visible delight, which he had to be extreamly admired, and his resolution, to reduce all religion to humane Reason, made me apt to feare him little, and to like him lesse' (149). Of the clergyman 'Mr Crashaw', presumably William Crashaw, Matthew opined 'there is not a more intollerable kinde of man, then an ignorant, audacious, lowde, and false vndertaker, such as he euer was'—there was a good deal more of this attack on Crashaw, but Matthew deleted twenty-three lines (145–6).[19] The adventurer Captain Edmund Whitelocke 'would be talking to me, like a mad man, as he was, both profanely against Pietie, and licentiously against Modestie', but 'he did it after so iollie and wittie a manner that he would tempte a man almost to forgiue him, euen in spight of his hart' (154–5). The jurist Dr Alberico Gentili, sent by his father, thought Matthew should take the oath of allegiance, just as he had taken the oath of believing the Council of Trent in Italy: it was 'Giusto come pigliarei vn scudello di Brodetto, Just as I would take a mease [mess] of Broath'. Matthew retorts that 'for my part, I durst not be so easie in swearing to things, concerning Religion, which were against my Conscience' (153). But his most violent reaction was reserved for another of his father's men, a lawyer named Mr Cooper, to whom Mathew alleged that passages from Augustine supported the Catholic Church's abstinence from some meats and clerical celibacy. 'Doth St. Austen, said the Lawyer, write this? Yes, sayd I; and I can shew it you, when you will. St. Austen, sayd he, was a Villaine. By that time, the Lawyer was neer the Stares', Matthew recalls, 'and I confesse, I was half tempted, to throwe him downe, and breake his neck' (157–8). A final debate with Dr Lancelot Andrewes, of a thankfully more intellectual nature, fills over thirty pages of Matthew's manuscript (158–189)—a tribute to the elderly bishop of Chichester's tenacity, but apparently with no effect on Matthew. Freed through Bacon's intervention when the plague hits London, Matthew is sent, in a last-ditch attempt to convince him, to the Catholic 'archpriest' George Blackwell, now in the Clink prison, who had gone against papal authority and taken the oath of allegiance to King James. That too backfired: Matthew 'pittyed the poore old man; and I pardoned his great feare, his desire of life, and, in a word, all his frayltie much more easily, then I could doe his not permitting, that a man might forbeare, with a good Conscience, to take that Oath, which had been condemned, ouer and ouer by the Sea Apostolick' (200).

The sojourn in England ends abruptly: 'After this, the clowdes came thick vpon me; needie persons, were looking after me; and I was aduised by some friends, rather to retire my self handsomely out of the way, for the safetie of the poore fortune, which I enjoyed, then still to be shutt-vp in prison, and to expose my whole Estate, to the first Beggar'. Matthew makes a 'hastie Sale' (203–4) of his estate, losing 'aboue ten in the hundred' (205), and after spending two months with his friend Edward Jones, he leaves for 'forraine Parts, where', he writes, 'I continued above twelue years togeather'. We hear nothing of those twelve years, not even that on 20 May 1614, in Rome, Cardinal Bellarmine ordained Matthew to the priesthood—all that matters in this narrative is Matthew's relationship with England. An encounter in Paris with George Villiers, soon to become the king's 'Fauorite of the time' (206), proves serendipitous: as the earl of Buckingham, Villiers persuades James to allow Matthew to return (in May 1617). But Matthew again refuses to take the oath; faced with 'the malice of two or three back-friends of mine, who were both great men, and great Puritans', he was 'fayne, after staying in England almost two yeares, to retire my self once againe beyond the seas' (in early 1619) (207). But before too long (in December 1621), 'the times grew a little more easie; and a noble, and effectuall reall friend and fauourer of mine, my lord of Bristol, had both so much good will, and so much power, as to obtaine my absolute returne home; where I haue continued euer since' (207–8). Now his only journey abroad was in 1623 with Prince Charles and Buckingham to Madrid as part of the abortive negotiations to marry the prince to the Spanish Infanta, after which 'King James was pleased to putt a visible marke of particular honour vpon me, at the instance, as I thinke, of his Maiestie, that now is; and partly also by meanes of the late duke of Buckingham, who testifyed to King James, how honestly I had carried myself in that iournie' (208).

Matthew's knighting by King James on 20 October 1623, at the instigation of the next sovereign, Charles I, and the most powerful favourite of both, Buckingham, should constitute the climactic moment of his 'Relation': the remarkable approbation of an ordained Roman Catholic priest by a British Protestant king as the most spectacular sign of the 'extraordinarie mercie' granted by God. But, for Matthew, the story has not yet finished—and once again, his parents constitute the obstacle. His success at court encouraged his parents to 'grow on apace, in being good to me many wayes'; but they 'were not only kinde, but carefull too'. Matthew describes how, at his father's house, he was ambushed by what he calls 'a kinde of lustie knott, if it might not rather goe for a little Colledge, of certaine eminent Clergie-men' (209), who stage a kind of ecclesiastical intervention. Matthew's obstinate answers physically affect the clerics: 'it was strange enough to see, how they wrung their hands, and how their whites of eyes were turned vp, and their deuout sighes were sent abroad, to testifye both their wonder and grief, that I would vtter myself after that manner' (215). After Matthew—in his own account—wins the argument, there is no further attempt made to convince him; if his parents broach the subject, 'they would rather doe it by sighes, and short wishes, then long discourses' (219–20). Matthew even suggests that his father was, in truth, sympathetic to his argument: 'we seldome parted, but that, I thought, he was full of difficultie, about knowing, how to proceede, between that, which he found to be easiest, and that, which he iudged to be best; which Best, not only in my Conscience, but in his own also (as I verily thinke) was to embrace my Belief' (221–2). Dr Matthew died (in 1628) 'in the self same manner, as he had liued; leauing matter of much grief to my hart; for I doubte his case is not the better now, for his hauing seene, and heard that from me, which I presumed to declare to him then' (223).

But it is Matthew's mother who completes the story—and there is not the slightest sign that she is ever won over to her son's belief. Frances Matthew, he writes, 'was much more feruent towards the Puritanicall & sole-Scripture way; and was euer vpon all occasions, wont to be as busie with scripture, as if it had been some gloue, vpon her fingers ends'. But despite being 'held in a mightie kind of opinion, with that sort of people' (223), she died 'in a most miserable manner', refusing to think of death or even to pray—despite the fact that 'during her health, she would be still talking of it'. Remaining 'of perfect sense, and vnderstanding, throughout her whole sicknes', she did not prepare for death but instead 'would be still diuerting, and entertayning herself otherwise, and still be calling for her silkes, and workes, with other toyes and trinckets, of that kinde. so that finally she went out of the world, more like an ignorant childe of foure yeares old, then like a talking Scripturist of almost fourescore' (224–5). Matthew's image of his mother—the 'talking Scripturist' reduced to a preliterate child—has strong echoes of the sonnet he wrote to Augustine's mother St Monica, in which he implored the saint to 'let my mother thy best daughter bee | and make her learne at last, that tis no shame | to put Christes crosse, before her A.B.C.'.[20] For Matthew, his mother's fate is vivid proof that 'the most forward and talking Protestants and Puritans, haue but the barke of the tree, without the iuice; and the shell, without the kernell' (225–6). Meanwhile, after his mother's death (in May 1629), despite a few losses, Matthew now has his country and his friends, 'amongst whom, I enjoy it, with as much honour and aduantage of manie kindes, as anie man of my poore Condition hath receaued; yea and, in my conscience, I thinke, with more than I should haue been admitted to, if I had been a Protestant' (231–2). His success proves that his conversion to Catholicism does not prevent him from being an Englishman of honour and advantage.

1640: A Funerall Aduise to the Reader

From 1621, Tobie Matthew became a familiar face at the English court, and remained so for the next nineteen years.[21] By his own reckoning, he was the intimate friend of influential figures including Sir Francis Bacon, George Villiers, duke of Buckingham, and John Digby, earl of Bristol, and the recipient of royal favour, including the knighthood, and rumours that he had been received into Charles I's privy chamber or even bedchamber in 1633.[22] To his detractors, Matthew was at best a running joke: one court informant alleged that 'neither the king nor queen maketh any esteeme of him and as often as ther is any speech of him they gyre [jeer?] and mocke at him'.[23] Some were less indulgent, claiming that Matthew was not only a recusant Catholic, but an ordained priest (which was true) and a Jesuit (which was not true, although Matthew did not mind people believing it was). Sir John Suckling spoke for many annoyed by his ubiquity: '*Toby Mathews* (pox on him) how came he there? | Was whispering nothing in some-bodies ear: | When he had the honour to be nam'd in Court.'[24]

That Sir Tobie Matthew had a well-known and colourful personality is clear from the lampoon in the satirical comedy *Hierarchomachia or The Antibishop*, a probably unperformed play by a knowledgeable Catholic of the opposing, non-Jesuit camp, where he appears as the anagrammatized 'Bitomattus'.[25] Bitomattus is depicted as 'a concealed Gibellin [Jesuit]', with a very close 'politick friend' Aggeus (George Gage), and flamboyantly dressed: 'Were you to judge me by my outward garb', he says, 'You'd swear I were a wanton or a knight | Of most affected vanity'. One woman strikes a telling blow at his textual activities:

> Though I never could translate
> Saint Augustine's *Confessions*, or express
> Count Troilus' legend to the reader's tears,
> And set forth books of cabinets and knacks,
> Yet can I say my creed, believe the church,
> And be as sensible of any wrong
> Done to her in her pastors as the best.

Evidently the playwright knew Matthew to be the anonymous translator of Augustine's *Confessions*, Biondi's life of Troilo Savelli, and de Avila's *Audi filia*, which

Matthew had subtitled '*a rich cabinet full of spirituall iewells*'—and equally the writer was unimpressed by the translator's alleged piety. The play attacks Bitomattus as a busybody, always intruding into political business: why, he's asked, is he 'so officious in the court? | So fawning on the great ones? so extreme | In visiting ambassadors, as some | Do call you troublesome, intruding, rude, | Importunate, nay imprudent?' And he is specifically attacked for becoming inappropriately intimate with beautiful women, in order to influence them—'Amongs the ladies... such a burr | Especially the rich ones, as you stick | At ev'ry turn upon their sleeves, and strive | To rule their families'—and for making crude remarks about their breasts, 'Words more befitting Aretine than you'. Matthew had a sturdy reputation for becoming intimate with women—as a means to their conversion. During his 1617–19 return to England, it was rumoured that he had helped convert the earl of Exeter's wife, Frances Brydges: the newsletter-writer John Chamberlain claimed to have 'heard yt now two severall [separate] wayes that he hath perverted her to become a Romane Catholique'.[26] Matthew's intimacy with Lucy, countess of Carlisle, was grist to the gossip mill.[27] And it was widely believed in 1637—wrongly, as it turned out—that he had converted Anne Boteler, wife of Mountjoy Blount, earl of Newport; the king's anger against Matthew was such that Secretary Conway quipped that 'Don *Tobiah* was in such Perplexity, that I find he will make a very ill Man to be a Martyr'.[28]

The constant trickle of attacks left Matthew acutely vulnerable to the rumours that engulfed him in the autumn of 1640. In August, he was identified as 'a Iesuited Priest' involved in a supposed plot to murder the king and the archbishop of Canterbury, William Laud, and characterized as 'a man principally noxious, and himselfe the Plague of the King and Kingdom of England; a most impudent man, who flies to all banquets, and feasts, called or not called; never quiet, alwaies in action & perpetuall motion; thrusting himselfe into all conversations of Superiours; he urgeth conferences familiarly, that he may fish out the minds of men'—and then passes intelligence to the Pope's legate, or even to the Pope himself.[29] From then on, Matthew was fair game. He was named in September in a satirical libel, alongside the queen's secretary Sir John Winter, Sir Kenelm Digby, and Endymion Porter, as 'birdes of a feather' who 'blow the Coales of dissension'.[30] The Privy Council discussed him on 7 October.[31] In November, a 1639 papal bull was discovered in which Urban VII exhorts Matthew, his 'beloved Son', to 'enkindle the Catholicks with a divine zeal', especially 'those *Amazones* and *Virago*'s for the Catholick cause'.[32] On 23 November, the City of London complained to the Commons that despite being 'convicted Recusants', Matthew, Digby, and Walter Montagu, son of the earl of Manchester, were still living in the city.[33] In December, a young man named Benjamin Hammond alleged that 'certaine Jesuites', including Sir Tobie, had 'seduced himselfe and his brother', persuading them 'to passe over his estate to the disherison [disinheriting] of his name'. In February 1641, Matthew was one of four 'English papists' named in the Commons as 'dangerous instruments in the Queenes Court' with 'dailie neare accesse to her Majestie'; a committee headed by Edmund Waller called for the 'Banishing of Englishe and Scotche Papists from the Courte', again naming Matthew. But by the time the Lords debated the issue on 15 March, the planned banishment was moot, since 'they are all goeing away save Winter'.[34] Indeed, Matthew had been in the wind since mid-December; by the time he was declared delinquent in late April 1641 for failing to turn himself in, he was safely in the Low Countries, where he would spend the last fourteen years of his life.[35]

It was during these frantic months, which Matthew must have realized might be his last in England, that he had the Folger manuscript written and witnessed—and once again, he revised and expanded his text. The determinedly upbeat tone of the end of the 'True historicall Relation' is notably tempered by the shorter tract that follows, the tellingly named 'Posthumus, or The Survivor' (239). Here, Matthew finds himself 'so daily subiect to indispositions and infirmities, and so full also of yeares, which now passe three-score [he was 63], as to giue me good assurance, that my life is not to last very long'. He claims 'I haue fully resolved...to leaue behinde me a Protestation of some things, concerning myself' (2:1); while currently in good health, 'My purpose...is, that, if it please God to call me to him, by the way of sicknes, and if that happen to me at home; and if [I] shall then remember, that I haue written such a Paper as this, to call for the sayd Paper into my hands, and then, and there, to proteste vpon my death-bed, that I haue spoken nothing in it but truth; and that I aske so much right of the world, as to be belieued therin' (2:3). Throughout the 'Posthumus', Matthew uses his supposed deathbed status to authenticate his words: 'the words of a dying man, may well deserue to be belieued' (2:12); it ends, 'This was then the substance of that which I was desirous to relate, or rather, as it were, to sign and seal with my last blood, since I write it as with the hand of a dying man' (2:18).

The 'Posthumus' starts as a confession of faith, in which Matthew declares that he 'liue[s] in the Profession of the Romane Catholick Fayth' (2:3), but it has two further goals: to provide support for the narrative of his life, and to address the current rumours against him. Knowing that 'it hath been doubted by manie, whether really, when I professed it first, I were, indeed a Catholick, or no; and whether also, I had not left my Protestant Religion, vpon discontentments, and ends', he takes the opportunity to 'affirme most truly, that when I became first a Catholick; I did it with all sinceritie of minde; and so fare I was from being wrought to it, by anie temporall respects, that I found, they were all directly crosse to my intention' (2:4). He spends more time rebutting the more topical charge, namely the 'diuers great Obiections against Catholicks...as if we were Pensioners to forraine Princes; as not being good subiects to the King; and as if we had designes against the State & c.' (2:7). Matthew's response is emphatic: 'I take God to witness, that I have neuer, in my whole life, knowne anie one subiect of the King's, in this Kingdome, receaue anie one Pension, or anie other pecuniarie profitt, of anie Prince in Europe...' (2:7–8), nor had he heard of 'anie disloyall purpose' by any of the king's subjects (2:9). He further denies that there are 'strange differences, euen amongst Catholicks themselues, concerning certaine doctrines', namely equivocation, obedience to princes, and whether or not to keep faith with heretics, and charges that 'some of vs, heer in England, are much more blameable, then the rest, for being more opposite, then others, to the wayes of temper and moderation' (2:11). In particular, he denies that there are schisms between Catholic clergy in England and abroad; and between the regular and secular clergy in England (2:12–13). Here we sense the battles being waged in English Catholic circles during the difficult days of the late 1630s and early 1640s.

The final section of the manuscript (2:22–59) is headed 'A Protestant Soule, which is piously affected, and procures to be saued, must not faile to consider, and consider wel, the Particulers, which follow heer', and contains twenty-five points, which he describes as 'motives of my Conuersion to Catholick Religion' (2:19). In the 'Posthumus', he implies that these have been added in some haste:

> I will doe it after a Summarie manner; for I must but touche, and goe. These heads I putt togeather heretofore; and I haue communicated them to some friend, vpon a certaine occasion, though independently vpon anie such discourse, as I haue held in this Paper hitherto. But now, I will annexe them heer to this; and they shall last after me...And though formerly they were reflected vpon by me, as Reasons and Motives but to myself; yet heer I send them out in form of a funerall aduise to the Reader, that he may vouchsafe to looke vpon them with a carefull eye. (2:20–1)

In September 1640, then, Matthew is writing as a dying man, wrapping up his affairs in haste, buffeting the 'True historicall Relation' with assurances of his sincerity—both in his personal piety, and in his account of his life. But despite his insistence on his imminent demise, Matthew in fact survived for another decade and a half, spending his time mainly in Brussels, Antwerp, and Ghent.[36] In that time his interest in life-writing only intensified, expanding to take on new forms. In 1642, Matthew published his translation from Spanish of the life of St Teresa de Avila, under the title *The Flaming Hart*. As he wrote in a lengthy preface, while the lives of saints can be written by men 'who are onlie eminent in the Historicall way', and men who are 'great Seruants of Mightie God', the ultimate is 'when Saints themselues write their own Liues; as the Incomparable S. *Augustin* did a great part of his, in the Diuine Booke of his *Confessions*'. These 'Relations of such Liues' are 'incomparably, of the most credit of all', since 'no bodie knowes so well, what passes concerning a man, as himself', and saints tell the truth, especiall those 'endued with verie great natural parts, of Witt, and Memorie, and Iudgement'.[37]

Matthew developed the idea that 'Saints themselues' should 'write their own Liues' in his manuscript life of Lucy Knatchbull, of the English Benedictine convent at Ghent, written between 1642 and 1652.[38] Acting as a confessor, Matthew required Knatchbull to commit to paper some of her life-story. He encouraged her to utilize models, and was not shy about recommending some of his own: at one point, Knatchbull describes how she 'thought upon divers Penitents; and in particular upon Troilo Savelli, whose help amongst the rest I desired', a reference to Matthew's translation of the life of the penitent bandit. Most thoroughgoing, however, is her identification with Teresa de Avila, whose life Matthew had just translated. Matthew himself stresses the similarity, remarking 'how deeply she was wont to wade in those Supernatural Waters where St Teresa used to bathe and swim'; their writings 'are as like one another, I mean not for Quantity... but for Quality and Kind, as even two drops of water can be'. As editor David Knowles puts it, 'practically any page of Dame Lucy's Relations could be paralleled from St. Teresa', while Nicky Hallett has noted that 'it is difficult to know whether coincidences are due to Teresian influence on Knatchbull or on Matthew'.[39] I would suggest that the parallels are due to Teresa's influence on Matthew, and Matthew's subsequent influence on Knatchbull, and that they are precisely not coincidences. Knatchbull's 'Life' reveals the complex interaction of biographical and autobiographical models on the writing of one's own life, and the use of those autobiographical writings to form a biography—which will then go on to serve as a new model for further autobiography.[40]

There were yet more writings that Matthew wanted published. In his final will, signed in Antwerp on 12 October 1647, he claims that he has 'translated the most part' of 'all the workes of my glorious Mother St Teresa', and asks that his 'deare and noble friend' Walter Montagu arrange for the manuscripts to be printed. And his fascination with Augustine continued to the end. Matthew also bequeaths to Montagu, 'all those papers, which I have written of the life of the glorious Saint Austin, which if God grant me life, I will finish', especially because 'I have wondered, that in so many lives which so many worthy and learned men have written of him, there is scarce any touch at all of the hyest favours which he received from allmighty God'. Sadly, the works of St Teresa and the life of Augustine are lost; among Matthew's papers, only a collection of letters to and from 'severall persons of honour' (notably Donne and Bacon), on which he had been working since the 1630s, was to reach print, in 1660, edited by Donne's son John, and prefaced with yet another piece of life-writing, his 'character of the most excellent lady, Lucy, Countesse of Carleile', his most important later patron.[41]

Matthew also mentions in his will that 'I have written the historical relation of my own conversion to the Catholique religion', but he makes no request for Montagu to publish it. His own life is evidently a different kind of life-writing. Why does Matthew have his 'True historicall Relation' so solemnly signed, sealed, and witnessed in the autumn of 1640? We get a hint, I would suggest, in the records of Antwerp's English Carmelite community. Matthew had a strong relationship with the order, leaving £600 to the convent in his will, and at one point had plans to be buried there.[42] When in 1642 Matthew presented the nuns with his translation of the life of St Teresa, he also gave them a portion of her pierced heart, with a message attached that vouchsafed that the reliquary was given to him in 1610 by Fray Diego de Guevara of the Augustinians at Salamanca, who had taken it from his own neck and placed it round Matthew's. Ever since, wrote Matthew, he had 'perpetually worne [it] next mine owne hart, above these thirtie years. And having lately translated that Life which she wrote, with her owne holie hand, into English particularly for the joy and comfort of the English Monasterie of the Teresian Religious women in Antwerp…I have thought fit to give them my aforesaid, undoubted Relick of the verie hart of the Glorious St. Teresa, their Holie Mother, and mine.' And then he authenticated the message:

> All this, I say, I affirme, and declare to be expressly true; and I will heer signe, and assure it, under my hand and seal; and am readie to take my oath that it is most true.
>
> Signed and Sealed, by me underwritten, in Antwerp, upon the One and Twentieth day of September in the yeare of our Lord God, One Thousand Six Hundred Fourtie Two.[43]

We hear again the language with which he endorsed the 1640 'Relation': 'I take God humbly to wittness, *that* all this Relation aforesaid, is entirely true', 'Signed by me in London, as in *the* presence of Almighty God, for most certeinly, and intirely true, vpon *the* 8th day of 7^{ber} [September] 1640. Tobie Matthew'. And he will use this language again, speaking of his own autobiography in his will: 'Withall I signify heere that whereas I have written the historical relation of my own conversion to the Catholique religion, I take allmighty God to witness, as at the houre and instant of my death, that I have delivered nothing therein, but the exact truth.'[44]

Coming from a man who did so much to disseminate the life-writings of Catholic men and women in print, this is a deliberate move. Matthew wanted his 'True historicall Relation' to survive, like the pierced fragment of Teresa's heart, as a kind of relic, within the closed Catholic communities with whom he spent his final years. And that is why, even with his parents long dead, Matthew's last will made sure to specify that his executor must be 'not of my owne blood: for as I have no obligation to comply with any of them in the disposition of my estate, in regard that my father and Mother did absolutely disinherit me of all their estate, in favour of them, and by reason of my religion; and besides for divers solide private reasons why I take none of them now into my care, who are nearest unto me, in this kind; I allso desire not to entrust any of them, in anything which may concern me, after my death'.[45] Instead, he entrusts his old friend Walter Montagu with his 'Relation', perhaps already sensing that Montagu will spend his life in these religious communities. (Montagu became abbot of the Benedictine monastery of Nanteuil in Metz.[46]) And with this final, emphatic rejection of his family, Tobie Matthew's conversion was complete.

10

The Familial Lives of Martha Moulsworth and Constance Lucy

'It is the Wont of all good Writers of Histories to begyn with his Birth and Linage, whose Life and Deedes they do discribe.' So says Sir James Perrot of 'The life, deedes and death of Sir John Perrott, Kt', his father, writing shortly after Perrot's death in 1592, and indeed he begins his biography with an account of 'the lineal Discent and Pedegree of Sir *John Perrott*, and his Auncestors'.[1] Almost a century later, John Aubrey concurs, noting at the opening of his 'Life of Mr Thomas Hobbes' that 'the writers of the Lives of the ancient philosophers used to, in the first place to speake of their Lineage'.[2] Robert Boyle even apologizes for *not* starting his own life with a pedigree: 'Not needlesly to confound the Herald with the Historian, & begin a Relation by a Pedigree, I shall content my selfe to informe yow, that the immediate Parents of our Philaretus [Boyle], were…'[3]

This genuflection to family lineage, utterly commonplace in men's life-writings of the period, deserves attention. Many of the life-writings that we understand as pertaining to an individual are, in important ways, life-writings of family lines.[4] Among the most famous of seventeenth-century English autobiographies, Edward, Lord Herbert of Cherbury's *Life* starts with a backward foray into family genealogy. Embarking on an account of 'those passages of my life, which I conceive may best declare me, and be most useful' to his posterity, Herbert suddenly turns to his forebears: 'Before yet I bring my Self to this accompt, it will be necessary I say somewhat concerning my Ancestors…'–and he writes, at some length, of his father, and his paternal grandfather and great-grandfather. This discussion could easily have been longer: pointing out that 'I am descended of Talbot, Devoreux, Gray, Corbet, and many other Noble Families' on his mother's side, he claims that 'I could say much more of my Ancestors of that side likewise, but that I should exceed my proposed scope'; he therefore limits himself to 'only say somewhat more of my Mother, my Brothers; and Sisters'.

It may seem natural to see Herbert's life proper starting with his birth—'I was borne at Eyton, in Shropshire…betweene the houres of twelve and one of the Clocke in the Afternoone'—and this genealogical exploration as simply grafted on as a preface: but the family history is, I would argue, a constitutive part of his life. For Herbert is acutely aware of hereditary influences. During his infancy, he suffers from a 'defluction at my ears'; when that clears up at the age of seven, he considers it 'left me free of the disease my ancestors were subject unto, being the epilepsy'. He returns to the subject of inherited illness when giving advice on the treatment of children: 'Breefely, what disease soeuer it be That is deriued from Anncestors of either side, it will be necessary first to giue such medicines to the Nurse as may make her milk effectuall for those purposes, As also afterwards to giue unto the Childe it selfe such specifique remedies as his age and Constitution will beare… I will recommend againe to my posterity the Curing of hereditary diseases in this very Infancy, otherwise without much difficulty they will neuer bee Cured'. For Herbert, his family history is not external to his life, but just as much a part of his formation as the sickly infancy and the precocious talking with servants during his early years with which he continues his account—which, indeed, carries on through to 'my Posterity', his descendants, for whom the life is written.[5]

Although perhaps the best known life-writings of early modern women are lives they wrote of their husbands, there was also a sturdy tradition of married women writing about their birth families. In 1610, at the age of eighty-four, the twice-married Rose Throckmorton opened her memoir with the heading 'Of my father', and tells of how 'In Hollinsheds chronicle I find this story'—of a papal curse 'set vp in the town of Dunkirk in flanders' and 'taken down by William Locke of London mercer'. This is Rose's cue to add to Holinshed: 'Now I his daughter Rose Throckmorton widow late wife of Simon Throckmorton Esq. and first the wife of Anthony Hickm*a*n a merch*a*nt of London, reading this of my father have thought good to leaue to my children this addition to it'—namely, '*tha*t for *tha*t act *the* king gaue him 100^{li} [pounds] a yeere & made him a gent*leman* of his privy chamber, and he was the kings mercer, and his ma*ies*ty vouchsafed to dine at his house'.[6] Although defining herself as 'widow late wife' in relation to two husbands, Throckmorton effectively sets herself up as a direct line between 'my father' and 'my children'. We see this repeated in other women's autobiographical writings. Margaret Cavendish opens 'A true Relation of my Birth, Breeding, and Life' with the statement 'My Father was a Gentleman, which Title is grounded and given by Merit, not by Princes', and then embarks on an account of her natal family, the Lucases, with whom she clearly still identifies.[7] And most famously—and relentlessly—Lady Anne Clifford wrote the lives of herself and her family as part of her campaign to reclaim her father's estates, which had passed to her male cousin when her father died with no male heir.[8]

It is, of course, hardly surprising that such 'family histories' are so numerous among surviving life-writings: these are precisely the kind of documents that were carefully handed down from generation to generation, often remaining physically in the same place, the muniments room of the family seat. But they do not represent the entire range of familial life-writings. There are also life-writings in which biological family relationships are challenged and even trumped by other, non-biological, affective relationships. As historians are exploring, in early modern England the notion of a household—either nuclear or extended—comprising only blood relatives was unlikely.[9] With mortality rates high, particularly in childbirth, and multiple marriages common, many households were of 'hybrid' families, comprising not only parents and children, but what we would now call step-parents, step-children, and foster-children. This chapter seeks out these non-biological relationships in the writings of two seventeenth-century women, Martha Moulsworth and Elizabeth Lucy, and shows how they come into intriguing conflict with the women's natal and marital commitments.

My Name Was Martha

Near the end of a seventeenth-century manuscript miscellany now housed in Yale University's Beinecke Library there survives a poem dated 'Nouember the 10th 1632' and entitled 'The Memorandum of Martha Moulsworth Widdowe'[10] (Fig. 17). The 'Memorandum' declares that its fifty-five slightly stumbling heroic couplets were written on the author's fifty-fifth birthday: 'The tenth day of the winter month Nouember' was the day which 'did open first theis eies, and shewed this light', and 'Now on thatt day vppon thatt daie I write'—'thatt clocke by ffiftie fiue retourns hath gonn'—providing a shared 'birth day of my selfe, & of theis lynes'. A marginal note puns that 'my muse is a tell clocke, & echoeth euerie stroke with a coupled ryme so many tymes viz 55'.

Moulsworth starts her life with baptism at a day old, when she was given the name 'Martha'—her biblical forebear is made explicit in marginal annotations to Luke 10:14 and Revelations 3:20:

> My Name was Martha, Martha tooke much payne
> our Sauiour christ her guesse [guest] to entertayne
> God gyue me grace my Inward house to dight
> that he with me may supp, & stay all night[.]

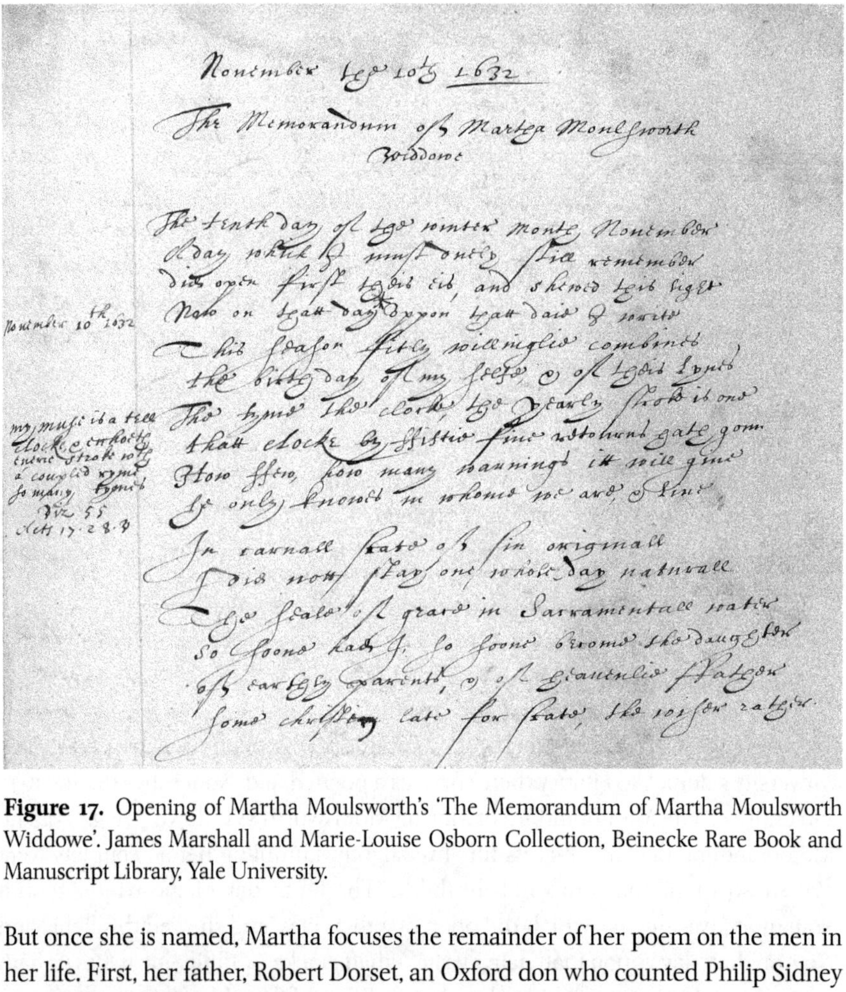
November the 10th 1632

The Memorandum of Martha Moulsworth
Widdowe

The tenth day of the winter month November
A day which I must onely still remember
did open first theis eis, and shewed this light
Now on that day upon that daie I write
This season fitly willinglie combines
the birth day of my selfe, & of theis lynes
The tyme the clocke, the yearly stroke is one
that clocke by ffiftie five retourns hath gone
How ffew, how many warnings itt will give
he only knowes in whome we are, & live

In carnall state of sin originall
I did nott stay one whole day naturall
The seale of grace in Sacramentall water
So soone had I, so soone become the daughter
of earthly parents, & of heavenlie ffather
some christen late for state, the wiser rather.

November 10th 1632

my muse is a tell clocke, & echoes everie stroke with a coupled ryme so many tymes Viz 55

Acts 17.28.9

Figure 17. Opening of Martha Moulsworth's 'The Memorandum of Martha Moulsworth Widdowe'. James Marshall and Marie-Louise Osborn Collection, Beinecke Rare Book and Manuscript Library, Yale University.

But once she is named, Martha focuses the remainder of her poem on the men in her life. First, her father, Robert Dorset, an Oxford don who counted Philip Sidney among his pupils:

> My ffather was a Man of spottles ffame
> of gentle Birth, & Dorsett was his name
> He had, & left lands of his owne possession
> he was of Leuies [Levi's] tribe by his profession [i.e. a clergyman]
> His Mother oxford knowenge well his worth
> arayd him in scarlett Robe did send him fforth.

Dorset raised her not only 'in godlie pietie | In modest chearefullnes, & sad sobrietie' but also, 'Beyond my sex & kind | he did with learning Lattin decke mind'. 'And whie nott so?' Moulsworth asks,

the muses ffemalls are
and therfore of Vs ffemales take some care
Two Vniuersities we haue of men
o thatt we had but one of women then
O then thatt would in witt, and tongs surpasse
All art of men thatt is, or euer was[.]

Despite her call for a women's university, her own education proved of limited value—'But I of Lattin haue no cause to boast | ffor want of vse, I longe ago itt lost'—and in another marginal gloss, Moulsworth puns that 'Lattin is not the most marketable mariadge mettall'. 'Had I no other portion to my dowre', Moulsworth muses, 'I might have stood a virgin to this houre.'

Instead, Martha married three times: 'Thrice this Right hand did holly wedlocke plight | And thrice this Left with pledged ringe was dight.' She describes her first marriage to 'Mr Nicolas Prynne, Aprill 18 1598' as coming 'late' at twenty-one; this 'first knott held fiue yeares, & eight months more', followed by 'a yeare sett on my mourning score'. Next was 'Mr Tho*mas* Througood ffebruary 3 1604': 'My second bond ten years nine months did last', after which 'three years eight Months I kept a widowes ffast'. The third husband was 'Mr Beuill Moulswoorth June 15, 1619', and here Martha is effusive in her praise: 'The third I tooke a louely man, & kind | such comelines in age we seldome ffind.' For both bride and groom, this was a third marriage: 'third wife I was to him, as he to me | third husband was, in number we agree'. The marriage lasted 'eleuen years, & eight months'—Moulsworth's 'autume' and yet 'a second spring'. To Martha's regret, 'to[o] soone awaie it hasted':

was neuer man so Buxome to his wife
with him I led an easie darlings life.
I had my will in house, in purse in Store
what would a women old or yong haue more?

Martha writes now on 10 November 1632, 'Two years Almost outwearinge since he died | And yett, & yet my tears ffor him nott dried'. After fifty lines devoted to her father and husbands, she deals with her children in a single brutal couplet: 'I by the ffirst, & last some Issue had | butt roote, & fruite is dead, w*hi*ch makes me sad.'[11] The poem ends with Martha avoiding the question as to which husband she would spend eternity with:

In vayne itt were, prophane itt were ffor me
With Sadnes to aske w*hi*ch of theis three
I shall call husband in *the* Resurrection

> ffor then shall all in glorious perfection
> Like to th'immortall heauenlie Angells liue
> who wedlocks bonds doe neither take nor giue[.]

Moulsworth's 'Memorandum', first published in 1993, instantly prompted an outpouring of critical analyses, and within seven years was installed in the *Norton Anthology of English Literature*.[12] A rare example of an early modern Englishwoman telling her own life-story in verse, the poem was hailed for its use of biblical allusion, its complex numerology, its deployment of archetypes and rhetorical figures, and its witty puns. But there is a palpable sense of disappointment in some of its feminist commentaries that, despite her call for a women's university, Moulsworth 'chooses to define herself only in her relationships with men as daughter, wife and widow', as Germaine Greer puts it.[13] Indeed, as Mary Ellen Lamb points out, this definition even structures the poem's material form: 'page breaks in the manuscript coincide with its division into thirds (or almost thirds) corresponding to the three periods of Moulsworth's life; before her marriages, during her marriages, and after her marriages'.[14] But Martha Moulsworth was a great deal more than daughter, wife, and widow.

An Acount of the Lady Lucy

To show how, I turn to a slim manuscript volume of thirty-eight pages, measuring five inches by four, with margins carefully ruled in red ink and page numbers, and written in a neat, consistent italic hand. Now at the Folger Shakespeare Library, this manuscript records the life-stories of two seventeenth-century gentlewomen, whose lives touched on Moulsworth's.[15] The first, unsigned, is entitled 'An Acount of the Lady Lucy, write to a pertickular friend of hers, Mrs. Moore'; it does not specify the identity of its author, although we understand that the biographer counts her- or himself as one of Lady Lucy's 'children'. But it is immediately followed by another short life, signed 'Mar. Eyre', which informs us that 'The Foregoing Account was writ by Mrs Lucy, Daughter In-law to the said Lady, who Liued diuerse Year with her, and Merited as larg A Character herself, as could be giuen of any of her Sex, hauing well Copyed after her, for whome she had so Great A Value, and Veneration'. From these clues, we can identify the first piece as a life of Lady Constance Lucy (1566–1637) written by her daughter-in-law, Elizabeth (d. 1690/1?), who married her sixth and youngest son Francis Lucy; the second is an account of Elizabeth Lucy by her third daughter Martha (*c.* 1645–1728), wife of the judge Sir Samuel Eyre.[16] The 'pertickular friend' to whom the life of Lady Lucy is addressed I shall identify as Marie Moore, a gentlewoman with whom she had become intimate 'in her declineing Time' (11).[17] Martha Eyre, or her amanuensis, appears to have copied out her mother's life of Lady Lucy from another source, and appended her own life of her mother, sometime after 1694.[18]

The volume opens with the words 'From the Time of her Sickness, to the Time of her Death' (1), and both lives, Constance Lucy's and Elizabeth Lucy's, devote much of their length to unremitting descriptions of the women's painful last days. Before we reach that point, however, Elizabeth Lucy starts by detailing Constance Lucy's acts of piety and charity, both domestic and civic, including erecting a lecture in the 'Desolate and poor Town near her in Hamshire', opening 'A School to teach Children to Read, and Write, and Cast Account', and paying for the apprenticeship of 'Ten poor children' (6–9). But after twelve pages, the 'Acount' takes a different tack. Lady Lucy, we are informed, 'used often to say, she thought it the best Duty belonging to her Sex, and hardest to do well, to be A Good Mother In-law; which she her self did Excel in'. Elizabeth Lucy recalls that 'I my self Reciued more kindness from her, *than* I think it possable by any Obserueance to gain from any Person now Liueing; but my Husband' (12–13). It is then that we hear Lady Lucy's life-story, which explains why the question of being 'A Good Mother In-law' is of such consequence.

Constance was born in 1566, the sole heir of Sir Richard Kingsmill (*c.* 1528–1600), of Highclere in Hampshire, who went on to hold the posts of attorney (1573) and surveyor (1590) of the Court of Wards.[19] Her mother died when Constance was no more than eight years old; when Sir Richard remarried, in or around 1574, Constance was placed in the household of the principal secretary of state, Sir Francis Walsingham, to act as a companion for his daughter Frances, about two years younger than herself.[20] Worth some forty thousand pounds, Constance was married, sometime after 1580, to Thomas Lucy, who was knighted in 1593. Together, the couple had fourteen children; ten were still alive at Sir Thomas's death in 1605. As a widow, Lady Lucy seems to have lived primarily in her London house in St Giles Cripplegate: in November 1624, she had two leading physicians, Sir William Paddy and Dr Thomas Mountford, vouch that she was 'verie aged, sickly, weake, and thereby enforced to keepe her Chamber', and that any attempt to move to the Lucys' country seat at Charlecote in Warwickshire—as a recent proclamation had required for all 'persons of qualitie'—would endanger her life.[21] Nevertheless, this aged, sickly, and weak lady managed to totter on for another thirteen years, outliving both her doctors. In her final illness, she was attended by Sir Theodore de Mayerne and Sir Simon Baskerville; when she died in 1637, her body was transported to Charlecote, where she was buried with great solemnity in her husband's tomb at St Leonard's church.

As Elizabeth Lucy tells it, Constance Lucy's life was a series of negotiations with other people's households. At a young age, Constance was thrust into very socially and politically elevated circles, 'brought up at Sir Francis Walsinghams, and to him uery Respectfull, and Extraordinarily kindly used, and being then one of the Places of Greatest Resort, of Persons of Quality in this Kingdome'. Despite Walsingham's prominence, Elizabeth Lucy insists, Sir Francis 'would put of[f] his Hatt to her as often as she passed by him, what, or with whome soeuer his Busyness was' (13–14). From being a companion in Walsingham's household, Constance moves directly to being a stepmother in the household of her husband. Thomas Lucy had already been married, from 1574 to his wife's death in 1580, to Dorothea Arnold; their son, Thomas, died young, but a daughter named Joyce, baptized on 8 July 1578, survived.[22] Now Constance Lucy was expected to be a mother to this stepdaughter.

Step-parents had a poor reputation. A stepfather might do as Sir Thomas Bodley was accused of doing: marry a rich widow, live off her money, and then effectively disinherit the children from her first marriage.[23] With stepmothers, the potential damage was affective as well as financial. Motherless children were at the mercy of a stepmother 'who in all probability wil less befriend them', as the earl of Clare put it in 1631.[24] Patricia Crawford has sketched the deteriorating relationship of a stepmother and stepdaughter, as recorded in the journal of Elizabeth Turner. In 1668, the child, Betty, was 'a goad in my side and pricks in mine eyes'; when Betty married in 1676, Elizabeth prayed for her stepdaughter's happiness, 'notwithstanding her continued hatred & malignant endeavour towards mee & mine'. It is indicative of the pressures on families that, even while dealing with the continuous hatred of one child, the Turners in 1674 adopted an orphaned niece and nephew, which proved a 'great charge' to them.[25]

But there is evidence that many on both sides of the relationship made a real effort. Lady Elizabeth Delaval recorded of her grandmother, Jane, Lady Gorges, that 'to her dying day, severall children that her lord had by a former wife pay'd her the same duty as iff she had been there own mother'.[26] Bathsua Makin in 1664 paid tribute to her former student, Lady Elizabeth Langham, highlighting her love for the children of her husband's first marriage: 'So good in all relations, so sweet | A daughter, such a lovely wife, discreet | A mother; though not hers, not partial | She loved as if they had been natural.'[27] And, as she recorded in her autobiography, Mary Rich, countess of Warwick, in 1659 assured her brother-in-law, Robert Rich, third earl of Warwick, that she would look after his three daughters:

> which, upon his deathbed, I promised to have while I lived as great a care of as if they had been my own, and that promise I can truly say I have performed, for I have from the time of their father's death, that I took them home to me, with the same care bred those three ladies,

who were all left to my care young, as I could have done if they had been my own children, studying and endeavouring to bring them up religiously, that they might be good, and do good afterwards, in their generation; and I am sure I have the affection of a mother for those sweet, hopeful young ladies, which I beseech God to bless.[28]

While the countess of Warwick actively volunteered to take on her nieces, Constance Lucy was 'as unprepared for such A Care, as One could posseable [possibly] be'. Nevertheless, she rose to the challenge, as Elizabeth Lucy writes: 'I haue heard her say that she euer demeaned herself to her [her stepdaughter], as she would wish should be dun to her Own, if so left, and with such Kindness euer to her and hers, as if she had ben her Own Mother: and so was allways Hono*red* of her, and *them*' (15). Constance gives pre-eminence to her husband's child, and treats Joyce as if she were her own daughter—on the grounds that this is what she would wish if she herself died, and her own children were presented with a new stepmother. It is a telling sentence, speaking to the quite reasonable fear of a mother that she would die while her children were still young, and they would find themselves at the mercy of a stepmother. The biographer is at pains to show that Constance Lucy's generosity to her stepdaughter went beyond maternal kindness to a young girl, to involve Joyce's children when they were adults. She recalls '[o]ne instance of her Loue and Kindness [that] Fell in my Rememberance': one of Joyce Lucy Cook's younger sons, a soldier, informed Lady Lucy that he planned to sell some reversions he possessed 'to put Mony in his Purse' as he raised a company to go to Sweden; when he could not secure a good price, Lady Lucy gave him the money he would have raised—and told him to keep the reversions (15–16).

Having established Constance's situation as a ward and a stepmother, Elizabeth turns to her performance as a mother-in-law. Lady Lucy was also warm '[t]o those that Marryed to any of her Children': 'her Carrage was in such A Wining way, as she was Reuerenced by *them* all, as thare own Parent, *wh*ich I can speak largly of towards my self' (16). Elizabeth gives 'one instance': 'not long before she Dyed, percuieing me with Child, she Charged me, *that* if my Husband did let me Want any thing I did use to haue, or should desire, I should let her know: and to the half of her Kingdome, *that* was her Phraise, she would precure [*sic*] it for me' (17). Elizabeth Lucy describes this devotion to sons- and daughters-in-law as '*the* hardest and Best Duty of A Woman'. Significantly, 'not so Hard', by contrast, was the task of being 'A Good Mother to her own Children'. Here, Constance Lucy showed great ingenuity. At the death of her husband, she was 'Left many and Smale upon her Hands'—six sons and four daughters—'of which but one Daughter Marryed, and none of her Sons *then* out of her House, but *the* Eldest, who had *then* bin at Oxford, and the Inns of Court, yet left under Age'. Even the eldest was not home and dry: 'for his Estate he might haue ben put to some trouble, but *that* through her Prudence, Kindness, and Wisdome, she had Compounded for it before almost any notice was taken of it', while 'towards her Younger Children, she was such A Phenex Mother, as if they had had no other Parent' (18–19).

In fact, Constance Lucy's campaign for her children had started before her husband's death:

> First in her Husbands Life Time, who was much in Debt, and now but newly come to his Estate, before he Dyed, more senceable of her own Sicklyness, *than* his, she so importuned him to make some Prouision for *them*, that all of *them* had somthing setteled upon them by him; but so in hast, that thare was little left to any of *the* Younger Children, *that* was not Subiect to some question. (19)

After Sir Thomas's death, Constance Lucy 'took *the* Education of *them* upon herself, and Spent not so littel, as Four or Fiue times so much as she had alowed to do it with, and was not sattisfyed til she had seen what was so imperfectly Setteled by thare Father, made sure unto *them*, and after, Doubled the ualue to all of *them*, to many of *them* Trebeled it'. This remarkable feat was achieved by an adept piece of property manoeuvring that also benefited her eldest son. When she was newly widowed, Lady Lucy 'made A Lease in trust of her Inheritance to some Friends for the Prouision of her Younger Children, which when through her own Sauing, she had done as she intended, out of *that* she Bequeathed that Lease to her Eldest Son, and all her Stock upon her Ground, thair, so that tho she dealt so Bountyfully to all her Younger Children, she in *that* manner inlarged her Eldest Sons Estate'—indeed, 'she left her Eldest Son A greater Eastate, and freer from Incumberance, *than* it was left to her, Brauely Wooded, and bestowed in Building near A Thousand Pound, at Highclear, *that* Cheife Seat of her Inheritance, and left it him Brauely Furnished, which will be A Thousand Pound A Year Inheritance' (21–2, 20–1).

Elizabeth Lucy claims that it would be 'to[o] much for my Book' to convey 'how all [Lady Lucy's] Sons ware broaght up in the University, some of the Inns of Court, some abroad in Trauel; how, and in what manner she directed and prouided for *them*, in thaire seuerall Courcs' and to relate 'how she Marryed her Daughters, and what she did for *them* after Marrage'; and 'what Honour, for Loue or her Children, she refusied in her Widdowhood, many Great Marryages *that* she might haue had' (23). We know that this direction and provision extended to some of her grandchildren: Patricia Phillippy has traced how Lady Lucy commissioned tombs in her local London church of St Giles Cripplegate for seventeen-year-old Constance Whitney, who died in her London house in 1628, after Lady Lucy had 'bred her since she was eight yeeres of age'; and Margaret Lucy, who died in 1634, mourned by 'her old

Grandmother, the Lady Constance Lucy, under whose Governement shee died'.[29] (One hopes that there were other grandchildren bred or governed by Lady Lucy who did not die during the process.)

It is only in the final sentence of the 'Acount' that Constance Lucy is presented as the wife of Sir Thomas Lucy, in what sounds like a rather grudging afterthought: 'not to Omite, what is worthy to be admired in her, and her Husband, as Wife and Husband, *that* in all *that* Time they Liued together, I haue heard her say, noe Man, Woman, nor Child, could euer say that they heard Angre or Hasty word betwen *them*'. And then, equally briefly, Constance becomes the child of her parents: 'as Excelent A Child she was, as Wife, or Mother, for I haue heard her speak with as thankfull A kind Rememberance of her Father and Mother, as was Posscible' (23–4). Superficially, this might seem to be the Constance Lucy portrayed on her father's tomb in St Michael's church at Highclere, kneeling alongside her husband, while their ten children serve as 'weepers' below their grandfather.[30] But in Elizabeth Lucy's telling, Constance Lucy's duty as wife and daughter is best seen—characteristically—in her generosity to her daughter-in-law. Lady Lucy did 'endeauour to procure A thankfull rememberance of her Father whore [*sic*—i.e. whose] only Child she was, to after Ages' by standing as godmother to the biographer's eldest son, 'and was pleased to Christen my Eldest Son, Kingsmel'—Lady Lucy's family name—'in Great Fauiour and Loue to my Husband and me, in Rememberance of him; and Charged me not to let any other Child get the Loue from him' (24). Elizabeth Lucy followed Constance's wishes in naming her first son Kingsmill, in honour of the family not of her husband, but of her mother-in-law.

Elizabeth Lucy's depiction of her mother-in-law speaks emphatically to the strong affective familial relationships that were possible beyond bloodlines. What is striking about Elizabeth's account of her mother-in-law, however, is that she refuses to flatten these relationships as if they were all similar in kind. For Elizabeth Lucy, it is precisely her mother-in-law's sensitivity to 'in-law' relationships that makes her such an impressive woman.

The manuscript's second life, the 'Character' of Elizabeth Lucy, promises initially to proceed on similar lines. Born in Hoddesdon in Hertfordshire, 'Daughter and Heir of Mr Moulsworth', Elizabeth, like Constance, was not to know her birth mother: 'her Mother dying in Child-bed of her, she was brought up under A Mother In-law' (25). This 'Mother In-law', or stepmother in modern terms, was none other than Mr Moulsworth's third wife Martha, author of the 'Memorandum', but in this case, there is no strong emotional connection evident between stepdaughter and stepmother; Elizabeth, we are told, 'Payed all Filiall obedience' to Martha (25), a polite phrase that suggests an acceptance of duty rather than anything more.

Instead, Martha Eyre presents her mother in terms of her marriage and her own children and grandchildren. Elizabeth, she tells us, 'was Marryed uery Young, to this Lady Lucys Youngest Son...She was his Wife Fifty Six Year, and A Mother to Nine Children; whereof only Tow [two] Daughters Suruiued her, the loss of her Children, Especially Three of *them*, Two Sons Men and One Daughter, who left Thirteen Children, ware uery great Afflictions to her; Tho she bore them with most becomeng Christian Patiance'. Eyre's account of her mother focuses almost entirely on her final years. After her fifty-six-year marriage, Elizabeth Lucy 'Buryed the best of Husbands'. During his final illness, she was inseparable from him: 'he lay some time Sick; she neuer stired from him, and tho she was uery Ill herself, would not be preswaded on to remoue, but lay in the Bed with him, til it was doubtfull whose Glass would First be out'. In bed with her husband when he died, Elizabeth 'Lay at least Four Hours by him after he was Dead', forbidding the attendants to cover his face; 'her whole Life had ben A Preparation to *that* great Work of Dying' (27, 28).

Eyre recounts her mother's final days in great and touching detail, through to the sudden end:

> she waked, stil desired to Rise; at lenght [*sic*] her Bodice ware brought her; she raised herself in the Bed, and sent *them* on; but grew A littel Faint, so thay layed her back upon her Pillow, and she recouered, and said, sure no Person euer had so weak A Back; She was preualed on not to Rise. Aboute seuen of the Clock she called her Children, gaue them her Blessing, and dismissed them: *then* bid her Woman draw the Curtane of her Bed, she kneeling withen the Curtanes, found she fetched her Breath A littel shorter then ordnary; I Droped some Palsy Watter on Crumbs of Bread, and brought to her; she put it away with her hand, but teling her what it was, and *that* she had promised the *Doctor* to take it, she took the Spoon in her hand and swallowed *them* down; *then* she desired to be turned: Turn me says she for A littel while; fetching her breath Louder *than* ordnary, her Woman Asked her how she did, she said A littel Pain in my Stomack, and immediately Dyed. (36–7)

She was, concludes Eyre, 'the Best Daughter, Wife, Mother, Mistress, Freind, and what Crowned all the rest, the most Exemplary Christian whose Charity was diffusiue, and whilst she Cherished the Body, improued the Soul' (38).

The copying out together of these two lives into a single manuscript makes a connection between them that is, in reality, almost circumstantial. We have Elizabeth Lucy's 'Acount' of Constance Lucy because Elizabeth presumably kept a copy, which was later copied out by her daughter Martha Eyre. It therefore becomes incorporated into a Lucy/Eyre family document, passed from mother to daughter. But that was not the stated intention behind Elizabeth Lucy's writing. The title declares that the 'Acount' was 'write to a pertickular friend of hers, Mrs. Moore', and the text elaborates that chief among Constance Lucy's consolations was '*that* she had *the* Loue and Friendship of so many Worthy and Religious Freinds; and not without Admireation *that* now in her declineing Time (as she Called it) she had found your Exellent self A Friend, whome she did realy call the Friend, as such she had published her Estemation of you: in her Will' (10–11). A marginal note reiterates that the 'Exellent self' to whom the text is addressed is 'Mrs Moor', and Constance Lucy's will indeed singles out a Mistress Moore. On 16 May 1635, she writes,

Item I doe giue to my deere freind that truly religious and worthie gentlewooman M*istris* Marie Moore, six of my trenchard*es* desiringe that she will continually vse them for herself to cutt vpon as a remembrance of her whoe in her life time did both loue and honor her And I doe giue vnto her alsoe my Clock of my chamber And I desire my children all to acknowledge my obligacion vnto her.[31]

On 3 May 1636, in failing health—'Excuse my bad writeing my sight is soe bad'—Lady Lucy returns to the same bequest, elaborating some of the details:

I will this to be annexed to the schedule of my will, I doe giue to that discreete and truly religious gentlewoman my sister M*istris* Mary Moore six of my greate trencher plates of silver that hath my armes graven vpon with a littell gold salte [i.e. salt-cellar], and a knyfe with a gould handle vpon both which her armes and myne are engraven I desire her to vse continually if there be noe cause to the contrary, in remembrance of her whoe affectionately loved her person, and vnfainedly honored her many vertues and shall doe, acknowledging a great obligacion to her many waies, I also giue her my Chamber Clock, with the [*blank*] that hath something written vpon it…[32]

This bequest raises several questions. Who is this Mistress Marie Moore? Why does Constance Lucy refer to her as 'my sister'? She is not a biological or a step-sister, since Constance Kingsmill was an only child. She is not a sister-in-law by marriage, since Constance's husband Thomas Lucy had only a sister. It would seem, then, that the sisterhood is affective rather than legal. But why then are Constance Lucy's arms engraven with Marie Moore's in gold on the handle of a knife? Beyond the intrinsic value of the items, the bequest—trencher plates, a salt cellar, a knife, a chamber clock—speaks to a domestic scene of a shared table and a shared chamber: Marie Moore is urged to 'vse them for herself to cutt vpon as a remembrance' of Constance Lucy. What is the 'great obligacion to her many waies' that Constance Lucy feels? And how would her children 'acknowledge my obligacion vnto her'?

Perhaps that obligation was acknowledged by one of those children, Elizabeth Lucy, in writing the 'Acount'.[33] Her life of Constance Lucy depicts only in passing a daughter and wife: she is more importantly a ward, a mother, a stepmother, a mother-in-law, and a friend—a woman for whom blood lineage is less important than the affective affinities she creates in the households in which she lives.

Martha Moulsworth, Widdowe

With Constance Lucy's life in mind, we can take another look at Martha Moulsworth's 'Memorandum'. As Martha Eyre tells us, Martha Moulsworth was the stepmother to Elizabeth Moulsworth Lucy, so she experienced the kind of in-law relationships in which Constance was so invested—but no stepchildren are mentioned in her verse. Yet, viewed through the evidence of other archival documents, Martha Moulsworth's life turns out to be very different from the one she outlines in the 'Memorandum', where she presents herself as little more than the daughter of a man named Dorset, and the wife of three other men. To see Moulsworth that way is to miss the third and final page in her life—as she titles the poem, this is 'The Memorandum of Martha Moulsworth, *Widdowe*'. Having enumerated her husbands, she concludes the poem: 'But in the meantime this must be my care | of knittinge here a fourth knott to beware'; citing Ecclesiastes 4:12 ('A threefold cord though hardly yet is broken'), she asks 'whie should I | then putt my Widowehood in jeopardy?' The 'Memorandum' ends with a sly note that Moulsworth knows she cannot do better: 'the Virgins life is gold, as Clarks vs tell | the Widowes siluar, I loue siluar well'. Moulsworth lived the silver life for another fourteen years after writing her 'Memorandum', and the evidence of her existence during that period—from her will, and the funeral sermon penned by her old friend Thomas Hassell—presents a distinctly different version of Martha Moulsworth, widow.

According to Moulsworth, her father not only raised her 'in godlie pietie | In modest chearefullnes, & sad sobrietie', but also 'Beyond my sex & kind | he did with learning Lattin decke mind [*sic*]'. In truth, however, Robert Dorset died on 29 May 1580, when Martha was two and a half years old, so any instruction he could have given her in Latin would have been severely limited; her widowed mother (another Martha) died probably early in 1581, leaving Martha and her brother Robert to be raised by her maternal grandmother, Helen, and Helen's husband Ralph Johnson until they reached the age of maturity (twenty-one).[34] In his funeral sermon for Moulsworth, Thomas Hassell noted that since she was 'left as an Orphane, to the care of others / (her parents dijing, whilst shee was yongue)', 'shee receiued the benefitt of her Education from others'—and that, in effect, she returned the favour by educating those who were not her own offspring: 'so shee thankfully communicated the same blessing to those, who beinge not her owne, were by mariage of their fathers committed to her tuition'.[35] Her will supports this image of a Martha Moulsworth fully immersed in complex networks of kinship and friendship.[36] In addition to legacies to children and grandchildren of various kinsmen and cousins,[37] she is still tightly linked to relatives and connections from her three marriages: 'to

William Pryn of Lincolnes Inn…hee being my husband Pryns godson', harking back to her first marriage (this being the Puritan William Prynne who 'lost his ears for defying king and bishops');[38] and 'I give to my daughter in law Elizabeth Lucey my gold ring with five Diamonds in itt, and to Martha her daughter my greate chaine of gold' (that is, her stepdaughter from her third marriage, Elizabeth Moulsworth Lucy, and Elizabeth's daughter Martha, later Martha Eyre, the author of the life of Elizabeth Lucy).[39]

But the strongest relationship is the one Martha has with her executrix, Elizabeth Rawdon—her stepdaughter by her second marriage to Thorowgood—and with Rawdon's children Marmaduke, Bevill, Robert, and Martha, her grandson Marmaduke, and her son-in-law Edmond Forster and his two daughters, Elizabeth and Martha. In the middle of her will, Moulsworth takes time to explain why she has selected Elizabeth Rawdon to inherit so much of her estate:

> And I doe hereby intimate declare and publishe that the reasons which doe enduce and cause mee to be so liberall and beneficiall vnto my said daughter in lawe Rowdon, and to her children, and grandchildren before named in bestoweing the most parte of my estate on them, and giveing my inheritance as aforesaid are as followeth That Thomas Thorowgood my late deceased husband, and ffather of the said Dame Elizabeth Rawdon left mee a plentifull estate of chattles and lands and other hereditaments, which I have enioyed thees manie yeares, And for that the said Dame Elizabeth and her said children, and grandchildren have ever bene loveing and kinde vnto mee and allwaise diligent & carefull of mee both in sicknes and in health, in soe much that shee and they have gayned and deserve my love, and I doe love her the said Dame Elizabeth as if shee were my owne child, and I love the said children, and grandchildren as if they were my owne.[40]

Partly, then, it is as repayment for the financial security Martha has enjoyed from the Thorowgood family; but primarily it is for the love, kindness, diligence, and care shown towards her by Elizabeth, her children, and grandchildren, whom she loves as if they were her own children and grandchildren.

The intimate relationship between Moulsworth and the Rawdons is given physical form in various manuscript documents. When Martha Moulsworth died in 1648, a copy of her funeral sermon by Thomas Hassell, vicar of Amwell parish for fifty-nine years, was presented to Elizabeth Rawdon. It occupies the second half of the manuscript in which it survives—the first half is given over to John Joanes's sermon commemorating Marmaduke Rawdon, Elizabeth's husband, a prominent London merchant and royalist, who died a few months earlier (28 April 1646).[41] In his dedication, Hassell laments that 'The two principall pillours of these two Houses are fallen both together…Their bodyes are reposed in a smale parcell of ground; And their memorye recorded into this little Manuell'.[42] If we take this literally, then it would seem that Moulsworth was buried alongside her stepdaughter's husband.

This *post mortem* closeness was also evident during the lives of Moulsworth and Rawdon, for the manuscript that contains the only known copy of Martha's autobiographical poem was a miscellany kept by Marmaduke Rawdon. Rawdon, or more likely a secretary, used the volume to compile texts dealing with London, parliament, and public offices, as well as more topical pieces such as the 1629 Star Chamber action against various luminaries for seditious discourse against King Charles; an incomplete copy of Sir Francis Vere's *Battle of Newport*; and 'The true Coppies of all the gentlemen bearing Armes in the Artillarie Garden taken out of the Roule deliuered to my Mr. Captayne Marmaduke Rawdon' (1631). There is also a copy of a letter from Rawdon to all the king's public officers guaranteeing protection against its bearer, Richard Swinarton.[43] Martha Moulsworth's contribution might seem out of place in this company, but its presence bears witness to her assured place in the Rawdon household.

By contrast, the life of Constance Lucy, specifically written for her friend Marie Moore, has survived through the Lucy family line. As we have seen, what we now have at the Folger is a copy, by Elizabeth Lucy's daughter Martha Eyre. In 1821, that volume was in the possession of the Salisbury judge, Deputy Recorder, and local historian Robert Benson, who 'descends from the Lucys', according to the antiquary Joseph Hunter, who was lent the manuscript by Benson around that time.[44] As if to re-place the life in its proper archive, back with the Lucy family, Benson made a copy for Sir George Lucy in 1831, a copy that now survives in the Warwickshire County Record Office.[45] This kind of archival reappropriation should give us pause when dealing with life-writings, and especially those by women: are we seeing a document in the form and place its author intended? or have multiple processes of copying, filing, and archiving served to obscure that intention? While many later readers seem to want to keep Constance Lucy as a wife, a mother, and a grandmother—and to ensure that her 'Life' 'descends from the Lucys', Elizabeth Lucy was much more concerned to present Constance Lucy as a ward, a stepmother, a mother-in-law, and finally as a friend to Marie Moore.

11

The Collected Lives of Samuel Clarke

In the afternoon of 4 February 1635, John Carter was buried. Eighty-one years old at his death, Carter was one of the last of Richard Rogers's generation, educated at Clare College, Cambridge under such men as Laurence Chaderton and Ezekiel Culverwell, before going on to preach at Bramford and then Belstead in Suffolk. Among the 'great confluence from all parts thereabouts', Richard Rogers's stepson, 'Old Mr. *Samuel Ward*, that famous Divine, and the glory of *Ipswich*, came to the Funerall, brought a mourning Gowne with him, and offered very respectively to Preach his funerall Sermon'. But Carter's son and daughter declined the offer, citing their father's injunction 'that no Sermon should be at his buryall. For, sayd he, it will give occasion to speak some good of me that I deserve not, and so false things will be uttered in the Pulpit.' Ward acquiesced to their wishes on the day, but the following Friday, back in his home parish, he delivered a funeral sermon for John Carter, 'to the great satisfaction of the whole Auditory'.[1]

Despite his insistence that his father should have no funeral sermon, some eighteen years later John Carter Jr. decided to raise his own memorial: a life of his father that he published as *The Tomb-Stone, or, a broken and imperfect monument, of that worthy man (who was just and perfect in his generations;) Mr John Carter*. The 'Life' itself is what had become by 1653 the standard anecdotal biography of a godly man, but Carter prints a more remarkable document among the prefatory materials: a letter 'To his Reverend Brother, and Fellow-Labourer in the Lords *Uineyard*, Mr. *Samuel Clark*, Pastor of *Bennet Fink*, London'. Carter admits that he does not know Clarke—'I never saw your face, otherwise then in the *Frontispice* of your learned Bookes'—but he has a strong sense of what Clarke does: 'you cease not to shew kindnesse to the living, and to the dead. To the living; by your preaching and Ministry, you make Saints daily. To the dead Saints you shew kindnesse, by perpetuating their Names, to their honours, and the good of many.'[2] The 'learned Bookes' of 'dead Saints' to which

Carter refers are four collections of lives that Clarke had published since 1650, specializing variously in the Church 'fathers, and other learned men', 'Christian emperors, kings, and soveraign princes', 'Christians of an inferiour rank', and, centrally, divines: 'famous divines', 'sundry modern divines', and 'our English divines'.[3] It was the first of these volumes, published in 1650, that most inspired Carter. As he writes to Clarke,

> In your first part of *the marrow of Ecclesiasticall History,* We had information, that you did resolve to add a second part; and to put in the Lives of such godly Divines, and others, as were eminent in these latter times, if you were furnished with faithfull information. Hereupon, divers did set upon me with very great importunity, to write the life of my deare Father, and to send it up to you. Truely, Worthy Sir! I was desirous of the thing, but durst not undertake the work: I was sensible of mine own weaknesse; and also that his sayings, and doings had so far slipped the memories of this Generation, that I should have brought to light such an imperfect thing, as rather would have been a blemish to so eminent a Saint, then an honour.

But after setting the task aside as impossible, Carter had very recently reconsidered:

> Some few daies since, I went about to make a new Diary for my selfe. I was desirous in the first place, to set down some passages of my Father, for mine own satisfaction, and use. I began so; and before I was aware, it amounted to so much, as I thought better that published, then nothing at all: and at the last my Spirit grew restlesse; I could not satisfie my selfe, till I had digested it into some order, and made it publike. And now, Sir, here it is; I present it to your judicious view: accept it in good part from a meer stranger. Because it was so short, therefore I joyned it to a weak and unworthy piece of mine own, to make it a Book.

Despite bolstering the 'Life' with one of his own sermons, Carter is unsure of the lasting power of this book, and so he turns to Clarke:

> My humble request to you, worthy Sir, is this, that (though I slipped the last opportunity, yet) if you shall set forth any more lives; or if you shall have a new Impression of any of the former: that you would extract so much of my precious Fathers life, as you shal judge fit, and place it where you please, in your *Ecclesiasticall* History. Your Monuments will bee lasting in after ages, when my poore *Pamphlet* will bee worne out with time.[4]

Carter had to wait nine years, but his humble request was answered: Clarke included the life of his father in his *A Collection of the Lives of Ten Eminent Divines* in 1662, where John Carter headed the list of recently deceased 'ministers, and others'.[5]

For the younger John Carter in 1653, it was not enough simply to remember his father in print. He was inspired more by the idea of his father being commemorated as part of something bigger—physically so, bound not in a 'poore Pamphlet' that will 'bee worne out with time', but in a solid book that 'will bee lasting in after ages'; but also metaphorically so, inside a 'Collection' of 'eminent divines', which would pass down to posterity. In so doing, Carter was sensing a new direction for life-writing that took hold during the 1650s: the preservation of the memory of individuals as a new collective entity, a new community.

Samuel Clarke: A Life in Print

Of the various men who published collections of lives in the second half of the seventeenth century—a list that would include Thomas Fuller, Izaak Walton, and Anthony Wood, among others—none was as prolific as Samuel Clarke. From early 1650 to his death in 1683, Clarke published an astonishing number of volumes of collected lives—in addition to many stand-alone lives. To explain the particular impact of Clarke's collections, I turn to his attempt to write his own life. In November 1660 Clarke penned what he titled, typically enough for a minister, 'A Brief Narrative of my Life, and of the most remarkable Acts of Gods Providence in guiding and governing of the same'. But the form that most of this 'Narrative' takes departed from the norm:

> About the year 1646. I published my first Book of Examples; which then contained but 12, or 14 sheets.
>
> *Anno* 1649. I published my first Parts of the Marrow of Ecclesiastical History, which contained but 63 sheets.
>
> *Anno* 1650. I contained my second Part of the Marrow of Ecclesiastical History, which contained 44 sheets.
>
> *Anno* 1651. I published my General Martyrology, which contained about 140 sheets.
>
> *Anno* 1652. I published my English Martyrology, which contained above 100 sheets.
>
> *Anno* 1654. I published again my first Part of the Marrow of Ecclesiastical History, much enlarged, to above 120 sheets in a Pica Letter.
>
> *Anno* 1655. I published my Mirror the second time, enlarged to 42 sheets of large Paper.
>
> *Anno* 1657. I published my Mirror the third time, enlarged to 240 sheets.
>
> *Anno* 1659. I published my first Part of Cases of Consciences, containing 144 sheets.
>
> *Anno* 1660. I published my General Martyrology, enlarged to above 100 sheets.
>
> Besides these greater, I was one of the four Ministers that made the *Jus Divinum regiminis Eclesiastici*; which was Printed three times, and enlarged.
>
> Also Printed a Sermon, which I Preached at our first *Warwick-shire* Feast.
>
> Another Sermon which I preached at the Funeral of Mr. *Tho. Beuley*.
>
> Another Book against Toleration, which I called Golden Apples.
>
> The Life of *Tamerlane*.
>
> A Sheet in defence of Tythes.

> All these contained above a Thousand Sheets; all which I wrote with my own hand, and was through God's mercy enabled thereunto, notwithstanding all my Ministerial employments, private and publick, Blessed be his Name for it.
>
> I have besides at this time, *November* 1660. above 300 sheets ready for the Press.[6]

At first glance, this seems nothing more than the list of works that John Bale appended to each of his short bio-bibliographies of English writers. But it is not strictly a list of writings: it is a list of Clarke's printed publications. Although he proudly boasts that he 'wrote with my own hand' all the works here listed, the chronology is strictly pegged to when he 'published' or 'printed' those works; the books are described not in terms of a word-count but in terms of the number and size of sheets of paper on which each was printed—or even, in the case of his 1654 volume, by the type employed ('a Pica Letter'). The provenance of this 'Brief Narrative' itself is telling: it was not willed to Clarke's children, but 'found in his Study' by his publisher, and printed, so he claimed, 'for the private information and edification of his Children'.[7] In short, Clarke's autobiography is that of a man *in print*, an author who understands and records his writings through the material form of their print publication, a man whose life is printed publicly before it can be read privately by his children.

As Clarke records, his first collection of lives appeared in 1649—in fact, January 1649/50—with the publication of *The Marrow of Ecclesiastical Historie*, which marrow he found 'conteined in the lives of the fathers, and other learned men, and famous divines, which have flourished in the Church since Christ's time, to this present age'. The *Marrow* is a substantial volume that confidently trumpets its own importance, with an endorsement from the licenser of books on divinity, Edmund Calamy, and congratulatory verse (albeit of woeful quality) provided by London ministers John Fuller and William Jenkyn, and Clarke's two sons Samuel and John, then both at Pembroke Hall in Cambridge. Interestingly, most of these contributors seem to believe the book will be called 'Lives' or 'Book of Lives'. His son John writes: 'How! *Lives*! They're dead. No: death they did evade | By their good *Lives*, which them immortal made...since good Lives are in this book so rife, | I make no doubt to call't a Book of Life.' The selling-point is not the novelty of the materials, but the fact that the volume brings them together: Clarke claims that readers 'shall finde gathered into one book those things which before laie scattered in manie...Here they shall have contracted into one little volume the substance of that, which if it had been translated, or transcribed according to the Originals would have filled manie such books as this, and yet (as I suppose) nothing of worth or weight omitted'—or as his son and namesake Samuel puts it, 'Contracted worth! Much in a little space: | Tis *Homer's Iliads* in a Nut-shel case'; 'Here's manie Saints; one Book: thus Schools do tell | *Ten thousand Angels in one Point may dwel*'.[8]

Why the fanfare? For decades now, English readers had relied on John Foxe for Protestant biography: continually revised and republished, the *Actes and Monuments* cast its huge shadow over any attempt to produce a new collection of life-writing. As Patrick Collinson put it, 'for the three generations which intervened between the Elizabethan settlement and the puritan commonwealth the bible and Foxe between them entirely satisfied the demand for edifying biographical history. Foxe was their Plutarch. He was read not once but repeatedly, and devotionally.'[9] Among the casualties of Foxe's success was Foxe himself. Around 1611, his son Simeon wrote a memoir of his father in which he lamented the strange lack of biographies of Foxe and others: 'Few are found in this age to write the lives of those illustrious men with whom our lands abounds. I am sorry for this. I have always thought it unfair to rob of their future memory these great men whose labours have won for us the blessings we enjoy.'[10] It was not until 1641 that the life of Foxe reached print, prefacing the second volume of a new edition of his own *Actes and Monuments*, over half a century after his death.[11]

True enough, since Foxe there had been attempts to produce alternative 'edifying biographical history', but they tended to be institutional in nature. Archbishop of Canterbury Matthew Parker, for example, presided over the 1571 publication of a set of Latin lives of the archbishops of Canterbury.[12] In 1601, Bishop Francis Godwin—now better known for his proto-science fiction *The Man in the Moon*—published a *Catalogue of the Bishops of England*, which worked through the seventy-two archbishops of Canterbury from Augustine to the present incumbent John Whitgift, before doing the same for each bishopric; the archdiocese of York followed. In his epistle to the reader, Godwin admitted that 'My collections the one way (I meane concerning matters ecclesiasticall) can adde nothing vnto that large and painefull worke of Master *Foxe*'.[13] The dullness of Godwin's efforts was only rendered more vivid by a 'supplie or addicion to the catalogue of bishops to the yeare 1608' presented by the courtier Sir John Harington to Prince Henry: a copy of Godwin's *Catalogue* adorned with extensive annotations in Harington's hand, and eighty-eight extra leaves where Harington helpfully 'supplied' what he felt Godwin—less worldly, more inhibited—had missed.[14] With his secular, courtly, private licence, Harington was able to poke some mildly scurrilous fun at living clerics.

From another tradition—and printed abroad, in St Omer—came John Wilson's *English Martyrologe* in 1608, the first printed collection devoted to British Catholic saints' lives; the Benedictine Jerome Porter produced *The Flowers of the Liues of the Most Renowned Saincts of the Three Kingdoms* in 1632.[15] The direct precedents to Clarke's volume also came from the Continent, which witnessed a steady procession of collections of lives, predominantly of Protestant churchmen. In 1597, the press of Theodor de Bry produced *Icones*, by the French antiquary Jean-Jacques

Boissard, in which each biography was matched by a full-page portrait.[16] Similarly illustrated (with previously published engravings by Hendrik Hondius), Jacobus Verheiden's 1602 catalogue of leading opponents of the Roman Antichrist included four Britons: John Wyclif, Thomas Cranmer, the Scot John Knox, and John Bale (whose entry was largely lifted from his own 1558 *Catalogus*).[17] Heidelberg scholar Melchior Adam produced multiple volumes of biographies between 1610 and 1620, covering German philosophers, German theologians, foreign theologians, jurists and politicans, and medical specialists,[18] while Joannes Meursius' *Athenæ Batavæ* (1625) contained short lives of Leiden worthies, largely from the university.[19]

In 1620, Henry Holland produced the first volume of this type to concentrate on English subjects, and to be printed partly in London—although, like its continental counterparts, it was written in Latin. The two-volume *Herοologia Anglica* [*History of English Heroes*] featured 'the most illustrious and learned Englishmen' from 1500 to 1620, and included sixty-five portraits: its first volume covered royals, aristocrats, politicians, and adventurers; the second a range of Protestant divines.[20] (Shortly before Holland's *Heroologia* appeared, Ben Jonson allegedly told William Drummond of Hawthornden that 'he had ane intention to perfect ane Epick Poeme intitled Heroologia of the Worthies of his Country, rowsed by fame, and was to dedicate it to his Country, it is all in Couplets, for he detesteth all other Rimes';[21] sadly, this epic life-writing verse never appeared.) It was only in the last years of Charles I's reign that this genre—with its engraved portrait, character sketch, and list of writings of each subject—was englished, and even then it was clearly indebted to its continental forebears. Donald Lupton's *The History of the Moderne Protestant Divines* (1637), devoted to the lives of 'great Antagonists *to the* Roman cause', was in fact a selection and translation of lives from the collections by Verheiden (for the 'Out-landish Writers') and Holland (for the 'English Writers'): Lupton believed 'it might bee some profit to our times to make them speake English'. The illustrations, Lupton makes clear, are also second-hand, inspired by Albrecht Durer and Hendrik Hondius, but redone 'in lesser Plates, for the profit of the Buyer'.[22]

With *The Marrow of Ecclesiastical Historie*, Clarke was attempting a history of the English Protestant Church that was not dependent on martyrs. Another budding life-writer, Thomas Fuller, soon realized its potential. Fuller had already enjoyed considerable success with his *The Holy State* (1642), a collection of 'characters'—sketches of social types, a genre popularized by Sir Thomas Overbury, among others—paired with short biographies of historical exemplars: 'The good Wife' was explained through the life of Augustine's mother Monica; 'The good Husband' through the life of Abraham; 'The good Servant' through the life of Abraham's steward Eliezer, and so on. Some of the examples were more recent: 'The Controversiall Divine' was figured by Dr William Whitaker; 'The generall Artist' by Julius Scaliger;

'The faithfull Minister' by William Perkins; and 'The good Sea-Captain' by Sir Francis Drake. Perhaps the most entertaining sequence came in the fifth book, covering 'The Profane State', where 'the Harlot' was cast as Joan, Queen of Naples; 'the Witch' as Joan of Arc; and 'the Atheist' as Cesare Borgia. But the pairing of character and real-life figure often proved an awkward fit: while Fuller's archetypal 'Harlot' is barren, whorish, poverty-ridden, and syphilitic, the fourteenth-century Joan[na], Queen of Naples turns out to be a canny political player who survives political turmoil by marrying four times.[23]

Now Fuller saw a more effective format in Clarke's collection. The title page of his anonymously published 1651 *Abel Redevivus: or, The dead yet speaking. The lives and deaths of the modern divines* claimed that the volume was 'Written by severall able and learned Men whose names ye shall finde in the Epistle to the Reader', and indeed the Epistle, signed by Fuller, attributed lives to Daniel Featley, Thomas Gataker, Peter Smith, William Bedell, bishop of Kilmore, and Henry Isaacson, claiming that 'my meannesse wrote' several of the others, while confessing that 'The rest the Stationer got transcribed out of Mr *Holland* and other Authors'.[24] But in admitting these appropriations, Fuller neglected to mention other, more extensive debts—debts that were quickly noticed by Samuel Clarke. In his next publication, *A Generall Martyrologie*, Clarke devoted an entire page to a mere six lines of text:

> There is lately come forth a Book called *Abel Redivivus*, or *The Lives of Modern Divines*, wherein there are threescore and nine Lives Printed *verbatim* out of my first Part of *The Marrow of Ecclesiastical History*, and divers more, with very little variation; which I thought fit to give the Reader notice of, that so he may not be deceived in buying the same thing twice.[25]

Clarke's helpful tip to the reader is, of course, in reality a direct attack on the editor of *Abel Redivivus* for plagiarizing sixty-nine of his lives. In the posthumously published *History of the Worthies of England*, Fuller admitted reading Clarke's works, but continued to deny any further indebtedness:

> I say Mr. *Clark* whose Books of our *modern Divines* I have perused, as *Travellers* by the *Levitical Law* were permitted to pass thorow other *mens Vineyards*. For they must eat their fill on conditions they put no Grapes up in their Vessels. I have bene satisfied with reading his works, and informed my self in Places and Dates of some mens *births* and *deaths*. But never did nor will (whatever hath been said of me, or done by others) incorporate any considerable quantity of his Works in my own, detesting such *Felony*, God having given me (be it spoken with thanks to him, and humility to man) plenty of my own, without being *plagiary* to any Author whatsoever.[26]

Nevertheless, the charge of plagiarism evidently touched Fuller, who returned to it later in the volume: 'I say Master *Samuel Clark*, with whose pen mine never did, nor shall *interfere*. Indeed as the flocks of *Jacob* were distanced *three days journeys* from those of *Laban*, so (to prevent *voluntary* or *casuall commixtures*) our *styles* are set more then a *Months* journey asunder.'[27]

Not that *The Marrow of Ecclesiastical Historie* was wholly a work of original scholarship itself. Clarke included in his collection 'A Catalogue of the Authors out of which these Lives were collected', acknowledging how some fifteen lives were lifted from Foxe's *Actes and Monuments*;[28] those of 'the *Germane, French, Switzers, &c.* Divines' had been 'collected out of the Continental collections' by Adam, Boissard, Holland, Verheiden, and Meursius; and 'Som of the *English* out of Dr *Holland's Horologia* [*sic*] *Anglicana*'. Nine of the lives had been published individually: Bernard Gilpin's life is by his former student George Carleton;[29] John Jewel's life had appeared 'before his *Apologie*', a 1609 English redaction by Daniel Featley of Laurence Humphrey's earlier Latin life;[30] William Whitaker's life is credited to 'Dr Humphrede', presumably Laurence Humphrey; John Foxe's life is by his son Simeon, published in 1641;[31] Andrew Willet's life is by Peter Smith, added to a posthumous edition of his *Synopsis Papismi*;[32] that of William Cowper, bishop of Galloway, is his autobiography, first published in 1619 and then prefixed to his 1623 *Workes*;[33] the German theologian David Pareus's life was published by his son Johann Philipp in 1633, and later prefixed to his 1647 *Opera*;[34] Robert Bolton's is drawn from the 'Life and death of Mr. Bolton' prefixed to his former student Edward Bagshaw's 1632 edition of Bolton's 'worke of the foure laste things';[35] William Whately's is from his funeral sermon by Henry Scudder.[36] Going beyond reprinting, Clarke explains that 'Some things I have added to divers these Lives which I met with in other good Autors'.[37] Among the good authors Clarke does *not* name is Thomas Fuller, from whose earlier work *The Holy State* his life of William Perkins was largely drawn, nor does he name Donald Lupton, whose *The History of the Moderne Protestant Divines* (1637) also contributed to the *Marrow*'s text and images.

What the row between Fuller and Clarke exposes is the fact that, despite their title-page billing, these men were not in fact creating the vast majority of their materials: they were collecting and compiling existing texts. The generic range of these 'lives'—discrete biographies, 'lives' appended to works, funeral sermons, autobiographies—suggests the miscellaneity that Clarke is drawing on. But in pulling them together in a volume headed by his name and image, Clarke is laying claim to a very particular grouping of men and women.

Gathering Relations

While Clarke's name loomed large over his collection, he expected his compilation to be both collaborative and accretive. In his first collection, he had John Wall and Simeon Ashe, with whom he had studied under Thomas Hooker at Emmanuel

College, Cambridge, call for further materials. Wall and Ashe informed the reader that Clarke 'resolv's (if God give life and health) to add a second part, unto this now published': so, 'if anie one will bee pleased to furnish him, with full and faithfull relations, of the godlie life and death, of anie their Christian friends (whether Ministers, or others) who have been eminent in their daies, their Names may hereby bee perpetuated, unto the service of posteritie'–it was this appeal that first attracted the attention of John Carter.[38]

But a call for 'Gods Worthies' is hardly neutral. In making the first call, Wall and Ashe took the opportunity to start the bidding with a list of prominent nonconformists of whom they 'might have given in a true, though short Character', starting with Richard Rogers and his friend Ezekiel Culverwell, and including John Bruen's biographer William Hinde and such recently deceased figures as Julines Herring, John Dod, and William Rathband.[39] Evidently aware that their wish list might be controversial, Wall and Ashe assure the reader that these men 'lived, and died Non- conformists[,] yet they alwaies kept a due distance from *Brownistical* separation, and were zealously affected towards the *Presbyterial* Government of the Church, as the works of som of them do sufficiently witness'.[40] In time, they got their wish: most (but not all) of Wall and Ashe's *desiderata* were included in Clarke's volumes.

Even in the materials that were written specifically for them, the various editions of *Lives* were a collective endeavour. While most of these entries are unsigned, and therefore presumably the work of Clarke himself, a few are credited to others. The life of Richard Rothwell 'was drawn up by my reverend friend Master *Stanley Gower* of Dorchester'.[41] Clarke drafted a brief life of John Preston, but was happy to replace it with a much fuller account 'written by my Revrrend [*sic*] friend, Master *Thomas Ball* of *Northampton*'.[42] In memorializing the master of Trinity College, Cambridge, Dr Thomas Hill (d. 1653), Clarke notes that 'He was a great friend to the publication of the lives of godly and eminent Masters, and Christians, and assisting to me in procuring information concerning the Lives of some of those Worthies whom I have formerly printed'.[43] Individual entries could also be collaboratively written. In piecing together the life of the Staffordshire puritan minister John Ball (d. 1640), one of the men that Wall and Ashe wanted to commemorate, Clarke noted that

> The materials of this Narrative...were received from these Ministers of the Gospel, and men of known integrity (*viz.* Master *Iohn Tailor* of *Checkley* in *Staffordshire*, (who was his Countryman and of his most ancient acquaintance.) Master *Thomas Langley* of *Middlewich* in *Cheshire*, (who besides his former intimatenesse, continued under his Ministry above five years, he being taken off from the exercise of his own Ministry by Episcopal power,) Master *Simeon Ashe* of *Bassy-shaw London*, (who for the space of many years had been his bosome friend,) and from Master *George Crosse* of *Clifton* in *Stafford-shire*, (who daily conversed with him for sundry

months, both before, and in the time of his last sicknesse,) who all of them do acknowledge themselves obliged to God, for the spiritual good, gained by their dearly respected, and much honoured friend and brother, who since his death, have been very sensible for their great losse by his removal.[44]

It is notable here that while Ball's 'bosome Friend' Ashe, as his literary executor, brought at least five manuscript treatises by Ball to the press, and provided prefatory materials concerning Ball for two, he chose not to write the life himself.[45] (Including a life of Ball in his *Worthies of England* in 1662, Thomas Fuller seems to have learned his lesson: he made sure to include a marginal note stressing that 'The substance of his Character is taken out of his life written by Mr. *Samuel Clarke*'[46]–ironically enough, since the life is not by Clarke.)

Subsequent volumes repeated the call to add further materials. In 1650, Clarke asserted that 'I intend not... to sit downe here, but to make some further progress in writing the lives of others of Gods Worthies: Wherefore my request is to all such as can furnish me with materials for the continuance of the blessed Memorials of their deceased friends, and for the publick good, and utility of the Church, to send them in to me'.[47] And, when he reprinted John Carter's letter in 1677, Clarke notes 'I have the rather inserted [it] to provoke, and stir up others, who can in this way, revive the memories of the Dead Saints, to do it, which will be a more lasting Monument to them, and far more beneficial, and advantageous to the Church of God, than any sumptuous, and costly Funerals, or Grave-stones whatsoever'.[48] We know that some readers responded, besides John Carter. Including a life of Dr William Gouge (d. 1653), Clarke notes that 'My Reverend Friend Master *Thomas Gouge*, eldest Son to this famous Doctor, desired me to insert this Life, amongst these other Worthies contained in this Volume'.[49] In a letter, the Scottish theologian Robert Baillie urged Clarke to include a life of Robert Boyd, pointing out that 'There is so much, before his Commentarie on the Epistle to the Ephesians [in his Latin works] as will be ground enough for a compleat narrative of his life'–although Baillie had also contacted 'Mr. Dowglass, who, I suppose, against the tyme yow speak of, may have a more perfect narration at yow'. Baillie also put in his plea for a life of 'your sometime good friend Mr. [Alexander] Hendersone, a truely heroick divine, for piety, learning, wisdome, eloquence, humilitie, single life, and every good part, for some yeares the most-eyed man of the three Kingdoms'.[50] (Neither Boyd nor Henderson made it into Clarke's *Lives*.)

Clarke's initial impulse was to celebrate modern divines, especially those with puritan leanings, and the historians who have written on him, notably Patrick Collinson, Jacqueline Eales, and Peter Lake, have rightly stressed that investment.[51] Certainly, his supporters and critics saw him that way. For Oliver Heywood, Clarke was simply the most recent in a canon of godly collectors: 'I do find that the Servants of God have been very careful and critical in Writing the Lives of Eminent Men, as Camerarius wrote the Life of Luther, Junius of Ursin, Beza of Calvin, Antonius Jaius [Faius] of Beza, Josias Simlerus of Peter Martyr, Dr. Humphry of Bp. Jewell, &c. Melchior Adamus hath summed them up together, and Mr. Samuel Clark hath made many Collections.'[52] When Heywood published his *A Narrative of the Holy Life, and Happy Death of*...*Mr. John Angier* (1685), a preface advised those who wished to be ministers to 'read their lives in Mr. *Clarks* Collections...and be ashamed of your selves, and provoked to a holy Emulation in true piety and Zeal; get into a corner, and tremble to see your selves thus outstript, and implore more Grace from Heaven'.[53] By contrast, in 1662, the Anglican Henry Foulis singled out Clarke's collections in his attack on presbyterianism, *The History of the Wicked Plots and Conspiracies of Our Pretended Saints*, saying that 'If we believe every thing in Mr. *Sam. Clarke*'s Story-Books, we shall with him, make wicked men, Saints; Rebels, good Subjects; and Schismaticks, the best Church-men; which, all should desire to be really perform'd, who wish the Honour of his Majesty, Peace of the Church, Prosperity and Happiness of the Nation'.[54]

But Clarke's ambitions went beyond a local confessionalism. As early as 1650, Clarke produced *The Second Part of the Marrow of Ecclesiastical History* featuring 'the lives of Christians of inferiour ranks'; of its eleven subjects, however, most were decidedly not of 'inferiour rank'–Sir John Oldcastle, Lord Cobham; Zisca, 'a noble Bohemian'; Pico della Mirandola, styled here 'John Picus, Earl of Mirandula'; Galeacius Caracciolus, Marquess of Vico; Lady Jane Grey; Sir Philip Sidney; John Harington of Exton; and Philippe de Mornay, sieur du Plessis-Marly. The only two who could claim 'inferiour rank' were the sibling icons of lay piety, John Bruen and Katherine Brettergh, the latter the first in a series of suffering godly women memorialized by Clarke.[55] This rather Catholic taste continued throughout his career, as Clarke published a bewildering selection of lives: of Tamerlane the Great, Gustavus, king of Sweden, Herod, Jesus, Nebuchadnezzar, Alexander, Cyrus, Hannibal, Julius Caesar, Pompey, Sir Francis Drake, William the Conqueror, Edward the Black Prince, Elizabeth I, and his own wife Katherine, in *A Looking Glass for Good Women to Dress Themselves* (1677). These might seem far removed from the church fathers and modern divines for which he is known, but Clarke had a plan for them.

In 1675, he published a new edition of *The Marrow of Ecclesiastical History*, the volume with which he had started his collections. Now the first part contained 'the Life of our Blessed Lord & Saviour Jesus Christ; with The Lives of the Ancient Fathers, School-men, First-Reformers, and Modern Divines'. Clarke noted that, 'If to these Lives the Reader shall please to add the *Martyrologies* twice formerly Printed, and now going to the Press again, together with the Lives at the end thereof, he may find a *Compendium* of the History of the Church from the beginning of the World, especially from the Apostles times to our present Age'. A second part, containing 'The Lives of Christian Emperors, Kings, and Sovereign Princes' as well as 'The Lives of Inferiour Christians, who have lived in these latter Centuries', would show 'what Eminent Emperors, Kings and Princes, God hath raised up in several Ages and Places to be, not only *Nursing-Fathers*, but strenuous Defenders of the Church and Flock of Christ, and Propagators of his Glorious Gospel'. The third part, comprising 'the Lives of many of those, who by their vertue and valor obtained the Sir-name of great' (a handy means of including Tamerlane, Alexander, Pompey, et al.), served to show 'how punctual God hath been in the accomplishment of those Predictions and Prophesies concerning the Rise, Growth, and Ruine of the four *Great Monarchies*, set down in sundry places of the Sacred Scriptures'. And if anyone wondered exactly how a non-Christian 'the great' might fit, Clarke explains that this demonstrates 'how wisely and powerfully He Rules and Over-rules the affairs of the World, even among the Heathen'.[56] Clarke had found a way to cast the whole of world history through the lens of the modern divines he admired so much.

Clarke's Lives: The Legacy

Clarke wrote his last letter to the reader 'From my Study in *Isleworth, March* 25. 1682', proudly noting that 'my former Labours in this kind, have been accepted with the Saints, and in the Church of Christ; which is apparent, for that they have been Printed four times in a few years space, and yet never less than a Thousand at a time'—again evaluating his writing in terms of print-run and number of editions. He signed off with what can only be read as a valediction: 'I am now in the Eighty third year of my Life, and therefore am never like to do more in this kind: but hope that God will raise up some more able person to carry on this so useful a work; and if my Judgment be of any value, these Lives are generally the best that ever I published.'[57]

Clarke died on 25 December of that year, before his final volume was completed. The 1683 *Lives of Sundry Eminent Persons* was seen through the press by his publisher with the help of the author's son, also Samuel Clarke, and the prolific religious writer Richard Baxter. Baxter's letter to the reader is informative. He admits that he hasn't read Clarke's volume itself—although he checked some of the figures whom he knew well, and points out that the volume contains some of his own work ('*John Janewaies* life, and *Joseph Allens* I had a hand in Publishing, and Prefacing heretofore'). It's clear that Clarke published without asking—Baxter even claims that 'I knew not of his Epitomizing my Wives life', but he approves of Clarke's redaction: 'the manner of that tells me he is like to be faithful in the rest'. And he talked Thomas Simmons into including one more addition to the *Lives*: 'I have desired the Book-seller to Reprint the Life of the Countess of *Suffolk*, Daughter to the Earl of *Holland*, written by Bishop *Rainbow*, yet living, as an excellent pattern to Ladies; the Book being not easily to be got.'[58]

Baxter had previously praised collections of lives for their moral value: 'The many Volumes of holy Lives, of antient Docters, Martyrs, and later Divines, Philosophers and others in *Germany, England* and other Lands, have done much good, and are still very useful, and a pleasant and profittable recreation, (O how much better than play-Books and Romances)?'[59] Here, however, he admitted more cautiously that anthologized lives were by no means consistent. '*Melchior Adam* hath done in my judgment very great Service to the Church in his four Volumes, the Lives of the *German* Divines, Philosophers, Lawyers and Physicians: But some he hath done copiously and excellently, and very many (of the three last sort) so exactly as to be next to nothing: And how could he help it? To have made Stories himself had been unworthy a Historian.' Clarke was similar to Adam—'so is it in this case'[60]—and Baxter ventriloquizes a criticism of Clarke's venture:

> Some Enemies deride him for Writing Lives with no more Art: But I take that to be his Commendation; He did not make the Histories, but take them made by faithful acquaintance of the dead: And he was not to patch or paint the dead, nor to add any thing of his own, but to deliver naked truth: some good men say, that many of the Lives of excellent men in his first Book, are short and dry: That's our loss, but none of his fault: If all had done as Mr. *Thomas Ball* did by his Tutor Dr. *Preston*, that defect had been fully satisfied: I was going to get from old *Sam. Hildersham*, some additions to his Father *Arthur's* Life, but his death frustrated me.[61]

Still, despite the variable quality of the lives themselves, Baxter sees the format of Clarke's collections as a model to be emulated—and a possible solution to a dilemma he had recently faced. In 1681, Baxter had published a 'breviate of the life' of his late wife, Margaret, written 'under the power of melting Grief, and therefore perhaps with the less prudent judgment; but not with the less, but the more Truth: For passionate Weakness poureth out all, which greater Prudence may conceal'. Inspired by writing this 'breviate', Baxter had embarked on two more, one of his 'excellent holy Mother-in-law' [stepmother], Mary Hunks Baxter, and the other of 'my old Friend and Housekeeper, *Jane Matthews*', soon adding a fourth, 'a *Breviate* of the Life and Death of that worthy Mother of my Wife, as to the time since I knew her'. But he had been persuaded by the 'Counsel of wise Friends' not to publish these three, and even to jettison much of his wife's life, 'as things which they think that Strangers will not make so great a matter as *Love* and *Nearness* made me do'. Although Baxter was clearly torn, he claimed to be 'convinced by the judgement of my Friends, that publick things are fittest for publick notice...Affection makes us think our own or our Friends affairs to be such, as the world should be affected with: I perceive this weakness, and submit.'[62] Now with Clarke's model he saw a way of preserving these and other lives: 'I have in Funeral Sermons and Epistles described truly many excellent persons, whose Examples would be useful to this depraved Age; were it not for the charge of Printing, I would wish them Bound all together as these be'—the *Lives* in Clarke's 1683 volume—'*viz.*, Mrs. *Bakers* of *Worcester*, Mrs. *Coxes*, Mrs. *Hanmers*, my Wives Mother, Alderman *Ashhursts*, Mr. *Waddesworth*, Mr. *Stubbs*, Mr. *Corbets*, *&c*....'[63] The collection, in other words, permits the inclusion of lives that might not be deemed worthy of individual publication.

Like many of Baxter's good ideas, this one came to nothing. But the influence of Clarke's collections can be seen elsewhere—and often in the works of men who did not share his religious politics. In 1660, William Winstanley brought together forty-seven of *England's Worthies*, 'our English Heroes, the greatest Princes, the most Reverend Cleargy-men, eminent States-men, and valiant Souldiers all deceast', from Constantine the Great to Oliver Cromwell. Five years later, he published *The Local Martyrology*, which included 'Brief catalogues and characters'—short, sometimes single-sentence, sketches of those 'loyal' to the king and those 'dregs of treachery' who betrayed him.[64] In 1661 Clement Barksdale entered the fray, with his *Memorials of Worthy Persons Two Decads*, which sought to commemorate the moderate churchman of 'this blessed *Restauration* of Church and State'. Barksdale published biographies of learned men and one woman (Lady Falkland) of the seventeenth century, drawn out of previously published biographies, autobiographies, 'lives' affixed to works, funeral sermons, materials from John Gauden's recent *Ecclesiae Anglicanae suspiria*, and in one case—Thomas Brandeston, of Barfold—'From Tradition of good hands'. The casual reader might be forgiven for not realizing that the writing was not Barksdale's: as he sheepishly admits, 'Know, that the *Authours* at the end, should have been cited at the beginning of every *Memorial* respectively'. (Even 'at the end', the attribution is not always as accurate as it might be: Izaak Walton's life of John Donne is ascribed to one 'Ierem. Walton'.[65]) By 1663, four 'Decads' had been published, with certain figures (James Ussher, George Herbert) included twice with different versions of their lives. The point is not the life-writing per se, but the claiming of individuals for Barksdale's Church.

After answering Clarke with his *Abel Redivivus*, Thomas Fuller spent his last years working on the posthumously published *History of the Worthies of England* (1662), a massive, county-by-county chorography of England. Whereas William Camden and John Speed had 'discribed the *rooms*' in the house of England, Fuller explained, 'so is it our intention, God willing to discribe the *Furniture* of those *rooms*; such

Eminent Commodities, which every County doth produce, with the Persons of Quality bred therein, and some other observables coincident with the same subject'. In introducing his work, Fuller was disarmingly direct about his reasons for taking on this massive piece of life-writing:

> I propound *five ends* to my self in this Book: First, *To gain some Glory to God.* Secondly, *To preserve the Memories ef the Dead.* Thirdly, *To present Examples to the Living.* Fourthly, *To entertain the Reader with Delight.* And lastly, (which I am not ashamed publickly to profess) *To procure some honest profit to my self.*[66]

The short biographical accounts that Fuller provided were distinguished by their social inclusiveness: as Allan Pritchard puts it, Fuller 'brings in not only courtiers but a court porter, alchemists, theatre people, and many other classes of persons who had previously been ignored by biographers, even a blacksmith'.[67]

Other collections made their focus more specific. During the 1660s, Anthony Wood started work on a remarkable compendium of short lives of those associated with Oxford, although the finished project—the *Athenæ Oxonienses* of 1691—cast its net far wider. In 1667, he took on as a collaborator the antiquarian John Aubrey, who would later embark on his own collections of *Brief Lives* (see Chapter 13). In 1668, David Lloyd published his collection of biographies of Anglicans and Royalist loyalists, under the title *Memoires of the lives, actions, sufferings & deaths of those noble reverend and excellent parsonages that suffered by death, sequestration, decimation, or otherwise, for the Protestant religion and the great principle thereof, allegiance to their soveraigne, in our late intestine wars*, covering over 1,000 lives in over 700 pages.[68] He followed it with two editions of *State-worthies, or, The States-Men and Favourites of England since the Reformation. Their prudence and policies, successes and miscarriages, advancements and falls.*[69] With his *Theatrum Poetarum, or a compleat collection of the poets, especially the most eminent of all ages* (1675), Edward Phillips provided a critical survey of a plethora of writers in Latin, Greek, French, Spanish, Italian, and English. A local focus was provided, again by William Winstanley, who ransacked Fuller's *Worthies* and Phillips's collection to produce *The Lives of the Most Famous English Poets, or the honour of Parnassus* (1687), covering over 200 writers. Four years later, Gerard Langbaine published his *An Account of the English Dramatick Poets* (1691), which provided bibliographies and quotations from the literary works as well as biographical sketches.[70] And Izaak Walton, who had been drafting prefatory lives for authors' works since 1640, first came to publish his collected *Lives* in 1670 (see Chapter 12).

All these writers had learned what John Carter had intuited in 1653: that a life in a collection stood a better chance of survival. In his last letter to the reader, Clarke took the opportunity to respond to an objection that he had evidently heard more than once: 'That many of them [the lives] have been Printed already, and in a more large and copious manner than we find them here'. Clarke answered, "Tis true, and yet I judge it necessary thus to Print them again. For I have observed, that being generally Printed in little Volumes, few of them come to a second Impression, but after a little time, are thrown aside and forgotten; whereas, when many excellent Lives are collected into one or more Volumes, they do continue, and will so do, till Printing shall be no more: Witness *Plutarchs* and *Melchior Adams, &c.* Lives.'[71] And witness now Clarke's *Lives*.

12

Izaak Walton's Lives and Works

Readers of Izaak Walton's *Lives*, as published in 1670 and 1675, are greeted with a polished, handsome book. The title page boasts that these are 'THE LIVES Of Dr. *John Donne*, Sir *Henry Wotton*, Mr. *Richard Hooker*, Mr. *George Herbert*. Written by *IZAAK WALTON*'. The collection is dedicated by Walton to George Morley, bishop of Winchester; Walton explains the book in an 'Epistle to the Reader'; a letter to Walton from Henry King, bishop of Chichester gives his 'Approbation of your Work'; and (in 1675) a lengthy poem praising Walton is contributed by Charles Cotton. Each life is prefaced by an engraved frontispiece of its subject–except Donne, whose portrait is elevated to face the volume's title page.[1] The inclusion of the senior ecclesiastics Morley and King and the poet Cotton serves to underline the choice of subjects for these *Lives*: Donne, Wotton, Hooker, and Herbert are all writers, but they are primarily churchmen–even Wotton, who took orders when he was appointed provost of Eton College.

There are strong links between three of the men: Donne and Wotton were almost lifelong friends; Donne was a close friend of Lady Magdalen Herbert, mother of George; and 'betwixt this *George Herbert* and Dr. *Donne* there was a long and dear friendship, made up by such a Sympathy of inclinations, that they coveted and joyed to be in each others Company' (E4^{v}). Walton moves on the edges of these circles.[2] From 1624, he was one of Donne's parishioners in St Dunstan's, and through Donne he met Wotton; Wotton in turn provided access to the so-called 'Great Tew' circle associated with the Cotswold seat of Lucius Cary, second viscount Falkland, which included Charles Cotton (father and namesake of the poet who contributed to the *Lives*), Gilbert Sheldon, later archbishop of Canterbury, and George Morley, to whom the *Lives* are dedicated, and in whose household Walton lived after the Restoration. Even the ostensible odd man out in the *Lives*, Richard Hooker, who died when Walton was a child, was, with Hugo Grotius, one of the inspirations behind the philosophy of the Great Tew set; it was Sheldon who commissioned

Walton to write the *Life of Hooker*. (This circle was also connected to Walton's fifth life, of Robert Sanderson, bishop of Lincoln, published separately in 1678; Sanderson was close to Morley.[3]) At the end of his *Life of Donne*, Walton hints at this community as he lists Donne's friends: Sir Henry Goodere, Sir Robert Drury, Lady Magdalen Herbert, Sir Henry Wotton, Joseph Hall, bishop of Norwich, Brian Duppa, bishop of Salisbury, and Henry King, bishop of Chichester, describing them as 'men [*sic*], in whom there was such a Commixture of general *Learning*, of natural *Eloquence*, and Christian *Humility*, that they deserve a Commemoration by a pen equal to their own, which none have exceeded. And in this enumeration of his friends, though many must be omitted, yet that man of primitive piety, Mr. *George Herbert* may not' (E4^{r}). These men and women are carefully curated for a post-Restoration readership. As Ian Donaldson has written, 'Charles II's return to England in 1660 initiated a period of intense interest in the chronicling of lives, especially of those who had played a major part in the great political and religious events of the preceding decades, or who now were regarded as significant or aspiring figures within the new society forming under the restored monarchy'.[4] Walton's *Lives* present a roll-call of those now regarded as significant by the restored Church of England, and provide an act of what Jessica Martin has aptly described as 'conformist commemoration'.[5]

The coherence and power of the 1670 and 1675 *Lives*, however, obscure their more piecemeal origins. For these lives had not been thought of as a unit: on occasion, they even appeared without acknowledging Walton as their author. The *Life of Donne* was written to preface the 1640 edition of Donne's *LXXX Sermons*, before being revised several times.[6] The *Life of Wotton* was written to introduce the 1651 edition of Wotton's writings, the *Reliquiae Wottonianae*.[7] The *Life of Hooker* was issued separately in 1665, but by 1666 had become the preface for a new edition of his *Laws of Ecclesiastical Polity*.[8] The *Life of Herbert* similarly existed as an independent piece, but provided a preface for Herbert's *The Temple*.[9] It is only in 1670 that 'Walton's *Lives*' appears, and Walton becomes the authorizing figure of his *Lives*. These are, in reality, *prefatory* lives, lives designed to preface an edition of an author's works. Walton was one of the pioneers of this long-standing subgenre—and also the creator of something entirely novel: a life that came drenched in the works.

How Walton Became a Life-Writer

As he tells it in 1670, Walton was the most reluctant of life-writers. The *Life of Donne* was meant to be written by Donne's friend Sir Henry Wotton, but Wotton died without penning a word; Walton took it on to ensure that Donne's *LXXX Sermons* (1640) were properly prefaced. But that selfless act 'begot a like necessity' of writing another life, 'of his and my ever-honoured friend, Sir *Henry Wotton*': in short, 'I became like those men that enter easily into a *Law-sute*, or a *quarrel*, and having begun, cannot make a fair retreat, and be quiet, when they desire it' (A4^{v}-A5^{r}). Walton had hoped that one of Wotton's 'many surviving friends, some one of higher parts and imployment, had been pleas'd to have commended his to Posterity', but 'since some years are now past, and they have all (I know not why) forborn to do it', Walton was moved by 'gratitude to the memory of my dead friend, and the renewed request of some that still live solicitous to see this duty performed' (G7^{v}). Although persuaded to write the *Life of Wotton*, so that the posthumous *Reliquiae Wottonianae* (1651) would not be Life-less, it was still 'with some distrust of mine own Abilities'. A life of Hooker had already been written—by John Gauden, bishop of Exeter—and published with Hooker's *Works*, but Gilbert Sheldon, the new archbishop of Canterbury, deemed it filled 'with so many dangerous mistakes, both of him and his *Books*' that he commissioned his old friend Walton 'to examine some Circumstances, and then rectifie the Bishops mistakes, by giving the World a fuller and a truer account of *Mr. Hooker* and his *Books*, then that Bishop had done'. Walton's *Life* replaced Gauden's in the 1666 edition (Gauden having helpfully died in the meantime): 'And, let me tell the Reader', insists Walton, 'that till *his Grace* had laid this injunction upon me, I could not admit a thought of any fitness in me to undertake it' (1670, A6^{r}). Only with the *Life of Herbert*, published in 1670, does Walton claim any agency: this life, he is happy to assert, is a 'Free-will-offering…writ, chiefly to please my self' (1675, A5^{v}).

But Walton is being disingenuous. He may not have intended to pen a life of Donne, but he was intimately involved in the planning of that life-writing. Publisher Richard Marriot had indeed commissioned Sir Henry Wotton to write a prefatory life for his edition of Donne's *LXXX Sermons*—the perfect choice, Walton insisted, since between the two men 'there was so mutual a knowledge, and such a friendship contracted in their Youth, as nothing but death could force a separation' (1675, B4^{v}-B5^{r}). But Walton was already involved in the volume, apparently in some editorial capacity, writing to Wotton in 1639 'requesting him to perform his promise of writing the Life of Dr. Donne'. Wotton's belated reply acknowledges 'the pleasure I have taken in your style and conceptions, together with a meditation of the subject you propound', suggesting that Walton had already supplied Wotton with both ideas ('conceptions') for the 'Life' and a proposed manner of executing them ('style'). Wotton promises 'to write at large to you by the next messenger…and then I shall set down certain general heads, wherein I desire information by your loving diligence', again suggesting Walton's further involvement: Wotton was expecting Walton to supply him with further 'information' prompted by 'certain general heads'.[10] And indeed, this is the scenario that Walton would later recall. Wotton asked Walton 'to inquire of some particulars that concern'd it, not doubting but my knowledge of the Author, and love to his memory, might make my diligence useful'. Walton affirms that he 'did most gladly undertake the employment, and continued it with great content 'till I had made my Collection ready to be augmented and completed by his [Wotton's] matchlesse Pen'. It would seem from this that Walton always planned to provide a substantial 'Collection' that Wotton would write up, augment, and complete.

Wotton declared that 'I will endeavour to perform my promise', although he thought the task, 'my age considered, almost hopeless from my pen'[11]—which proved to be prescient, as he died in early December 1639. The thought that Donne's sermons might be published without a life was too much for Walton, he claimed: 'Indignation or grief (indeed I know not which) transported me so far, that I reviewed my forsaken-Collections, and resolv'd the World should see the best plain Picture of the *Authors Life* that my artless Pensil, guided by the hand of truth, could present to it' (1675, B5^{r}). In other words, Walton retrieved the 'Collections' that he had sent to Wotton, and wrote them up himself, replacing Wotton's 'matchlesse Pen' with his 'artless Pensil'. But Walton did not put down his artless pencil after sketching his life of Donne in 1640. Instead, he returned to it multiple times, publishing new versions in 1658, 1670, and 1675.[12]

A Prefatory Life: Donne in 1640

In his study of English biography in the seventeenth century, Allan Pritchard claims that 'The practice of publishing prefatory lives of notable religious figures had already become so well established in England before the middle of the seventeenth century that Walton in 1640 was moved to write the first of his biographies, that of Donne, by the thought that it would be a pity if Donne's collected sermons appeared without such a life'.[13] Certainly, Walton tells us of his 'indignation and griefe' when he learns that Wotton's death means 'that these Sermons were to be publisht without the Authors life' (1640, A5^{v}). But was this intense reaction warranted?

By 1640, the practice of including a prefatory life in an edition of an author's works was well established on the Continent, but still something of a rarity in England. Thomas Speght included an antiquarian 'life' of Geoffrey Chaucer in his 1598 edition of the *Workes*, but posthumous editions of the works of Philip Sidney, Edmund Spenser, and William Shakespeare did not follow suit.[14] In 1609, the *Works* of the Elizabethan divine John Jewel had been prefaced by Daniel Featley's 'Life of the Worthie Prelate'—although Featley merely translated and retooled an existing

Latin life by Laurence Humphrey.[15] In 1614, Thomas Lodge's translation of the works of Seneca boasted a life of the author penned by the Low Countries humanist Justus Lipsius, but Lodge was in effect englishing Lipsius' 1605 Antwerp edition, which included this life.[16] Other collected works included funeral sermons, rather than formal biographies: Lancelot Andrewes's *XCVI Sermons* included John Buckeridge's sermon on Andrewes,[17] and Thomas Prior's 1624 sermon on Miles Smith, bishop of Gloucester, was belatedly appended to a collection of Smith's *Sermons* in 1632[18]—in each case, the funeral sermon was placed last in the volume and given its own title page, separating out the life from the works.

Perhaps the first tailor-made prefatory English life was 'A short view of the life and vertves of the avthovr', which appeared before a collection of Arthur Lake's collection of ninety-nine *Sermons, with Some Religious and Divine Meditations* in 1629. In his will, Lake desired that his sermons should be 'perfected... soe as they maye be worth the printinge for the good of younger Studentes', and the panegyrical 'Life' was authored by an older student, John Harris, who had studied under Lake at New College, Oxford.[19] In this way, Harris follows in the footsteps of other 'insider' life-writers, such as George Cavendish, writing the life of his former employer Thomas Wolsey, or William Roper, writing the life of his father-in-law Sir Thomas More. If Wotton had written Donne's life, we might have been given something of this ilk.

In the same year, 1629, a more intriguing prefatory life was provided by Sir Edward Coke in his edition of the fifteenth-century lawyer Thomas Littleton. Coke provides an account of Littleton's life and an engraving of Littleton's portrait—but claims that the true Littleton is to be found in his writings:

> He that is desirous to see his picture, may in the Churches of Frankley and Hales Owen see the graue and reuerend countenance of our Author, the outward man, but he hath left this Book, as a figure of that higher and nobler part (that is) of the excellent and rare endowments of his minde, especially in the profound knowledge of the fundamentall Lawes of this Realme. He that diligently reades this excellent Worke, shall behold the childe and figure of his mind, which the more often he beholds in the vitall line, & well obserues him, the more shall he iustly admire the iudgement of our Author, and increase his owne.[20]

A comparable move—contrasting the monumental effigy of a dead man with the 'childe and figure of his mind' in his written works—is made in a verse that was added to the 1635 edition of Donne's *Poems*:

> I see in his last preach'd, and printed Booke,
> His Picture in a sheete; in *Pauls* I looke,
> And see his Statue in a sheet of stone,

And sure his body in the grave hath one:
These sheets present him dead, these if you buy,
You have him living to Eternity.[21]

The poet here alludes to the startling frontispiece to Donne's late sermon, *Deaths Duell* (Fig. 18), based on his funeral monument in St Paul's, where Donne is depicted in a winding sheet (hence the punning on sheets).[22] This hexastichon is credited to the publisher 'Jo[hn] Ma[rriot]', but it speaks directly to what Walton will make of Donne over the next forty years. For Walton does not leave it for Donne's own work

Figure 18. John Donne's effigy portrayed in the frontispiece of *Deaths Duell* (1633). Beinecke Rare Book and Manuscript Library, Yale University.

to give 'the childe and figure of his mind': he injects that mind into the 'Life' he tells. And in so doing, he meshes the man's life and the man's writings inextricably.

The 1640 'Life' opens with short paragraphs, some no longer than a sentence, each recapping one element of Donne's early years: his birth and his father's family; his mother's family; his education at home and at Oxford; the refusal of his degree because his Catholic friends advised against taking it; his move to Cambridge at fourteen; and at seventeen to London's Lincoln Inn, where his tutors brought him under the sway of 'particular principles of the Romish Church'. This almost note-like quality sees us through his sea voyages with Robert Devereux, earl of Essex; his secretaryship to Lord Keeper Ellesmere; his falling in love with Ellesmere's niece, the daughter of Sir George More; their secret marriage, and his subsequent firing from Ellesmere's service and imprisonment. With no job security, Donne and his wife are taken in by a kinsman, Sir Francis Wally of Pirford; after Wally's death, the Donnes take a house in Mitcham, Surrey. Eventually, his friends persuade him to return to London, where his talents attract the attention of several leading figures, including the king, James I, who commissions him to write a defence of his Oath of Supremacy and Allegiance, Donne's *Pseudo-Martyr*. James urges Donne to enter holy orders; Donne takes three years to study and ponder before agreeing.

It is the turning point in the narrative. 'Now the English Church had gained a second S. *Augustine*', proclaims Walton, 'for I think none was so like him before his conversion, none so like S. *Ambrose* after it. And if his youth had the infirmities of the one Father, his age had the excellencies of the other, the learning and holinesse of both' (B2^{r}). We now enter into an account of Donne's successful Church career; the death of his wife; his lectureship at Lincoln's Inn; his place on the embassy of Viscount Doncaster into Germany; and, on his return, his appointment as dean of St Paul's and other ecclesiastical endowments, including Prolocutor to the Convocation. Only once is he 'clouded with the Kings displeasure'–when James hears a rumour that Donne had preached against his directions about Sunday evening lectures; Donne convinces the king that he is innocent of the charge. At fifty-four, Donne falls ill, and on his sickbed writes *A Composition of Holy Extasies*, 'occasioned, and appliable to the Emergencies of that sicknesse'. Five years later, another illness proves fatal.

It is during his subject's final sickness that Walton allows himself to move beyond the chronology that has thus far propelled the 'Life'. The shift is firmly signposted:

> This sicknesse continued long, not onely weakning, but wearing him so much, that my desire is, he may now take some rest: And that thou judge it no impertinent digression (before I speake of his death) to looke backe with me upon some observations of his life, which (while a gentle slumber seises him) may (I hope fitly) exercise thy Consideration. (B3^{v})

These 'observations' permit Walton to forward some opinions on his subject. Until about the age of twenty, 'The recreations of his youth were Poetry', which Walton appraises through its metaphysics: 'it may appeare by his choice Metaphors, that all the Arts joined to assist him with their utmost skill'. In his later 'penitentiall yeares', however, 'vieweing some of those pieces loosely scattered in his youth, he wisht they had been abortive, or so short-liv'd, that he had witnessed their funeralls'. Now, by contrast, Donne turned to 'many divine Sonnets, and other high, holy, and harmonious composures'; Walton quotes as an example 'A Hymne to God the Father', which Donne had written 'even on his former sick bed', and cites 'A Hymne to God my God in my sicknesse', which he wrote on 'his Death-bed' ($B4^{r}$). Lest his readers feel that writing poetry on one's deathbed is inappropriate, Walton sketches a dying Donne whose life 'was a continued studie', and who left as 'the visible fruits of his labours' a huge body of writing, which he itemizes. Walton goes on to quote at length from Donne's will and testament, detail his charitable work before and at his death, and quote from the prayers he wrote for the poor ($B4^{r-v}$).

In this closing section, Walton reserves his greatest criticism for Donne's clandestine marriage to Anne More:

> His marriage was the remarkable error of his life, which (though he had a wit apt enough, and very able to maintaine paradoxes; And though his wives competent yeares, and other reasons might be justly urged to moderate severe censure; yet) he never seemed to justifie, and doubtlesse had repented it, if God had not blest them with a mutuall, and so cordiall an affection, as in the midst of their sufferings made their bread of sorrow taste more pleasantly then the banquet of fooles. ($B3^{v}$–$B4^{r}$)

This is a remarkable sentence—not least because, with its constant qualifications ('though', 'though', 'yet', 'if'), it does not seem to know where it is going. In Walton's eyes, there is no doubt that 'His marriage was the remarkable error of his life'; the only problem is that Donne himself never sought to justify it, and never 'repented' it. All Walton can do is to suggest that Donne lived with this error because his wit was 'very able to maintaine paradoxes'.

'But I returne from my digression.' With Donne still 'sick in Essex', the rumour spreads that he has died, which prompts a letter (dated 7 January 1630) to a friend, which Walton quotes *in toto*. Donne travels in London to preach on the first Friday in Lent: 'when (to the amazement of some beholders) he appeared in the Pulpit, many thought he presented himselfe, not to preach mortification by a living voice, but morality by a decayed body, and dying face'. As Donne spoke on '*To God the Lord belong the issues from death*', many in the congregation 'profess[ed] they thought the Text Prophetically chosen, and that D. *Donne* had preacht his owne Funerall Sermon' ($B6^{r}$).[23] It was to be his last. Donne returned to his home, and the following day spoke to an unnamed friend in one of the very few pieces of direct speech in the 'Life'. Here Donne claims, 'I am not sad; I am in a serious contemplation of the mercies of my God to me.' Now he sees that it was God's hand that 'prevented me from all temporall employment', who ensured that he 'should never settle nor thrive untill I entred into the Ministery'. He is thankful that this ministry has enabled him 'to requite most of those friends that shewed me kindnesse when my fortunes were low', notably his father-in-law Sir George More; and to maintain his mother, whose old age saw 'a great decay'. He concludes: 'I cannot plead innocencie of life, (especially of my youth) but I am to be judged by a mercifull God, who hath given me (even at this time) some testimonies by his holy Spirit, that I am of the number of his Elect. I am ful of joy, and shall die in peace' (B6^{r}). The death comes after almost a folio page of his final sufferings, which Walton summarizes: 'Thus *variable*, thus *vertuous* was the life, thus *memorable*, thus *exemplary* was the *death* of this most excellent man' (B6^{v}). After Donne is buried in St Paul's, a generous donation allows his executors to purchase a marble monument for him. Walton closes with an impressionistic account of Donne's stature, body, aspect, eye, fancy, wit and judgement, and mind, and a transcription of his epitaph (C1^{v}).

It is, in many ways, a curious piece of life-writing. Walton had known Donne, as his parishioner in St Dunstan's, from March 1624. When his neighbour and friend John Marriot had published the posthumous 1633 collection of *Poems by J. D.*, Walton had contributed an elegy, which in the second (1635) edition was used to comment on the engraving of Donne by William Marshall. Donne's friend, fellow poet, and executor Henry King, bishop of Chichester, even recalled that Walton was 'your self...present at his bed-side' three days before Donne's death.[24] But in the 1640 'Life', precisely where one might want to make much of the personal contact, all of this is downplayed: Walton mentions 'my knowledge of the Author, and love to his memory' (A3^{r}), and avows that 'his conversation made me (and many others) happy' (A3^{v}), but refrains from placing himself directly in Donne's life.

Instead, Walton finds a new way of making Donne vivid in his 'Life'. In the 1640 version, Walton quotes Donne's writings directly only three times: once in verse ('A Hymne to God the Father', B4^{r}) and twice in prose, in the letter of 7 January 1630 and a passage from *Pseudo-Martyr*, where the direct quotation is typographically signalled clearly in italics and credited in a marginal note (A4^{r}).[25] But, as David Novarr and Jessica Martin have demonstrated, there are traces of Donne all over Walton's prose.[26] Walton's favourite technique is to drop a charged word or phrase in unannounced, thereby imbuing the narrative with some Donnean colour. So when we first see and hear Donne in the pulpit, Walton depicts him as 'A Preacher in earnest, weeping sometimes for his Auditory, sometimes with them, alwayes preaching to himselfe, like an Angel in a cloud, though in none' (B2^{r}); admirers of

Donne's verse would recognize the phrase 'Angel in a cloud' in this context as drawing on a line from his poem 'To Mr. Tilman after he had taken orders': 'As Angels out of clouds, from Pulpits speake'.[27] When Donne buries 'with his teares all his sublunary joys in his most deare and deserving Wives grave' (B2^{v}), there is a clear reference to 'Dull sublunary lovers love' from 'A Valediction forbidding mourning'.[28] When Donne preaches his final sermon with his 'decayed body, and dying face', Walton comments that 'doubtlesse many did secretly ask that question in *Ezekiel, Doe these bones live?*' (B6^{r}). But it is not the congregation that asked this question; it was Donne himself, in that very sermon: '*God* seems to haue caried the declaration of his *power* to a great height, when hee sets the *Prophet Ezechiel* in the *valley of dry bones*, & says, *Sonne of man can these bones liue?*'[29] Having delivered that final sermon, Walton declares, 'Now he had nothing to doe but die' (B6^{v}), a line lifted not from Donne's sermon but from the epistle 'To the Reader' appended to its 1632 printing: 'there remained nothing for him to doe, but to die'.[30]

This habit informs the final words of Walton's 'Life', as he imagines what will happen to Donne's body, '*now become a small quantity of Christian dust. But I shall see it re-inanimated*' (C1^{r}). As Martin argues, he is here drawing on Donne's Easter Day 1626 sermon (published in the same volume as Walton's 'Life'):

> God that knowes in which Boxe of his Cabinet all his seed Pearle lies, in what corner of the world every atome, every graine of every mans dust sleeps, shall recollect that dust, and then recompact that body, and then re-inanimate that man, and that is the accomplishment of all.

But Donne does not leave the 'accomplishment' there. Instead, he uses it as the starting point for his argument that this resurrection, which he calls 're-efformation', comes from recollection:

> In this resurrection, from this Dispersion and scattering in sin, the way is by Recollection too: That this sinner recollect himselfe, and his own history, his own annals, his own journalls, and call to minde where he lost his way, and with what tendernesse of conscience, and holy startling he entred into some sins at first, in which he is seared up now...[31]

It is in this 'Recollection'—drawing, tellingly, on history, annals, and journals—that Walton sees particular value for his work of life-writing.

These Times: Donne in 1658

In the mid-1650s, Walton started to revise his 1640 *Life of Donne*. The new version, published alone (without the sermons) in 1658, is notably updated, and very much of its moment. Walton had been an enthusiastic supporter of Archbishop Laud and an ardent royalist: his subsequent sadness and frustration after the civil wars at the state of the country, and the Church of England in particular, is evident in several of his writings.

The message is far from subtle—but the means by which Walton constructs this message is more intricate. Rather than shoehorning in a comment on contemporary politics with nothing to do with John Donne, Walton uses Donne himself to make his case for him by lacing his prose with Donne's own words. A sense of Walton's working methods can be gleaned from the notes he made on the inside cover of his copy of Eusebius' histories, now in Salisbury Cathedral. Writing sometime after 1651, Walton reminds himself:

At his conversion take out of Jeremy the ways of man are not in his owne powr
loke doc dones letter to Tilman
& on Sir Philip Sidnys psalms
on this booke folyo 28. of hims and psalms w*hich* was his holy recreation the latter part of his life and is now his imployment in heven where he makes new ditties in the praise of that god in 3 persons to whome be glorie

And his better part is now doing that in heaven which was most of his imployment on earth magnifying the mercies and making hims and singing them to that god to whome be glory and honer and[32]

These five notes inform two passages that Walton adds to his 1658 *Life of Donne*, both of which comment on the situation of the late 1650s. The first is an account of Donne being approached by the new dean of Gloucester, Thomas Morton, in 1607, with the offer of a benefice, which Donne ultimately turns down. Walton takes the opportunity to give us 'a short, but true character of this good man':

God hath been so good to his Church, as to afford it in every age some such men to serve at his Altar as have been piously ambitious of doing good to mankind... These times he did blesse with many such; some of which still live to be patterns of Apostolicall Charity, and of more than Humane Patience. I have said this because I have occasion to mention one of them in my following discourse; namely, Dr. *Morton*, the most laborious and learned Bishop of *Durham*, one that God hath blessed with perfect intellectuals, and a cheerfull heart at the age of 94 yeares (and is yet living) one that in his dayes of plenty used his large Revenue to the encouragement of *Learning* and *Vertue*; and is now (be it spoken with sorrow) reduced to a narrow estate, which he embraces without repining; and still shews the beauty of his mind by so liberall a hand, as if this were an age in which *to morrow were to care for it self.* (1658, B11^{r-v})

Morton establishes for Walton a 'then' and 'now': 'These times', Donne's times, were blessed with many men like Morton; now, the elderly Morton, and by extension the Church, is 'reduced to a narrow estate'. The Morton–Donne exchange comprises two pieces from Morton to Donne, and Donne's response. But in fact 'Morton' ventriloquizes Donne himself. When he says, 'Remember, Mr Donne, no mans education or parts make him too good for this employment, which is to be an Ambassador for him who by a vile death opened the gates of life to mankind', he is paraphrasing Donne's poem 'To Mr *Tilman* after he had taken orders', which Walton has reminded himself to use ('note doc dones letter to Tilman'):

> What function is so noble, as to bee
> Embassadour to God and destinie?
> To open life, to give kingdomes to more
> Than Kings give dignities; to keepe heavens doore?[33]

The Morton anecdote also poses something of a narrative conundrum: how can Donne be properly convinced by Morton's argument, but fail to take him up on it? The answer, as Walton notes in his Eusebius, lies in 'Jeremie', and specifically a paraphrase of Jeremiah 10:23, 'O Lord, I know that the way of man is not in himself: it is not in man that walketh to direct his steps': 'This was his present resolution', writes Walton, 'but the heart of man is not in his own keeping.'

The third and fourth notes extend the 'then and now' contrasts by focusing on a topical controversy: whether or not music should be used in church.[34] Music had been banned from church services by the Puritans; at the moment that Walton was writing, a group of musicians was petitioning to set up 'a college of musicians, with power to practise music publicly' to make up for 'the dissolution of the choirs in cathedral' which meant that 'many of us have died in want'.[35] Walton's note, '& on Sir Philip Sidnys psalms', refers us to Donne's verse 'Upon the Translation of the Psalms by Sir Philip Sidney and the Countess of Pembroke his Sister', which alleges that the Sidney siblings 'tell us [the English] *why*, and teach us *how* to sing' with their psalm translations, combining the song of Heaven, the music of the spheres ('Their harmony is rather danc'd than sung'), and 'our third Quire' on earth: 'This Quire hath all. The Organist is hee | Who hath tun'd God and Man, the Organ we.'[36] The fourth note, an internal reference to 'on this booke folyo 28', takes us to the leaf numbered 28 of Eusebius, concerning 'Psalmes and Hymnes', which quotes Philo Judaeus writing about the holy men of his Egypt: '*They contemplate not onely divine things, but they make grave canticles, and hymnes unto God in a more sacred rime, of every kind of meter and verse*'; Eusebius takes this as evidence that Christians in first-century Egypt 'newly compiled and collected Psalmes'.[37]

These two pieces by Donne and Eusebius inform perhaps the most passionate moment in Walton's 'Life', in a passage that he adds after quoting Donne's 'An Hymne to God the Father' ('Wilt thou forgive that sin where I begunne'):[38]

I have the rather mentioned this *Hymne*, for that he [Donne] caus'd it to be set to a most grave and solemn tune, and to be often sung to the *Organ* by the *Choristers* of that *Church*, in his own hearing, especially at the Evening Service; and at his return from his Customary Devotions in that place, did occasionally say to a friend, The words of this *Hymne* have restored to me the same thoughts of joy that possest my soul in my sicknesse when I composed it. And, Oh the power of Church-musick! that Harmony added to it has raised the affections of my heart, and quickned my graces of zeal and gratitude; *and I observe*, that I alwaies return from paying this publick duty of *Prayer* and *Praise to* God with an unexpressible tranquillity of mind, *and a willingnesse to* leave the world.

After this manner did the Disciples of our Saviour, and the best of Christians in those Ages of the Church nearest to his time, offer their praises to Almighty God. And the reader of St. *Augustines* life may there find, that towards his dissolution he wept abundantly, that the enemies of Christianity had broke in upon them, and prophaned and ruin'd their *Sanctuaries*, and because their *Publick Hymns* and Lauds were lost out of their Churches. And after this manner have many devout soules lifted up their hands and offered acceptable Sacrifices unto Almighty God in that place where Dr. *Donne* offered his.

But now oh Lord–(1658, E1^{r}–E2^{r})

The passage breaks off dramatically, but the emphatic 'now' has done its work. Walton is explicitly comparing earlier representatives of the Church–Christ's disciples, the early Christians, St Augustine, and Donne–with the men of 'now', and his focus is on 'the power of Church-musick'. The power of psalms and hymns, as registered by Donne's verse on the Sidneys' psalter, and the antiquity of its use, as vouched for by Eusebius, are here brought to bear on the situation of the late 1650s. The historical specificity of this passage is underscored in its 1670 revision, when Walton amends the final line to 'But now oh Lord–1656'. By 1670, Walton is part of the dominant faction in the Church of England; the moment of crisis has passed, church music plays once again, and his uncharacteristic outburst can be dated and safely filed for posterity.

Lean, Pale, and Death-Like: Donne's Slow Death

As he returned to his 'Life of Donne' in 1658, and again in 1670 and 1675, Walton added elements that produced a distinctly different Donne than the one he had sketched in 1640. The latter half of the narrative had always been weighted towards his death, which was relentlessly trailed. Increasingly, however, Walton added elements that presented Donne as a man almost obsessed with his demise.

Donne had been buried in St Paul's Cathedral beneath a striking white marble monument by Nicholas Stone, which depicts its subject draped in a funeral shroud, pulled together at the head and feet—but whereas one might expect a shrouded corpse to be lying down, Donne is apparently standing on his funerary urn. In 1640, Walton had simply noted that an unnamed 'some good body' had sent 100 marks to Donne's executors 'towards the making of a Monument for him, which I think is as lively a representation, as in dead marble can be made of him' (1640, C1^{r}). Now, in 1658, he changes the story. Rather than the result of an anonymous, posthumous gift, the monument is part of Donne's deathbed narrative. In his final illness, persuaded by his physician Dr Simeon Foxe (son and biographer of John Foxe), Donne 'yielded at this very time to have a Monument made for him' (1658, F6^{r}). The direction, however, 'was left to Dr. *Donne* himself':

> Dr. *Donne* sent for a Carver to make for him in wood the figure of an *Urn*, giving him directions for the compasse and height of it, and to bring with it a board of the height of his body. These being got, and without delay a choice Painter was in a readiness to draw his picture, which was taken as followeth.—Severall Charcole-fires being first made in his large study, he brought with him into that place his winding-sheet in his hand, and having put off all his clothes, had his sheet put on him, and so tied with knots at his head and feet, and his hands so placed as dead bodies are usually fitted for the grave. Upon this Urn he thus stood with his eyes shut, and so much of the sheet turned aside as might shew his lean, pale, and death-like face, which was purposely turned toward the East, from whence he expected the second coming of our Saviour. Thus he was drawn at his just height; and when the picture was fully finished, he caused it to be set by his bed-side, where it continued, and became his hourly object till his death, and was then given to his dearest friend and Executor Dr. *King*, who caused him to be thus carved in one entire piece of white Marble, as it now stands in the Cathedrall Church of S. *Pauls*. (F6^{r}–F7^{r})

As Helen Gardner points out in a merciless dissection of the passage, it is extremely unlikely that the terminally ill Donne managed to stand inside a knotted sheet for any length of time to be sketched—indeed, she speculates that the figure should not be seen as 'standing' at all: the sculptor embarked on a reclining figure for an altar tomb, but plans were changed, and the effigy ended up standing in a niche. (Gardner allows that Donne may have commissioned a painter to depict him in his final days.[39]) Whatever the circumstances of the effigy's creation, Walton's account presents Donne, not content with delivering his own funeral sermon, prefiguring, and effectively authoring, the details of his own death.

When Walton returns to Donne for his 1670 *Lives*, he projects this death-obsessed Donne back into his earlier life. Walton includes in his narrative for the first time what appear to be two letters by Donne, carefully dated 10 August and 7 September, that express his troubled state of mind while living at 'my hospital at Micham' (i.e. during the Donnes' early marriage at Mitcham, *c.* 1606–11). Walton introduces the first letter to the reader: 'that you may the better now judge of the then present Condition of his minde and fortune, I shall present you with an extract collected out of some few of his many Letters' (1670, C6^{v}–C7^{r}). The 10 August letter describes the illness of his family: 'I have already lost half a Child, and with that mischance of hers, my wife is fallen into such a discomposure, as would afflict her too extremely, but that the sickness of all her children stupifies her'. It ends, 'if God should ease us with burials, I know not how to performe even that: but I flatter my self with this hope, that I am dying too: for, I cannot waste faster then by such griefs'. Moving to the second letter, Walton editorializes: 'Thus he did bemoan himself: And thus in other letters…' (C7^{r}).

As R. E. Bennett demonstrated in 1937, these letters are in truth concoctions by Izaak Walton.[40] Walton draws on Donne's words, bringing together eight passages from five different letters, all of which had appeared in print in the 1651 collection (and some, indeed, in the letters Walton appended to his 1658 life). So when Walton writes, 'And thus in other letters', he is technically telling the truth: these words are from other letters, plural. But much of this letter is misleading. The date and place of composition are fabrications. And Walton provides nuanced rewritings that turn Donne's general thoughts into Donne's personal revelations. Thus, in an original letter to Henry Goodere, Donne had written:

> but to be no part of any body, is to be nothing. At most, the greatest persons, are but great wens, and excrescences; men of wit and delightfull conversation, but as moales for ornament, except they be so incorporated into the body of the world, that they contribute something to the sustentation of the whole.[41]

Walton's appropriation reads:

> but to be no part of my body, is as to be nothing, and so I am, and shall so judge my self, unless I could be so incorporated into a part of the world, as by business to contribute some sustentation to the whole. (1670, C7^{v})

Walton's Donne speaks in the first person so that 'any body' becomes emphatically 'my body', and 'the body of the world' becomes 'a part of the world', losing the resonance of 'body', and the pun on 'incorporated'. And the passage's most striking words—with the 'greatest persons' being 'great wens, and excrescences' and 'moales for ornament'—are lost.

The image of Donne's ailing wife and dying children also informs one of the most famous passages in the *Life of Donne*, which was not added until 1675, and marks a new departure for Walton.[42] In the 1670 version, following the sad time at Mitcham,

Walton has Donne moving into a house next door to Sir Robert Drury on Drury Lane, and becoming a noted interlocutor of learned men and leading divines. In 1675's account, after moving into Drury's 'own large house on *Drewry-lane*' (C6^{v}), Donne is called by Drury to accompany the embassy of Lord Hay to the French king, Henri IV. Hearing this news, Donne's pregnant wife 'profest an unwillingness to allow him any absence from her; saying, *her divining soul boded her some ill in his absence*; and therefore, desired him not to leave her'. But Donne heads for France anyway. In Paris, Drury 'as he left, so he found Mr. *Donne* alone; but, in such an Extasie, and, so alter'd as to his looks, as amaz'd Sir *Robert* to behold him' (C7^{r}). When pressed as to what had happened, Donne

> was not able to make a present answer: but, after a long and perplext pause, did at last say, *I have seen a dreadful Vision since I saw you: I have seen my dear wife pass twice by me thorough this room, with her hair hanging about her shoulders, and a dead child in her arms: this, I have seen since I saw you.* (C7^{v})

Drury suggests that Donne must have fallen asleep, and that '*this is the result of some melancholy dream, which I desire you to forget*'. But Donne is adamant: '*I cannot be surer that I now live, then, that I have not slept since I saw you: and am, as sure, that at her second appearing, she stopt, and look'd me in the face, and vanisht.*' To placate Donne's anxieties, Drury sends a messenger back to Drury House, who reports 'That he found and left Mrs. *Donne* very sad, and sick in her bed: and, that after a long and dangerous labor she had been deliver'd of a dead child. And, upon examination, the abortion prov'd to be the same day, and about the very hour that Mr. *Donne* affirm'd he saw her pass by him in his Chamber' (C7^{v}).

As Walton immediately points out, 'This is a relation that will beget some wonder: and, it well may; for, most of our world are at present possest with an opinion that *Visions* and *Miracles* are ceas'd' (C7^{v}–C8^{r}). But he goes on to argue for the existence of a '*sympathy* of *souls*', employing what sounds like a Donnean conceit: ''tis most certain, that two Lutes, being both strung and tun'd to an equal pitch, and then, one plaid upon, the other, that is not totcht, being laid upon a Table at a fit distance, will (like an Eccho to a trumpet) warble a faint audible harmony, in answer to the same tune'. He also cites various scriptural and classical precedents, and the fact that both St Augustine (already established as a model for Donne) and his mother Monica 'had visions in order to his Conversion'. He cites the opinion of 'many pious and learned men' that God assigns to each man 'a particular *guardian angel*' (C8^{r}). As Carole Levin notes, it was indeed '[a] commonly held belief... that, if one had "secret passages of sympathy" with someone, one could learn of their death through a dream'[43]—but the coordinates of the vision story are all awry. Donne lived near to Drury's house, not in Drury House; he moved there after the embassy, not before; while Donne was on that embassy, his wife and children were on the Isle of Wight, not London, and so on. But more startlingly, the story is full of the kind of hackneyed phrases and motifs—divining souls, dreadful visions, trance-like ecstasy—reminiscent of romance or Restoration tragedy. The account is also highly patterned—the wife's premonition followed by the husband's sympathetic vision; a twelve-day journey from London to Paris followed by the messenger's twelve-day return journey. Once again, Walton interlaces hints of Donne's verse: so when Anne Donne says '*her divining soul boded her some ill in his absence*' ($C7^r$), we hear the lines of Donne's 'Song': 'Let not thy divining heart | Forethinke me any ill'.[44]

Walton cannot help but signal the improbability of the vision. Despite including this episode, as narrator he attempts to distance himself from either believing or 'proving' it, by having an anonymous (and now, presumably, deceased) source vouch for its truth:

> I forbear, least, I that intended to be but a Relator, may be thought to be an ingag'd person for the proving what was related to me...though it was not told me by Mr. *Donne* himself; it was told me (*now long since*) by a Person of Honour, and of such intimacy with him, that he knew more of the secrets of his soul, then any person then living; and I think they [*sic*] told me the truth; for, it was told with such circumstances, and such asseveration, that (to say nothing of my own thoughts) I verily believe he that told it me, did himself believe it to be true. ($C8^v$)

But Walton then prints Donne's 'A Valediction, forbidding to Mourn', claiming that these are 'Verses given by Mr. *Donne* to his wife at the time that he then parted from her' ($D1^r$). The reader is tacitly encouraged to see this poem as an illustration of the story: of 'two souls...which are one', which despite the poet's absence 'indure not yet | A breach, but, an expansion, like gold, to aiery thinness beat'; souls that are two like 'stiff twin-compasses', so that while the poet's soul 'far does rome', his beloved's sits 'in the Center', leaning and hearkening after his ($D1^{r-v}$). Written *before* Donne leaves for France, it also makes the poet a prophet of his own life-story.

Over a period of thirty-five years, Walton adapts and points his life of Donne so that it serves different functions. In 1640, it does the journeyman work of providing the life to explain the sermons: the narrative hinges neatly on Donne's regally inspired conversion to the ministry. In 1658, Donne becomes the (entirely anachronistic) spokesman against puritan impositions on the Church of England. In 1670, Donne's familiar voice is introduced through his letters—albeit letters concocted to provide him with a voice of pessimism. And by 1675, Donne's story has taken on elements of the supernatural, with Walton's narrative voice registering the dissonances of genre and register that have crept in. Where would Walton have gone next? There is the tantalizing suggestion that Walton may not have seen the 1675 *Lives* as his final word on John Donne. In a copy of the printed book now in the Albert H. Childs Memorial Collection at Yale University we find Walton's hand, still making notes, still correcting, still revising.[45]

The case could be made that Walton was a trendsetter. In 1640, when he claimed that it would be unseemly if Donne's sermons were published without a prefatory life, he was stretching the truth. But if he said the same thing in 1675, he would be on firmer ground, and by the century's end the combination of 'life and works' was becoming the norm. Following Walton's 1640 life of Donne, many authors—both spiritual and lay, recently deceased and long gone—found themselves the subjects of prefatory lives: from Francis Quarles in 1644 (by 'Vrsvla Quarles, his sorrowful widow') through to writers as diverse as poet and playwright Aphra Behn, book collector Robert Cotton (appended to a catalogue of his library), and political philosopher James Harrington in the last years of the century.[46] But none of these lives does what Walton did with his *Lives*: in seeking to add prefatory biographies to printed collections of his subjects' writings, Walton ended up by creating *Lives* that stood alone, under the name not of Donne or Wotton or Herbert or Hooker, but of Izaak Walton.

13

John Aubrey's Minutes of Lives

As he embarked on his life of John Donne, Izaak Walton issued an apology for the limitations of his art:

If I shall be demanded, as once *Pompeys* poore Bondman was, (whilest he was alone on the Sea shore gathering the pieces of an old Boat to burne the body of his dead Master) What art thou that preparest the funeralls of *Pompey* the great? Who am I that so officiously set the Authors memorie on fire? I hope the question hath in it more of wonder then disdaine.[1]

Alluding to an episode in Plutarch's *Parallel Lives*, Walton compares himself to Philip, the enfranchised bondman of the Roman leader Pompey, who, following Pompey's assassination at Pelusium in Egypt, recovers his master's decapitated, abused body on the beach.[2] Walton casts himself as the dutiful former slave—his own *Lives* feature several loyal dependents at key moments[3]—who uses whatever is at hand on the beach to 'set the Authors memorie on fire'. It is an act of loyalty and respect in which the ship's wreckage and the desecrated body are transmuted into the purity of fire.[4]

John Aubrey also insistently uses the image of the wreckage of an old boat to describe his life-writing: he may well have read Plutarch, but he uses the image to utterly different ends. The Latin phrase 'Tanquam Tabula[ta] Naufragii [like the plank[s] of a shipwreck]' appears on the first pages of his 'Wiltshire Antiquities' and two of the three volumes of his 'Brief Lives'.[5] But Aubrey explains it best in the third draft of his 'Life' of his long-time friend Thomas Hobbes:

Amongst innumerable Observations of Him w*h*ich had deserued to be sett downe these few (that haue not scapt my memory) I hu*m*bly offer to *the* p*re*sent Age & Posterity, tanquam Tabula*m* naufragii; & as plankes & lighter things swimme, & are p*re*serued, where the more weighty sinke & are lost.

Aubrey had forgotten where he'd picked up the phrase 'tanquam Tabul*am* naufragii'—in a marginal note he reminds himself that he should '*Vide* [See] Erasmi Adagia', always a good bet when searching for a classical tag, or failing that, '*quaere* Dr Bl', ask Dr Blackburne, who was preparing the Latin *vita* of Hobbes for him.[6] But most likely, as a man of pronounced 'Verulamian Designes',[7] Aubrey found the phrase when reading Francis Bacon's *The Advancement of Learning* (1605), as Bacon delineates the kinds of histories, as 'MEMORIALLS, PARFITE HISTORIES, and ANTIQVITIES', where 'ANTIQVITIES are Historie defaced, or some remnants of History, which have casually escaped the shipwrack of time':

> ANTIQVITIES, or Remnants of History, are, as was saide, *tanquam Tabula Naufragij*, when industrious persons by an exact and scrupulous diligence and obseruation, out of Monum*ents*, Names, Wordes, Prouerbes, Traditions, Priuate Recordes, and Euidences, Fragments of stories, Passages of Bookes, that concerne not storie and the like, doe saue and recouer somewhat from the deluge of time.[8]

Aubrey turns Bacon's simile into something new. Bacon looks back to the past, seeing the planks from a shipwreck as the fragmentary remnants of history that have floated ashore by chance. Aubrey instead looks forward to the future, and 'offers to *the* p*re*sent Age and Posterity', his 'innumerable Observations' of Hobbes, which are like planks, because 'plankes & lighter things swimme, and are p*re*served, where the more weighty sinke & are lost'—it is precisely the ability of these fragments to survive that interests him. 'Men think', he writes,

> because euery body remembers a memorable Accident shortly after 'tis donne, 'twill never be forgotten, w*hi*ch for want of registring at last is drowned in Oblivion. This reflection has been a hint, that by my meanes many Antiquities have been reskued, & p*re*servd; I my selfe now inclining to senescens - or els utterly lost & forgotten.[9]

Whereas Walton uses the planks of a shipwreck to 'set the Authors memorie on fire', Aubrey has 'Reskued' them from the past '& p*re*servd' them for the future in their own right. What Bacon calls 'ANTIQVITIES, or Remnants of History', Aubrey sees as 'Minutes of Lives'.

'Minutes of Lives' is perhaps a better description of Aubrey's surviving life-writing than the standard title under which they have been known for over a century: *Brief Lives*. The phrase derives from his own short title for the first volume, 'Σχεδιασματα. Brief Lives' (1:3), but the first word, *Schediasmata*, is perhaps preferable—a 'schediasm' in early modern English is 'a sudden invention, or a work extempore',[10] and Aubrey's 'lives' do not, for the most part, provide life-narratives of his subjects, but rather a series of notes *on* the life. While this is true of the *Brief Lives*, however, this may not have been how Aubrey initially understood his project. For the *Brief Lives*, commenced in 1680, was not Aubrey's first attempt at writing lives.

The Road to the *Brief Lives*

John Aubrey (1626–97) was born and raised largely in Wiltshire, a county for which he retained a keen interest.[11] Although he attended Trinity College, Oxford, and the Middle Temple, he did not complete his studies at either. When his father died in 1652, Aubrey became responsible for his debts, and was by 1662 forced to sell some of his properties; a broken marriage agreement in 1666 cost him dearly; in 1671 he gave up what was left of his inheritance; he was even forced to sell some of his books in 1677. Despite this, Aubrey remained an industrious researcher and scholar, with a remarkable collection of friends, which included such luminaries as Hobbes, Samuel Hartlib, Sir Kenelm Digby, John Wilkins, Robert Hooke, James Harrington, Sir William Petty, Sir Christopher Wren, and his long-time collaborator, Anthony Wood; like many of them, Aubrey was a member of the Royal Society (from 1663). Although in his lifetime Aubrey published only one work in print—'a collection of hermetick philosophy' entitled *Miscellanies*[12]—his surviving manuscripts reveal a startling range of interests and expertise: works on multiple aspects of his native Wiltshire; a 'Perambulation of Surrey'; a study of English place names; analyses of burial monuments and ancient megaliths such as Avebury and Stonehenge; Britain's traces of Roman culture; British folklore and customs; magic rites; and astrology. He penned a treatise on educational reform, expatiated on the principles of neoclassical architecture, made calculations in arithmetic, mathematics, and algebra, collected 'approved receipts' (proven recipes), and kept a scientific commonplace book—a 'fol[io] an inch thick' by 1692.

Undoubtedly Aubrey's best-known work, however, is his *Brief Lives*, which survives in three manuscript volumes at Oxford's Bodleian Library, and has been published several times over the past two centuries—most recently in Kate Bennett's landmark 2015 edition. *Brief Lives* is usually regarded as a belated result of Aubrey's collaboration with Anthony Wood, whom he met in Oxford in August 1667. When Wood started to write his biographical sketches of Oxford University alumni—which would result in his *Historia et antiquitates Universitatis Oxoniensis* (1674) and later his *Athenæ Oxonienses* (1691–2)—Aubrey undertook much of the primary research, providing information to Wood by letter while keeping his own records. The shift from researcher to life-writer occurred when his friend Thomas Hobbes died on 4 December 1679. Aubrey was keen to memorialize Hobbes as soon as possible, opining that 'no body knew so many particulars of his Life as my selfe',[13] and decided to write a supplement to Hobbes's autobiography. A life of a man like Hobbes, however, needed to be cast in Latin, and for that job Aubrey chose a young doctor named Richard Blackburne, whom he deemed among 'the best schol*ars* in London of his age' and, crucially, a 'φιλο [*philo*] Hobbist'.[14]

In an undated letter, we find Aubrey excitedly advising Blackburne how to lay out Hobbes's life:

> Dr Blackbourne!
> Pray advise me whether 'twould not shew handsomest to begin with a description of Malmesbury, and then to place Mr. H. pedigre?
> But, with all, should not
> Thomas Hobbes was borne at Malmesbury, Apr. [*space*] 1688 [*sic*]
> be the initiall and, as it were, textuall line?

The shape of the entire volume was still undecided:

> Shall I in the first place putt Mr. H. life donne by himself? (If so, whether in Latin, or English, or both?)[15] Or else, shall I intersperse it with these animadversions?
> I could begin with a pleasant description of Malmesbury, etc. (all new and untoucht) 14 leaves in 8vo [octavo], which his verses will lead me to, and which Ant. Wood seems to desire.

Aubrey calls on Blackburne to exercise his judgement: 'Pray be my Aristarchus [the editor of Homer], and correct and marke what you thinke fit.'[16] Blackburne took the invitation seriously, but corrected his text with greater assiduity than Aubrey envisioned. In its final form, the volume does not open with a description of Malmesbury or Hobbes's pedigree; Hobbes's autobiography comes not first, but last; and, ignoring Wood's desire, the proposed 'pleasant description of Malmesbury' did not make it into print. Aubrey's initial enthusiasm for Blackburne—he gushed to Wood that Blackburne's style made it seem 'as if Mr Hobbes's soule were come into his body'—soon soured. What Aubrey had initially acclaimed as a 'delicate style'[17] he soon decried: Blackburne, he worried, 'would putt in the High Style',[18] better suited to panegyric.

More important than style was the question of content. Aubrey complained to Wood that 'the D*octo*r is a great iudge, & consequently magisteriall: he is much ag*ains*t Minutiæ [small details]',[19] and claimed that if the life were done according to Blackburne, 'there will be the trueth, but not the whole':

> Now I say the Offices of a Panegyrist & Historian, are much different. A life, is a short Historie: and there minutenes of a famous person is gratefull. I never yet knew a Witt (unles he were a piece of an Antiquary) write a proper Epitaph, but leave the reader ignorant, what countryman &c: only tickles his eares with Elogies.[20]

Blackburne was supported in his objections by two scholarly friends, John Dryden and John Lord Vaughan—they seem especially to have insisted that the fact that Hobbes had served as a page should be omitted.[21] Dryden was himself thinking through these issues, as he prepared a 'Life of Plutarch' to preface the new translation of Plutarch's *Parallel Lives*. Comparing the 'three species' of history, '*Commentaries* or *Annals*; *History* properly so called; and *Biographia*, or the Lives of particular Men', he explained that while the third, '*Biographia*', was 'in dignity inferiour to *History* and *Annalls*, in pleasure and instruction it equals, or even excels both of them':

> there is withal, a descent into minute circumstances, and trivial passages of life, which are natural to this way of writing, and which the dignity of the other two will not admit. There you are conducted only into the rooms of state; here you are led into the private Lodgings of the Heroe: you see him in his undress, and are made Familiar with his most private actions and conversations. You may behold a *Scipio* and a *Lelius* gathering Cockle-shells on the shore, *Augustus* playing at bounding stones with *Boyes*; and *Agesilaus* riding on a Hobby-horse among his Children. The Pageantry of Life is taken away; you see the poor reasonable Animal, as naked as ever nature made him; are made acquainted with his passions and his follies, and find the *Demy-God* a *Man*.[22]

It might seem that Dryden is here defending 'minute circumstances' but, as Kelsey Jackson Williams has argued, in the cases of Scipio, Laelius, Augustus, and Agesilaus, 'the private action illustrated served to illuminate the character of the subject in such a way as to teach a moral or social lesson, harking back to Dryden's initial praise of biography for the "pleasure and instruction" it gives'.[23] No such instruction would be forthcoming from the 'minute' that Hobbes had served as a lowly page. Two months later, Aubrey was less considered in his criticism: 'Pox take your orators & poets, they spoile liues & histories. The D*octo*r says that I am too minute; but a hundred yeare hence that minutenesse will be gratefull'—and he had supporters: 'Sir W*illiam* Petty ordered me to be so'.[24]

The breakdown of relations with Blackburne, however, sparked a new thought: Aubrey decided to write his own, new 'Life' of Hobbes in English, indulging his conviction that even 'the recrementa [dross] of so learned a Person [as Hobbes] are valueable'.[25] This life was to contain 'nothing that is in the Latin one': 'I have writt 3 copies (improved) of TH. Life', Aubrey reported to Wood on 10 February 1680; 'I did not think I could have been so copious, it will be at least 8 sheets.'[26] It was not long before he had moved beyond Hobbes.[27] On 17 February he wrote that while smoking some tobacco the previous Sunday night, 'it came into my mind to scribble a sheet of paper close which I shall enlarge (much) viz: the Lives of *the* worthy & ingeniose K*nigh*t Sir W. Petty from his cradle; Sir Chr. Wren the like. as also Mr. Rob. Hooke'.[28] Little more than a month later, he declared to Wood that 'I have to my

Booke of Lives made a Kalendar of 55 persons, & have donne 10 of them: 3 or 4 leaves a foli*o* a piece.... 'twill be a pretty thing, & I am glad you putt me on it'. Aubrey boasted of his facility in his new undertaking: 'I doe it playingly. This morning being up by 10 I writt two, one was Sir J*ohn* Suckling, of whom I wrote a leafe & ½ in foli*o*.'[29] Two months more, and he could write: 'My Memoirs of Lives [66] a book of 2 qu*ires* close written, and after I had begun it I had such an impulse on my spirit that I could not be at quiet till I had donne it.' By the end of September, he was expecting to write 'in all about six score'.[30] In fact, by 1693 Aubrey had completed more than 400 entries—including a companion 'Lives of our English mathematical writers'—in four folio volumes, which he presented to the Ashmolean.[31]

Although he seems to have taken the initiative in writing these lives, in a letter of 15 June 1680 Aubrey credited Wood for the shape of the project: 'I have according to your desire, putt in writing these Minutes of LIVES, tumultuarily, as they occurr'd to my thoughts: or as occasionally I had information of them... 'Tis a Taske that I never thought to have undertaken, till you imposed it upon me.' According to Aubrey, Wood said that he was 'fitt for it, by reason of my generall acquaintance', since during his fifty years, he had 'been much tumbled up and downe in it; which hath made me much knowne' (1:37). It is easy to be dismissive of the fifty-four-year-old Aubrey's insistent claims to senescence and longevity. But Aubrey was intensely sensitive to the passage of time, and saw himself as possessing memories that would disappear if he did not set them down. He mourned the dispersal of the library from Malmesbury Abbey after the dissolution of the monasteries in the 1530s, when manuscripts 'flew-about like butterflies'; in his youth, he suffered to see gloves 'wrapt-up...in many good pieces of Antiquity', medieval manuscripts recycled as waste papers in book bindings, and used by the rector of the abbey to stop up his barrels of 'Speciall Ale'. Aubrey visited the abbey in 1647, but 'by that time [the manuscripts] were lost and disperst', not least thanks to the rector's sons, 'Gunners and soldiers', who 'scoured their Gunnes with 'em'.[32] As he wrote to Wood, ''Tis pitty that such Minutes had not been taken 100 yeares since or more: for want thereof many worthy mens Names and Notions are swallowd-up in oblivion: as much of these would also, had it not been through your Instigation: and perhaps this is one of the usefullest pieces that I have scribbl*ed*' (1:38).

This would become his mission. Aubrey would commit to paper any 'minute' of a life that he felt might otherwise be lost, firmly believing that his minutes were potentially more valuable than the published biographies, as he suggested to Wood:

> What uncertainty doe we find in printed Histories? they either treading too neer on the heeles of trueth, that they dare not speake plaine; or els for want of intelligence (things

being antiquated) become too obscure and darke! I doe not here repeat any thing already published (to the best of my remembrance) and I fancy my selfe all along discoursing with you; alledgeing those of my Relations and acquaintance (as either you knew or have heard of) ad faciendam Fidem [to inspire confidence]. So that you make me to renew my acquaintance with my old and deceased Friends, and to rejuvenescere [become young again] (as it were) which is the pleasure of old men. (1:38)

But the downside to this plain speaking was that the materials could be delicate:

I here lay-downe to you (out of the conjunct friendship between us) the Trueth, the naked and plain trueth (and as neer as I can, and that religiously as a Pœnitent to his Confessor) nothing but the trueth: which is here exposed so bare that the very *pudenda* are not hid, and affords many passages that would raise a Blush in a young Virgins cheeke. So that after your perusall, I must desire you to make a Castration (as [the editor] Raderus to Martial) and to sowe-on some Figge-leaves i.e. to be my Index expurgatorius [arbiter of what material must be deleted from a printed work]. (1:38)

Aubrey's minutes certainly needed fig-leaves, tending as some of them do to the sensational and salacious. Scurrilous rumours are recorded with no evidence: Sir John Denham's second wife was 'poysoned at the hands of the Countess of Rochester, with Chocolatte' (1:350); 'Some suspect that' poet Andrew Marvell 'was poysoned by the Jesuites, but I cannot be positive' (he later scored out his uncertainty) (1:345); Sir John Suckling, exiled and destitute in France, 'tooke poyson, which killed him miserably with vomiting' (1:369). Aubrey does not shy away from his subjects' alleged fornication, adultery, and illegitimate offspring. There is a hint of incest in his minute of Richard Corbet, bishop of Norwich, who married the twenty-years-younger Alice Hutton, 'whom 'twas sayd he begott. she was a very beautifull woman, and so was her mother' (1:355). William Petty, still alive when Aubrey wrote his minutes, 'has a naturall daughter, that much resembles him, no legitimate child so much, that acts at the Dukes play-house' (1:44). The unmarried French philosopher René Descartes 'kept a good conditioned hansome woman, that he liked, and by whom he had some Children (I thinke 2 or 3.)'; Aubrey comments that ''tis pity', but even-handedly reasons that 'comeing from the Loines of such a father, they should be well cultivated' (1:104–5). Other outcomes could be less welcome. The playwright Sir William Davenant 'gott a terrible clap of a Black handsome wench that lay in Axe-yard Westminster... which cost him his Nose' (1:141–2). In a notable departure from Izaak Walton's life of George Herbert, Aubrey focuses on his third marriage to Jane Danvers, to whom he was related; since Herbert 'was a very fine complexion and consumptive', Aubrey writes, this 'marige [marriage] I suppose hastened his death', since 'my kinswoman was a handsome bona roba [courtesan]: and ingeniose' (1:694). And Sir Philip Sidney, injured in a skirmish in the Low Countries, loved his wife so well 'he could not (contrary to the injunction of his Physitians and Chirurgions) forbeare his carnall knowledge of her, which cost him his Life' (1:258).

As will by now be evident, much of this material is overtly misogynist. Despite Aubrey's tribute that Mary Sidney Herbert, countess of Pembroke, 'was the greatest patronesse of witt and learning of any Lady in her time', he reserves for her the most prurient depiction of female sexuality:

> She was very salacious: and she had a contrivance that in the Spring of the yeare when the Stallions were to leape the Mares, they were to be brought before such a part of the house, where she had a vidette to look on them, and please her selfe with their sport: and then she would act the like sport herself with her stallions. one of her great Gallants was Crooke-back't Cecill Earl of Salisbury. (1:251)

One is hardly surprised that among the 'stallions' at the Herberts' Wiltshire estate of Wilton was her own brother: 'Sir Philip Sydney was much here, and there was so great love between him and his faire Sister, that I have heard old Gentlemen say that they lay together, and 'twas thought the first Philip Earle of Pembroke was begot by him: but he inherited not the witt of either the brother or sister.' (Aubrey later thought better of these two passages, and scored out much of them.) And as a parting blow, Aubrey casts doubt on the countess's second marriage to Sir Matthew Lister: 'Jack Markham saies they were not maried' (1:252). Good reason, then, as Aubrey warned Wood, that 'These *Arcana* are not fitt to lett flie abroad, till about 30 yeares hence; for the author and the Persons (like Medlars) ought first to be rotten' (1:35).

These are the *Brief Lives* as they are best known today—not the exemplary lives we expect from Samuel Clarke or Izaak Walton, but an endlessly entertaining miscellany of fun facts about the great and the good (and the neither great nor good) of seventeenth-century English society. It is this image that prompted Harold Love to claim that Aubrey is 'an anecdotalist' trading in entertaining gossip, 'primarily interested in telling a good story', whose lives 'frequently turn their subject into a species of monster'; but, as Allan Pritchard insists, Aubrey includes this ephemeral information because he believed in 'the importance of preserving a wide range of information from the present for the future'.[33] As Kate Bennett's edition has demonstrated beyond doubt, the *Brief Lives* are a treasure trove of otherwise lost information on a whole host of topics, many of them highly erudite.[34] But this was not Aubrey's first attempt at life-writing—and there is every reason to believe that his earlier attempt looked very different.

The Life of Verulam

In his *Ephemerides* for 1655, Samuel Hartlib, a great admirer of Francis Bacon, recorded that 'Mr Aubrey is writing the life of Verulam'.[35] He repeated the news in a letter to Dr John Worthington on 12 December: 'One Mr. Aubrey an English gentleman is about to write the Life of that Noble Scholar. I wish he may do it to the life.'[36] For anyone who knew the John Aubrey of 1655, the choice of subject would seem only natural. Aubrey's interest in Francis Bacon started in his childhood when he 'mett accidentally' with his mother's copy of Bacon's *Essays*, and it 'first opened my understanding as to Moralls' (1:431). A clergyman and Eton scholar named Theophilus Wodenote, who spent two years with the Aubrey family at Broad Chalke, furthered his interest: '[h]e did me much good in opening of my understanding; advised me to read Lord Bacons Essayes' (1:527). His writings prove that Aubrey also knew Bacon's *Advancement of Learning*, *Novum Organum*, and *Historia vitae et mortis*, and his copies of the *Historia naturalis & experimentalis de ventis* and the *Remaines*, purchased in 1650 and 1651 respectively, survive.[37] The pervasive influence of Bacon is best seen in his *Idea of Education* as Aubrey sketches his ideal school, which should contain 'All my Lord Chancellor Bacons Writings'; its hall is modelled on the hall of Bacon's Hertfordshire estate of Gorhambury and its chambers should follow the décor of Bacon's chambers at Gray's Inn ('hung with grass green say').[38]

Aubrey was not alone in his fascination with Bacon in the three decades after his death. The correspondence of several learned figures reveals that there was a spirited search for unpublished Bacon manuscripts, involving, in the Netherlands, the Dutch scholars Isaac and Jacob Gruter, and the English ambassador in The Hague, Sir William Boswell; in France, the translator Pierre Amboise; and in England, Bacon's amanuensis and chaplain William Rawley, Sir Thomas Browne, and Samuel Hartlib, among others.[39] In December 1652, Aubrey paid a visit of his 'owne accord' to Hartlib, who recorded in his diary, the *Ephemerides*, that Aubrey 'seemd to be a very witty man and a mighty favorer and promoter of all Ingen*ious* and Verulamian Designes'.[40] The following March, Hartlib wrote to Aubrey to boast that he had received 'a piece of the L*ord* Verulam's w*hich* was never yet extant in print';[41] and a few months later, Aubrey had been recruited to Hartlib's campaign to track down Bacon's writings: 'My Lady Mitton is said to have the remainder of all Verul*am's* MS. *which* Aubrey will labor to get from her.'[42] This search for Bacon's manuscripts was a long-term endeavour: in 1680, Aubrey records that he had 'not long since' obtained a letter supposedly in Bacon's hand from Dr Walter Charleton (1:205–6).

So when Hartlib noted that 'Mr Aubrey is writing the life of Verulam',[43] Aubrey already had in place some of the raw materials. He had known Bacon's erstwhile amanuensis Thomas Hobbes since he was just eight years old. In 1650, he had visited Bacon's servant Thomas Bushell at his house in Lambeth, and viewed 'Bushell's rocks', a Bacon-inspired hydraulic grotto and waterworks, in Enstone, Oxfordshire.[44] His relative Sir John Danvers was another helpful source. Now, in preparation for the life, Aubrey visited Bacon's former estate at Gorhambury and wrote '4 leves in folio close written of the 2 houses, gardens, woods &c.: and of his Lordships manner of Living, & grandarie' in his 'liber B'.[45] And yet, after all this work, Aubrey did not bring that 'Life of Bacon' to fruition in the 1650s.

Why did Aubrey abandon his life of Bacon? I suggest that he lost momentum when another life was published in 1657—one written by Bacon's chaplain, amanuensis, and editor, William Rawley, and prefaced to a collection of unpublished works entitled *Resuscitatio*.[46] Following Bacon's death in April 1626, Rawley had taken it on himself to bring his master's works to fruition as 'a Seruant, to the Labours, and Memory of that Noble Lord, the Lo. *Viscount S. Alban*'.[47] In early 1627, he published the *Sylva Sylvarum* together with the *New Atlantis*, explaining to the dedicatee, Charles I, that he did so 'as one that was trusted with his *Lordships Writings*, euen to the last'.[48] To the reader, Rawley elaborated that 'Hauing had the Honour to be continually with my *Lord*, in compiling of this *Worke*; And to be employed therein; I haue thought it not amisse, (with his Lordships good leaue and liking,) for the better satisfaction of those that shall reade it, to make knowne somewhat of his Lordships Intentions, touching the Ordering, and Publishing of the same'. In explaining Bacon's intentions, Rawley constantly draws attention to his intimate access to his master, sometimes lapsing into the present tense, as if Bacon were still alive: 'I haue heard his Lordship often say…I haue also heard his Lordship discourse…I haue heard his Lordship speake complainingly…his Lordship hath often in his Mouth…his Lordship is wont to say…I haue heard his Lordship say also…I will conclude with an vsuall Speech of his Lordships…'. Rawley claims familiarity with Bacon's thoughts: 'his Lordship thought good…his *Lord*ship perswadeth Himselfe…He did consider likewise…'. At the end of the epistle 'To the Reader', Rawley adds an odd marginal note: 'This Epistle is the same, that should haue been prefixed to this Booke, if his Lordship had liued.' This is, at face value, nonsensical—if Bacon had lived, the epistle would have been written and signed by Bacon—but it speaks to Rawley's insistence that he is effectively ventriloquizing Bacon.

Over the following years, Rawley established himself as the gatekeeper to Bacon's legacy. In 1629, he edited *Certaine Miscellany Works*, a collection of minor pieces, and then, in 1638, a volume of Bacon's writings in Latin translation, and a new English translation of the *Historia vitae et mortis*.[49] But after 1638, Rawley went quiet. Samuel Hartlib noted in his 1655 *Ephemerides* that 'Dr Rawlins [*sic*] hath a very thick Book (which will make a folio) of Lord Verulam containing Miscellany Speeches which hee keepes vnpublished. Dr Wats'–Gilbert Watts, who had translated Bacon's *De augmentis* into English–'had it for some times in his keeping but hee was called vpon by the *said* Dr and restored the same'.[50] So why did William Rawley suddenly publish these 'Miscellany Speeches *which* hee keepes vnpublished' in the 1657 *Resuscitatio*, and preface them with a 'Life' of Bacon, something he had never attempted before? One possible answer, I would suggest, is that he had heard that John Aubrey was writing a life of Bacon, and wanted to stake his prior claim.

Rawley's 'Life' is brief and to the point.[51] Starting with his subject's birthplace and date, and his parents, he moves quickly through the 'first, and childish' years where Bacon's adult wit is presaged and Queen Elizabeth dubs him 'The young Lord Keeper'. Moving to university at Cambridge under John Whitgift, by sixteen Bacon has developed a dislike for the philosophy of Aristotle (foreshadowing his attempt to write a new *Organon*). While he is in Paris with the English ambassador Amias Paulet, his father dies unexpectedly, and Bacon receives only a meagre inheritance. Taking up the study of common law, Bacon becomes 'Queen's Counsel Learned, Extraordinary' and at Gray's Inn erects 'Lord Bacons Lodgings'. But his true calling is political life; there is a brief mention of his relationship with Robert Devereux, second earl of Essex, but greater time is given to his access to Elizabeth, and the lack of any tangible reward for his service. Under James I, Bacon finally attains to offices and dignities, and marries Alice Barnham, though the couple have no children. Rawley then jumps to the last five years of his life, withdrawn from civil society, when Bacon composes most of his works, which are listed.

Moving away from chronology, Rawley then treats a series of topics: Bacon's abilities, writing style, habits as a reader, preferred modes of relaxation, meals, conversation, opinions and assertions, his humane performance as a prosecutor, his conduct towards the sovereign, his faith ('This Lord was Religious'), his freedom from malice. Rawley claims that Bacon's fame was greater overseas than at home, quoting a letter from Italy addressed to William Cavendish, the future earl of Devonshire, and citing the multiple translations of his works, and his foreign visitors. Local praise is forthcoming from Fulke Greville, Lord Brooke, and Dr Samuel Collins, provost of King's College, Cambridge. Claiming that 'It hath been desired; That something should be signified, touching his *Diet*; And the *Regiment*, of his *Health*', Rawley returns to those topics at greater length, before speculating about the role of the moon in his nativity (eclipses of the moon caused Bacon to faint). Finally, he speaks of Bacon's final illness and death, his burial, and his monument, erected by his secretary Sir Thomas Meautys with an inscription by Sir Henry Wotton. This, then, is the approved life of Bacon by the man who guards Bacon's reputation. His 'Life' notably omits any mention of the two major scandals of Bacon's life, which have obsessed biographical work on Bacon since the eighteenth century: Bacon's apparent betrayal of his erstwhile patron and friend Essex, whom he prosecuted in 1600 and 1601; and his ignominious fall from grace in 1621, when he was accused of accepting bribes as Lord Chancellor, imprisoned, fined, and banished from the court.

We cannot know for sure what Aubrey had put together for his life of Francis Bacon. 'Liber B', the manuscript that contained his notes for the project, was borrowed from the Ashmolean by his brother William in 1703, and subsequently lost.[52] One might assume that it would resemble the life of Hobbes that he wanted Blackburne to write: perhaps the opening line 'Francis Bacon was born at York House, January 22 1560/1', and a description of Gorhambury, or Bacon's pedigree. But certainly, when Aubrey returned to Francis Bacon, over a quarter century after he first worked on his life, he was doing something new. Reading Aubrey's entry on Bacon against Rawley's 'Life', it becomes clear that Aubrey does not touch on any of the topics that Rawley has covered. Indeed, this approach evolves into a policy of Aubrey's contribution to life-writing. Describing another early work, he claimed 'I have writt Memorandums of Sir Walter Ralegh... not yet toucht by any one, for I meddle not with any Memorandum that is already printed'.[53] Accordingly, he entitled his later work on Thomas Hobbes 'Supplementum Vitae THOMAE HOBBES Malmesburiensis', since it was only meant to supplement Hobbes's own verse autobiography; it was Wood who insisted he retitle it: 'what need you Supplimentum, pray say The Life of Thomas Hobbs'.[54] And with Bacon, Rawley's 'Life' is taken as a given—indeed, Aubrey's first marginal note on his life is 'vide [see] his Life writt by Dr William Rawley before Baconi Resuscitatio. in folio' (1:205)—although one senses Aubrey's annoyance in his description of *Resuscitatio* as 'A piece of Philosophy halfe as thick as a Grammar set forth By Dr Rawley' (1:220–1).

In writing a supplement to Rawley's 'Life', Aubrey is freed from having to provide a chronology. As a result, however, the 'Brief life' can seem to readers confusingly miscellaneous: multifarious pieces of information (very often witty 'apophthegmata' or *bon mots*) somehow relating to Bacon but with no discernible order—an impression strengthened by the manuscript itself, where Aubrey has evidently added material at many different times, sometimes writing perpendicular to the main text in the margins of his page (Fig. 19). At the end of his entry, Aubrey attempts a list of Bacon's publications, and transcribes writings about or related to Bacon from publications by Ben Jonson, Thomas Blundeville, and Thomas Farnaby, as well as an inscription by Bacon to his friend Jeremiah Bettenham on a summer house in Gray's Inn gardens.

Aubrey gives over much of his account to the places where Bacon lived, with a lengthy description of the family seat of Gorhambury and the nearby Verulam House, built by Bacon, which Aubrey had visited in 1656. By the time Aubrey

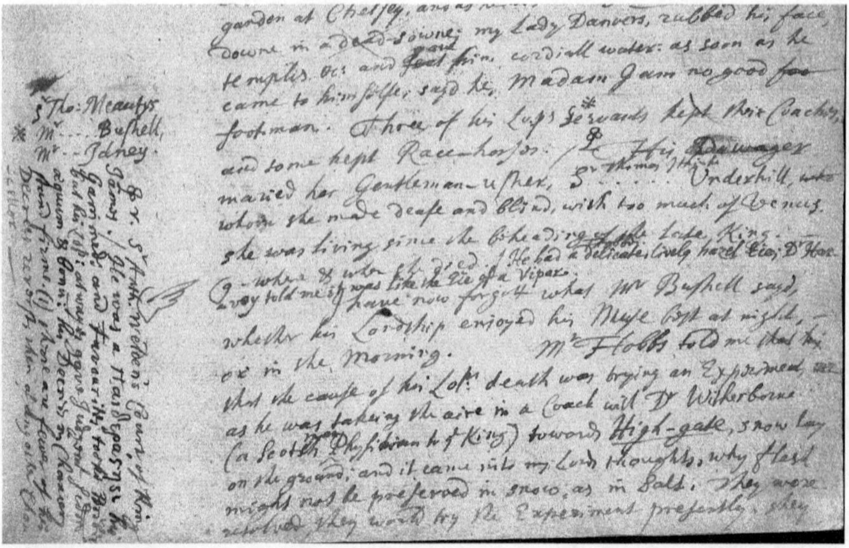

Figure 19. John Aubrey's minutes on Francis Bacon. The Bodleian Libraries, The University of Oxford, MS Aubrey 6, fo. 68r.

returned to these materials for his 'Minute' of Bacon, much had already gone: Verulam House was 'sold about 1665, or 1666 by Sir Harbottle Grimston Baronet (now Master of the Rolles) to two Carpenters for fower hundred poundes: of which they made eight hundred poundes' (1:213). There are details he cannot recall: of Verulam House, he writes, 'I doe not well remember, if on the East-side were Bay-windowes', and draws a 'Model' of the house *'by memorie'*. Even at Gorhambury, much is lost: the 'elegant Sommer-houses well built of Roman-architecture: well wainscoted and cieled' are 'yet standing, but defaced. so that one would have thought the Barbarians had made a Conquest here' (1:219).

As we might expect, Aubrey's notes go places that Rawley would not deign to visit. While Rawley avoided any mention of Bacon's scandalous fall in 1621, Aubrey alludes to it obliquely, claiming that it was his servants who took bribes—'The East-India Merchants presented his Lordship with a Cabinet of Jewells, which his Page Mr Cockaine recieved, and decieved his Lord' (1:208)—and lived extravagantly—'Three of his Lordships Servants kept their Coaches, and some kept Race-horses' (1:209–10). In the process of exonerating Bacon of judicial corruption, however, Aubrey charges him with another crime, that of sodomy: 'He was a *Παιδεραστηστι* [pederast] his Ganimeds and Favourites tooke Bribes but his Lordship alwayes gave Judgement secundum æquum et bonum [according to what was equitable and good]; his Decrees in Chancery stand firme. i.e. there are fewer of his Decrees reverst, then of any other

Chancellor' (1:210). The logic in this strange sequence seems to be that, although Bacon was overindulgent towards his male servants, who were indeed guilty of taking bribes, Bacon himself dispensed justice impartially as Lord Chancellor. Far from suggesting that Bacon might be sexually interested in male 'Ganimeds and Favourites', Rawley had been keen to present a rosy picture of Bacon's marriage to Alice Barnham. The lack of children, he insisted, did not 'detract from his good usage, of his *Consort*, during the *Intermarriage*: whom he prosecuted, with much *Conjugall Love*, and *Respect*; with many Rich *Gifts*, and *Endowments*; Besides a *Roab* of *Honour*, which he invested her withal; which she wore, untill her *Dying Day*; Being twenty years, and more, after his Death'.[55] For Aubrey, by contrast, Lady Bacon was not the grieving widow eternally draped in her robe of honour, but a sexually lascivious woman who could not wait to replace her pederast husband with one of her own servants: 'His Dowager married her Gentleman-usher, Sir Thomas I thinke Underhill, whom she made deafe and blind, with too much of Venus' (1:210).

Aubrey's most famous contribution to the Bacon biography concerns his death. In 1657, Rawley wrote that Bacon had 'casually repaired' to the house of the earl of Arundel in Highgate, then still a village north of London, and a week later died there 'Of a gentle *Feaver*, accidentally accompanied, with a great *Cold*; whereby the *Defluxion* of *Rheume*, fell so plentifully upon his *Breast*, that he died by *Suffocation*'.[56] Aubrey has a much better story:

> Mr Thomas Hobbes told me that the cause of his Lordships death was trying an Experiment, viz as he was takeing the aire in a Coach with Dr. Witherborne. (a Scotch man Physitian to the King) towards *High-gate*, snow lay on the ground; and it came into my Lords thoughts, why flesh might not be preserved in snow, as in Salt. They were resolved, they would try the Experiment presently. they alighted out of the Coach, and went into a poore womans howse at the bottome of Highgate hill, and bought a Hen, and made the woman exenterate [eviscerate] it, and then stuffed the bodie with Snow, and my Lord did help to doe it himselfe. The Snow so chilled him, that he immediately fell so extremely ill, that he could not returne to his lodgeings (I suppose then at Grayes Inne) but went to the Earle of Arundells howse at High-gate, where they had putt him into a good bed warmed with a panne, but it was a damp bed that had not been layn-in about a yeare before, which gave him such a cold that that [*sic*] in 2 or 3 dayes as I remember he told me, he dyed of Suffocation. (1:210–11)

The location and the nature of Bacon's death (Arundel's Highgate house, a 'Suffocation') are the same, and Hobbes, Bacon's amanuensis and Aubrey's friend, would seem a trustworthy source. Even if the vagaries of the British climate mean there might indeed have been snow on the ground in April, that does not explain why Bacon would suddenly feel the need to perform a refrigeration experiment when he had published on the phenomenon years earlier. And yet Aubrey's story functions perfectly to portray Bacon as an inveterate hands-on experimenter, whose passion for knowledge leads inevitably to his demise—and to this day it remains one of the facts people remember about Francis Bacon.

Antiquities 'Reskued' from the past '& preservd' for the future: this is the goal that Aubrey sets for himself. We may want to read his collections as 'Brief lives'—and indeed, past editors have mangled and misrepresented his writings so that they *read* as 'Brief lives'—but Aubrey saw them instead as raw materials for future life-writing. And these materials bring with them a huge amount of information about how they should be read. As Kate Bennett puts it, 'Aubrey was adept at preserving the atmosphere in which stories were told and memories transmitted; but not in cracking these accounts open to draw out the facts. He offers a different kind of biographical truth, suggesting that we may be able to hear, through him, the seventeenth century talking to and about itself.'[57] For all Rawley's vaunted intimacy with Bacon, there is nothing in his 'Life' of the vividness that Aubrey achieves. Thomas Hobbes told Aubrey that Bacon 'had a delicate, lively hazel Eie'; William Harvey 'told me it was like the Eie of a Viper' (1:210). Bacon's servants all wore Spanish leather boots, for if they wore less expensive footwear 'he would smell the neates-leather, which offended him'. Bacon often had 'Musique in the next roome where he meditated'. His table was 'strewed with Sweet Herbes and Flowers, which he sayd did refresh his spirits and memorie' (1:207). Sir John Danvers informed Aubrey that Bacon 'would often drinke a good draught of strong Beer (March-beer) to bedwards, to lay his working Fancy asleep: which otherwise would keepe him from sleeping great part of the night' (1:209).

The point is not the 'fact' that Francis Bacon had green eyes: it is that Aubrey allows us to hear Thomas Hobbes telling him that Bacon had a delicate, lively hazel eye, and Dr William Harvey telling him that it was like the eye of the viper. From Thomas Bushell, we see Bacon meditating and dictating to him in the coppice-wood in the west of his Gorhambury estate, where he planted peonies and tulips under every tree. Harold Love has suggested that Aubrey's lives can be seen as part of a new form of 'biography as a written-down derivative of gossip, conversation, and oral legend'.[58] But it is not merely oral: through Aubrey's eyes, and with Aubrey's memory, we also see the remains of the places where Bacon lived and worked—Gray's Inn, Verulam House, Gorhambury—and mourn with him already the summer houses 'yet standing, but defaced', the 'Paradise' that 'now is a large ploughed field' (1:219). These are the planks of the shipwreck that Aubrey keeps afloat through the centuries.

Walton and Aubrey: The Lives of John Hales

We can see the distinctiveness of Aubrey's approach in a very particular comparison with the work of Izaak Walton. Walton's *Lives* were known to Aubrey: in 1680, Aubrey wrote to the then eighty-seven-year-old Walton to ask a series of five questions about various figures, including Ben Jonson; Walton dutifully replied, and Aubrey included Walton's letter, 'in his owne handwriting', in his manuscript before his life of Jonson (1:357–9, facsimile on 1:360). There is nothing in Walton's letter, or anywhere else, to suggest that he knew Aubrey well.

On occasion, however, the two men occupied the same territory. Each attempted to write a life of John Hales (1584–1656), fellow of Corpus Christi College, Oxford, where he was also Regius Professor of Greek (and had delivered Sir Thomas Bodley's funeral oration), fellow of Eton College, and canon of Windsor. It was Hales who had failed to write the life of Sir Henry Wotton that Walton inherited; it could be seen as some form of justice that his own life-writing had a similar fate. The divine Anthony Faringdon, who had worked with Hales at Windsor—'there was none to whom Mr. *Hales* was so throughly known as unto him'—was supposed to write a life to prefix a collection of Hales's *Golden Remains* (1659), but died in 1658 before he could do the work: he noted wryly, in a prefatory letter, that 'I have drawn in my minde the *Model* of his *Life*, but I am like Mr. *HALES* in this, which was one of his *defects*, not to pen any thing, till I must needs'.[59] John Pearson, who had been a schoolboy at Eton under Hales, stepped in, but begged the reader, 'being deprived of the proper Plutarch', to excuse him for providing no more than a perfunctory character sketch.[60] When in 1673 a second edition of the *Golden Remains* was planned, the publisher Richard Marriot and his long-time associate Izaak Walton—in their time-honoured fashion—undertook much of the research for the antiquary and Corpus Christi fellow William Fulman to pen the biography. But Fulman, though a vicious critic of others' life-writing, was incapable of producing his own, and failed to do so here;[61] the *Golden Remains* went into its second impression still bearing its now fourteen-year-old apology by Pearson. It would be Anthony Wood who published the first full 'Life of Hales' in 1692, in the second volume of his *Athenæ Oxonienses*, drawing heavily on research undertaken by Aubrey, while Aubrey included Hales in his unpublished *Brief Lives* (1:398–9). But efforts continued (and continued to fail) into the eighteenth and nineteenth centuries, as the antiquary and natural philosopher William Stukeley (1687–1765) gathered notes on Hales's life and works, and the archival scholar Joseph Hunter (1783–1861) collected materials for a biography: neither project came to fruition.[62]

Walton's involvement in the quest to write Hales's life can be reconstructed from the papers of William Fulman at Corpus Christi, and those of Church of England historian John Walker, now at the Bodleian.[63] In a letter dated 24 August 1673 to Marriot, Walton describes his contribution.[64] From Anthony Faringdon's executor John Millington he had obtained 'so much of mr Hales his life as mr faringdon had writ'; he had made enquiries of 'many that knew' Hales, including 'mrs Powny of windesor (at whose howse he dyed)', and set down what he had learned; and he had commissioned the Eton schoolmaster Thomas Mountague to write down his memories. If Fulman could now 'make his queries concerning the part of his life spent in oxford', Walton continues, 'he will haue many, and good, I mene trew informations from mr ffaringdon till he come thither', and then 'by me and my meanes' comparable information on Hales's life 'since he came to Eaton'.[65] Between the Faringdon notes, Walton's information, and his own knowledge of the Oxford years, then, Fulman could piece together Hales's life.

Two months later, on 20 October, Walton wrote to Fulman directly, handing over a substantial trove of materials on Hales. As promised, he included Faringdon's opening gambit on 'The Authours Life', which he had had copied out ('for, it was very foule writ and much interlined', as he warns Fulman).[66] Walton also included a letter dated 22 June 1673 written—'to me and now to you'—by the dean of Chichester Cathedral, George Stradling, in answer to 'inquiries' Walton had made about Hales.[67] Most importantly, Walton provided Fulman with a lengthy letter containing many of his own researches, advising him that 'you may note that what follows will not be set downe in order, but backward and forward, as I have Colected them in my queries and possibly twice'. What this document contains, then, is Walton's own researches, written up (and heavily emended—the letter is full of deletions and insertions), but not inserted into the roughly chronological sequence one might expect of a finished 'life'. Occasionally, Walton interjects his own personal knowledge of Hales. Discussing how foreign scholars, including Hugo Grotius, would write to Hales 'for solutions of learned questions', Walton notes that 'I have beine shewed by him the picture of *grotius* which he kept in his study, and to me he spake highly of his greate and usefull learning'. Sometimes, Walton condenses the words of multiple informants ('severall have told me of his greate abstinance that is from Thursday noone to Satterday noone with out taking a bit of bread or drinking a spoonful of drinke'). For Hales's views on religious controversy, Walton suggests further reading—'Concerning this vew doctor parkers last booke folio—135. and you are to reade do*ctor* pearson his preface to mr Hales his sermons and fragments' while offering 'in probabillitie that he was of an other opinion nerer his end'. Walton's notes can be emphatic: 'Concerning his booke of scisme you may note that whatever his opinion was he kept it to him selfe as to the Controverted parts of it...You may note that when the Lady Salter wood have had him stay longer, he said it might bring her in danger...'—'you may note' is less of a suggestion, and more an instruction.[68]

For much of his letter, though, Walton is relaying oral testimony by individual informants, among them the man originally commissioned to write the life, Anthony Faringdon: Walton describes how two or three months before Hales's death, Faringdon 'went to se him at the towne of Eaton wher he found him gravely

Cherfull at the howse of mrs or goody powny where a very mene Lodging Contented him'. Another key witness is Henry King's sister Anne (by 1673 Lady How), who spent time with Hales during the Interregnum at Richings Park, near Eton, the home of Lady Salter. Lady How, whom Walton deemed 'a most generose and ingenious lady', provided several testimonials to Hales's character. He lived for fourteen days on 'bere and bred and tosts' to test how he would fare if sequestered; he was 'neuer out of Humor but always euen, and humble, and quiet', 'alwayes reddy to resolue questions', 'kept his opinions to himselfe'. In his latter days at Richings, 'he was visually reading Tho*mas* a kempis w*hi*ch of a small print he read without spectakells'.[69]

While Lady How's reminiscences give us a pious, reserved John Hales, the picture suddenly changes with the voice of another of Walton's informants. When the college rents were being sequestered, Walton is told, Hales hid for nine weeks 'to preserue the Collage writings and keyes'—but 'this concelement was so nere the collage or highway that he said after pleasantly those that searcht for him might haue smelt him if he had eaten garlick'. This gem, Walton relates, 'was told me by mrs powny from whome or mr montague it may be had more perfectly'. It was in Mrs Powney's Eton house that Hales died; Walton elaborates that 'this woman was the widow of—powny some time mr Hales his servant: but he dyed before mr Hales was in his distress. and she was affectionately dilligent to atend him in all his necessities and at her poore howse the good man dyed'. Walton sorely needed local witnesses like Mrs Powney and Thomas Mountague. The notes he provided to Fulman are full of holes, signalled by the frequent appearance of the letter 'q' ('quaere', or 'inquire'): 'he liud - q - yeares afer he was sequesterd he dyed the 19° of my Anno - q - mrs powny' and so on. He advised Fulman that Mountague 'or mrs powny will answere all the q as to the yeare of his deth, and who was at the charge of his monument [Walton's nearest guess was "some frend"], how long he lay sick his behauior then: and what ells is defectiue in theise colections gatherd by me'.[70]

Walton's collections were to remain defective: Marriot died in 1679, Walton in 1683, and Fulman in 1688, their life still unwritten. But they were not the only men chasing a life of Hales. As an Oxford man, Hales was an important figure in Anthony Wood's *Athenæ Oxonienses* project—and so he became the concern of Wood's collaborator, John Aubrey. In Aubrey's researches, we can see how his working methods resembled Walton's—but, more importantly, how he had an eye for different details. Like Walton, Aubrey drew on memories of a meeting with Hales, 'within a yeare before he deceased': 'a prettie little man, sanguine, of a cheerfull countenance, very gentile, and courteous, I was recieved [*sic*] by him with much humanity: he was in a kind of violet-colourd cloath Gowne with buttons and loopes (he wore not a black gowne) and was reading Thomas à Kempis'—the same reading material that Lady

How had recalled to Walton. But Aubrey also noted Hales's favourite tipple: 'he loved Canarie; but moderately to refresh his spirits' (1:398–9).

Aubrey's initial informant was his local vicar in Broad Chalke, Wiltshire, John Sloper, who had sterling familial connections: 'his mother was Mr Hales's sister; and he [Hales] bred him [Sloper] at Eaton' (1:398). But just as Walton's notes change as they move from Lady How to Mrs Powney, so Aubrey's view of Hales changes when he journeys to Eton in July 1682 to interview Hales's landlady, as he related to Wood in a letter. 'Mr J. Hales dyed at M*ist*ris Powneys howse [a widowe woman] in Eaton opposite the churchyard adjoyning to the Christopher Inne southwards.' The house was familiar to Aubrey, since ''Tis the howse where I sawe him': 'a handsome darke old fashioned house: the hall (after the old fashion) above the wainscot painted cloath, with godly sentences, out of the Psalmes &c.: according to the pious custome of old times', with 'a convenient garden and orchard'. Mrs Powney painted a positive picture of her lodger: 'she told me, that when she was maried, Mr Hales was very bountifull to them in setting them up to live in the world: she was very carefull of him, & respectfull to him'. According to Mrs Powney, 'Mr Hales was the common Godfather' in Eton, 'and 'twas pretty to see, as he walked to Windsor, how his Godchil*dren* fell on their knees' to ask 'his blessing'. Moreover, 'When he was Burser [at Eton], he still gave away all his Groates for the acquittances to his Godchildren, & by that time he came to Windsor Bridge, he would have never a groate left'. She also filled in some of Aubrey's queries about Hales's library: 'Cornelius Bee bought his Library for 700*li* w*hich* cost him not lesse than 2500*li*. M*ist*ris Powney told me, that she was much ag*ain*st the sale because she knew it was his Life & ioy.'[71]

Between her sketches of Hales as bountiful benefactor, Mrs Powney took the opportunity to correct the information from Aubrey's earlier informant. 'This M*ist*ris Powney assured me that the poor were more relievable (that is to say) that he recieued [*sic*] more kindnesse from them, then from the Rich.' She was particularly keen to point out what Aubrey had been told 'of my Lady Salter (from her nephew Sloper vicar of Chalk) is false'. Lady Salter, Mrs Powney claimed, 'had him [Hales] to her howse indeed, but twas to teach her sonne; who was such a blockhed he could not read well'. Sloper was not only a false informant, she insisted; despite the fact that Hales 'bred up our Vicar', Sloper, '(she told me) never sent him a Token'. The animosity between Sloper and Mrs Powney was only exacerbated by Hales's death: 'he is angry with her, thinks he left her too much'. (Hales did indeed bequeath Mrs Powney 'All my English books, together with the remainder of all monies, goods, and utensils whatsoever'.) In sum, Mrs Powney made quite an impression on Aubrey: 'She is a very good woman and of a gratefull spirit... she is a woman primitively good, & deserues to be remembred... She haz been handsome.

a good understanding, neate and cleanly.' He regretted one lapse in his research, however: 'I wish I had her *Christian* name.'[72]

Mrs Powney's Christian name was Hannah. We know this because Anthony Wood, taking Aubrey's cue, wrote to John Roswell, a Corpus alumnus, canon of Windsor and master at Eton, to check.[73] And when he published the first full 'Life of Hales' in 1692, in the second volume of his *Athenæ Oxonienses*, Wood drew liberally on Aubrey's notes, in the process giving us more details of the Eton landlady:

> retiring to *Eaton*, [Hales] took up his quarters and sojourned in an house next to the *Christopher Inn*, belonging then to *Hannah* the widow of *John Dickenson*, (a Servant from his youth to our Author *Hales*) and afterwards the wife and widdow of one *Sim. Powney*; which *Hannah* was very careful of, and respectful to, him, as having formerly at her Marriage received of his bounty.[74]

A year apart, Aubrey and Walton make their way to Mrs Powney's house in Eton. But whereas Walton treats her, along with the schoolmaster Mountague, as a useful source of information, a local authority from whom details may be had 'more perfectly', Aubrey paints a warm and admiring portrait of 'a woman primitively good' who 'deserues to be remembred' in her own right. As Kate Bennett has argued, by including figures like Hannah Powney, Aubrey's life-writing 'did justice to the experience, observation, and contribution of persons without the social position, the masculine sex, or even on occasions, the talents to make their voice heard'.[75] Walton collects his shipwrecked planks to build a funeral pyre for John Hales; Aubrey collects those planks not only to memorialize Hales, his ostensible subject, but also to ensure that Hannah Powney is remembered over 300 years later.

14

Samuel Pepys's Life in Shorthand

Late in 1659, Samuel Pepys bought a new paper book from his stationer, ruled margins on each page in red ink, and penned a short analysis of the current fortunes of himself, his household, and his country. Then, on 1 January 1660, or shortly afterwards, Pepys wrote the first daily entry in his new diary. With a few exceptions, he would provide entries for every day between then and 31 May 1669, when he brought the diary to an end, citing his failing eyesight as the reason for its demise. The 3100 manuscript pages he filled in the intervening nine years and five months are now a classic of British prose. Pepys had the good fortune–as a diarist, at least–to write during a period of fascinating turmoil for the London in which he lived: a decade that saw the Restoration of the Stuart monarchy, the Great Plague of 1665, the Great Fire of 1666, and the Second Anglo-Dutch War–and his position high in the Navy bureaucracy meant that he had access to its defining moments: Pepys accompanied Charles II on his return to England; he was the first to inform the king and his brother of the state of the Great Fire. In recounting these events, Pepys writes with remarkable immediacy:

> all over the Thames, with one's face in the wind you were almost burned with a shower of Firedrops - this is very true - so as houses were burned by these drops and flakes of fire, three or four, nay five or six houses, one from another... We stayed till, it being darkish, we saw the fire as only one entire arch of fire from this to the other side of the bridge, and in a bow up the hill, for an arch of above a mile long. It made me weep to see it. The churches, houses, and all on fire and flaming at once, and a horrid noise the flames made, and the cracking of houses at their ruine.[1]

Yet his diary is most prized for its intimate portrait of its writer and for its frank exposition of his weaknesses, physical and moral. As Pepys's most recent biographer, Claire Tomalin, puts it, the diary 'allows us to experience the world from inside his skin, and for all its huge, Shakespearean cast of characters, it is always essentially a rhapsody on himself at the centre'.[2] Yet being inside his skin means we also witness his public masturbation and his constant assaults on female servants, shop assistants, and the wives and daughters of men suing for his patronage.[3] These incidents, I shall suggest, Pepys did not intend for all of us to know.

The diary survives in six calf-bound volumes with gilt crests in the Pepys Library at Magdalene College, Cambridge.[4] Its modern editors, Robert Latham and William Matthews, calculate that the diary 'contains about 1,250,000 words'[5]—only strictly the diary does not contain many 'words' but instead shorthand symbols, with only a few scattered words, mainly proper names, written out in longhand. For most of its extraordinary length, the diary is remarkably clear and legible... but only if the reader understands the shorthand. Pepys scholars do of course note that the diary is written in shorthand—but the acknowledgement is usually fleeting. In his 1974 biography, Richard Ollard writes that it is 'important' to know that the diary 'was written in shorthand under the strictest secrecy' but does not explain why; Tomalin's 2001 study devotes only one paragraph of its nearly 500 pages to a consideration of shorthand.[6] It's easy to see why the shorthand gets sidelined—why sacrifice all that immediacy and vividness in favour of opaque symbols that are everything that our Pepys is not: hidden, secretive, neurotically private? But the shorthand is more than an annoying detail that we can push to one side: it is the very fabric of the diary. Pepys himself understood this well: when he deposited his diaries in his 'Bibliotheca Pepysiana' at Magdalene, he catalogued them under the titles: 'My own Diary MSS in Short-hand' and 'Pepys - Diary in Shorthand'.[7] Pepys's interest in shorthand was more than casual: he amassed the largest collection of books on shorthand of his day. And, as this chapter will show, the diary is written not in a single shorthand, but rather in an evolving experiment with shorthand—one that, by May 1669, ultimately proved too cumbersome for even this most conscientious of record keepers.

Swift or Secret? The Uses of Early Modern Shorthand

When Timothy Bright published the first English shorthand manual in 1588, he entitled it *Characterie. An arte of shorte, swifte, and secrete writing by character.*[8] Over a century later, John Locke stressed that shorthand, which is 'known only in *England*, may perhaps, be thought worth the Learning, both for Dispatch in what Men write for their own Memory, and Concealment of what they would not have lie open to every Eye'. Dispatch and concealment, swiftness and secrecy: these are the two great assets of shorthand. Locke also hints at a third: the facility with which a shorthand can be adapted to any person's 'own private use or phancy'.[9]

By the time Locke came to write this, there were dozens of English shorthands available for writers to use and adapt.[10] Bright's 1588 *Characterie* was followed by a series of manuals by the famed calligrapher Peter Bales in the closing years of the sixteenth century, and then by other early systems by John Willis, Edmond Willis, W. Folkingham, and Henry Petre. Pepys's shorthand is in essence the one promulgated by Thomas Shelton in two works, *Short Writing* (1620) and *Tachygraphy* (1635). Shelton drew his inspiration primarily from John Willis's *An Abreuiation of Writing by Character* (1602), which provided him with an alphabet comprising curves and straight lines, and a system of representing vowels within words by spatial arrangement; he streamlined Willis's system by simplifying the representation of diphthongs, and reducing the number of symbols for key words and suffixes to around 300.[11] Shelton's system proved particularly popular with students–the *Tachygraphy*'s 1641 title page boasted it was 'approoued by both Vnyuersities'[12]– and Pepys probably learned it while at Magdalene College from 1650 to 1654, to take down lecture notes.

Shorthand was by no means the sole preserve of academia, however. As early as 1616 George Buck noted that among the writing arts taught in London, there was now 'the art of *Brachygraphie*, which is an Art newly discouered, or newly recouered, & is of very goode & necessarie vse being well and honestly exercised: for by the meanes & helpe therof (they which know it) can readily take a Sermon, Oration, Play, or any long speech, dictated, acted, & vttered in the instant'.[13] The emphasis here is on dispatch, the speedy taking down of oral presentation in real time. The future parliamentarian Simonds d'Ewes (1602–50) recalled being 'directed…to take notes in writing at sermons' at the school of Henry Reynolds between 1614 and 1616–and since Reynolds was himself a deviser of shorthands, this instruction probably included the teaching of shorthand. (D'Ewes was more impressed by the achievements of Reynolds's daughter Bathsua, who also invented a shorthand, the *Index radiographia*;[14] as a law student, D'Ewes kept his own diary in cipher rather than shorthand.[15]) The shorthand masters stressed the pious application of their art to the taking of notes during sermons, and there is evidence that the practice was widespread. John Aubrey writes that John Graunt, born in 1620, was 'bred-up, (as the fashion then was) in the Puritan way', which meant among other things that he 'wrote Short-hand dextrously' and spent 'many yeares constant hearing, and writing sermon-notes'.[16] In 1641, the Bohemian educationalist Jan Amos Komenský (Comenius) noted with surprise the ubiquity of note-taking at sermons in England: 'Some thirty years since (in King James's reign) they discovered an art which has now come into vogue even among the country folk, that of tachygraphy which they call stenography.' Komenský went so far as to claim that 'Almost all of them acquire this, as soon as they have learnt at school to read the Scriptures in the vernacular. It takes them about another year to learn the art of shorthand.'[17] Beyond sermons, men and women used shorthand to record all kinds of materials, even practising various shorthands for pleasure. Henry Oxinden copied out Shelton's shorthand version of the Lord's Prayer and Creed into his personal manuscript. In 1639, Katherine Packer took down recipes in shorthand for her miscellany entitled 'A Booke of very Good medecines for seuerall deseases wounds and sores both new and olde'.[18] By 1641, John Wilkins could write in his *Mercury* that 'This short-hand writing, is now so ordinary in practice (it being usuall for any common Mechanick both to write and invent it) that I shall not neede to set downe any particular example of it'.[19]

Shorthand became especially useful in political circles. Parliamentary debates of the 1620s were taken down by Bulstrode Whitelocke (using a system devised by John Willis) and Edward Nicholas (adapting Edmond Willis's).[20] Roger Williams, the future founder of Rhode Island, allegedly launched his career recording cases in Star Chamber for Sir Edward Coke, who had observed his facility in taking down sermons in shorthand.[21] Sometimes the motive for the shorthand-taker was to preserve worthy orations: Lord Keeper John Williams's speeches on 'grave and weighty Causes' were reportedly so 'admirable' that they were 'taken in short-hand by several'.[22] From the 1640s, high-level trials (including Archbishop William Laud's and John Lilburne's) and scaffold speeches (notably those of the earl of Strafford and Charles I) were captured in shorthand, a practice common enough that John Evelyn could write in his 'Kalendarium' that 'it was not my Custome or delight, to be often present at any *Capital Trials*, we having them commonly, so exactly published by those who take them in shorthand'.[23]

Shorthand also provided a level of confidentiality–albeit one that could be decrypted. The army secretary William Clarke used shorthand to take down the New Model Army's Putney Debates of 1647,[24] and to correspond privately with his secretariat, including John Rushworth, who later used the same shorthand to mark up books in the Fairfax library when preparing his *Historical Collections*.[25] This ability to render writing at least somewhat secret was also prized in domestic settings, especially for women seeking to conceal their life-writings from their husbands.[26] In 1686, Sarah Henry (later Sarah Savage) started her diary by registering her concern that she lacked 'the advantage of writing characters' (the shorthand symbols that would allow her a measure of privacy); her solution was to write in longhand but 'to endeavour to keep it private'.[27] Others were more successful at preserving their privacy: when Samuel Bury came to publish fragments of the diary of his late wife Elizabeth in 1720, he admitted that 'betwixt Twenty and Thirty Years, she conceal'd her Accounts in Short Hand, which cannot be recovered by me, nor, I believe by any other, because of many peculiar Characters and Abbreviations of her own'; he could only publish what she wrote in longhand, starting in 1690.[28]

Some male relatives and editors, however, went to considerable lengths to discover the codes with which women's papers could be read. The 1659 funeral sermon for Mary Bewley recorded that in the last six months of her life, she had extended her pious 'Closet duties' by 'commit[ting] to writing' her 'pondering and meditation', although this work 'being in short-hand writing can hardly be read, some of the Characters being of her own invention'. It was only 'after much importunity' Bewley 'read to her husband and friends, to their great satisfaction'—that is, she read from her shorthand—'for therein she discovered her gifts and graces, knowledge and affection, excellent matter, handsomely composed, and all in Scripture-language'.[29] Similarly, Elizabeth Dunton, who died in 1697, having 'kept a Diary for near on Twenty Years', specifically 'desired that all those large Papers might be burnt, though even much of what she writ was in a Short-hand of her own Invention'; her editor Timothy Rogers noted that 'That part of the Diary, which I have Extracted several Things that were written with her own Hand, was with great Difficulty obtain'd from her by her Husband in her last Sickness; in which, as she express'd it, She thought it her Duty to deny him nothing'.[30] Mary Bewley and Elizabeth Dunton revealed their shorthands only under pressure and *in extremis*: their hope had been to write in secret, for no future audience.

Some writers used shorthand in a more varied way. In his diary, the merchant and amateur astrologer Samuel Jeake of Rye (1652–99) provided a chronology of his educational milestones: in February 1657, he 'entred reading in the Bible'; in 1661 or 1662, he 'learned to write' and by 1663 'could write well, severall hands'; in 1663 he 'entered into the Greek Grammar; having before learned the Latine Authors' and 'began to learn Rhetorick'; by April 1664 'I could draw pictures indifferent well, learn'd of my self'; and on 9 September 1665, he noted, 'By this time I had learned to write Shorthand'. At the same time he 'began to learn Hebrew', and on 18 July 1666, he 'began to set down Memorandums of my Life in a Diary'.[31] One extract of that diary, from 28 March to 19 October 1699, which survives among his family papers in the Rye Museum, is written in shorthand, with only a few phrases in longhand. But there is precious little in the entries that would require any degree of secrecy: most are simply records of his purchases, precisely timed to facilitate astrological readings. It seems likely that this was the preferred initial form of his daily diary, with shorthand used for speed. But a more extensive diary, now at the Clark Library, written up in 1694 from memoranda, deploys shorthand in a more strategic manner.[32] Here, Jeake designates as deserving of shorthand treatment such painfully personal matters as 'the void[ing of] a great worm downwards', the tribulations caused by an anal fistula (including a disastrous attempt to operate), bouts of melancholy, and—charmingly—the failed marriage negotiations that he undertook with several women before his successful match with

Elizabeth Hartshorne in 1680. Once married, Jeake uses shorthand to record sexual encounters with his wife and details of her pregnancies; perhaps more surprisingly, his struggle with poor eyesight is also assigned to shorthand, as is the note that he 'Had my hair cut'.[33]

Shelton's shorthand seems to have been particularly popular with Cambridge-and Harvard-educated men. In the summer of 1662, the nineteen-year-old Trinity College undergraduate Isaac Newton (1642–1727) used Shelton's shorthand to write lists of his personal sins—which hid the shocking revelation that he ate an apple in church, or made a mousetrap on a Sunday, and more understandably, 'Threatning my father and mother Smith to burne them and the house over them. Wishing death and hoping it to some'.[34] Newton also includes a catch-all reference to 'Having uncleane thoughts words and actions and dreamese [*sic*]', and this area, which we might now designate as 'sexual', was a favourite topic for shorthand.[35] Two years later, in December 1655, the Bermuda-born, Harvard-educated alchemist George Starkey (1628–65) embarked during a stay in Bristol on 'A perfect day booke of all material passages of my life from Dec 11 and so forward'.[36] Written in shorthand, the perfect day book contained some very imperfect passages detailing Starkey's rampant drinking (and hangovers), gambling, 'idle discourse', and what he refers to—abbreviated and in shorthand—as 'lf pollut': 'self-pollution', either masturbation or involuntary emission of semen. On the second day, Wednesday, after Starkey 'rose about seven in the morning' and 'committed <se>lf pollut<ion>', as usual, he makes a covenant with God, pledging moderation in tavern drinking; abstention from gambling, lying, self-pollution, fornication, and adultery; and a commitment to daily prayer and attendance at sermons. Sad to report, Starkey did not make it to the afternoon, getting carried away in an argument at the Star Tavern. But the nights were the real challenge: on Thursday he was 'much troubled in the night with filthy dream', and on Friday that he 'was defiled twise this night by <se>lf pollut<ion>'. The day book does not continue beyond Friday, but the five days' entries suffice to show that Starkey felt that his battle with alcohol and 'self-pollution' warranted a level of obfuscation not required even in his alchemical notebooks.

Starkey's Harvard contemporary, the poet and minister Michael Wigglesworth (1631–1705), deployed the same shorthand in his diary, but with more nuance. Wigglesworth's surviving diary opens when he is tutoring at Harvard, with an entry that sets the tone for what is to follow:

> If *the* unloving carriages of my pupils can goe so to my heart as they doe; how they doe my vain thoughts, my detestable pride, my *unnatural filthy lust that are so often and even this day in some measure stirring in me* how do these griev my lord Jesus that loves me infinite more then I do them? (3)

The phrase here in italics is in the manuscript in Shelton's shorthand, and presumably it was redacted that way because of the reference to 'unnatural filthy lust'. This interpretation is borne out by other shorthand passages in the pages that follow:

> *I find such unresistable torments of carnal lusts or provocation unto the ejection of seed that I find my self unable to read any thing to inform me about my distemper because of the prevailing or rising of my lusts.* (4)
>
> *The last night a filthy dream and so pollution escaped me in my sleep...* (5)
>
> *Some filthiness escaped me in a filthy dream, the lord notwithstanding.*[37] (6)

Wigglesworth also drops into shorthand when discussing some non-sexual sins, especially pride, and often when he mentions other people, as if protecting them. But shorthand is most emphatically deployed to discuss Wigglesworth's 'old sins' (93).

On 15 September 1655, Wigglesworth lists, in two columns, his current blessings and trials as winter approaches. Concluding that 'God will guide and provide', he decides that 'In Memoriall of his former mercys received in answer to prayer and off all his goodnes hitherto I will erect...A pillar to the prayse of his grace'. But the pillar he draws is unsettlingly phallic (Fig. 20), and is followed immediately by a lapse into shorthand:

> some *night pollution escaped me notwithstanding my earnest prayer to the contrary which brought to mind my old sins now too much forgotten (as near as I remember the thoughts that then I had) together with my later sins unto seeming one that had received so many mercies from the Lord O unthankfulness unthankfulness when shall I get rid of thee.*[38]

Whatever 'old sins' Wigglesworth was alluding to, there is no doubt that he saw shorthand as a means to obscure from others, and to highlight for himself, aspects of his thought and behaviour that he found disturbing. It was a technique that, several thousand miles away, Samuel Pepys would elaborate in his own idiosyncratic style.

Pepys's Uses of Shorthand

Pepys was an inveterate shorthand writer. He kept many documents relating to his official duties in shorthand—we still have a letterbook from 1664 to 1668; entries he made in the 'Navy White Book' before July 1665; and an account of debates before the Privy Council between December 1670 and February 1671 about a report by

Figure 20. Drawing of a pillar and shorthand text in the diary of Michael Wigglesworth. Massachusetts Historical Society.

the Brooke House Commissioners, all taken down in a Sheltonian shorthand.[39] Shorthand notes exist from his service to the 1677 Parliament, with a reminder that they were subsequently 'To be transcribed in longhand'.[40] Pepys was evidently known for his skill: in 1680, Charles II summoned him to Newmarket to take down an account of his escape from the battle of Worcester in 1651.[41] Pepys ensured that his servant Will Hewer mastered the art, ordering him to take down their parish preacher's first sermon when he returned to London after the 1665 plague.[42] Although Hewer's version of Shelton's system is slightly different to Pepys's, Pepys could read it: composing a sensitive letter to James, duke of York about the poor condition of the Navy, Pepys noted 'It was a great convenience tonight, that what I had writ fowle in shorthand, I could read to W. Hewer and he take it fair in shorthand so as I can read it tomorrow to Sir W. Coventry, and then come home and he read to me, while I take it in longhand to present - which saves me much time' (7:374). In other circumstances, however, it seems only Pepys knew how to make sense of his shorthand. In 1683, on his mission to Tangier, he writes of being 'with my Lord in his cabin, for him to write, in long-hand, from my short-hand notes, which I read, my arguments for destroying Tangier'.[43]

Pepys's interest in shorthand went deep; he assembled what he called 'A Collection of the Principal Short-hands hitherto published, & now to be recovered, in England, March 25th 1693', which remains the most extensive collection of seventeenth-century English shorthand books. The subject catalogue that Pepys compiled for his library gives us some sense of how he viewed these shorthands. In the section under 'Arts and Sciences', 'Short-hand' is given an entry, but cross-referenced: 'vid. [see] Writing'. 'Writing' is then divided into three categories: 'Secretly', 'Faire', and 'Swiftly'. Under 'Secretly', Pepys lists three books: Blaise de Vigenère's *Traité des chiffres* (1586), John Wilkins's *Mercury* (1641), and Claude Comiers's *L'art d'écrire et de parler occultement* (1690). By contrast, the shorthand collection is catalogued under 'Swiftly'.

Yet in its form his shorthand diary belies that categorization. Pepys's diary was not written 'Swiftly'; rather, all the evidence suggests that it was composed carefully in a series of stages. On 10 November 1665, for example, Pepys records: 'Up, and enter all my Journall since the 28th of October, having every day's passages well in my head, though it troubles me to remember it'—on this occasion, he was 'forced to, being kept from my lodging, where my books and papers are, for several days' (6:295). On 22 December following, he again noted 'making up my Journall for 8 or 9 days; and so my mind being eased of it' (6:337).[44] In 1668, Pepys twice failed to write up his diary (for periods of eleven and thirteen days), but—conscientious administrator that he was—kept his notes so that he could do it later.[45] In some cases these notes, also in shorthand, are primarily lists of expenses with some *aide-mémoire* phrases interspersed. Thus Friday 10 April 1668 reads:

All morning at office. At noon with *W P* to *D Y* and attended council. So to piper's. And Duck-lane and there kissed book- seller's wife and bought *Legend*	0 - 14 - 0	
So home coach	0 - 4 - 0	to *S*r. *W P* Carrier. Mrs Hann dead.[46]

The expense amounts have been scored through, presumably when Pepys transferred them to an account book.

From these rare failures to write it up, it is obvious that—despite the easy spontaneity of its prose—Pepys's diary was a labour-intensive undertaking, composed over time from notes (and sometimes from external documents, such as the Bills of Mortality whose statistics Pepys quotes). Shorthand, though perhaps chosen for its swiftness to take initial notes, is not used for speed in the diary's final form. We must look elsewhere for its function—but helpfully, the diary leaves us some clues.

Why Pepys Ended his Diary

Samuel Pepys is one of the very few writers who formally ends his diary. Most diaries are left hanging, as their authors simply fail to continue them—sometimes because of illness or death, sometimes out of a lack of time or commitment. Pepys, by contrast, gives formal notice that he will no longer write his diary, at least in its present format, and more importantly, he tells us why (Fig. 21):

And thus ends all that I doubt I shall ever be able to do with my own eyes in the keeping of my journall, I being not able to do it any longer, having done now so long as to undo my eyes almost every time that I take a pen in my hand; and therefore, whatever comes of it, I must forbear; and therefore resolve from this time forward to have it kept by my people in long-hand, and must therefore be contented to set down no more then is fit for them and all the world to know; or if there be anything (which cannot be much, now my amours to [Deb] are past, and my eyes hindering me in almost all other pleasures), I must endeavour to keep a margin in my book open, to add here and there a note in short-hand with my own hand. And

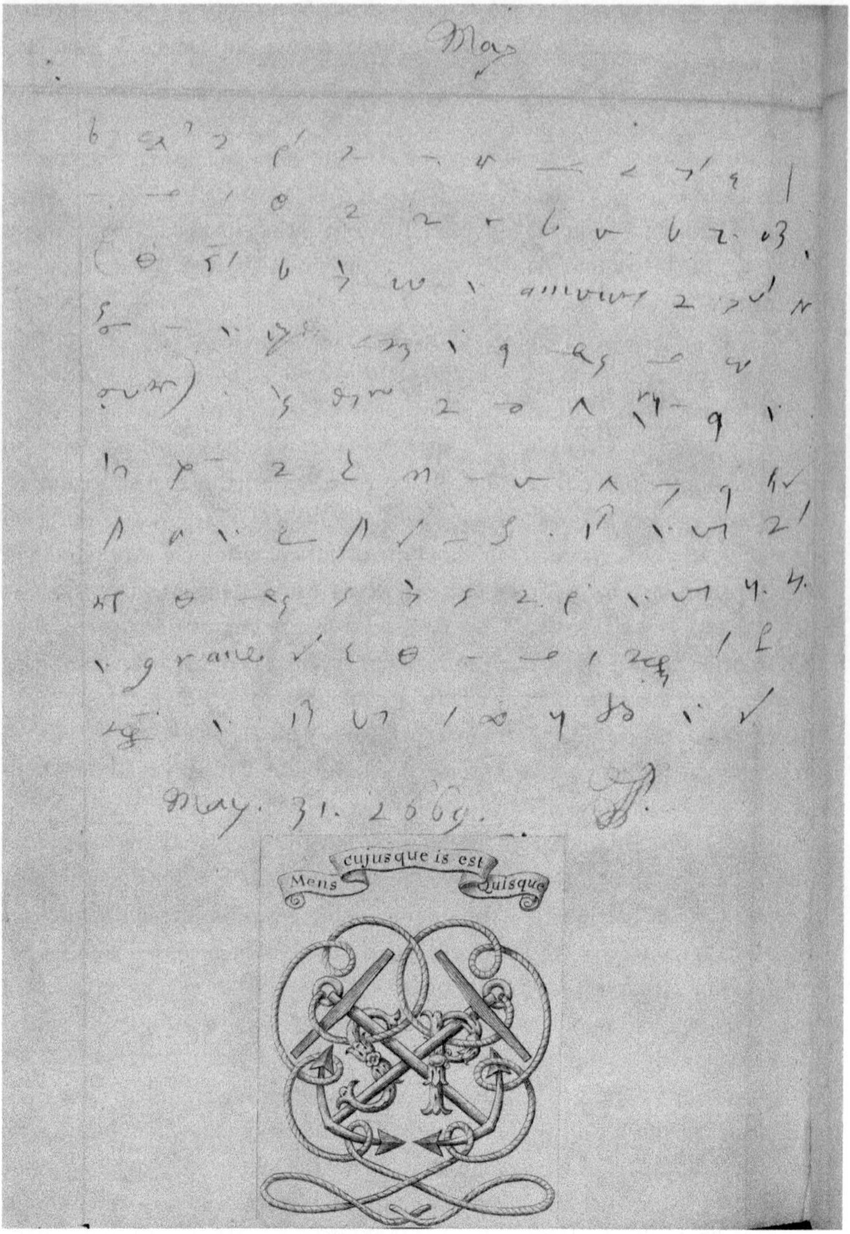

Figure 21. Last page of Samuel Pepys's diary in shorthand. By permission of the Pepys Library, Magdalene College, Cambridge.

so I betake myself to that course which [is] almost as much as to see myself go into my grave - for which, and all the discomforts that will accompany my being blind, the good God prepare me. May. 31. 1669. S.P. (9:564–5)

And there the diary ends—Pepys left blank the last fifty-four pages, their red margins already ruled.[47]

It is an extraordinary entry, full of prime Pepysian disingenuousness. His eyesight did not fail him: he continued to function visually for another thirty-four years. He was even able to write in shorthand, as a so-called 'second diary', detailing a mission to Tangier in 1683, proves.[48] Pepys claims that 'now my amours to Deb are past', there 'cannot be much' material in his diary that would not be 'fit' for his 'people' to set down: we can be sceptical of this claim, given that the very same entry includes an account of going to a Mrs Michell's, knowing 'her husband to be out of town. And here yo did besar ella [I did kiss her], but have not opportunity to para hazer mas [to do more] with her as I would have offered if yo [I] had had it' (9:564). But what we do get here is a clear statement about the politics of writing in shorthand and longhand. Shorthand is necessary, Pepys writes, because of material that is not 'fit for [my people] and all the world to know', material like 'my amours to Deb'. If he hands over the writing of his diary to servants, this aspect of his activities will be lost, or at least reduced to the state where he can only 'add here and there a note in short-hand with my own hand' in a margin purposefully kept clean.

According to this entry, Pepys's use of shorthand is inextricably bound up with his illicit, extramarital sexual liaisons. It is these 'other pleasures' that require the labour-intensive coding of his diary: he must record these incidents in his own hand, in shorthand, and (as the reference to Mrs Michell suggests) in foreign and quasi-foreign languages.[49] We might see here similarities with Michael Wigglesworth's recourse to shorthand for passages that record details of his lusts. But Pepys's relationship with shorthand is, I would suggest, more complex than that of his contemporaries, and it evolves over time, according to the nature and seriousness of his philandering.

When he starts his diary in January 1660, Pepys does not record any advances towards women. During a visit that year to the Netherlands, away from his wife, he does kiss the hand of a Dutch woman 'but had not the face to offer anything more' (1:150). But in September 1660, Pepys records an encounter in a manner which prefigures the technique he will develop in future years. While he is standing at the door of his now empty former residence in Axe Yard, 'Mrs. Diana comes by, whom I took into my house upstairs and there did dally with her a great while, and find that in Latin, nulla puella negat [the girl denies nothing]' (1:239). Here Pepys archly moves into another language to describe the sexual encounter—but he also signals that move explicitly, and his subsequent encounters with Diana are recounted in English.[50]

In January 1664, an encounter with the haberdasher Betty Lane prompts some new concerns—and the turn to a new language:

> I by water to Westminster-hall and there did see Mrs Lane, and de là, elle and I to the cabaret at the Cloche in the street du roy; and there, after some caresses, je l'ay foutée sous de la chaise deux times, and the last to my great pleasure; mais j'ai grand peur que je l'ay fait faire aussi elle même. Mais after I had done, elle commençait parler as before and I did perceive that je n'avais fait rien de danger à elle. Et avec ça, I came away; and though I did make grand promises à la contraire, nonobstant je ne la verrai pas long time.

Pepys has used French in passing before—in referring to his wife Elizabeth's 'old pain in the lip of her chose', for example (1:213)—but here his use of the language goes much further. He puts into French not merely the details of the athletic sexual act ('after some caresses, I fucked her twice under the chair'), but also its location ('from there, she and I to the cabaret at the Bell in King Street') and, most strikingly, its aftermath, with his attendant worries: 'I was much afraid that I had done to her the same. But after I had done, she started to speak as before and I did perceive that I had done nothing dangerous to her. But with that, I came away; and though I did make large promises to the contrary, nevertheless I won't see her again for a long time.' In turning to French, Pepys self-consciously marks the encounter as exotic, continental, and erotic—but French is also the native tongue of his wife. Perhaps that explains why when his mind returns to the incident with some remorse while he's in bed, his diary returns to the French: 'with my mind un peu trouble pour ce que j'ai fait today. But I hope it will be la dernière de toute ma vie' (5:16).

It was not. For about sixteen months, his liaisons are in French, be they with Bagwell's wife, Mrs Martin in Bow Street, Jervas's daughter, or Jervas's maid Jane Welsh.[51] Then, on 15 May 1665, we hear a hint of a new linguistic turn when he describes Mary, the maid at the Harp-and-Ball, as 'formosa' ('beautiful'). This Spanish mode is elaborated on 20 June, the 'Thankesgiving day for Victory over the Dutch'. After dinner, Pepys walks to Herbert's, 'and there spent a little time avec la mosa [Sarah], sin hazer algo con ella que kiss and tocar ses mamelles, que me haza hazer la cosa a mi mismo con gran Plaisir' (6:132). Here, still under cover of Shelton's tachygraphy, Pepys moves between English, French, and Spanish, with Spanish predominating. This quickly becomes Pepys's standard device,[52] with the three languages occasionally peppered with words from Dutch, Italian, Latin, and Greek.[53]

The use of this multilingual shorthand establishes some distinctions in Pepys's erotic repertoire. In describing his nocturnal erotic 'fancy' involving leading court ladies, he keeps to English: 'I have used of late, since my wife went, to make a bad use of my fancy with whatever woman I have a mind to - which I am ashamed of and shall endeavour to do no more' (4:204); 'to bed - before I sleep, fancying myself to sport with Mrs Steward [Frances Stuart] in great pleasure' (4:230); 'to bed, sporting in my fancy with the Queen' (4:232). But he deploys the polyglot to record episodes of orgasm in public places. Sailing home from Billingsgate on 16 December 1665, he conjures up images of Betty Howlet: 'lying down close in my boat, and there, without use of my hand, had great pleasure, and the first time I did make trial of my strength of fancy of that kind without my hand, and had it complete avec la fille que I did see au-jour-dhuy in Westminster hall' (6: 331). On 11 November 1666, he records 'Here at church (God forgive me), my mind did courir upon Betty Michell, so that I do hazer con mi cosa in la eglisa meme' (7:365), Betty being the young daughter of a friend. On 3 May 1668, he goes after dinner 'to church again where I did please myself con mes ojos shut in futar in conceit the hook-nosed young lady, a merchant's daughter, in the upper pew in the church under the pulpit' (9:184). And on Christmas Eve, 1667, during high mass at the Queen's Chapel in Whitehall, he observes the queen with some of her ladies: 'But here I did make myself to do la cosa by mere imagination, mirando a jolie mosa and with my eyes open, which I never did before - and God forgive me for it, it being in the chapel' (8:588). As Joseph Roach notes, 'masturbating during religious services made Pepys feel more guilty but also more excited'.[54]

Even by Pepys's standards, August 1665 sticks out as a month of polyglot polyamory. The month's entries are particularly striking because they take place against the macabre backdrop of London's great plague at its zenith. Pepys's fumbling sexual exploits alternate with reports of who's dead and dying, the statistics from the Bills of Mortality (on the 10th, 4000 deaths within the last week, 3000 from the plague), the drafting of his will ('the town growing so unhealthy that a man cannot depend upon living two days to an end'; 6:187), and his 'seeing a coffin with a dead body therein, dead of the plague, lying in an open close' (6:201). On Sunday 6th, Pepys 'had my head combed by my little girl', his servant Susan, an activity he found arousing:

> to whom I confess que je sum demasiado kind, nuper ponendo sæpe mes mains in su dos choses de son breast. Mais il faut que je leave it, lest it bring me to alguno major inconvenience. (6:185)

On Monday 8th, 'after dinner Bagwell's wife waited at the door, and went with me to my office, en lequel jo haze todo which I had a corasón a hazer con ella' (6:186). In the morning of the 11th, a 'pleasant rancontre' occurred when 'old Delkes' brought his married daughter Mrs Robins with him, attempting to get her husband excused from naval duty: 'Uno ombre pouvait avoir done any cosa cum ella, but I did natha sino besar her' (6:187). The next day, Saturday 12th, 'old Bagwell' invited Pepys into his daughter's house; when he left, 'ego had my volunté de su hija' (6:189). He returned to the house on the 22nd, 'and fasebam la cosa que ego tenebam a mind to con ella' (6:201). Mrs Robins's return on the 23rd prompted a rhapsody of Spanish, French, English, Latin, and Greek:

And jo haze ella mettre su mano upon her pragma hasta hazerme hazer la cosa in su mano. Pero ella no voulut permettre que je ponebam meam manum a ella, but I do not doubt but *αλλω χ[ρ]όνω* de obtenir le.

It loses pretty much everything in translation: 'And I made her put her hand on her thing until she made me do the thing in her hand. But she would not let me put my hand to her, but I do not doubt but another time I will get it.'

One might think that five languages interwoven and put in shorthand[55] might be cover enough for Pepys's extramarital affairs. But even this is complicated still further on 31 May 1667:

Up, and there came young Mrs Daniel in the morning as I expected, about business of her husband's; I took her into the office to discourse with her getting some imployment for him. And there I did punt mini harand toli hemr benleri, so as to malak mimi senelf do; but shere ilis somo leanen that I had no greaset plelesonure with hener.[56]

Here he uses English, but obscures his words by adding superfluous letters (r, l, m, n) or syllables (ar, er, li, al, mi, ne, mo)—decluttered of these, the sentence reads 'And there I did put my hand to my belly, so as to make myself do; but she is so lean that I had no great pleasure with her' (8:244). Not coincidentally, it is at this point in the diary that Pepys severely reduces his use of longhand, which he has used primarily for proper names.[57]

The stakes were raised when Pepys became involved with his wife's maid and companion, Deb Willet. On 31 March 1668, he ends his day by describing, in his shorthand + polyglot + additional letters and syllables, how Deb undressed him, 'and there I did give her good advice and beso la, ella weeping still; and yo did take her, the first time in my life, sobra mi genu and did poner mi mano sub her jupes and toca su thigh, which did hazer me great pleasure; and so did no more, but besando-la went to my bed' (9:143). A blank page follows before the day dawns on 1 April, when he continues:

Up and to dress myself; and called, as I use, Deb to brush and dress me and there I did again as I did the last night con mi mano, but would have tocado su thing; but ella endeavoured to prevent me con much modesty by putting su hand there about, which I was well pleased with and would not do too much, and so con great kindness dismissed la... (9:144)

From then on, there is little mention of sexual contact with Deb—perhaps because Pepys was able to absorb their encounters within the daily routine between master and maid. (In the summer of 1668, only one incident is recorded, which takes place, significantly, outside the household, in a coach.) This would explain the shock of Sunday 25 October 1668:

and after supper, to have my head combed by Deb, which occasioned the greatest sorrow to me that ever I knew in this world; for my wife, coming up suddenly, did find me imbracing the girl con my hand sub su coats; and endeed, I was with my main in her cunny. (9:337)

Elizabeth's long-lasting anger ensured that Deb left the Pepys household; although Pepys stalked his former maidservant for several months, eventually he realized his 'amours to Deb' were over.

By the time he wrote his final entry on 31 May 1669, Pepys had become nervous about his diary. On the previous 9 March, there is a telling entry in which he encounters his friend Sir William Coventry, now a prisoner in the Tower of London:

Up, and to the tower and there find Sir W. Coventry alone, writing down his journall, which he tells me he now keeps of the material things; [upon] which I told him, and he is the only man that I ever told it to I think, that I have kept it most strictly these eight or ten years; and I am sorry almost that I told it him - it not being necessary, nor may be convenient to have it known. (9:475)

Pepys's regret at telling Coventry about his diary is all the more striking because Coventry is generous in revealing his own. As Pepys records, Coventry tells him about the petition he has written, and its passage to the king; Pepys then adds, 'But by this discourse he was pleased to take occasion to show me and read to me his jour—'—Pepys here replaces what was clearly going to be 'journall' with 'account'—'his account, which he hath kept by him under his own hand, of all his discourse...'. Pepys concludes, 'And really, I was mighty proud to be privy to this great transaction' (9:475–6). And yet, at the same time that Coventry shares his diary with him, Pepys worries that it will not be 'convenient' to have the existence of his own diary known. This attitude is a far cry from Pepys's proud boast back in April 1660 when he kept the lieutenant of his ship in his cabin 'late, showing him my manner of keeping a Journall' (1:107).

Bibliotheca Pepysiana

Pepys knew which books and papers he wanted to keep, and which he wanted to destroy. One of the most charged episodes in his diary comes in January 1663, during a quarrel with his wife. The previous November, distressed at her lack of company, Elizabeth 'in her discontent' sent Pepys 'a letter, which I am in a quandary what to do, whether to read it or not; but I purpose not, but to burn it before her face, that I may put a stop to more of this nature' (3:257–8). Now, Elizabeth takes from her locked trunk 'a bundle of papers' including a copy of the letter she sent her husband:

> She now read it, and was so picquant, and wrote in English, and most of it true, of the retirednesse of her life, and how unpleasant it was, that being writ in English and so in danger of being met with and read by others, I was vexed at it and desired her and then commanded her to teare it. (4:9)

When Elizabeth fails to obey, Pepys embarks on an orgy of paper-tearing:

> I forced it from her and tore it, and withal took her other bundle of papers from her and leapt out of the bed and in my shirt clapped them into the pockets of my breeches, that she might not get them from me; and having got on my stockings and breeches and gown, I pulled them one by one and tore them all before her face, though it went against my heart to do it, she crying and desiring me not to do it. But such was my passion and trouble to see the letters of my love to her, and my Will, wherein I had given her all I have in the world when I went to sea with my Lord Sandwich, to be joyned with a paper of so much disgrace to me and dishonor if it should have been found by anybody.

Pepys 'tore them all' except a bond, their marriage licence and his first letter to her, and then—keeping the pieces of her letter and his will—he 'burnt all the rest' (4:9–10). The terms in which Pepys relates these outbursts are revealing. His anger about his wife's letter does not primarily concern its content, but the fact that it is 'writ in English' and therefore 'in danger of being met with and read by others'. He is then further chafed by the fact 'a paper of so much disgrace to me and dishonour' is 'joyned' to his love-letters and his will in which he leaves everything to Elizabeth. The letter would become part of his posterity—and that is what he is at such pains to avoid.

Another incident occurs in January 1668. On 13 January, visiting his bookseller Martin in the Strand, Pepys 'saw the French book which I did think to have had for my wife to translate, called *L'Escholle de Filles*'—presumably believing it to be an educational work[58]—'but when I came to look into it, it is the most bawdy, lewd book that ever I saw, rather worse then *putana errante*—so that I was ashamed of reading in it' (9:21–2). *L'escolle des filles, ou La philosophie des dames, divisée en deux dialogues*—an erotic exchange between two women, one a virgin, the other more sexually experienced—had been a sensation since it appeared in Paris in 1655. On 8 February, after spending an hour in the bookseller's shop, Pepys finally 'bought that idle, roguish book, *L'escholle des Filles*, which I have bought in plain binding (avoiding the buying of it better bound) because I resolve, as soon as I have read it, to burn it, that it may not stand in the list of books, nor among them, to disgrace them if it should be found' (9:57–8). The following day (a Sunday), he spent considerable time 'reading a little of *L'escolle des Filles*', which he deemed 'a mighty lewd book' but talked himself into believing that it was 'yet not amiss for a sober man once to read over to inform himself in the villainy of the world' (9:58). After entertaining a group of friends who 'drank my good store of wine', Pepys returns alone to his chamber, 'where I did read through *L'escholle des Filles*; a lewd book, but what doth me no wrong to read for information sake (but it did hazer my primick para stand all the while, and una vez to decharger); and after I had done it, I burned it, that it might not be among my books to my shame' (9:59).

Pepys's insistence that his wife's letter should not be 'found by anybody' and that this 'lewd book' should feature neither 'among my books' or even 'in the list of books' (he had started cataloguing his collection a few years earlier) stands in stark contrast to his plans for his diary, in which of course he leaves us the details of his wife's letter, and of his masturbatory reading of French pornography.[59] He went to remarkable lengths to ensure the survival of the six volumes: they were bound with the title 'Journall' printed on the spines, placed among the printed books in Pepys's library, and entered 'in the list of books' in 1693. In a 1703 codicil to his will, Pepys left exacting instructions to his nephew John Jackson on how to prepare his collection, which, after Jackson's death, was to be 'placed and for ever Settled' in Magdalene College, Cambridge and to 'be called by the name of Bibliotheca Pepysiana'. Jackson died in 1723, and the library was moved to the 'New Building' at Magdalene the following year.[60]

This might seem a dangerously public venue for Pepys's diary. But access to and readership of the manuscripts has always been limited; even in today's climate of digitization, only a few openings of the diaries have been published in facsimile. Instead, the world turns to the superb modern edition by Latham and Matthews, where one is able to get a general sense of the ratcheting up of Pepys's treatment of his 'amours'. But in seeking to right the wrongs of previous expurgated, bowdlerized versions, the modern edition makes the text more transparent than it was ever meant to be. The text is rendered into modern spelling; punctuation is added (Pepys provides only full stops and parentheses); no indication is given as to which words were originally in longhand; and, one footnote aside, Pepys's habit of adding nonsense syllables to words is silently emended: 'For the reader's comfort, these passages are transcribed into ordinary spelling'.[61] What we lose here, in the modern edition's bracing frankness, is Pepys's increasingly layered coding of his 'amours', a retreat from a readable English shorthand, into a foreign language in shorthand, into a mélange of foreign words in shorthand, before finally degenerating into a nonsense baby-talk describing the ways in which he attempted 'to malak mimi senelf do'.

Why does Pepys go to these lengths? As we have seen, many seventeenth-century writers knew that penning a diary in shorthand affords some level of privacy and secrecy: it could well be, then, that this is simply a conflicted or guilt-ridden Pepys signalling his discomfort.[62] But that does not strike me as telling the whole story. Using Shelton's *Tachygraphy*, or a slight variant of it, leaves the diary open to too many readers—even in Pepys's household, Will Hewer would have been able to make it out. It seems rather that the use of shorthand signals a reassuring secrecy *to its writer*—and that the subsequent moves into multiple foreign languages and superfluous characters serve to intensify this sense of secrecy. Pepys was a great re-reader: in February 1668, he wrote of 'looking over my Memorandum-books, which are now of great use to me and do fully reward me for all my care in keeping them' (9:91)—while this refers to his office memorandum-books,[63] the same must have been true of his diaries. When Pepys uses his polyglot shorthand for passages of his diary, he not only hides them from others, but also makes them visible to himself. The coding is for Pepys the reader: these are passages of a charged, illicit sexuality to which he will return—and which he goes out of his way to preserve.

15

The Dangerous Lives of Thomas Dangerfield

In late April 1685, an odd piece of printed life-writing went on sale in London. What the title page proclaimed as *Dangerfield's Memoires, Digested into Adventures, Receits, and Expences* resembled Richard Stonley's pecuniary reckonings or Samuel Pepys's rough notes: a daily record of income and expenditure from Tuesday 2 December 1684 to Thursday 19 March 1685, containing only the blandest of information about each day—where Dangerfield went, where he dined, where he lodged.[1] Why should anyone want to know such minute detail about this 'Capt. Dangerfield'?

A prefatory notice explained why. '*Dangerfield Himself*', we learn, '*is at present a Prisoner in Newgate.*' The reader is advised that the publication covers the months of an '*Expedition*' during which '*DANGERFIELD* went by the Name of *FIELD*', and that this publication has been sent 'into All the Places where he made his *Progress*' in the hope that memories would be jogged, prompting 'some Further Discovery of so Notorious a *Cheat*'. To this end, a description is provided of the cheat Dangerfield—'He's a *Proper, Black, Handsome-Fellow.* He was in *Second Mourning*, and a *Short Periwig*, for the Greater Part of the Time'—and of his servant Mark, and their horses (A2^{v}). Dangerfield, we're told, had a habit of keeping '*Distinct Diaries* of his *Motions, Receits, and Expences*', and 'his Papers of Disbursements' recorded the remarkable sum of 'Fourteen Hundred and Fifty Pound, Fifteen Shillings, and a Half-penny, Well told' in 'the Space of *Two Years*, and betwixt *Eight and Nine Months*' (A2^{r}). The present diary—written 'By his Own Hand', according to the title page—merely records the Newgate prisoner's most recent activities.

The Dangerfield of the *Memoires* is a man almost continually on the move, spending most of his nights in inns before moving swiftly on in the morning. In December he rides through Buckinghamshire, Oxfordshire, Gloucestershire, and Worcestershire, before settling for Christmas week in Shrewsbury; the New Year sees him in north Wales, Cheshire, heading back through Shropshire and

Worcestershire to the West Midlands, Warwickshire, Leicestershire, Bedfordshire, Middlesex, and Kent, ending up in London. At least twenty-five individuals are mentioned, most identified only by their initials. The most constant presence is his servant, Mark, who is temporarily replaced in February (after he 'grew saucy') by Robin (E1^{r}). There is also a 'sister Judith' and a 'Sister *Nesse*', and others simply referred to as 'my friend', 'my Dame', and 'my Dear'. There are walk-on parts for a tailor, a carrier, a surgeon, a butcher, a coachman, and a succession of female inn-keepers: Mrs Hilton, Mrs Marget, Dame Thynne in Hackney, Mrs Lowen at Waltham Cross, Mrs Walker in Brentwood, and 'Mrs *Billings*, who entertain'd me very Generously' for five hours (F3^{v}). More unexpected is Dangerfield's friendship with a Mr Wesley of Exeter College, Oxford, who sold him a copy of Lucretius for two shillings (B2^{r}, B2^{v}, B3^{r}, B4^{r}).

Most of the expenses recorded are for lodging and dining, and the needs of the horses: payments for new shoes and the re-shoeing of 'removes' (old shoes), 'frosting' the shoes to gain traction in snow, purchasing of a bit, girths, and a saddle cloth, fees for ostlers (the horse-keepers at inns), saddlers, and veterinary care: 'To the Smith for Bleeding him in the Tayle, & a Cataplasme' (C2^{v}). There are also some luxuries: 'a Hat for my self' (C2^{r}), a neck-cloth, chocolate, shoes, a periwig, a pair of cotton stockings, a tortoiseshell comb, and 'a Shaggerin Case to my Cizors' (F3^{r}). But the nature of the 'receits' is less transparent, with the sums raised varying widely, from 15 shillings on Tuesday 2 December to 109 on Saturday 13 December (Fig. 22). The income is broken down into individual items, each with its contributor revealed not by a personal name but by a more general description. On Monday 15 December, for example, a day he deems a 'Tolerable Success' (and which he celebrates by getting 'Foxed with my Landlord'), Dangerfield records 'receits' of 87 shillings, a considerable sum, raised from nine people: six shillings 'Of a farmer', twenty shillings 'Of a Gentleman', six shillings 'Of a Farmers Wife', and so on. Also noted are failures to raise funds: even on this successful day there are '6 Refuses' and a further opportunity 'Lost by *Mark*'s Folly' (B4^{v}).

In order to comprehend how this itinerant man could be making significant income from people whose names he does not know, we are required to join the dots. One early reader, John Aubrey's collaborator Anthony Wood, saw Dangerfield as a confidence trickster, playing on the sympathies of provincial men and women with sob stories: he noted in his copy of *Dangerfield's Memoires* that 'All the su*mm*s of money *wh*ich he rec*eived* (as they followe in this book) Dangerfied [*sic*] borrowed und*er* the guise of a decayed gent. or a k*nigh*t *tha*t had been rob'd on the high way & c.'[2] A few decades later, the biographer Roger North agreed: 'It is wonderful by what Art he deluded those poor People, and made them part with their Money by Angels, Crowns, and Half-Crowns, as they did to him.'[3] But there are hints of a

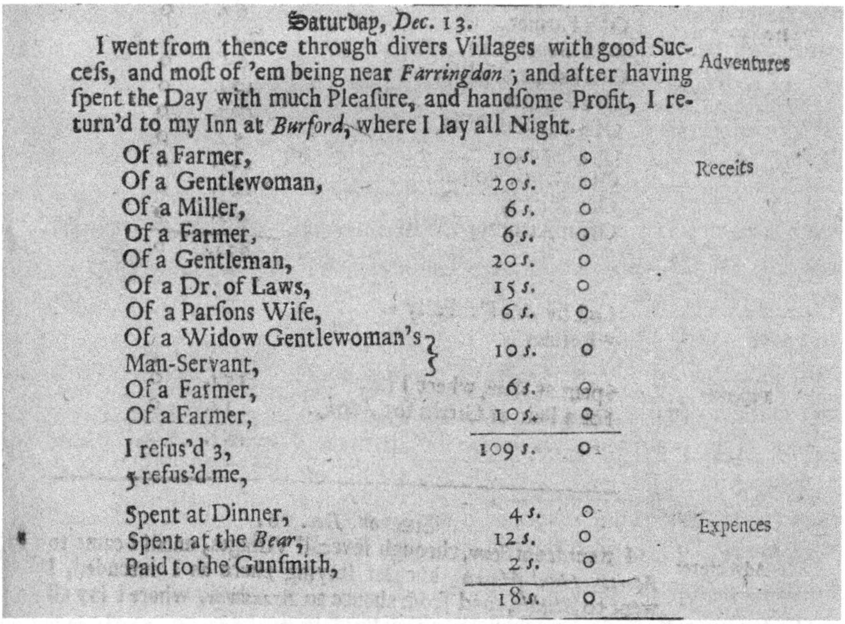

Saturday, *Dec.* 13.

I went from thence through divers Villages with good Succeſs, and moſt of 'em being near *Farringdon*; and after having ſpent the Day with much Pleaſure, and handſome Profit, I return'd to my Inn at *Burford*, where I lay all Night. — Adventures

Of a Farmer,	10 *s.*	0	Receits
Of a Gentlewoman,	20 *s.*	0	
Of a Miller,	6 *s.*	0	
Of a Farmer,	6 *s.*	0	
Of a Gentleman,	20 *s.*	0	
Of a Dr. of Laws,	15 *s.*	0	
Of a Parſons Wife,	6 *s.*	0	
Of a Widow Gentlewoman's Man-Servant,	10 *s.*	0	
Of a Farmer,	6 *s.*	0	
Of a Farmer,	10 *s.*	0	
I refus'd 3,	109 *s.*	0	
5 refus'd me,			
Spent at Dinner,	4 *s.*	0	Expences
Spent at the *Bear*,	12 *s.*	0	
Paid to the Gunſmith,	2 *s.*	0	
	18 *s.*	0	

Figure 22. Receipts and expenses for 13 December 1584. *Dangerfield's Memoires* (1685). The Bodleian Libraries, The University of Oxford, Firth e. 30 (18), sig. B4r.

violent edge to Dangerfield's fund-raising. He was usually armed: on 26 January, Dangerfield records that he 'Lost my Pistolls' (D1r). At noon on 3 February, about ten miles from Burton-on-Trent, Dangerfield and Mark encounter difficulties that prompt the diary's longest entry:

> we were over-taken at the End of a Narrow Lane by 7 Horse-men, one of them bid me Stand, and drew forth his Sword; But a fair Heath offering in it's Prospect Better Tearms, Call'd to me to Whip and Ride for it; and accordingly we did, and by much out-Rode all the Pursuers for the space of an hour Whip and Spur: By this time finding our Horses much Impaired, and perceiving no more than 4 of the 7 in sight that Chased us, we e'en resolved to Turn Back and give 'em Battel; which was accordingly done, and after a Smart dispute as ever I met with, which held about a quarter of an hour, My Self, My Horse, and *Mark*, being wounded, we having put all 4 of 'em to Flight, whipped forwards, afresh...

Dangerfield's wound was serious enough that it had to be dressed by a surgeon (D3r), and this 'Smart dispute' interrupts his cash-flow: it is over three weeks until he next records any income. Shortly after, he and Mark rearm themselves, spending forty shillings for two pistols from a gunsmith in the Minories on 13 March (F3r). The incident has led modern critics to assume, no doubt correctly, that Dangerfield was a highwayman:[4] the seven horsemen that encounter them were presumably a rival gang.

The *Memoires* were never meant to tell the whole story. In the book's epistle 'To the Reader', we are told that 'The Entire Life of This *Hero* is Reserv'd for a Better Pen, and Leisure: The Intent of These Papers being only to Pick up, and to Furnish Fresh Matter toward the Just History of his Adventures'. But, we are assured, 'His *Treasons, Cheats, Perjuries*, and Other *Publique Misdemeanors*, are All upon *Record*, and Needless to be here Inserted'.[5] The writer is here alluding to the fact that Dangerfield's crimes have already been the subject of a notable book–indeed, that is probably the reason that the reader picked up *Dangerfield's Memoires*. For, five years earlier, Dangerfield had been the hero of a biography which related 'the juvenile rambles of Thomas Dangerfield', and cast him as a glamorously exotic alter ego: Don Tomazo.[6] The existence of *Dangerfield's Memoires* proves the success of *Don Tomazo*: as Kate Loveman puts it, 'Through its mundane reportage *Dangerfield's Memoires* testifies to the interest surrounding the informer and the compelling nature of rogue literature in general. The lure of rogue biography was such that readers were prepared to buy what was essentially an accounts book.'[7] But *Dangerfield's Memoires* would itself lead–by a series of accidents, but still inexorably–to the real-life death of Don Tomazo.

English Guzmans: The Rise of Rogue Biography

In the mid-seventeenth century, England witnessed the rise of a new form of biography, one specializing in the notorious criminals of the day. This genre of rogue biography looked back to Spanish picaresque novels such as the anonymous *La vida de Lazarillo de Tormes* (1554) and especially Mateo Alemán's *Guzmán de Alfarache* (1599, 1604), which had enjoyed new popularity in English as James Mabbe's *The Rogue* (1622), whose anti-hero moves from town to town, performing tricks and duping the gullible. While these texts were clearly fictional, however, the 1650s introduced a 'real-life' counterpart, in which the Guzmán formula was welded onto the career of historical persons.[8] In 1652, George Fidge published *The English Gusman; or the history of that unparallel'd thief James Hind*, a highwayman hanged in Worcester that September. *The English Gusman* combined accounts of Hind's arrest, interrogation, imprisonment, and Old Bailey appearance with a chapbook-like 'full Relation of all the severall Robberies, madd Pranks, and handsom Jests done by Him', and added for good measure the tale of how 'at Hatfield he was Enchanted by a Witch for three years space; and how She Switch'd His Horse with a white Rod, and gave him a thing like a Sun-dial, the Point of which should direct him which way to take when persued'.[9] The combination of gleeful recounting of crimes, romance-like incidents, and real-life judicial comeuppance proved a winning formula, and many other such books followed.

The most popular was *The English Rogue* (1665), a first-person narrative of the career thief Meriton Latroon, 'a witty extravagant' who authored many 'eminent cheats'. Its title paid homage to Mabbe's *The Rogue* but the book essayed something new: while nominally fictional, Latroon's life-story—born in Ireland to a Church of England vicar murdered in the Irish rising of 1641—sounded tantalizingly close to that of its author, Richard Head.[10] According to Francis Kirkman, who published a sequel, Head 'reaped a great deal of ignominy by writing' the first volume, 'for many people were so ignorant, as to believe that it was a true and exact account of the Authors life', and subsequently 'lookt on him as a dangerous person, and shunned and avoided his company'.[11] Head was not mistaken: even John Aubrey, in his *Brief Lives*, treats 'Meriton' as a real person, while noting that 'his true name was Head'. Meriton, he writes, 'had been amongst the Gipsies. He looked like a knave, with his gogling eies. He would transforme himselfe into shape'—all details Aubrey gleaned from *The English Rogue*: he never met Head (let alone the fictional Meriton).[12] Kirkman titillates the reader with the admission that Head 'was indeed guilty of some petty waggeries', just not 'guilty of the whole', and that he was 'guilty of many female frauds, his inclination leading him to be a lover (though Mercurial and unconstant) of the Female sex'.[13] This no doubt helped sell the many sequels to *The English Rogue*, two of which Head co-wrote, despite his supposed outrage at the readers' response to his original.

Truth and fiction merged in various other ways. The ne'er-do-well Charles Croke (*fl.* 1656–86) rewrote his own life adventures—including eventful stints in Oxford, Virginia, and Portugal—as the picaresque *Fortune's Uncertainty, or Youth's inconstancy* (1667), casting himself as 'Rodolphus', apparently hewing close to the truth.[14] The serial con artist Mary Carleton (1632?–73) achieved such notoriety for trying to pass herself off as a German noblewoman that she inspired a play at Drury Lane (in which she starred), a visit in jail from Samuel Pepys, and some twenty-five publications, including a supposed autobiography, *The Case of Madam Mary Carleton* (1663).[15] After Carleton was eventually hanged at Tyburn in 1673, Francis Kirkman published a lengthy biography, *The Counterfeit Lady Unveiled*, that gloried in its fictionality: as Kirkman puts it, 'If I should promise to give you a true account of her whole life I should deceive you, for how can Truth be discovered of her who was wholly composed of Falsehood?'[16]

The life-writing-as-Guzmán-picaresque genre gained enough traction for an irritated Margaret Cavendish to parody it in one of her sociable letters, published in 1664, in which 'Sir F.O.' has declared that he will write his own life in this mode:

> for he saies, he knows no reason, but he may write his own life as well as Guzman: and since you desire my opinion of his intended work, I can onely say, that his Life for anything I know

to be the contrary, hath ben as evil as Guzman's, but whether his Wit be as good as Guzman's, I know not, yet I doubt the worst, and to write an Evil life without Wit, will be but a dull and tedious Story, indeed so tedious and dull, as I believe none will take the pains to read it, unless he himself read of himself: but it is to be hoped, that he will be tir'd of himself, and so desist from his self Story.[17]

Cavendish hoped in vain. Indeed, these new genres took a hold so strong that they became part of the fabric of political intrigue over the coming years, in particular fuelling the 'Popish Plot', the alleged Catholic conspiracy to assassinate Charles II that was initially 'exposed' by Titus Oates in 1678. The endless twists and turns of the simultaneously fact-and-fiction Plot naturally gave themselves to the possibly-true-possibly-not genres of criminal life-writing, and played out on London booksellers' stands as much as in Westminster's courts.

Thomas Dangerfield entered this world in March 1679, when he was incarcerated in Newgate on counterfeiting charges. Believing him to be a sympathetic fellow Catholic, a midwife named Elizabeth Cellier, almoner to Elizabeth, countess of Powis, bailed him from jail, and put Dangerfield to work, gathering intelligence.[18] At this point, Dangerfield 'revealed' to Cellier that the Popish Plot was in truth a myth spread by Presbyterians as part of a plan to capture the state, a revelation eagerly believed by Cellier and Lady Powis, who introduced Dangerfield to the earl of Peterborough, James, duke of York (the king's Catholic younger brother), and finally King Charles himself. When these men declined to act on Dangerfield's intelligence, he simply invented more, planting and then discovering incriminating documents in the rooms of the Whig Colonel Roderick Mansell; but Mansell defended himself, and it was Dangerfield who ended up back in jail, this time for coining (fabricating false money). After Cellier bailed him out again Dangerfield made an incredible *volte-face*: not only was there no Presbyterian plot, he now alleged, but that supposed conspiracy hid a *Catholic* plot involving Cellier, the countess of Powis, Peterborough, and Roger Palmer, earl of Castlemaine, among others, to murder King Charles and the earl of Shaftesbury. Documents supporting Dangerfield's allegations were conveniently discovered in Cellier's meal-tub.[19] For his loyal service to the crown, Dangerfield was pardoned and given a pension; he then laid out his accusations in two books, *Mr. Tho. Dangerfields Particular Narrative of the Late Popish Design* (October/November 1679) and *Mr. Tho. Dangerfield's Second Narrative* (February 1679/80).[20]

When Cellier was arraigned for treason in the King's Bench in June 1680, she launched a campaign to undermine Dangerfield as a witness, declaring 'If I can prove he was whipped and transported, pilloried, perjured, &c. he is no witness'. She claimed that Dangerfield had previously been indicted for burglary, that he was guilty of forgery, and that he had perjured himself. Although the witnesses she produced were unable to claim with certainty that the man in court was the Thomas Dangerfield they knew to be a criminal, Cellier did obtain a copy of a record that showed Dangerfield had been pilloried in Salisbury 'for uttering counterfeit guineas', and another 'Record of an Outlawry for Felony'. Dangerfield's value as a witness was fatally compromised: the case against Lady Powis was thrown out, and Castlemaine was found not guilty.[21]

Buoyed by her success in court, Cellier continued her attack with a pamphlet entitled *Malice Defeated* (1680). This was to be her undoing, landing her back in jail for libel after she claimed that Catholic prisoners were being tortured in Newgate; she was later fined and pilloried.[22] But *Malice Defeated* also contained the seeds of a new direction for the life-writing of Thomas Dangerfield. His own account, *Dangerfields Particular Narrative*, had started in March 1679, just before his first meeting with Cellier; it gave no information about his past. Cellier decided to make good that lack in an appendix to *Malice Defeated*, which—influenced by the Guzmán genre—she entitled 'The matchless picaro; or, A short essay of the fortune and virtues of Seignior Don Tomaso Ganderfieldo, alias Francisco de Corombona', in which she provides 'an Abstract of *Seignior Don Thomazo Ganderfieldo, Francisco de Corombona*, & c. his *Recorded Virtues*, and what himself hath told to many Persons that are ready to attest it upon Oath'. This 'Abstract' stretches from Dangerfield's childhood in Waltham Abbey, through a precocious criminal career that resulted in multiple jail sentences, transportation, a branding in Puerto Ferrara, and an aborted hanging in Antwerp. In addition to court appearances in London, Essex, Wiltshire, and Middlesex, Cellier 'found his Name Recorded in 28 places, having been Transported, Burnt in the Hand, five times Adjudged to the Pillory, seven times Fin'd, twice Out-law'd for Fellony, and broke the Goal in several places eight times'. Modesty, she claims ironically, led Dangerfield to omit most of 'his strange and unparallell'd Adventures in *England, Scotland, Ireland, France, Spain, Flanders*, and *Holland*, and elsewhere on the Coast of *Guiny* and *Barbadoes*', and especially 'the Just and Generous Entertainments he found in the Inchanted Castles of *Chelmsford, Newgate, Antwerp, York, Callice, Salisbury, Winbourn, West-chester, Reading, Abbington*, the *Gate-house, Dublin*, the *Counter*, the *Kings-bench*, with many more'—all in all a life 'so remarkable, that it exceeds all the Worthies of his quality that have gone before him'—like 'the *Spanish Guzman*, the *English Rogue*, and the *Italian Bandetto mengone*' (who spent his last twenty years on the top of a tower in an iron cage, before he 'beat out his Brains against the Bars of the Cage').[23]

Cellier ended her account by stating that 'I understand that the Gentleman is going to Publish his life at large, by the name of *Don Francisco de Corombona*' ($M2^v$),[24] but no book of that title was forthcoming. Dangerfield instead responded with a point-by-point rebuttal of certain parts of *Malice Defeated* 'wrote by the hand of

Thomas Dangerfield', in which he accused Cellier of having multiple extramarital affairs, including one with a Negro servant that produced 'a brave *Tawny Face'd Boy*'.[25] He did not address Cellier's charges about his pre-1679 life. That was left to another, anonymous book that appeared within weeks: a 'life at large' entitled *Don Tomazo, or the Juvenile Rambles of Thomas Dangerfield.*

The Juvenile Rambles of Thomas Dangerfield

Don Tomazo justifies its publication by its precursors: 'Had it not been for the high misdemeanours of *Clavel* we had miss'd a neat and excellent Poem, and the Discovery of a great Mystery of Iniquity. The Cheats and cunning Contrivances of *Gusman* and *Lazarillo de Tormes* have been made *English* out of the *Spanish* Language, as well to instruct, as to delight' (A2^{v}–A3^{r}). The author tellingly cites John Clavell's *A Recantation of an Ill Led Life* (1628), an autobiographical poem written by an imprisoned highwayman who, while claiming repentance, also betrayed some fascinating professional details of his erstwhile trade.[26] The apogee of the autobiographical tradition is also invoked: 'the way to amendment is never out of date. St. Austin himself had occasion enough to repent the Follies of his Youth' (A3^{r}). It's an audacious comparison: Clavell, Lazarillo, Guzmán–and St Augustine. *Don Tomazo* thus claims to sit somewhere between the fictional picaresque novel and the repentant spiritual autobiography, while taking the form of a third-person biography.

The narrative voice is breezy yet learned, liberally dropping classical allusions. Don Tomazo is 'this young Gusman' (C7^{v}) embarking on 'his first Essays of Gusmanry' (B6^{r}), and the narrator develops an entire Gusman mythology, complete with axioms: 'it is not for Clowns and Men of sullen tempers, but for Persons of accute complyance, and airy behaviour, to be *Gusmans*' (D3^{r-v}); 'true Gusmans never mind Morality' (F6^{v}); 'Gusmans call that Necessity, when they want Fewel to feed the heat of their Prodigality' (G6^{r}); 'Such is the Fate of Gusmanry, sometimes to abound, and sometimes to want Bread' (H4^{v}–H5^{r}). Fortune lets him know that 'he was yet but a young Gusman, and that there were others superior to him, whose Art was not to be learnt by Rules of *Accidence* or *Grammar*, but by a suffering Experience' (E7^{v}). But while its inspiration is Spanish, Don Tomazo's elaboration of Gusmanry has a notably patriotic agenda. London is 'the grand Receptacle of all the most refin'd Virtuosi in Gusmanry' (G6^{r}), and English Gusmanry thinks big: as Don Tomazo sets out intent on 'no less then the intended Destruction of the whole *Guiney* Trade', the narrator comments, 'See here the difference between a *Spanish* and an *English Gusman*; the one pursuing a poor hungry Plot upon his penurious

Masters Bread and Cheese; the other designing to grasp the Riches of the fourth part of the World by the Ruine of a National Commerce' (G6^{v}).

Cellier's narrative is recognizable in this telling, but the chronology is different, and the story much longer and more detailed. Born in Essex, Don Tomazo rebels against a severe father, and is easy pickings for 'a pure Satanical Privy-Counsellour' (B3^{r}), his father's Scottish servant Jemmy. Believing Jemmy's tales of his father's 'stately Mansion' (B4^{v}), Don Tomazo runs away with him, only to find that Jemmy's father lives with his family, livestock, and various 'sharp-set Vermine' in a hovel. His time in Scotland sees him alternately as the victim of crime and the recipient of generous-hearted philanthropy by the local lairds. But in Peebles, Don Tomazo decides 'not to laze under hedges, not to go whining from door to door, to court penurious Charity; but to cheat the Crafty, out-knave the Knave in grain'—and more specifically, 'to white-wash Boatles' (copper coins worth one sixth of a penny) to pass them off as 'a certain Scotch piece of Silver, call'd a Forty-peny Piece', worth some 'twenty Boatles in Copper'. Within a week, Don Tomazo has made about five pounds, proving the moral: 'the wide World is no dangerous Sea for one that can swim' (D1^{r}). The Scottish interlude encapsulates the strangely shifting register of Don Tomazo: while, as one critic writes, 'there is an air of reality about the description of this Scottish visit',[27] there are some scenes that stretch credulity. Near Dumfries, Don Tomazo becomes convinced that a woman who curses him is a witch, and disables her power by cutting off her thumb (D4^{r}-D5^{r}), an episode that plays too neatly on a recent witch-hunt in Dumfries, and recalls James Hind's enchantment by a Hatfield witch in *The English Gusman*.

His Scottish adventures at an end, Don Tomazo returns to his father, but is thrown out after sneaking out to sleep with his mistress. He uses his father's name to cheat one of his friends for thirty pounds, an adventure in which the narrator memorably dubs the hapless apprentice whom Don Tomazo dupes as 'the Knight of the burning Pestle', 'Monsieur Blunderbus', 'City-Dromedary', 'Boobie', 'Nickapoop', 'the tame Dottrell', 'young Nicodemus', 'Tot Tottie', and 'the dejected Counter-scrubber' (E6^{v}-E8^{r}). Our hero then sets sail for Cadiz in southern Spain, from where he embarks on an itinerant life, spending time in Leghorn, Scanderoon, Grand Cairo, Genoa, and Dublin, with longer stretches in the Low Countries and the west of England. He is, at various times, a soldier, a thief, a 'Pickaroon' with designs on the Guinea trade, a merchant, a spy, and a sea-rover, falling back on coining when other plans fail; his protean nature allows him to personate a German ('humouring that pretence with broken English'; H1^{r}), a Spanish count, a jockey, a Flanders 'Boor', a captain in the prince of Orange's army, a merchant, and a woman—a disguise which leaves him vulnerable to assault by a 'lascivious Horse Officer, mad to be riding a fresh County Wench' (N5^{r}).

So who wrote this picaresque life of Thomas Dangerfield? Its basic plot-line is close to Cellier's 'The matchless Picaro', which has led more than one critic to argue that Cellier was basing her text on this one.[28] But while Cellier evidently knew the story–in a marginal note, she cites as witnesses 'Margaret Jenkins, and others to whom he told it'–the chronology demands that Cellier's publication pre-dated *Don Tomazo*.[29] By contrast with 'The matchless Picaro', *Don Tomazo* exalts the criminal reputation of its hero, whose 'rambles' take him close to such important figures as the prince of Orange; he is represented as the inspiration for the 1667 siege of Oudenaarde; and serving in the duke of Luxemburg's army, he is captured at the battle of Seneffe in August 1674 (O8^{r}). Conversely, the account pointedly excludes some of the low points in Cellier's narrative. Although Don Tomazo spends time in Puerto Ferrara, there is no suggestion here that he is branded in the hand there, as Cellier suggests. Neither does *Don Tomazo* refer to Dangerfield's Old Bailey trial for burglary, which left him branded in the left hand–although Dangerfield himself discusses this affair in *The Case of Tho. Dangerfield*.[30] There is no lashing in Reading–or anywhere else, for that matter. Only at Sarum (Salisbury) is there a hint that Don Tomazo is in real trouble: we're told that 'he was convicted, and suffer'd the penalty of his Sentence', although the penalty remains unspecified. (In the King's Bench in 1680, it was established that Dangerfield had been sentenced to stand 'in the pillory for uttering counterfeit guineas' at Salisbury; in *Don Tomazo*, our hero 'purchas'd the Liberty of his Heels' from Salisbury after being visited by a 'full handed' female friend, while in court it was heard that he had been 'outlawed upon a felony'.) In short, the Don Tomazo that emerges from this narrative is resourceful, ruthless, and–despite his criminality–appealing: the reader is compelled to root for him.

It seems likely that Dangerfield was at the very least involved in its composition. While the story is told in the third person, there are slips into the first person: 'all weather-beaten as we were, at length we arrived at Jemmy's Father's Palace' (B6^{r}); 'So soon as we came to this unfortunate Apartment' (B7^{r}); 'we heard of good Philips being transported to the other World' (G4^{r}). Are these slips proof that the text was originally written in the first person? Or are they entirely deliberate, designed to make the reader feel that this is a thinly disguised first-person narrative? While youths need to sow their wild oats, says the letter 'To the Reader', Don Tomazo 'has sow'd his already, and finding it such ill husbandry to deal in that sort of Grain, has resolv'd to give over' (A2^{r}). The author has therefore 'thought it convenient to give the World an account of his Transgressions, to the end that People, as many have done, may not think him worse than he was, what ever self-interest would have made him' (A2$^{r\text{-}v}$). The next sentence implies that Dangerfield is himself party to this publication: 'Nor does he expect that any man will henceforth upbraid him for what is past, as being under the Protection of his Sovereigns Pardon, to which all true Subjects ought to give an awful respect and obedience' ($A2^v$). Despite the claims to Augustine-like atonement, any possibility of repentance is swiftly taken back: 'Not that he goes about to excuse his Offences; but this he hopes he may presume to say, That it was not his custom to put any man in danger of his life, but himself. He only impos'd upon the belief and understandings of others, which being deluded, misguided their Wills' ($A3^{r-v}$). All these hints suggest that this book in some way derives from the Dangerfield camp, and that Don Tomazo is making a case for Thomas Dangerfield.

But more importantly, Don Tomazo turned Thomas Dangerfield into a fictional hero, fit for emulation. Within a year, Dangerfield had appeared in the anonymous *The Perplex'd Prince* as Delego, 'a bold daring and adventerous Blade' (in his copy, the annalist Narcissus Luttrell annotated the reference in the margin as 'Thomas Dangerfeild').[31] To some others, he embodied an anti-hero worthy of emulation. In *The Whole Life of William Fuller*, published in 1703, Fuller, a rogue and informer himself, wrote fondly of how he had read *Don Tomazo* at the age of fourteen: 'a Gentlewoman lent me a Book to read, which was *Dangerfield's* Rambles: I read it over 8 times; and one Evening, as I was walking in the Garden, a Thought came into Mind, that I should have almost the same fate, as that Man had.' It was, he said, a 'strange Omen' of his own career.[32]

Half a century later, the biographer and theorist of biography Roger North saluted 'The noble Captain *Dangerfield*' as not only a champion of the 'sham-plot', but the coiner of the term itself.[33] Despite North's status as a biographer, he sees Dangerfield here as something closer to a literary author—and later critics have followed suit. In his alternative history of the novel, Steve Moore praises *Don Tomazo* for 'its mercurial wit..., its Wodehousian mix of elegant diction and slang, and its playful appropriation of literary genres'.[34] Paul Salzman includes *Don Tomazo* in his *Anthology of Seventeenth-Century Prose Fiction*, alongside fictions by Mary Wroth, Margaret Cavendish, John Bunyan, William Congreve, and Aphra Behn.[35] He also inspired works important to the history of life-writing, albeit fictional life-writing. John Dunton's anonymously published *A Voyage round the World: or, a Pocket-Library Divided into Several Volumes* (1691) has as its first volume 'the Rare Adventures of Don Kainophilus, From his Cradle to his 15th. Year', presented as a series of 'rambles' made by 'a Rambler', just like Dangerfield's 'juvenile rambles'—and Dunton even lifts lines, without credit, from *Don Tomazo*.[36] In 1705, Dunton would produce a remarkable work entitled *The Life and Errors of John Dunton Late Citizen of London; written by himself in solitude. With an idea of a new life*, which has been identified as an important next step in the history of (fictional) autobiography.[37] And Don Tomazo has been seen as the stepping stone from the picaresque criminal lives of the earlier seventeenth century to the string of eighteenth-century literary heroes and heroines that have no real-life counterpart[38]—and especially the criminals whose autobiographies were ghosted by Daniel Defoe: the pirate Captain Singleton, the pickpockets Colonel Jack and Moll Flanders, and the courtesan Roxana.[39]

It would be all too easy to end my account of early modern English life-writing here, as the providential spiritual autobiography merges with the criminal life to become something altogether more crafted and literary—but that would be a mistake. For Thomas Dangerfield could not remain Don Tomazo. And whatever its merits as a work of fiction, *Don Tomazo* breaks off in a most unsatisfying manner. With our hero once again in prison, we hear that Mrs Cellier 'gave him her first Visits, which produc'd those Transactions between them, that have lately made so great a Noise in the World. For an account whereof, the Reader is refer'd to the Narratives themselves. *FINIS.*' (P8^{v}). Don Tomazo is not allowed a fictional ending: instead we are thrust back into the transactions and narratives of Thomas Dangerfield, a jolting shift back to the real world that would ultimately cost Dangerfield his life.

Duke Dangerfield

Dangerfield's Memoires lurch to an abrupt halt on Thursday 19 March 1685. On that day, Dangerfield and 'sister Judith' ride to London, making stops at 'the Cheescake-house' in Mile End and with 'Dame Thynne' in Hackney, before walking to Aldgate to take a coach across town. Having dropped Judith 'in the Middle of Pater-Noster-Row', Dangerfield visits his barber, his tailor, and his shoemaker, meets with 'Charles B–' and 'Dr F–' to consult about his injured arm, and then returns 'to my Inn'.[40] He has time to record the day's expenses, but does not note how much the night cost him—because he was soon under arrest. For on that same day, 19 March, secretary of state Robert Spencer, earl of Sunderland issued a warrant to apprehend Dangerfield for 'seuerall treasonable & dangerous practises against his Majesty and his Government', and to seize his papers.[41] Assuming the diary is genuine, it would presumably have been on his person or in his chamber, and seized when Dangerfield was arrested.[42]

In the King's Bench before Lord Chief Justice George Jeffreys on 30 May, Dangerfield was charged with perjury, relating to claims in his 1679 *Particular Narrative* that he had been paid to murder Charles II by his brother, the then duke of York, who in February 1685 had become King James II.[43] His trial on 29 June saw a parade of those he had harmed—including the earl of Peterborough, Elizabeth Cellier's husband, and Lady Powis—testify against him; even his own witnesses had nothing positive to say about him. Dangerfield blustered that his 'Evidence was the Prop of the Protestant Religion (which made great laughter in the Court)', and was 'sharply reproved by my Lord Chief Justice and kept within his bounds, which was observed to put him a little out of his Newgate Rethorick'. The jury found him guilty of libel without needing to retire.[44] Dangerfield's sentence was 'That he should pay the Fine of 500 l. That he should stand twice in the Pillory, and go about the Hall with a Paper in his Hat signifying his Crime; That on Thursday next he should be whipped from Al[d]gate to Newgate; and on Saturday following from Newgate to Tyburn'.[45]

It was a sensational enough case but, oddly, this was not the narrative that proved most popular with the reading public: instead a fake news story took flight. It was broadcast in broadsheets and pamphlets that Dangerfield had been charged for impersonating James Scott, duke of Monmouth, the eldest illegitimate son of the late king, Charles II, now living in exile on the Continent, but constantly rumoured to be gathering Protestant forces to invade England and oust his Catholic uncle, James II. In one broadsheet, *Duke Dangerfield declaring how he represented the D. of Mon–*, Dangerfield thinks back over his storied criminal career—'Am I he that laid so many profound Plots? that famous *Danger field* that writ the Legend, the Inconvincible Narrative! that laid the Foundation of a deep Plot in the bottom of a Meal-Tub? He that offer'd to kill his King for 20 *l.*'—and decides on a new stratagem: 'shall I now be afraid to take upon me the person of a Duke? The D. of M—A Duke out of Fashion, and out at heels, no place nor being in the Earth, and but a Vagabond, no more then my self?' And, perhaps in time, he'd be king himself: 'and why shou'd I not? I am an *English* Man as well as he, I am as good a Subject as he, and for ought I know, have as good a Title to the Crown'. Dangerfield buys himself 'a Star and a Purple Livery Coat' in Long Lane, and departs for Staffordshire, 'keeping the Star close cover'd under a Campain Coat'. By dropping hints of his exile—'ever and anon talking of *Flanders, Brussels,* and the unkindness of the *M. de Grana* in banishing him his Territories'—and occasionally flashing 'the Star and blew Garter', Dangerfield 'made the People believe he was not only the D– of M. but ador'd him as a King'.

To confirm his 'Royal Extraction', Dangerfield takes it on himself to cure the King's Evil, scrofula, by the 'Miracle of Touching'—a habit to which he was well suited, 'for he generally Touched all Night, besides once or twice a day as the patient presented'. He tied round his afflicted subjects' necks 'Counterfeit half Geanies which he Coyned himself for that purpose, fastned in halfpeny Tape', receiving two guineas per person for his troubles. He then further confirmed his sovereignty, when he 'falls a Knighting all the Scum of the Country'—creating 'Sir *Simon Smut*, Blaksmith', 'Sir *Solomon Sole*, Cobler', 'Sir *Brason Nose*, Kettle Tinker', et al.—in the process bringing some 400 pounds' worth of 'Fees into the Treasury'. His downfall came when he returned to London to dispose of 'six blank Patents for Baronets'. At Mile End, he was spotted by John Sing, whom he had previously denounced as a

Jesuit; Sing trailed him to his Whitechapel lodgings, and then informed '*Madam Celier*, who glad to catch the old Badger in his own Trap, went with a strong Guard and secured his Grace in the presence, which was the Kitching, under a Canopie in the Chimney Corner'. The pamphlet provides a dramatic re-enactment of the unhappy reunion between Dangerfield and Cellier, in which Dangerfield confesses that 'The Meal Tub Plot was mine', and that he now scorns death: 'If I had been hang'd when I was *Dangerfield*, and a poor Devil, no had pitty'd me, But now I have liv'd to be a Duke, I dye with Honour, a Fig for the World.' And off he is carried to Whitehall.[46] Another contemporary ballad, *Wish upon Wish, or Dangerfields lamentation*, is less upbeat, as a despairing Dangerfield laments his fate, and resolves to stop pretending to be Monmouth: 'No *M–th*, no, no, | No more ile disguise, | The Cloak, and the Star | Ile leave off and be wise.'[47]

Further confusion is evident in a broadsheet ballad entitled *Dangerfields Dance*, licensed for publication on 2 July, the day of the first flogging, presumably to cash in on the event (Fig. 23). The ballad is illustrated by a woodcut in which Dangerfield is depicted in the pillory 'For a Seditious libel', and being whipped 'at the carts arse', according to his King's Bench verdict. Yet the heading claims instead that Dangerfield was punished for 'several notorious crimes by him committed, viz. he pretended to be a Duke, and feigned himself to be Monmouth, with several other pranks'. There is an odd detail here, however, that deserves attention: in his plan 'Poor Women to deceive, and get their Coyn', Dangerfield, he is charged, made 'the World believe thou wert some Spark | Who had such Honour from thy Servant *Mark*'.[48] Why would anyone know the name of Dangerfield's servant?

Figure 23. Woodcut detail from *Dangerfields Dance* (1685). The Bodleian Libraries, The University of Oxford, Ashm. G. 16 (68).

The answer lies back in *Dangerfield's Memoires*, where Mark is mentioned frequently. And, as Kate Loveman has suggested, it is the *Memoires* that also fuelled the Monmouth story. From Christmas Day 1684 to New Year's Day a week later, Dangerfield lodged at the Raven in Shrewsbury. On Friday 26 December, he 'had the Taylor to make me a Suit of Cloaths', laying out some forty-nine shillings for three and a half yards of cloth and twenty-nine shillings for four yards of black satin. The tailoring turned out to have some hidden costs: 'after he had taken Measure of me, we went to the *Pheasant-Tavern*, and Drank two Bottles of Sack'—two more shillings, and three shillings for 'the fiddlers there'—'after which I went home to the *Raven* to Dinner; then after I had Slept a little I went to the Coffee-house, where I found a deal of good Company, with whom I stay'd, and play'd at Back-Gammon and Hazzard untill two a Clock the Next Morning'—losing fifteen shillings at hazard, his expenses reveal. It was a heavy day of drinking, and the hangover was worse. 'The Taylor made me sit within [inside] all day for want of my Cloaths', Dangerfield reported on Saturday 27th, 'so that that day nothing hap'ned more then his coming to me very Drunk, and so became very Troublesome, and that it was Commonly reported about *Shrewsbury*, that I was the *Duke of Monmouth*'.

It seems, then, that Dangerfield's secluded presence in the Raven at Shrewsbury—brought about because he had nothing to wear—gave rise to a rumour that he was, in fact, the duke of Monmouth returned from exile. It's not even too implausible an idea: Monmouth and Dangerfield were born within months of each other; Dangerfield had money to spend, and an apparent need for secrecy. As Loveman puts it, the readers of the broadsheet ballads 'may well have been under the impression that Dangerfield had earned his punishment because of his (fictional) roguish pranks. The rogue literature about Dangerfield had created an alternate history which was more entertaining and less divisive than the actual series of events.'[49] So while the public's desire to read more about Don Tomazo led them to purchase *Dangerfield's Memoires*, a chance diary entry in the *Memoires* prompted the notion that Dangerfield had embarked on yet another feat of disguise and deception—a notion that was fuelled by his punishment for a wholly different crime dating from six years earlier.

The End of Dangerfield

In truth, there was no need to fictionalize the life of Thomas Dangerfield: what happened next was more sensational than any of his rambles. 4 July saw the execution of the second and final bout of whipping and pillorying, at Tyburn (Fig. 24). But, as Sir John Bramston recorded in his autobiography,

Figure 24. Detail from *A True Relation of the Sentence and Condemnation of Thomas Dangerfield* (1685). The Bodleian Libraries, The University of Oxford, Firth b.27 (1), fo. 6ʳ.

In the returne from Tyburne, in a coach, guarded with the Sheriff's officers, in Holborne, one Mr Francis, of Grey's Inn, came to the coach side to see and speake with him, with whome yet he had noe busines nor acquaintance. He asked Daingerfeild 'how he liked his race, and how he did after his heats;' to whome Daingerfeild replyed, 'You are the sonn of a whore.' Francis thervpon, haueinge a small caine in his hand, thrust at him, which rann into his eye, and he died next day.[50]

After Dangerfield died, Robert Francis was brought in, indicted, found guilty of wilful murder, and sentenced to hang.[51] His fate led Francis to be featured in what was fast becoming a hugely popular form of life-writing: the biographies of those sentenced to death, as written by the Chaplain in Ordinary of Newgate, who brought them to life 'With many remarkable Passages and Transactions, during the Series of their lives, taken from their own Mouths, after their Condemnation', with the stated aim 'to deter others from such rash and lawless Enterprizes, as must inevitably end in their Ruin and disgrace'. On returning to Newgate, the Ordinary wrote, Francis 'began seriously to consider what he had done, becoming more Melancholly than ever, and as much as stood with conveniency, retired from company, seriously reflecting upon his latter end'. He claimed that 'what he had done was rashly, and altogether without any premeditated Malice': happening to pass by, he was 'pressed into the Croude out of curiosity to see the Prisoner, of whom he had little or no knowledge only by report'. After 'an unhappy word passing' between them, Francis 'pushed at him with his *Cane*, not imagining it would have proved of fatal consequence'. The event was entirely out of character, Francis claimed: 'he had lived in credit and reputation, not being given to quarrel, nor transported with passion to a degree of mischiefeing any person before this unhappy Accident, hoping the God of Mercys would pardon his sins'.[52]

Francis was executed at Tyburn on 24 July 1685, an event that, as Roger Morrice notes, provoked 'great variety of discourses thereupon'.[53] Some, like Sir John Bramston, were sympathetic to him:

> It may well be presumed Francis had noe designe of killinge, for he had a sword by his side, which was a more likely thing to kill him then that litle caine, indeed, the smallest that euer I see vsed, and without any iron ferule or any thinge at the end; and Francis his wife was by too. But Daingerfeild was under protection of the Kinge and his officers, and had sufferd the law, and there was a great aggrauation of the crime, I suppose, for certeinly there was noe intent to kill him.

For Bramston, the true criminal was Thomas Dangerfield: 'This fellow had binn a highway theife and a cheat, had binn burnt in the hand, and whipt; a wittie rogue too, and now at last pretended religion. But there is an end of him!'[54]

Bramston spoke too soon. Dangerfield proved to have a powerful afterlife—and even a rehabilitation. Shortly after he was killed, another broadsheet ballad appeared, entitled *Dangerfield's Ghost to Jefferys*, George Jeffreys being the notorious 'hanging judge' who sentenced him. '*Revenge! Revenge!* my injur'd *Shade* begins | To haunt thy guilty Soul, and scourge thy sins', Dangerfield warns Jeffreys, before confronting him with the gory mess that is his body, repeatedly flogged and then stabbed by Francis:

> [S]ee the dismal *shape* in which I dy'd!
> My Body all deform'd with putrid Gore,
> Bleeding my *Soul* away at every *Pore*;
> Pusht faster on by *Francis*, less unkind;
> My *Body* swoln, and bloated as thy *Mind*.
> This dangling *Eye-ball* rolls about in vain,
> Never to find its proper *seat* again,
> The hollow *Cell* usurpt by Blood and *Brain*:
> The trembling *Jury's* Verdict ought to be
> *Murder'd at once, by* Francis, *and by Thee.*[55]

Robert Francis is here the 'less unkind' party only because his action hastened Dangerfield's death and thus limited his suffering; Dangerfield's murder lies equally at the judicial hand of Jeffreys.

This version of events was elaborated by Roger Coke in his popular 1697 *A Detection of the Court and State of England*, where he claimed that Robert Francis was 'a fierce Papist', and that Dangerfield died of Francis's wound, along 'with the Agony of his Whipping...his Body was so swoln and martyr'd...that 'twas a question whether he died of the Whipping, or Wound in his Eye'.[56] Coke's suggestion was elaborated four years later in *The Merciful Assizes* (1701), a self-styled mock 'panegyric on the late Lord Jeffreys hanging so many in the west', by the writer and publisher John Dunton—the man who had lifted the 'rambles' and a couple of sentences from *Don Tomazo*. Condemning Francis as 'a Red-Hot *Papist*', Dunton also claimed that Dangerfield's body 'was so swoln and *Martyr'd* with his *Whipping*, that it was a Question whether he Dyed of that, or of the Wound in his Eye, for which *Francis* however was justly Hang'd, the *King* thinking it wou'd appear to be too Base a Partiality, to Pardon him for so Foul a Fact'. He then went further to rehabilitate Dangerfield, claiming 'his Father was a Gentleman, who Liv'd in good Fashion, at *Waltham-Abby*' while Dangerfield himself 'was a Man of Business and Courage, and therefore employ'd by the *Papists* (while among 'em) in their *Desperate and most Dangerous Concerns*, and was then of a Religion that excus'd, and encouraged the worst things he, or any other Man, cou'd be Guilty of'. Before going to his final whipping, Dangerfield 'had *Strong Bodings* of his Death, and chose a Text for his Funeral Sermon...Saying he was confident they had such a Particular malice against him, he shou'd ne'er return alive'.[57] When Dangerfield does indeed die, Dunton recalls,

> Mr. *Dangerfield*'s Body was convey'd to *Waltham-Abby*, with several Coaches attending it; and there Honourably Bury'd, and 'twas what he deserv'd: For the worst of his Enemies have own'd he was a Man of Wit, Courage, and Business; all which he reconcil'd the best of any one: He had as much Address, as perfect and great a Presence of Mind, in whatever Exigencies, as can be met with: He was the best Companion, the best Friend, in the World; and as Generous an Enemy: He did nothing but what lookt very handsome; and there was a Charm in the meanest, and something most bewitchingly pleasant, in the most indefensible of his Actions. He cou'd do almost every thing, and 'tis hard to say what he did with the greatest Grace - In a Word, all that knew him must say, that he wanted nothing but an Estate, to have made him as Compleat a Gentleman, as most in England.[58]

What Dunton fails to disclose in this unexpected panegyric is that he and Dangerfield were in fact brothers-in-law. In 1682, Dunton married Elizabeth Annesley, daughter of the dissenting minister Dr Samuel Annesley. The following March, Dangerfield married Elizabeth's sister Sarah, 'without her fathers knowledge', as Roger Morrice recorded in his 'entering booke'; in early April, Dangerfield went to her parents' house, 'claimed her and has her, it makes a great deale of discourse in town'.[59] It was a close-knit group: a third Annesley sister, Judith, is the 'sister Judith' mentioned repeatedly in *Dangerfield's Memoires*; a fourth, Susannah, married Samuel Wesley, from whom Dangerfield had purchased his Lucretius in Oxford in December 1684;[60] Dunton would publish Wesley's first poetry collection, the wonderfully titled *Maggots*, in 1687.[61] In his account of Dangerfield's death, Dunton betrays his active involvement: he claims that 'the Murderer [Francis] Fled, but was Pursu'd by the Rabble, and *taken by my means in Holborn*'. He also reveals that 'Attempts were made to *bribe* Mr. *Dangerfield's Wife*, that she might Consent to the Pardon of her Husband's Murderer, but she wou'd not *sell his Blood*, and had an *Appeal* ready against him, had he been Pardon'd'.[62]

In Sarah Dangerfield's principled refusal to pardon her husband's murderer, and John Dunton's posthumous defence of his brother-in-law, we see how the rambles of Don Tomazo did real and lasting damage not only to Thomas Dangerfield, but also to those close to him. And we see this again when the memory of Dangerfield's strange death was revived one last time in the 24 June 1721 issue of *Applebee's Journal* in an anonymous piece entitled 'Against Reviling Public Criminals'. Its author writes that 'I know nothing of its kind that savours of more Inhumanity than to insult Men under Trouble, and especially such as fall into the Hands of Publick Justice'. 'Men in the Hands of the Law', he continued, 'should be left to the Law', and not have their load 'made heavier by the Reproaches of the People'. He brings in as 'an eminent Example of the Resentment of the Government in *England*' the case of Dangerfield, who was fatally wounded 'by an officious Wretch, as the Officers of Justice were bringing him back to Newgate'; 'The Murderer was immediately apprehended, and being condemn'd, no Intercession could prevail with the King to pardon him; but he was hang'd, as he deserv'd, all Men abhorring the barbarous Action'.[63] This angry anonymous *Applebee's* writer has been identified as Daniel Defoe, the foremost English novelist of the early eighteenth century. It might be wondered why Defoe would allude to this case, now some thirty-six years old—but Defoe was also close to the circles around Dangerfield, Dunton, and the Annesley family into which they married. He was born in 1660 in Dr Annesley's parish of St Giles Cripplegate; when Annesley was ejected two years later, the Foe family followed him to his meeting house at Little St Helens in Bishopsgate, and Defoe wrote an anonymous elegy on the minister.[64]

So Thomas Dangerfield does indeed meet John Dunton and Daniel Defoe—but not in the way we might expect. The life-writing connections between Dangerfield, Dunton, and Defoe are of course intriguing and seductive: many of Dunton's and Defoe's works take cues from Dangerfield, subject of multiple autobiographies, a fictional biography, and a printed diary. But if we are to see the influence of

Don Tomazo on Defoe's creations, then we should also consider the influence of Thomas Dangerfield and his 'barbarous' death on Defoe himself. Whereas Defoe's anti-heroes are fictional, Dangerfield occupies a place somewhere between fact and fiction—or perhaps, more dangerously, in fiction and fact simultaneously. He serves as a final reminder that in the England of the sixteenth and seventeenth centuries, life-writing was not simply a literary exercise or a personal indulgence. Like Thomas More's a century and a half earlier, but in an entirely different register, Dangerfield's story is one of familial and parochial loyalties, overlaid with partisan politics and religious controversy, and competing claims of criminality and conspiracy—the complex webs that produce so much of the life-writing of early modern England.

Notes

Introduction

1. On Bodley, see Clennell, 'Bodley, Sir Thomas (1545–1613)'; Clennell, 'Introduction'.
2. Sir Ralph Winwood, though married to Bodley's stepdaughter, inherited nothing but some worthless armoury. See Chamberlain to Alice Carleton, 4 February 1612/13. TNA, SP 14/72, fo. 34^{v}. Winwood's servant John More also denounced Bodley's 'miserable avarice', criticized his treatment of his stepchildren 'whose father did provide the materials wherewith his wealth and honour is erected', and negotiated with executors for a better deal for his master. See More to Winwood, ? January 1613; 6 February 1612/13; 8 February 1612/13; 1/2 March 1612/13; 7 August 1613, in Historical Manuscripts Commission, *Report on the Manuscripts of the Duke of Buccleuch and Queensberry*, 123, 123–4, 124–5, 125–6, 128, 141–2. See also Sir Henry Savile to Winwood, 29 January 1612/13, ibid., 123.
3. Chamberlain to Dudley Carleton, 23 June 1613. TNA, SP 14/74, fo. 20^{r}.
4. Chamberlain to Carleton, 25 March 1613. TNA, SP 14/72, fo. 162^{r}.
5. Chamberlain to Carleton, 23 June 1613. TNA, SP 14/74, fo. 20^{r}.
6. Chamberlain to Winwood, 10 February 1612/13. *The Letters of John Chamberlain*, ed. McClure, 1:420. Chamberlain later wrote, 'Sir Henry Sauile shewed me the last weeke his notes taken in the reading of Sir Thomas Bodleys life, written by himself in seuen sheets of paper with vanitie enough.' Chamberlain to Carleton, 25 February 1612/13. TNA, SP 14/72, fo. 103^{r}.
7. Bodley, *The Life of S[i]r Thomas Bodley*, C4^{r}, C4^{v}. See Wooden, 'Sir Thomas Bodley's *Life of Himself* (1609) and the Epideictic Strategies of Encomia'.
8. Chamberlain to Carleton, 25 February 1612/13. TNA, SP 14/72, fo. 103^{r}.
9. *The Diary of John Manningham of the Middle Temple, 1602–1603*, ed. Sorlien: the Bodley story at 186 (on 6 February 1602/3), and another at 100–1, printed from BL Harley MS 5353.
10. Chamberlain to Winwood, 10 February 1612/13. *The Letters of John Chamberlain*, ed. McClure, 1:420. It is possible that Abbot is acting as one of the three overseers of Bodley's will, as Clennell suggests ('Introduction', 27), but, as Cyndia Susan Clegg writes, from 1610, 'although he did not personally license books for the press, [George Abbot] concentrated authority for licensing in his own household and that of John King, Bishop of London'. Clegg, *Press Censorship in Jacobean England*, 63.
11. Traces of the influence of the 'Life' can, however, be felt in the Latin funeral oration that John Hales delivered at Merton on 29 March. Hales, 'Oratio funebris'; Blank, ed. and Whittington, trans., 'John Hales' Funeral Oration for Sir Thomas Bodley: an Edited Translation'; on Hales's debt to Bodley's *Life*, see 178 n. 9.
12. Anon [Langbaine?], 'To the Reader' in Bodley, *Life*, A2^{r-v}.
13. According to Anthony Wood, Hakewill 'translated into Latine *The life of Sir Tho. Bodley*, his Kinsman, which is in MS. in the publick Library'. *Athenæ Oxonienses*, 1:F1^{v} (col. 67).

14. Lloyd, *The States-Men and Favourites of England since the Reformation*, 2Q1^{v}–2Q4^{r}; Lloyd, *State-Worthies, or, The States-Men and Favourites of England since the Reformation*, 2nd edn, 3F3^{r}–3F5^{r}; Wood, *Athenæ Oxonienses*, 2: N3^{v}–N4^{r} (cols. 326–9).
15. Hearne, 'To the Reader', in *Reliquiæ Bodleianæ: Or Some Genuine Remains of Sir Thomas Bodley* [ed. Hearne], A2^{r}–A8^{v}, at A8^{r}, A8^{v}. The 'Life' is at B1^{r}–B8^{r}.
16. Hearne, 'The Publisher's Preface', xlv–xlvi.
17. Bacon, *The Two Bookes…Of the Proficience and Aduancement of Learning, Diuine and Humane*, 2D1^{v}.
18. Manton, 'To the Christian Reader', b9^{r}; Manton was publishing some 'remarkable passages in the holy life and happy death' of Mrs Dorothy Shaw, wife of a Kingston-upon-Hull preacher. For lives of children, see Vernon, *The Compleat Scholler; or, a Relation of the Life, and Latter End Especially of Caleb Vernon*; Davis, *A Sermon at the Funeral of the Vertuous and Truly Religious Lady, Mrs. Margaret Andrewes*; Anon., *The Life and Death of Mrs. Margaret Andrews.*
19. Calamy, 'The Introduction': largely concerned with continental lives, Calamy admits that 'yet several natives of our British Isles have also written their own lives, as well as the inhabitants of other countries' (1:41), citing attempts by George Buchanan, Sir James Melville, Bishop Joseph Hall, Dr John Forbes, Samuel Parker, Richard Baxter, and Gilbert Burnet—with a special mention that 'a certain ingenious gentleman [i.e. Thomas Hearne] has published a great many curiosities, in which he has generally met with good acceptance' (1:45), including the life of Sir Thomas Bodley. North, *General Preface and Life of Dr John North*, ed. Millard.
20. Nicolson, *The Development of English Biography*, 69, 36, 37; Epstein, *Recognizing Biography*, 13–33; Altick, *Lives and Letters: A History of Literary Biography in England and America*, 20; Butt, *Biography in the Hands of Walton, Johnson, and Boswell*. See also de Sola Pinto, *English Biography in the Seventeenth Century: Selected Short Lives*, whose canon is literary, weighted towards the Restoration, and entirely male.
21. Shumaker, *English Autobiography: Its Emergence, Materials, and Form*; Pascal, *Design and Truth in Autobiography*. Bottrall, *Every Man a Phoenix*, focuses on Herbert of Cherbury, Bunyan, Thomas Browne's *Religio medici* and Richard Baxter's 'Narrative of the most memorable passages of his life and times'. Bunyan is also the starting point for Morris, *Versions of the Self: Studies in English Biography from John Bunyan to John Stuart Mill*; and he is the sole early modern subject of Bruss, *Autobiographical Acts: the Changing Situation of a Literary Genre*, 33–60, and Spengemann, *The Forms of Autobiography: Episodes in the History of a Literary Genre*, 44–51. Weintraub, *The Value of the Individual: Self and Circumstance in Autobiography*, devotes its only English chapter to 'the Puritan unification of the personality' (Bunyan, Baxter, and Benjamin Franklin).
22. Spalding, *Self-Harvest: A Study of Diaries and the Diarist*, 9, 34, and *passim*; see also Fothergill, *Private Chronicles: A Study of English Diaries*, 13–14; Dobbs, *Dear Diary…: Some Studies in Self-Interest*, has chapters on Evelyn and Pepys.
23. Gittings, *The Nature of Biography*, 23, 26, 29; Anderson, *Biographical Truth.*
24. Osborn, *The Beginnings of Autobiography in England: A Paper Delivered…at the Fifth Clark Library Seminar 8 August 1959*; Heale, *Autobiography and Authorship in Renaissance Verse*; Skura, *Tudor Autobiography: Listening for Inwardness.*

25. For Rogers and Ward, see *Two Elizabethan Puritan Diaries*, ed. Knappen; for Hoby, see *Diary of Lady Margaret Hoby 1599–1605*, ed. Meads, and *The Private Life of an Elizabethan Lady: The Diary of Lady Margaret Hoby 1599–1605*, ed. Moody.
26. Tindall, *John Bunyan Mechanic Preacher*, 22–41; Starr, *Defoe & Spiritual Autobiography*, x, vii, x; Ebner, *Autobiography in Seventeenth-Century England: Theology and the Self*; Watkins, *The Puritan Experience: Studies in Spiritual Autobiography*; Hindmarsh, *The Evangelical Conversion Narrative: Spiritual Autobiography in Early Modern England*; Lynch, *Protestant Autobiography in the Seventeenth-Century Anglophone World*.
27. On New England, see Matthews, *American Diaries in Manuscript, 1580–1594: A Descriptive Bibliography*; Shea, *Spiritual Autobiography in Early America*; Caldwell, *The Puritan Conversion Narrative: The Beginnings of American Expression*; Payne, *The Self and the Sacred: Conversion and Autobiography in Early American Protestantism*; Brekus, 'Writing as a Protestant Practice: Devotional Diaries in Early New England'; Lynch, *Protestant Autobiography*; Rivett, *The Science of the Soul in Colonial New England*. On Catholic houses, see Hallett ed., *Lives of Spirit: English Carmelite Self-Writing of the Early Modern Period*; *English Convents in Exile, 1600–1800*, vol. 3, *Life Writing I*, ed. Hallett; vol. 4, *Life Writing II*, ed. Daemen-de Gelder.
28. See Graham, Hinds, Hobby, and Wilcox eds, *Her Own Life: Autobiographical Writings by Seventeenth-Century Englishwomen*; Hinds, *God's Englishwomen: Seventeenth-Century Radical Sectarian Writing and Feminist Criticism*; Garman et al., *Hidden in Plain Sight: Quaker Women's Writings, 1650–1700*; Booy ed., *Autobiographical Writings by Early Quaker Women*; Botonaki, *Seventeenth-Century English Women's Autobiographical Writings: Disclosing Enclosures*; Seelig, *Autobiography and Genre in Early Modern Literature: Reading Women's Lives, 1660–1680*; Dowd and Eckerle eds, *Genre and Women's Life Writing in Early Modern England*; Eckerle, *Romancing the Self in Early Modern Englishwomen's Life Writing*.
29. Spufford, 'First Steps in Literacy: The Reading and Writing Experiences of the Humblest Seventeenth-Century Spiritual Autobiographers'; Amelang, *The Flight of Icarus: Artisan Autobiography in Early Modern Europe*; Seaver, *Wallington's World: A Puritan Artisan in Seventeenth-Century London*; Fumerton, *Unsettled: The Culture of Mobility and the Working Poor in Early Modern England*.
30. Bottrall, *Every Man a Phoenix*, 3; Clifford, 'Introduction', xi; Ebner, *Autobiography in Seventeenth-Century England*, 17; Mascuch, *Origins of the Individualist Self: Autobiography and Self-Identity in England, 1591–1791*, 8.
31. In 1661, the anonymously published *Life of that Reverend Divine, and Learned Historian, Dr. Thomas Fuller* (probably by John Fell) refers to itself as 'This biography' (H5^{r}), and two years later James Heath's *Flagellum* describes itself as 'this *Biography* of *Oliver Cromwell*' and 'this Memoir of him, which pretends to an exact Biography' (A5^{v}, B4^{v}). Robert Crosse was alleged to have 'writ a Book call'd *Biographia*, which gives Rules, how Lives are to be writ' in the early 1670s (Glanvill, *A Praefatory Answer to Mr. Henry Stubbe*, P2^{r}), although sadly no such book survives. And most famously, John Dryden used '*Biographia*' to denote 'the Lives of particular Men' in the 'Life of Plutarch' with which he prefaced the 1683–5 translation of Plutarch's *Lives* (G2^{r}, and G4^{v}, G7^{r}).
32. [Cavendish], marchioness of Newcastle, *CCXI Sociable Letters*, A4^{v}; North, 'General Preface', in North, *General Preface and Life of Dr John North*, ed. Millard, 78. 'Idiography'

draws on 'idiograph', which Thomas Blount defines as 'a private writing; or of ones own hand writing' (*Glossographia*, 2nd edn, X1^v).

33. In his 1796 *Miscellanies; or Literary Recreations*, Isaac D'Israeli offered 'Some observations on diaries, self-biography and self-characters' (95); reviewing the book the following year, William Taylor wrote that 'We are doubtful whether [self-biography] be legitimate: it is not very usual in English to employ hybrid words partly Saxon and partly Greek: yet *autobiography* would have seemed pedantic' ('Art. IV. *Miscellanies*; or Literary Recreations. By I. D'Israeli...', 375). Despite the linguist's doubts, however, the pedantic 'autobiography' caught on over the following years: Robert Southey used it in 1809 without comment (*Quarterly Review* 1 (1809), 283: 'This very amusing and unique specimen of autobiography'). See Folkenflik, 'Introduction: The Institution of Autobiography', in *The Culture of Autobiography: Constructions of Self-Representation*, 3–6, although his claim that Anne Yearsley used the term 'autobiographical' is mistaken.
34. Skura, *Tudor Autobiography*, quoted at 3; Smyth, *Autobiography in Early Modern England*.
35. 'Life-writing' has recently achieved some currency in early modern discussions, though without a clear or agreed definition. For Judith Anderson, it is what we should call early modern biography 'with greater historical accuracy' (*Biographical Truth*, 2); for Michelle Dowd and Julie Eckerle, by contrast, it provides a handy catch-all category covering 'both traditional autobiographical writing and also a wide range of genres that involve writing about the self and theorizing about self-writing' ('Recent Studies in Early Modern English Life Writing', 132).
36. Stauffer, *English Biography before 1700*; Delany, *British Autobiography in the Seventeenth Century*; Pritchard, *English Biography in the Seventeenth Century: A Critical Survey*, 7 n. 2. To see how prevalent genre-specific studies have become, see the Bibliography, Section C. For a rare exception, see Kendall, *The Art of Biography*.
37. Gusdorf, 'Conditions and Limits of Autobiography', 35.
38. Kassell, *Medicine & Magic in Elizabethan London: Simon Forman: Astrologer, Alchemist, & Physician*, 19–24, quoted at 21, 22, 19; for a bibliography of Forman's life-writings, see ibid., 233.
39. *The Autobiography of Henry Newcome, M.A.*, ed. Parkinson, 1:1–2, 2.
40. *Autobiography of Henry Newcome*, 1:7, 305. For John Angier's diary, see Heywood, *Oliver Heywood's Life of John Angier of Denton together with Angier's Diary, and Extracts from his 'An Helpe to Better Hearts': also Samuel Angier's Diary*, ed. Axon.
41. *Autobiography of Henry Newcome*, 1:1, 48, 146, 229, 247–8, 261, 270.
42. *Autobiography of Henry Newcome*, 14.
43. *Autobiography of Henry Newcome*, 1:287, referring to Adam, *Vitae Germanorum Theologorum*.
44. For similar appraisals within autobiographical texts, see Smyth, *Autobiography*, 2; Whitehouse, 'Structures and Processes of English Spiritual Autobiography from Bunyan to Cowper', 103.
45. Isham, 'Booke of Remembrance', Princeton University Library, Robert Taylor Collection, RTCO1 (no. 62); Isham, Diary, Northamptonshire Record Office, IL 3365; for a digital edition of both, see *Constructing Elizabeth Isham* (www2.warwick.ac.uk/fac/arts/ren/projects/isham). See Aughterson, 'Isham, Elizabeth (*bap.* 1608, *d.* 1654)'; Eardley, '"Like hewen stone": Augustine, Audience and Revision in Elizabeth Isham's "Booke of Remembrance" (c. 1639)'; Stephens, '"My cheefest work": The Making of the Spiritual

Autobiography of Elizabeth Isham'; Stephens, *The Gentlewoman's Remembrance: Patriarchy, Piety, and Singlehood in Early Stuart England.*

46. *The Diary of Ralph Josselin 1616–1683*, ed. Macfarlane, 15.
47. An almanac from 1637, with Evelyn's notes, survives in Balliol College, Oxford.
48. Two versions survive: *De Vita Propria* (*Of My Own Life*), which takes Evelyn's life-story only to 1644 (in an eighteenth-century transcription, BL Add. MS 78326), and, recycling some material, the *Kalendarium*, which goes through to 1697 (BL Add. MSS 78323–78325); further loose sheets survive covering the last years of Evelyn's life. *The Diary of John Evelyn*, ed. de Beer. For discussions of the writing process, see de Beer, in Evelyn, *Diary*, 1:87–101; Chambers, 'Evelyn, John (1620–1706)'.
49. Ezell, 'Ann Halkett's Morning Devotions: Posthumous Publication and the Culture of Writing in Late Seventeenth-Century Britain', 217, 219.
50. Heywood, *The Rev. Oliver Heywood, B.A. 1630–1702; His Autobiography, Diaries, Anecdote and Event Books*, ed. Horsfall Turner.
51. *An Account of the Life and Death of Mrs. Elizabeth Bury* [ed. Samuel Bury], A3^{r}.
52. Mendelson, 'Stuart Women's Diaries and Occasional Memoirs', 188, discussing Savage, *Memoirs of the Life & Character of Mrs. Sarah Savage*, ed. Williams; [Rich], *Autobiography of Mary Countess of Warwick*, ed. Croker; Thornton, *The Autobiography of Mrs. Alice Thornton, of East Newton, Co. York*, ed. Jackson.
53. Norbrook, '"But a copie": Textual Authority and Gender in Editions of *The Life of John Hutchinson*', 110, 117, 115; Hutchinson, *Memoirs of the Life of Colonel Hutchinson Governor of Nottingham by his Widow Lucy*, ed. Hutchinson, rev. Firth.
54. For Pepys's diary, see Chapter 14; Dee, *The Private Diary and Catalogue of his Library of Manuscripts*, ed. Halliwell; Dee, *The Diaries of John Dee*, ed. Fenton.
55. See *infra*, p. 293, n. 11.
56. Wood, *Athenæ Oxonienses*, 2:N4^{r} (col. 327). See Bodley, *Autobiography*, ed. Clennell, 55 n. 1: for copies, see Bodl. MS Arch. Selden A. 76 (*c.* 1615); Bodl. MS Add. A. 186, fos. 1^{r}–8^{v}, with some pages missing, copied with his will (fos. 9^{r}–20^{r}, with a codicil, 21^{r}–22^{v}); BL Sloane MS 1786. BL Cotton MS Titus C. vii, fos. 173^{r}–174^{v} comprises selected passages, 'Ex vita Thomæ Bodlei sua manu discripta'.
57. Burr, *The Autobiography: A Critical and Comparative Study* sees 'the three great archetypes' as Julius Caesar, Augustine, and Cardano and devotes fewer than three pages (417–19) of her 400-plus-page book to a cursory listing of English-language texts. The key early modern texts of Whittemore, *Pure Lives: The Early Biographers* are Vasari's *Lives* and, idiosyncratically, Raphael Holinshed's *Chronicles* (1577, 1587).
58. *The Diary of Sir Henry Slingsby, of Scriven, Bart.*, ed. Parsons, 54–5, alluding to Montaigne, *The Essayes or Morall, Politike and Millitarie Discourses*, trans. Florio, L2^{r}.
59. The exception is St Teresa de Avila, whose autobiography was translated into English by Tobie Matthew (Chapter 9); even then, the translation was not published in England.
60. For the belated translation of life-writings, see Braden, 'Biography'.
61. For the phrase 'sacred biography', see Heffernan, *Sacred Biography: Saints and their Biographers in the Middle Ages*, quoted at 19.
62. Voragine, [*Legenda aurea*]; Kempe, *Here begynneth a shorte treatyse of contemplacyon taught by our lorde Jhesucryste, or taken out of the boke of Margerie Kempe of Lyn*; Bradshaw, *Here begynneth*

the holy lyfe and history of Saynt Werburge very frutefull for all Christen people to rede; Bradshaw, *Here begynneth the lyfe of Saynt Radegunde*.

63. Voragine, [*Legenda aurea*] (1527).
64. Pico della Mirandola, *Here is conteyned the lyfe of Johan Picus Erle of Myrandula*, trans. More; see Edwards, 'Introduction' [to *Life of* Pico], in *The Complete Works of St Thomas More*, vol. 1, ed. Edwards, Rodgers, and Miller, xxxv–lix. For the lives of Richard III, see *The Complete Works of St. Thomas More*, vol. 2, ed. Sylvester.
65. Seeking to redress the negative portrayal in Edward Hall's *Chronicle* of his former employer Cardinal Thomas Wolsey, George Cavendish wrote a 'Life' which circulated heavily in manuscript—over fifty copies are known to survive today. For manuscript witnesses, see *CELM*, CvG4–CvG57; Cavendish, *The Life and Death of Cardinal Wolsey*, ed. Sylvester.
66. Houlbrooke, 'Funeral Sermons', in *Death, Religion, and the Family in England, 1480–1750*, 295–330, at 298; see also Appendix 2, at 386–7.
67. Kilby, *Hallelu-iah: Praise yee the Lord, for the Vnburthening of a Loaden Conscience*.
68. *The Diary of Samuel Rogers, 1634–1638*, ed. Webster and Shipps, 1; printed from Queen's University, Belfast, Percy MS 7 A.
69. *The Diary of Ralph Josselin 1616–1683*, ed. Macfarlane, 1–15.
70. Baker, 'Johnson, Cicely (*fl.* 1617/18–1636/7)'; see *Scripture Women: Rose Thurgood, 'A Lecture of Repentance' & Cicely Johnson, 'Fanatical Reveries'*, printed from John Rylands Library, Manchester, English MS 875, fos. 201–27, and 247–74.
71. *The Journal of Richard Norwood, Surveyor of Bermuda*, ed. Craven and Hayward, printed from Bermuda Archives, P.A. 307; Bendall, 'Norwood, Richard (1590–1675)'.
72. For lives of lay women, see Rowlands, 'Recusant Women 1560–1640', 162–3, 175.
73. Gerard, *The Autobiography of a Hunted Priest*, trans. Caraman; Weston, *William Weston: The Autobiography of an Elizabethan*, trans. Caraman.
74. Kenny ed., *The Responsa Scholarum of the English College, Rome*; Hallett, *Lives of Spirit*.
75. Donaldson, 'National Biography and the Arts of Memory: From Thomas Fuller to Colin Matthew', 67; Wilcox, 'Selves in Strange Lands: Autobiography and Exile in the Mid-Seventeenth Century'; Murphy, 'Revised Lives: Lineage and Dislocation in Seventeenth-Century English Autobiography', unpublished PhD dissertation, 2014.
76. *The Memoirs of Anne, Lady Halkett and Ann, Lady Fanshawe*, ed. Loftis; [Cavendish] *The Life of the Thrice Noble, High and Puissant Prince William Cavendishe, Duke, Marquess and Earl of Newcastle*; Hutchinson, *Memoirs of the Life of Colonel Hutchinson*, ed. Sutherland; *Lady Anne Halkett: Selected Self-Writings*, ed. Trill.
77. Evans, *An Eccho to the Voice from Heaven, or, A Narration of the Life, and Manner of the Special Calling, and Visions of Arise Evans*; Smith, *Wonderfull Prophecyes Revealed to Nicholas Smith Shoe-Maker*; Trapnel, *A Legacy for Saints; Being Several Experiences of the Dealings of God with Anna Trapnel, in, and after her Conversion* [ed. Proud and Ingold]; Coppin, *Truths Testimony and a Testimony of Truths Appearing*.
78. See Graham, Hinds, Hobby, and Wilcox eds, *Her Own Life: Autobiographical Writings by Seventeenth-Century Englishwomen*; Hinds, *God's Englishwomen: Seventeenth-Century Radical Sectarian Writing and Feminist Criticism*; Garman et al., *Hidden in Plain Sight: Quaker Women's Writings, 1650–1700*; Booy ed., *Autobiographical Writings by Early Quaker Women*.

79. See Tindall, *John Bunyan: Mechanick Preacher*, 22–41; Starr, *Defoe & Spiritual Autobiography*, x, vii, x; Ebner, *Autobiography in Seventeenth-Century England: Theology and the Self*; Watkins, *The Puritan Experience: Studies in Spiritual Autobiography*; Hindmarsh, *The Evangelical Conversion Narrative: Spiritual Autobiography in Early Modern England*; Lynch, *Protestant Autobiography in the Seventeenth-Century Anglophone World.*
80. See, for example, Powell, *Spirituall Experiences, of Sundry Beleevers*. From New England, John Eliot sent back 'confessions' of the Christianity of the native Americans, although they were translated and vouchsafed only by Eliot himself: see Eliot, *A Further Account of the Progress of the Gospel Amongst the Indians in New England.*
81. See especially Bourcier, *Les journaux privés en Angleterre de 1600 à 1660*; McKay, 'The Diary Network in Sixteenth and Seventeenth Century England'; Clarke, 'Diaries'; McKay, 'English Diarists: Gender, Geography and Occupation, 1500–1700'.
82. *The Diary of Ralph Josselin 1616–1683*, ed. Macfarlane; Macfarlane, *The Family Life of Ralph Josselin, a Seventeenth-Century Clergyman; An Essay in Historical Anthropology*. See also *The Diary of Thomas Crosfield*, ed. F. S. Boas (1935), printed from Queen's College, Oxford, MS 390.
83. *The Diary of Robert Woodford, 1637–1641*, ed. Fielding; *The Journal of William Dowsing: Iconoclasm in East Anglia during the English Civil War*, ed. Cooper; *The Notebooks of Nehemiah Wallington, 1618–1654: A Selection*, ed. Booy. For Savage, see Mendelson, 'Stuart Women's Diaries and Occasional Memoirs', 203, citing CCRO D/Basten/8, and Bodl. MS Eng. Misc. e. 331.
84. *The Diary of Roger Lowe of Ashton-in-Makerfield, Lancashire 1663–74*, ed. Sachse. The diary is now held at the Wigan Archives Service, Leigh.
85. Mendelson, 'Stuart Women's Diaries and Occasional Memoirs', 183, citing a fragment, Bodl. MS Rawlinson Q. e. 28, and a contemporary transcript, Bodl. MS Rawlinson D. 1262–3.
86. *The Diary of Anne Clifford, 1616–1619*, ed. Acheson; *Katherine Austen's Book M: British Library, Additional Manuscript 4454*, ed. Ross, printed from BL Additional MS 4454.
87. *The Diary of John Manningham of the Middle Temple, 1602–1603*, ed. Sorlien, printed from BL Harley MS 5353; *The diary of Sir Simonds D'Ewes (1622–1624): journal d'un étudiant londonien sous le règne de Jacques Ier*, ed. Bourcier, printed from BL Harley MS 421; *The Journal of Sir Simonds D'Ewes from the Beginning of the Long Parliament to the Opening of the Trial of the Earl of Strafford*, ed. Notestein; *The Diary of Sir Henry Slingsby, of Scriven, Bart.*, ed. Parsons, 55.
88. *The Diary of John Evelyn*, ed. de Beer.
89. Jonson, *Volpone or the Foxe*, I3r (4.1).
90. Digby, *Loose Fantasies*, ed. Gabrieli; the manuscript is BL Harley MS 6758, fos. 5–169. For the story of this work, see Moshenska, *A Stain in the Blood: The Remarkable Voyage of Sir Kenelm Digby.*
91. Boyle, 'An Account of Philaretus', quoted at 4, 6, 7, 8, 12, 14, 15, 16.
92. Eckerle, *Romancing the Self in Early Modern Englishwomen's Life Writing.*
93. *Memoirs of the Life of Colonel Hutchinson with the Fragment of an Autobiography of Mrs. Hutchinson*, ed. Sutherland, 114.

Chapter 1

1. Manuscript note, Emmanuel College, Cambridge, MS 76, fo. [4]^{v}; Harpsfield's dedicatory epistle is at fos. [5]^{r}-[6]^{r}, and the life at fos. 1^{r}-57^{r} (misnumbered: it should be 1-60). See Rhodes James ed., *The Western Manuscripts in the Library of Emmanuel College: A Descriptive Catalogue*, 69. Printed as Harpsfield, *The Life and Death of Sr Thomas Moore, Knight, Sometimes Lord High Chancellor of England*, ed. Hitchcock and Chambers, xiii-xiv. On 8 April 1582, the Privy Council ordered Essex justices of the peace to cooperate fully with Topcliffe's mission. TNA, PC 2/13, fo. 67.
2. 'The moiety of the pourparty of the manor of Estwestham and Plais with all rents, & c., in the parish of Estham in co. Essex, now or late in the occupation of *Arden Waferer*, esq': 'Inquisitions: 1589', in *Abstracts of Inquisitiones Post Mortem for the City of London: Part 3*, ed. Fry, 129-43. On Waferer, see Trimble, *The Catholic Laity in Elizabethan England 1558-1603*, 58, 86, 192, 251; Parmiter, *Elizabeth Popish Recusancy in the Inns of Court*, 9-13, 22, 46, 51-2.
3. Thomas More of Barnbrough (1532-1606) lived in the next parish, Low Leyton. On this identification of 'Mr. Thomas Moare', see Harpsfield, *Life and Death*, 294-6.
4. Fleetwood to Burghley, 14 April 1582. BL Lansdowne MS 35, fos. 87-89, at 87^{r}; *A True Reporte of the Death & Martyrdome of M. Campion Jesuite and Preiste, & M. Sherwin, & M. Bryan Preistes, at Tiborne the First of December 1581.*
5. Fleetwood to Burghley, 14 April 1582. BL Lansdowne MS 35, fos. 87^{r}.
6. Hulse, 'Dead Man's Treasure: The Cult of Thomas More', 208, 217-20; Marotti, 'Manuscript Transmission and the Catholic Martyrdom Account in Early Modern England', 172.
7. Topcliffe is already noted as an ill-tempered torturer in a letter of 25 October 1582 from 'G. B.'. Caraman ed., *The Other Face: Catholic Life under Elizabeth I*, 243. On Topcliffe, see Bindoff, 'Topcliffe, Richard (1531-1604), of Somerby, Lincs. and Westminster'; Rowse, 'The Truth about Topcliffe'; Richardson, 'Topcliffe, Richard (1531-1604)'.
8. Gerard, *The Autobiography of a Hunted Priest*, trans. Caraman, 68, 69.
9. Jessopp, *One Generation of a Norfolk House: A Contribution to Elizabethan History*, 70-1.
10. Topcliffe to Elizabeth, 'Good or Evil Friday, 1595', quoted in Jessopp, *One Generation*, 71.
11. See, for example, Huntington RB60060, Topcliffe's copy of [Allen], *A True, Sincere, and Modest Defense of English Catholics*; Sherman, *Used Books*, xvii-xix.
12. Folger MS K.b.1; see Sherman, *Used Books: Marking Readers in Renaissance England*, xvii.
13. Harpsfield, *Life and Death*, 209, 212, 213, 214, 217.
14. Emmanuel MS 76, fos. 2^{r}, 9^{v}, 25^{v}, 10^{v}, 14^{r}, 18^{r}, 18^{v}.
15. Emmanuel MS 76, fos. 19^{v}-20^{r}.
16. The scribe of Emmanuel MS 76, fo. [5]^{v} mangles the joke; see Harpsfield, *Life and Death*, 4.
17. Emmanuel MS 76, fo. [6]^{r}.
18. Chambers, 'The Continuity of English Prose from Alfred to More and his School', xlvi, xlvii.
19. Roper, *The Mirrour of Vertue in Worldly Greatnes. Or the Life of Syr Thomas More Knight, Sometime Lo. Chancellour of England*, *1^{r}-*2^{v}.
20. Stapleton, 'Vita D. Thomæ Mori'; Ba:, *The Lyfe of Sir Thomas More, Sometimes Lord Chancellor of England*, ed. Hitchcock and Hallett, with Reed.; [More], *D.O.M.S. The Life and Death of*

Sir Thomas Moore Lord High Chancellour of England. For an account of these texts, see Anderegg, 'The Tradition of Early More Biography', esp. 9–25.

21. Lewis, *English Literature in the Sixteenth Century excluding Drama*; Gittings, *The Nature of Biography*, 23; Gittings also cites George Cavendish's life of Cardinal Wolsey, another product of the 1550s. See also Stauffer, *English Biography before 1700*, 129–33; Kendall, *The Art of Biography*, 80–7.
22. Anderegg, 'The Tradition of Early More Biography', 6.
23. Roper, *The Lyfe of Sir Thomas Moore, Knighte*, ed. Hitchcock, 3. Future references to this edition are in the main text.
24. Some manuscripts qualify this sentence as 'knowing at this daye no man *living*' (my emphasis).
25. See especially Sylvester, 'William Roper's *Life of More*'.
26. Maguire, 'William Roper's *Life of More*: The Working Methods of a Tudor Biographer', 60–1.
27. More, *The Workes… Wrytten by Him in the Englyshe Tonge*, ed. Rastell, 2Z2^{v}–2Z3^{v} at 2Z3^{r} (More to Margaret Roper). See also 2X4^{v}–2X6^{v} at 2X5^{v} (to Cromwell), and 2Y6^{r}–2Y7^{v} at 2Y6^{v} (to Watson).
28. More, *Workes*, 2X4^{r-v}, at 2X4^{r}; see Maguire, 'Roper's *Life of More*', 61.
29. Lewis, *English Literature in the Sixteenth Century excluding Drama*, 287.
30. Other manuscripts explained how this had happened with more specificity: 'which, although he had in the foresaid conveyaunce reserued, as he did the reste, for tearme of life to him self, neuer the lesse, vpon further consideracion, two dayes after, by another conveyaunce, he gaue the same immediatlye to my wife and me in possession' (79–80).
31. Other manuscripts describe Margaret as 'like one that had forgotten herselfe, being all ravished with the entyre loue of her deere father' (98).
32. More, *Workes*, 2Z5^{r-v}.
33. Conrad, 'Manipulating Reputations: Sir Thomas More, Sir Thomas Elyot, and the Conclusion of William Roper's *Lyfe of Sir Thomas Moore, Knighte*', 140–3.
34. Emmanuel MS 76, fo. 4^{r}.
35. Emmanuel MS 76, fo. 23^{r-v}.
36. Emmanuel MS 76, fos. [5]^{v}–[6]^{r}.
37. On Harpsfield, see Hitchcock, 'Life and Works of Nicholas Harpsfield', clxxv–ccxiv; Freeman, 'Harpsfield, Nicholas (1519–1575)'.
38. Foxe, *Actes and Monuments of these Latter and Perillous Dayes Touching Matters of the Church* (1563), 1546.
39. Emmanuel MS 76, fo. [60]^{r} (misfoliated as 57^{r}).
40. Cope [*pseud.* Harpsfield], *Dialogi sex contra summi pontificatus, monasticae vitae, sanctorum, sacrarum imaginum oppugnatores, et pseudomartyres*; Sander [and Rishton], *De origine ac progressu schismatis Anglicani, liber*; Pollini, *L'historia ecclesiastica della rivoluzion d'Inghilterra, divisa in libri quattro*.
41. Topcliffe, marginalia in Pollini, *L'historia ecclesiastica della rivoluzion d'Inghilterra, divisa in libri quattro*, Exeter University, Special Collections, ROWSE/POL. The marginalia is commented on in Neale, *Elizabeth I and her Parliaments*, vol. 2, 1584–1601, 153 and n. 2; Rowse, 'Truth', 181–2, 185–6, 188–92 (Rowse owned the book); and Merriam, 'Unremarked Evidence against Anderegg's Conjecture'.

42. Topcliffe, marginalium in Pollini, *L'historia ecclesiastica*, 2D4^{r}.
43. Harpsfield, 'A Treatise of Doctor Nicholas Harpesfeilds Concerning Marriage, Occasioned by the Pretended Diuourse betweene King Henry the Eight and Queene Katherine', BL Additional MS 33737, fos. 2^{r}–314^{v}; see also Harpsfield, *A Treatise on the Pretended Divorce between Henry VIII. and Catharine of Aragon*, ed. Pocock.
44. Topcliffe, marginalia in Pollini, *L'historia ecclesiastica*, b3^{r}.
45. Harpsfield, 'A Treatise', BL Additional MS 33737, fo. 177^{v}. For the discovery of this manuscript at Carter's house, see ibid., fo. 314^{v}: 'This Coppie was taken from the originall which was found by M$^{r.}$ Topliffe [*sic*] in the house of Williams [*sic*] sometime seruant to the said Doctor Nicholas Harpesfeild who confessed that two leaues of the said originall were of his said *Masters* owne hand writing.'
46. Harpsfield, 'A Treatise', BL Additional MS 33737, fo. 14^{r}.
47. Questier, 'Catholicism, Kinship, and the Public Memory of Sir Thomas More', 490; Woods, '"Strange discourse": The Controversial Subject of *Sir Thomas More*', 4–5.
48. Topcliffe, marginalia in Pollini, *L'historia ecclesiastica*, 3D1^{r}. On Carter, see Gadd, 'Carter, William (*b.* in or before 1549, *d.* 1584)'; Birrell, 'William Carter (c. 1549–84): Recusant Printer, Publisher, Binder, Stationer, Scribe - and Martyr'.
49. Now BL Harley MS 422. See annotations: 'tayken in Carters hovse, a printer: in the presence of mr. Payne mr. Norris, etc: [signed] Ric: Topcliffe' [Topcliffe's hand]; 'I had this of Whiting of Lancashire William Carter' [Carter's hand] (both on fo. 136^{r}); 'Confessed by Carter to bee vallendgers hande' [third hand]; '[t]ayken in Carters hovse. | a printer in the presence | of Mr Payne Mr Norrice | the persevant etc. |[signed] Ric. Topclyffe' [Topcliffe's hand]; 'I had this of Whyting. William Carter' [Carter's hand] (all fo. 161^{r}). See *A Jesuit Challenge: Edmund Campion's Debates at the Tower of London in 1581*, ed. Holleran, 225–7.
50. Arblaster, *Antwerp & the World: Richard Verstegan and the International Culture of Catholic Reformation*, 21.
51. Topcliffe, marginalia in Pollini, *L'historia ecclesiastica*, 3D1^{r}.
52. [Gibbons], *Concertatio Ecclesiae Catholicae in Anglia*, 2I3^{r}–2L1^{r}.
53. O'Sullivan, 'R. W. Chambers: A Tribute'.

Chapter 2

1. Happé and King, 'Introduction' to their edn, *The Vocacyon of John Bale*, 1.
2. 'me inter ceteros interfero, omnium minimus, vt sciant posteri inter hos me non semper fuisse ociosum.' Bale, 'Cronica seu fasciculus temporum ordinis Carmelitarum ex varijs' [hereafter 'Fasciculus'] in Bodl. MS Selden Supra 41, fos. 107^{r}–195^{v}, life at fo. 195$^{r–v}$, quoted at fo. 195^{r}; see also Bale, 'Anglorum Heliades', BL Harley MS 3838, fos. 111^{v}–112^{v} (facsimile printed in Harris, *John Bale*, 132–4); Bale, *Illustrium maioris Britanniae…summarium* [hereafter *Summarium*], 3P2^{v}–3P4^{v}; Bale, *Scriptorum illustrium maioris Brytannicae… catalogus* [hereafter *Catalogus*], 2T3^{v}–2T5^{r}. On these treatments, see Wort, *John Bale and Religious Conversion*, ch. 2.
3. Stauffer, *English Biography before 1700*, 178. Bale, *The Vocacyon of Iohan Bale to the Bishoprick of Ossorie in Irelande*; for a modern edition, see Bale, *Vocacyon* ed. Happé and King.
4. Fuller, *The History of the Worthies of England*, ed. Fuller, 3H2^{v}–3H3^{r} at 3H2^{v}.

5. On Bale, see Davies, 'A Bibliography of John Bale'; Harris, *John Bale*; McCusker, *John Bale: Dramatist and Antiquary*; Fairfield, *John Bale, Mythmaker for the English Reformation*; Happé, *John Bale*; King, 'Bale, John'; Wort, *John Bale and Religious Conversion in Reformation England*; *CELM* s. v. John Bale.
6. Fuller, *History of the Worthies*, 3H3^r^.
7. Most notably, Bale wrote a life of St Anne, the mother of the Virgin Mary: see Chapter 3 of this volume.
8. Sharpe, 'The English Bibliographical Tradition from Kirkestede to Tanner'.
9. Jotischky, *The Carmelites and Antiquity: Mendicants and their Pasts in the Middle Ages*, 202.
10. As noted in Hudson, '*Visio Baleii*: An Early Literary Historian', 316.
11. Copsey, 'The Wandering Doctoral Student: An Analysis of MS. Harley 1819 John Bale's Notebook of his Visit to France and Italy in 1526–1527'.
12. 'Nam cum certis argumentis præuidissem anno Christi .M.D.xxxiij. Anglorum cœnobijs iustissimam, ob nefanda inhabitantium scelera ac ueritatis contemptum, imminere destructionem. Ad eorum statim singulari Dei dono, me contuli Bibliothecas, qui mihi tunc magis erant familiares ac beneuoli, utpote Carmelitarum & Augustinensium... Quod & apud Dominicanos ac Minoritas, Carthusianos, Brigidanos, aliosque sectarios fecissem quoque, si non inciuiliter introitum mihi negassent.' Bale, *Summarium*, 3Q2^v^; Carley 'Introduction' to Leland, *De uiris illustribus. On Famous Men*, cvii–cviii.
13. 'triennio fere laboraui in colligendis diuersorum librorum autoribus & titulis, cum quorundam eorum initijs'. Bale, *Summarium*, 3Q2^v^; Carley, 'Introduction', cviii.
14. Leland, *De uiris illustribus*. For the licence, see Leland, *The Laboryouse Iourney [and] Serche of Iohan Leylande, for Englandes Antiquitees*, ed. Bale, B8^r^.
15. '...mihi prouintiam iniungis ut Carmelitarum in Angliam ingressum, progressum, et tandem illustrium uirorum cathologum tibi depingam.' Bale, 'Anglorum Heliades', fo. 3^v^.
16. Indeed, in one entry, Leland cites a fact as being 'As the Englishman John Bale of Covehithe records in a certain hurriedly assembled collection on the Carmelites' ('ut Ioannes Baleus Conensis, homo Anglus, refert in quodam collectaneo de Carmelitis tumultuaria opera consuto'). Leland, *De uiris illustribus*, 578 and trans., 579.
17. Leland, *Laboryouse Journey*, B4^v^, B5^v^.
18. 'Ioannes Sharpaeus, ut ueteres testantur bibliothecae, inter philosophos et theologos sui saeculi illustris habitus est. Sed et controuersia quae illi magna fuit cum Vicocliuianis aliquid ad splendorem nominis attulit. Nam Lernas teterrimas quidem illas, noua uirulentarum dissertationum de eucharistiae sacramento capita alte exerentes, gladio euangelico acerrime insectatus est.' Leland, *De uiris illustribus*, 650 and trans., 651.
19. 'Perpende praeposterum Lelandi iudicium hoc loco. Barbarissimum sophistam theologum illustrem uocat, pios doctores lernas, et papistarum commenta frigidissima, immo iniquissima, gladium Euangelicum. Tu interim qualis hic atque sui similes fuerint ex scripta nosce'. Cambridge, Trinity College, MS R. 7. 15 (753), fo. 122^r^, as quoted in Carley, 'Introduction', cxlvii, n. 627, and trans., clxvi–clxvii.
20. Bale, *Catalogus*, 1:2S1^r–v^ (505–06).
21. Marshall, 'Evangelical Conversion in the Reign of Henry VIII', esp. 14–16.
22. Pollmann, 'A Different Road to God: The Protestant Experience of Conversion in the Sixteenth Century', 58.

23. 'pro adipiscendis bonarum atrium disciplinis, cantabrigie, louanij, et tholose operam dedit.' Bale, 'Fasciculus', fo. 195^{r}.
24. 'Parentum meorum partim superstitione, partim inopia, quod numerosa nimis premerentur liberorum familia, duodecim annorum puer, in Carmelitani monachatus barathrum Nordouici detrudebar. Varijs dogmatum turbinibus illic & Cantabrigiæ, sine aut perito paedotriba aut docto mecœnate interim fluctuabam.' Bale, *Summarium*, 3P2^{v}–3P3^{r}.
25. 'Effulgescente tandem euangelica veritate, papistica voti cum Iohanne baret, thoma egidio, andrea bassano, Iohanne stermano, aliisque sincerioribus theologis decretum mutauit.... Ceteros suos quondam commilitanes in sua babilone cum suis papisticis decretis relinquerunt hij quos dixi.... Ferre enim nequibant cristiani homines, que tunc apud eos fiebant mala.... Quos anno domini – 1538 – funditus in anglia vomere verbi sui eradicauit dominus iuxta cristi uaticinium, Math. 15.' Bale, 'Fasciculus', fo. 195^{r-v}.
26. 'Effulgscere tandem cepit Euangelica Veritas. Cuius inardescens amore. Sinistri voti cum prefato Bareto mutaui quoque decretum, traditionibus humanis diuina preferens iura.' Bale, 'Anglorum Heliades', fo. 111^{v}.
27. 'donec apparente Dei uerbo, reuocari cœperint ecclesiae ad ueræ theologiæ fontes. In ea autem luce, seu splendore ortus nouæ Hierusalem, deformitatem meam uidi, atque inde per Dei bonitatem eum transferebar in portum, quo omnia erant supera solidam ædificata petram. Horribillis bestiæ, seu execrabilis Antichristi maledictum characterem deinceps erasi, extirpaui, deleui. Non enim ab homine, neque per hominem, sed ex speciali Christi et uerbo et dono, uxorem fidelissimam accepi Dorotheam, ut non amplius essem papæ creatura, sed Dei iubentis, Qui non continet, nubat in domino.' Bale, *Summarium*, 3P3^{r}.
28. 'Et ne deinceps in aliquo essem tam execrabilis bestiæ creatura.' Bale, *Catalogus*, 2T3^{v}.
29. See Stewart, *Close Readers: Humanism and Sodomy in Early Modern England*, ch. 2.
30. Bale to Cromwell, [1537?]. BL Cotton Cleopatra E.iv, fo. 167^{r}.
31. On Wentworth, see Dale, 'Wentworth, Sir Thomas I (by 1500–1551)'; Carter, 'Wentworth, Thomas, first Baron Wentworth (1501–1551)'. The two martyrs were John Kerby and Roger Clarke. John Foxe writes that Wentworth 'did shrowd him self behinde one of the posts of the gallery, and wept' during Kerby's execution. Foxe, *Actes and Monuments* (1563), 2N4^{r}.
32. 'IOANNES Baroetus...inter primos...quodam Euangelicum dogma suscepit. Nunc autem, quo uertiginis spiritu ductus nescio, tanquam uilissimus canis, ad uomitum est reuersus...' Bale, *Catalogus*, suppl. 112.
33. Elsewhere, he credits Henry VIII: 'Ego certe id ei honoris post Deum meum debeo, quod sim Euangelij regni Dei (ut spero) per eius administrationem particeps, cumante illius in Romanum pontificum edictum, obstinatissimus papista fuerim' (*Summarium*, 3M2^{r}).
34. On Bale in Ireland, see Ellis, 'John Bale, Bishop of Ossory, 1552–3'; Tanner, *Ireland's Holy Wars: The Struggle for a Nation's Soul, 1500–2000*, 79–83; Walsh, 'Deliberate Provocation or Reforming Zeal? John Bale as First Church of Ireland Bishop of Ossory (1552/53–1563)'; Jefferies, *The Irish Church and the Tudor Reformations*, 98–102.
35. On the *Vocacyon*, see Fairfield, 'The *Vocacyon of Johan Bale* and Early English Autobiography'; Hadfield, 'Translating the Reformation: John Bale's Irish *Vocacyon*'; Happé, '*The Vocacyon*

of Johan Bale: Protestant Rhetoric and the Self'; Skura, *Tudor Autobiography: Listening for Inwardness*, 49-72.

36. On Browne, see Bradshaw, 'George Browne, First Reformation Archbishop of Dublin, 1536-1554'; Murray, 'Ecclesiastical Justice and the Enforcement of the Reformation: The Case of Archbishop Browne and the Clergy of Dublin'; Murray, 'The Diocese of Dublin in the Sixteenth Century: Clerical Opposition and the Failure of the Reformation'.
37. Murray, *Enforcing the English Reformation in Ireland: Clerical Resistance and Political Conflict in the Diocese of Dublin, 1534-1590*, 145.
38. Walsh, 'Deliberate Provocation', 42. See Bradshaw, 'The Edwardian Reformation in Ireland, 1547-53', 86.
39. Walsh, 'Deliberate Provocation', 49-50.
40. Edward VI noted the need for 'The placing of one in a bishopric in Ireland which Turner of Canterbury hath refused'. See 'Memorandum for the Council of State', 13 October 1552, in Edward VI, *The Chronicle and Political Papers*, ed. Jordan, 178-80 at 179.
41. Bale to Parker, 30 June 1560, Canterbury, printed in Graham and Watson, *The Recovery of the Past in Early Elizabethan England: Documents by John Bale and John Joscelyn from the Circle of Matthew Parker*, 17-30, at 17-18.
42. Lambert is named only in the Preface, where Bale writes that 'by me [he] was delyvred from hys vayne belue of purgatorye / and of other Popysh peltryes' ($A6^{v}$).
43. Innocent III, *Een zuverlic boucxkin vander ketyvigheyt der menschelicker naturen*, trans. van Muelen. See Luborsky and Ingram, *A Guide to English Illustrated Books 1536-1603*, 1:51-2 (entry on STC 1207), and 2: fig. 68.
44. See Fairfield, 'The *Vocacyon of Johan Bale*'; Hadfield, 'Translating the Reformation', 45; Happé, '*The Vocacyon of Johan Bale*', 48.
45. Skura, *Tudor Autobiography*, 57-61.
46. Cancellar, *The Pathe of Obedience*, $D3^{r}$, $D3^{v}$, $D5^{r-v}$, $D4^{v}$, $D5^{r}$.
47. Baskerville, 'A Religious Disturbance in Canterbury, June 1561'; the manuscript is at Lambeth Palace Library, London, MS 2001.

Chapter 3

1. Grace Mildmay, journal, Northamptonshire Central Library, Northamptonshire Studies Collection, Accession No. 7839, consulted on CD-ROM at the British Library, quoted at 2:30, 1:1, 1:3, 1:2. Mildmay's journal is partially printed in Pollock, *With Faith and Physic: The Life of a Tudor Gentlewoman, Lady Grace Mildmay, 1552-1620*, and Martin, 'The Autobiography of Grace, Lady Mildmay'. The other recommended texts are Musculus, *Common Places of Christian Religion*, trans. Man; and a version of Thomas à Kempis's *Imitatio Christi*, perhaps *The Folowinge of Chryste*, trans. Whitford, ed. Peto.
2. Evenden and Freeman, *Religion and the Book in Early Modern England: The Making of Foxe's 'Book of Martyrs'*, 229.
3. 'But indeed even now I hear that there is also muttering by some who say that they are seized by long expectation until this [book]—our *Golden Legend* as they call it—is set forth' ('Quin & iam nunc mussitari etiam audio a nonnullis audio, qui longa sese tenere dicant

expectatione, quoad hæc tandem, (*Legenda nostra vt appellant Aurea*) euulganda sit…'). Foxe, 'Ad doctum Lectorem', Foxe, *Actes and Monuments of these Latter and Perillous Dayes Touching Matters of the Church* (1563), B3^{r}–B4^{r}, at B3^{r}; trans. Evenden and Freeman, *Religion and the Book*, 114. Further references to this edition are in the main text.

4. Voragine, [*Legenda aurea*] (1483). Further editions and extracts were published in 1487?, 1493, 1498, 1500?, 1503/4, 1507, 1512 (*bis*), and 1527; see STC 24874–24880.5. On the *Golden Legend* in England, see White, *Tudor Books of Saints and Martyrs*.
5. Kisby, 'Books in London Parish Churches before 1603: Some Preliminary Observations', 311 (Table 2), 312.
6. Gnapheus, *A Myrrour or Glasse for Them that be Syke [and] in Payne*, trans. Coverdale?, F5^{v}–F6^{r}.
7. Wyse, *A Consolacyon for Chrysten People to Repayre Agayn the Lordes Temple*, E1^{v}–E2^{r}.
8. Voragine, [*Legenda aurea*] (1527). While the *Legenda* 'fell victim to the Reformation' in Britain, it continued to be published elsewhere in Europe, despite attacks from Catholic scholars. See Reames, *The Legenda aurea: A Reexamination of its Paradoxical History*, 28 and *passim*.
9. As described in Harryson [*pseud.* Bale], *Yet a Course at the Romyshe Foxe*, L6^{r-v}. See Rex, 'John Bale, Geoffrey Downes and Jesus College', 490–2; Rex, 'Friars in the English Reformation', 42.
10. Bale, *A Mysterye of Inyquyte Contayned within the Heretycall Genealogye of Ponce Pantolabus*, I4^{v}. See also Harryson [*pseud.* Bale], *Yet a Course*, G8^{r}, where he satirizes the hostile reaction to a prayerbook written by Luther that contained only 'the lordes prayer, the commaundementes, and crede. It ys moche maruele to me, yf they are now become heresye, and legenda aurea, with sancta Maria ora pro nobis out of your ordynarye pye and portas becometh ageyne so wholsom lernynge.'
11. In 'Fasciculus Carmelitarum': 'Diue Anne vitam' (Bodl. MS Selden supra 41, fo. 195^{r}). The entry in 'Anglorum Heliades' includes the incipit: 'Diue Anne vitam, Li. i. In Ephesina Synodo' (BL Harley MS 3838, fo. 110^{v}). See Oliver Wort, 'The Double Life of Anne: John Bale's "Examinations," and "Diue Anne Vitam" (sic)'. On St Anne's appeal to the Carmelites, see Nixon, *Mary's Mother: Saint Anne in Late Medieval Europe*, 12, 29–30.
12. Bale, *A Brefe Chronycle concernynge the Examinacyon and Death of the Blessed Martyr of Christ Syr Iohan Oldecastell the Lorde Cobham*.
13. Bale, *Brefe Chronycle*, A3^{v}–A4^{r}.
14. Netter of Walden, 'Fasciculi Zizaniorum Magistri Johannis Wyclif', Bodl. MS e. Musaeo 86; Bale's index is at fos. iii^{r}–viii^{r}. For a printed edition (without Bale's index), see *Fasciculi Zizaniorum Magistri Johannis Wyclif, Ascribed to Thomas Netter of Walden*, ed. Shirley.
15. Bale, *Brefe Chronycle*, G4^{v}–G5^{r}, G5^{v}.
16. Askew, *The First Examinacyon of Anne Askewe, Lately Martyred in Smythfelde*, ed. Bale; Askew, *The Lattre Examinacyon of Anne Askewe, with the Elucydacyon of J. Bale*, ed. Bale. For a modern edition, see *The Examinations of Anne Askew*, ed. Beilin.
17. Askew, *First Examinacyon*, ♠6^{v}.
18. Askew, *Lattre Examinacyon*, B6^{v}, B7^{r-v}.
19. Askew, *First Examinacyon*, F8^{r}.

20. Foxe, *Commentarii rerum in ecclesia gestarum.*
21. The two men were reunited in Basel by the end of September 1555, living in a colony of English exiles in the Klarakloster, an abandoned convent of the Poor Clares. Mozley, *John Foxe and his Book*, 51; Evenden and Freeman, *Religion and the Book*, 62–3, 71.
22. Bodl. MS e Musaeo 86: see annotations at fos. 61^{v}–63^{v}, 105^{v}–110^{v}, 161^{v}, 292^{r-v}, cited in Evenden and Freeman, *Religion and the Book*, 40–6. When Bale set off for Ireland in 1552, he must have left the 'Fasciculi Zizaniorum' with Foxe.
23. In Machyn's spelling, 'bornyd for a ronyus a[pinions]'. Machyn, journal, BL Cotton MS Vitellius F.v, fo. 42^{v}. For an online edition see *A London Provisioner's Chronicle, 1550–1563, by Henry Machyn: Manuscript, Transcription, And Modernization*, ed. Bailey, Miller, and Moore (http://quod.lib.umich.edu/m/machyn/).
24. Foxe, *Rerum in ecclesia gestarum*, discussed in Evenden and Freeman, *Religion and the Book*, 85–94.
25. Ridley, *A Frendly Farewel…vnto all his True Louers and Frendes in God*, (:)1^{r}–3^{v}, at (:)1^{r}–(:)2^{r}.
26. Brice, *A Compendiou[s Regi]ster in Metre Contei[ning the] Names, and Pacient Suffry[ngs of the] Membres of Iesus Christ, a[nd the Tor]mented; and Cruelly Burned [within] Englande.*
27. Foxe, *The First Volume of the Ecclesiasticall History contaynyng the Actes and Monumentes* (1570), 2O5^{v} (p. 694).
28. Askew, *First Examinacyon*, O7^{r-v}.
29. Foxe, *Actes and Monumentes* (1570), 3U3^{v}.
30. Jewel, *A Replie vnto M. Hardinges Answeare*, 3B6^{v}.
31. *New Light on Drake: A Collection of Documents Relating to his Voyage of Circumnavigation*, ed. Nuttall, 347–59 at 354, 348, 356–7. See also Kelsey, *Sir Francis Drake: The Queen's Pirate*, 167–9.
32. Wolton, *The Castell of Christians and Fortresse of the Faithfull Beseiged, and Defended*, M1^{r-v}.
33. Harding, *A Confvtation of a Booke Intitvled An Apologie of the Chvrch of England*, D1^{v}, D2^{r}, D1^{v}, D2^{r}.
34. Harding, *A Reioindre to M. Iewels Replie against the Sacrifice of the Masse*, 2Y4^{r}, 2Y4^{v}–2Z1^{r}, 2Z1^{v}.
35. D[oleman] [pseud. Persons], *A Treatise of Three Conuersions of England from Paganisme to Christian Religion*, 2b8^{v}–2c1^{r}.
36. Jewel, *Replie vnto M. Hardinges Answeare*, 3B6^{v}–3C1^{r}.
37. Harding, *Reioindre*, Y2^{r-v}.
38. Harding, *Reioindre*, 2Z4^{v}, 2Z4^{v}–3A1^{r}, 3A1^{v}, 3A2^{r}.
39. Foxe, *Actes and Monumentes* (1570), 5L2^{v}, 5L1^{r}. On Jores, see Ogier, *Reformation and Society in Guernsey*, 53; see also Mullaney, 'Reforming Resistance: Class, Gender, and Legitimacy in Foxe's *Book of Martyrs*', 238.
40. Foxe, *Actes and Monumentes* (1570), 5K5^{v}–5K6^{r}.
41. Evenden and Freeman, *Religion and the Book*, 205.
42. Privy Council to the archbishops of Canterbury and York and the bishop of London, 27 November 1570, cited in Evenden and Freeman, 'John Foxe, John Day and the Printing of the "Book of Martyrs"', 30.
43. Wallington, 'A Record of Gods Marcys, or a Thankfull Remembrance', in *The Notebooks of Nehemiah Wallington, 1618–1654: A Selection*, ed. Booy, 86–8, at 88; printed from Guildhall Library, London, Manuscript 204, fo. 474^{r}.

44. Walker, *The Vertuous Wife: or, the Holy Life of Mrs. Elizab[e]th Walker*, E4^r.
45. Salter, *A Mirrhor Mete for All Mothers, Matrones, and Maidens, Intituled the Mirrhor of Modestie*, C4^r. On women reading Foxe, see Charlton, *Women, Religion and Education in Early Modern England*, 66; Freeman, '"The good ministrye of godlye and vertuouse women": The Elizabethan Martyrologists and the Female Supporters of the Marian Martyrs', 31–2; Eckerle, *Romancing the Self in Early Modern Englishwomen's Life Writing*, 29, 35.
46. Some of the following examples are drawn from King, *Foxe's Book of Martyrs and Early Modern Print Culture*, 284–320; Evenden and Freeman, 'John Foxe, John Day', 48; and Collinson, '"A magazine of religious patterns": An Erasmian Topic Transposed in English Protestantism', 507.
47. Clarke, *A Collection of the Lives of Ten Eminent Divines* (1662), 3M4^r.
48. Eyre, *A Dyurnall or Catalogue of All My Accions and Expenses from the 1st of January 1646–[7]*, ed. Morehouse 79, 104.
49. *The Diary of Roger Lowe of Ashton-in-Makerfield, Lancashire 1663–74*, ed. Sachse, 98.
50. Hoby, *The Private Life of an Elizabethan Lady: The Diary of Lady Margaret Hoby 1599–1605*, ed. Moody, 22, 26, 151.
51. *The Diary of Robert Woodford, 1637–1641*, ed. Fielding, 107 and n. 50.
52. Clarke, *Ten Eminent Divines* (1662), 2T2^v.
53. Morrill, 'William Dowsing, the Bureaucratic Puritan', esp. 180, 182, 187–8 and 188 n. 92.
54. See Lady Tresham to her cousin, 8 May 1583 (drafted by Tresham). Historical Manuscripts Commission, *Report on Manuscripts in Various Collections, III, The Manuscripts of T. B. Clarke-Thornhill, Esq., Sir T. Barrett-Lennard, Bart., Pelham R. Papillon, Esq., and W. Cleverly Alexander, Esq.*, 29–30, at 30. See also 'Reasons for and against a Petition to the Queen', 1584/1585?, in Tresham's collection, arguing that subjects can appeal to their prince for mercy and relief, giving as example 'the Protestantes in Queen Marie's tyme to her, as appeareth in Foxe, &c.'. Ibid., 34–7 at 34.
55. Pounds ed., 'William Carnsew of Bokelly and his Diary, 1576–7', 38, 40.
56. *The Autobiography of Henry Newcome, M.A.*, ed. Parkinson, 1:48.
57. Grace Mildmay, journal, Northamptonshire Central Library, Northamptonshire Studies Collection, Accession No. 7839, 2:2–3. Further references are in the text.
58. Narveson, *Bible Readers and Lay Writers in Early Modern England: Gender and Self-Definition in an Emergent Writing Culture*, 44–5.
59. This is a composite reconstruction from several drafts: the sentence has been revised multiple times in the manuscript, and no single version of it makes grammatical sense.

Chapter 4

1. Bodl. MS Eng. Misc. c. 330, title page. See *The Autobiography of Thomas Whythorne*, ed. Osborn (1961), and the slightly abridged *The Autobiography of Thomas Whythorne: Modern Spelling Edition*, ed. Osborn (1962). References in the text are to Osborn's 1961 edition, unless otherwise stated. In cases where the text is no longer extant or visible—the first two lines of the title now read 'A book…ng…ts, | with lo..ge discoor….ett with'—I follow Osborn's reconstruction of the text.
2. On the manuscript's history, see Osborn, 'Introduction', lx–lxi.

3. Osborn, 'The Osborn Collection, 1934–1974', 162; Osborn, 'Some Experiences of a Scholar-Collector', 4–6.
4. D[avey], 'Whithorne, Thomas (*fl.* 1590)'.
5. Whythorne, *Songes of Three, Fower and Five Voyces*; Whythorne, *Duos, or Songs for Two Voices*.
6. Burney, *A General History of Music, from the Earliest Ages to the Present Period*, 3:119. For similar negative appraisals, see Walker, *A History of Music in England*, 58 n. 1; Davey, *History of English Music*, 138. On Whythorne's varying reputation, see Osborn, 'Introduction', xiii–xvii.
7. Fellowes, *The English Madrigal Composers*, 35–6.
8. Warlock [pseud. Heseltine], *Thomas Whythorne: An Unknown Elizabethan Composer*, 4, 8, 11.
9. Anon., [*In this boke ar conteynyd .xx. songes. ix. of .iiii. partes, and xi. of thre partes*]; Byrd, *Psalmes, Sonets, & Songs of Sadnes and Pietie*; see McQuillan, 'Introduction', ii. See also Boyd, *Elizabethan Music and Musical Criticism*, 100–3.
10. As Whythorne realized: 'ther hath not any one of our nation published in print any Musick for two voices (as diuers strangers in forrein countries haue don heretofore)'. *Duos*, 2nd leaf, recto.
11. McQuillan, 'Introduction', iv.
12. Nelson, 'Love in the Music Room: Thomas Whythorne and the Private Affairs of Tudor Music Tutors'; Page, *The Guitar in Tudor England: A Social and Musical History*, 150–65.
13. Osborn, *The Beginnings of Autobiography in England*. See also Heale, *Autobiography and Authorship in Renaissance Verse*, 41–56; Skura, *Tudor Autobiography: Listening for Inwardnesss*, 98–125; Heale, 'Thomas Whithorne and First-Person Life-Writing in the Sixteenth Century'.
14. Helen Wilcox similarly notes: 'This disarming mixture of tradition and individual talent is typical of Whythorne's *Book*, and of early modern autobiographical writing in general, in which shared history and personal anecdote merge and generate a kind of double authority.' Wilcox, 'Of Music and Silence: The Harmonies of Thomas Whythorne and Rose Tremain', 293–4.
15. Palmer, *Thomas Whythorne's Speech: The Phonology of a Sixteenth-Century Native of Somerset in London*. On this debate, see Scragg, *A History of English Spelling*, 93–5; Blank, *Broken English: Dialects and the Politics of Language in Renaissance Writings*, 23–9; Salmon, 'Orthography and Punctuation', 16–21, 30–1. Whythorne refers to Sir John Cheke to Sir Thomas Hoby, 16 July 1557, in Castiglione, *The Courtyer*, trans. Hoby, [3A]1^{r-v}; Hart, *An Orthographie*. See also Smith, *De recta et emendata linguæ Anglicæ scriptione dialogus*, and, for a different view, see Baret, *An Alvearie or Triple Dictionarie, in Englishe, Latin, and French*.
16. Aelfric, Abbot of Eynsham, *A Testimonie of Antiquitie*, [ed. Joscelyn and Parker]. The Anglo-Saxon investments of Parker, Day, and Whythorne deserve further study.
17. Bodl. MS Eng. Misc. c. 330, fo. 92^{r-v}; compare with fo. 34^{r-v}.
18. For Whythorne's biography, see Osborn, 'Introduction', xvii–liii; Osborn, 'Whythorne, Thomas' (1980), 20: 393–4; Bennell, 'Whithorne, Thomas (*c.*1528–1596)'.
19. Bloxam, *A register of the presidents, fellows, demies, instructors in grammar and in music, chaplains, clerks, choristers, and other members of Saint Mary Magdalen College in the University of Oxford, The demies*, 1:99: 'Whitehorne, Thomas, aged 16' [in 1544].
20. Wyatt, *Certayne psalmes chosen out of the psalter of Dauid, commonlye called the .vii. penytentiall psalms*; Sternhold, *Al such psalmes of Dauid as Thomas Sternehold ... didde in his life time draw*

into English metre; Howard, earl of Surrey et al., *Songes and Sonettes, Written by Henry Haward Late Earle of Surrey, and Other*.
21. Adams, 'Dudley, Ambrose, Earl of Warwick (*c*.1530–1590)'.
22. The others are Thomas Covert, Adrian Schaell, and Henry Thorne.
23. Elizabeth Evenden argues that work was delayed by Whythorne's late delivery of his manuscript, and the death in 1569 of music proof-reader Thomas Caustun. Evenden, *Patents, Pictures, and Patronage: John Day and the Tudor Book Trade*, 142–3.
24. On Heywood's later years, see Flynn, '*When all that is to Was ys brought*: John Heywood's "rythme declaringe his own life and nature"'.
25. Misacmos [i.e. Harington], *A New Discourse of a Stale Subiect, Called the Metamorphosis of Aiax*, D3^{r-v}.
26. See Wiggins with Richardson, *British Drama 1533-1642: A Catalogue, I, 1533-1566*, 169–70 (#159).
27. Howard et al., *Songes and Sonettes*.
28. STC 13861-13868.
29. Googe, *Eglogs, Epytaphes and Sonettes*; Turbeville, *Epitaphes, Epigrams, Songs and Sonets*.
30. See Shore, 'The *Autobiography* of Thomas Whythorne: An Early Elizabethan Context for Poetry'; Shore, 'Whythorne's *Autobiography* and the Genesis of Gascoigne's *Master F. J.*'.
31. [Gascoigne], *A Hundreth Sundry Flowres*, A3^{r} (p. 205).
32. The manuscript is torn at this point, so it is possible he may have gone on to name his good friend, but it seems more likely that the friend simply provides him with a reason for writing.
33. Shakespeare, *As You Like It* (2.7) in *Comedies, Histories, & Tragedies*, R1^{v} (p. 194). See Dove, *The Perfect Age of Man's Life*.
34. Elyot, *The Castel of Helth*, C3^{r}.
35. On Whythorne's portraits, see Whythorne, *Autobiography*, 305–6; Tassi, *The Scandal of Images: Iconoclasm, Eroticism and Painting in Early Modern English Drama*, 102–4; Tittler, *The Face of the City: Civic Portraiture and Civic Identity in Early Modern England*, 27–8; Tittler, *Portraits, Painters, and Publics in Provincial England, 1540-1640*, 22, 29, 77; Cooper, *Citizen Portrait: Portrait Painting and the Urban Elite of Tudor and Jacobean England and Wales*, 14–16, 52, 56–8, 167–8; Orlin, 'Personhood in the Age of Reformation', 32–3.
36. George Gower, *Portrait of Thomas Whythorne, Musician.* Yale University, Beinecke Library, callmark 1980.389, painting on board oil, 42.3 × 36.4 cm, misdated to *c.* 1590. The Beinecke catalogue follows Osborn's suggestion that the portrait is by Gower; it would date from three years before his earliest known portrait. Tittler, by contrast, dismisses it as being 'as we might expect a vernacular work of no great aesthetic distinction' (*The Face of the City*, 35 n. 30).
37. Page, *Guitar in Tudor England*, 155.
38. See Hodgkin, 'Thomas Whythorne and the Problems of Mastery'.
39. See Legh, *The Accedens of Armony*, Q2^{r-v}: 'The fowerth, what he is of condicion, whether clene or life, iust in promise, a keeper of hospitalitie, conning in al, or anye one of the vii. artes liberal, or of Diuinitie, Cosmographi, Historiographi, Phisike, Lawe … and whether he be a Philosopher.'
40. Strype, *The Life and Acts of Matthew Parker*, 2:434. Strype misreads Whythorne as 'Whitheare'.

41. Whythorne, *Songes*, 3A3^{v}.
42. Whythorne here cites Wilson, 'A Brief Declaration in Meter, of the vij. Liberal Artes', in *The Rule of Reason, Conteinyng the Arte of Logique*, B2^{r}.

Chapter 5

1. Holinshed et al., *The First and Second Volume of Chronicles* (1587), 6K6^{v}, 6L1^{v} (1311, 1313). John Dee recorded the first event in his ephemerides: 'Earthquake towards 6 in the afternoon. It lasted for two minutes. It began at exactly 10 minutes before 6 or thereabouts.' *The Diaries of John Dee*, ed. Fenton, 8–9 (6 April 1580).
2. Holinshed, *Chronicles* (1587), 6K6^{v}–6L1^{v} (1311–13), quoted at 6L1^{v} (1313).
3. Morrill, 'William Dowsing, the Bureaucratic Puritan', 198–9.
4. Gordon and Rist eds, *The Arts of Remembrance in Early Modern England: Memorial Cultures of the Post Reformation*.
5. Holinshed, *Chronicles* (1587), 6K6^{v} (1311). It is indeed only an extract: later, the writer notes that 'This gentlemans distributions are so diuerse, and so manie, that the rehersall of them requireth a large discourse' (6L1^{r}, 1312).
6. Lambe is listed among Members of the Chapel present at the 'enterview *with* the frenche king' at the Field of the Cloth of Gold in June–July 1520. *Records of English Court Music*, Vol. 7, (1485–1558), ed. Ashbee, 55 (from TNA, SP 1/19, fo. 267^{v}). See Kisby, 'Officers and Office-Holding at the English Court: A Study of the Chapel Royal, 1485–1547', 25, 58. On the various offices of the Chapel Royal, see Baldwin, *The Chapel Royal Ancient & Modern*.
7. *Two Tudor Subsidy Assessment Rolls for the City of London: 1541 and 1582*, ed. Lang, 68.
8. Archer, 'Lambe, William (*d.* 1580)'.
9. Archer, 'Lambe, William'. Lambe's philanthropy is the culminating example in White, *Social Criticism in Popular Religious Literature of the Sixteenth Century*, 282–5. W. K. Jordan mentions Lambe in his landmark study *Philanthropy in England 1480–1660: A Study of the Changing Pattern of English Social Aspirations*, 221–2, promising that 'We shall deal at length with the career and notable charities of this great merchant in the second volume of this study' (222 n. 1), but no second volume appeared.
10. For Sutton Valence School, see Blatchley-Hennah, *A Short History of Sutton Valence School*, esp. 1–19.
11. Stow, *The Chronicles of England from Brute vnto this Present Yeare of Christ. 1580* (1580), 4E6^{v}–4E7^{v} (1188–90).
12. For the Clothworkers' involvement, see Girtin, *The Golden Ram: A Narrative History of the Clothworkers' Company, 1528–1958*, 189–95 and *passim*.
13. The site was surveyed by Ralph Treswell in 1612 for the Clothworkers. See *The London Surveys of Ralph Treswell*, ed. Schofield, esp. 58–64, 97–9; Schofield, *The Building of London from the Conquest to the Great Fire*, 56–7; Howell, *Londinopolis, an Historicall Discourse or Perlustration of the City of London*, 2B1^{r}.
14. Fleming, *An Epitaph, or Funerall Inscription, vpon the Godlie Life and Death of the Right Worshipfull Maister William Lambe Esquire*.
15. The only other known instance of this doubling of memorial publication is John Phillips's writings on Margaret Douglas, countess of Lennox, in 1578: *An Epitaphe on the Death of the*

Right Noble and Most Vertuous Lady Margarit Duglasis Good Grace, Countisse of Lininox, and *A Commemoration of the Right Noble and Vertuous Ladye, Margrit Duglasis Good Grace, Countis of Lennox*. See Livingston, *British Broadside Ballads of the Sixteenth Century: A Catalogue of the Extant Sheets and an Essay*, 461–3 (Phillips on Douglas) and 195–7 (Fleming on Lambe).

16. Arber ed., *A Transcript of the Registers of the Company of Stationers of London, 1554–1640 A.D.*, 2:369.
17. Fleming, *A Memoriall of the Famous Monuments and Charitable Almesdeedes of the Right Worshipfull Maister William Lambe Esquire*. All references in the main text are to this publication.
18. On Fleming, see Clegg, 'Fleming, Abraham'; Painting Stubbs, 'Abraham Fleming: Writer, Cleric and Preacher in Elizabethan and Jacobean London', unpublished PhD dissertation, 2011; Heal and Summerson, 'The Genesis of the two Editions', 13–15.
19. See Marshall, *Beliefs and the Dead in Reformation England*, 276.
20. R. M., *An Epytaphe vpon the Death of M. Rycharde Goodricke Esquier*; Awdelay, *An Epitaphe vpon the Death [of] Mayster Iohn Viron Preacher*; Bro[ke], *An Epitaphe Declaryng the Lyfe and End of D. Edmund Boner & c.*; Newton, *An Epitaphe vpon the Worthy and Honorable Lady, the Lady Knowles*; [Phillips], *An Epitaph on the Death of the Vertuous Matrone, the Lady Maioresse, Late Wyfe to the Right Honorable Lorde, (Alexander Auenet) Lord Maior of the Citie of London*; [Churchyard], *The Epitaphe of the Honorable Earle of Penbroke, Baron of Cardiffe, and Knight of the Most Noble Order of the Garter*; Lloyd, *An Epitaph vpon the Death of the Honorable, Syr Edward Saunders Knight*; [Painter], *A Moorning Diti vpon the Deceas of the Most Nobl Prins Henry Earl of Arvndel…*; [Philllips], *An Epitaph on the Death, of the Right Honorable and Vertuous Lord Henry Wrisley, the Noble Earle of South Hampton.*
21. [R. D.], *An Epitaph vpon the Death of Richard Price Esquier (the Second Sonne of Sir Iohn Price Knight, Deceased)*; the exemplar is Huntington HN 18287. See Livingston, 'The Provenance of Three Early Broadsheets', 54–6.
22. Anon., *A Liuing Remembrance of Master Robert Rogers, Marchant Aduenturer & Leatherseller of London Deceased*, discussed in Gordon, *Writing Early Modern London: Memory, Text and Community*, 5–6, and reproduced on 7.
23. Will of William Lambe, 10 March 1579/80. TNA, PROB 11/62, fo. 157^{r}.
24. Stow, *The Summarie of the Chronicles of England. Diligently Collected, Abridged & Continued vnto this Present Yeare of Christ. 1579* (1579), 2E3^{v}–2E4^{v} (438–40) at 2E4^{r} (439).
25. Stow, *The Chronicles of England* (1580), 4E6^{v}–4E7^{v} (1188–90) at 4E7^{r} (1189).
26. Clare Painting Stubbs has argued alternatively that Lambe's executor Sir William Cordell 'commissioned the godly and learned Fleming to write *Epitaph* and *Memoriall* in approximate accordance of Lambe's wishes and to the exclusion of all other writers' ('Abraham Fleming', 153; see also 24, 37 n. 64, 68, 142–3, 151, 154, 233). As I shall suggest, *Lambes Conduit of Comfort* demonstrates a working relationship between Lambe and Fleming before Lambe's death.
27. [Fleming], [*Lambes Conduit of Comfort*]. Only one copy survives (BL C.194.a.209), with its first two leaves (the title page and the opening of the dedicatory epistle) missing. Publication details are supplied from the colophon.
28. Fleming and Lambe may have met through their mutual acquaintance Sir William Cordell, Lambe's executor and Fleming's three-time dedicatee. See Painting Stubbs, 'Abraham Fleming', 24 and n. 41.
29. Will of William Lambe, TNA, PROB 11/62, fo. 157^{r}.

30. Llewellyn, 'Honour in Life, Death and in the Memory: Funeral Monuments in Early Modern England', 191. See also Marshall, *Beliefs and the Dead in Reformation England*; Sherlock, *Monuments and Memory in Early Modern England.*
31. Dugdale, *The History of St. Pauls Cathedral in London from its Foundation untill these Times*, 2G1^{v}, 2H2^{r}.
32. Fleming, *Memoriall*, E2^{r-v}. The transcriptions in Stow, *Survey of London*, rev. Munday, 2H4^{r-v} (355–6) and Dugdale, *History of St Pauls*, 2H2^{r}, have some minor variants. Ramie Targoff includes this epitaph in her discussion of tombs where a man is buried with multiple spouses (*Posthumous Love: Eros and the Afterlife in Renaissance England*, 13); there is, however, no evidence that Lambe's three wives were buried with him.
33. On punning in Lambe's epitaph text as a mnemonic device, see Sherlock, *Monuments and Memory in Early Modern England*, 211: 'Names could be made into words and words into images, in mnemonics that helped the living recall the dead.'
34. Fleming, *Memoriall*, D1^{r-v}, E2^{v}.
35. Dugdale, *History of St Pauls*, 2I2^{r}, 2K1^{r-v}.
36. For the sermons to 1596, see Arber, *Transcript of the Registers*, 1: 494 (Gilpin), 498, 504, 509, 514, 519, 525 (all Henry Trippe), 533, 539 (no preacher named), 546, 554, 560, 566, 572, 578 (Trippe); for the dinner, see ibid., 1:533, 539, 546; subsequently 'mistres Judsons money' paid for the dinner.
37. Fleming, *Epitaph.*
38. Archer, 'The Arts and Acts of Memorialization in Early Modern London', 95.
39. On Fleming's contribution to the 1587 *Chronicles*, see also Miller, 'Abraham Fleming: Editor of Shakespeare's Holinshed'; Donno, 'Abraham Fleming, a Learned Corrector in 1586–87'; Summerson, 'Sources: 1587', 80–3; Woodcock, 'Narrative Voice and Influencing the Reader'; Marshall, 'Religious Ideology', 419–22.
40. I owe the two references following to Matthew Woodcock, who generously claims that 'It would be unfair to suggest that Fleming was over-fond of the sound of his own voice in the *Chronicles*...' ('Narrative Voice', 343).
41. Holinshed, *Chronicles* (1587), III, N3^{r} (149).
42. Holinshed, *Chronicles* (1587), III, R3^{r} (197). The reference is to Nausea, *Of All Blasing Starrs in Generall, as Well Supernaturall as Naturall*, trans. Fleming.
43. Holinshed, *Chronicles* (1587), 6K6^{v} (1311).
44. Woodcock, 'Narrative Voice', 342. See also Benbow, 'The Providential Theory of Historical Causation in *Holinshed's Chronicles*: 1577 and 1587'.
45. Holinshed, *Chronicles* (1587), 6K6^{v} (1311). The Latin tag is from Book VI ('Virgo') of Marcellus Palingenius Stellatus, *Zodiacus vitae sive de hominis vita* (1536).
46. Holinshed, *Chronicles* (1587), 6L1^{r} (1312). The Latin tag is by Hieronymus Wolf, 'In Germaniae stuporem'.
47. Fleming, *The Conduit of Comfort Containing Sundrie Comfortable Prayers, to the Strengthening of the Faith of a Weak Christian* (1627). This edition is 'The fifth impression'; the others have not survived.
48. Hakluyt received 6s 8d as a fee and £1 6s 8d for 'his charges up and down from Oxford'. Girtin, *The Golden Ram*, 55.
49. Liu, 'Jackson, Arthur (*c.* 1593–1666)'.

50. 'The Maner & Vsuage of Lambs Chappell', [1648?]. TNA, SP 16/520, fo. 84r.
51. Girtin, *The Golden Ram*, 40–1, 238; for John Wykeham Archer's 1851 drawing of the bust of Lambe in the Chapel of the Clothworkers' Almshouses, Cripplegate, and Rebus of Lamb, formerly on the Conduit, Lambs Conduit Street, 1851, see British Museum 1874,0314.1*. The Clothworkers' Hall has a painting of Lambe, a pastiche, probably painted around 1892 by Edith Sprague at the Clothworkers' commission, based on the Lambe's Chapel effigy. Wickham, *Clothworkers' Hall Portraits*, 94–5 (# 47). I am grateful for advice on this from Hannah Dunmow, Archivist at Clothworkers' Hall (personal communication, 24 February 2017).
52. The inscription, in Long Yard, reads 'Lambe's Conduit the property of the City of London, this Pump is Erected for the Benefit of the Publicke'. See http://www.londonremembers.com/memorials/lambs-conduit-pump; Painting Stubbs, 'Abraham Fleming', 151.a.

Chapter 6

1. Folger MS V.a.459–461. For the discovery, see Anon., '[Illustration]: Diary of Richard Stonley'; Schoenbaum, *William Shakespeare: A Compact Documentary Life*, 176n. On the volumes, see W[olfe], 'Richard Stonley (ca. 1520–1600)'.
2. Folger MS V.a.460, fo. 9r (12 June 1593).
3. Shakespeare, *Venus and Adonis*; Eliot, *The Suruay or Topographical Description of France*.
4. Schoenbaum, *William Shakespeare*, 176.
5. An undated missive from Douce to Steevens notes that while 'Mr Malone, speaking of Shakespeare's Venus & Adonis, observes that it was entered in the Stationers books by R. Field in 1593 and again by Harrison in 1594 in which year he supposes it to have been published', this assumption is belied by 'a Manuscript diary which has lately passed through Mr D's hands there is the following entry upon the 12th. *June* 1593.' (Douce to Steevens, n.d. Folger MS C.b.10, no. 66). In 1796 Malone recorded the purchase, noting that 'the following entry having been found in an ancient MS. Diary, which some time since was in the hands of an acquaintance of Mr. Steevens, by whom it was communicated to me' (Malone, *An Inquiry into the Authenticity of Certain Miscellaneous Papers and Legal Instruments*..., 67 n. 39).
6. Owners included the architect William Niven of Kingwood, Berkshire (then living in Marlow Place, Great Marlow; Niven died in 1921) (bookplate in Folger MS V.a.459) and John Adair Hawkins (bookplate in Folger MS V.a.460). The three volumes were purchased from Stanford, CA collector William Wreden in 1972.
7. Matthews, *British Diaries: An Annotated Bibliography of British Diaries Written between 1442 and 1942*. See also Spalding, *Self-Harvest: A Study of Diaries and the Diarist*; Fothergill, *Private Chronicles: A Study of English Diaries*; Bourcier, *Les journaux privés en Angleterre de 1600 à 1660*; Mendelson, 'Stuart Women's Diaries and Occasional Memoirs'; Clarke, 'Diaries'; Lenox-Conyngham, *Diaries in Ireland: An Anthology 1590–1987*.
8. Guylforde, *This is the begynnynge, and contynuaunce of the pylgrymage of Sir Richarde Guylforde knyght*; *The Pylgrymage of Sir Richarde Guylforde*, ed. Ellis.
9. John Taylor, diary, 1513. BL Cotton MS Cleopatra C. v, fos. 65–96.

10. Torkington, *Ye Oldest Diarie of Englysshe Travell: being the hitherto unpublished narrative of the pilgrimage of Sir Richard Torkington to Jerusalem in 1517*, ed. Loftie, based on BL Additional MSS 28561 and 28562.
11. Archbold, 'A Diary of the Expedition of 1544', based on CUL MS Dd. 14. 30 (3).
12. *An Elizabethan in 1582: The Diary of Richard Madox, Fellow of All Souls*, ed. Donno.
13. *Literary Remains of King Edward the Sixth*, ed. Nichols, 2: 209–474, based on BL Cotton MS Nero C.x, discussed by Nichols at 1:x–xv; Walsingham, 'Journal of Sir Francis Walsingham, from Dec. 1570 to April 1583', ed. Martin; Melville, *The Diary of Rev. James Melville*, ed. Kinloch; Melville, *The Autobiography and Diary of Rev. James Meville*, ed. Pitcairn.
14. 'dyd [sit] all the sermon tyme monser henry de machyn ffor ij [words] the wyche was told hym *that* veron the ffrenche[man] *the* precher was taken *with* a wenche by *the* rep[orting] by on wylliam laurans clarke of sant mare maud[lins] in mylkstrett *the* wyche *the* sam hare knellyd down [be]ffor M veron & *the* bysshope & yet wold nott for[give] hym ffor all is fryndes *that* he had worshephull'. Machyn, journal, BL Cotton MS Vitellius F.v., fo. 144^r. On Veron, see Denis, 'John Veron: The First Known French Protestant in England'.
15. Dee, 'The Compendious Rehearsall of John Dee his Dutifull Declaracion', in *Autobiographical Tracts of Dr. John Dee*, ed. Crossley, 1–45 at 5; Dee, notes in Abū Ali Yahyā al-Khayyāt, *Albohali*...*de iudiciis nativitatem* (Nuremberg: Johann von Berg, 1546), now at the Royal College of Physicians, shelfmark D1/45-g-21(1); discussed in Brian Levack, *Renaissance Magic*, 15.
16. Dee, 'Compendious rehearsall', 5; Stadius, *Ephemerides novae, auctae et repurgatae*...*secundum Antverpiae longitudinem. ab anno 1554. usque ad annum 1600*, now Bodl. MS Ashmole 487; Magini, *Ephemerides coelestium motuum*..., *ad annos xl. ab anno Domini 1581 usque ad annum 1620*, now Bodl. MS Ashmole 488. For modern transcriptions, see Dee, *The Diaries of John Dee*, ed. Fenton.
17. Dee, *Diaries*, ed. Fenton, 4, 276.
18. Hubrigh, *An almanacke, and prognostication, for the yeare of our Lorde God. 1565. seruing for al Europia [sic], and almost most necessary for all students, marchantes, mariners and trauellers, both by sea, and lande*, cited in Stallybrass, 'Printing and the Manuscript Revolution', 114.
19. Both cited in Smyth, *Autobiography in Early Modern England*, 19–20.
20. Smyth, *Autobiography*, 20.
21. *The Diary of Walter Powell of Llantilio Crossenny in the County of Monmouth, Gentleman. 1603–1654*, ed. Bradney, xi. As the diary entries start, Powell reiterates: 'these memorandums are to be seene in my blank Allmanacks wch are filed together one yeare after th'other' (5).
22. Stallybrass, 'Printing and the Manuscript Revolution', 114.
23. TNA, SP 46/16. Rowse, *Tudor Cornwall: Portrait of a Society*, 19, 426–33, and, especially, Rowse, 'The Diary of William Carnsew, Country Gentleman'. The text of the diary is printed in Pounds, 'William Carnsew of Bokelly and his Diary, 1576–7'.
24. Diary of R[ichard] C[arnsew], TNA, SP 46/15, fo. 212.
25. Cato, *Catonis disticha moralia*, ed. Erasmus, trans. Taverner; Taverner, *The Garden of Wysdome*.
26. Poovey, *A History of the Modern Fact: Problems of Knowledge in the Sciences of Wealth and Society*, ch. 2; Sullivan, *The Rhetoric of Credit: Merchants in Early Modern Writing*.

27. Pacioli, *Summa de arithematica, geometria, proportioni et proportionalita*. For a survey and extracts of English accountancy manuals, see Yamey, Edey, and Thomson, *Accounting in England and Scotland: 1543–1800: Double Entry in Exposition and Practice*.
28. Smyth, *Autobiography in Early Modern England*, esp ch. 2; Smyth, 'Money, Accounting, and Life-Writing, 1600–1700: Balancing a Life'; Scott-Warren, 'Accounting'.
29. Ryrie, *Being Protestant*, 299.
30. Scott-Warren, 'Books in the Bedchamber', 249.
31. Perkins, *A Treatise of the Vocations, or, Callings of Men*, I1[v], I2[r], I2[v].
32. For Stonley's biography, see F[uidge], 'Stoneley, Richard (*c*. 1520–1600), of Itchington, Warws., Doddington, Essex, and London'; and Heal, 'Stonley, Richard (1520/21–1600)'. See also Cameron, 'John Heywood and Richard Stonley'; Hotson, 'The Library of Elizabeth's Embezzling Teller'; Scott-Warren, 'Books in the Bedchamber'; Scott-Warren, 'Early Modern Bookkeeping and Life-Writing Revisited: Accounting for Richard Stonley'. I am grateful to Dr Scott-Warren for generously allowing me to read his unpublished work on Stonley.
33. Houlbrooke, 'Dun, Sir Daniel (1544/5–1617)'.
34. Elton, 'The Elizabethan Exchequer: War in the Receipt', 355–6, 359.
35. Fuidge, 'Stoneley, Richard', 3:450.
36. Fuidge, 'Stoneley, Richard', 3:450.
37. Stonley to Burghley, 28 February 1587/8. CP 165/41 and 43.
38. Richard Taillor to Burghley, 23 September 1588. TNA, SP 12/216, fo. 61[r].
39. See Stonley to Burghley, 20 December 1588. CP 166/79.
40. I am here correcting my earlier assertion that 'the diaries bear almost no trace of' Stonley's professional woes. See Stewart, 'The Materiality of Early Modern Life-Writing: The Case of Richard Stonley', 173–4.
41. Folger MS V.a.460, fo. 29[v] (3 October 1593).
42. Folger MS V.a.460, fo. 32[r] (10 October 1593).
43. Folger MS V.a.460, fo. 32[v] (12 October 1593).
44. Folger MS V.a.460, fo. 34[v], 35[r] (*bis*), 35[v] (24, 25, 26, 27 October 1593).
45. Skynner to Burghley, 27 October 1593. CP 23/100.
46. Folger MS V.a.460, fo. 58[r] (21 January 1593/4).
47. *Pace* John Guy, who claims optimistically that 'his diaries illuminate the range and extent of his dealings' (*Tudor England*, 394).
48. Scott-Warren, 'Books in the Bedchamber', 249.
49. Sybil M. Jack observes that 'Stonley kept the various interests he was recording separate by using different hands, so that under each entry there may be as many as three or four hands'. Jack, 'A Capital Display: Initials in Exchequer Documents', 66 n. 6.
50. Folger MS V.a.459, fo. 3[v] (18 June 1581).
51. Folger MS V.a.459, fos. 6[r], 10[r] (30 June 1591, 21 July 1581).
52. Stow, *A Summarie of the Chronicles of Englande* (1587), 3A8[v] (p. 704); Holinshed et al., *The First and Second Volumes of Chronicles* (1587), 3: 6L6[r] (p. 1322).
53. I am grateful to Margreta de Grazia for this observation.
54. Tavener, *Garden of Wysdome*.
55. Folger MS V.a.461, fo. 74[v] (29 April 1598).

56. Folger MS V.a.461, fo. 36^{r} (29 June 1597).
57. *OED* s.v. daybook. Neither of Stonley's terms has yet found its way into the *OED*.
58. Smyth, *Autobiography*, 63 and ch. 2 *passim*.

Chapter 7

1. Foxe, *Actes and Monuments of these Latter and Perillous Dayes Touching Matters of the Church* (1563), 3M5^{v}.
2. Sampson, 'To the Christian Reader', A4^{r-v}, A6^{v}–A7^{r}.
3. Alec Ryrie has also suggested Bradford as the earliest citation of this style of diary-keeping: 'If we must pick a winner, the best candidate is probably John Bradford, who was martyred in 1555.' *Being Protestant in Reformation Britain*, 298.
4. Clarke, *Holy Incense for the Censers of the Saints*, H8^{r-v}, H8^{r}.
5. Byfield, *The Marrow of the Oracles of God*, Z1^{r-v}, citing Job 36:24 and 37:14 and Psalms 78:7.
6. Harris, *Peters Enlargement vpon the Prayers of the Church*, A4^{r}.
7. Dyke, 'A Treatise of Repentance', in *Two Treatises*, D5^{r}. A marginal note explicitly credits 'M. *Samson* preface to his Sermon of Repentance'. Cf. also F4^{r}.
8. Webster, *Godly Clergy in Early Stuart England: The Caroline Puritan Movement c. 1620–1643*, 122.
9. Rogers, *Seuen Treatises*, title page; Rogers, Perkins, Greenham, Mosse, and Webbe, *A Garden of Spirituall Flowers*.
10. Haller, *The Rise of Puritanism*, 36.
11. Rogers, *Seuen Treatises*, 2E4^{v}–2E5^{r}.
12. Rogers, *Seuen Treatises*, 2E4^{v}–2E5^{r}, 2N3^{r}.
13. Rogers, *Seuen Treatises*, 2E5^{r}.
14. Dr Williams's Library, London, Baxter MS 61.13, partially published in *Two Elizabethan Puritan Diaries*, ed. Knappen, 53–102. References in the text are to the manuscript. Only a portion of the original diaries survived, by virtue of being inserted into the manuscripts of Richard Baxter. The volume was deposited in Dr Williams's Library by Baxter's literary executor Roger Morrice, whose amanuensis transcribed portions of one volume into a manuscript entitled 'Morrice I'. Benjamin Brook published some extracts of a later diary in *The Lives of the Puritans*, 2: 231–4. The volume in its current state was reconstructed by W. H. Black in 1858 (Knappen, 'Introduction', *Two Elizabethan Puritan Diaries*, vii–viii).
15. Black thought the author might be Paul Baine; for Knappen's identification of Rogers, see Knappen, 'Introduction', viii.
16. On Rogers, see Knappen, 'Introduction', 17–35; Bremer, 'Rogers, Richard (1551–1618)'; Collinson, Craig, and Usher, 'Rogers, Richard (1551–1618)', 224–6.
17. For analyses of Rogers's diary, see Haller, *Rise of Puritanism*, 38–46.
18. Interestingly, 'Ezech[iel]' is added later in a different ink.
19. Knappen, *Two Elizabethan Puritan Diaries*, 100 n. 64.
20. This passage is changed to delete 'knowledge seeking' and 'neglected' in favour of '[illegible]' and 'hindrance'.
21. Bremer, *Congregational Communion: Clerical Friendship in the Anglo-American Puritan Community, 1610–1692*, 50–7 and *passim*.

22. Further research is needed on the reading of other men's diaries during their lifetimes. Nehemiah Wallington wrote his first notebook 'in Roman hand that others mite benifet by it as well as I'; and he notes that he read it over with his son-in-law (*The Notebooks of Nehemiah Wallington, 1618-1654: A Selection*, ed. Booy, 269, 29). When Vavasor Powell is ill and in despair, he wants to read over his 'little Diary, which Book I then desired to see, but having lent it to a Christian Friend that was far distant, could not' (quoted in Bagshaw, *The Life and Death of Mr. Vavasor Powell*, B6^{v}).
23. Watkins, *The Puritan Experience: Studies in Spiritual Autobiography*, 18.
24. See especially Webster, 'Writing to Redundancy: Approaches to Spiritual Journals and Early Modern Spirituality'; and also Watkins, *The Puritan Experience*, 22, 23; Murray, 'Introduction'; Ryrie, *Being Protestant in Reformation Britain*, 298.
25. Ambrose, *Media: The Middle Things, in Reference to the First and Last Things*, K3^{r}-K4^{r}, with entries, K4^{r}-M3^{r}.
26. Beadle, *The Journal or Diary of a Thankful Christian*, a2^{r-v}.
27. Samuel Ward, diary, Sidney Sussex College, Cambridge, College MS 45; for a partial modern edition, see Knappen, *Two Elizabethan Puritan Diaries*, 103–23.
28. Margaret Hoby, diary, BL Egerton MS 2614; printed as *Diary of Lady Margaret Hoby 1599-1605*, ed. Meads; *The Private Life of an Elizabethan Lady: The Diary of Lady Margaret Hoby 1599-1605*, ed. Moody.
29. Kilby, *Hallelu-iah: Praise yee the Lord, for the Vnburthening of a Loaden Conscience*, from E6^{r}.
30. Jeremiah Dyke to Lucy, countess of Bedford, 5 May 1614, in Dyke, *The Mystery of Selfe-Deceiuing*, ed. Dyke, A2^{r}-A6^{r}, at A5^{r}.
31. Stock, *The Churches Lamentation for the Losse of the Godly*, F7^{v}-G2^{r}; Healy, 'Harington, John, Second Baron Harington of Exton (*bap.* 1592, *d.* 1614)'.
32. Clarke, *Lives* (1683), Y1^{v}.
33. Carter, *The Tomb-Stone, and A Rare Sight*, D6^{v}.
34. Wilson, 'The Life of Mr. Arthur Wilson the Historian', 2:475; the manuscript is CUL MS Add. 33.
35. McKay, 'The Diary Network in Sixteenth and Seventeenth Century England', para. 3.
36. I here exclude Scottish examples: future Church of Scotland minister Robert Blair was at Glasgow University in the 1610s when he 'heard of the practice of some diligent Christians, who daily took brief notes of the condition of their souls, marking both what failings and escapes they were overtaken with, as also what speed they came and progress they made in the ways of God'; Blair takes up the practice for the next sixteen years. *Robert Blair of Bangor, Containing his Autobiography from 1593 to 1636*, ed. McCrie, 81.
37. Todd, 'Puritan Self-Fashioning: The Diary of Samuel Ward'.
38. Collinson, 'Dyke, Daniel (*d.* 1614)'.
39. Stock, *The Churches Lamentation*, F7^{v}-G2^{r}; Healy, 'Harington, John'.
40. *The Autobiography of Henry Newcome, M.A.*, ed. Parkinson, 1:14.
41. Donagan, 'Fairclough, Samuel (1594–1677)'.
42. Lee, 'Carter, John (1554–1635)', rev. Yiannikkou.
43. On Rhodes, see Marchant, *The Puritans and the Church Courts in the Diocese of York 1560-1642*, 37, 48, 271–2.
44. Cambers, 'Readers' Marks and Religious Practice: Margaret Hoby's Marginalia', 213.

45. Crawford, 'Reconsidering Early Modern Women's Writing: or, how Margaret Hoby Read her De Mornay'.
46. Jenkyn, *An Exposition of the Epistle of Jude, together with Many Large and Usefull Deductions... The Second Part*, 3M3^{r-v}. For Jenkyn's relationship to Rogers, see *The Diary of Samuel Rogers*, ed. Webster and Shipps, 99 n. 402.
47. Mather, *Magnalia Christi Americana; or, the Ecclesiastical History of New-England*, ed. Robbins, 1:303-4, 306. See also Webster, *Godly Clergy in Early Stuart England*, 3, 20-2, 37.
48. Shepard, quoted in Alexander ed., *American Personal Religious Accounts 1600-1980*, 56-60, at 58.
49. Will of Richard Rogers, 15 April 1618. 'The Rogers family: the will of Rev. Richard Rogers of Wethersfield, Co. Essex, England. The will of Rev. John Rogers of Dedham, Co. Essex, England', 326-30, at 327. Collinson, Craig, and Usher suggest that this refers to 'a copy of the *Seven Treatises*', but the context (a discussion of his writings and papers, the proposed division of the seven) makes that unlikely ('Rogers, Richard', 246). The will is at London Metropolitan Archives DL/C/360, fos. 314^{r}-16^{r}.
50. Gataker, *The decease of Lazarus Christ's friend A funerall sermon on Iohn. chap. 11. vers. 11. preached at the buriall of Mr. John Parker merchant and citizen of London*, G4^{r}.
51. *The Diary of Samuel Rogers, 1634-1638*, ed. Webster and Shipps, printed from Queen's University, Belfast, Percy MS 7 A.
52. Heywood, *Life of John Angier of Denton together with Angier's Diary, and extracts from his 'An Helpe to Better Hearts': also Samuel Angier's Diary*, ed. Axon, 50.
53. Rogers, 'Sixty Memorials for a Godly Life', 3:112; Webster, *Godly Clergy in Early Stuart England*, 122-3.
54. Mather, *Magnalia Christi Americana*, 1:408-13, quoted at 412.
55. Brekus, 'Writing as a Protestant Practice: Devotional Diaries in Early New England', 20.
56. Mather, *Magnalia*.
57. Wintrop, quoted in Alexander, *American Personal Religious Accounts*, 49-55, at 50.
58. Shepard, quoted in Alexander, *American Personal Religious Accounts*, 56.
59. Mather, *Magnalia*, 1:521-5.
60. Mather, *Magnalia*, 1:414-22; Wright, 'Rogers, John (1630/31-1684)'.
61. Mather, *Magnalia*, 1:420-1.
62. Collinson, 'Puritan Emmanuel', 189-91.
63. Collinson, Craig, and Usher, 'Rogers, Richard', 245-6.

Chapter 8

1. Dickinson ed., *The Registers of the Parish of Childwall. Part I. 1557-1680*, 132, 133.
2. These events chime with the complaints about the 'Manifolde popishe Superstition vsed in the Buriall of the dead' in Lancashire, recorded in 1590. See [Carter], 'A description of the state, civil and ecclesiastical, of the county of Lancaster, about the year 1590, by some of the clergy of the diocese of Chester', printed from Bodl. MS Tanner 144.
3. TNA, STAC 5/A8/31, discussed in Dottie, 'The Recusant Riots at Childwall in May, 1600: A Reappraisal', 9-11.
4. Dickinson ed., *Registers of the Parish of Childwall. Part I*, 133.

5. Segar and Holme, 'The Book of ffuneralls in Chesshiere, Lanc. Salop. & Northwales, & c.', BL Lansdowne MS 879, fo. 7^{r}, printed in *Lancashire Funeral Certificates*, ed. King with Raines, 37, with commentary at 38–40.
6. Harrison and Leigh, *Deaths advantage little regarded, and the soules solace against sorrow... Whereunto is annexed, the Christian life and godly death of the said Gentlewoman* (1602).
7. STC 12867, 12868, 12868a, 12869; STC 12864, 12865, Wing C3946 and C3946A. The edition published in 1606 is dated as '1605'. A facsimile edition of a British Library exemplar of the 1602 edition with an 'Introduction' (7–40) by Warnicke and Doebler was published in 1993; its pages are misordered, so the introductory 'To the Christian Reader' and the chart of Harrison's sermon are placed at the end.
8. Clarke, *The Second Part of the Marrow of Ecclesiastical History* (1650), 3P4^{v}–3R1^{r}.
9. Phillippy, *Women, Death and Literature in Post-Reformation* England, 99–103.
10. *The Booke of Common Prayer*, U1^{r}–U4^{r}. On controversies over burial rites, see Maltby, *Prayer Book and People in Elizabethan and Early Stuart England*, 56–63.
11. On funeral sermons, see Tromly, '"Accordinge to sounde religion": The Elizabethan Controversy over the Funeral Sermon'; Gittings, *Death, Burial and the Individual in Early Modern England*; Houlbrooke, *Death, Religion, and the Family in England, 1480–1750*, 295–330; Green, *Print and Protestantism in Early Modern England*, 203–5; Marshall, *Beliefs and the Dead in Reformation England*, ch. 7.
12. Anderson, *A Sermon of Sure Comfort Preached at the Funerall of Master Robert Keylwey Esquire*, A2^{r-v}.
13. Sparke, *A Sermon Preached at Cheanies at the Buriall of the Right Honorable the Earle of Bedford*, F2^{r}–F4^{r}, at F2^{r}, F3^{v}.
14. White, *A Godlie Sermon Preached the xxj. Day of Iune, 1586. at Pensehurst in Kent, at the Buriall of the Late Right Honourable Sir Henrie Sidney Knight*, B3^{v}–B4^{v}.
15. Chamberlain, *A Sermon Preached at Farington in Barkeshire, the Seuenteene of Februarie, 1587 at the Buriall of the Right Honorable the Ladie Anne Countes of Warwicke*, A5^{v}.
16. Babington, *A Funerall Sermon Preached by the Reuerend Father in God, Geruase Babington, then Bishop of Landaue*, A2^{r}, A2^{v}, A3^{r}, A4^{r-v}, A4^{v}.
17. Shute, *Corona charitatis, the crowne of charitie: a sermon preacht in Mercers Chappell, May 10. 1625. at the solemne funerals of his euer-renowmed friend... Mr Richard Fishbvrne*, D4^{v}.
18. Fitz-Geffry, *Elisha his lamentation, for his owne, and all Israels losse, in Elijah: The subiect of a sermon, preached at the funeralls of the Right Worshipfull Sir Anthony Rous, late of Halton in Cornwall, Knight*, F3^{r}.
19. Scott, *The Saints Privilege, or, Gain by Dying*, C4^{r}.
20. Guy, *Pieties Pillar: or, A sermon preached at the funerall of mistresse Elizabeth Gouge... With a true narration of her life and death*, C8^{r}.
21. Ferebe, *Lifes Farewell. Or A funerall sermon preached at Saint Iohns in the Deuises in Wilshiere, the 30. of August last 1614 at the funerall of Iohn Drew Gentleman*, D4^{v}–E1^{r}, E2^{r}.
22. Featley, Day, Sibbs, Taylor, et al., *ΘΡΗΝΟΙΚΟΣ. The House of Movrning*.
23. Hinde, *A Faithfull Remonstrance of the Holy Life and Happy Death, of Iohn Bruen of Bruen-Stapleford*; Clarke, *Second Part*, 3Y1^{r}–4C3^{r}. On Bruen, see Hindle, 'Bruen, John (1560–1625)'.
24. Hinde, *Faithfull Remonstrance*, N5^{r-v}.
25. Richardson, *Puritanism in North-West England: A Regional Study of the Diocese of Chester to 1642*, 90.

26. Hinde, *Faithfull Remonstrance*, P1v–P2v.
27. Hinde, *Faithfull Remonstrance*, F7v–F8r.
28. Richardson, *Puritanism*, 123, quoting Chester, County and Diocesan RO. Quarter sessions records. QSF 1/80. 1603. Bruen sponsored another assault on seven crosses in the winter of 1613–14: see Hindle, *The State and Social Change in Early Modern England, c.* 1550–1640, 66–7.
29. Hinde, *Faithfull Remonstrance*, D8r.
30. Dickinson, *Registers of the Parish of Childwall. Part I*, 9. Scholastica Brettergh was baptized on 23 February 1582/3 (ibid., 37).
31. The date and place of their marriage are unknown; their only daughter Anne was baptized on 8 June 1600. Dickinson, *Registers of the Parish of Childwall. Part I*, 52.
32. A further Foxe brother, John, married another puritan, Judith. Richardson, *Puritanism*, 95–6; Hindle, 'Bruen, John'; Guscott, 'Hinde, William (1568/9–1629)'.
33. See Richardson, *Puritanism*; Haigh, *Reformation and Resistance in Tudor Lancashire*; Dottie, 'Recusant Riots'; Quintrell, 'Government in Perspective: Lancashire and the Privy Council, 1570–1640'.
34. [Carter], 'A Description of… Lancaster'.
35. Haigh, *Reformation and Resistance*, 327.
36. See Axon, 'The King's Preachers in Lancashire, 1599–1845', 69.
37. Vaughan to Cecil, 6 March 1598/9. CP 176/115.
38. Vaughan to Cecil, 20 February 1599/1600. CP 68/44.
39. Axon, 'King's Preachers', 72–3; Richardson, *Puritanism*, 20; Warnicke and Doebler, 'Introduction', 35 n. 12.
40. Dottie, 'Recusant Riots', 8. An undated declaration by one Greenloe claimed that 'Mr William Bretter or his disciples haue said that if her maiestie should graunt any toleration vnto the papists'—a suggestion that apparently was 'greately in vre' at the time—'*that* she was not worthye to be queen and asone that should be, they would geue bobb*es*, or there should be bobbes geaven'. Greenloe also alleged that Brettergh had claimed '*that* the Earle of Essex was worthiest to be kynge. And *that* whereas the papist looke for a change, there would be change by Michaelmas daye as neare as it was [7 or 8 days before], but little to there good'. Declaration by Greenloe, [November 1599 or 1600?]. TNA, SP 15/34, fo. 38r. The threat here is murky, but it is clear that Brettergh's views attracted fierce criticism and opposition from local recusants.
41. Dottie, 'Recusant Riots', 9–11.
42. 'Ryottes in Lancashire' [after 15 August 1600]. CP 79/79; Vaughan to Cecil, 28 May 1600. CP 180/100.
43. The rhetoric of riot was required for the case to come under the jurisdiction of the Star Chamber, and may overstate the real level of violence in these incidents.
44. 'Ryottes in Lancashire' [after 15 August 1600]. CP 79/79. William Brettergh's maternal grandmother, Ann Chisenhall, had been born Ann Wrightington.
45. 'Ryottes in Lancashire' [after 15 August 1600]. CP 79/79.
46. Vaughan to Cecil, 16 September 1600. CP 181/18. See also the interrogations about the 20 August attack in TNA, SP 12/275, pp. 105–10 (art. 64).
47. Haigh, *Reformation and Resistance*, 327–9.
48. The future New England minister Richard Mather (1596–1669) later boarded in Aspinall's household.

49. See, for example, *Lancashire Funeral Certificates*, ed. King and Raines, 40; Phillippy, *Women, Death and Literature*, 85 and *passim*.
50. Guscott, 'Hinde, William (1568/9–1629)'.
51. 'Good Sir, after I had read with comfort, that which I gained from you with much intreaty, I meane a copie of your Sermon preached at my wiues Funerall; I was so ful and pregnant of the birth, that I could beare no longer must needs bring foorth the same... Happily you will deem I do you wrong, to publish the same, without your futher [*sic*] warrantie...'. Brettergh to Leigh, 20 November 1601 (G4^{r-v}).
52. This is assumed by the poet T. H. in 1630: 'See the life & death of Mistris *Brettergh* by *Mr. Harrison*, Preacher of Hyton in Lancashire.' T.H. A.B. C.C.C., 'To his Friend the Author', in Wadsworth, *Further Obseruations of the English Spanish Pilgrim*, A4^{v}–B1^{v}, at B1^{r}.
53. Harrison, *The Difference of Hearers, or An Exposition of the Parable of the Sower.*
54. Vaughan to Cecil, 16 April 1601. CP 181/140.
55. These phrases are from the title page of the second edition: Stubbes, *A Christal Glasse for Christian Women*. For a comparative account of Stubbes and Brettergh, see Phillippy, *Women, Death and Literature*, 81–108. For female piety in funeral sermons more generally, see Carlson, 'English Funeral Sermons as Sources: The Example of Female Piety in Pre-1640 Sermons'; Shami, 'Women and Sermons'.
56. Arber ed., *A Transcript of the Registers of the Company of Stationers of London: 1554–1640, A.D.*, 3:77.
57. Bolton, *Instructions for a Right Comforting Afflicted Consciences*, G2^{v}, G3^{r}.
58. Nalton, *Twenty Sermons Preached upon Several Texts*, K5^{r}.
59. Brooks, *A Cabinet of Choice Jewels, or, A Box of Precious Ointment*, 2D1^{r}.
60. Traughton, *Of the Causes and Cure of Sad Disconsolate Thoughts in Christians*, C8^{v}–C12^{r}.
61. Glascock, *Mary's Choice, or, The choice of the truly godly person opened, and justified, in a sermon preached at the funeral of Mrs. Anne Petter*, C4^{v}. The speech was also quoted at length in White, *A Treatise of the Power of Godlinesse*, 2B1^{r-v}, and Walker, *The Preciousness of Christ to the Believing-Christian*, B8^{r}.

Chapter 9

1. Folger MS V.a.269. A printed edition, *A true historical relation of the conversion of Sir Tobie Matthew to the holy Catholic faith; with the antecedents and consequences thereof*, ed. Mathew, has some minor omissions. All references in the text are to the manuscript, which has two sequences of pagination. Matthew's signature appears on the unpaginated title page as 'Tobie Matthew', and on 1:232. On 1:1, the title is repeated, but another hand has supplied 'Sir Tobie Matthews' [*sic*]. 'Posthumus' is at 2:1–21; 'Considerations' at 2:22–59 is signed at 2:59 by James Louth on 29 July 1641. Louth may have been the scribe.
2. On Matthew's engagement with life-writing, see Lynch, *Protestant Autobiography in the Seventeenth-Century Anglophone World*, 31–46, 65–70; Murray, 'The Radicalism of Early Modern Spiritual Autobiography', 48–52.
3. The fullest biography of Matthew is Feil, 'Sir Tobie Matthew and his *Collection of Letters*', unpublished PhD dissertation. See also Mathew and Calthrop, *The Life of Sir Tobie Matthew, Bacon's Alter Ego*; Mathew, *Sir Tobie Mathew*; S[utherland], 'Matthew, Tobias (1577–1655), of

London'; Loomie, 'Matthew, Sir Toby (1577–1655)'; D[avidson] and S[groi], 'Matthew, Tobie (1577–1665), of Durham House, The Strand, Westminster'.

4. Gerard, *The Autobiography of a Hunted Priest*, trans. Caraman, xvii, xxiv, xvii.
5. Weston, *William Weston: The Autobiography of an Elizabethan*, trans. Caraman.
6. Murray, *The Poetics of Conversion in Early Modern English Literature*, 38–43; translation by Murray at 39–40: for the Latin, see Kenny ed., *The Responsa Scholarum of the English College, Rome*, 1:xi.
7. Murray, *Poetics of Conversion*, 42–3, 40; Murray, '"Now I ame a Catholique": William Alabaster and the Early Modern Catholic Conversion Narrative'. Alabaster's autobiography and Persons's unfinished translation are in the English College at Rome, Liber 1394 and Liber 1395 respectively.
8. Amelang, 'Tracing Lives: The Spanish Inquisition and the Act of Autobiography', 38.
9. Puccini, *The Life of the Holy and Venerable Mother Suor Maria Maddalena de Patsi*, [trans. Matthew]; Biondi, *A relation of the death of the most illustrious Lord, Sigr. Troilo Sauelli*, [trans. Matthew]; de Auila, *The audi filia, or a Rich Cabinet Full of Spirituall Iewells*, [trans. Matthew].
10. Matthew to Mary Gage, 16 August 1611, Paris. Archivum Britannicum Societatis Iesu [hereafter ABSI] MS 949 (copy in modernized spelling), 306. This transcript (probably early twentieth century) was taken from a letter then at Stonyhurst College: its current location remains unknown. I am grateful to Heather Wolfe and Elizabeth DeBold at the Folger, David Knight at Stonyhurst, and Rebecca Somerset at the Jesuit Archives for helping me to track down this letter. Mathew and Calthrop, *Life*, quotes from the letter, but without specifying its location.
11. On Gage, see Revill and Steer, 'George Gage I and George Gage II'; Loomie, 'Gage, George (*c*.1582–1638)'; Vander Motten and Daemen-de Gelder, 'Sir Toby Matthew and his "fidus Achates" George Gage, 1607–1620'. For the sonnets (in Huntington HM 198, fos. 88–95), see Petti, 'Unknown Sonnets by Sir Toby Matthew'. Will of Tobie Matthew, 7 June 1614; pr. in Mathew and Calthrop, *Life*, 128–34; the original is in the Venerable English College at Rome.
12. On Mary Gage, see 'Who Were the Nuns', http://wwtn.history.qmul.ac.uk/counties/details.php?uid=BB080, accessed 17 March 2016.
13. Thoresby, *Vicaria Leodiensis: or, the History of the Church of Leedes in Yorkshire*, 174. See also Cross, 'Matthew, Frances (1550/51–1629)'.
14. Quoted in Thoresby, *Vicaria Leodiensis*, 174.
15. 'Tobias Matthew ex Ecclesia Christi natus 18 annos [*sic*, he was nineteen] incidit in epilepticos insultus partim ex vitio ventriculo partim lienis habuit curande rationem que sequitor: decem: 18, 1596'. Bodl. Rawlinson A 369/52 (a medical receipt book), as quoted in Feil, 'Sir Tobie Matthew', 9 n. 1.
16. Carleton to John Chamberlain, 10 January [1596/7]. TNA, SP 12/266, fo. 16^{r}.
17. Carleton to Mr Hickes, [January? 1596/7]. TNA, SP 12/256, fos. 29^{r}–30^{r}.
18. Matthew to Carleton, [January 1596/7?]. TNA, SP 12/266, fo. 30^{r}.
19. Matthew may have tempered his attack on William Crashaw after his son, the poet Richard Crashaw, converted to Roman Catholicism in or around 1645.
20. Petti, 'Unknown Sonnets', 128.

21. On Matthew's years at court, see Albion, *Charles I and the Court of Rome: A Study in 17th Century Diplomacy*; Hibbard, *Charles I and the Popish Plot*, esp. 36, 40, 52–6; *Newsletters from the Caroline Court, 1631–1638*, ed. Questier.
22. On the rumours, see *Newsletters*, 157, 159, 157 n. 729.
23. Fountayne [George Leyburn] to [Peter Biddulph], 1 March 1633; *Newsletters*, 159–61 (#47) at 159.
24. Suckling, 'A Sessions of the Poets', in *Fragmenta aurea*, A4^{r}–A6^{r}, at A5^{r}.
25. 'Reyerardus', *Hierorachomachia or The Anti-Bishop*, ed. Gossett, from a manuscript at the Venerable English College at Rome.
26. Chamberlain to Sir Dudley Carleton, 10 January 1618. *The Letters of John Chamberlain*, ed. McClure, 2:128.
27. Suckling claimed that Carlisle's patronage had given Matthew his *entrée* into society: 'But Sir, you may thank my Lady *Carleil* for't: | For had not her care furnisht you out | With something of handsome, without all doubt | You and your sorry Lady Muse had been | In the number of those that were not let in'. 'Sessions of the Poets', A5^{r}.
28. Conway to Thomas Wentworth, earl of Strafford, [1637]. *The Earl of Straffordes Letters and Dispatches*, ed. Knowler, 2:125.
29. Prynne, *Romes Master-Peece, or, The Grand Conspiracy of the Pope and his Iesuited Instruments*, C3^{r-v}, and *passim*; see also Hibbard, *Charles I and the Popish Plot*, 157–62.
30. TNA, SP 16/468, fo. 266^{r}.
31. Notes by Windebank of business transacted by the Council this day, 7 October 1640. TNA, SP 16/49, fo. 104^{r}. See also Windebank to Charles I, 6 October 1640, concerning Mathew: TNA, SP 16/464, fo. 101^{r}.
32. Urban VII to Matthew, 14 May [1640?], printed in Rushworth, *Historical Collections of Private Passages of State*, pt. 2, 1324–6, at 1325.
33. Rawlinson C 956, fo. 77^{r-v}, quoted in *The Journal of Sir Simonds D'Ewes*, ed. Notestein, 541.
34. D'Ewes, *Journal*, 112, 357, 359 n. 9, 360 and n. 10, 393 n. 16, 488, 494–5 n. 16, 498, quoted at 488 n. 9.
35. Feil, 'Sir Tobie Matthew', 245–7.
36. Feil, 'Sir Tobie Matthew', 247–55.
37. Teresa de Avila, *The Flaming Hart, or, The Life of the Gloriovs S. Teresa*, trans. [Matthew], *7^{v}–*8^{r}.
38. Matthew, *The Life of Lady Lucy Knatchbull*, ed. Knowles, from a manuscript at Oulton College. For another, shorter version, from a manuscript of the Canonesses of the Holy Sepulchre, Colchester, see *Life Writing I*, ed. Hallett, 159–222. On this phenomenon more generally, see Hallett, *Lives of Spirit*.
39. Knowles, 'Introduction' to Matthew, *Life of Lady Lucy Knatchbull*, xxiii; Hallett, *Life Writing I*, 159.
40. Matthew also wrote a 'little relation' of Sister Agnes of Saint Albert [née Agnes Vivine Roosendael] of the English Teresian monastery at Antwerp in 'Short Colections of the Beginings of Our English Monastery of Teresians in Antwerp with some few perticulars of our Dear Deceased Religious', 'writ by Sr Tobie Matthew who was a Jesuett but not publikely known to be so one who had a singular love and affection for the Community and a great devout of our Holy Mother St Teresa'. *Life Writing II*, ed.

Daemen-de Gelder, 1–310; the manuscript is at Felixarchief Antwerp, KK 1018 ('Engelse Theresianen, Kloosterkronieck'), 298–315, quoted at 315. See also Vander Motten and Daemen-de Gelder, 'A Cloistered Entrepôt: Sir Tobie Matthew and the English Carmel at Antwerp', 552–7.

41. Matthew, *A Collection of Letters* [ed. Donne].
42. Mathew and Calthrop, *Life*, 399.
43. Quoted in Hardman, *English Carmelites in Penal Times*, 76–7. On 23 May 1688, the prioress at Antwerp, Mary of the Holy Ghost, sent a letter to James II's pregnant queen, Mary of Modena, including a relic of Teresa, 'a peece of her flesh...beseeching your maiesty to weare it in your labour'. BL Additional MS 28225, fos. 276–7, quoted in Hallett, *The Senses in Religious Communities, 1600–1800*, 113.
44. Will of Tobie Matthew, 12 October 1647, Antwerp, printed in Mathew and Calthorp, *Life*, 337–41 at 339–40, 340. The original is in the Venerable English College at Rome.
45. Ibid., 338.
46. Cooper, 'Montagu, Walter (1604/5–1677)', rev. Metzger. The fate of the manuscript after 1655 is unclear. The hagiographer priest Alban Butler used it as the basis for his *The Life of Sir Tobie Matthews* [*sic*]; and it was at some point owned by the Irish antiquarian William Chadwick Neligan: *A brief description of a curious manuscript in the collection of the Rev. Dr. Neligan, entitled A true historicall relation of the conversion of Sir Tobie Matthew to the holie Catholic fayth, with the antecedents & consequents thereof* ([Cork?]: privately printed, [1835?]). See also Smith, *Bacon and Shakespeare. An inquiry touching players, playhouses, and play-writers in the days of Elizabeth...to which is appended an abstract of an MS. respecting Tobie Matthew*, 155–62.

Chapter 10

1. Perrot, *The History of that Most Eminent Statesman, Sir John Perrott, Knight of the Bath, and Lord Lieutenant of Ireland*, ed. Rawlinson, B6v, B7v. Perhaps not coincidentally, Perrot, as the illegitimate son of Sir John, waged a long legal battle to be included in this ancestry: see Thrush, 'Perrot, Sir James (1571/2–1637)'.
2. Bodl. MS Aubrey 9, fo. 30r.
3. Boyle, 'An Account of Philaretus during his Minority', 2. The manuscript is at the Royal Society, Boyle Papers 37, fos. 170–84.
4. See Pritchard, *English Biography in the Seventeenth Century: A Critical Survey*, ch. 10 ('Biography as Family History').
5. Herbert of Cherbury, *The Life of Edward, First Lord Herbert of Cherbury Written by Himself*, ed. Shuttleworth, 1, 8, 11, 18.
6. Throckmorton, 'Certaine Old Stories Recorded by an Aged Gentlewoman...about the Yeer our Lord 1610', BL Additional MS 43827, fos. 1r–18v, at fos, 2r–3r (consulted on Perdita).
7. [Cavendish], marchioness of Newcastle, 'A True Relation of my Birth, Breeding, and Life', 3A4v, 3D4r.
8. See Clifford, *Anne Clifford's Great Books of Record*, ed. Malay.
9. Chaytor, 'Household and Kinship: Ryton in the Late 16th and Early 17th Centuries', 29; Cressy, 'Kinship and Kin Interaction in Early Modern England'; Tadmor, 'The Concept of

Household-Family in Eighteenth-Century England'; O'Hara, *Courtship and Constraint: Rethinking the Making of Marriage in Tudor England*, 38; Tadmor, *Family and Friends in Eighteenth-Century England: Household, Kinship, and Patronage*, 34, 137, 140, 143, 153–4; Crawford, *Blood, Bodies and Families in Early Modern England*, 3-6 and *passim*. I am grateful to Julie Crawford for advice on this bibliography.

10. Moulsworth, 'The Memorandum of Martha Moulsworth', 1632. Beinecke Library, Osborn MS fb150, item 6. For old and modern spelling editions and multiple critical perspectives, see *'The Muses Female Are': Martha Moulsworth and Other Women Writers of the English Renaissance*, ed. Evans and Little.
11. Martha had two children by first husband Nicholas Prynne: Richard, baptized on 13 June 1602, and Martha, baptized on 15 April 1604 (after her father's death). She may well have been the mother of Bevill Moulsworth, junior: her third husband asked 'to bee buried in Broxburne Church vnder that stone where my deare sonne Bevill Molesworth lyeth'. See Grundy, 'Identity and Numbers in Martha Moulsworth's "Memorandum"', 11; will of Bevill Molesworth, 17 February 1631/2. TNA, PROB 11/159, pr. in Evans and Little eds, *'The Muses Female Are'*, 224–7, at 225.
12. *'My Name Was Martha': A Renaissance Woman's Autobiographical Poem*, ed. Evans and Wiedemann; Evans, 'A Silent Woman Speaks: "The Memorandum Of Martha Moulsworth, Widowe"'; *'The Muses Female Are'*, ed. Evans and Little; *'The Birthday of my Self': Martha Moulsworth, Renaissance Poet*, ed. Depas-Orange and Evans; Evans, 'Deference and Defiance: The "Memorandum" of Martha Moulsworth'; Sterling, commentary in *Reading Early Modern Women: An Anthology of Texts in Manuscript and Print, 1550-1700*, ed. Ostovich and Sauer, 258–61, at 260–1. See also Evans, 'Moulsworth, Martha (1577–1646)'.
13. Greer, '"Backward springs": The Self-Invention of Martha Moulsworth', 3.
14. Lamb, 'The Poem as a Clock: Martha Moulsworth Tells Time Three Ways', 92.
15. Folger MS V.a.166. Further references to this manuscript (which is paginated rather than foliated) are given in the main text.
16. Lewin, 'Eyre, Sir Samuel (*bap.* 1638, *d.* 1698)'.
17. Will of Lady Constance Lucy, 3 and 16 May 1635. TNA, PROB 11/174.
18. The *terminus ante quem* is provided by Eyre's reference to 'Doctor Tenison, sence Arch Bishope of Canterbury'; Thomas Tenison's predecessor John Tillotson died on 22 November 1694; Tenison was enthroned on 16 May 1695. Marshall, 'Tenison, Thomas (1636–1715)'.
19. H[arding], 'Kingsmill, Richard (*c.* 1528-1600), of Highclere, Hants.'; Fritze, 'Kingsmill family (*per. c.*1480–1698)'.
20. Fairfax-Lucy, *Charlecote and the Lucys: The Chronicle of an English family*, 101, claims that Kingsmill sold the wardship of his daughter to the Crown, and Constance subsequently became Walsingham's ward.
21. James I, warrant for Lady Constance Lucy to stay in London, 26 November 1624. TNA, SP 14/175, fo. 72. For the proclamation, of 19 October 1624, see James I, *A Proclamation Commanding Persons of Qualitie to Reside in their Countreys*.
22. Around 1597, Joyce Lucy married William Cook, by whom she had three sons and six daughters, including the future Sir Robert Cook—hence Elizabeth Lucy's description that Thomas Lucy 'by A Formar Wife, had Sir Robert Cooks Mother, *then* but A Girl'. Folger

V.a.166, p. 14. See J[ones], 'Cooke, William II (1572–1619), of Gray's Inn and Highnam Court, Glos.'.

23. See pp. 1–2 in this volume.
24. Letter book of the earl of Clare (21 November 1631), Nottingham University Library Ne C 15 404, p. 272, as quoted in Crawford, *Blood, Bodies and Families*, 98.
25. Journal of Elizabeth Turner, 14 July 1672, Centre for Kentish Studies, as quoted in Crawford, *Blood, Bodies and Families*, 99.
26. *The Meditations of Lady Elizabeth Delaval Written between 1662 and 1671*, ed. Greene, 75, cited in Crawford, *Blood, Bodies and Families*, 99.
27. Makin, 'Upon the Much Lamented Death of the Right Honourable the Lady Elizabeth Langham', edited from Huntington MS H.A, 8799.
28. [Rich], *Autobiography of Mary Countess of Warwick*, ed. Croker, 27, cited in Crawford, *Blood, Bodies and Families*, 99.
29. Phillippy, '"Herselfe living, to be pictured": "Monumental circles" and Women's Self-Portraiture', 142–5.
30. See Phillippy, '"Herselfe living, to be pictured"', 139–40, and Fig. 5.
31. Will of Lady Constance Lucy, 16 May 1635. TNA, PROB 11/174.
32. Will of Lady Constance Lucy, 3 May 1636. TNA, PROB 11/174.
33. Phillippy suggests 'The publication of Lady Lucy's friendship with Mrs Moore in her will is a textual counterpart of [*sic*] her publication of relationships with female kin on her monuments. In response to this commemorative gesture, Elizabeth publishes the friendship once again in her account of her mother's [*sic*] life'. '"Herselfe living, to be pictured"', 145.
34. Will of Martha Dorsett, 19 January 1580/1. TNA, PROB 11/63.
35. Thomas Hassell's funeral sermon on Martha Moulsworth, 28 October 1646. Bodl. MS Don.g.9, here at 51^{r}, printed in *'The Muses Female Are'*, 243–61, at 252. See Shami, 'Women and Sermons', 159–60.
36. Will of Martha Moulsworth, 19 July 1646. TNA, PROB 11/197, pr. in *'The Muses Female Are'*, 221–4. Greer notes that Moulsworth 'painstakingly lists a series of considerable legacies to a horde of other people's unmarried grandchildren and great grandchildren' ('"Backward springs"', 3).
37. She leaves legacies 'to the children and grandchildren that are vnmarried nowe of my loving kinsman Symon Edmondes of London Alderman', 'To Hugh Wood the sonne of my cozen Hugh Wood and Martha his wife', 'To Christopher Parke the sonne of my Cozen Christopher Parke, and Anne his wife', 'my cozen Thomas Willys of London Chaundler', Will of Martha Moulsworth, 19 July 1646. TNA, PROB 11/197, pr. in *'The Muses Female Are'*, 221–2.
38. Evans, 'Deference and Defiance', 176.
39. Will of Martha Moulsworth, 19 July 1646. TNA, PROB 11/197, pr. in *'The Muses Female Are'*, 221–4 at 223.
40. Will of Martha Moulsworth, 19 July 1646. TNA, PROB 11/197, pr. in *'The Muses Female Are'*, 223.
41. Bodl. MS Don.g.9; the Moulsworth sermon is at fos. 31^{r}–55^{r}, pr. in *'The Muses Female Are'*, 243–54.
42. Bodl. MS Don.g.9, fo. 31^{v}.

43. See Orbis catalogue entry for Beinecke, Osborn MS fb150; *CELM*, MhM1; Appleby, 'Roydon, Sir Marmaduke (1583–1646)'.
44. The first unfoliated leaf has the ownership mark 'Robert Benson. | Close Salisbury | 1821'. See Cooper, 'Benson, Robert (1797–1844)', rev. Mooney. Joseph Hunter gives a detailed account of and extracts from the manuscript in BL Additional MS 24475, fo. 56^{r-v}, noting 'A small MS. has been lent to me by Robert Benson Esq Deputy Recorder of Salisbury, containing a short account of the Character of Lady Lucy (born Kingsmill) wife of Sir Thomas Lucy of Charlcote, written by her daughter in lawe Mrs Lucy, born Moulsworth, & addressed to Mrs Moore' (fo. 56^{r}). This manuscript miscellany was 'Begun at Bath, about 1819' (fo. 1^{r}). In 1845, Hunter wrote: 'I have seen a manuscript account of this lady [Constance Lucy] written by the wife of one of her descendants…The original is in the possession of Robert Benson, Esquire, recorder of Salisbury, who descends from the Lucys.' Hunter, *New Illustrations of the Life, Studies, and Writings of Shakespeare*, 1:61 and 1:61 n.*. The manuscript was later in the possession of the Shakespeare scholar James Halliwell-Phillipps. See [Halliwell-Phillipps], *A Calendar of the Shakespearean Rarities, Drawings and Engravings, Preserved at Hollingbury Copse, near Brighton*, 42 (#98).
45. Warwickshire County Record Office, L6/1246; I am grateful to Karen Moulder at the Warwickshire CRO for information on this manuscript (personal communication, 25 February 2016).

Chapter 11

1. Carter, *The Tomb-Stone, and A Rare Sight*, D6^{v}–D7^{r}, D7^{r}. This revises the account in Lee, 'Carter, John (1554–1635)', rev. Yiannikkou.
2. Carter to Clarke, in Carter, *The Tomb-Stone*, B6^{v}–B8^{r}, at B7^{r}, B7^{r-v}.
3. Clarke, *The Marrow of Ecclesiastical Historie* (1650); Clarke, *The Second Part of the Marrow of Ecclesiastical History* (1650); Clarke, *A Generall Martyrologie, containing a collection of all the greatest persecutions which have befallen the Church of Christ From the Creation to our present Times. Whereunto are added, The Lives of sundry Modern Divines* (1651); Clarke, *A Martyrologie* (1652).
4. Carter to Clarke, in Carter, *The Tomb-Stone*, B7^{r-v}.
5. Clarke, *A Collection of the Lives of Ten Eminent Divines* (1662).
6. Clarke, *The Lives of Sundry Eminent Persons in this Later Age* (1683), a1^{r-v}.
7. Clarke, *Lives* (1683), A1^{v} (unsigned note).
8. Clarke, *Marrow* (1650), c4^{r}, b1^{v} [=c1^{v}], b3^{v} [=c3^{v}].
9. Collinson, '"A magazine of religious patterns": An Erasmian Topic Transposed in English Protestantism', 507.
10. Simeon Foxe, preface to the Latin life of John Foxe: quoted in Mozley, *John Foxe and his Book*, 4, from BL Lansdowne MS 388.
11. Foxe, *Acts and Monuments of Matters Most Special and Memorable Happening in the Church* (1641), 2: A4^{r}–B6^{v} (English) and A2^{r}–B4^{v} (Latin).
12. Parker, Acworth, and Joscelyn, *De antiquitate Britannicae ecclesiae & priuilegiis ecclesiae Cantuariensis cum Archiepiscopis eiusdem* 70.
13. G[odwin], *A Catalogue of the Bishops of England*, A3^{r}.

14. Harington, *A Supplie or Addicion to the Catalogue of Bishops, to the Yeare 1608*, BL Royal MS 17 B. XXII, published as *A Briefe View of the State of the Church of England*, [ed. Chetwynd]; for a modern edition, see Harington, *A Supplie or Addicion to the Catalogue of Bishops to the Yeare 1608*, ed. Miller.
15. Wilson, *The English Martyrologe Conteyning a Summary of the Liues of the Glorious and Renowned Saintes of the Three Kingdomes, England, Scotland, and Ireland*; Porter, *The Flowers of the Liues of the Most Renowned Saincts of the Three Kingdoms England Scotland, and Ireland*. For these, and manuscript collections, see Rhodes, 'English Books of Martyrs and Saints of the Late Sixteenth and Early Seventeenth Centuries', 11–12.
16. Boissard, *Icones quinquaginta virorum illustrium doctrina et eruditione praestantium ad vivum effictae*.
17. Verheiden, *Praestantium aliquot theologorum, qui Rom. Antichristum præcipuè oppugnarunt, effigies*.
18. Adam, *Vitae Germanorum philosophorum*; Adam, *Decades duae continentes vitas theologorum exterorum principium*; Adam, *Vitae Germanorum medicorum*; Adam, *Vitae Germanorum theologorum*; Adam, *Vitae Germanorum iureconsultorum et politicorum*.
19. Meursius, *Athenæ Batavæ. Sive, de vrbe Leidensi, & academiâ, virisque claris; qui utramque ingenio suo, atque scriptis, illustrarunt: libri dvo*.
20. Holland, *Heroologia Anglica, hoc est, clarissimorum et doctissimorum aliquot Anglorum*.
21. Drummond, 'Informations be Ben Johnston to W. D.', ed. Donaldson, quoted in Donaldson, 'National Biography and the Arts of Memory: From Thomas Fuller to Colin Matthew', 73.
22. Lupton, *The History of the Modern Protestant Divines*, A8^{v}, a1^{v}, a1^{r-v}. Adopting the same format, Lupton's *The Glory of their Times. Or The Liues of the Primitiue Fathers* provided images and lives of figures from Philo Judaeus to Thomas Aquinas. See also Porter, 'Lupton, Donald (*d.* 1676)'.
23. Fuller, *The Holy State*.
24. [Fuller], *Abel Redevivus: or, The Dead Yet Speaking. The Lives and Deaths of the Modern Divines*, title page, A3^{v}–A4^{r}.
25. Clarke, *Generall Martyrologie* (1651), b4^{r}.
26. Fuller, *History of the Worthies*, 5G4^{r} (Montgomeryshire, 47).
27. Fuller, *History of the Worthies*, 2A1^{r} (Cheshire, 181).
28. 'The *Lives* of *Wickleif, Huss, Hierom of Prague, Frith, Bilney, Tindal, Rogers, Saunders, Hooper, Tailor, Bradford, Ridley, Latimer, Philpot*, and *Cranmer*, are collected out of the Book of *Martyrs*.' Clarke, *Marrow* (1650), c4^{v}.
29. Carleton, *Vita Bernardi Gilpin viri sanctissimi, famaque apud Anglos aquolinares* [sic] *celeberrimi*; Carleton, *The Life of Bernard Gilpin a Man Most Holy and Renowned among the Northerne English*.
30. [Featley], 'The Life of the Worthie Prelate and Faithfvll Servant of God Iohn Iewel Sometimes Bishop of Sarisbvrie'.
31. Foxe, *Acts and Monuments* (1641).
32. Willet, *Synopsis papismi*.
33. Cowper, *The Life and Death of... Mr. William Cowper, Bishop of Galloway*.

34. Pareus, *Narratio historica de curriculo vitae, & obitu reverendissimi patris D. Davidis Parei*, republished in Pareus, *Opera theologica exegetica*.
35. B[agshaw], 'The Life and Death of Mr. Bolton'.
36. Scudder, 'The Life and Death of M. Whately'.
37. Clarke, *Marrow* (1650), c4^{v}.
38. Wall and Ashe, 7 December 1649, in Clarke, *Marrow* (1650), b2^{r}, b2^{v}.
39. '*viz*. Doctor [John] *Preston*, [Richard] *Sibs*, [Thomas] *Tailor*, [John] *Stoughton* & c. Mr. [Richard] *Rogers*, [Richard] *Stock*, [Ezekiel] *Culverwel*, [William] *Pemble* & c. As also Mr. [Arthur] *Hildersham*, [John] *Dod*, [Thomas] *Pierson*, [Julines] *Herring*, [John] *Ball*, [Josias] *Nicols*, [William] *Hinde*, and [William] *Rathband*', Wall and Ashe, 7 December 1649, in Clarke, *Marrow* (1650), b2^{v}.
40. Wall and Ashe, 7 December 1649, in Clarke, *Marrow* (1650), b2^{v}-b3^{r}.
41. Clarke, *Generall Martyrologie* (1651), 3N3^{r}.
42. For Clarke's version of the life, see BL Harley MS 6037, fo. 15^{v}; Clarke, *Generall Martyrologie* (1651), 3U4^{r}; Moore, *English Hypothetical Universalism: John Preston and the Softening of Reformed Theology*, 3–4 n. 2.
43. Clarke, *The Lives of Thirty-Two English Divines*, 3rd edn (1677), 2G4^{v}. Hill edited William Fenner's works with Edmund Calamy from 1651. Knighton, 'Hill, Thomas (*d*. 1653)'.
44. Clarke, *Generall Martyrologie*, 3M1^{v}-3M2^{r}.
45. Sutton, 'Ball, John (1585–1640)'. See Ball, *The Power of Godliness*; Ball, *A Treatise of Divine Meditation*.
46. Fuller, *The History of the Worthies of England*, 3X1^{r}.
47. Clarke, *Second Part of the Marrow* (1650), A2^{v}.
48. Clarke, *The Lives of Thirty-Two English Divines* (1677), T2^{r}.
49. Clarke, *The Lives of Thirty-Two English Divines* (1677), 3I3^{r}.
50. Baillie to Clarke, 27 July 1653. *Letters and Journals of Robert Baillie, A. M., Principal of the University of Glasgow, M.DC.XXXVII-M.DC.LXII*, ed. Laing, 3:226–7.
51. Collinson, '"A magazine of religious patterns"'; Eales, 'Samuel Clarke and the "Lives" of Godly Women in Seventeenth-Century England'; Lake, 'Reading Clarke's *Lives* in Political and Polemical Context'.
52. [Heywood?], *Some Remarks upon the Life of that Painful Servant of God, Mr. Nathanael Heywood*, A7^{v}-A8^{r}.
53. Heywood, 'A Narrative of the Holy Life, and Happy Death of...Mr. John Angier' (1685), printed in *Oliver Heywood's Life of John Angier of Denton together with Angier's Diary, and Extracts from his 'An Helpe to Better Hearts': also Samuel Angier's Diary*, ed. Axon, 43–122 at 46.
54. Foulis, *The history of the wicked plots and conspiracies of our pretended saints representing the beginning, constitution, and designs of the Jesuite*, (b 2)^{v}.
55. Eales, 'Samuel Clarke and the "Lives" of Godly Women in Seventeenth-Century England'.
56. Clarke, *The Marrow of Ecclesiastical History*, 3rd edn (1675), (g)1^{r}.
57. Clarke, *The Lives of Sundry Eminent Persons* (1683), A1^{r-v}.
58. [Baxter], 'To the Reader', 16 January 1682/3, in Clarke, *The Lives of Sundry Eminent Persons* (1683), a3^{r}-a4^{v}, at a4^{r}, a3^{v}, Simmons also added lives of Sir Nathaniel Barnardiston, Richard Blackerby, and Samuel Fairclough.

59. Baxter to 'Christian Reader', 28 August 1672, in Janeway, *Invisibles, Realities, Demonstrated in the Holy Life and Triumphant Death of Mr. John Janeway*, A3^{r}–A8^{v}, at A4^{v}.
60. [Baxter], 'To the Reader', in Clarke, *The Lives of Sundry Eminent Persons* (1683), a4^{r}.
61. [Baxter], 'To the Reader', in Clarke, *The Lives of Sundry Eminent Persons* (1683), a4^{r}.
62. Baxter, *A Breviate of the Life of Margaret, the Daughter of Francis Charlton . . . and Wife of Richard Baxter*, A1^{v}, A2^{r}, A3^{v}.
63. [Baxter], 'To the Reader', in Clarke, *The Lives of Sundry Eminent Persons* (1683), a4^{v}.
64. Winstanley, *England's Worthies. Select Lives of the Most Eminent Persons from Constantine the Great, to the Death of Oliver Cromwel Late Protector*, A3^{r}; Winstanley, *The Loyal Martyrology*.
65. Barksdale, *Memorials of Worthy Persons Two Decads*, *2^{v}, *3^{v}, *1^{v} *4^{r-v}, B12^{v}.
66. Fuller, *Worthies*, B1^{r}.
67. Pritchard, *English Biography in the Seventeenth Century: A Critical Survey*, 22.
68. Lloyd, *Memoires of the Lives, Actions, Sufferings & Deaths of Those Noble Reverend and Excellent Parsonages* (1668); 2nd edn (1677).
69. Lloyd, *The Statesmen and Favourites of England since the Reformation*; Lloyd, *State-Worthies, or, The States-Men and Favourites of England since the Reformation* (1670); 2nd edn with additions (1679).
70. Phillips, *Theatrum poetarum*; Winstanley, *The Lives of the Most Famous English Poets*; Langbaine, *An Account of the English Dramatick Poets*.
71. Clarke, *The Lives of Sundry Eminent Persons* (1683), A1^{r}.

Chapter 12

1. Walton, *The Lives of Dr. John Donne, Sir Henry Wotton, Mr. Richard Hooker, Mr. George Herbert* (1670); Walton, *The Lives of Dr. John Donne, Sir Henry Wotton, Mr. Richard Hooker, Mr. George Herbert* (1675).
2. On Walton, see Stanwood, *Izaak Walton*; Martin, *Walton's Lives*; Martin, 'Walton, Izaak (1593–1683)'.
3. Walton, *The Life of Dr. Sanderson, Late Bishop of Lincoln*.
4. Donaldson, 'National Biography and the Arts of Memory: From Thomas Fuller to Colin Matthew', 67.
5. Martin, *Walton's Lives: Conformist Commemoration and the Rise of Biography*.
6. Walton, 'The Life and Death of Dr Donne, Late Deane of St Pauls London' (1640). See also Walton, *The Life of John Donne, Dr. in Divinity, and Late Dean of Saint Pauls Church* (1658).
7. Wa[lton], 'The Life of Sir Henry Wotton' (1651). Further editions followed in 1654, 1672, and 1685.
8. Walton, *The Life of Mr. Rich. Hooker* (1665). See also Walton, 'The Life of Mr. Richard Hooker' in *The Works of that Learned and Judicious Divine Mr. Richard Hooker*, [ed. Gauden] (1666); further editions of the *Works* followed in 1676 and 1682.
9. Walton, *The Life of Mr. George Herbert* (1670). See also Walton, 'The Life of Mr. George Herbert' in Herbert, *The Temple* (1674), 1–59.
10. Wotton to Walton, <6 February–December> 1639. *The Life and Letters of Sir Henry Wotton*, ed. Pearsall Smith, 2:404–5.

11. Wotton to Walton, <6 February-December> 1639. Wotton, *Life and Letters*, 2:404–5.
12. On the multiple versions, see Butts, 'A Bibliography of Izaak Walton's *Lives*', and especially Novarr, *The Making of Walton's Lives.*
13. Pritchard, *English Biography in the Seventeenth Century: A Critical Survey*, 20; see also his ch. 4, *passim*.
14. Speght, 'The Life of Geffrey Chaucer'.
15. [Featley], 'The Life of the Worthie Prelate and Faithfvll Servant of God Iohn Iewel Sometimes Bishop of Sarisbvrie'.
16. Lipsius, 'The Life of Lvcivs Annævs Seneca, Described'.
17. Buckeridge, 'A Sermon Preached at the Funeral of the Right Honorable and Reverend Father in God Lancelot Late Lord Bishop of Winchester'.
18. Prior, 'A Sermon at the Fvnerall of the Right Reverend Father in God, Miles, Late Lord Bishop of Glovcester'.
19. Harris, 'A short view of the life and vertues of the avthovr'; will of Arthur Lake, 27 December 1625: TNA, PROB 11/152/99.
20. Coke, 'The Preface'.
21. Jo. Mar., 'Hexastichon bibliopolae', in Donne, *Poems…with Elegies on the Authors Death* (1635), A4^{v}.
22. Donne, *Deaths Duell, or, A Consolation to the Soule, against the Dying Life, and Living Death of the Body.*
23. On its title page, Donne's *Deaths Dvell* is described as being given 'at White Hall, before the Kings Maiesty…and called by his Maiesties household the doctors owne funerall sermon'. The sermon is also introduced in this way: 'This Sermon was, by Sacred Authoritie, stiled the Authors own funeral Sermon' (A4^{r}).
24. King to Walton, 13 November 1664. Walton, *Life of Hooker* (1665), A2^{v}–A3^{r}.
25. Walton here quotes Donne, *Pseudo-Martyr*, B3^{r}.
26. Novarr, *Making*, chs. 1–4; Martin, *Walton's Lives*, 167–203.
27. Donne, *Poems* (1635), 2a7^{r-v}, at 2a7^{v}; Martin, *Walton's Lives*, 177.
28. Donne, *Poems…with Elegies on the Authors Death* (1633), 2C1^{v}; Martin, *Walton's Lives*, 188–9.
29. Donne, *Deaths duell*, D3^{v}–D4^{r}; Martin, *Walton's Lives*, 180–1.
30. R., 'To the Reader', in Donne, *Deaths Duell*, A4^{r-v} at A4^{r}; Martin, *Walton's Lives*, 181.
31. Donne, *LXXX Sermons*, T5^{v}; Martin, *Walton's Lives*, 181–3.
32. *The ancient ecclesiasticall histories of the first six hundred yeares after Christ, written…by three learned historiographers, Eusebius, Socrates and Evagrius.* Salisbury Cathedral, R. 4. 7 (*CELM* *Wtl 165). The notes are printed in Novarr, *Making*, 499, and dated to 1655–8 ('Appendix A. The Date of Walton's Notes in his Copy of *Eusebius*', 499–502).
33. Donne, *Poems* (1635), 2a7^{v}.
34. Novarr, *Making*, 500–1.
35. John Hingston et al. to the Committee of Council for Music, 19 February 1656/7. TNA, SP 18/153, fo. 253; see Novarr, *Making*, 95 n. 181.
36. Donne, 'Vpon the Translation of the Psalmes by Sir *Philip Sydney*, and the Countesse of Pembroke his Sister', *Poems* (1635), 2A5^{v}–2A6^{r}.
37. Eusebius, *Ancient Ecclesiasticall Histories*, C1^{v}.

38. Donne, *Poems* (1633), 2Y3^{v}.
39. Gardner, 'Dean Donne's Monument in St. Paul's'.
40. Bennett, 'Walton's Use of Donne's Letters'.
41. Donne, *Letters to Severall Persons of Honour*, ed. Donne, H2^{r}.
42. On this passage, see Vaught, *Masculinity and Emotion in Early Modern English Literature*, 177–90.
43. Levin, *Dreaming the English Renaissance: Politics and Desire in Court and Culture*, 36.
44. Donne, *Poems* (1633), 2D4^{r}; Martin, *Walton's Lives*, 189.
45. Yale University, Beinecke Library, BEIN Ij W175 A670L Copy 2. Novarr notes corrections, not entirely legible, on p. 31 and 'somewhat later in the vision' (*Making*, 123).
46. Quarles, 'A Short Relation of the Life and Death of M^{r}. Francis Quarles'; Anon, 'The History of the Life and Memoirs of Mrs. Behn'; Smith, 'Vita D. Roberti Cottoni'; Toland, 'The Life of James Harrington'.

Chapter 13

1. Walton, 'The Life and Death of Dr Donne, Late Deane of St Pauls London', A3^{r}.
2. Plutarch, *The Lives of the Noble Grecians and Romanes*, trans. North, 3O5^{v} (p. 718): 'Then hauing washed his body with salt water, and wrapped it vp in an old shirt of his, bicause be had no other shift to lay it in: he sought vpon the sands, & found at the length a peece of an old fishers bote, enough to serue to burne his naked bodie with, but not all fully out. As he was busie gathering the broken peeces of this bote together, thither came vnto him an old ROMANE, whom his youth had serued vnder *Pompey* and sayd vnto him: O frend, what art thou that preparest the funeralls of *Pompey* the great?'
3. See Walkden, 'The Servant and the Grave Robber: Walton's *Lives* in Restoration England', 331–3.
4. Walton insisted that this *apologia* be added to every subsequent edition: 'when *Doctor Donn*'s Sermons were first printed, this was then my excuse for daring to write his life; and, I dare not now appear without it'. Walton, *The Lives of Dr. John Donne, Sir Henry Wotton, Mr. Richard Hooker, Mr. George Herbert* (1675), B5^{v}.
5. Bodl. MS Aubrey 6, fo. 2^{r}; Bodl. MS Aubrey 8, fo. 4^{r}; Bodl. MS Aubrey 3, fo. 10^{r}; Aubrey, *Brief Lives with an Apparatus for the Lives of our English Mathematical Writers*, ed. Bennett, 1:6, 1:271; see also Bennett's note, 2: 761–2. References to Aubrey's *Brief Lives* in the main text are to Bennett's edition.
6. Bodl. MS Aubrey 9, fo. 29^{r}.
7. The phrase is Samuel Hartlib's, to whom Aubrey 'seemd to be…a mighty favorer and promoter of all Ingen*ious* and Verulamian Designes'. Sheffield University Library, Hartlib Papers [HP] 28/2/42B–43A (*Ephemerides*, 1652), quoted in Jackson Williams, 'Training the Virtuoso: John Aubrey's Education and Early Life', 167. For an online edition of the Hartlib Papers, see http://www.hrionline.ac.uk/hartlib/index.html.
8. Bacon, *The Two Bookes…of the Proficience and Aduancement of Learning, Diuine And Humaine*, 2C2^{v}, 2C3^{r}. Riccardo Fubini has suggested that Bacon's source may be Biondi Flavio's *Italy Illuminated*: see Fubini, *Storiografia dell'Umanesimo in Italia da Leonardo Bruni ad Annio da Viterbo*, XVI–XVII, 47–8.

9. Bodl. MS Aubrey 9, fo. 29^{r}.
10. Blount, *Glossographia, or, A dictionary interpreting all such hard words of whatsoever language now used in our refined English tongue*, $2M7^{v}$, quoted in *OED* s.v. *schediasm*.
11. On Aubrey, see Powell, *John Aubrey and his Friends*; Hunter, *John Aubrey and the Realm of Learning*; Tylden-Wright, *John Aubrey: A Life*; Fox, 'Aubrey, John (1626–1697)'; Bennett, 'General Introduction'; Jackson Williams, *The Antiquary: John Aubrey's Historical Scholarship*.
12. Aubrey, *Miscellanies upon the Following Subjects*.
13. Bodl. MS Aubrey 9, fo. 29^{r}.
14. Aubrey to Wood, 10 February 1679/80. Bodl. MS Ballard 14, fo. 125^{r}. On the working relationship between Aubrey and Blackburne, see Powell, *Aubrey and his Friends*, 178–80; Hunter, *Aubrey and the Realm of Learning*, 78–80; Parkin, 'Blackburne, Richard (1651/2–1716)'; Jackson Williams, *The Antiquary*, 100–4.
15. See Anon., 'The Autobiographies of Thomas Hobbes', *Mind* 48 (1939), 403–5.
16. Aubrey to Blackburne, n.d. Bodl. MS Aubrey 9, fo. 28^{v}.
17. Aubrey to Wood, 7 March 1679/80. Bodl. MS Tanner 456a, fo. 23^{r}.
18. Aubrey to Wood, 22 May 1680. Bodl. MS Wood F. 39, fo. 340^{r}.
19. Aubrey to Wood, 7 March 1679/80. Bodl. MS Tanner 456a, fo. 23^{r}.
20. Aubrey to Wood, 27 March 1680. Bodl. MS Ballard 14, fo. 131^{r}.
21. Hunter, *John Aubrey*, 79. Jackson Williams, *The Antiquary*, 101 n. 29, notes 'Evidence for the involvement of Dryden and Vaughan comes for Aubrey's letter to Wood of 27 March' (Bodl. MS Ballard 14, fo. 131^{r}).
22. Dryden, 'The Life of Plutarch', $G2^{r}$, $G5^{r}$, $G7^{r}$, $G7^{v}$.
23. Jackson Williams, *The Antiquary*, 102. See also Zwicker, 'Considering the Ancients: Dryden and the Uses of Biography'.
24. Aubrey to Wood, 22 May 1680. Bodl. MS Wood F 39, fo. 340^{r}.
25. As Jackson Williams notes, 'Recrementa' can also mean (after Aulus Gellius) 'human excrement'. Aubrey made a note to 'meliorate this word' but failed to. Jackson Williams, *The Antiquary*, 103, commenting on Bodl. MS Aubrey 9, fo. 29^{r}, marginal note.
26. Aubrey to Wood, 10 February 1680. Bodl. MS Ballard 14, fo. 125^{r}.
27. On the genesis of the *Brief Lives*, see Powell, 181–4; Tylden-Wright, *John Aubrey: A Life*, 216–20; and especially Bennett, 'General Introduction'.
28. Aubrey to Wood, 17 February 1680. Bodl. MS Ballard 14, fo. 126^{r}.
29. Aubrey to Wood, 27 March 1680. Bodl. MS Ballard 14, fo. 131^{r}.
30. Aubrey to Wood, 22 May 1680. Bodl. MS Wood F.39, fo. 340^{r}.
31. Now Bodley MSS Aubrey 6–9.
32. Bennett, 'John Aubrey and the Printed Book', 394–5, quoting Aubrey, 'The Naturall Historie of Wiltshire', Bodl. MS Aubrey 2, fos. 18, 19^{v}.
33. Love, 'Gossip and Biography', 93 and *passim*; Pritchard, *English Biography in the Seventeenth Century: A Critical Survey*, 181, and ch. 9, *passim*.
34. Aubrey, *Brief Lives*, ed. Bennett.
35. HP 29/5/54B (*Ephemerides*, 1655).
36. Hartlib to Worthington, 12 December 1655. *The Diary and Correspondence of Dr. John Worthington*, ed. Crossley, vol. 1, 65–79 at 68–9. See also Hartlib to Worthington, 10 March

1655/6: 'Mr. Aubrey is not writing Sir W. Boswell's but the Lord Bacon's life.' Worthington, *Diary and Correspondence*, 79–84 at 82.

37. As Bodl. Ashmole A 42, and Bodl Ashmole 1621 (1).
38. Bodl. MS Aubrey 10, quoted at fos. 105^{r}, 124^{r}.
39. For the Gruter connection, see Rees, 'Introduction', lxxv–lxxxv.
40. HP 28/2/42B–43A (*Ephemerides*, 1652). On Aubrey and Hartlib, see Turnbull, 'Samuel Hartlib's Acquaintance with John Aubrey'.
41. Hartlib to Aubrey, 8 March 1652/3. Bodl. MS Aubrey 12, fo. 155^{r}. The manuscript remains unidentified.
42. HP 28/2/49B (*Ephemerides*, 1653). Lady Mitton (presumably Mytton) remains unidentified.
43. HP 29/5/54B (*Ephemerides*, 1655).
44. Aubrey, *Lives*, 1:314. See Bennett, 'John Aubrey's Oxfordshire Collections: An Edition of Aubrey's Annotations to his Presentation Copy of Robert Plot's *Natural History of Oxford-shire*, Bodleian Library Ashmole 1722'; Bennett, 'John Aubrey and the Printed Book', 395.
45. Bodl. MS Aubrey 9, fo. 34^{v}.
46. Aubrey seems not to have been aware of Pierre Amboise's French life, published in 1631; Rawley, who was attacked in the prefatory material, probably chose to ignore it. Amboise, 'Discovrs svr la vie de Mre Francois Bacon, chancelier d' Angleterre'. For the attack see 'Advertissement [au Lecteur]' in Bacon, *Histoire natvrelle*, ed./trans. Amboise, ā4^{r}–ā7^{r}, at ā6^{v}–ā7^{r}.
47. Bacon, *Certaine Miscellany Works of the Right Honovrable, Francis Lo. Verulam, Viscount S. Alban*, ed. Rawley, A3^{r}.
48. Bacon, *Sylua syluarum: or A Naturall Historie in Ten Centuries*, ed. Rawley, ¶^{v}.
49. Bacon, [O]*perum moralium et civilium tomus*, ed. Rawley; Bacon, *Historie Naturall and Experimentall, of Life and Death*, ed. [and trans.?] Rawley.
50. HP 29/5/57A (*Ephemerides*, 1655).
51. On Rawley's 'Life', see also Pritchard, *English Biography in the Seventeenth Century*, 117–20.
52. On 'Liber B', see Bennett, 'General Introduction', lxix.
53. Bennett, 'Aubrey and the Printed Book', 397, quoting Bodl. MS Ballard 14, fo. 130^{v}.
54. Bennett, 'Aubrey and the Printed Book', 397, quoting Bodl. MS Aubrey 9, fo. 28^{r}.
55. Rawley, 'The Life of the Honourable Author', (b4)^{v}.
56. Rawley, 'The Life of the Honourable Author', (c4)^{v}.
57. Bennett, 'General Introduction', xlvi.
58. Love, 'Gossip and Biography', 102.
59. Faringdon to Garthwait, September [1658], in Hales, *Golden Remains*, ed. Gunning a3^{v}–a4^{r}, at a4^{r}; I am grateful to Daniel Blank for this reference.
60. Pearson, 'To the Reader', in Hales, *Golden Remains*, ed. Gunning, a1^{r}–a3^{r} at a1^{r}.
61. On Fulman, see Sherlock, 'Fulman, William (1632–1688)'.
62. Stukeley's notes are in BL Additional MS 4222; Hunter's in BL Additional MS 24481. See Elson, *John Hales of Eton*, 160–1; I owe this reference to Daniel Blank.
63. See Butt, 'Izaak Walton's Collections for Fulman's Life of John Hales'; King, *The Poems of Henry King*, ed. Crum, 21; and especially Bevan, 'Izaak Walton's Collections for Fulman's Life of John Hales: the Walker Part'.

64. On Walton's relationship with Marriot, see Bevan, 'Izaak Walton and his Publisher'.
65. Walton to Marriott, 24 August 1673, Winchester. Corpus Christi College, Oxford, Fulman MS 10, fo. 78^{r}, printed in Bevan, 'Walton's Collections', 267–8.
66. Faringdon, 'The Authors Life' (copy). Bodl. MS J. Walker, c. 2, fos. 198–9, printed in Bevan, 'Walton's Collections', 167–9. The paper notes the additions are 'by M^{r}. Walton, *the* scrawl his own hand'.
67. Stradling to Walton, 22 June 1673, Chichester. Bodl. MS J. Walker c. 2, fo. 196^{r}, printed in Bevan, 'Walton's Collections', 165–6. Bevan suggests that the scribe was Izaak Walton, Jr.
68. Walton to Fulman, 20 October 1673. Bodl. MS J. Walker c. 2, fo. 199^{r-v}.
69. Walton to Fulman, 20 October 1673. Bodl. MS J. Walker c. 2, fo. 199^{r-v}. On Anne King, see Larminie, 'King, Anne [*married names* Anne Dutton; Anne Howe, Lady Howe] (*b.* in or before 1621, *d.* 1684 × 1701)'.
70. Walton to Fulman, 20 October 1673. Bodl. MS J. Walker c. 2, fo. 199^{r-v}. Some of these queries were answered by another Eton man, Nathaniel Ingelo: see Ingelo to Marriot, 29 October 1673. Fulman MS 10, fos. 81–2, discussed in Butt, 'Walton's Collections', 269–70.
71. Aubrey to Wood, St Anne's Day 1682. Bodl. MS Wood F 39, fo. 368^{r-v}.
72. Ibid. For Hales's will, 10 May 1656, see Bayle, *A General Dictionary Historical and Critical*, ed. Bernard, Birch, John, et al., vol. 8, 3O2^{v} (p. 236).
73. Roswell to Wood, 10 January 1682/3. Bodl. MS Wood F 43, fo. 312^{r}, quoted in Aubrey, *Brief Lives*, ed. Bennett, 2:1319. Similarly, Ingelo confirmed to Marriot that Mrs Powney was Hannah, and her husband Simon.
74. Wood, *Athenæ Oxonienses*, 2: I3^{v}–I4^{r}.
75. Bennett, 'John Aubrey and the Rhapsodic Book', 332.

Chapter 14

1. Pepys, *The Diary of Samuel Pepys: A New and Complete Transcription*, ed. Latham and Matthews, 7:271 (2 September 1666). References in the text are to this edition.
2. Tomalin, *Samuel Pepys: The Unequalled Self*, xxxviii.
3. On Pepys' sexual life, see the indulgent Wilson, *The Private Life of Mr. Pepys*; Turner, *Fashioning Adultery: Gender, Sex and Civility in England, 1660–1740*, 29–35.
4. Magdalene College, Cambridge, Pepys Library, MS 1836–41.
5. Pepys, *Diary*, 1:xli.
6. Ollard, *Pepys: A Biography*, 21: Ollard briefly mentions that Pepys learned shorthand for taking lecture notes at Cambridge (30); Tomalin, *Samuel Pepys*, 40–1.
7. 'Catalogue Supeller Literaria Samuelis Pepys; containing The Catalogue of my Books; adjusted to Michaelmass 1700', 93; and 'Alphabet Suppeller Literaria Samuelis Pepys; containing The Alphabet to my Books, adjusted to Michaelmas 1700', 180. Facsimiles of both are published in Pepys, *Catalogue of the Pepys Library at Magdalene College Cambridge*, volume VII, *Facsimile of Pepys' Catalogue*, ed. McKitterick.
8. Bright, *Charac[terie.] An Ar[te] of Shorte, Swift[e], and Secrete Writing by Character*.
9. Locke, *Some Thoughts Concerning Education*, T7^{r-v}.
10. Alston, *Treatises on Short-Hand, A Bibliography of the English Language from the Invention of Printing to the Year 1800*, viii. For a brief survey, see Henderson, '"Swifte and secrete writing" in Seventeenth-Century England, and Samuel Shelton's *Brachygraphy*'.

11. See Carlton, *Bibliotheca Pepysiana. A Descriptive Catalogue of the Library of Samuel Pepys*, 4 vols, *Part IV. Shorthand Books*, 29–46; Chappell, 'Introduction' to Pepys, *Shorthand Letters*; [Matthews], 'The Shorthand'.
12. Shelton, *Tachygraphy the most exact and compendious methode of short and swift writing*.
13. Buck, 'An Appendix or Corollary of the Foundations and Descriptions of the Three Most Famous Vniuersities of England', 4O1[v].
14. D'Ewes, *The Autobiography and Correspondence of Sir Simonds D'Ewes*, ed. Halliwell, 1:95, 63. On Makin, see Salmon, 'Bathsua Makin (1600–c.1673): A Pioneer Linguist and Feminist', esp. 242–3; Teague, *Bathsua Makin, Woman of Learning*, 30, 35–7.
15. D'Ewes, *The diary of Sir Simonds D'Ewes (1622-1624): journal d'un étudiant londonien sous le règne de Jacques I*[er], ed. Bourchier.
16. Aubrey, *Brief Lives with an Apparatus for the Lives of our English Mathematical Writers*, ed. Bennett, 1:310.
17. 'Juvenum et virorum bona pars conciones calamo excipiunt, et quidem verbo tenus. Inventa enim hic est ante annos 30 (sub Jacobo) et jam etiam inter rusticos invaluit *tachygraphiae* ars, quam illi *stenographiam* vocant, quâ (non literarum, sed characterum voces integras significantium beneficio) lingvae celeritatem manu imitantur. Discunt autem illam in urbibus propemodum omnes, simul atque vulgatam scripturam in schola didicerint, annum circiter addentes ad steganographiam addiscendam.' Komenský ad amicos Lesnae in Polonia agentes, 8/18 October 1641. Komensky, *Dílo Jana Amose Komenského*, vol. 14, ed. Svoboda, Borská, and Nováková, 113–16 at 113–14; trans. Young, *Comenius in England*, 65.
18. Folger MS V.b.110, fo. 2[v] and Folger MS V.a.38, cited in Wolfe, 'Thomas Shelton's Shorthand Version of the Lord's Prayer'.
19. Wilkins, *Mercvry, or, The Secret and Swift Messenger*, H1[v]–H2[r].
20. Mendle, 'The "Prints" of the Trials: The Nexus of Politics, Religion, Law and Information in Late Seventeenth-Century England', 126.
21. Bremer, 'Williams, Roger (c.1606–1683)'.
22. Philips, *The Life of John Williams, Ld. Keeper of the Great Seal, Bp. of Lincoln, and Abp. of York*, F4[v].
23. Mendle, '"Prints" of the Trials', 126–7; Evelyn, *The Diary of John Evelyn*, ed. de Beer, 4:175 (18 July 1679).
24. Henderson, 'Reading, and Writing, the Text of the Putney Debates'; Henderson, 'Appendix C: A Note on William Clarke's Shorthand'.
25. Henderson, '"Posterity to judge"—John Rushworth and his "Historicall Collections"'.
26. On women's use of shorthand, see Mendelson, 'Stuart Women's Diaries and Occasional Memoirs', 183–4; and Ezell, 'Domestic Papers: Manuscript Culture and Early Modern Women's Life Writing', 40–1.
27. Mendelson, 'Stuart Women's Diaries', 184, quoting Chester Record Office, D/Basten/8, fo. 1.
28. *An Account of the Life and Death of Mrs. Elizabeth Bury… Chiefly Collected out of Her Own Diary* ed. [Bury], B4[r].
29. [Reynolds], *Imitation and Caution for Christian Woman: or, The Life and Death of that Excellent Gentlewoman, Mrs. Mary Bewley*, B2[v], B3[r].
30. Rogers, *The Character of a Good Woman…occasion'd by the decease of Mrs. Elizabeth Dunton…with an account of her life and death, and part of the diary writ with her own hand*, e5[r–v].

31. Jeake, *An Astrological Diary of the Seventeenth Century: Samuel Jeake of Rye 1652–1699*, ed. Hunter and Gregory, 86–9.
32. Jeake, *Astrological Diary*, printing Rye Museum, Selmes MS 52 as appendix I, 253–9, with illustration (Fig. 2) at 252; and William Andrews Clark Memorial Library, Los Angeles, MS J43M3/D540, at 83–250.
33. Jeake, *Astrological Diary*, 86 (13 June 1657).
34. Fitzwilliam Museum, Cambridge, MS.1-1936, fos. 3^{r-v}, 4^{v}; transcribed in Westfall, 'Short-Writing and the State of Newton's Conscience, 1662', 13–15.
35. By contrast, Robert Hooke coded his sexual encounters with the symbol for Pisces. *The Diary of Robert Hooke...1672–1680*, ed. Robinson and Adams, 3; see examples at 38, 41, 42, 44, 45, 46.
36. BL Sloane MS 3711, fo. 68; printed in Starkey, *Alchemical Laboratory Notebooks and Correspondence*, ed. Newman and Principe, 124–5 (document 10A).
37. Michael Wigglesworth, diary, Massachusetts Historical Society, Ms. SBd-20, printed as *The Diary of Michael Wigglesworth, 1653–1657: The Conscience of a Puritan*, ed. Morgan, quoted at 3, 4, 5, 6. For Wigglesworth and Starkey, see Newman, *Gehennial Fire: The Lives of George Starkey, an American Alchemist in the Scientific Revolution*, 173–4. On the diary, see Cherniavsky, 'Night Pollution and the Floods of Confession in Michael Wigglesworth's Diary'; Hughes, '"Meat out of the eater": Panic and Desire in American Puritan Poetry'; Bray, 'To Be a Man in Early Modern Society: The Curious Case of Michael Wigglesworth'.
38. Wigglesworth, *Diary*, 93.
39. National Maritime Museum, LBK/8; see Pepys, *Shorthand Letters of Samuel Pepys. From a Volume Entitled S. Pepys's Official Correspondence* 1662–1679, ed. Chappell. Navy White Book, Pepys Library MS 2581, printed in Pepys, *Samuel Pepys and the Second Dutch War: Pepys's Navy White Book and Brooke House Papers*, transcribed by Matthews and Knighton, ed. Latham, at 1–167. The Brooke House Journal is lost, but printed in Pepys, *Samuel Pepys and the Second Dutch War*, 334–435, from a copy, Pepys Library MS 2874, pp. 385–503.
40. Bodl. Rawlinson MS C 869; see Howarth, 'Introduction', xii.
41. Pepys Library MS 2141.
42. Hewer's shorthand notebook, reporting the sermon, is at Houghton Library, Harvard, MS Eng. 991.1. See Pepys, *Diary*, 7:35 (4 February 1666) and n. 3.
43. Pepys, 'Second Diary', 13 September 1683; *Letters and the Second Diary of Samuel Pepys*, ed. Howarth, 390.
44. For other such references, see 3:162 (10 August 1662): 'And I to my closet in my office, to perfect my Journall'; 7:170 (18 June 1666): 'in my chamber most of the morning, setting things to right there, my Journall and accounts with my father and brother'. Smyth, *Autobiography in Early Modern England*, 209–10.
45. Pepys, *Diary* 9:160–8 (10–19 April 1668), and 9:224–43 (5–17 June 1668); see Smyth, *Autobiography*, 59.
46. Pepys, *Diary*, 9:160–1 (notes for 10 April 1668). The italicized letters are in longhand. *W P* is William Petty, and *D Y* the Duke of York. *Legend* is probably a 1527 edition of the *Legenda aurea*. Pepys, *Diary*, 9:161 n. 1.
47. Pepys, *Diary*, 9:565 n. *a*.

48. Bodl. MS Rawlinson C 859, with a further portion in Bodl. MS Rawlinson A 190; printed in Pepys, *Second Diary*, 379–449.
49. Pepys scholars usually follow Latham and Matthews in writing of Pepys's 'lingua franca', 'a mixture of foreign languages' (Pepys, *Diary*, 1:lxi–lxii). My objective here is to show how the use of foreign languages is more subtle and dynamic than this catch-all phrase allows.
50. Pepys, *Diary*, 1:246 (16 September 1660), 1:252 (23 September 1660).
51. For Mrs Bagwell, see 15 and 16 December 1664, 23 January 1665, 20 and 21 February 1665; Mrs Martin, 2 January 1665; Jervas's daughter, 23 January 1665; Jane Welsh, 27 January 1665.
52. See *Diary*, 6:145 (3 July 1665); 6:162 (19 July 1665).
53. Pepys, *Diary*, 1:lxi.
54. Roach, 'Celebrity Erotics: Pepys, Performance, and Painted Ladies', 219. See also Laqueur, *Solitary Sex: A Cultural History of Masturbation*, 180–2.
55. James Grantham Turner claims that the foreign words were 'written in longhand, and blaze forth from the page of shorthand', and David Turner writes 'these phrases were written in longhand', but Latham and Matthews insist that 'The passages are all written in shorthand'. Turner, 'Pepys and the Private Parts of Monarchy', 97; Turner, *Fashioning Adultery*, 30; Pepys, *Diary*, lxi. See also *The Illustrated Pepys: Extracts from the Diary*, ed. Latham, 8, where the 'private polyglot' is 'still in shorthand'.
56. Pepys, *Diary*, 8:244 and n. a-a (31 May 1667).
57. Pepys, *Diary*, 8:245 n. a.
58. Loveman, *Samuel Pepys and his Books: Reading, Newsgathering, and Sociability, 1660–1703*, 117–18.
59. As Ian Frederick Moulton observes, Pepys 'not only consumed *L'école des filles* in private, he also kept a private record of that consumption, in which he attempted to explain to himself why he took pleasure from the text and why he subsequently destroyed it'. *Before Pornography: Erotic Writings in Early Modern England*, 37.
60. Wheatley, *Pepysiana or Additional Notes on the Particulars of Pepys's Life and on Some Passages in the Diary with Appendixes*, 251–68; Pepys, *Diary*, 2:lxxii.
61. Pepys, *Diary*, 8:244 n. a-a.
62. I am grateful to an anonymous reviewer for this suggestion.
63. Pepys, *Diary*, 9:91 n. 2.

Chapter 15

1. Dangerfield, *Dangerfield's Memoires, Digested into Adventures, Receits, and Expences by his Own Hand.* Anthony Wood wrote on his copy that it was 'published in the latter end of Apr.'. Bodl. Wood 372 (16), title page; Kiessling, *The Library of Anthony Wood*, 201, #2155. On *Dangerfield's Memoires*, see Gladfelder, *Criminality and Narrative in Eighteenth-Century England: Beyond the Law*, 72–7; and Loveman, '"Eminent cheats": Rogue Narratives in the Literature of the Exclusion Crisis', 119. This chapter is indebted to Loveman's chapter, which deals with many of the same materials, although not through the perspective of life-writing.
2. Wood, marginal note in his copy of *Dangerfield's Memoires*, Bodl. Wood 372 (16), A2^{v}; Kiessling, *The Library of Anthony Wood*, 201, #2155; quoted in Loveman, '"Eminent cheats"', 119.

Wood also attempted to identify some of the men mentioned in the diary: see marginalia at B1^{v}, B4^{v}, C2^{r}.

3. North, *Examen: or, an Enquiry into the Credit and Veracity of a Pretended Complete History*, 265.
4. See Sergeant, 'Duke Dangerfield', 187; Gladfelder, *Criminality and Narrative*, 73.
5. *Dangerfield's Memoires*, A2^{r}.
6. *Don Tomazo, or, the Juvenile Rambles of Thomas Dangerfield*. On Dangerfield, see Sergeant, 'Duke Dangerfield'; Petherick, 'Handsome Thomas and the Popish Midwife', esp. 237–41, 258–64; Marshall, 'Dangerfield, Thomas (1654–1685)', although the entry misses some pertinent information, including his marriage; Loveman, '"Eminent cheats"', 115–21.
7. Loveman, '"Eminent cheats"', 119.
8. On the criminal biography vogue, see Peterson ed., *The Counterfeit Lady Unveiled and Other Criminal Fiction of Seventeenth-Century England: A Selection*; McKeon, *The Origins of the English Novel 1600–1740*, 96–100; Faller, *Turned to Account: The Forms and Functions of Criminal Biography in Late Seventeenth and Early Eighteenth-Century England*; Gladfelder, *Criminality and Narrative*.
9. F[idge], *The English Gusman; or the History of that Unparallel'd Thief James Hind*. See Faller, *Turned to Account*, 6–16; White, 'Hind, James (bap. 1616, d. 1652)'.
10. [Head], *The English Rogue Described, in the Life of Meriton Latroon, a Witty Extravagant*; Pritchard, 'Head, Richard (c.1637–1686?)'.
11. Kirkman, 'To the Reader', *The English Rogue Continued*, A4^{r}.
12. Aubrey, *Brief Lives*, ed. Bennett, 1:474, 1:27 (Meriton as index entry), and notes at 2:1396–7.
13. Kirkman, 'To the Reader', A4^{r}, A5^{r}.
14. [Croke], *Fortune's uncertainty, or, Youth's unconstancy wherein is contained a true and impartial account of what hapned in the space of a few years to the author, whom you will know in this ensuing discourse by the name of Rodolphvs*; Larminie, 'Charles Croke (*fl.* 1652–1686)' in 'Croke, Unton (1594/5–1670/71)'.
15. On Carleton, see Bernbaum, *The Mary Carleton Narratives 1663–1673: A Missing Chapter in the History of the English Novel*; Todd, 'Carleton, Mary (1634×42–1673)'; Kietzman, *The Self-Fashioning of an Early Modern Englishwoman: Mary Carleton's Lives*. For Pepys's visit, see *The Diary of Samuel Pepys: A New and Complete Transcription*, ed. Latham and Matthews, 4:163 (29 May 1663).
16. K[irkman], *The Counterfeit Lady Unveiled*, B2^{r}.
17. [Cavendish], marchioness of Newcastle, *CCXI Sociable Letters*, A3^{r}.
18. On Cellier, see Weil, '"If I did say so I lyed": Elizabeth Cellier and the Construction of Credibility in the Popish Plot Crisis'; Richards, 'A Life in Writing: Elizabeth Cellier and Print Culture'; King, 'Cellier, Elizabeth (*fl.* 1668–1688)'.
19. See Luttrell, *A Brief Historical Relation of State Affairs from September 1678 to April 1714*, 1:23–4, 25, 29.
20. Dangerfield, *Mr. Tho. Dangerfields Particular Narrative of the Late Popish… Written by Himself*; Dangerfield, *Mr. Tho. Dangerfield's Second Narrative*, [A1]^{v}.
21. [Howell] ed., *Cobbett's Complete Collection of State Trials and Proceedings for High Treason and Other Crimes and Misdemeanors from the Earliest Period to the Present Time*, vol. 7, cols. 1043–67 at cols. 1049–51; Luttrell, *Brief Historical Relation*, 1:47–8.
22. Robert Hooke notes on 13 September 1680: 'Celier condemned £1000 and Pillory'. *The Diary of Robert Hooke… 1672–1680*, ed. Robinson and Adams, 454.

23. Cellier, 'The Matchless Picaro' in *Malice Defeated*, M1^{r}–M2^{v}, at M1^{v}–M2^{r}, M2^{v}. This was republished as *The Matchless Rogue; or, a Brief Account of the Life of Don Thomazo, the Unfortunate Son*.
24. Cellier, 'Matchless Picaro', M2^{v}.
25. Dangerfield, *Tho. Dangerfield's Answer to a Certain Scandalous Lying Pamphlet Entituled, Malice Defeated*, D2^{v}.
26. Clavell, *A Recantation of an Ill Led Life, or, A Discouerie of the High-Way Law*; Bellany, 'Clavell, John (1601–1643)'.
27. Sergeant, 'Duke Dangerfield', 136; Donovan, *Women and the Rise of the Novel, 1405–1726*, 147 (Donovan refers to Cellier's *The Matchless Rogue* reprint).
28. Sergeant, 'Duke Dangerfield', 143.
29. Cellier, *Malice Defeated*, N1^{r}.
30. Dangerfield, *The Case of Tho. Dangerfield* (London: for the author, 1680), G2^{r-v}. A list of those tried at the London and Middlesex Sessions on 26 February 1673 includes 'Thomas Daingerfield', convicted of robbery, who pleaded his clergy, and was burned in the hand ('Clergie burn'd'). TNA, SP 29/334, fo.19^{r}.
31. Anon., *The Perplex'd Prince*, E7^{v}, E8^{r}–E9^{r}. In Luttrell's copy (BL 292.a.34), the annotation is on E7^{v}.
32. Fuller, *The Whole Life of William Fuller*, B2^{v}.
33. North, *Examen: or, an Enquiry into the Credit and Veracity of a Pretended Complete History*, 231; see also 256–71.
34. Moore, *The Novel: An Alternative History: 1600 to 1800*, 598–600, at 599.
35. Salzman ed., *An Anthology of Seventeenth-Century Fiction*.
36. [Dunton], *A Voyage round the World, or, A Pocket-Library Divided into Several Volumes*. As Don Tomazo tries to sleep in Scotland, 'There were no shady Woods for Nightingales to lull him into soft slumbers; no murmuring Rills, to which he might make his sorrowful complaints; no kind Hermits to invite him to their Cells. All his comfort was in Hope, and the Compassion of his Guardian Angel' (C1^{r}). Dunton writes, ''Tis true, there were in my way no shady Woods for Nightingales to lull me into soft slumbers, no murmuring Rills to which I might make my sorrowful Complaints, no kind Hermits to invite me to their Cells; all my comfort was in HOPE, and the Compassion of my *Guardian-Angel*' (*Voyage*, D3^{r}). The resemblance was perhaps recognized by Anthony Wood who bound *Don Tomazo* with Dunton's *Voyage*, in a volume entitled 'Travells Rambles'. Bodl. Wood 155(5), cited in Loveman, '"Eminent cheats"', 118.
37. Dunton, *Life and Errors*. See Mascuch, *Origins of the Individualist Self: Autobiography and Self-Identity in England, 1591–1791*, 135–61.
38. See, for example, Colahan, 'Dangerfield's Picaresque *Don Tomazo*: English Novelists as Spanish (Anti-Heroes)'; Kuhlisch, 'The Ambivalent Rogue: Moll Flanders as Modern *Pícara*', 354 n. 7; Parrinder, *Nation and Novel: The English Novel from its Origins to the Present Day*, 46–7; Garrido Ardila, 'The Picaresque Novel and the Rise of the English Novel: From Baldwin and Delony to Defoe and Smollett', 126; Bayer, *Novel Horizons: The Genre Making of Restoration Fiction*, 262 n. 147.
39. Defoe, *The Life, Adventures, and Pyracies, of the Famous Captain Singleton*; Defoe, *The Fortunes and Misfortunes of the Famous Moll Flanders*; Defoe, *The History of the Most Remarkable Life, and Extraordinary Adventures, of the Truly Honorable Colonel Jaque, Vulgarly Call'd, Colonel Jack*;

Defoe, *The Fortunate Mistress: or. a History of the Life and Vast Variety of Fortunes of…Lady Roxana*. On Defoe's criminal writings, see Faller, *Crime and Defoe: A New Kind of Writing*.

40. *Dangerfield's Memoires*, F4r.
41. Robert Spencer, 2nd earl of Sunderland, warrant to Thomas Beake, 19 March 1684/5. TNA, SP 44/336, fo. 45r. Luttrell dates the arrest to 21 March 1685: 'Dangerfeild, the late evidence of the popish plot, is apprehended and committed to Newgate'. *Brief Historical Relation*, 1:336.
42. Luttrell notes on 21 March 1684/5 that Dangerfield 'is apprehended and committed to Newgate'. Luttrell, *Brief Historical Relation*, 336.
43. *The Entering Booke of Roger Morrice 1677–1691*, vol. 3, *The Reign of James II 1685–1687*, ed. Harris, 10 (6 June 1685): 'Dangerfield was upon Saturday May 30 tryed in Westminster Hall, and convicted of Perjury in his first Narrative'; Luttrell, *Brief Historical Relation*, 1:344–5.
44. Anon., *A true narrative of the arraignment, tryal, and conviction of Thomas Dangerfield for high-misdemeanors against His Present Majesty, James the Second, at the King's-Bench-Barr, at Westminster, on Saturday, May the 30th, 1685*.
45. [Court of King's Bench], *The Third Part of Modern Reports Being a Collection of Several Special Cases in the Court of Kings-Bench*, K2v. See also Morrice, *Entering Booke*, 3:23 (2 July 1685); Luttrell, *Brief Historical Relation*, 350.
46. Anon., *Duke Dangerfield declaring how he represented the D. of Mon– in the country with his miraculous gift of touching, making knights, and other pranks in Staffordshire*.
47. Anon., *Wish upon wish, or Dangerfields lamentation. Being a true relation, of a discovery of all the rogueries of Captain Dangerfield*. Another contemporary broadsheet specifies only that 'I turn'd a Coiner by my Trade, | And *Mountibank* of State': Anon., *The doleful lamentation of Thomas who was lately apprehended and imprisoned in Newgate, for high misdemeaner & c.*
48. Anon., *Dangerfields Dance giving an account of several notorious crimes by him committed, viz, he pretended to be a Duke, and feigned himself to be Monmouth, with several other pranks*. Another broadsheet, *A true relation of the sentence and condemnation of Thomas Dangerfield, at the King's Bench Bar, for his horrid crimes and perjuries*, was also published on 2 July. Although it alludes to 'perjury' and 'his whole Libelous Narrative', the uninformed reader would be hard pressed to work out for what heinous crime Dangerfield was being sentenced.
49. Loveman, '"Eminent cheats"', 121.
50. *The Autobiography of Sir John Bramston, K.B., of Skreens, in the Hundred of Chelmsford*, ed. Bramston, 194–5. See also Morrice, *Entering Booke*, 3:25 (9 July 1685): 'Upon Saturday after Dangerfield had been Whipt to Tyburn, and was ready to enter into Newgate back, Mr. Francis a Baraster of Greys Inn a Kentish man came to Dangerfield, and asked him some questions, to which he returned not such an answer as pleased, therefore Francis run him into the eye with a stafftuck, and Francis is apprehended, and now in Newgate. And Dangerfield dyed upon Lords day about one a Clock'; Luttrell, *Brief Historical Relation*, 351.
51. Morrice, *Entering Booke*, 3:30 (23 July 1685); Luttrell, *Brief Historical Relation*, 1:354.
52. *The behaviour, confession, and execution, of the four prisoners at Tyburn William Blower, for high treason; Robert Francis for the murther of Tho. Dangerfield, Henry Anthony, and John Morgan for two several burglarys and fellonies. On Friday the 24 of this instant July, 1685*, A1r.
53. Morrice, *Entering Booke*, 3:31 (30 July 1685); Luttrell, *Brief Historical Relation*, 1:355.
54. Bramston, *Autobiography*, 195.

55. Anon., *Dangerfield's Ghost to Jefferys.*
56. Coke, *A Detection of the Court and State of England*, 2R7^{v} (p. 638).
57. [Dunton], *The Merciful Assizes: or, a Panegyric on the Late Lord Jeffreys Hanging so Many in the West*, P3^{v}–P4^{v}.
58. [Dunton], *The Merciful Assizes*, Q2^{r-v}.
59. Morrice, *The Entering Booke of Roger Morrice 1677–1691*, vol. 2, *The Reign of Charles II 1677–1685*, ed. Spurr, 361 (7 April 1683). See also Young, 'Sources for the Annesley Family', 53. Dunton later wrote that Sarah (by now remarried as 'Madam *Fromantle*') 'is the only person I ever knew, whom an Estate made more humble, and condescending: Her Life is one continued Act of Tenderness, WIT, and Piety'. Dunton, *The Life and Errors of John Dunton Late Citizen of London; Written by Himself in Solitude. With an Idea of a New Life*, 2H4^{r}.
60. *Dangerfield's Memoires*, B2^{r}.
61. Wesley, *Maggots, or, Poems on Several Subjects, Never Before Handled by a Scholar.*
62. [Dunton], *Merciful Assizes*, Q1^{v}.
63. Anon. [Defoe], 'Against Reviling Public Criminals', *Applebee's Journal*, 24 June 1721, printed in Lee, *Daniel Defoe: His Life, and his Recently Discovered Writings: Extending from 1716 to 1729*, 2:393–6.
64. [Defoe], *The Character of the Late Dr. Samuel Annesley, by Way of Elegy.*

Bibliography

This bibliography is divided into six sections:

A. Manuscripts and printed books with marginalia
B. Editions from pre-1750 manuscript materials
C. Pre-1750 printed books
D. Critical works on life-writing (in chronological order)
E. Other post-1750 printed books
F. Unpublished dissertations
G. Electronic resources

A. *Manuscripts and printed books with marginalia*

Archivum Britannicum Societatis Iesu, London

MS 949: Tobie Matthew to Mary Gage, 16 August 1611 (copy) (pp. 305–53)

Beinecke Library, Yale University, New Haven, CT

Osborn MS fb150: Martha Moulsworth, 'The Memorandum of Martha Moulsworth', 1632 (item 6)

Bodleian Library, Oxford

Add. A. 186: documents relating to Thomas Bodley

Aubrey 2: John Aubrey, 'A Naturall Historie of Wiltshire'

Aubrey 3: John Aubrey, 'An Essay Towards the Description of the North Division of Wiltshire'

Aubrey 6–8: John Aubrey, 'Brief Lives'

Aubrey 9: John Aubrey, 'The Life of Mr Thomas Hobbes of Malmesbury'

Aubrey 10: John Aubrey, 'An Idea of Education of Young Gentlemen'

Aubrey 12: correspondence, Samuel Hartlib to John Aubrey, 1653 (fo. 155^{r}).

Ballard 14: correspondence, John Aubrey to Anthony Wood, 1680 (fos. 125^{r}, 126^{r}, 131^{r})

Don.g.9: Thomas Hassell, funeral sermons (on Martha Moulsworth, fos. 31^{r}–55^{r})

e Musaeo 86: Thomas Netter of Walden, 'Fasciculi Zizaniorum Magistri Johannis Wyclif', with annotations and index by John Bale

Eng. Misc. c. 330: Thomas Whythorne, 'A Book of Songs and Sonetts'

J. Walker c. 2: papers connected to a projected life of John Hales, by Anthony Faringdon, George Stradling, and Izaak Walton (fos. 196^{r}, 198–9)

Selden Supra 41: works by John Bale

Tanner 456a: correspondence, John Aubrey to Anthony Wood, 1680 (fo. 23^{r})

Wood F. 39: correspondence, John Aubrey to Anthony Wood, 1680–2 (fos. 340^{r}, 347^{r}, 368^{r-v})

Wood F. 43: correspondence, Edward Roswell to Anthony Wood, 1683 (fo. 312^{r})

British Library, London

Additional 24475: Joseph Hunter, notes (from 1819)

Additional 33737: Nicholas Harpsfield, 'A Treatise…Concerning Marriage, Occasioned by the Pretended Diuourse betweene King Henry the Eight and Queene Katherine' (fos. 2^{r}–314^{v})

Additional 43827: Rose Throckmorton, 'Certaine Old Stories Recorded by an Aged Gentlewoman…about the Yeer our Lord 1610' (fos. 1^{r}–18^{v})

Cotton Cleopara C. v: John Taylor, diary, 1513 (fos. 65–96)

Cotton Cleopatra E. iv: John Bale to Thomas Cromwell, [1537?] (fo. 167^{r})

Cotton Titus C.vii: 'Ex vita Thomæ Bodlei sua manu discripta' (fos. 173^{r}–174^{v})

Cotton Vitellius F.v: Henry Machyn, journal

Egerton 2614: Lady Margaret Hoby, diary, 1599–1605

Harley MS 421: Simonds D'Ewes, diary, 1622–4

Harley MS 422: Edmund Campion's debates, with Richard Topcliffe's marginalia (fos. 136^{r}–147^{r}, 136^{r}–147^{r})

Harley 3838: John Bale, various works

Harley 5353: John Manningham, diary

Harley 6037: Samuel Clarke, draft life of John Preston (fo. 15^{v})

Lansdowne 35: correspondence, Fleetwood to Burghley, 14 April 1582 (fos. 87–9)

Lansdowne 879: William Segar and Randle Holme, 'The Book of ffuneralls in Chesshiere, Lanc. Salop. & Northwales, & c.' (fo. 7^{r})

Dr Williams's Library, London

Baxter 61.13: diary of Richard Rogers

Emmanuel College, Cambridge

MS 76: writings by Nicholas Harpsfield, including 'The Life of Sir Thomas More', fos. 1^{r}–57^{r}, with Richard Topcliffe's marginalia

Exeter University Library, Exeter

Special Collections, ROWSE/POL: Girolamo Pollini, *L'historia ecclesiastica della rivoluzion d'Inghilterra, divisa in libri Quattro* (Rome: Guglielmo Facciotti, 1594), with Richard Topcliffe's marginalia

Folger Shakespeare Library, Washington, DC

C.b.10, no. 66: Francis Douce to George Steevens, n.d.

K.b.1: Richard Topcliffe, examination reports of Jesuits (1587)

V.a.38: Katherine Packer, 'A Book of Very Good Medecines for Several Diseases Wounds and Sores Both New and Old' (1639)

V.a.166: life of Lady Constance Lucy by Elizabeth Lucy; life of Elizabeth Lucy by Martha Eyre

V.a.269: Tobie Matthew, 'A true historicall Relation' (1640)

V.a.459–461: Richard Stonley, diaries

V.b.110: Henry Oxinden, miscellany

Hatfield House

CP 23/100: correspondence, Vincent Skynner to William Cecil, lord Burghley, 1593

CP 68/44, 176/115, 180/100, 181/18, 181/140, correspondence, Richard Vaughan to Robert Cecil, 1599–1601

CP 79/79: 'Ryottes in Lancashire', [1600]

CP 165/41, 165/43, 166/79, correspondence, Richard Stonley to William Cecil, lord Burghley, 1588

Massachusetts Historical Society, Boston, MA

Ms. SBd-20: Michael Wigglesworth, diary

The National Archives, Kew

PC 2/13: Privy Council minutes, 8 April 1582 (fo. 67^{r})

PROB 11/62: will of William Lambe, 10 March 1579/80

PROB 11/63: will of Martha Dorsett, 19 January 1580/1

PROB 11/152/99: will of Arthur Lake, 27 December 1625

PROB 11/159: will of Bevill Molesworth, 17 February 1631/2

PROB 11/174: will of Lady Constance Lucy, 3 and 16 May 1635

PROB 11/197: will of Martha Moulsworth, 19 July 1646

SP 12/216: correspondence, Richard Tailor to William Cecil, lord Burghley, 1588 (fo. 61^{r})

SP 12/256: correspondence, Dudley Carleton to Mr Hickes, [1596/7] (fos. 29^{r}–30^{r})

SP 12/266: correspondence, Dudley Carleton to John Chamberlain, [1596/7] (fo. 16^{r}); Tobie Matthew to Carleton, [1596/7?] (fo. 30^{r})

SP 12/275: interrogations about the 20 August 1601 attack in Lancashire (pp. 105–10, art. 64)

SP 14/72: correspondence, John Chamberlain to Alice Carleton (fo. 34^{v}); Chamberlain to Dudley Carleton (fo. 162^{r}), 1613

SP 14/74: correspondence, John Chamberlain to Dudley Carleton, 1613 (fo. 20^{r})

SP 14/175: James I, warrant for Lady Constance Lucy, 1624 (fo. 72)

SP 15/34: declaration by Greenloe, [November 1599 or 1600?] (fo. 38^{r})

SP 16/49: notes by Windebank of business transacted by the Privy Council, 7 October 1640 (fo. 104^{r})

SP 16/464: correspondence, Thomas Windebank to Charles I, 1640 (fo. 101^{r})

SP 16/468: libel against Tobie Matthew et al., 1639 (fo. 266^{r})

SP 16/520: 'The Maner & Vsuage of Lambs Chappell', [1648?] (fo. 84^{r})

SP 18/153: John Hingston et al. to the Committee of Council for Music, 1656/7 (fo. 253)

SP 29/334: list of those tried at the London and Middlesex Sessions, 26 February 1673 (fo. 19^{r})

SP 44/336: Robert Spencer, 2nd earl of Sunderland, warrant to Thomas Beake, 19 March 1684/5 (fo. 45^{r})

SP 46/15: diary of R[ichard] C[arnsew] (fos. 212^{r}–219^{v})

SP 46/16: diary of William Carnsew (fos. 38^{r}–52^{v})

STAC 5/A8/31: papers relating to Lancashire riots, 1601

Northamptonshire Central Library, Northampton

Northamptonshire Studies Collection, Accession No. 7839: Grace Mildmay, journal [consulted on CD-ROM at the British Library]

Sheffield University Library

Hartlib Papers [HP] 28/2/42B–43A, 49B (*Ephemerides*, 1652, 1653) [consulted online]

Hartlib Papers [HP] 29/5/54B, 57A (*Ephemerides*, 1655) [consulted online]

B. *Editions from pre-1700 manuscript materials*

Alexander, Jon ed., *American Personal Religious Accounts 1600–1980: Toward an Inner History of America's Faiths* (New York: The Edwin Mellen Press, 1983).

Arber, Edward ed., *A Transcript of the Registers of the Company of Stationers of London, 1554–1640 A.D.*, 5 vols (London: privately printed, 1875–94).

Archbold, W. A. J. ed., 'A Diary of the Expedition of 1544', *English Historical Review* 16 (1901), 503–7.

Ashbee, Andrew ed., *Records of English Court Music*, vol. 7, (1485–1558) (Aldershot: Scolar Press, 1993).

Aubrey, John, *Brief Lives with an Apparatus for the Lives of our English Mathematical Writers*, ed. Kate Bennett, 2 vols (Oxford: Oxford University Press, 2015).

Austen, Katherine, *Katherine Austen's Book M: British Library, Additional Manuscript 4454*, ed. Sarah C. E. Ross (Tempe, AZ: ACMRS [Arizona Center for Medieval and Renaissance Studies], 2011).

Ba, Ro, *The Lyfe of Sir Thomas More, Sometimes Lord Chancellor of England*, ed. Elsie Vaughan Hitchcock and P. E. Hallett, with A. W. Reed (London: Early English Text Society, 1950).

Baillie, Robert, *Letters and Journals of Robert Baillie, A.M., Principal of the University of Glasgow, M.DC.XXXVII–M.DC.LXII*, ed. David Laing, 3 vols (Edinburgh: Robert Ogle, 1842).

Blair, Robert, *Robert Blair of Bangor, Containing his Autobiography from 1593 to 1636*, ed. Thomas McCrie (London: Woodrow Society, 1848).

Bloxam, John Rouse ed., *A register of the presidents, fellows, demies, instructors in grammar and in music, chaplains, clerks, choristers, and other members of Saint Mary Magdalen College in the University of Oxford, from the foundation of the College to the present time, The demies*, vol. I (Oxford and London: James Parker, 1873).

Boyle, Robert, 'An Account of Philaretus during his Minority', in Robert Boyle et al., *Robert Boyle by Himself and his Friends, with a Fragment of William Wotton's Lost Life of Boyle*, ed. Michael Hunter (London: William Pickering, 1994), 2–22.

Bramston, John, *The Autobiography of Sir John Bramston, K.B., of Skreens, in the Hundred of Chelmsford*, ed. Thomas William Bramston (London: Camden Society, 1845).

Brook, Benjamin, *The Lives of the Puritans*, 3 vols (London: James Black, 1813).

Calamy, Edmund, 'The Introduction' to *An Historical Account of My Own Life, with Some Reflections on the Times I Have Lived in.* (1671–1731), ed. John Towill Rutt, 2 vols (London: Henry Colburn and Richard Bentley, 1829), 1:1–51.

Campion, Edmund, *A Jesuit Challenge: Edmund Campion's Debates at the Tower of London in 1581*, ed. James V. Holleran (New York: Fordham University Press, 1999).

Caraman, Philip ed., *The Other Face: Catholic Life under Elizabeth I* (New York: Sheed and Ward, 1960).

Carnsew, William, 'William Carnsew of Bokelly and his Diary, 1576–7', ed. N. J. G. Pounds, *Journal of the Royal Institution of Cornwall* n. s. 8 (1978), 14–60.

[Carter, Oliver], 'A description of the state, civil and ecclesiastical, of the county of Lancaster, about the year 1590, by some of the clergy of the diocese of Chester', in *Chetham Miscellanies* V, ed. F. R. Raines (Manchester: Chetham Society, 1875), 5–7.

Cavendish, George, *The Life and Death of Cardinal Wolsey*, ed. Richard S. Sylvester (London: Oxford University Press, 1959).

Chamberlain, John, *The Letters of John Chamberlain*, ed. Norman Egbert McClure, 2 vols (Philadelphia: The American Philosophical Society, 1939).

Clifford, Anne, *The Diary of Anne Clifford, 1616-1619*, ed. Katherine O. Acheson (New York: Garland, 1995).

Clifford, Anne, *Anne Clifford's Great Books of Record*, ed. Jessica L. Malay (Manchester: Manchester University Press, 2015).

Daemen-de Gelder, Katrien ed., *Life Writing II*, vol. 4 of *English Convents in Exile, 1600-1800*, general ed. Caroline Bowden, 6 vols (London: Pickering & Chatto, 2013).

Dallam, Thomas, 'The Diary of Master Thomas Dallam, 1599-1600', *Early Voyages and Travels in the Levant*, ed. J. T. Bent, Hakluyt Society, 87 (1893), 1-98.

Dee, John, *Autobiographical Tracts of Dr. John Dee*, ed. James Crossley, in *Remains Historical & Literary Connected with the Palatine Counties of Lancaster and Chester* 24 (Manchester: Chetham Society, 1851), 1-45.

Dee, John, *The Private Diary and Catalogue of his Library of Manuscripts*, ed. James Orchard Halliwell (London: Camden Society, 1868).

Dee, John, *The Diaries of John Dee*, ed. Edward Fenton (Charlbury, Oxon: Day Books, 1998).

Delaval, Elizabeth, *The Meditations of Lady Elizabeth Delaval Written between 1662 and 1671*, ed. Douglas G. Greene (Gateshead: Northumberland Press for the Surtees Society, 1978).

D'Ewes, Simonds, *The Autobiography and Correspondence of Sir Simonds D'Ewes*, ed. James O. Halliwell, 2 vols (London: Bentley, 1845).

D'Ewes, Simonds, *The Journal of Sir Simonds D'Ewes from the Beginning of the Long Parliament to the Opening of the Trial of the Earl of Strafford*, ed. Wallace Notestein (New Haven, CT: Yale University Press, 1923).

D'Ewes, Simonds, *The diary of Sir Simonds D'Ewes (1622-1624): journal d'un étudiant londonien sous le règne de Jacques Ier*, ed. Elisabeth Bourcier, Publications de la Sorbonne, Littératures 5 (Paris: Didier, 1974).

Dickinson, Robert ed., *The Registers of the Parish of Childwall. Part I. 1557-1680* (Leyland, Preston: Lancashire Parish Register Society, 1967).

Digby, Kenelm, *Loose Fantasies*, ed. Vittorio Gabrieli (Rome: Edizioni di Storia e Letteratura, 1968).

Dowsing, William, *The Journal of William Dowsing: Iconoclasm in East Anglia during the English Civil War*, ed. Trevor Cooper (Woodbridge, Suffolk: Boydell & Brewer, 2001).

Drake, Francis, *New Light on Drake: A Collection of Documents Relating to his Voyage of Circumnavigation*, trans./ed. Zelia Nuttall (London: Hakluyt Society, 1914).

Drummond, William, 'Informations be Ben Johnston to W. D.', ed. Ian Donaldson, in *The Cambridge Edition of the Works of Ben Jonson Online* (Cambridge: Cambridge University Press, 2014-15).

Edward VI, *Literary Remains of King Edward the Sixth*, ed. John Gough Nichols, 2 vols (London: Roxburghe Club, 1857).

Edward VI, *The Chronicle and Political Papers*, ed. W. K. Jordan (Ithaca, NY: Cornell University Press for the Folger Shakespeare Library, 1966).

Evelyn, John, *The Diary of John Evelyn*, ed. E. S. de Beer, 6 vols (Oxford: Clarendon Press, 1955).

Fanshawe, Ann, *The Memoirs of Anne, Lady Halkett and Ann, Lady Fanshawe*, ed. John Loftis (Oxford: Clarendon Press, 1979).

Fry, E. A. ed., *Abstracts of Inquisitiones Post Mortem for the City of London: Part 3* (London, 1908).

Garman, Mary et al., *Hidden in Plain Sight: Quaker Women's Writings, 1650-1700* (Wallingford, PA: Pendle Hill Publications, 1996).

Gerard, John, *The Autobiography of a Hunted Priest*, trans. Philip Caraman (New York: Pellegrini & Cudahy, 1952).

Graham, Elspeth, Hilary Hinds, Elaine Hobby, and Helen Wilcox eds, *Her Own Life: Autobiographical Writings by Seventeenth-Century Englishwomen* (London: Routledge, 1989).

Graham, Timothy and Andrew G. Watson, *The Recovery of the Past in Early Elizabethan England: Documents by John Bale and John Joscelyn from the Circle of Matthew Parker* (Cambridge: Cambridge Bibliographical Society, 1998).

Halkett, Anne, *The Memoirs of Anne, Lady Halkett and Ann, Lady Fanshawe*, ed. John Loftis (Oxford: Clarendon Press, 1979).

Halkett, Anne, *Lady Anne Halkett: Selected Self-Writings*, ed. Suzanne Trill (Aldershot: Ashgate, 2007).

Hallett, Nicky ed., *Lives of Spirit: English Carmelite Self-Writing of the Early Modern Period* (Aldershot: Ashgate, 2007).

Hallett, Nicky ed., *Life Writing I*, vol. 3 of *English Convents in Exile, 1600-1800*, general ed. Caroline Bowden, 6 vols (London: Pickering & Chatto, 2012).

Harington, John, *A Supplie or Addicion to the Catalogue of Bishops to the Yeare 1608*, ed. R. H. Miller (Potomac, MD: José Porrúa Turanzas, 1979).

Harpsfield, Nicholas, *A Treatise on the Pretended Divorce between Henry VIII. and Catharine of Aragon*, ed. Nicholas Pocock (London: Camden Society, 1878).

Harpsfield, Nicholas, *The Life and Death of Sr Thomas Moore, Knight, Sometimes Lord High Chancellor of England*, ed. Elsie Vaughan Hitchcock and R. W. Chambers (London: Oxford University Press for the Early English Text Society, 1932).

Herbert, Edward, Lord Herbert of Cherbury, *The Life of Edward, First Lord Herbert of Cherbury Written by Himself*, ed. J. M. Shuttleworth (London: Oxford University Press, 1976).

Heywood, Oliver, *The Rev. Oliver Heywood, B.A. 1630-1702; His Autobiography, Diaries, Anecdote and Event Books; Illustrating the General and Family History of Yorkshire and Lancashire*, ed. J. Horsfall Turner, 4 vols (Brighouse: A.B. Bayes for the editor, 1882, A.B. Bayes, 1881; Bingley: T. Harrison, 1883, T. Harrison for the editor, 1885).

Heywood, Oliver, *Oliver Heywood's Life of John Angier of Denton together with Angier's Diary, and Extracts from his 'An Helpe to Better Hearts': also Samuel Angier's Diary*, ed. Ernest Axon (Manchester: Chetham Society, 1937).

Historical Manuscripts Commission, *Report on the Manuscripts of the Duke of Buccleuch and Queensberry, K.G., K.T., Preserved at Montagu House, Whitehall* (London: HMSO, 1899).

Historical Manuscripts Commission, *Report on Manuscripts in Various Collections, III, The Manuscripts of T. B. Clarke-Thornhill, Esq., Sir T. Barrett-Lennard, Bart., Pelham R. Papillon, Esq., and W. Cleverly Alexander, Esq.* (London: HMSO, 1904).

Hoby, Margaret, *Diary of Lady Margaret Hoby 1599-1605*, ed. Dorothy M. Meads (London: George Routledge, 1930).

Hoby, Margaret, *The Private Life of an Elizabethan lady: The Diary of Lady Margaret Hoby 1599-1605*, ed. Joanna Moody (Thrupp: Sutton, 1998).

Honywell, William, 'A Devonshire Yeoman's Diary', ed. F. J. Snell, *The Antiquary* 26 (1892) 254-9.

Hooke, Robert, *The Diary of Robert Hooke...1672-1680*, ed. Henry W. Robinson and Walter Adams (London: Taylor & Francis, 1935).

Howell, T. B. ed., *Cobbett's Complete Collection of State Trials and Proceedings for High Treason and Other Crimes and Misdemeanors from the Earliest Period to the Present Time*, vol. 7 (London: T. C. Hansard, 1810).

Hutchinson, Lucy, *Memoirs of the Life of Colonel Hutchinson Governor of Nottingham by his Widow Lucy*, ed. Julius Hutchinson, rev. C. H. Firth, 2 vols (London: John C. Nimmo, 1885).

Hutchinson, Lucy, *Memoirs of the Life of Colonel Hutchinson with the Fragment of an Autobiography of Mrs. Hutchinson*, ed. James Sutherland (London: Oxford University Press, 1973).

Jeake, Samuel, *An Astrological Diary of the Seventeenth Century: Samuel Jeake of Rye 1652-1699*, ed. Michael Hunter and Annabel Gregory (Oxford: Clarendon Press, 1988).

Johnson, Cicely *see* Thurgood, Rose and Cicely Johnson.

Josselin, Ralph, *The Diary of Ralph Josselin 1616-83*, ed. Alan Macfarlane (Oxford: Oxford University Press, 1976).

Kenny, Anthony ed., *The Responsa Scholarum of the English College, Rome*, 2 vols ([Bromley]: Catholic Record Society, 1962).

King, Henry, *The Poems of Henry King*, ed. Margaret Crum (Oxford: Clarendon Press, 1965).

King, Thomas William with F. R. Raines, eds, *Lancashire Funeral Certificates* in *Remains Historical and Literary Connected with the Palatine Counties of Lancaster and Chester*, vol. 75 (Manchester: Chetham Society, 1869).

Komensky, Jan Amos, *Dílo Jana Amose Komenského*, vol. 14, ed. Ludvík Svoboda, Jarmila Borská, and Julie Nováková (Prague: Academia, 1974).

Lang, R. G. ed., *Two Tudor Subsidy Assessment Rolls for the City of London: 1541 and 1582* (London: London Record Society, 1993).

Leland, John, *De uiris illustribus. On Famous Men*, ed./trans. James P. Carley with Caroline Brett (Toronto: Pontifical Institute of Mediaeval Studies/Bodleian Library, 2010).

Lenox-Conyngham, Melosina ed., *Diaries in Ireland: An Anthology 1590-1987* (Dublin: The Lilliput Press, 1998).

Lowe, Roger, *The Diary of Roger Lowe of Ashton-in-Makerfield, Lancashire 1663-74*, ed. William L. Sachse, foreword by Wallace Notestein (New Haven, CT: Yale University Press, 1938).

Luttrell, Narcissus, *A Brief Historical Relation of State Affairs from September 1678 to April 1714*, 6 vols (Oxford: at the University Press, 1857).

Madox, Richard, *An Elizabethan in 1582: The Diary of Richard Madox, Fellow of All Souls*, ed. Elizabeth Story Donno (London: Hakluyt Society, 1976).

Makin, Bathsua, 'Upon the Much Lamented Death of the Right Honourable the Lady Elizabeth Langham', in *Early Modern Women Poets (1520-1700): An Anthology*, ed. Jane Stevenson and Peter Davidson (Oxford: Oxford University Press, 2001), 221-2.

Manningham, John, *The Diary of John Manningham of the Middle Temple, 1602–1603*, ed. R. P. Sorlien (Hanover, NH: University Press of New England for the University of Rhode Island, 1976).

Mather, Cotton, *Magnalia Christi Americana; or, the Ecclesiastical History of New-England*, ed. Thomas Robbins, 2 vols (Hartford, CT: Silas Andrus & Son, 1853).

Matthew, Tobie, *A true historical relation of the conversion of Sir Tobie Matthew to the holy Catholic faith; with the antecedents and consequences thereof*, ed. A. H. Mathew (London: Burns & Oates, 1908).

Matthew, Tobie, *The Life of Lady Lucy Knatchbull*, ed. David Knowles (London: Sheed and Ward, 1931).

Melville, James, *The Diary of Rev. James Melville*, ed. G. R. Kinloch (Edinburgh: Bannatyne Club, 1829).

Melville, James, *The Autobiography and Diary of Rev. James Meville*, ed. R. Pitcairn (Edinburgh: Wodrow Club, 1842).

Mildmay, Grace, *With Faith and Physic: The Life of a Tudor Gentlewoman, Lady Grace Mildmay, 1552–1620*, ed. Linda Pollock (London: Collins & Brown, 1993).

Mildmay, Grace, 'The Autobiography of Grace, Lady Mildmay', ed. Randall Martin, *Renaissance and Reformation/Renaissance et Réforme* n.s. 18 (1994), 33–81.

Morrice, Roger, *The Entering Booke of Roger Morrice 1677–1691*, vol. 2, *The Reign of Charles II 1677–1685*, ed. John Spurr (Woodbridge, Suffolk: The Boydell Press/The Parliamentary History Yearbook Trust, 2007).

Morrice, Roger, *The Entering Booke of Roger Morrice 1677–1691*, vol. 3, *The Reign of James II 1685–1687*, ed. Tim Harris (Woodbridge, Suffolk: The Boydell Press/The Parliamentary History Yearbook Trust, 2007).

Moulsworth, Martha, *'My Name Was Martha': A Renaissance Woman's Autobiographical Poem*, ed. Robert C. Evans and Barbara Wiedemann (West Cornwall, CT: Locust Hill Press, 1993).

Moulsworth, Martha, *'The Muses Female Are': Martha Moulsworth and Other Women Writers of the English Renaissance*, ed. Robert C. Evans and Anne C. Little (West Cornwall, CT: Locust Hill Press, 1995).

Netter, Thomas, *Fasciculi Zizaniorum Magistri Johannis Wyclif, Ascribed to Thomas Netter of Walden*, ed. Walter Waddington Shirley, Rolls Series 5 (London, 1858).

Newcome, Henry, *The Diary of the Rev. Henry Newcome, from September 30, 1661, to September 29, 1663*, ed. Thomas Heywood (Manchester: Chetham Society, 1849).

Newcome, Henry, *The Autobiography of Henry Newcome*, ed. R. Parkinson, 2 vols (Manchester: Chetham Society, 1852).

North, Roger, *General Preface and Life of Dr John North*, ed. Peter Millard (Toronto: University of Toronto Press, 1984).

Norwood, Richard, *The Journal of Richard Norwood, Surveyor of Bermuda*, ed. Wesley Frank Craven and Walter B. Hayward (New York: Scholars' Facsimiles & Reprints for the Bermuda Historical Monuments Trust, 1945).

Pepys, Samuel, *Letters and the Second Diary of Samuel Pepys*, ed. R. G. Howarth (London: J. M. Dent and Sons, 1932).

Pepys, Samuel, *Shorthand Letters of Samuel Pepys. From a Volume Entitled S. Pepys's Official Correspondence 1662–1679*, ed. Edwin Chappell (Cambridge: University Press, 1933).

Pepys, Samuel, *The Diary of Samuel Pepys: A New and Complete Transcription*, ed. Robert Latham and William Matthews, 10 vols (London: G. Bell and Sons, 1970–83).

Pepys, Samuel, *The Illustrated Pepys: Extracts from the Diary*, ed. Robert Latham (Berkeley, CA: University of California Press, 1978).

Pepys, Samuel, *Catalogue of the Pepys Library at Magdalene College Cambridge*, volume VII, *Facsimile of Pepys' Catalogue*, ed. David McKitterick, photographs by Gerry Bye, 2 pts (Cambridge: D. S. Brewer, 1991).

Pepys, Samuel, *Samuel Pepys and the Second Dutch War: Pepys's Navy White Book and Brooke House Papers*, transcribed by William Matthews and Charles Knighton, ed. Robert Latham (Aldershot: Scolar Press for the Navy Records Society, 1995).

Perrot, James, *The history of that most eminent statesman, Sir John Perrott, Knight of the Bath, and Lord Lieutenant of Ireland... Now first published from the original manuscript, written about the latter end of the reign of Queen Elizabeth*, ed. Richard Rawlinson (London: n.pub., 1728).

Powell, Walter, *The Diary of Walter Powell of Llantilio Crossenny in the County of Monmouth, Gentleman. 1603–1654*, ed. Joseph Alfred Bradney (Bristol: John Wright, 1907).

Questier, Michael ed., *Newsletters from the Caroline Court, 1631–1638: Catholicism and the Politics of the Personal Rule* (Cambridge: Cambridge University Press for the Royal Historical Society, 2005).

'Reyerardus', *Hierorachomachia or The Anti-Bishop*, ed. Suzanne Gossett (East Brunswick, NJ: Bucknell University Press, 1982).

[Rich], Mary, countess of Warwick, *Autobiography of Mary Countess of Warwick*, ed. T. Crofton Croker (London: Percy Society, 1848).

Rogers, John, 'Sixty Memorials for a Godly Life', in Cotton Mather, *Antiquities. The First Book of the New-English History* (London: Thomas Parkhurst, 1702), 3:109–13.

Rogers, Richard, 'The Rogers Family: The Will of Rev. Richard Rogers of Wethersfield, Co. Essex, England. The Will of Rev. John Rogers of Dedham, Co. Essex, England', *The New-England Historical and Genealogical Register* 17 (1847–8), 326–30.

Rogers, Richard, 'The Diary of Richard Rogers', in *Two Elizabethan Puritan Diaries*, ed. M. M. Knappen (Chicago: The American Society of Church History, 1933), 53–102.

Rogers, Samuel, *The Diary of Samuel Rogers, 1634–1638*, ed. Tom Webster and Kenneth Shipps (Woodbridge, Suffolk: The Boydell Press/Church of England Record Society, 2004).

Roper, William, *The Lyfe of Sir Thomas Moore, Knighte*, ed. Elsie Vaughan Hitchcock (London: Early English Text Society, 1935).

Savage, Sarah, *Memoirs of the Life & Character of Mrs. Sarah Savage*, ed. J. B. Williams (London: Holdsworth and Ball, 1828).

Shepard, Thomas, *God's Plot: The Paradoxes of Puritan Piety; Being the Autobiography & Journal of Thomas Shepard*, ed. Michael McGiffert ([Amherst, MA]: University of Massachusetts Press, 1972).

Slingsby, Henry, *The Diary of Sir Henry Slingsby, of Scriven, Bart.*, ed. Daniel Parsons (London: Longman et al., 1830).

Starkey, George, *Alchemical Laboratory Notebooks and Correspondence*, ed. William R. Newman and Lawrence M. Principe (Chicago: University of Chicago Press, 2004).

Strafford, earl of *see* Wentworth, Thomas, earl of Strafford.

Thoresby, Ralph, *The Diary of Ralph Thoresby, F. R. S. Author of the Topography of Leeds (1677–1624). Now First Published from the Original Manuscript*, ed. Joseph Hunter, 2 vols (London: Henry Colburn and Richard Bentley, 1830).

Thornton, Alice, *The Autobiography of Alice Thornton of East Newton, Co. York*, ed. Charles Jackson (Durham: Surtees Society, 1875).

Thurgood, Rose and Cicely Johnson, *Scripture Women: Rose Thurgood, 'A Lecture of Repentance' & Cicely Johnson, 'Fanatical Reveries'*, ed. Naomi Baker (Nottingham: Trent Editions, 2005).

Torkington, Richard, *Ye Oldest Diarie of Englysshe Travell: being the hitherto unpublished narrative of the pilgrimage of Sir Richard Torkington to Jerusalem in 1517*, ed. W. J. Loftie (London: Field & Tuer, 1884).

Treswell, Ralph, *The London Surveys of Ralph Treswell*, ed. John Schofield (London: London Topographical Society, 1987).

Wallington, Nehemiah, *The Notebooks of Nehemiah Wallington, 1618–1654: A Selection*, ed. David Booy (Aldershot: Ashgate, 2007).

Walsingham, Francis, 'Journal of Sir Francis Walsingham, from Dec. 1570 to April 1583', ed. Charles Trice Martin, in *Camden Miscellany* 6 (London: Camden Society, 1870).

Ward, Samuel, 'The Diary of Samuel Ward', in *Two Elizabethan Puritan Diaries*, ed. M. M. Knappen (Chicago: The American Society of Church History, 1933), 103–23.

Warwick, Mary, countess of, *see* [Rich], Mary, countess of Warwick.

Wentworth, Thomas, earl of Strafford, *The Earl of Strafforde's Letters and Dispatches*, ed. William Knowler, 2 vols (London: William Bowyer, 1739).

Weston, William, *William Weston: The Autobiography of an Elizabethan*, trans. Philip Caraman (London: Longmans, Freen, 1955).

Whythorne, Thomas, *The Autobiography of Thomas Whythorne*, ed. James M. Osborn (Oxford: Clarendon Press, 1961).

Whythorne, Thomas, *The Autobiography of Thomas Whythorne: Modern Spelling Edition*, ed. James M. Osborn (Oxford: Clarendon Press, 1962).

Wigglesworth, Michael, *The Diary of Michael Wigglesworth, 1653–1657; The Conscience of a Puritan*, ed. Edmund S. Morgan (New York: Harper Row, 1965).

Wilson, Arthur, 'The Life of Mr. Arthur Wilson the Historian', in *Desiderata curiosa: or, a collection of divers scarce and curious pieces relating chiefly to matters of history*, ed. Francis Peck, rev. edn, 2 vols (London: Thomas Evans, 1779), 2:460–83.

Woodford, Robert, *The Diary of Robert Woodford, 1637–1641*, ed. John Fielding (Cambridge: Cambridge University Press for the Royal Historical Society, 2012).

Worthington, John, *The Diary and Correspondence of Dr. John Worthington*, ed. James Crossley, vol. 1 (Manchester: Chetham Society, 1847).

Wotton, Henry, *The Life and Letters of Sir Henry Wotton*, ed. Logan Pearsall Smith, 2 vols (Oxford: Clarendon Press, 1907).

C. Pre-1750 printed books, and later editions

Adam, Melchior, *Vitae Germanorum philosophorum*, 2nd edn (Heidelberg: impensis Ionæ Rosæ, 1615).

Adam, Melchior, *Decades duae continentes vitas theologorum exterorum principium* (Frankfurt am Maim: sumptibus J. Rosae, 1618).

Adam, Melchior, *Vitae Germanorum iureconsultorum et politicorum* (Heidelberg: heredum Ionæ Rosæ, 1620).

Adam, Melchior, *Vitae Germanorum medicorum* (Heidelberg: heredum Ionæ Rosæ, 1620).

Adam, Melchior, *Vitae Germanorum theologorum* (Heidelberg: impensis Ionæ Rosæ, 1620).

Aelfric, Abbot of Eynsham, *A Testimonie of Antiquitie*, [ed. John Joscelyn and Matthew Parker] (London: John Day, 1566), STC 159.5.

Amboise, Pierre, 'Discovrs svr la vie de Mre Francois Bacon, chancelier d' Angleterre', in *Histoire natvrelle de Mre Francois Bacon, Baron de Verulan, Vicomte de sainct Alban, & Chancelier d'Angleterre*, ed./trans. Pierre Amboise (Paris: Antoine de Sommaville & André Sovbron, 1631), A1^{r}–B5^{v}.

Ambrose, Isaac, *Media: The Middle Things, in Reference to the First and Last Things: or, The means, duties, ordinances, both secret, private and publike, for continuance and increase of a godly life, once begun, till we come to Heaven* (London: John Field for Nathanaell Webb and William Grantham, 1650 [i.e. 1649]), Wing A2958.

Anderson, Anthony, *A Sermon of Sure Comfort Preached at the Funerall of Master Robert Keylwey Esquire, at Exton in Rutland, the 18. of Marche 1580.* (London: H. Middleton, 1581), STC 569.

Anon., [*In this boke ar conteynyd .xx. songes. ix. of .iiii. partes, and xi. of thre partes*] (London: 'At the signe of the black Mores', 1530), STC 22924.

Anon., *A true reporte of the death & martyrdome of M. Campion Jesuite and preiste, & M. Sherwin, & M. Bryan preistes, at Tiborne the first of December 1581. Observid and written by a Catholike preist, which was present therat. Whereunto is annexid certayne verses made by sundrie persons* ([London]: [R. Rowlands or Verstegan], 1582), STC 4537.

Anon., *A Liuing Remembrance of Master Robert Rogers, Marchant Aduenturer & Leatherseller of London Deceased* (London: M. Allde, 1601), STC 21224.

Anon., *The Life and Death of Mrs. Margaret Andrews* (London: Nathaniel Ponder, 1680), Wing L2004.

Anon., *Don Tomazo, or, the Juvenile Rambles of Thomas Dangerfield* (London: William Rumbald, 1680), Wing D185.

Anon., *The behaviour, confession, and execution, of the four prisoners at Tyburn William Blower, for high treason; Robert Francis for the murther of Tho. Dangerfield, Henry Anthony, and John Morgan for two several burglarys and fellonies. On Friday the 24 of this instant July, 1685* ([London: E. Mallet, [1685]), Wing B1705.

Anon., *Dangerfields Dance giving an account of several notorious crimes by him committed, viz, he pretended to be a Duke, and feigned himself to be Monmouth, with several other pranks: for which he was sentenced stand in the pillory, to be whip'd at the carts arse, and to be sent back to prison* (London: J. M., 1685), Wing D194.

Anon., *Dangerfield's Ghost to Jefferys* (n.p.: n.pub., [1685?]), Wing D194A.

Anon., *The doleful lamentation of Thomas who was lately apprehended and imprisoned in Newgate, for high misdemeaner & c.: to the tune of 'Tis for mine own offence I must dye* (London: J. Huzzey, 1685), Wing D1838.

Anon., *Duke Dangerfield declaring how he represented the D. of Mon– in the country with his miraculous gift of touching, making knights, and other pranks in Staffordshire: how he was brought to town, examin'd before the King and counsell, and committed to Newgate* (London: J. Smith, 1685), Wing D2506.

Anon., *A true narrative of the arraignment, tryal, and conviction of Thomas Dangerfield for high-misdemeanors against His Present Majesty, James the Second, at the King's-Bench-Barr, at Westminster, on Saturday, May the 30th, 1685* (London: E. Mallet, 1685), Wing T2776.

Anon., *A true relation of the sentence and condemnation of Thomas Dangerfield, at the King's Bench Bar, for his horrid crimes and perjuries* ([London: Walter Davis], 1685), Wing T3044.

Anon., *Wish upon wish, or Dangerfields lamentation. Being a true relation, of a discovery of all the rogueries of Captain Dangerfield, who now is a close prisoner in his Majestys gaol of Newgate, for acting the D. of M. in several countries in England. To the tune of, The old mans wish* (London: Absalom Chamberlain, [1685]), Wing D1797aA.

Anon., 'The History of the Life and Memoirs of Mrs. Behn', in Aphra Behn, *All the Histories and Novels* (London: Samuel Briscoe, 1698), Wing B1712, a6^r–d3^v.

Askew, Anne, *The First Examinacyon of Anne Askewe, Lately Martyred in Smythfelde*, ed. John Bale (Marpurg in the lande of Hessen [i.e. Wesel]: [D. van der Straten], 1546), STC 848.

Askew, Anne, *The Lattre Examinacyon of Anne Askewe, with the Elucydacyon of J. Bale* (Marpurg in the lande of Hessen [i.e. Wesel]: [D. van der Straten], 1547), STC 850.

Askew, Anne, *The Examinations of Anne Askew*, ed. Elaine V. Beilin (New York: Oxford University Press, 1996).

Aubrey, John, *Miscellanies upon the Following Subjects* (London: Edward Castle, 1696), Wing A4188.

Awdelay, John, *An Epitaphe vpon the Death [of] Mayster Iohn Viron Preacher* (London: John Awdelay, 1563), STC 992.

Babington, Gervase, *A funerall sermon Preached by the reuerend father in God, Geruase Babington, then bishop of Landaue, a little before his translation to Exeter, in the hearing of most of the knights and gentlemen of that diocesse* ([London]: I. Roberts, for Thomas Charde, 1595), STC 1089.

Bacon, Francis, *The Two Bookes... Of the Profiencie and Aduancement of Learning, Diuine and Humaine* (London: Henry Tomes, 1605), STC 1164.

Bacon, Francis, *Sylua syluarum: or A Naturall Historie In Ten Centuries*, ed. William Rawley (London: I[ohn] H[aviland and Augustine Mathewes] for William Lee, 1626 [i.e. 1627]), STC 1168.

Bacon, Francis, *Certaine Miscellany Works of the Right Honovrable, Francis Lo. Verulam, Viscount S. Alban*, ed. William Rawley (London: J. Haviland for Humphrey Robinson, 1629), STC 1124.

Bacon, Francis, *Histoire natvrelle de Mre Francois Bacon, Baron de Verulan, Vicomte de sainct Alban, & Chancelier d'Angleterre*, ed./trans. Pierre Amboise (Paris: Antoine de Sommaville & André Sovbron, 1631).

Bacon, Francis, *Historie Naturall and Experimentall, of Life and Death*, ed. [and trans.?] William Rawley (London: John Haviland for William Lee and Humphrey Mosley, 1638), STC 1158.

Bacon, Francis, *Operum moralium et civilium tomus*, ed. William Rawley (London: Edward Griffin[, John Haviland, Bernard Norton, and John Bill] for Richard Whitaker [and John Norton], 1638), STC 1110.

Bagshaw, Edward ed., 'The Life and Death of Mr. Bolton', in Robert Bolton, *Mr Boltons Last and Learned Worke of the Foure Last Things... Together with the Life and Death of the Author*, ed. E[dward] B[agshawe] (London: George Miller, 1632), STC 3242, a6^r–d2^r.

Bagshaw, Edward, *The Life and Death of Mr. Vavasor Powell* ([London]: n.pub., 1671), Wing L2003.

Bale, John, *A Brefe Chronycle Concernynge the Examinacyon and Death of the Blessed Martyr of Christ Syr Iohan Oldecastell the Lorde Cobham* ([Antwerp: Hans Luft?], 1544), STC 1276.

Bale, John, *A Mysterye of Inyquyte Contayned within the Heretycall Genealogye of Ponce Pantolabus* (Geneva [i.e. Antwerp]: Mycheal Woode [i.e. A. Goinus], 1545), STC 1303.

Bale, John, *Illustrium maioris Britanniae…summarium* (Wesel: Dirik van der Straten, 1548), STC 1295.

Bale, John, *The Vocacyon of Iohan Bale to the Bishoprick of Ossorie in Irelande* ([Wesel?: Joos Lambrecht and Hugh Singleton?], 1553), STC 1307.

Bale, John, *Scriptorum illustrium maioris Brytannicae…catalogus* (Basel: Johannes Oporinus, 1557), STC 1296 Variant.

Bale, John, *The Vocacyon of John Bale*, ed. Peter Happé and John N. King (Binghamton, NY: Medieval & Renaissance Texts & Studies/Renaissance English Text Society, 1990).
see also Askew, Anne; Harryson, Johan; Leland, John.

Ball, John, *The Power of Godlines, Both Doctrinally, and Practically Handled*, ed. Simeon Ashe (London: Abraham Miller for George Sawbridge, 1657), Wing B561.

Ball, John, *A Treatise of Divine Meditation*, ed. Simeon Ashe (London: H. Mortlock, 1660), Wing B575.

Baret, John, *An Alvearie or Triple Dictionarie, in Englishe, Latin, and French* ([London: Henry Denham, 1574]), STC 1410.

Barksdale, Clement, *Memorials of Worthy Persons Two Decads* (London: I. R., 1661), Wing B800.

Baxter, Richard, *A Breviate of the Life of Margaret, the Daughter of Francis Charlton…and Wife of Richard Baxter* (London: B. Simmons, 1681), Wing B1194.

Bayle, Pierre, *A General Dictionary Historical and Critical*, ed. John Peter Bernard, Thomas Birch, John Lockman, et al., vol. 8. (London: James Bettenham for G. Strahan et al., 1739).

Beadle, John, *The Journal or Diary of a Thankful Christian* (London: E. Cotes for Tho. Parkhurst, 1656), Wing B1557.

Biondi, Giuseppe, *A relation of the death of the most illustrious lord, Sigr. Troilo Sauelli, a Baron of Rome who was there beheaded, in the castle of Sant-Angelo, on the 18. of April, 1592*, [trans. Tobie Matthew] ([Saint Omer: English College Press], 1620), STC 3134.

Blount, Thomas, *Glossographia*, 2nd edn (London: Thomas Newcombe for George Sawbridge, 1661), Wing B3335.

Bodley, Thomas, *The Life of S*[i]*r Thomas Bodley, the Honourable Founder of the Publique Library in the Vniversity of Oxford* (Oxford: Henry Hall, 1647), Wing B3392.

Bodley, Thomas, *Reliquiæ Bodleianæ: or Some Genuine Remains of Sir Thomas Bodley*, [ed. Thomas Hearne] (London: John Hartley, 1703).

Bodley, Thomas, *The Autobiography of Thomas Bodley*, ed. William Clennell (Oxford: Bodleian Library, 2006).

Boissard, Jean-Jacques, *Icones quinquaginta virorum illustrium doctrina et eruditione praestantium ad vivum effictae* (Frankfurt am Main: Matthaeus Becker, haer. Theodor de Bry, 1597).

Bolton, Robert, *Instructions for a Right Comforting Afflicted Consciences* (London: Felix Kyngston for Thomas Weaver, 1631), STC 3238.

Book of Common Prayer, *The Booke of Common Prayer, and Administracion of the Sacramentes, and other Rites and Ceremonies in the Church of England* (London: Richard Jugge and John Cawood, 1559), STC 16293.3.

Booy, David ed., *Autobiographical Writings by Early Quaker Women* (Aldershot: Ashgate, 2004).

Bradford, John, *Two Notable Sermons...the One of Repentance, and the Other of the Lordes Supper*, ed. Thomas Sampson (London: John Awdely, and John Wyght, 1574), STC 3500.5.

Bradshaw, Henry, *Here begynneth the holy lyfe and history of Saynt Werburge very frutefull for all Christen people to rede* (London: Richard Pynson, 1521), STC 3506.

Bradshaw, Henry, *Here begynneth the lyfe of Saynt Radegunde* (London: Richard Pynson, 1525), STC 3507.

Brice, Thomas, *A Compendiou[s Regi]ster in Metre Contei[ning the] Names, and Pacient Suffry[ngs of the] Membres of Iesus Christ, a[nd the Tor]mented; and Cruelly Burned [within] Englande* ([London: John Kingston for Richard Adams], 1559), STC 3726.

Bright, Timothy, *Charac[terie.] An Ar[te] of Shorte, Swift[e], and Secrete Writing by Character* (London: J. Windet, 1588), STC 3743.

Bro[ke], Tho[mas], *An Epitaphe Declaryng the Lyfe and End of D. Edmund Boner & c.* (London: John Day, 1569), STC 3817.4.

Brooks, Thomas, *A Cabinet of Choice Jewels, or, A Box of Precious Ointment* (London: John Hancock, 1669), Wing B4937.

Buck, George, 'The third vniversitie of England', in John Stow, *The Annales, or a Generall Chronicle of England...vnto the Ende of this Present Yeere 1614*, rev. Edmond Howes (London: [Thomas Dawson] for Thomas Adams, 1615), STC 23338, $4L5^r$-$4O3^v$.

Buckeridge, John, 'A Sermon Preached at the Funeral of the Right Honorable and Reverend Father in God Lancelot late Lord Bishop of Winchester', in Lancelot Andrewes, *XCVI. Sermons*, ed. William Laud and John Buckeridge (London: George Miller for Richard Badger, 1629), STC 606, $5Q1^r$-$5R6^v$.

Bunyan, John, *Grace Abounding to the Chief of Sinners* (London: George Larkin, 1666), Wing B5523.

Burnet, Gilbert, *The Memoires of the Lives and Actions of James and William, Dukes of Hamilton and Castleherald* (London: J. Grover for R. Royston, 1677), Wing B5832.

Burnet, Gilbert, *The Life and Death of Sir Matthew Hale, Kt* (London: William Shrowsbery, 1681), Wing B5827.

Bury, Elizabeth, *An Account of the Life and Death of Mrs. Elizabeth Bury, who Died, May the 11th, 1720. Aged 76. Chiefly Collected out of Her Own Diary* ed. [Samuel Bury] (Bristol: J. Penn, 1720).

Byfield, Nicholas, *The Marrow of the Oracles of God, or, Divers Treatises, Containing Directions about Six of the Waightiest Things Can Concerne a Christian in this Life* (London: Ralph Rounthwaite, 1622), STC 4220.5.

Byrd, William, *Psalmes, Sonets, & Songs of Sadnes and Pietie* (London: Thomas East, 1588), STC 4253.3 and 4253.7.

Cancellar, James, *The Pathe of Obedience* (London: John Wailande, [1556?]), STC 4565.

Carleton, George, *Vita Bernardi Gilpin viri sanctissimi, famaque apud Anglos aquolinares [sic] celeberrimi* (London: William Jones, 1628), STC 4646.

Carleton, George, *The Life of Bernard Gilpin a Man Most Holy and Renowned among the Northerne English* (London: William Jones, 1629), STC 4647.

Carleton, Mary, *The Case of Madam Mary Carleton* (London: Samuel Speed and Henry Marsh, 1663), Wing C586A.

Carter, John, *The Tomb-Stone, and A Rare Sight* (London: Tho. Roycroft, for Edw. Dod, and Nath. Ekins, 1653) Wing C656A.

Castiglione, Baldessare, *The Courtyer of Count Baldessar Castilio Diuided into Foure Bookes*, trans. Thomas Hoby (London: William Seres, 1561), STC 4778.

Cato, *Catonis disticha moralia*, ed. Desiderius Erasmus, trans. Richard Taverner (London: Nicholas Hill for Robert Toy, 1583), STC 4843.

[Cavendish], Margaret, marchioness of Newcastle, 'A True Relation of My Birth, Breeding, and Life', in *Natures Pictures Drawn by Fancies Pencil to the Life* (London: J. Martin and J. Allestrye, 1656), Wing N855, 3A4^{v}–3D4^{r}.

[Cavendish], Margaret, marchioness of Newcastle, *CCXI Sociable Letters* (London: William Wilson, 1664), Wing N872.

[Cavendish], Margaret, marchioness of Newcastle, *The Life of the Thrice Noble, High and Puissant Prince William Cavendishe, Duke, Marquess and Earl of Newcastle* (London: A. Maxwell, 1667), Wing N853.

Cellier, Elizabeth, *Malice Defeated, or, A Brief Relation of the Accusation and Deliverance of Elizabeth Cellier* (London: Elizabeth Cellier, 1680), Wing C1661.

Cellier, Elizabeth, *The Matchless Rogue; or, A Brief Account of the Life of Don Thomazo, the Unfortunate Son* (London: Elizabeth Cellier, 1680), Wing C1662.

Chamberlain, Bartholomew, *A Sermon Preached at Farington in Barkeshire, the Seuenteene of Februarie, 1587 At the Buriall of the Right Honorable the Ladie Anne Countes of Warwicke*... (London: John Wolfe, 1591), STC 4952.

[Churchyard, Thomas], *The Epitaphe of the Honorable Earle of Penbroke, Baron of Cardiffe, and Knight of the Most Noble Order of the Garter* (London: William Griffith, 1570), STC 5227.

Clarke, John, *Holy Incense for the Censers of the Saints. Or, A Method of Prayer with Matter, and Formes in Selected Sentences of Sacred Scripture* (London: [A. Mathewes] for Robert Milbourne, 1634), STC 5357.

Clarke, Samuel, *The Marrow of Ecclesiastical Historie* (London: William Du-gard, 1650), Wing C4543.

Clarke, Samuel, *The Second Part of the Marrow of Ecclesiastical History* (London: Robert White and William Wilson, 1650), Wing C4556.

Clarke, Samuel, *A Generall Martyrologie, containing a collection of all the greatest persecutions which have befallen the Church of Christ from the Creation to our present times. Whereunto are added, The lives of sundry modern divines* (London: A. M. for Thomas Underhill and John Rothwell, 1651), Wing C4513.

Clarke, Samuel, *A Martyrologie* (London: T. Ratcliffe and E. Mottershed for John Browne, 1652), Wing C4546.

Clarke, Samuel, *A Collection of the Lives of Ten Eminent Divines* (London: William Miller, 1662), Wing C4506.

Clarke, Samuel, *The Marrow of Ecclesiastical History*, 3rd edn (London: W. B. for Thomas Sawbridge and William Birch, 1675), Wing C4545.

Clarke, Samuel, *The Lives of Thirty-Two English Divines*, 3rd edn (London: William Birch, 1677), Wing C4359.

Clarke, Samuel, *The Lives of Sundry Eminent Persons in this Later Age. In Two Parts, I. Of Divines. II. Of Nobility and Gentry of Both Sexes* (London: Thomas Simmons, 1683), Wing C4538.

Clavell, John, *A Recantation of an Ill Led Life, or, A Discouerie of the High-Way Law* (London: 'for the autous [*sic*] vse', 1628), STC 5369.2.

Coke, Edward, 'The Preface', in *The First Part of the Institutes of the Lawes of England. Or, A Commentarie vpon Littleton* (London: [Miles Flesher, John Haviland, and Robert Young,] the assigns of John More for Richard More, 1629), STC 15785, ₵3^{r}–₵6^{v}.

Coke, Roger, *A Detection of the Court and State of England during the Four Last Reigns and the Inter-Regnum*, 2 vols (London: Andr. Bell, 1697), Wing C4975.

Cope, Alan [*pseud.* Nicholas Harpsfield], *Dialogi sex contra summi pontificates, monasticae vitae, sanctorum, sacrarum imaginum oppugnatores, et pseudomartyres* (Antwerp: Christoper Plantin, 1566).

Coppin, Richard, *Truths Testimony and a Testimony of Truths Appearing* (London: n.pub., 1655), Wing C6105.

[Court of King's Bench], *The Third Part of Modern Reports Being a Collection of Several Special Cases in the Court of Kings-Bench* (London: Charles Harper, 1700), Wing T911.

Cowper, William, *The Life and Death of the Reuerend Father, and Faithfull Seruant of God, Mr. William Cowper, Bishop of Galloway* (London: George Purslowe for John Budge, 1619), STC 5945.

[Croke, Charles], *Fortune's uncertainty, or, Youth's unconstancy wherein is contained a true and impartial account of what hapned in the space of a few years to the author, whom you will know in this ensuing discourse by the name of Rodolphvs* (London: Thomas Dring, 1667), Wing C7008.

[D., R.], *An epitaph vpon the death of Richard Price Esquier (the second sonne of Sir Iohn Price Knight, deceased) which Richard left this life the fifth day of Ianuarie, 1586* (London: John Charlewood, [1587?]), STC 6178.

Dangerfield, Thomas, *Mr. Tho. Dangerfields Particular Narrative of the late Popish…Written by Himself* (London: Henry Hills et al., 1679), Wing D192.

Dangerfield, Thomas, *Mr. Tho. Dangerfield's Second Narrative* (London: Thomas Cockerill, 1680), Wing D193.

Dangerfield, Thomas, *The Case of Tho. Dangerfield* (London: for the author, 1680), Wing C1181.

Dangerfield, Thomas, *Tho. Dangerfield's Answer to a Certain Scandalous Lying Pamphlet Entituled, Malice Defeated* (London: for the author, 1680), Wing D183.

Dangerfield, Thomas, *Dangerfield's Memoires, Digested into Adventures, Receits, and Expences by His Own Hand* (London: J. Bennet for Charles Brome, 1685), Wing D190.

Davis, Isaiah, *A Sermon at the Funeral of the Vertuous and Truly Religious Lady, Mrs. Margaret Andrewes* (London: n.pub., 1680), Wing D418A.

de Auila, Juan, *The audi filia, or A Rich Cabinet Full of Spirituall Iewells*, [trans. Tobie Matthew] ([Saint-Omer: English College Press], 1620), STC 983.

Defoe, Daniel, *The Character of the late Dr. Samuel Annesley, by Way of Elegy: With a Preface Written by One of His Hearers* (London: E. Whitlock, 1697), Wing D829B.

Defoe, Daniel, *The Life, Adventures, and Pyracies, of the Famous Captain Singleton* (London: J. Brotherton et al., 1720).

[Defoe, Daniel], 'Against Reviling Public Criminals', *Applebee's Journal*, 24 June 1721.

Defoe, Daniel, *The Fortunes and Misfortunes of the Famous Moll Flanders* (London: W. Chetwood et al., 1722).

Defoe, Daniel, *The History of the Most Remarkable Life, and Extraordinary Adventures, of the Truly Honorable Colonel Jaque, Vulgarly Call'd, Colonel Jack* (London: J. Applebee, 1722).

Defoe, Daniel, *The Fortunate Mistress: or, A History of the Life and Vast Variety Of Fortunes of... Lady Roxana* (London: T. Warner et al., 1724).

D[oleman], N. [*pseud.* Robert Persons], *A Treatise of Three Conuersions of England from Paganisme to Christian Religion*, 3 vols ([Saint-Omer]: [François Bellet], 1603[-1604]), STC 19416.

Donne, John, *Pseudo-Martyr* (London: W. Stansby for Walter Burre, 1610), STC 7048.

Donne, John, *Deaths Duell, or, A Consolation to the Soule, against the Dying Life, and Liuing Death of the Body* (London: Thomas Harper, for Richard Redmer and Benjamin Fisher, 1632), STC 7031.

Donne, John, *Poems... With Elegies on the Authors Death* (London: M[iles] F[lesher] for John Marriot, 1633), STC 7045.

Donne, John, *Poems... with Elegies on the Authors Death* (London: M. F. for John Marriot, 1635), STC 7046.

Donne, John, *LXXX Sermons* (London: Richard Royston and Richard Marriot, 1640), STC 7038.

Donne, John, *Letters to Severall Persons of Honour*, ed. John Donne, Jr. (London: J. Flesher for Richard Marriot, 1651), Wing D1864.

Dryden, John, 'The Life of Plutarch', in *Plutarch's Lives*, trans. John Dryden et al. (London: Jacob Tonson, 1683), Wing P2635. B1^{r}–I8^{v}.

Dugdale, William, *The History of St. Pauls Cathedral in London from its Foundation untill These Times* (London: Thomas Warren, 1658), Wing D2482.

Dunton, John, *A Voyage round the World, or, A Pocket-Library Divided into Several Volumes* (London: Richard Newcome, [1691]), Wing V742.

Dunton, John, *The Merciful Assizes: or, A Panegyric on the Late Lord Jeffreys Hanging so Many in the West* (London: Elizabeth Harris, 1701).

Dunton, John, *The Life and Errors of John Dunton Late Citizen of London; Written by Himself in Solitude. With an Idea of A New Life* (London: S. Malthus, 1705).

Dyke, Daniel, *The Mystery of Selfe-Deceiuing*, ed. Jeremiah Dyke (London: Edward Griffin for Ralph Mab, 1614), STC 7398.

Dyke, Daniel, *Two Treatises. The One, of Repentance, the Other, of Christs Temptations* (London: Edward Griffin for Ralph Mab, 1616), STC 7408.

Eliot, John, *The Suruay or Topographical Description of France* (London: John Wolfe, 1592), STC 7575.

Eliot, John, *Tears of Repentance: or, A Further Narrative of the Progress of the Gospel Amongst the Indians in New-England* (London: Peter Cole, 1653), Wing E524.

Eliot, John, *A Further Account of the Progress of the Gospel Amongst the Indians in New England* (London: John Macock, 1660), Wing E510.

Elyot, Thomas, *The Castel of Helth* (London: Thomas Berthelet, 1539), STC 7643.

Erasmus, Desiderius *see* Cato.

Eusebius, Socrates, and Evagrius, *The Ancient Ecclesiasticall Histories of the First Six Hundred Yeares after Christi* (London: George Miller [and Thomas Cotes] for Michael Sparke, 1636), STC 10576.

Evans, Arise, *An Eccho to the Voice from Heaven, or, A Narration of the Life, and Manner of the Special Calling, and Visions of Arise Evans* (London: for the author, 1652), Wing E3457.

[Featley, Daniel], 'The Life of the Worthie Prelate and Faithfvll Servant of God Iohn Iewel Sometimes Bishop of Sarisbvrie', in John Jewel, *The works of the very learned and reuerend father in God Iohn Iewell, not long since Bishop of Sarisburie. Newly set forth with some amendment of diuers quotations: and a briefe discourse of his life* (London: [Eliot's Court Press for] John Norton, 1609), STC 14579, ¶¶1r–¶¶6v.

Featley, Daniel, Martin Day, Richard Sibbs, Thomas Taylor, et al., *ΘΡΗΝΟΙΚΟΣ. The House of Movrning* (London: John Dawson for R. M., 1640), STC 24049.

[Fell, John], *The Life of that Reverend Divine, and Learned Historian, Dr. Thomas Fuller* (London: J. W., H. B., and H. M., 1661), Wing F616.

Ferebe, George, *Lifes Farewell. Or A funerall sermon preached at Saint Iohns in the Deuises in Wilshiere, the 30. of August last 1614 At the funerall of Iohn Drew Gentleman* (London: Edw. Griffin, for Ralph Mab, 1615), STC 10818.

F[idge], G[eorge], *The English Gusman; or the History of that Unparallel'd Thief James Hind* (London: T. N. for George Latham, Jr., 1652), Wing F852.

Fitz-Geffry, Charles, *Elisha his lamentation, for his owne, and all Israels losse, in Elijah The subiect of a sermon, preached at the funeralls of the Right Worshipfull Sir Anthony Rous, late of Halton in Cornwall, Knight* (London: William Stansby for John Parker, 1622), STC 10942.

Fleming, Abraham, [*Lambes Conduit of Comfort*] (London: Henry Denham, 1579), STC 11037.3.

Fleming, Abraham, *An Epitaph, or Funerall Inscription, vpon the Godlie Life and Death of the Right Worshipfull Maister William Lambe Esquire* (London: Henry Denham for Thomas Turner, 1580), STC 11038.

Fleming, Abraham, *A Memoriall of the Famous Monuments and Charitable Almesdeedes of the Right Worshipfull Maister William Lambe Esquire* (London: Henry Denham for Thomas Turner, 1580), STC 11047.

Fleming, Abraham, *The Conduit of Comfort Containing Sundrie Comfortable Prayers, to the Strengthening of the Faith of a Weak Christian* (London: A[ugustine] M[athewes] for Fr[ancis] Grove, 1627), STC 11037.5.

see also Nausea, Friedrich.

Foulis, Henry, *The history of the wicked plots and conspiracies of our pretended saints representing the beginning, constitution, and designs of the Jesuite* (London: E. Cotes for A. Seile, 1662), Wing F1642.

Foxe, John, *Commentarii rerum in ecclesia gestarum* (Strasbourg: Wendelin I Rihel, 1554).

Foxe, John, *Rerum in ecclesia gestarum* (Basel: Johann Oporinus & Nikolaus Brylinger, 1559).

Foxe, John, *Actes and Monuments of these Latter and Perillous Dayes Touching Matters of the Church* (London: John Day, 1563), STC 11222.

Foxe, John, *The First Volume of the Ecclesiasticall History Contaynyng the Actes and Monumentes* (London: John Day, 1570), STC 11223.

Foxe, John, *Acts and Monuments of Matters Most Special and Memorable Happening in the Church, with an Universall Historie of the Same*, 3 vols (London: Company of Stationers, 1641), Wing F2035.

Fuller, Thomas, *The Holy State* (Cambridge: Roger Daniel for John Williams, 1642), Wing F2443.

[Fuller, Thomas], *Abel Redevivus: or, The Dead Yet Speaking. The Lives and Deaths of the Modern Divines* (London: Tho. Brudenell for John Stafford, 1651), Wing F2400.

Fuller, Thomas, *The History of the Worthies of England*, ed. John Fuller (London: J. G., W. L., and W. G., 1662), Wing F2440.

Fuller, William, *The Whole Life of William Fuller* (London, 1703).

[Gascoigne, George], *A Hundreth Sundry Flowres* (London: Henrie Bynneman [and Henry Middleton] for Richard Smith, 1573), STC 11635.

Gataker, Thomas, *The decease of Lazarus Christ's friend A funerall sermon on Iohn. chap. 11. vers. 11. preached at the buriall of Mr. John Parker merchant and citizen of London* (London: E[dward] G[riffin] for Edward Brewster and Fulke Clyfton, 1640), STC 11656.

[Gibbons, John], *Concertatio ecclesiae catholicae in Anglia*, 2nd edn (Trier: Heinrich Bock, 1588).

Glanvill, Joseph, *A Praefatory Answer to Mr. Henry Stubbe* (London: A. Clark for J. Collins, 1671), Wing G821.

Glascock, John, *Mary's Choice, or, The choice of the truly godly person opened, and justified, in a sermon preached at the funeral of Mrs. Anne Petter* (London: J. H. for Samuel Gellibrand, 1659), Wing G842.

Gnapheus, Wilhelm, *A Myrrour or Glasse for Them that be Syke [and] in Payne. Translated out of Dutche in English*, trans. Miles Coverdale? ([Southwark: James Nicolson for Ian Gough, 1536]), STC 11470.5.

G[odwin], F[rancis], *A Catalogue of the Bishops of England* (London: [Eliot's Court Press] for George Bishop, 1601), STC 11937.

Googe, Barnabe, *Eglogs, Epytaphes and Sonettes* (London: T. Colwell for R. Newbery, 1563), STC 12048.

Guy, Nicholas, *Pieties Pillar: or, A sermon preached at the funerall of mistresse Elizabeth Gouge*... *With a true narration of her life and death* (London: George Millar [*sic*], 1626), STC 12543.

Guylforde, Richard, *This is the begynnynge, and contynuaunce of the pylgrymage of Sir Richarde Guylforde knyght* (London: Richard Pynson, 1511), STC 12549.

Guylforde, Richard, *The Pylgrymage of Sir Richarde Guylforde*, ed. Henry Ellis (London: Camden Society, 1851).

Hales, John, 'Oratio funebris', in *Bodleiomnema* (Oxford: Joseph Barnes, 1613), STC 19048, $L3^r$–$N3^r$.

Hales, John, *Golden Remains of the Ever Memorable Mr. Iohn Hales of Eton College & c.*, ed. Peter Gunning (London: Timothy Garthwait, 1659), Wing H629.

Hales, John, 'John Hales' Funeral Oration for Sir Thomas Bodley: an Edited Translation', ed. Daniel Blank, trans. Leah Whittington, *Bodleian Library Record* 25 (2012), 144–82.

Harding, Thomas, *A Confvtation of a Booke Intitvled An Apologie of the Chvrch of England* (Antwerp: Johannes de Laet, 1565), STC 12762.

Harding, Thomas, *A Reioindre to M. Iewels Replie against the Sacrifice of the Masse* (Louvain: John Fowler, 1567), STC 12761.

Harington, John, *A Briefe View of the State of the Church of England*, [ed. John Chetwynd] (London: Jos. Kirton, 1653), Wing H770.
see also Misacmos.

Harpsfield, Nicholas *see* Cope, Alan.

Harris, John, 'A short view of the life and vertues of the avthovr' in Arthur Lake, *Sermons, with Some Religious and Divine Meditations* (London: W. Stansby for Nathaniel Butter, 1629), STC 15134, ¶4^r–$A2^r$.

Harris, Robert, *Peters Enlargement vpon the Prayers of the Church* (London: John Haviland for John Bartlet, 1624), STC 12840.

Harrison, William, *The Difference of Hearers, or An Exposition of the Parable of the Sower* (London: William Bladon, 1614), STC 12870.

Harrison, William and William Leigh, *Deaths advantage little regarded, and the soules solace against sorrow… Whereunto is annexed, the Christian life and godly death of the said Gentlewoman* (London: Felix Kyngston, 1602), STC 12866.

Harrison, William and William Leigh, *Deaths advantage little regarded, and the soules solace against sorrow… A facsimile reproduction with an introduction*, ed. Retha M. Warnicke and Bettie Anne Doebler (Delmar, NY: Scholars' Facsimiles & Reprints, 1993).

Harryson, Johan [*pseud.* John Bale], *Yet a Course at the Romyshe Foxe* ([Zurich [i.e. Antwerp]: Oliver Jacobson [i.e. A. Goinus], 1543]), STC 1309.

Hart, John, *An orthographie conteyning the due order and reason, howe to write or paint thimage of mannes voice, most like to the life or nature* (London: [Henry Denham? for] William Seres, 1569), STC 12890.

[Head, Richard], *The English rogue described, in the life of Meriton Latroon, a witty extravagant. Being a compleat history of the most eminent cheats of both sexes* (London: Henry Marsh, 1665), Wing H1246.

Hearne, Thomas, 'The Publisher's Preface', in *Peter Langtoft's Chronicle (as illustrated by Robert of Brunne) from the Death of Cadwalader to the End of K. Edward the First's Reign*, ed. Thomas Hearne, 2 vols (Oxford: at the Theater, 1725), 1: ix–xciii.

Hearne, Thomas, 'To the Reader', in Thomas Bodley, *Reliquiæ Bodleianæ: or Some Genuine Remains of Sir Thomas Bodley*, [ed. Thomas Hearne] (London: John Hartley, 1703), A2^r–A8^v.

Heath, James *see* T., S., Gent.

[Heywood, Oliver], *Some Remarks upon the Life of that Painful Servant of God, Mr. Nathanael Heywood* (London: Tho. Cockerill, 1695), Wing A3975.

Hinde, William, *A Faithfull Remonstrance of the Holy Life and Happy Death, of Iohn Bruen of Bruen-Stapleford* (London: R. B. for Philemon Stephens, and Christopher Meredith, 1641), Wing H2063.

Holland, Henry, *Heroologia Anglica, hoc est, clarissimorum et doctissimorum aliquot Anglorum* ([Arnhem: Jan Jansson at the expenses of Crispijn van de Passe and Jan Jansson for Henry Holland, London, 1620]), STC 13582.

Howell, James, *Londinopolis, an Historicall Discourse or Perlustration of the City of London* (London: J. Streater for Henry Twiford, George Sawbridge, Th. and John Place, 1657), Wing H3090.

Hoby, Thomas *see* Castiglione, Baldassare.

Holinshed, Raphael, et al., *The First and Second Volumes of Chronicles* ([London]: John Harrison, George Bishop, Rafe Newberie, Henry Denham, and Thomas Woodcock, [1587]), STC 13569.

Howard, Henry, earl of Surrey et al., *Songes and Sonettes, Written by Henry Haward Late Earle of Surrey, and Other* (London: Richard Tottel, 1557), STC 13860.

Hubrigh, Joachim, *An almanacke, and prognostication, for the yeare of our Lorde God. 1565. seruing for al Europia, and almost most necessary for all students, marchantes, mariners and trauellers, both by sea, and lande* ([London]: Henry Denham for William Pick[e]ring, [1565]), STC 462.5.

Innocent III, *Een zuverlic boucxkin vander ketyvigheyt der menschelicker naturen*, trans. Andries van Muelen (Ghent: Joos Lambrecht, 1543).

James I, *A Proclamation Commanding Persons of Qualitie to Reside in their Countreys* (London: Bonham Norton and John Bill, 1624), STC 8741.

Janeway, James, *Invisibles, Realities, Demonstrated in The Holy Life and Triumphant Death of Mr. John Janeway, Fellow of King's Collegde in Cambridge* (London: Tho. Pankhurst, 1674), Wing J471.

Jenkyn, William, *An Exposition of the Epistle of Jude, together with Many Large and Usefull Deductions... The Second Part* (London: Tho. Maxey, for Samuel Gellibrand, 1654), Wing J642.

Jewel, John, *A Replie vnto M. Hardinges Answeare* (London: Henry Wykes, 1565), STC 14606.

Jonson, Ben, *Volpone or The Foxe* (London: [George Eld for] Thomas Thorpe, 1607), STC 14783.

Kempe, Margery, *Here begynneth a shorte treatyse of contemplacyon taught by our lorde Jhesucryste, or taken out of the boke of Margerie Kempe of Lyn* (London: Wynkyn de Worde, 1501), STC 14924.

Kempis, Thomas à, *The Folowinge of Chryste*, trans. Richard Whitford, ed. William Peto (London: John Cawood, 1556), STC 23966.

Kilby, Richard, *Hallelu-iah: Praise Yee the Lord, for the Vnburthening of a Loaden Conscience* (Cambridge: Cantrell Legge, 1618), STC 14955.

Kirkman, Francis, *The Counterfeit Lady Unveiled* (London: Peter Parker, 1673), Wing K630A.

Kirkman, Francis, 'To the Reader', in *The English Rogue Continued...* (London: Francis Kirkman, 1671), Wing H2149, A4^r–B4^v.

Langbaine, Gerard, *An Account of the English Dramatick Poets* (Oxford: L. L. for George West and Henry Clements, 1691), Wing L373.

Legh, Gerard, *The Accedens of Armony* (London: Richard Tottel, 1576), STC 15390.

Leland, John, *The Laboryouse Iourney [and] Serche of Iohan Leylande, for Englandes Antiquitees*, ed. John Bale ([London: S. Mierdman for John Bale], 1549), STC 15445.

Lipsius, Justus, 'The Life of Lvcivs Annævs Seneca, Described', in *The Workes of Lucius Annaeus Seneca, both Morrall and Naturall*, trans. Thomas Lodge (London: William Stansby, 1614), STC 22213, c1^r–d8^v.

Lloyd, David, *The States-Men and Favourites of England since the Reformation* (London: J. C. for Samuel Speed, 1665), Wing L2648.

Lloyd, David, *Memoires of the Lives, Actions, Sufferings & Deaths of Those Noble Reverend and Excellent Parsonages that suffered by death, sequestration, decimation, or otherwise, for the Protestant religion* (London: Samuel Speed, John Wright, John Symmer, and James Collins, 1668), Wing L2642.

Lloyd, David, *State-Worthies, or, The States-Men and Favourites of England since the Reformation*, 2nd edn (London: Thomas Milbourne for Samuel Speed, 1670), Wing L2646.

Lloyd, David, *Memoires of the Lives, Actions, Sufferings & Deaths of Those Noble Reverend and Excellent Parsonages that suffered by death, sequestration, decimation, or otherwise, for the Protestant religion*, 2nd edn (London: Dorman Newman, 1677), Wing L2643.

Lloyd, Lodowick, *An Epitaph vpon the Death of the Honorable, Syr Edward Saunders Knight, Lorde Cheefe Baron of the Exchequer, Who Dyed the. 19. of Nouember. 1576* (London: H. S[ingleton] for Henry Disle, [1576]), STC 16620.

Locke, John, *Some Thoughts Concerning Education*, 5th edn (London: A. and J. Churchill, 1705).

Lupton, Donald, *The History of the Modern Protestant Divines* (London: N. and John Okes, 1637), STC 24660.

Lupton, Donald, *The Glory of Their Times. Or The Liues of the Primitiue Fathers* (London: John Okes, 1640), STC 16943.

M., R., *An Epytaphe vpon the Death of M. Rycharde Goodricke Esquier* ([London: n.pub., 1562]), STC 17145.3.

Manton, Thomas, 'To the Christian Reader', in [John Shawe], *Mistris Shawe's Tomb-Stone. Or, the saints remains. Being a brief narrative, of some few (amongst many) remarkable passages in the holy life and happy death of that precious servant of the Lord Mrs. Dorothy Shaw, (late the dearly beloved wife of Mr. John Shaw preacher of the Gospell at Kingstone upon Hull,) who sweetly slept in the Lord Decemb. 10th and was interred at Trinity Church, in Hull Decemb. 12. 1647* (London: Nathanael Brooks, 1658), Wing S3029, b8^{r}–b11^{v}.

Mather, Cotton, *Magnalia Christi Americana: or, The Ecclesiastical History of New-England*, ed. Thomas Robbins, 2 vols (Hartford, CT: Silas Andrus & Son, 1853).

Matthew, Tobie, *A Collection of Letters…with a Character of the Most Excellent Lady, Lucy, Countesse of Carleile*, [ed. John Donne, Jr.] (London: Henry Herringman, 1660 [i.e. 1659]), Wing M1319.

see also Augustine; Biondi, Giuseppe; Puccini, Vincenzio; Teresa de Avila.

Meursius, Joannes, *Athenæ Batavæ. Sive, de vrbe Leidensi, & academiâ, virisque claris; qui utramque ingenio suo, atque scriptis, illustrarunt: libri dvo* (Leiden: Andreas Cloucquius and the Elseviers, 1625).

Misacmos [*pseud.* John Harington], *A New Discourse of a Stale Subiect, Called the Metamorphosis of Aiax* (London: Richard Field [and Eliot's Court Press], 1596), STC 12772.

Montaigne, Michel de, *The Essayes or Morall, Politike and Millitarie Discourses*, trans. John Florio (London: Valentine Sims for Edward Blount, 1603), STC 18041.

[More, Cresacre, *pseud.* T. M.], *D.O.M.S. The Life and Death of Sir Thomas Moore Lord High Chancellour of England* ([Douai: B. Bellière, 1631?]), STC 18066.

More, Thomas, *The Workes…Wrytten by Him in the Englyshe Tonge*, ed. William Rastell (London: John Cawood, John Waly, and Richard Tottel, 1557), STC 18076.

More, Thomas, *The Complete Works of St. Thomas More*, vol. 2, ed. Richard S. Sylvester (New Haven, CT: Yale University Press, 1963).

see also Pico della Mirandola, Giovanni Francesco.

Musculus, Wolfgang, *Common Places of Christian Religion*, trans. John Man (London: [Reginalde Wolfe], [1563]), STC 18308.

Nalton, James, *Twenty Sermons Preached upon Several Texts* (London: Dorman Newman, 1677), Wing N124.

Nausea, Friedrich, *Of all Blasing Starrs in Generall, as Well Supernaturall as Naturall*, trans. Abraham Fleming (London: [H. Middleton?] for Thomas Woodcocke, 1577), STC 18413.

Newton, Thomas, *An Epitaphe vpon the Worthy and Honorable Lady, the Lady Knowles* (London: William How for Richard Jones, 1569), STC 18512.

North, Roger, *Examen: or, An Enquiry into the Credit and Veracity of a Pretended Complete History* (London: Fletcher Gyles, 1740).

Pacioli, Luca, *Summa de arithematica, geometria, proportioni et proportionalita* (Venice: Paganino de Paganini, 1494).

[Painter, William], *A Moorning Diti vpon the Deceas of the Most Nobl Prins Henry Earl of Arvndel…*(London: John Allde, [1580]), STC 10932.

Pareus, David, *Opera theologica exegetica*, 4 vols (Frankfurt am Main: J. Roos's widow, 1647).

Pareus, Johann Philipp, *Narratio historica de curriculo vitae, & obitu reverendissimi patris D. Davidis Parei*, (Frankfurt am Main: Wolfgang Hofmann for Wilhelm Fitzer, 1633).

Parker, Matthew, assisted by George Acworth and John Joscelyn, *De antiquitate Britannicae ecclesiae & priuilegiis ecclesiae Cantuariensis cum Archiepiscopis eiusdem 70* (London: John Day, 1571), STC 19292.

Perkins, William, *A Treatise of the Vocations, or, Callings of Men* ([London]: John Legat, 1603), STC 19751.

see also Rogers, Richard.

Persons, Robert, *see* D[oleman], N.

Peterson, Spiro ed., *The Counterfeit Lady Unveiled and Other Criminal Fiction of Seventeenth-Century England: A Selection* (Garden City, NY: Anchor Books/Doubleday & Company, 1961).

Philips, Ambrose, *The Life of John Williams, Ld. Keeper of the Great Seal, Bp. of Lincoln, and Abp. of York in the Reigns of King James and King Charles the First* (Cambridge: The University Press for A. Bosvile, 1700), Wing P2025.

Phillips, Edward, *Theatrum poetarum, or, A Compleat Collection of the Poets Especially the Most Eminent, of All Ages* (London: Charles Smith, 1675), Wing P2075.

[Phillips, John], *An epitaph on the death of the vertuous matrone, the Lady Maioresse, late wyfe to the right honorable Lorde, (Alexander Auenet) Lord Maior of the citie of London. Who deceased the vii. daie of Iuly. 1570* (London: Richard Jones, 1570), STC 19868.

[Phillips, John], *A Commemoration of the Right Noble and Vertuous Ladye, Margrit Duglasis Good Grace, Countis of Lennox* (London: John Charlewood, 1578), STC 19864.

[Phillips, John], *An Epitaphe on the Death of the Right Noble and Most Vertuous Lady Margarit Duglasis Good Grace, Countisse of Lininox* (London: Edward White, 1578), STC 19866.

[Phillips, John], *An epitaph on the death, of the Right honorable and vertuous Lord Henry Wrisley, the noble Earle of South hampton: who lieth interred at Touchfeelde in the countie of Hamshyre, the 30. day of Nouember 158* ([London: n.pub., 1581), STC 19867.

Pico della Mirandola, Giovanni Francesco, *Here is conteyned the lyfe of Johan Picus Erle of Myrandula*, trans. Thomas More (London: John Rastell, 1510), STC 19897.7.

Plutarch, *The Lives of the Noble Grecians and Romanes*, trans. Thomas North (London: Thomas Vautrollier and John Wight, 1579), STC 20066.

Pollini, Girolamo, *L'historia ecclesiastica della rivoluzion d'Inghilterra, divisa in libri Quattro* (Rome: Guglielmo Facciotti, 1594).

Porter, Jerome, *The Flowers of the Liues of the Most Renowned Saincts of the Three Kingdoms England Scotland, and Ireland written and collected out of the best authours and manuscripts of our nation, and distributed according to their feasts in the calendar* (Douai: 'With licence, and approbation of the Ordinary', 1632), STC 20124.

Powell, Vavasor, *Spirituall experiences, of sundry beleevers Held forth by them at severall solemne meetings, and conferences to that end* (London: Robert Ibbitson, 1653), Wing P3095.

Prior, Thomas, 'A Sermon at the Fvnerall of the Right Reverend Father in God, Miles, Late Lord Bishop of Glovcester', in Miles Smith, *Sermons* (London: Elizabeth Allde for Robert Allot, 1632), STC 22808, 2N5^{r}–2Q2^{r}.

Prynne, William, *Romes Master-Peece, or, The Grand Conspiracy of the Pope and his Iesuited Instruments*, 2nd edn (London: Michael Sparke, Senior, 1644), Wing P4056.

Puccini, Vincenzio, *The Life of the Holy and Venerable Mother Suor Maria Maddalena de Patsi*, [trans. Tobie Matthew] ([Saint Omer: English College Press], 1619), STC 20483.

Quarles, Ursula, 'A Short Relation of the Life and Death of M^{r}. Francis Quarles', in Francis Quarles, *Solomons Recantation, Entituled Ecclesiastes, Paraphrased* (London: M. F. for Richard Royston, 1645), Wing Q116, A2^{r}–A4^{v}.

Rawley, William, 'The Life of the Honourable Author', in Francis Bacon, *Resuscitatio, or, Bringing into Publick Light Severall Pieces of the Works...Hitherto Sleeping*, ed. William Rawley (London: Sarah Griffin for William Lee, 1657), Wing B319, (b2)^{r}–(c4)^{v}.

[Reynolds, Edward], *Imitation and Caution for Christian Woman: or, The Life and Death of that Excellent Gentlewoman, Mrs. Mary Bewley* (London: E. M. for George Calvert, 1659), Wing I55.

Ridley, Nicholas, *A Frendly Farewel...vnto all His True Louers and Frendes in God* (London: John Day, 1559), STC 21051.

Rogers, Richard, *Seuen Treatises* (London: Felix Kyngston, for Thomas Man, and Robert Dexter, 1603), STC 21215.

Rogers, Richard with William Perkins, Richard Greenham, Miles Mosse, and George Webbe, *A Garden of Spiritual Flowers*, 5th edn (London: Thomas Pavier, 1609), STC 21205.

Rogers, Timothy, *The Character of a Good Woman, both in a single and marry'd state...occasion'd by the decease of Mrs. Elizabeth Dunton, who died May 28, 1697: with an account of her life and death, and part of the diary writ with her own hand* (London: J. Harris, 1697), Wing R1846.

Roper, William, *The Mirrour of Vertue in Worldly Greatnes. Or The Life of Syr Thomas More Knight, Sometime Lo. Chancellour of England* (Paris [i.e. Saint-Omer]: [The English College Press], 1626), STC 21316.

Rushworth, John, *Historical Collections of Private Passages of State*, pt. 2 (London: J. D. for J. Wright and R. Chiswell, 1680), Wing R2318.

Salter, Thomas, *A Mirrhor Mete for all Mothers, Matrones, and Maidens, Intituled the Mirrhor of Modestie* (London: [J. Kingston] for Edward White, [1579]), STC 21634.

Salzman, Paul ed., *An Anthology of Seventeenth-Century Fiction* (Oxford: Oxford University Press, 1991).

Sampson, Thomas, 'To the Christian Reader', in John Bradford, *Two Notable Sermons...the One of Repentance, and the Other of the Lordes Supper*, ed. Thomas Sampson (London: John Awdely, and John Wyght, 1574), STC 3500.5, A2^{r}–A8^{v}.

Sander, Nicholas [and Edward Rishton], *De origine ac progressu schismatis Anglicani, liber* (Cologne [i.e. Rheims: Jean Foigny], 1585).

Scott, Chr[istopher], *The Saints Privilege, or, Gain by Dying* (London: [n.pub.], 1673), Wing S2034.

Scudder, Henry, 'The Life and Death of M. Whately', in William Whately, *Prototypes, or, The Primarie Precedent Presidents out of the Booke of Genesis* (London: G. M. for George Edwards, 1640), STC 25317.3, a1^{r}–a7^{r}.

Shakespeare, William, *Venus and Adonis* (London: Richard Field, 1593), STC 22354.

Shakespeare, William, *Comedies, Histories, & Tragedies* (London: Isaac Jaggard and Ed. Blount 1623), STC 22273.

Shelton, Thomas, *Tachygraphy the most exact and compendious methode of short and swift writing that hath ever yet beene published by any* (London: Samuel Cartwright, 1641), Wing S3074.

Shute, Nat[haniel], *Corona charitatis, the crowne of charitie: a sermon preacht in Mercers Chappell, May 10. 1625. at the solemne funerals of his euer-renowmed friend . . . Mr Richard Fishbvrne* (London: W. Stansby for Samuel Man, 1626), STC 22466.

Smith, Nicholas, *Wonderfull prophecyes revealed to Nicholas Smith shoe-maker, living at Tillington neer Petworth in Sussex, as he was about 30 years agoe in the house of one Vickers living in the Stert at Abbington in Barkshire* (London: n.pub., 1632), Wing S4141.

Smith, Thomas, *De recta et emendata linguæ anglicæ scriptione dialogus* (Paris: Robert Estienne, 1568).

Smith, Thomas, 'Vita D. Roberti Cottoni', in *Catalogus librorum manuscriptorum Bibliothecae Cottonianae* (Oxford: e Theatro Sheldoniano, 1696), Wing S4233, §a2^{r}–§d2^{v}.

Sparke, Thomas, *A Sermon Preached at Cheanies at the Buriall of the Right Honorable the Earle of Bedford, the 14. of September. 1585* (London: [John Windet], 1585), STC 23022.

Speght, Thomas, 'The Life of Geffrey Chaucer', in Geoffrey Chaucer, *The Workes of Our Antient and Lerned English Poet, Geffrey Chaucer, Newly Printed* (London: [Adam Islip] for George Bishop, 1598), STC 5077, b2^{r}–c3^{v}.

Stapleton, Thomas, 'Vita D. Thomæ Mori', in *Tres Thomae, seu: de sancti Thomae apostoli rebus gestis* (Douai: Jean Bogard, 1588), a2^{r}–r5^{v}.

Sternhold, Thomas, *Al such psalmes of Dauid as Thomas Sternehold late grome of [the] kinges Maiesties robes, didde in his life time draw into English metre* (London: Edward Whitchurch, 1549), STC 2420.

Stock, Richard, *The Churches Lamentation for the Losse of the Godly* (London: John Beale, 1614), STC 23273.

Stow, John, *The Summarie of the Chronicles of England. Diligently collected, abridged & continued vnto this present yeare of Christ. 1579* (London: Richard Tottel and Henry Bynneman, [1579]), STC 23325.7.

Stow, John, *The Chronicles of England from Brute vnto this Present Yeare of Christ. 1580* (London: [Henry Bynneman for] Ralph Newbery, 1580), STC 23333.

Stow, John, *A Summarie of the Chronicles of Englande* (London: Ralph Newberie and Henrie Denham, [1587]), STC 23326.

Stow, John, *Survey of London*, rev. Anthony Munday (London: Nicholas Bourn, 1633), STC 23345.5.

Stubbes, Philip, *A Christal Glasse for Christian Women* (London: Richard Jones, 1592), STC 23382.

Suckling, John, *Fragmenta aurea: A Collection of all the Incomparable Peeces* (London: [Ruth Raworth and Tho. Walkley] for Humphrey Moseley, 1646), Wing S6126A.

T., S., Gent. [*pseud.* James Heath], *Flagellum, or, The Life and Death, Birth and Burial of Oliver Cromwel* (London: L. R., 1663), Wing H1328.

Taverner, Richard, *The Garden of Wysdome* (London: Richard Taverner, 1539), STC 23711a.
see also Cato.

Teresa de Avila, *The Flaming Hart, or, The Life of the Gloriovs S. Teresa*, [trans. Tobie Matthew] (Antwerp: Johannes Meursius, 1642), Wing T753.

Thoresby, Ralph, *Vicaria Leodiensis: or, The History of the Church of Leedes in Yorkshire* (London: Joseph Smith, 1724).

Toland, John, 'The Life of James Harrington', in James Harrington, *The Oceana . . . and His Other Works*, ed. John Toland (London: n.pub., 1700), Wing H816, a2^{r}–e2^{r}.

Trapnel, Anna, *A Legacy for Saints; Being Several Experiences of the Dealings of God with Anna Trapnel, in, and after Her Conversion*, [ed. John Proud and Caleb Ingold] (London: T. Brewster, 1654), Wing T2032.

Traughton, W[illiam], *Of the Causes and Cure of Sad Disconsolate Thoughts in Christians* (London: Benjamin Harris, 1677), Wing T2317.

Turbeville, George, *Epitaphes, Epigrams, Songs and Sonets* (London: H. Denham, 1567), STC 24326.

Verheiden, Jacobus, *Praestantium aliquot theologorum, qui Rom. Antichristum præcipuè oppugnarunt, effigies* (The Hague: B. C. Nieulandt, 1602).

Vernon, John, *The Compleat Scholler; or, A Relation of the Life, and Latter End Especially of Caleb Vernon* (London: John Vernon, 1666), Wing V250B.

Voragine, Jacobus de, [*Legenda aurea*] (Westminster: William Caxton, 1483), STC 24873.

Voragine, Jacobus de, [*Legenda aurea*] ([London]: Wynkyn de Worde, 1527), STC 24880.

Wadsworth, James, *Further Obseruations of the English Spanish Pilgrime* (London: Felix Kyngston for Nathaniel Butter, 1630), STC 24928.

Walker, Anthony, *The Vertuous Wife: or, The Holy Life of Mrs. Elizab[e]th Walker, Late Wife of A. Walker, D.D. Sometime Rector of Fyfield in Essex* (London: N. R., 1694), Wing W311A.

Walker, William, *The Preciousness of Christ to the Believing-Christian* (London: Anne Maxwel for Joseph Clark, 1667), Wing W432A.

Walton, Izaak, 'The Life and Death of Dr Donne, Late Deane of St Pauls London', in John Donne, *LXXX Sermons* (London: Richard Royston and Richard Marriot, 1640), STC 7038, A3^{r}-C1^{v}.

Walton, Izaak, 'The Life of Sir Henry Wotton', in Henry Wotton, *Reliquiae Wottonianae or, A Collection of Lives, Letters, Poems* (London: Thomas Maxey, for R. Marriot, G. Bedel, and T. Garthwait, 1651), Wing W3648, b1^{r}-c12^{v}.

Walton, Izaak, *The Life of John Donne, Dr. in Divinity, and Late Dean of Saint Pauls Church* (London: J. G. for R. Marriot, 1658), Wing W668.

Walton, Izaak, *The Life of Mr. Rich. Hooker* (London: J. G. for Rich. Marriot, 1665), Wing W670.

Walton, Izaak, 'The Life of Mr. Richard Hooker', in *The Works of that Learned and Judicious Divine Mr. Richard Hooker*, [ed. John Gauden] (London: Thomas Newcomb for Andrew Crook, 1666), Wing H2361, a1^{r}-d3^{v}.

Walton, Izaak, *The Lives of Dr. John Donne, Sir Henry Wotton, Mr. Richard Hooker, Mr. George Herbert* (London: Tho. Newcomb for Richard Marriot, 1670), Wing W671.

Walton, Izaak, *The Life of Mr. George Herbert* (London: Tho: Newcomb for Richard Marriot, 1670), Wing W669.

Walton, Izaak, 'The Life of Mr. George Herbert', in George Herbert, *The Temple: Sacred Poems and Private Ejaculations*, 10th edn (London: W. Godbid, for R. S, 1674), 1–59, Wing H1521, A1^{r}-C6^{r}.

Walton, Izaak, *The Lives of Dr. John Donne, Sir Henry Wotton, Mr. Richard Hooker, Mr. George Herbert* (London: Thomas Roycroft for Richard Marriot, 1675), Wing W672.

Walton, Izaak, *The Life of Dr. Sanderson, Late Bishop of Lincoln* (London: Richard Marriot, 1678), Wing W667.

Wesley, Samuel, *Maggots, or, Poems on Several Subjects, Never Before Handled by a Scholar* (London: John Dunton, 1685), Wing W1374.

White, Thomas, *A Godlie Sermon Preached the xxj. Day of Iune, 1586. at Pensehurst in Kent, at the Buriall of the Late Right Honourable Sir Henrie Sidney Knight*...(London: Henrie Midleton, 1586), STC 25404.

White, Thomas, *A Treatise of the Power of Godlinesse* (London: R. I. for Joseph Cranford, 1658), Wing W1848.

Whythorne, Thomas, *Songes of Three, Fower and Five Voyces* (London: John Day, 1571), STC 22584.

Whythorne, Thomas, *Duos, or Songs for Two Voices* (London: T. Este, the assigne of W. Byrd, 1590), STC 25583.

Whythorne, Thomas, *Songes for Five Voyces*, ed. Robert McQuillan (Moretonhampstead: Antico Edition, 2000).

Wilkins, John, *Mercvry, or, The secret and swift messenger shewing, how a man may with privacy and speed communicate his thoughts to a friend at any distance* (London: I. Norton for Iohn Maynard and Timothy Wilkins, 1641), Wing W2202.

Willet, Andrew, *Synopsis papismi* (London: John Haviland, [John Legat, Thomas Cotes, and other] for John Grismond, 1634), STC 25700a.5.

Wilson, John, *The English martyrologe conteyning a summary of the liues of the glorious and renowned saintes of the three kingdomes, England, Scotland, and Ireland* ([St Omer: English College Press], 1608), STC 25771.

Wilson, Thomas, *The Rule of Reason, Conteinynge the Arte of Logique* (London: Richard Grafton, 1553), STC 25809.

Winstanley, William, *England's Worthies. Select Lives of the Most Eminent Persons from Constantine the Great, to the Death of Oliver Cromwel Late Protector* (London: Nath. Brooke, 1660), Wing W3058.

Winstanley, William, *The Loyal Martyrology* (London: Thomas Mabb for Edward Thomas, 1665), Wing W3066.

Winstanley, William, *The Lives of the Most Famous English Poets, or, The Honour of Parnassus* (London: H. Clark for Samuel Manship, 1687), Wing W3065.

Wolton, John, *The castell of Christians and fortresse of the faithfull beseiged, and defended, now almost sixe thowsand yeares* (London: J. C[harlewood] for Thomas Sturrup, 1577), STC 25975.

Wood, Anthony, *Athenæ Oxonienses*, 2 vols (London: Thomas Bennet, 1691–2), Wing W3383A.

Wyatt, Thomas, *Certayne psalmes chosen out of the psalter of Dauid, commonlye called the .vii. penytentiall psalms* (London: Thomas Raynald [for] Iohn Harryngton, 1549), STC 2726.
see also Howard, Henry, earl of Surrey.

Wyse, Nicholas, *A Consolacyon for Chrysten People to Repayre Agayn the Lordes Temple* (London: John Waylande, 1538), STC 26063.

D. Critical works on life-writing (in chronological order)

Burr, Anne Robeson, *The Autobiography: A Critical and Comparative Study* (Boston: Houghton Mifflin, 1909).

Nicolson, Harold, *The Development of English Biography* (New York: Harcourt, Brace and Company, 1928).

Stauffer, Donald A., *English Biography before 1700* (Cambridge, MA: Harvard University Press, 1930).

Spalding, P. A., *Self-Harvest: A Study of Diaries and the Diarist* (London: Independent Press, 1949).

de Sola Pinto, Vivian ed., *English Biography in the Seventeenth Century: Selected Short Lives* (London: George G. Harrap, 1951).

Shumaker, Wayne, *English Autobiography: Its Emergence, Materials, and Form* (Berkeley, CA: University of California Press, 1954).

Bottrall, Margaret, *Every Man a Phoenix: Studies in Seventeenth-Century Autobiography* (London: John Murray, 1958).

Osborn, James M., *The Beginnings of Autobiography in England: A Paper Delivered...at the Fifth Clark Library Seminar 8 August 1959* (Los Angeles: William Andrews Clark Memorial Library, University of California, Los Angeles, [1960]).

Pascal, Roy, *Design and Truth in Autobiography* (London: Routledge & Kegan Paul, 1960).

Clifford, James L. ed., *Biography as an Art: Selected Criticism 1560-1960* (London: Oxford University Press, 1962).

Altick, Richard D., *Lives and Letters: A History of Literary Biography in England and America* (New York: Knopf, 1965).

Kendall, Paul Muray, *The Art of Biography* (New York: W. W. Norton, 1965).

Starr, G. A., *Defoe & Spiritual Autobiography* (Princeton, NJ: Princeton University Press, 1965).

Butt, John, *Biography in the Hands of Walton, Johnson, and Boswell* (Los Angeles: University of California Los Angeles, 1966).

Morris, John N., *Versions of the Self: Studies in English Autobiography from John Bunyan to John Stuart Mill* (New York: Basic Books, 1966).

Matthews, William, *British Diaries: An Annotated Bibliography of British Diaries Written between 1442 and 1942* (Gloucester, MA: Peter Smith, 1967).

Shea, Daniel B., Jr., *Spiritual Autobiography in Early America* (Princeton, NJ: Princeton University Press, 1968).

Delany, Paul, *British Autobiography in the Seventeenth Century* (London: Routledge & Kegan Paul, 1969).

Ebner, Dean, *Autobiography in Seventeenth-Century England: Theology and the Self* (The Hague: Mouton, 1971).

Watkins, Owen C., *The Puritan Experience: Studies in Spiritual Autobiography* (New York: Schocken Books, 1972).

Dobbs, Brian, *Dear Diary: Some Studies in Self-Interest* (London: Elm Tree Books, 1974).

Fothergill, Robert A., *Private Chronicles: A Study of English Diaries* (London: Oxford University Press, 1974).

Matthews, William, *American Diaries in Manuscript, 1580-1954: A Descriptive Bibliography* (Athens, GA: University of Georgia Press, 1974).

Bourcier, Élisabeth, *Les journaux privés en Angleterre de 1600 à 1660* (Paris: Publications de la Sorbonne, 1976).

Bruss, Elizabeth W., *Autobiographical Acts: The Changing Situation of a Literary Genre* (Baltimore: Johns Hopkins University Press, 1976).

Gittings, Robert, *The Nature of Biography* (Seattle: University of Washington Press, 1978).

Weintraub, Karl Joachim, *The Value of the Individual: Self and Circumstance in Autobiography* (Chicago: University of Chicago Press, 1978).

Spufford, Margaret, 'First Steps in Literacy: The Reading and Writing Experiences of the Humblest Seventeenth-Century Spiritual Autobiographers', *Social History* 4 (1979), 407–35.

Gusdorf, Georges, 'Conditions and Limits of Autobiography', trans. James Olney, in *Autobiography: Essays Theoretical and Critical*, ed. James Olney (Princeton, NJ: Princeton University Press, 1980), 28–49.

Olney, James, ed., *Autobiography: Essays Theoretical and Critical* (Princeton, NJ: Princeton University Press, 1980).

Pomerleau, Cynthia S., 'The Emergence of Women's Autobiography in England', in *Women's Autobiography: Essays in Criticism*, ed. Estelle C. Jelinek (Bloomington, IN: Indiana University Press, 1980), 21–38.

Spengemann, William C., *The Forms of Autobiography: Episodes in the History of a Literary Genre* (New Haven, CT: Yale University Press, 1980).

Findley, Sandra and Elaine Hobby, 'Seventeenth Century Women's Autobiography', in *1642: Literature and Power in the Seventeenth Century: Proceedings of the Essex Conference on the Sociology of Literature, July l980*, ed. Francis Barker et al. (Colchester: University of Essex, 1981), 11–36.

Caldwell, Patricia, *The Puritan Conversion Narrative: The Beginnings of American Expression* (Cambridge: Cambridge University Press, 1983).

Anderson, Judith H., *Biographical Truth: The Representation of Historical Persons in Tudor-Stuart Writing* (New Haven, CT: Yale University Press, 1984).

Mendelson, Sara Heller, 'Stuart Women's Diaries and Occasional Memoirs', in *Women in English Society 1500-1800*, ed. Mary Prior (London: Methuen, 1985), 181-210.

Epstein, William H., *Recognizing Biography* (Philadelphia: University of Pennsylvania Press, 1987).

Faller, Lincoln B., *Turned to Account: The Forms and Functions of Criminal Biography in Late Seventeenth and Early Eighteenth-Century England* (Cambridge: Cambridge University Press, 1987).

Whittemore, Reed, *Pure Lives: The Early Biographers* (Baltimore: Johns Hopkins University Press, 1988).

Folkenflik, Robert, *The Culture of Autobiography: Constructions of Self-Representation* (Stanford, CA: Stanford University Press, 1993).

Mayer, Thomas F. and D. R. Woolf eds, *The Rhetorics of Life-Writing in Early Modern Europe: Forms of Biography from Cassandra Fedele to Louis XIV* (Ann Arbor, MI: University of Michigan Press, 1995).

Mascuch, Michael, *Origins of the Individualist Self: Autobiography and Self-Identity in England, 1591-1791* (Stanford, CA: Stanford University Press, 1996).

Sherman, Stuart, *Telling Time: Clocks, Diaries, and English Diurnal Form, 1660-1785* (Chicago: University of Chicago Press, 1996).

Amelang, James S., *The Flight of Icarus: Artisan Autobiography in Early Modern Europe* (Stanford, CA: Stanford University Press, 1998).

Payne, Rodger M., *The Self and the Sacred: Conversion and Autobiography in Early American Protestantism* (Knoxville, TN: University of Tennessee Press, 1998).

Dragstra, Henk, Sheila Ottway, and Helen Wilcox eds, *Betraying Our Selves: Forms of Self-Representation in Early Modern English Texts* (Houndmills: Macmillan, 2000).

McKay, Elaine, 'The Diary Network in Sixteenth and Seventeenth Century England', *Eras Journal* 2 (November 2001), http://artsonline.monash.edu.au/eras/the-diary-network-in-sixteenth-and-seventeenth-century-england/, accessed 17 December 2017.

France, Peter and William St Clair, eds, *Mapping Lives: The Uses of Biography* (Oxford: Oxford University Press for the British Academy, 2002).

Myers, Robin, Michael Harris, and Giles Mandelbrote eds, *Lives in Print: Biography and the Book Trade from the Middle Ages to the 21st century* (New Castle, DE and London: Oak Knoll Press & The British Library, 2002).

Clarke, Elizabeth, 'Diaries', in *A Companion to English Renaissance Literature and Culture*, ed. Michael Hattaway, paperback edn (Oxford: Blackwell, 2003), 609–14.

Heale, Elizabeth, *Autobiography and Authorship in Renaissance Verse* (Houndmills: Palgrave Macmillan, 2003).

Botonaki, Effie, *Seventeenth-Century English Women's Autobiographical Writings: Disclosing Enclosures* (Lewiston, NY: Edwin Mellen Press, 2004).

Hindmarsh, D. Bruce, *The Evangelical Conversion Narrative: Spiritual Autobiography in Early Modern England* (Oxford: Oxford University Press, 2005).

McKay, Elaine, 'English Diarists: Gender, Geography and Occupation, 1500–1700', *History* 90 (2005), 191–212.

Pritchard, Allan, *English Biography in the Seventeenth Century: A Critical Survey* (Toronto: University of Toronto Press, 2005).

Bedford, Ronald, Lloyd Davis, and Philippa Kelly eds, *Early Modern Autobiography: Theories, Genres, Practices* (Ann Arbor, MI: University of Michigan Press, 2006).

Brekus, Catherine A., 'Writing as a Protestant Practice: Devotional Diaries in Early New England', in *Practicing Protestants: Histories of Christian Life in America, 1630–1965*, ed Laurie F. Maffly-Kipp, Leigh E. Schmidt, and Mark Valeri (Baltimore: Johns Hopkins University Press, 2006), 19–34.

Seelig, Sharon Cadman, *Autobiography and Gender in Early Modern Literature: Reading Women's Lives, 1660–1680* (Cambridge: Cambridge University Press, 2006).

Bedford, Ronald, Lloyd Davis, and Philippa Kelly, eds, *Early Modern English Lives: Autobiography and Self-Representation, 1500–1660* (Aldershot: Ashgate, 2007).

Dowd, Michelle M. and Julie A. Eckerle eds, *Genre and Women's Life Writing in Early Modern England* (Aldershot: Ashgate, 2007).

Hodgkin, Katharine, *Madness in Seventeenth-Century Autobiography* (Houndmills: Palgrave Macmillan, 2007).

Sharpe, Kevin and Steven Zwicker eds, *Writing Lives: Biography and Textuality, Identity and Representation in Early Modern England* (Oxford: Oxford University Press, 2008).

Skura, Meredith Anne, *Tudor Autobiography: Listening for Inwardness* (Chicago: University of Chicago Press, 2008).

Smyth, Adam, *Autobiography in Early Modern England* (Cambridge: Cambridge University Press, 2010).

Dowd, Michelle M. and Julie A. Eckerle, 'Recent Studies in Early Modern English Life Writing', *ELR* 40 (2010), 132–62.

Collett, Anne and Louise D'Arcens eds, *The Unsociable Sociability of Women's Lifewriting* (Houndmills: Palgrave Macmillan, 2010).

Baggerman, Arianne, Rudolf Dekker, and Michael Mascuch eds, *Controlling Time and Shaping the Self: Developments in Autobiographical Writing since the Sixteenth Century* (Leiden: Brill, 2011).

Lynch, Kathleen, *Protestant Autobiography in the Seventeenth-Century Anglophone World* (Oxford: Oxford University Press, 2012).

Eckerle, Julie A., *Romancing the Self in Early Modern Englishwomen's Life Writing* (Farnham: Ashgate, 2013).

Leader, Zachary, ed., *On Life-Writing* (Oxford: Oxford University Press, 2015).

Smith, Robert F. W. and Gemma L. Watson eds, *Writing the Lives of People and Things, AD 500-1700: A Multi-Disciplinary Future for Biography* (Farnham: Ashgate, 2016).

Smyth, Adam, ed., *A History of English Autobiography* (Cambridge: Cambridge University Press, 2016).

E. *Other post-1750 printed books*

Adams, Simon, 'Dudley, Ambrose, earl of Warwick (*c.*1530–1590)', *ODNB*.

Albion, Gordon, *Charles I and the Court of Rome: A Study in 17th Century Diplomacy* (London: Burns, Oates & Washbourne, 1935).

Alston, R. C., *Treatises on Short-Hand, A Bibliography of the English Language from the Invention of Printing to the Year 1800*, viii (London: E. J. Arnold for the author, 1966).

Amelang, James S., 'Tracing Lives: The Spanish Inquisition and the Act of Autobiography', in *Controlling Time and Shaping the Self: Developments in Autobiographical Writing since the Sixteenth Century*, ed. Arianne Baggerman, Rudolf Dekker, and Michael Mascuch (Leiden: Brill, 2011), 33–48.

Anderegg, Michael A., 'The Tradition of Early More Biography', in *Essential Articles for the Study of Thomas More*, ed. R. S. Sylvester and G. P. Marc'hadour (Hamden, CT: Archon Books, 1977), 3–25, and notes, 583–9.

Anon., 'The Autobiographies of Thomas Hobbes', *Mind* 48 (1939), 403–5.

Anon., '[Illustration]: Diary of Richard Stonley', *Shakespeare Quarterly* 24 (1973), unnumbered pages (3–4).

Appleby, John C., 'Roydon, Sir Marmaduke (1583–1646)', *ODNB*.

Arblaster, Paul, *Antwerp & the World: Richard Verstegan and the International Culture of Catholic Reformation* (Leuven: Leuven University Press, 2004).

Archer, Ian W., 'The Arts and Acts of Memorialization in Early Modern London', in *Imagining Early Modern London: Perceptions and Portrayals of the City from Stow to Strype, 1598–1720*, ed. J. F. Merritt (Cambridge: Cambridge University Press, 2001), 89–113.

Archer, Ian W., 'Lambe, William (*d.* 1580)', *ODNB*.

Aughterson, Kate, 'Isham, Elizabeth (*bap.* 1608, *d.* 1654)', *ODNB*.

Axon, Ernest, 'The King's Preachers in Lancashire, 1599–1845', *Transactions of the Lancashire and Cheshire Antiquarian Society* 56 (1941–2), 67–104.

Baker, Naomi, 'Johnson, Cicely (*fl.* 1617/18–1636/7)', *ODNB*.

Baldwin, David, *The Chapel Royal Ancient & Modern* (London: Duckworth, 1990).

Baskerville, E. J., 'A Religious Disturbance in Canterbury, June 1561', *Historical Research*, 65 (1992), 340–8.

Bayer, Gerd, *Novel Horizons: The Genre Making of Restoration Fiction* (Manchester: Manchester University Press, 2016).

Bellany, Alastair, 'Clavell, John (1601-1643)', *ODNB*.

Benbow, R. Mark, 'The Providential Theory of Historical Causation in *Holinshed's Chronicles*: 1577 and 1587', *Texas Studies in Literature and Language* 1 (1959), 264–76.

Bendall, Sarah, 'Norwood, Richard (1590-1675)', *ODNB*.

Bennell, John, 'Whithorne, Thomas (*c*.1528–1596)', *ODNB*.

Bennett, Kate, 'John Aubrey's Oxfordshire Collections: An Edition of Aubrey's Annotations to His Presentation Copy of Robert Plot's *Natural History of Oxford-shire*, Bodleian Library Ashmole 1722', *Oxoniensia* 64 (1999), 59–86.

Bennett, Kate, 'John Aubrey and the Printed Book', *Huntington Library Quarterly* 76 (2013), 393–411.

Bennett, Kate, 'John Aubrey and the Rhapsodic Book', *Renaissance Studies* 28 (2014), 317–32.

Bennett, Kate, 'General Introduction' to John Aubrey, *Brief Lives with an Apparatus for the Lives of our English Mathematical Writers*, ed. Kate Bennett, 2 vols (Oxford: Oxford University Press, 2015), 1:xxi–cvi.

Bennett, R. E., 'Walton's Use of Donne's Letters,' *Philological Quarterly* 16 (1973), 30–4.

Bernbaum, Ernest, *The Mary Carleton Narratives 1663-1673: A Missing Chapter in the History of the English novel* (Cambridge, MA: Harvard University Press, 1914).

Bevan, Jonquil, 'Izaak Walton and His Publisher, *The Library* 32 (1977), 344–59.

Bevan, Jonquil, 'Izaak Walton's Collections for Fulman's life of John Hales: The Walker Part', *Bodleian Library Record* 13 (1989), 160–71.

B[indoff], S. T., 'Topcliffe, Richard (1531-1604), of Somerby, Lincs. and Westminster', in *The House of Commons* 1558-1603, ed. P. W. Hasler, 3 vols (London: HMSO for the History of Parliament Trust, 1981), 3:513–15.

Birrell, T. A., 'William Carter (c. 1549–84): Recusant Printer, Publisher, Binder, Stationer, Scribe - and Martyr', *Recusant History* 28 (2006), 22–42.

Blank, Paula, *Broken English: Dialects and the Politics of Language in Renaissance Writings* (London: Routledge, 1996).

Blatchley-Hennah, F. T. W., *A Short History of Sutton Valence School* (Maidstone: Kent Messenger, 1952).

Boyd, Morrison Comegys, *Elizabethan Music and Musical Criticism*, 2nd edn (Philadelphia: University of Pennsylvania Press, 1962).

Braden, Gordon, 'Biography', in *The Oxford History of Literary Translation in English*, vol. 2, 1550-1660, ed. Gordon Braden, Robert Cummings, and Stuart Gillespie (Oxford: Oxford University Press, 2010), 322–30.

Bradshaw, Brendan, 'George Browne, First Reformation Archbishop of Dublin, 1536-1554', *Journal of Ecclesiastical History* 21 (1970), 301–26.

Bradshaw, Brendan, 'The Edwardian Reformation in Ireland, 1547–53', *Archivium Hibernicum* 34 (1976/7), 83–99.

Bray, Alan, 'To Be a Man in Early Modern Society: The Curious Case of Michael Wigglesworth', *History Workshop Journal*, 41 (1996), 155–65.

Bremer, Francis J., *Congregational Communion: Clerical Friendship in the Anglo-American Puritan Community, 1610–1692* (Boston: Northeastern University Press, 1994).

Bremer, Francis J., 'Rogers, Richard (1551–1618)', *ODNB*.

Bremer, Francis J., 'Williams, Roger (c.1606–1683)', *ODNB*.

Brown, Nancy Pollard, 'Paperchase: The Dissemination of Catholic Texts in Elizabethan England', *English Manuscript Studies 1100–1700*, 1 (1988), 120–43.

Burney, Charles, *A General History of Music, from the Earliest Ages to the Present Period*, 4 vols (London: Payne & Son, 1776–89).

Butler, Alban, *The Life of Sir Tobie Matthews* [*sic*] (London: J. P. Coghlan, 1795).

Butts, J. E., 'A Bibliography of Izaak Walton's *Lives*', *Oxford Bibliographical Society Proceedings & Papers* 2 (1927–30), 327–40.

Butts, J. E., 'Izaak Walton's Collections for Fulman's Life of John Hales', *Modern Language Review* 29 (1934), 267–73.

Cambers, Andrew, 'Readers' Marks and Religious Practice: Margaret Hoby's Marginalia', in *Tudor Books and Readers: Materiality and the Construction of Meaning*, ed. John N. King (Cambridge: Cambridge University Press, 2010), 211–31.

Cameron, K. W., 'John Heywood and Richard Stonley', *Shakespeare Association Bulletin* 14 (1939), 55–6.

Carley, James P., 'Introduction' to John Leland, *De viris illustribus. On Famous Men*, ed./trans. James P. Carley with Caroline Brett (Toronto: Pontifical Institute of Mediaeval Studies/ Bodleian Library, 2010), xi–xxxv.

Carlson, Eric Josef, 'English Funeral Sermons as Sources: The Example of Female Piety in Pre-1640 Sermons', *Albion* 32 (2000), 567–97.

Carlton, William J., *Bibliotheca Pepysiana. A Descriptive Catalogue of the Library of Samuel Pepys*, 4 vols, *Part IV. Shorthand Books* (London: Sidgwick & Jackson, 1940).

Carter, P. R. N., 'Wentworth, Thomas, first Baron Wentworth (1501–1551)', *ODNB*.

Chambers, Douglas D. C., 'Evelyn, John (1620–1706)', *ODNB*.

Chambers, R. W., 'The Continuity of English Prose from Alfred to More and His School', in Nicholas Harpsfield, *The Life and Death of Sr Thomas Moore, Knight, Sometimes Lord High Chancellor of England*, ed. Elsie Vaughan Hitchcock and R. W. Chambers (London: Oxford University Press for the Early English Text Society, 1932), xlv–clxxiv.

Chappell, Edwin, 'Introduction' to Samuel Pepys, *Shorthand Letters of Samuel Pepys. From a Volume Entitled S. Pepys's Official Correspondence 1662–1679*, ed. Edwin Chappell (Cambridge: University Press, 1933), vii–xiv.

Charlton, Kenneth, *Women, Religion and Education in Early Modern England* (London: Routledge, 1990).

Chaytor, Miranda, 'Household and Kinship: Ryton in the late 16th and early 17th centuries', *History Workshop* 10 (1980), 25–60.

Cherniavsky, Eva, 'Night Pollution and the Floods of Confession in Michael Wigglesworth's Diary', *Arizona Quarterly* 45:2 (1989), 15–33.

Clegg, Cyndia Susan, *Press Censorship in Jacobean England* (Cambridge: Cambridge University Press, 2001).

Clegg, Cyndia Susan, 'Fleming, Abraham', *ODNB*.

Clennell, William, 'Introduction' to *The Autobiography of Thomas Bodley*, ed. William Clennell (Oxford: Bodleian Library, 2006), 9–31.

Clennell, W. H., 'Bodley, Sir Thomas (1545–1613)', *ODNB*.

Clifford, James L., 'Introduction' to *Biography as an Art: Selected Criticism 1560–1960*, ed. James L. Clifford (London: Oxford University Press, 1962), ix–xxii.

Colahan, Clark, 'Dangerfield's Picaresque *Don Tomazo*: English Novelists as Spanish (Anti-Heroes)', *Neohelicon* 25 (1998), 311–28.

Collinson, Patrick, '"A magazine of religious patterns": An Erasmian Topic Transposed in English Protestantism', in *Godly People: Essays on English Protestantism and Puritanism* (London: Hambledon Press, 1983), 499–525.

Collinson, Patrick, 'Puritan Emmanuel', in Sarah Bendall, Christopher Brooke, and Patrick Collinson, *A History of Emmanuel College, Cambridge* (Woodbridge, Suffolk: Boydell Press, 1999), 177–226.

Collinson, Patrick, 'Dyke, Daniel (*d.* 1614)', *ODNB*.

Collinson, Patrick, John Craig, and Brett Usher, 'Rogers, Richard (1551–1618)', in *Conference and Combination Lectures in the Elizabethan Church: Dedham and Bury St Edmunds 1582–1590*, ed. Patrick Collinson, John Craig, and Brett Usher (Woodbridge, Suffolk: Boydell Press, 2003), 224–6.

Conrad, F. W., 'Manipulating Reputations: Sir Thomas More, Sir Thomas Elyot, and the Conclusion of William Roper's *Lyfe of Sir Thomas Moore, Knighte*', in *The Rhetorics of Life-Writing in Early Modern Europe: Forms of Biography from Cassandra Fedele to Louis XIV*, ed. Thomas F. Mayer and D. R. Woolf (Ann Arbor, MI: University of Michigan Press, 1995), 133–61.

Cooper, Tarnya, *Citizen Portrait: Portrait Painting and the Urban Elite of Tudor and Jacobean England and Wales* (New Haven, CT: Yale University Press for the Paul Mellon Centre for Studies in British Art, 2012).

Cooper, Thompson, 'Benson, Robert (1797–1844)', rev. Hugh Mooney, *ODNB*.

Cooper, Thompson, 'Montagu, Walter (1604/5–1677)', rev. Edward Charles Metzger, *ODNB*.

Copsey, Richard, 'The Wandering Doctoral Student: An Analysis of MS. Harley 1819 John Bale's Notebook of His Visit to France and Italy in 1526–1527', in *Carmel in Britain: Studies on the Early History of the Carmelite Order*, III, *The Hermits from Mount Carmel* (Faversham and Rome: Saint Albert's Press & Edizioni Carmelitane, 2004), 283–307.

Crawford, Julie, 'Reconsidering Early Modern Women's Writing: or, How Margaret Hoby Read Her De Mornay', *Huntington Library Quarterly* 73 (2010), 193–223.

Crawford, Patricia, *Blood, Bodies and Families in Early Modern England* (Harlow: Pearson, 2004).

Cressy, David, 'Kinship and Kin Interaction in Early Modern England', *Past and Present* 113 (1986), 38–69.

Cross, Claire, 'Matthew, Frances (1550/51–1629)', *ODNB*.

D[ale], M. K., 'Wentworth, Sir Thomas I (by 1500–1551), of Nettlestead, Suff. and Westminster, Mdx.', in *The House of Commons 1509–1558*, ed. S. T. Bindoff, 3 vols (London: History of Parliament Trust, 1982), 3:584–5.

Davey, Henry, *History of English Music* (London: J. Curwen & Sons, [1895]).

Davey, Henry, 'Whithorne, Thomas (*fl.* 1590)', in *Dictionary of National Biography*, ed. Leslie Stephen and Sidney Lee, 63 vols (London, 1885–1900), 61:137–8.

D[avidson], A[lan] and R[osemary] C. L. S[groi], 'Matthew, Tobie (1577–1655), of Durham House, The Strand, Westminster', in *The House of Commons 1604–1629*, ed. Andrew Thrush & John P. Ferris, 6 vols (Cambridge: Cambridge University Press for the History of Parliament Trust, 2010), 5:286–8.

Davies, W. T., 'A Bibliography of John Bale', *Oxford Bibliographical Proceedings & Papers* 5 (1936–9) (Oxford, 1940).

Denis, Philippe, 'John Veron: The First Known French Protestant in England', *Proceedings of the Huguenot Society of London* 22 (1973), 257–63.

Depas-Orange, Ann and Robert C. Evans eds, *'The Birthday of My Self': Martha Moulsworth, Renaissance Poet*, special issue of *Critical Matrix* 10 (1996).

D'Israeli, Iaac, *Miscellanies; or, Literary Recreations* (London: T. Cadell and W. Davies, 1796).

Donagan, Barbara, 'Fairclough, Samuel (1594–1677)', *ODNB*.

Donaldson, Ian, 'National Biography and the Arts of Memory: From Thomas Fuller to Colin Matthew', in *Mapping Lives: The Uses of Biography*, ed. Peter France and William St Clair (Oxford: Oxford University Press for the British Academy, 2002), 67–82.

Donno, Elizabeth Story, 'Abraham Fleming, a Learned Corrector in 1586–87', *Studies in Bibliography* 42 (1989), 200–11.

Donovan, Josephine, *Women and the Rise of the Novel, 1405–1726*, 2nd edn (New York: Palgrave Macmillan, 2013).

Dottie, Roy G., 'The Recusant Riots at Childwall in May, 1600: A Reappraisal', *Transactions of the Historic Society of Lancashire and Cheshire* 132 (1982), 1–28.

Dove, Mary, *The Perfect Ages of Man's Life* (Cambridge: Cambridge University Press, 1989).

Eales, Jacqueline, 'Samuel Clarke and the "Lives" of Godly Women in Seventeenth-Century England', in *Women in the Church: Papers Read at the 1989 Summer Meeting and the 1990 Winter Meeting of the Ecclesiastical History Society*, ed. W. J. Sheils and Diana Wood (Oxford: Basil Blackwell for the Ecclesiastical History Society, 1990), 365–76.

Eardley, Alice, '"Like hewen stone": Augustine, Audience and Revision in Elizabeth Isham's "Booke of Remembrance" (c. 1639)', in *Women and Writing, c. 1340–1650: The Domestication of Print Culture*, ed. Anne Lawrence-Mathers and Philippa Hardman (York: York Medieval Press, University of York, 2010), 177–95.

Ellis, S. G., 'John Bale, Bishop of Ossory, 1552–3', *Journal of the Butler Society* 3:2 (1984), 282–93.

Elson, James Hinsdale, *John Hales of Eton* (Morningside Heights, NY: King's Crown Press, 1948).

Elton, G. R., 'The Elizabethan Exchequer: War in the Receipt' (1961), reprinted in *Studies in Tudor and Stuart Politics and Government: Papers and Reviews 1946–1972*, vol. 1, *Tudor Politics/Tudor Government* (Cambridge: Cambridge University Press, 1974), 355–88.

Evans, Robert C., 'Deference and Defiance: The "Memorandum" of Martha Moulsworth', in *Representing Women in Renaissance England*, ed. Claude J. Summers and Ted-Larry Pebworth (Columbia, MO: University of Missouri Press, 1997), 175–86.

Evans, Robert C., 'A Silent Woman Speaks: "The Memorandum of Martha Moulsworth, Widowe"', *Yale University Library Gazette* 69 (1995), 149–62.

Evans, Robert C., 'Moulsworth, Martha (1577–1646)', *ODNB*.

Evans, Robert C. and Anne C. Little eds, *'The Muses Female Are': Martha Moulsworth and Other Women Writers of the English Renaissance* (West Cornwall, CT: Locust Hill Press, 1995).

Evans, Robert C. and Barbara Wiedemann eds, *'My Name Was Martha': A Renaissance Woman's Autobiographical Poem* (West Cornwall, CT: Locust Hill Press, 1993).
see also Depas-Orange, Ann.

Evenden, Elizabeth, *Patents, Pictures and Patronage: John Day and the Tudor Book Trade* (Aldershot: Ashgate, 2008).

Evenden, Elizabeth and Thomas S. Freeman, 'John Foxe, John Day and the Printing of the "Book of Martyrs"', in *Lives in Print: Biography and the Book Trade from the Middle Ages to the 21st century*, ed. Robin Myers, Michael Harris, and Giles Mandelbrote (New Castle, DE and London: Oak Knoll Press & The British Library, 2002), 23–54.

Evenden, Elizabeth and Thomas S. Freeman, *Religion and the Book in Early Modern England: the Making of Foxe's 'Book of Martyrs'* (Cambridge: Cambridge University Press, 2011).

Ezell, Margaret J. M., 'Ann Halkett's Morning Devotions: Posthumous Publication and the Culture of Writing in Late Seventeenth-Century Britain', in *Print, Manuscript, & Performance: The Changing Relations of the Media in Early Modern England*, ed. Arthur F. Marotti and Michael D. Bristol (Columbus: Ohio State University Press, 2000), 215–31.

Ezell, Margaret J. M., 'Domestic Papers: Manuscript Culture and Early Modern Women's Life Writing', in *Genre and Women's Life Writing in Early Modern England*, ed. Michelle M. Dowd and Julie A. Eckerle (Aldershot: Ashgate, 2007), 33–48.

Fairfax-Lucy, Alice, *Charlecote and the Lucys: The Chronicle of an English Family* (London: Oxford University Press, 1958).

Fairfield, Leslie P., *John Bale, Mythmaker for the English Reformation* (West Lafayette, IN: Purdue University Press, 1976).

Fairfield, Leslie P., 'The *Vocacyon of Johan Bale* and Early English Autobiography', *Renaissance Quarterly* 24 (1971), 327–40.

Faller, Lincoln B., *Crime and Defoe: A New Kind of Writing* (Cambridge: Cambridge University Press, 1997).

Fellowes, Edmund Horace, *The English Madrigal Composers* (Oxford: Clarendon Press, 1921).

Finkelpearl, P. J., 'Manningham, John (*c.*1575–1622)', *ODNB*.

Flynn, Jane, '*When all that is to Was ys brought*: John Heywood's "rythme declaringe his own life and nature"', *British Catholic History* 33 (2017), 323–56.

Fox, Adam, 'Aubrey, John (1626–1697)', *ODNB*.

Freeman, Thomas S., '"The good ministrye of godlye and vertuouse women": The Elizabethan Martyrologists and the Female Supporters of the Marian Martyrs', *Journal of British Studies* 39 (2000), 8–31.

Freeman, Thomas S., 'Harpsfield, Nicholas (1519–1575)', *ODNB*.
see also Evenden, Elizabeth and Thomas S. Freeman.

Fritze, Ronald H., 'Kingsmill family (*per. c.*1480–1698)', *ODNB*.

Fubini, Riccardo, *Storiografia dell'Umanesimo in Italia da Leonardo Bruni ad Annio da Viterbo* (Rome: Edizioni di Storia e Letteratura, 2003).

F[uidge], N. M., 'Stoneley, Richard (*c.* 1520–1600), of Itchington, Warws., Doddington, Essex, and London', in *The House of Commons, 1558–1603*, ed. P. W. Hasler, 3 vols (London: HMSO for the History of Parliament Trust, 1981), 3:450–1.

Fumerton, Patricia, *Unsettled: The Culture of Mobility and the Working Poor in Early Modern England* (Chicago: University of Chicago Press, 2006).

Gadd, I., 'Carter, William (*b.* in or before 1549, *d.* 1584)', *ODNB*.

Gardner, Helen, 'Dean Donne's Monument in St. Paul's', in *Evidence in Literary Scholarship: Essays in Memory of James Marshall Osborn*, ed. René Wellek and Alvaro Ribeiro (Oxford: Clarendon Press, 1979), 29–44.

Garrido Ardila, J. A., 'The Picaresque Novel and the Rise of the English Novel: From Baldwin and Delony to Defoe and Smollett', in *The Picaresque Novel in Western Literature: From the Sixteenth Century to the Neopicaresque*, ed. J. A. Garrido Ardila (Cambridge: Cambridge University Press, 2015), 113–39.

Girtin, Thomas, *The Golden Ram: A Narrative History of the Clothworkers' Company, 1528–1958* (London: The Clothworkers' Company, 1958).

Gittings, Clare, *Death, Burial and the Individual in Early Modern England* (London: Croom Helm, 1984).

Gladfelder, Hal, *Criminality and Narrative in Eighteenth-Century England: Beyond the Law* (Baltimore: Johns Hopkins University Press, 2001).

Gordon, Andrew, *Writing Early Modern London: Memory, Text and Community* (Basingstoke: Palgrave Macmillan, 2013).

Gordon, Andrew and Thomas Rist eds, *The Arts of Remembrance in Early Modern England: Memorial Cultures of the Post Reformation* (Farnham: Ashgate, 2013).

Green, Ian, *Print and Protestantism in Early Modern England* (Oxford: Oxford University Press, 2000).

Greer, Germaine, '"Backward springs": The Self-Invention of Martha Moulsworth', in *'The Muses Female Are': Martha Moulsworth and Other Women Writers of the English Renaissance*, ed. Robert C. Evans and Anne C. Little (West Cornwall, CT: Locust Hill Press, 1995), 3–8.

Grundy, Isobel, 'Identity and Numbers in Martha Moulsworth's "Memorandum"', in *'The Muses Female Are': Martha Moulsworth and Other Women Writers of the English Renaissance*, ed. Robert C. Evans and Anne C. Little (West Cornwall, CT: Locust Hill Press, 1995), 9–16.

Guscott, S. J., 'Hinde, William (1568/9–1629)', *ODNB*.

Guy, John, *Tudor England* (Oxford: Oxford University Press, 1988).

Hadfield, Andrew, 'Translating the Reformation: John Bale's Irish *Vocacyon*', in *Representing Ireland: Literature and the Origins of Conflict, 1534–1660*, ed. Brendan Bradshaw, Andrew Hadfield, and Willy Maley (Cambridge: Cambridge University Press, 1993), 43–59.

Haigh, Christopher, *Reformation and Resistance in Tudor Lancashire* (Cambridge: Cambridge University Press, 1975).

Haller, William, *The Rise of Puritanism: or, The Way to the New Jerusalem as Set Forth in Pulpit and Press from Thomas Cartwright to John Lilburne and John Milton, 1570–1643* (New York: Columbia University Press, 1938).

Hallett, Nicky, *The Senses in Religious Communities, 1600–1800: Early Modern 'Convents of Pleasure'* (Farnham: Ashgate, 2013).

[Halliwell-Phillipps, J. O.], *A Calendar of the Shakespearean Rarities, Drawings and Engravings, Preserved at Hollingbury Copse, near Brighton* (London: privately printed, 1887).

Hambrick-Stowe, Charles, *The Practice of Piety: Puritan Devotional Disciplines in Seventeenth-Century New England* (Chapel Hill, NC: University of North Carolina Press, 1982).

Happé, Peter, *John Bale* (New York: Twayne, 1996).

Happé, Peter, '*The Vocacyon of Johan Bale*: Protestant Rhetoric and the Self', in *Betraying Our Selves: Forms of Self-Representation in Early Modern English Texts*, ed Henk Dragstra, Sheila Ottway, and Helen Wilcox (Houndmills: Macmillan, 2000), 45–58.

Happé, Peter and John N. King, 'Introduction' to John Bale, *The Vocacyon of John Bale* (Binghamton, NY: Medieval & Renaissance Texts & Studies/Renaissance English Text Society, 1990), 1–24.

H[arding], A[lan], 'Kingsmill, Richard (*c.* 1528–1600), of Highclere, Hants.', in *The House of Commons 1558–1603*, ed. P. W. Hasler, 3 vols (London: HMSO for the History of Parliament Trust, 1981), 2:400–1.

Hardman, Anne, *English Carmelites in Penal Times* (London: Burns Oates & Washbourne, 1936).

Harris, Jesse W., *John Bale* (Urbana, IL: University of Illinois Press, 1940).

Heal, Felicity, 'Stonley, Richard (1520/21–1600)', *ODNB* (2016).

Heal, Felicity and Henry Summerson, 'The Genesis of the Two Editions', in *The Oxford Handbook of Holinshed's Chronicles*, ed. Paulina Kewes, Ian W. Archer, and Felicity Heal (Oxford: Oxford University Press, 2013), 3–20.

Heale, Elizabeth, 'Thomas Whithorne and First-Person Life-Writing in the Sixteenth Century', in *The Oxford Handbook of Tudor Literature, 1485–1603*, ed. Mike Pincombe and Cathy Shrank (Oxford: Oxford University Press, 2009), 606–22.

Healy, Simon, 'Harington, John, second Baron Harington of Exton (*bap.* 1592, *d.* 1614)', *ODNB*.

Heffernan, Thomas J., *Sacred Biography: Saints and their Biographers in the Middle Ages*, (New York: Oxford University Press, 1988).

Henderson, Frances, '"Posterity to judge"–John Rushworth and his "Historicall Collections"', *Bodleian Library Record* 15 (1996), 247–59.

Henderson, Frances, 'Reading, and Writing, the Text of the Putney Debates', in *The Putney Debates of 1647: The Army, the Levellers, and the English State*, ed. Michael Mendle (Cambridge: Cambridge University Press, 2001), 36–50.

Henderson, Frances, 'Appendix C: A Note on William Clarke's Shorthand', in *The Clarke Papers: Further Selections from the Papers of William Clarke*, ed. Frances Henderson (Cambridge: Cambridge University Press for the Royal Historical Society, 2005), 375–82.

Henderson, Frances, '"Swifte and secrete writing" in Seventeenth-Century England, and Samuel Shelton's *Brachygraphy*', *electronic British Library Journal* (2008), article 7. https://www.bl.uk/eblj/2008articles/pdf/ebljarticle52008.pdf, accessed 17 December 2017.

Heseltine, Philip *see* Warlock, Peter.

Hibbard, Caroline M., *Charles I and the Popish Plot* (Chapel Hill, NC: University of North Carolina Press, 1983).

Hindle, Steve, *The State and Social Change in Early Modern England, c. 1550–1640* (Houndmills: Macmillan, 2000).

Hindle, Steve, 'Bruen, John (1560–1625)', *ODNB*.

Hinds, Hilary, *God's Englishwomen: Seventeenth-Century Radical Sectarian Writing and Feminist Criticism* (Manchester: Manchester University Press, 1996).

Hitchcock, Elsie Vaughan, 'Life and Works of Nicholas Harpsfield', in Nicholas Harpsfield, *The Life and Death of Sr Thomas Moore, Knight, Sometimes Lord High Chancellor of England*, ed. Elsie Vaughan Hitchcock and R. W. Chambers (London: Oxford University Press for the Early English Text Society, 1932), clxxv–ccxiv.

Hodgkin, Katharine, 'Thomas Whythorne and the Problems of Mastery', *History Workshop* 29 (1990), 20–41.

Hotson, Leslie, 'The Library of Elizabeth's Embezzling Teller', *Studies in Bibliography* 2 (1949–50), 49–61.

Houlbrooke, Ralph, *Death, Religion, and the Family in England, 1480–1750* (Oxford: Clarendon Press, 1998).

Houlbrooke, Ralph, 'Dun, Sir Daniel (1544/5–1617)', *ODNB.*

Howarth, R. G., 'Introduction' to Samuel Pepys, *Letters and the Second Diary of Samuel Pepys*, ed. R. G. Howarth (London: J. M. Dent and Sons, 1932), vii–xviii.

Hudson, Anne, '*Visio Baleii*: An Early Literary Historian', in *The Long Fifteenth Century: Essays for Douglas Gray*, ed. Helen Cooper and Sally Mapstone (Oxford: Clarendon Press, 1997), 313–39.

Hughes, Walter, '"Meat out of the eater": Panic and Desire in American Puritan Poetry', in *Engendering Men: The Question of Male Feminist Criticism*, ed. Joseph A. Boone and Michael Cadden (New York: Routledge, 1990), 102–21.

Hulse, Clark, 'Dead Man's Treasure: The Cult of Thomas More', in *The Production of English Renaissance Culture*, ed. David Lee Miller, Sharon O'Dair, and Harold Weber (Ithaca, NY: Cornell University Press, 1994), 190–225.

Hunter, Joseph, *New Illustrations of the Life, Studies, and Writings of Shakespeare*, 2 vols (London: J. B. Nichols and Son, 1845).

Hunter, Michael, *John Aubrey and the Realm of Learning* (London: Duckworth, 1975).

Jack, Sybil M., 'A Capital Display: Initials in Exchequer Documents', *Parergon* 13 (1996), 63–76.

Jackson Williams, Kelsey, 'Training the Virtuoso: John Aubrey's Education and Early Life', *The Seventeenth Century* 27 (2012), 157–82.

Jackson Williams, Kelsey, *The Antiquary: John Aubrey's Historical Scholarship* (Oxford: Oxford University Press, 2016).

Jefferies, Henry A., *The Irish Church and the Tudor Reformations* (Dublin: Four Courts Press, 2010).

Jessopp, Augustus, *One Generation of a Norfolk House: A Contribution to Elizabethan History*, 2nd edn (London: Burns and Oates, 1879).

J[ones], W. J., 'Cooke, William II (1572–1619), of Gray's Inn and Highnam Court, Glos.', in *The House of Commons* 1558–1603, ed. P. W. Hasler, 3 vols (London: HMSO for the History of Parliament Trust, 1981), 1:647–8.

Jordan, W. K., *Philanthropy in England 1480–1660: A Study of the Changing Pattern of English Social Aspirations* (London: George Allen & Unwin, 1959).

Jotischky, Andrew, *The Carmelites and Antiquity: Mendicants and their Pasts in the Middle Ages* (Oxford: Oxford University Press, 2002).

Kassell, Lauren, *Medicine & Magic in Elizabethan London: Simon Forman: Astrologer, Alchemist, & Physician* (Oxford: Oxford University Press, 2005).

Kelsey, Harry, *Sir Francis Drake: The Queen's Pirate* (New Haven, CT: Yale University Press, 1998).

Kiessling, Nicolas K., *The Library of Anthony Wood* (Oxford: Oxford Bibliographical Society, 2002).

Kietzman, Mary Jo, *The Self-Fashioning of an Early Modern Englishwoman: Mary Carleton's Lives* (Aldershot: Ashgate, 2004).

King, Helen, 'Cellier, Elizabeth (*fl.* 1668–1688)', *ODNB.*

King, John N., *Foxe's Book of Martyrs and Early Modern Print Culture* (Cambridge: Cambridge University Press, 2006).

King, John N., 'Bale, John', *ODNB*.

see also Happé, Peter and John N. King.

Kisby, Fiona, 'Officers and Office-Holding at the English Court: A Study of the Chapel Royal, 1485–1547', *Royal Musical Association Research Chronicle* 32 (1999), 1–61.

Kisby, Fiona, 'Books in London Parish Churches before 1603: Some Preliminary Observations', in *The Church and Learning in Later Medieval Society: Essays in Honour of R. B. Dobson*, ed. Caroline M. Barron and Jenny Stratford (Donington: Shaun Tyas, 2002), 305–26.

Knappen, M. M., 'The Life of Richard Rogers', in *Two Elizabethan Puritan Diaries by Richard Rogers and Samuel Ward*, ed. M. M. Knappen (Chicago: The American Society of Church History, 1933), 17–35.

Knighton, C. S., 'Hill, Thomas (*d.* 1653)', *ODNB*.

Knowles, David, 'Introduction' to Tobie Matthew, *The Life of Lady Lucy Knatchbull*, ed. David Knowles (London: Sheed and Ward, 1931), vii–xxvii.

Kuhlisch, Tina, 'The Ambivalent Rogue: Moll Flanders as Modern *Pícara*', in *Rogues and Early Modern English Culture*, ed. Craig Dionne and Steve Mentz (Ann Arbor, MI: University of Michigan Press, 2004), 337–60.

Lake, Peter, 'Reading Clarke's *Lives* in Political and Polemical Context', in *Writing Lives: Biography and Textuality, Identity and Representation in Early Modern England*, ed. Kevin Sharpe and Steven N. Zwicker (Oxford: Oxford University Press, 2008), 293–318.

Lamb, Mary Ellen, 'The Poem as a Clock: Martha Moulsworth Tells Time Three Ways', in *'The Muses Female Are': Martha Moulsworth and Other Women Writers of the English Renaissance*, ed. Robert C. Evans and Anne C. Little (West Cornwall, CT: Locust Hill Press, 1995), 91–100.

Lamb, Mary Ellen, 'Margaret Hoby's Diary: Women's Reading Practices and the Gendering of the Reformation Subject', in *Pilgrimage for Love: Essays in Early Modern Literature in Honor of Josephine A. Roberts*, ed. Sigrid King (Tempe, AZ: Arizona Center for Medieval and Renaissance Studies, 1999), 63–94.

Lancaster, Henry, 'Crosse, Robert (1604/5–1683)', *ODNB*.

Laqueur, Thomas W., *Solitary Sex: A Cultural History of Masturbation* (New York: Zone Books, 2003).

Larminie, Vivienne, 'Charles Croke (*fl.* 1652–1686)', in 'Croke, Unton (1594/5–1670/71)', *ODNB*.

Larminie, Vivienne, 'King, Anne [*married names* Anne Dutton; Anne Howe, Lady Howe] (*b.* in or before 1621, *d.* 1684×1701)', *ODNB* (2005).

Lee, Sidney, 'Carter, John (1554–1635)', rev. Jason Yiannikkou, *ODNB*.

Lee, William, *Daniel Defoe: His Life, and His Recently Discovered Writings: Extending from 1716 to 1729*, 3 vols (London: John Camden Hotten, 1869).

Levack, Brian, *Renaissance Magic* (New York: Garland, 1992).

Levin, Carole, *Dreaming the English Renaissance: Politics and Desire in Court and Culture* (New York: Palgrave Macmillan, 2008).

Lewin, C. G., 'Eyre, Sir Samuel (*bap.* 1638, *d.* 1698)', *ODNB*.

Lewis, C. S., *English Literature in the Sixteenth Century excluding Drama* (Oxford: Clarendon Press, 1954).

Little, Anne C. *see* Evans, Robert C. and Anne C. Little.

Liu, Tai, 'Jackson, Arthur (*c.*1593–1666)', *ODNB*.

Livingston, Carole Rose, 'The Provenance of Three Early Broadsheets', *The Library*, 6th ser., 2 (1980), 53–6.

Livingston, Carole Rose, *British Broadside Ballads of the Sixteenth Century: A Catalogue of the Extant Sheets and an Essay* (New York: Garland, 1991).

Llewellyn, Nigel, 'Honour in Life, Death and in the Memory: Funeral Monuments in Early Modern England', *Transactions of the Royal Historical Society*, 6th ser., 6 (1996), 179–200.

Loomie, A. J., 'Gage, George (*c.*1582–1638)', *ODNB*.

Loomie, A. J., 'Matthew, Sir Toby (1577–1655)', *ODNB*.

Love, Harold, 'Gossip and Biography', in *Writing Lives: Biography and Textuality, Identity and Representation in Early Modern England*, ed. Kevin Sharpe and Steven N. Zwicker (Oxford: Oxford University Press, 2008), 91–104.

Loveman, Kate, '"Eminent cheats": Rogue Narratives in the Literature of the Exclusion Crisis', in *Fear, Exclusion and Revolution: Roger Morrice and Britain in the 1680s*, ed. Jason McElligott (Aldershot: Ashgate, 2006), 108–22.

Loveman, Kate, *Samuel Pepys and His Books: Reading, Newsgathering, and Sociability, 1660–1703* (Oxford: Oxford University Press, 2015).

Luborsky, Ruth Samson and Elizabeth Morley Ingram, *A Guide to English Illustrated Books 1536–1603*, 2 vols (Tempe, AZ: Medieval & Renaissance Texts & Studies, 1998).

McCusker, Honor, *John Bale: Dramatist and Antiquary* (Bryn Mawr, PA: Bryn Mawr College, 1942).

Macfarlane, Alan, *The Family Life of Ralph Josselin, a Seventeenth-Century Clergyman; An Essay in Historical Anthropology* (Cambridge: Cambridge University Press, 1970).

McKeon, Michael, *The Origins of the English Novel 1600–1740* (Baltimore: Johns Hopkins University Press, 1987).

McQuillan, Robert, 'Introduction' to Thomas Whythorne, *Songes for Five Voyces*, ed. Robert McQuillan (Moretonhampstead: Antico Edition, 2000), ix–xi.

Maguire, John, 'William Roper's *Life of More*: The Working Methods of a Tudor Biographer', *Moreana* 23 (1969) 59–65.

Malone, Edmond, *An Inquiry into the Authenticity of Certain Miscellaneous Papers and Legal Instruments* (London: T. Cadell, Jun. and W. Davies, 1796).

Maltby, Judith, *Prayer Book and People in Elizabethan and Early Stuart England* (Cambridge: Cambridge University Press, 1998).

Marchant, Ronald A., *The Puritans and the Church Courts in the Diocese of York 1560–1642* (London: Longmans, 1960).

Marshall, Alan, 'Dangerfield, Thomas (1654–1685)', *ODNB*.

Marshall, Peter, *Beliefs and the Dead in Reformation England* (Oxford: Oxford University Press, 2002).

Marshall, Peter, 'Evangelical Conversion in the Reign of Henry VIII', in *The Beginnings of English Protestantism*, ed. Peter Marshall and Alex Ryrie (Cambridge: Cambridge University Press, 2002), 14–37.

Marshall, Peter, 'Religious Ideology', in *The Oxford Handbook of Holinshed's Chronicles*, ed. Paulina Kewes, Ian W. Archer, and Felicity Heal (Oxford: Oxford University Press, 2013), 411–26.

Marshall, William, 'Tenison, Thomas (1636–1715)', *ODNB*.

Martin, Jessica, *Walton's Lives: Conformist Commemoration and the Rise of Biography* (Oxford: Oxford University Press, 2001).

Martin, Jessica, 'Walton, Izaak (1593–1683)', *ODNB*.

Martin, Randall, 'The Autobiography of Grace, Lady Mildmay', *Renaissance and Reformation/Renaissance et Réforme* n.s. 18 (1994), 33–81.

Mathew, Arnold Harris and Annette Calthrop, *The Life of Sir Tobie Matthew, Bacon's Alter Ego* (London: Elkin Mathews, 1907).

Mathew, David, *Sir Tobie Mathew* (London: M. Parrish, 1950).

[Matthews, William], 'The Shorthand', in Samuel Pepys, *The Diary of Samuel Pepys: A New and Complete Transcription*, ed. Robert Latham and William Matthews, 10 vols (London: G. Bell and Sons, 1970–83), 1:xlviii–liv.

Mendle, Michael, 'The "Prints" of the Trials: The Nexus of Politics, Religion, Law and Information in Late Seventeenth-Century England', in *Fear, Exclusion and Revolution: Roger Morrice and Britain in the* 1680s, ed. Jason McElligott (Aldershot: Ashgate, 2006), 123–37.

Merriam, Thomas, 'Unremarked Evidence against Anderegg's Conjecture', *Notes and Queries* 60 (2013), 407–10.

Miller, William E., 'Abraham Fleming: Editor of Shakespeare's Holinshed', *Texas Studies in Literature and Language* 1 (1959), 89–100.

Moore, Jonathan D., *English Hypothetical Universalism: John Preston and the Softening of Reformed Theology* (Grand Rapids, MI: Eerdmans, 2007).

Moore, Steve, *The Novel: An Alternative History: 1600 to 1800* (New York: Bloomsbury, 2013).

Morrill, John, 'William Dowsing, the Bureaucratic Puritan', in *Public Duty and Private Conscience in Seventeenth-Century England: Essays Presented to G. E. Aylmer*, ed. John Morrill, Paul Slack, and Daniel Woolf (Oxford: Clarendon Press, 1993), 173–203.

Moshenska, Joe, *A Stain in the Blood: The Remarkable Voyage of Sir Kenelm Digby* (London: William Heinemann, 2016).

Moulton, Ian Frederick, *Before Pornography: Erotic Writings in Early Modern England* (Oxford: Oxford University Press, 2000).

Mozley, J. F., *John Foxe and His Book* (London: Society for Promoting Christian Knowledge, 1940).

Mullaney, Steven, 'Reforming Resistance: Class, Gender, and Legitimacy in Foxe's *Book of Martyrs*', in *Print, Manuscript, & Performance: The Changing Relations of the Media in Early Modern England*, ed. Arthur F. Marotti and Michael D. Bristol (Columbus: Ohio State University Press, 2000), 235–51.

Murray, Germaine Fry, 'Introduction' to John Beadle, *A Critical Edition of John Beadle's A Journall or Diary of a Thankfull Christian*, ed. Germaine Fry Murray (New York: Garland, 1996), ix–lxxi.

Murray, James, 'Ecclesiastical Justice and the Enforcement of the Reformation: The Case of Archbishop Browne and the Clergy of Dublin', in *As by Law Established: The Church of Ireland since the Reformation*, ed. Alan Ford, James McGuire, and Kenneth Milne (Dublin: The Lilliput Press, 1995), 33–51.

Murray, James, 'The Diocese of Dublin in the Sixteenth Century: Clerical Opposition and the Failure of the Reformation', in *History of the Catholic Diocese of Dublin*, ed. James Kelly and Dáire Keogh (Dublin: Four Courts Press, 2000), 92–111.

Murray, James, *Enforcing the English Reformation in Ireland: Clerical Resistance and Political Conflict in the Diocese of Dublin, 1534–1590* (Cambridge: Cambridge University Press, 2009).

Murray, Molly, '"Now I ame a Catholique": William Alabaster and the Early Modern Catholic Conversion Narrative', in *Catholic Culture in Early Modern England*, ed. Ronald Corthell, Frances E. Dolan, Christopher Highley, and Arthur F. Marotti (Notre Dame, IN: University of Notre Dame Press, 2007), 189–215.

Murray, Molly, *The Poetics of Conversion in Early Modern English Literature* (Cambridge: Cambridge University Press, 2009).

Murray, Molly, 'The Radicalism of Early Modern Spiritual Autobiography', in *A History of English Autobiography*, ed. Adam Smyth (Cambridge: Cambridge University Press, 2016), 41–55.

Narveson, Kate, *Bible Readers and Lay Writers in Early Modern England: Gender and Self-Definition in an Emergent Writing Culture* (Aldershot: Ashgate, 2012).

Neale, J. E., *Elizabeth I and Her Parliaments*, vol. 2, 1584–1601 (London: Jonathan Cape, 1957).

Neligan, William Chadwick, *A brief description of a curious manuscript in the collection of the Rev. Dr. Neligan, entitled* A true historicall relation of the conversion of Sir Tobie Matthew to the holie Catholic fayth, with the antecedents & consequents thereof ([Cork?]: privately printed, [1835?]).

Nelson, Katie M., 'Love in the Music Room: Thomas Whythorne and the Private Affairs of Tudor Music Tutors', *Early Music* 40 (2012), 15–26.

Newman, William R., *Gehennial Fire: The Lives of George Starkey, an American Alchemist in the Scientific Revolution* (Cambridge, MA: Harvard University Press, 1994).

Nixon, Virginia, *Mary's Mother: Saint Anne in Late Medieval Europe* (University Park, PA: The Pennsylvania State University Press, 2004).

Norbrook, David, '"But a copie": Textual Authority and Gender in Editions of *The Life of John Hutchinson*', in *New Ways of Looking at Old Texts, III*, ed. W. Speed Hill (Tempe, AZ: Arizona Center for Medieval and Renaissance Studies, 2004), 109–30.

Novarr, David, *The Making of Walton's Lives* (Ithaca, NY: Cornell University Press, 1958).

Ogier, D. M., *Reformation and Society in Guernsey* (Woodbridge, Suffolk: Boydell, 1996).

O'Hara, Diana, *Courtship and Constraint: Rethinking the Making of Marriage in Tudor England* (Manchester: Manchester University Press, 2000).

Ollard, Richard, *Pepys: A Biography* (London: Hodder and Stoughton, 1974).

Orlin, Lena Cowen, 'Personhood in the Age of Reformation', in *Elizabeth I and Her People*, ed. Tarnya Cooper with Jane Eade (London: National Portrait Gallery, 2014), 26–33.

Osborn, James M., 'Introduction' to Thomas Whythorne, *The Autobiography of Thomas Whythorne*, ed. James M. Osborn (Oxford: Clarendon Press, 1961), xiii–lxv.

Osborn, James M., 'The Osborn Collection, 1934–1974', *The Yale University Library Gazette* 49 (1974), 154–70.

Osborn, James M., 'Some Experiences of a Scholar-Collector', in James M. Osborn and Robert Vosper, *Building Book Collections: Two Variations on a Theme* (Los Angeles: William Andrew Clark Memorial Library, UCLA, 1977), 1–16.

Osborn, James M., 'Whythorne, Thomas', in *The New Grove Dictionary of Music and Musicians*, ed. Stanley Sadie, 20 vols (London: Macmillan, 1980), 20:393–4.

O'Sullivan, Richard, 'R. W. Chambers: A Tribute', *The Tablet*, 179/5321 (2 May 1942), 2.

Page, Christopher, *The Guitar in Tudor England: A Social and Musical History* (Cambridge: Cambridge University Press, 2015).

Palmer, Rupert E., Jr., *Thomas Whythorn's Speech: The Phonology of a Sixteenth-Century Native of Somerset in London* (Copenhagen: Rosenkilde and Bagger, 1969).

Parkin, Jon, 'Blackburne, Richard (1651/2–1716)', *ODNB*.

Parmiter, Geoffrey de C., *Elizabeth Popish Recusancy in the Inns of Court, Bulletin of the Institute of Historical Research* special supplement no. 11 (November 1976).

Parrinder, Patrick, *Nation and Novel: The English Novel from its Origins to the Present Day* (Oxford: Oxford University Press, 2006).

Petherick, Maurice, 'Handsome Thomas and the Popish Midwife', in *Restoration Rogues* (London: Hollis & Carter, 1951), 183–263.

Petti, Anthony G., 'Unknown Sonnets by Sir Toby Matthew', *Recusant History* 9 (1967), 123–58.

Phillippy, Patricia, *Women, Death and Literature in Post-Reformation England* (Cambridge: Cambridge University Press, 2002).

Phillippy, Patricia, '"Herselfe living, to be pictured": "Monumental circles" and Women's Self-Portraiture', in *The History of British Women's Writing, 1610-1690: volume three*, ed. Mihoko Suzuki (Houndmills: Palgrave Macmillan, 2011), 129–54.

Pollman, Judith, 'A Different Road to God: The Protestant Experience of Conversion in the Sixteenth Century', in *Conversion to Modernities: The Globalization of Christianity*, ed. Peter van der Veer (New York: Routledge, 1996), 47–64.

Pollock, Linda, *With Faith and Physic: The Life of a Tudor Gentlewoman, Lady Grace Mildmay, 1552-1620* (London: Collins & Brown, 1993).

Poovey, Mary, *A History of the Modern Fact: Problems of Knowledge in the Sciences of Wealth and Society* (Chicago: University of Chicago Press, 1998).

Porter, Stephen, 'Lupton, Donald (*d.* 1676)', *ODNB*.

Pounds, N. J. G., 'William Carnsew of Bokelly and his Diary, 1576–7', *Journal of the Royal Institution of Cornwall* n. s. 8 (1978), 14–60.

Powell, Anthony, *John Aubrey and his Friends* (New York: Charles Scribner's Sons, 1948).

Pritchard, Jonathan, 'Head, Richard (*c*.1637–1686?)', *ODNB*.

Questier, Michael, 'Catholicism, Kinship, and the Public Memory of Sir Thomas More', *Journal of Ecclesiastical History* 53 (2002), 476–509.

Quintrell, B. W., 'Government in Perspective: Lancashire and the Privy Council, 1570–1640', *Transactions of the Historic Society of Lancashire and Cheshire* 131 (1982), 36–63.

Reames, Sherry L., *The Legenda aurea: A Reexamination of its Paradoxical History* (Madison, WI: University of Wisconsin Press, 1985).

Rees, Graham, 'Introduction' to Francis Bacon, *Philosophical Studies c. 1611-1619*, ed. Graham Rees (Oxford: Clarendon Press, 1996), xvii–cx.

Revill, P. and F. Steer, 'George Gage I and George Gage II', *Bulletin of the Institute of Historical Research* 31/84 (1958), 141–58.

Rex, Richard, 'John Bale, Geoffrey Downes and Jesus College', *Journal of Ecclesiastical History* 49 (1998), 486–93.

Rex, Richard, 'Friars in the English Reformation', in *The Beginnings of English Protestantism*, ed. Peter Marshall and Alex Ryrie (Cambridge: Cambridge University Press, 2002), 38–59.

Rhodes, J. T., 'English Books of Martyrs and Saints of the Late Sixteenth and Early Seventeenth Centuries', *Recusant History* 22 (1994), 7–25.

Rhodes James, Montague ed., *The Western Manuscripts in the Library of Emmanuel College: A Descriptive Catalogue* (Cambridge: the University Press, 1904).
Richards, Penny, 'A Life in Writing: Elizabeth Cellier and Print Culture', *Women's Writing* 7 (2000), 411–25.
Richardson, R. C., *Puritanism in North-West England: A Regional Study of the Diocese of Chester to 1642* (Manchester: Manchester University Press, 1972).
Richardson, William, 'Topcliffe, Richard (1531–1604)', *ODNB*.
Rivett, Sarah, *The Science of the Soul in Colonial New England* (Chapel Hill, NC: University of North Carolina Press, 2011).
Roach, Joseph, 'Celebrity Erotics: Pepys, Performance, and Painted Ladies', *The Yale Journal of Criticism* 16 (2003), 211–30.
Rowlands, Marie B., 'Recusant Women 1560–1640', in *Women in English Society 1500–1800* ed. Mary Prior (London: Methuen, 1986), 149–80.
Rowse, A. L., *Tudor Cornwall: Portrait of a Society* (London: Jonathan Cape, 1941).
Rowse, A. L., 'The Diary of William Carnsew, Country Gentleman', in *Court & Country: Studies in Tudor Social History* (Brighton: The Harvester Press, 1987), 136–80.
Rowse, A. L., 'The Truth about Topcliffe', in *Court & Country: Studies in Tudor Social History* (Brighton: The Harvester Press, 1987), 181–210.
Ryrie, Alec, *Being Protestant in Reformation Britain* (Oxford: Oxford University Press, 2013).
Salmon, Vivian, 'Bathsua Makin (1600–c.1673): A Pioneer Linguist and Feminist', in *Language and Society in Early Modern England: Selected Essays 1981–1994*, ed. Konrad Koerner (Amsterdam and Philadelphia: John Benjamins, 1996), 239–60.
Salmon, Vivian, 'Orthography and Punctuation', in *The Cambridge History of the English Language*, vol. 3, *1476–1776*, ed. Roger Lass (Cambridge: Cambridge University Press, 1999), 13–55.
Schoenbaum, Samuel, *William Shakespeare: A Compact Documentary Life* (Oxford: Clarendon Press, 1977).
Schofield, John, *The Building of London from the Conquest to the Great Fire* (London: Colonnade Books, 1984).
Scott-Warren, Jason, 'Books in the Bedchamber: Religion, Accounting and the Library of Richard Stonley', in *Tudor Books and Readers: Materiality and the Construction of Meaning*, ed. John N. King (Cambridge: Cambridge University Press, 2010), 232–52.
Scott-Warren, Jason, 'Early Modern Bookkeeping and Life-Writing Revisited: Accounting for Richard Stonley', *Past and Present* 230 (2016), suppl. 11, 151–70.
Scragg, D. G., *A History of English Spelling* (Manchester: Manchester University Press, 1974).
Seaver, Paul S., *Wallington's World: A Puritan Artisan in Seventeenth-Century London* (Stanford, CA: Stanford University Press, 1985).
Sergeant, Philip W., 'Duke Dangerfield', in *Liars and Fakers* (London: Hutchinson & Co., [1926]), 133–98.
Shami, Jeanne, 'Women and Sermons', in *The Oxford Handbook of the Early Modern Sermon*, ed. Peter McCullough, Hugh Adlington, and Emma Rhatigan (Oxford: Oxford University Press, 2011), 155–77.
Sharpe, Richard, 'The English Bibliographical Tradition from Kirkestede to Tanner', in *Britannia Latina: Latin in the Culture of Great Britain from the Middle Ages to the Twentieth Century*,

ed. Charles Burnett and Nicholas Mann (London-Turin: The Warburg Institute-Nino Aragno Editore, 2005), 86–128.

Sherlock, Peter, *Monuments and Memory in Early Modern England* (Aldershot: Ashgate, 2008).

Sherlock, Peter, 'Fulman, William (1632–1688)', *ODNB*.

Sherman, William H., *Used Books: Marking Readers in Renaissance England* (Philadelphia: University of Pennsylvania Press, 2008).

Shore, David R., 'The *Autobiography* of Thomas Whythorne: An Early Elizabethan Context for Poetry', *Renaissance and Reformation* 17 (1981), 72–86.

Shore, David R., 'Whythorne's *Autobiography* and the Genesis of Gascoigne's *Master F. J.*', *Journal of Medieval and Renaissance Studies* 12 (1982), 159–78.

Smith, William Henry, *Bacon and Shakespeare. An inquiry touching players, playhouses, and play-writers in the days of Elizabeth... to which is appended an abstract of an MS. respecting Tobie Matthew* (London: John Russell Smith, 1857).

Smyth, Adam, 'Money, Accounting, and Life-Writing, 1600–1700: Balancing a Life', in *A History of English Autobiography*, ed. Adam Smyth (Cambridge: Cambridge University Press, 2016), 86–99.

[Southey, Robert], 'Art. XI. *The Memoirs of the Life and Writings of Percival Stockdale...*' [review], *Quarterly Review* 1 (1809), 371–86.

Stallybrass, Peter, 'Printing and the Manuscript Revolution', in *Explorations in Communication and Theory*, ed. Barbie Zelizer (London: Routledge, 2008), 111–18.

Stanwood, P. G., *Izaak Walton* (New York: Twayne, 1998).

Stephens, Isaac, '"My cheefest work": The Making of the Spiritual Autobiography of Elizabeth Isham', *Midland History* 34 (2009), 181–203.

Stephens, Isaac, *The Gentlewoman's Remembrance: Patriarchy, Piety, and Singlehood in Early Stuart England* (Manchester: Manchester University Press, 2016).

Sterling, Eric, commentary in *Reading Early Modern Women: An Anthology of Texts in Manuscript and Print, 1550-1700*, ed. Helen Ostovich and Elizabeth Sauer (New York: Routledge, 2004), 258–61.

Stewart, Alan, *Close Readers: Humanism and Sodomy in Early Modern England* (Princeton, NJ: Princeton University Press, 1997).

Stewart, Alan, 'The Materiality of Early Modern Life-Writing: The Case of Richard Stonley', in *On Life-Writing*, ed. Zachary Leader (Oxford: Oxford University Press, 2015), 161–79.

Strype, John, *The Life and Acts of Matthew Parker*, 3 vols (Oxford: Clarendon Press, 1821).

Sullivan, Ceri, *The Rhetoric of Credit: Merchants in Early Modern Writing* (Madison, NJ: Fairleigh Dickinson University Press, 2002).

Summerson, Henry, 'Sources: 1587', in *The Oxford Handbook of Holinshed's Chronicles*, ed. Paulina Kewes, Ian W. Archer, and Felicity Heal (Oxford: Oxford University Press, 2013), 76–92. *see also* Heal, Felicity.

S[utherland], N. M., 'Matthew, Tobias (1577–1655), of London', in *The House of Commons 1558-1603*, ed. P. W. Hasler, 3 vols (London: HMSO for the History of Parliament Trust, 1981), 3:36–7.

Sutton, John, 'Ball, John (1585–1640)', *ODNB*.

Sylvester, R. S., 'William Roper's *Life of More*', *Moreana* 36 (December 1972), 47–59.

Tadmor, Naomi, 'The Concept of Household-Family in Eighteenth-Century England', *Past and Present* 151 (1996), 111–40.

Tadmor, Naomi, *Family and Friends in Eighteenth-Century England: Household, Kinship, and Patronage* (Cambridge: Cambridge University Press, 2001).

Tanner, Marcus, *Ireland's Holy Wars: The Struggle for a Nation's Soul, 1500-2000* (New Haven, CT: Yale University Press, 2001).

Targoff, Ramie, *Posthumous Love: Eros and the Afterlife in Renaissance England* (Chicago: University of Chicago Press, 2014).

Tassi, Marguerite A., *The Scandal of Images: Iconoclasm, Eroticism and Painting in Early Modern English Drama* (Selinsgrove, PA: Susquehanna University Press, 2005).

[Taylor, William], 'Art. IV. *Miscellanies*; or Literary Recreations. By I. D'Israeli . . .', *Monthly Review*, 2nd ser., 24 (1796), 374–9.

Teague, Frances, *Bathsua Makin, Woman of Learning* (Lewisburg, PA: Bucknell University Press, 1998).

Thrush, Andrew, 'Perrot, Sir James (1571/2–1637)', *ODNB*.

Tindall, William York, *John Bunyan: Mechanick Preacher* (New York: Columbia University Press, 1934).

Tittler, Robert, *The Face of the City: Civic Portraiture and Civic Identity in Early Modern England* (Manchester: Manchester University Press, 2007).

Tittler, Robert, *Portraits, Painters, and Publics in Provincial England, 1540-1640* (Oxford: Oxford University Press, 2012).

Todd, Janet, 'Carleton, Mary (1634×42–1673)', *ODNB*.

Todd, Margo, 'Puritan Self-Fashioning: The Diary of Samuel Ward', *Journal of British Studies* 31 (1992), 236–64.

Tomalin, Claire, *Samuel Pepys: The Unequalled Self* (London: Viking, 2002).

Trimble, William Raleigh, *The Catholic Laity in Elizabethan England 1558-1603* (Cambridge, MA: Belknap Press of Harvard University Press, 1964).

Tromly, Frederic B., '"Accordinge to sounde religion": The Elizabethan Controversy over the Funeral Sermon', *Journal of Medieval and Renaissance Studies* 13 (1983), 293–312.

Turnbull, G. H., 'Samuel Hartlib's Acquaintance with John Aubrey', *Notes and Queries* 195 (1950), 31–3.

Turner, David M., *Fashioning Adultery: Gender, Sex and Civility in England, 1660-1740* (Cambridge: Cambridge University Press, 2002).

Turner, James Grantham, 'Pepys and the Private Parts of Monarchy', in *Culture and Society in the Stuart Restoration: Literature, Drama, History*, ed. Gerald Maclean (Cambridge: Cambridge University Press, 1995), 95–110.

Tylden-Wright, David, *John Aubrey: A Life* (London: HarperCollins, 1991).

Vander Motten, J. P. and Katrien Daemen-de Gelder, 'A Cloistered Entrepôt: Sir Tobie Matthew and the English Carmel at Antwerp', *English Studies* 92 (2011), 548–61.

Vander Motten, J. P. and Katrien Daemen-de Gelder, 'Sir Toby Matthew and his "fidus Achates" George Gage, 1607-1620', *ANQ* 23 (2010), 20–30.

Van Hyning, Victoria, 'Expressing Selfhood in the Convent: Anonymous Chronicling and Subsumed Autobiography', *Recusant History* 32 (2014), 219–34.

Vaught, Jennifer C., *Masculinity and Emotion in Early Modern English Literature* (Aldershot: Ashgate, 2008).

Walkden, Andrea, 'The Servant and the Grave Robber: Walton's *Lives* in Restoration England', in *Writing Lives: Biography and Textuality, Identity and Representation in Early Modern England*, ed. Kevin Sharpe and Steven N. Zwicker (Oxford: Oxford University Press, 2008), 319–36.

Walker, Ernest, *A History of Music in England* (London: Oxford University Press, 1907).

Walsh, Katherine, 'Deliberate Provocation or Reforming Zeal? John Bale as First Church of Ireland Bishop of Ossory (1552/53–1563)', in *Taking Sides: Colonial and Confessional Mentalités in Early Modern Ireland: Essays in Honour of Karl S. Bottigheimer*, ed. Vincent P. Carey and Ute Lotz-Heumann (Dublin: Four Courts Press, 2003), 42–62.

Warlock, Peter [*pseud.* Philip Heseltine], *Thomas Whythorne: An Unknown Elizabethan Composer* (London: Oxford University Press/Humphrey Milford, 1925).

Warnicke, Retha and Bettie Anne Doebler, 'Introduction' to William Harrison and William Leigh, *Deaths advantage little regarded, and the soules solace against sorrow…Whereunto is annexed, the Christian life and godly death of the said Gentlewoman*, facsimile edition, ed. Retha M. Warnicke and Bettie Anne Doebler (Delmar, NY: Scholars' Facsimiles & Reprints, 1993), 7–40.

Webster, Tom, *Godly Clergy in Early Stuart England: The Caroline Puritan Movement c. 1620–1643* (Cambridge: Cambridge University Press, 1997).

Webster, Tom, 'Writing to Redundancy: Approaches to Spiritual Journals and Early Modern Spirituality', *Historical Journal* 39 (1996), 33–56.

Weil, Rachel, '"If I did say so I lyed": Elizabeth Cellier and the Construction of Credibility in the Popish Plot Crisis', in *Political Culture and Cultural Politics in Early Modern England: Essays Presented to David Underdown*, ed. Susan D. Amussen and Mark A. Kishlansky (Manchester: Manchester University Press, 1995), 189–209.

Westfall, Richard, 'Short-Writing and the State of Newton's Conscience, 1662', *Notes and Records of the Royal Society of London* 18 (1963), 10–16.

Wheatley, George, *Pepysiana or Additional Notes on the Particulars of Pepys's Life and on Some Passages in the Diary with Appendixes* (London: George Bell & Sons, 1899).

White, Barbara, 'Hind, James (*bap.* 1616, *d.* 1652)', *ODNB*.

White, Helen C., *Social Criticism in Popular Religious Literature of the Sixteenth Century* (London: Macmillan, 1944).

White, Helen C., *Tudor Books of Saints and Martyrs* (Madison, WI: University of Wisconsin Press, 1963).

Whitehouse, Tessa, 'Structures and Processes of English Spiritual Autobiography from Bunyan to Cowper', in *A History of English Autobiography*, ed. Adam Smyth (Cambridge: Cambridge University Press, 2016), 103–18.

Wickham, D. E., *Clothworkers' Hall Portraits: The Portraits and Modelled Portrait Heads in the Collection of the Clothworkers' Company–A Summary Catalogue* ([London: The Clothworkers Company], 1997).

Wiedemann, Barbara *see* Evans, Robert C. and Barbara Wiedemann.

Wiggins, Martin with Catherine Richardson, *British Drama 1533–1642: A Catalogue*, I, 1533–1566 (Oxford: Oxford University Press, 2012).

Wilcox, Helen, 'Of Music and Silence: The Harmonies of Thomas Whythorne and Rose Tremain', in *Challenging Humanism: Essays in Honor of Dominic Baker-Smith*, ed. Ton Hoenselaars and Arthur F. Kinney (Newark, DE: University of Delaware Press, 2005), 290–310.

Wilcox, Helen, 'Selves in Strange Lands: Autobiography and Exile in the Mid-Seventeenth Century', in *Early Modern Autobiography: Theories, Genres, Practices*, ed. Ronald Bedford, Lloyd Davis, and Phillippa Kelly (Ann Arbor, MI: University of Michigan Press, 2006), 131–59.

Wilson, John Harold, *The Private Life of Mr. Pepys* (New York: Farrar, Straus and Cudahy, 1959).

Wolfe, Heather, 'Richard Stonley (ca. 1520–1600)', in *'The Pen's Excellencie': Treasures from the Manuscript Collection of the Folger Shakespeare Library*, ed. Heather Wolfe (Washington, DC: Folger Shakespeare Library, 2002), 75–6.

Wolfe, Heather, 'Thomas Shelton's Shorthand Version of the Lord's Prayer', *The Collation: A Gathering of Scholarship from the Folger Shakespeare Library* (blog), 24 May 2012, https://collation.folger.edu/2012/05/thomas-sheltons-shorthand-version-of-the-lords-prayer/, accessed on 17 December 2017.

Woodcock, Matthew, 'Narrative Voice and Influencing the Reader', in *The Oxford Handbook of Holinshed's Chronicles*, ed. Paulina Kewes, Ian W. Archer, and Felicity Heal (Oxford: Oxford University Press, 2013), 337–53.

Wooden, Warren W., 'Sir Thomas Bodley's *Life of Himself* (1609) and the Epideictic Strategies of Encomia', *Studies in Philology* 83 (1986), 62–75.

Woods, Gillian, '"Strange discourse": The Controversial Subject of *Sir Thomas More*', *Renaissance Drama* n.s. 39 (2011), 3–35.

Wort, Oliver, 'The Double Life of Anne: John Bale's "Examinations," and "Diue Anne Vitam" (sic)', *Review of English Studies* n.s. 58 (2007), 633–56.

Wort, Oliver, *John Bale and Religious Conversion in Reformation England* (London: Pickering & Chatto, 2013).

Wright, Conrad Edick, 'Rogers, John (1630/31–1684)', *ODNB*.

Yamey, B. S., H. C. Edey, and Hugh W. Thomson, *Accounting in England and Scotland: 1543–1800: Double Entry in Exposition and Practice* (London: Sweet & Maxwell, 1963).

Young, Betty, 'Sources for the Annesley Family', *Proceedings of the Wesley Historical Society* 45 (1985), 46–57.

Young, Robert Fitzgibbon, *Comenius in England* (Oxford: Oxford University Press, 1932).

Zwicker, Steven N., 'Considering the Ancients: Dryden and the Uses of Biography', in *Writing Lives: Biography and Textuality, Identity and Representation in Early Modern England*, ed. Kevin Sharpe and Steven N. Zwicker (Oxford: Oxford University Press, 2008), 105–24.

F. *Unpublished dissertations*

Feil, John P., 'Sir Tobie Matthew and his *Collection of Letters*', PhD dissertation, University of Chicago, 1962.

Murphy, Sara Ann, 'Revised Lives: Lineage and Dislocation in Seventeenth-Century English Autobiography', PhD dissertation, Columbia University, 2014.

Painting Stubbs, Claire Elizabeth, 'Abraham Fleming: Writer, Cleric and Preacher in Elizabethan and Jacobean London', PhD dissertation, Royal Holloway, University of London, 2011.

G. *Electronic resources*

The Acts and Monuments Online (johnfoxe.org)
Catalogue of English Literary Manuscripts (www.celm-ms.org.uk/)
Constructing Elizabeth Isham (www2.warwick.ac.uk/fac/arts/ren/projects/isham)
Early English Books Online (https://eebo.chadwyck.com/)
The English Broadside Ballad Archive (http://ebba.english.ucsb.edu/)
English Short-Title Catalogue (estc.bl.uk/)
A London Provisioner's Chronicle, 1550–1563, by Henry Machyn: Manuscript, Transcription, and Modernization, ed. Richard W. Bailey, Marilyn Miller, and Colette Moore (http://quod.lib.umich.edu/m/machyn)
LUNA: Folger Digital Image Collection (luna.folger.edu)
Oxford English Dictionary (www.oed.com/)
Oxford Dictionary of National Biography (www.oxforddnb.com/)
Perdita Manuscripts (http://www.perditamanuscripts.amdigital.co.uk)
The Samuel Hartlib Papers (http://www.hrionline.ac.uk/hartlib/index.html)
Universal Short Title Catalogue (www.ustc.ac.uk)
Who Were the Nuns? (https://wwtn.history.qmul.ac.uk/)

Index